Administering Relational Databases On Microsoft Azure

A detail paradigm to support SQL on Azure cloud, DP 300 study guide, and explore the hidden side of cloud databases

Administering Relational Database on Microsoft Azure

Prashanth Jayaram, TX, USA
ISBN- (pbk): **ISBN: 9798706128029**
Imprint: Independently published

About the Authors 17

Target Audience 19

How to use this book to study for the exam 20

Organization of this book 21

Acknowledgements 22

Learning Objective 25

Why become Microsoft Certified 26

Hardware and software requirements 28

Hardware requirements 28

Software requirements 28

Chapter 1 Azure Fundamentals and Concepts 30

Cloud Computing Concepts 32

Cloud Computing Models 33

Cloud Computing Services Types 35

Infrastructure as a Service (IaaS) 36

Platform as a Service (PaaS) 37

Serverless compute 39

Software as a Service (SaaS) 39

Azure architectural components 40

Azure Compute Service 43

Azure Network Services 44

Azure Storage Services 45

Summary 47

Chapter 2 Explore Azure Data Platform roles 48

Azure Data Engineer 48

Azure Database Administrator 49

Azure Data Analyst 49

Azure Data Scientist 50

Azure Artificial Intelligence Engineer 50

On-premise Database Administrator 50

How to move to Azure Database Administrator role 51

Migrate to the Cloud 52

Educate *53*

Explore the cloud management and migration tools *53*

Start your analysis to define the baseline metrics *53*

Build the confidence *53*

Assess the security *54*

Prepare migration *54*

Prepare for a live cutover *54*

Rollback strategy *55*

Perform continuous testing *55*

Understand the TCO (Total Cost of Ownership) and ROI (Return on Investment) 55

Summary 59

Chapter 3 Azure Database Platform choices in Azure **59**

Azure data categories *59*

Azure database services 60

SQL Server in an Azure VM *62*

Azure SQL Database *63*

Azure SQL Managed Instance *65*

Open-Source Databases on Azure SQL Platform *66*

Azure Synapse Analytics *67*

Azure Cosmos DB *69*

Summary 70

Chapter 4 Plan and implement data platforms resources in Azure **71**

Explain IaaS options for deploying SQL Server in Azure 71

Deploy SQL Server on Azure VM 75

SQL Server licensing models 75

VIRTUAL MACHINE FAMILIES 77

PROVISION AND DEPLOY SQL SERVER TO AZURE VIRTUAL MACHINES 81

Deployment using the Azure Marketplace 81

Deploying via Azure PowerShell 84

Deploying via Azure CLI 85

Deploying using the Azure Resource Manager templates 86

Lab 1: Provision a SQL Server on an Azure virtual machine 87

SQL SERVER TO SQL SERVER ON AZURE VMS MIGRATIONS 94

Assessment Overview 95

Assess 97

Migrate 97

Backup and restore method: 98

Backup to URL 98

Detach and attach 99

Log shipping 99

Database Migration Assistant (DMA) 101

Distributed availability group 101

Post-migration 102

PAAS OPTIONS FOR DEPLOYING SQL SERVER IN AZURE 102

Database Transaction Unit(DTU) model 103

vCores-based purchasing model 106

Hyperscale 107

Comparison between vCores and DTU based model 108

Azure SQL Database in Serverless configuration 109

Comparison between Provisioned and Serverless compute tier 111

LAB 2: DEPLOY A SINGLE SQL DATABASE 111

LAB 3: DEPLOYING AN AZURE SQL DATABASE VIA POWERSHELL/CLI 113

LAB 4: DEPLOYING AZURE SQL DATABASE USING AZURE RESOURCE MANAGER TEMPLATES 114

SQL ELASTIC POOLS 114

When should you consider a SQL Database elastic pool? 117

LAB 5: DEPLOY AN ELASTIC POOL FOR AZURE SQL DATABASE 119

SQL managed instance 122

Deploy MariaDB, MySQL, and PostgreSQL on Azure 126

Azure Database for MySQL *126*

Azure Database for PostgreSQL *129*

Lab 6: Create an Azure Database for the MariaDB server by using the Azure portal 134

Lab 7: Deploy a PostgreSQL database server to Azure 137

Summary 139

Chapter 5 Implement secure data platform environment in Azure. 140

SQL Server Authentication Methods 140

Configure Azure AD authentication 143

Configure Security Principals 146

Configure database authorization 156

Configure database and object-level permissions 156

Ownership chaining 159

Switch the Execution Context 160

Apply the principle of least privilege for all securable 161

Implement security for data at rest 162

Implement object-level encryption 167

Implement Dynamic Data Masking 172

Configure server and database-level firewall rules 175

Row-Level Security 178

Apply a data classification strategy 184

Advanced Threat Protection 186

Configure server and database audits 189

Implement data change tracking 197

Perform a vulnerability assessment 200

Summary 204

Chapter 6 Monitor and optimize Azure Data Platform resources 205

Monitoring Azure SQL Database and Azure SQL Managed instances 205

View Database data storage for Azure SQL Database 205

Compute utilization and chart formats 207
Chart timeline 209
Chart Metrics 209
ALERT RULES 210
Static vs Dynamic threshold 214
Actions groups 218
Actions 220
DIAGNOSTIC SETTINGS 221
Avg CPU utilization: 227
Log write percentage: 228
Deadlocks 229
Filter diagnostics data for an Azure SQL Database 230
Script for failed logins 231
QUERY PERFORMANCE INSIGHT 233
Resource Consuming Queries 234
Top 5 queries by CPU. Data IO and Log IO 235
By Data IO: 235
By Log IO: 236
Lists the top queries by their %CPU, Data IO (%), Log IO (%), Duration and execution count. 236
Recommendations: 237
Long-running queries 238
Custom dashboard 238
Review top queries per duration 239
Review top queries per execution count 240
CHAPTER 7 MONITORING AZURE RESOURCES USING THE AZURE MONITOR **241**
MONITOR AZURE SQL DATABASE USING AZURE MONITOR 242
AZURE SQL ANALYTICS 248
SQL DATABASE VIEW 252
SQL MANAGED INSTANCE VIEW 253
INTELLIGENT INSIGHTS REPORT 254
ELASTIC POOLS AND DATABASE REPORTS 257

Query reports 257

View Azure SQL Database Log analytics data using Power BI 258

Extended Events in Azure SQL Database 265

system_health extended event session in Azure SQL Database 268

Create an extended event to capture update statement 269

Capture Deadlock information using the extended event 272

Describe automatic tuning 277

Automatic plan correction *280*

Create Index *281*

Drop Index *281*

View performance recommendations for Azure SQL Database *282*

Optimize Azure SQL Server on VM 283

Virtual machines types *284*

Azure managed disks *285*

SQL Server storage configuration best practices *287*

SQL Server 2019 Memory-Optimized TempDB Metadata *289*

Summary 290

Chapter 8 Optimize query performance in SQL Server **291**

Execution Plans 292

Query lifecycle 292

Different format and types of the query execution plan 294

Graphical execution plan *294*

Estimated execution plan *299*

Actual execution plan *299*

Live Query Statistics *300*

Read a graphical query execution plan *301*

Lightweight query profiling *305*

lightweight query execution statistics profiling infrastructure – V1 305

Lightweight query execution statistics profiling infrastructure – V2 305

Lightweight query execution statistics profiling infrastructure – V3 306

The last query plans stats 307

IDENTIFY PROBLEM AREAS IN EXECUTION PLANS 309
Table scan Vs Index scan Vs Index seek *309*
RID Lookup and Key Lookup *310*
Sort operator *311*
Parallelism *312*
Warnings *312*
Inaccurate Row Estimates *312*
Missing Index *313*
SARGAbility *313*
Missing and out-of-date statistics *316*
PARAMETER SNIFFING 316
COLUMNSTORE INDEX 318
TABLE PARTITIONING 320
IN-MEMORY OLTP IN AZURE SQL DATABASE AND MANAGED INSTANCES 320
LAB 9: IDENTIFY ISSUES WITH A DATABASE DESIGN 322
DYNAMIC MANAGEMENT VIEWS AND FUNCTIONS FOR PERFORMANCE MONITORING 325
Dynamic Management Queries *326*
WAIT STATISTICS 328
AZURE SQL INDEXES AND STATISTICS MAINTENANCE 330
Detecting fragmentation *331*
AzureSQLMaintenance stored procedure *332*
MONITORING PERFORMANCE BY USING THE QUERY STORE 334
LAB 10: USE COVERING INDEX FOR IMPROVING QUERY EXECUTION PLAN 336
TempDB configuration for Azure SQL Database and Azure SQL Managed Instance *340*
Azure SQL Database TempDB configuration *340*
Azure SQL Managed Instance TempDB configuration *341*
MAX DEGREE OF PARALLELISM 342
LAB 11: USE QUERY STORE FEATURE TO RESOLVE THE PERFORMANCE ISSUE 344
SUMMARY 349

CHAPTER 9 PERFORM AUTOMATION OF TASKS **350**

AZURE CLOUD SHELL 351

AZURE CLI OVERVIEW 354
AZURE POWERSHELL 356
WHY DOES POWERSHELL CMDLETS SO EASY TO USE? 357
THE HISTORY OF POWERSHELL 359
AZ AND AZ CLI COMMANDS 362
SUPPORTED PLATFORMS 364
DIFFERENCES BETWEEN AZURE POWERSHELL AND AZURE CLI 364
AZURE AUTOMATION ACCOUNT 365
What is a runbook? *365*
Create Azure automation account *366*
Import a runbook *368*
How to load PowerShell modules *370*
How to create PowerShell workflow *371*
Publish the runbook *375*
LINKED SERVER TO RUN T-SQL ON AZURE SQL DATABASE 377
AZURE ELASTIC JOBS 381
Components *382*
Elastic jobs *383*
When should I use Elastic Jobs? *383*
Limitations *384*
Configure Elastic job steps *384*
Create an Elastic Job agent *384*
Once the deployment completes, you can see the elastic job is ready for the configuration.Creating database scoped credentials on the agent database *386*
Creating a target group and members *387*
Creating logins on target master *389*
Create a user on the target database *389*
Create a job and job step *390*
Run and monitor the job *391*
Schedule the job *391*
CREATE SCHEDULED JOBS USING LOGIC APP 392

Use-Case: Create a workflow to load the data by executing SP using Logic Apps. 392
Configure Logic Apps 393
Build Logic Apps 394
Provisioning an Azure SQL Server and SQL Database Using Azure PowerShell 399
Pre-requisites: 399
Prepare the deployment code 402
Azure Resource Manager Templates 405
The Benefits 406
Deploy template steps 406
How to find a JSON template? 407
Deploy Azure SQL database using a JSON template 410
The difference between declarative and imperative programming 414
Deploying an Azure ARM Template using PowerShell 415
Schedule jobs with SQL Server Agent 419
Multi-Server Automation 421
Configure Multi-server automation 421
Configure notifications for task success/failure/non-completion 423
Configure Database Mail 424
Configure Operator 429
Configure Maintenance jobs to send alerts 431
Use-case: How to set up an alert in SQL Server Agent jobs 437
Run PowerShell script steps in SQL Server Agent 438
Prerequisite: 438
Summary 441

Chapter 10 Plan and implement high availability and disaster recovery environments in Azure 443

Recovery Time Objective (RTO) and Recovery Point Objective(RPO) 443
Explore high availability and disaster recovery options 445
SQL Server HADR Features for Azure Virtual Machine 446
Windows Failover clustering 446
SQL Server Always On Availability Groups 446
Add a backend pool for the availability group listener 449

Configure the health probe 449
Configure Load balancing rules 449
EXPLORE THE HIGH AVAILABILITY AND DISASTER RECOVERY SOLUTION FOR IAAS 449
Availability Sets: 449
Availability zones 450
Azure Site Recovery 451
SINGLE REGION SQL SERVER ALWAYS ON AVAILABILITY GROUP 451
HYBRID SQL SERVER ALWAYS ON AVAILABILITY GROUP 452
DISTRIBUTED AVAILABILITY GROUP 453
DISASTER RECOVERY USING LOG SHIPPING 454
AZURE SITE RECOVERY 454
PAAS DEPLOYMENTS HIGH AVAILABILITY AND DISASTER RECOVERY OPTIONS 455
Standard availability model 456
General Purpose service tier zone redundant availability 457
Premium availability model locally redundant availability 458
Active geo-replication for Azure SQL databases 461
Auto-failover groups 462
DIFFERENCE BETWEEN ACTIVE-GEO REPLICATION AND AUTO-FAILOVER GROUPS 466
BACKUP AND RESTORE DATABASES 466
Backup and restore SQL Server running on Azure virtual machines 466
Automated Backup V2 for SQL Server 2016 onwards 469
Scenario 1: Weekly full backup 471
Scenario 2: Daily full backup 472
Azure Backup for SQL VMs 473
Manual backup – Backup To URL 475
Backup to block blob vs page blob 475
Microsoft Azure Blob Storage service components 476
Decision matrix 476
Backup and restore for an Azure SQL Database 477
Understand Long-term retention period policy 478
Backup storage redundancy for SQL Database and SQL MI on Azure 480

Locally-redundant storage(LRS) 481
Zone-redundant storage (ZRS) 482
Geo-redundant storage (RA-GRS) 483
Geo-zone-redundant storage(GZRS) 484
Data redundancy options comparisons 485
Durability and availability parameters 486
Durability and availability by outage scenario 486
Configure backup storage redundancy 487
LAB 12: CONFIGURE AN AZURE SQL DATABASE GEO-REPLICATION USING AZURE PORTAL 487
LAB 13: CONFIGURE AN AZURE SQL DATABASE AUTO-FAILOVER GROUPS USING AZURE PORTAL 494
Initiate a manual failover for auto-failover groups 497
LAB 14: CONFIGURE AN AZURE SQL DATABASE GEO-REPLICATION USING AZURE CLI 499
LAB 15: CONFIGURE AUTO-FAILOVER GROUP USING AZURE CLI 501
LAB 15: BACKUP DATABASE TO URL 503
Backup to URL using Storage account access key 504
Backup to URL using shared access signature 505
LAB 16: CONFIGURE AUTOMATIC BACKUP V2 FOR EXISTING VM 508
LAB 17: CONFIGURE SQL SERVER BACKUP IN AZURE VMS 511
Configure a backup in the default recovery service vault policy 513
Create a custom backup policy in the recovery service vault 515
LAB 18: CONFIGURE LTR POLICY FOR AZURE SQL DATABASE USING AZURE CLI 517
SUMMARY 519

CHAPTER 11 PERFORM ADMINISTRATION USING T-SQL AND POWERSHELL. 520

OVERVIEW OF AZURE SQL DATABASE 521
CREATE A DATABASE IN AZURE SQL USING T-SQL 522
CREATE A DATABASE WITH THE OPTIONS 522
CREATE AN ELASTIC POOL DATABASE 523
COPY AZURE SQL DATABASE 523
CHANGE THE SERVICE TIER USING T-SQL 524
PERFORMANCE MONITORING USING EXTENDED EVENTS T-SQL 525
How to use SSMS to read extend events log files 529

DYNAMIC MANAGED VIEWS IN AZURE SQL 533
HOW TO DETERMINE THE DATABASES WITH COMPUTE UTILIZATION OVER 75% LAST DAYS 534
HOW TO MEASURE RESOURCE CONSUMPTION OF A DATABASE USING SYS.DM_DB_RESOURCE_STATS 534
HOW TO CONFIGURE AUTOMATIC TUNING USING T-SQL 534
Manage automatic tuning in two ways: 535
Automatic index management 535
HOW TO ENABLE, MODIFY AND DISABLE CHANGE TRACKING 536
HOW TO RECOVER THE DELETED AZURE SQL DATABASES 537
LAB 19: HOW TO PROTECT THE ACCIDENTAL DELETES OF LOGICAL AZURE SQL SERVER? 538
Read-only lock 539
Delete lock 541
LAB 20: CONFIGURE LTR (LONG TERM RETENTION) FOR AZURE SQL SERVER 543
HOW TO VIEW BACKUPS USING AZURE POWERSHELL 544
MANAGE SECURITY USING T-SQL 547
Azure SQL Database Admin account 547
Azure SQL admin account limitation 547
Azure SQL special accounts 548
Dbmanager role 548
Login managers 548
Azure Active Directory administrator 549
Configure the firewall using T-SQL 549
Manage server-level firewall rules through Transact-SQL 549
Database-level firewall rules 550
Create a database role that owns a fixed database role 550
Azure SQL Database security management 551
How to view the roles and permissions in Azure SQL server instance 552
Data Integrity in Azure SQL Database 552
Query Azure SQL Database with AD Universal MFA Authentication using PowerShell 554
Use ADO.NET objects. 554
How to report free database space in Azure SQL Database 555
Data storage using Azure Portal 556
Data storage details using T-SQL 556

Accelerated Database Recovery (ADR 557
Summary 558

Chapter 12 Unified Azure SQL management 559

Automatic SQL VM resource provider registration 559
Pre-requisites: 560
Enable automatic registration 561
Register SQL Server VM with SQL IaaS Agent Extension 562
Update SQL on Azure VM to Full mode using Azure Portal 563
Update SQL on Azure VM to Full mode using PowerShell 564
Verify registration status using PowerShell 564
Look into the future. 565
Summary 565

Chapter 13 SQL Workload Migration to Microsoft Azure 566

Planning 566
Migration tools 567
Microsoft Assessment and Planning Toolkit 568
Data Migration Assistant (DMA) 569
Azure Migrate Service 571
Migrate to a SQL Server instance on an Azure VM 572
Migrate to an Azure SQL Database 573
Migrate to an Azure SQL Database Managed Instance 574
Summary 575

Chapter 14 Practice tests with direct and scenario related questions 576

Certificate Candidate 578
Study Guidelines 578
Plan and Implement Data Platform Resources 578
Recommend an appropriate database offering based on specific requirements: 580
Configure resources for scale and performance: 580
Evaluate a strategy for moving to Azure: 581

Implement a migration or upgrade strategy for moving to Azure: 582
Implement a Secure Environment 584
Implement security for data at rest: 584
Implement security for data in transit: 585
Implement compliance controls for sensitive data: 585
Monitor and Optimize Operational Resources 586
Implement performance-related maintenance tasks: 586
Identify performance-related issues: 587
Configure resources for optimal performance: 588
Configure a user database for optimal performance: 588
Optimize Query Performance 589
Evaluate performance improvements: 589
Review the database table and index design: 590
Perform Automation of Tasks 591
Evaluate and implement an alert and notification strategy: 591
Manage and automate tasks in Azure: 592
Plan and Implement a High Availability and Disaster Recovery (HADR) Environment 593
Test a HADR strategy by using platform, OS and database tools: 594
Perform backup and restore a database by using database tools: 594
Configure DR by using platform and database tools: 595
Configure HA using platform, OS and database tools: 595
Perform Administration by Using T-SQL 595
Monitor database configuration by using T-SQL: 596
Perform backup and restore a database by using T-SQL: 596
Manage authentication by using T-SQL: 597
Manage authorization by using T-SQL: 597

CHAPTER 15 Q&A **598**

WHAT IS THE NEXT STEP 647

About the Authors

Prashanth Jayaram is a Product Design and Automation Expert in database technology with 15 years of rich, extensive experience designing database solutions. He is a Microsoft Certified Professional with a Masters in Computers. He currently focuses on Azure SQL, Automation, SQL Server, MongoDB and MySQL.

His technical specialization has been in Azure SQL administration, designing and Implementing high availability solution, cross-platform database migrations, but the breadth of his expertise has allowed him to cover a plethora of topics in his writing, including SQL Server, PowerShell, Azure SQL, Azure Cosmos DB, Python, database replication, DevOps, and more.

His writing includes multi-part stairways on database backup, restore and entire series on introducing SQL for beginners. And published book including **PowerShell 6.0 Linux Administration Cookbook** and **The SQL Workshop**

R**ajendra Gupta** is a database consultant with 13 years of rich and extensive experience in database technologies. . He is the author of hundreds of authoritative articles(450+) on SQL Server, Azure, MySQL, Linux, Power BI, Performance tuning, AWS/Amazon RDS, Git, and related technologies that have been viewed by over 10m readers to date. He is Microsoft Certified Trainer, MCSA, and AWS Solution Architect – Associate. He writes technical articles for SQLSHACK, MSSQLTIPS, QUEST, DZONE popular blogs.

He is the creator of one of the most significant free online collections of articles on a single topic, with his 50-part series on SQL Server Always On Availability Groups. Based on his contribution to the SQL Server community, he has been recognized with various awards, including the prestigious “Best author of the year" continuously two years in a row 2019 and 2020 at the leading technical website SQLShack. Rajendra has also grabbed MSSQLTips – Champion award for his contribution.

Ahmad Yaseen is a Big Data engineer. As a full-stack technologist, he has knowledge and experience across a broad and deep array of subjects, demonstrated by extensive certifications and a large body of technical articles, stairways, and eBooks.

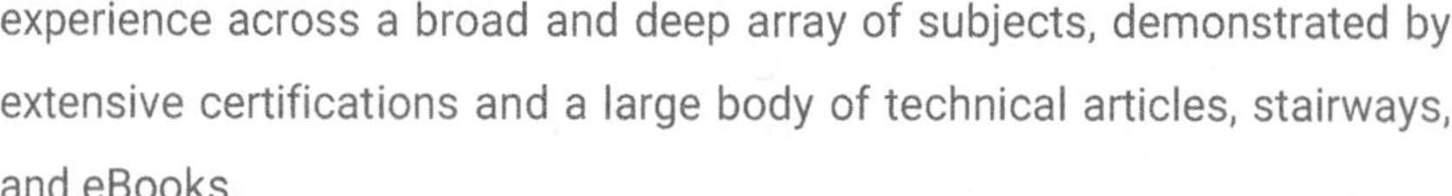

His authoritative writings have included many deep-dive topics for database administration like auditing, transaction logs and execution plans, and articles on client technologies and database development tools like Azure Data Studio. His recent focus has been Azure. Such work has received both industry and community recognition, including being awarded "Author of the year" two years in a row at SQL Shack, the leading technical journal for SQL Server database professionals.

His bona fides include Microsoft Certified Solution Expert in Data Management and Analytics, Microsoft Certified Solution Associate in SQL Database Administration and Development, Azure Data Engineer Associate, Azure AI engineer Associate, Azure Database Administrator Associate, Azure Data Analyst Associate, Azure Developer Associate, Azure Administrator Associate, Microsoft Certified Educator and Microsoft Certified Trainer.

Target Audience

Administering Relational Databases on Microsoft Azure takes readers through a complete tour of understanding of fundamental Azure concepts, Azure SQL administration, Azure Management tools and techniques. This book will give an edge over to clear DP 300 exam. Increasingly, we continue to be flooded with information about the importance of the cloud. Cloud computing is everywhere, but not everyone knows exactly what it is and where to get started.

1	This book audience is database professionals managing databases and interested in learning about administering the cloud data-platform technologies on Microsoft Azure.
2	This book is for those who are planning to become an Azure Database Administrator to manage the database infrastructure on the Azure relational data platform.

We try to focus more on Azure SQL platform and give you the foundational understanding of what the cloud is and tell you how some of these cloud technologies can work for you, and direct you to improve your knowledge and get certified using hassle-free learning. If you find it is for you, you will pick up useful tricks and tips for making a move to the cloud as seamless as possible.

1	Azure database administrator exam serves as an ideal ThinkPad for furthering your understanding of database cloud computing solutions on Microsoft Azure. With this book, you can build your cloud expertise and gain technical competency to prepare for the Exam DP-300.
2	This book provides the reader with advanced Azure database management knowledge for Azure SQL Database, SQL on Azure VM, SQL Server, PostgreSQL, and MySQL. It delivers a solid understanding of Cloud infrastructure with detailed expertise in implementing Azure cloud database solutions.
3	This book aims to give a different dimension to face the **DP 300: Administering-relational-databases-on-Microsoft-Azure**. If you have been looking to move from On-Premise DBA to Cloud DBA, this book definitely helps you with all the required information. This book is an attempt to give enough information with detailed information on the Cloud infrastructure.

This book covers the various areas of Administering databases on the Azure platform.

In the end, you get to see many best practices based scenarios associated with cloud operations, useful links to Microsoft documentation, exam format and guide.

How to use this book to study for the exam

The design of any certification exams is to validate your product knowledge. This book is an effort to prepare your readiness to take an exam. We organize this book to help you check your understanding of the skills tested by the exam. This book is a comprehensive guide and advice using this combination with the study materials. It helps you refresh your skills in specific areas; to give quick learning tips and tricks that you need to perform on-job-duties efficiently.

Microsoft Official Practice Tests are available for many exams at **https://aka.ms/practicetests**.

The content is curated based on our experience and publicly available information. This book intends to cover the major topics on the exam, but it does not cover every exam question. You should treat this book as a supplement to your on-job-duty experience and other study materials.

You can also find free online courses and live events from Microsoft Virtual Academy at https://www.microsoftvirtualacademy.com.

Organization of this book

We organized the book by the "Skills measured" list published for the exam. Each chapter in this book is an effort to curate the content more clearly and concisely. In addition, the book in-houses several use-case scenarios, our real-time experience, tips-and-tricks to manage the cloud databases more efficiently.

The book outline will give you the concepts, workflow or architectural diagram, real-time scenarios, and each chapter concluded by leading a thorough summary.

To access the code from Git Hub repository, refer to the link **https://github.com/AzureDP300/AzureDP300**

This book refers to few architectural diagrams from Microsoft official documentation site (**https://docs.microsoft.com/en-in/**).

It includes 20 Lab section and 150+ Q&A to assess your readiness for the DP 300 exam.

Acknowledgements

Rajendra Gupta:

First and foremost, I am incredibly thankful to God for blessing me and giving me strength, energy and patience, success in my life, and reaching this ambition.

I am forever grateful to my Parents (Mr Shyam Sunder Gupta and Mrs Krishna Gupta) to give me the support, confidence, and untiringly supported in my life and motivate me to explore a new direction in my life. I also appreciate the support of my in-laws Mr Heera Lal Agarwal, Mrs Prem lata Agarwal.

I am always grateful to my Wife, Dr Kusum Agarwal, for her love, understanding, tremendous moral support and help extended to me all the time. This achievement of my life would not be possible without the support and cooperation throughout this journey. I'm so blessed to have you. Thank you for your love, support, care, and every little effort you are doing for me is simply amazing. A special thanks to my sweet and charming Daughter (Akshita Gupta) for her capturing me while I spend extended hours in front of the screen. My daughter is most excited about the launch of my book.

I want to express my special appreciation and thanks to my colleagues Prashant Jayaram and Ahmad Yaseen for an outstanding effort in writing this book.

A special thanks to Stephen Norrod(Sr Mgr - Database Eng and Ops), Chetna Mhatre(Dir - DB Eng & Ops),Ramiro Zavala(MD - Platform & End User Eng), Brian Lockwood, Jeremy Kadlec,, SQLShack, MSSQLTips, United and Quest team.

Prashanth Jayaram

Jumping out of the comfort zone is never easy. I took up the challenge as a chance. Today, with "Administering Relational Databases on Microsoft SQL" book brings the feeling of gratitude and contentment that makes everything worthwhile.

First, I want to dedicate this book to all the teachers. A special thanks to my inspirational teachers, Victor.D'Souza, Late. Chinappa, Pushpalatha.S.Sukatankar, and Sudhindra P. Ananth,

Huge respect for my role model, my dad, R Jayaram. Thank you dad for everything!!

Second, I want to thank my love, my wife, Ambika S.G, who has stood by me through all my works. She gave me support and help and discussed several design ideas. She also supported the family during much of my unstoppable work. Believe me, it was never easy. Along with her, I want to acknowledge my 5-year-old twin angles, Prarvitha and Prarthana, my cheer girls. They had no idea, but they knew that dad is an author and expecting a comic book for them.

Third, my heartfelt gratitude to my parents R Jayaram and Indira M—my strength, for always being steadfast and supportive. My siblings Balu Jayaram and Gopinath J, my energizer and firm believer in my strength. My in-laws, Padmavathi K.L, for her immensity and selflessness and Govindappa A.V, and family from my side and my wife's side have all been wonderful.

Thanks to my friends, colleagues and the entire team of SQLShack. Special thanks to Brian Lockwood. He gave us the platform to perform—great mentor, fantastic human being!

Ahmad Yaseen

First and foremost, I would like to thank God. You gave me the power to believe in my passion and pursue my dreams. I could never have done this without the faith I have in you.

Writing a book is more challenging than I thought and more rewarding than I could have ever imagined. None of this would have been possible without the hard work and teamwork performed by Prashanth and Rajendra.

To my father, Mr.Zuhair Yaseen and my mother, Mrs.Tamam Adas: I am speechless! I can barely find the words to express all the wisdom, love and support you have given me, and keep saying, "I'm always proud of you".

To my wife, Mrs. Lamis: What can I say? I am so thankful that I have you in my corner pushing me when I am ready to give up. All the good that comes from this book I look forward to sharing with you! You are my first supporter and friend! Thanks for not just believing, but knowing that I could do this! I Love You Always & Forever!

I cannot forget who I started my writing journey with, Mr.Brian Lockwood and the whole MSSQLTips and SQLShack team!

Special thanks to my kids: Kenan, Kinda and Karen, my brothers, sisters, friends, who are always in my back... supporting and encouraging me. I Love You All!

Learning Objective

This book unlocks new learning opportunities for developers, administrators, cloud aspirants—help them discover SQL on Azure.

This book covers many answers to your questions in cloud infrastructure.

1. Why do we have to shift from traditional DBA to Cloud DBA?
2. How can an organization get started their journey into the cloud?
3. What are the best methodologies and techniques available for cloud adoption?
4. How to migrate from on-premise to cloud?
5. How to optimize the databases?
6. How to implement Automation?

This book provides the platform for learning the advanced Azure SQL database management concepts, delivering a solid understanding of cloud infrastructure and available tools, and explaining how to implement cloud database solutions. Upon completion of the book, readers will be able to:

- Understand Azure fundamentals and concepts
- Design cloud infrastructure solutions with a focus on databases in mind
- Design your environment with the right services models—DTU, VCore, Serverless Computing, SQL on Azure VM, etc.
- Learn to administer and manage Azure SQL with the best practices in mind
- Implement Azure PowerShell and Azure CLI solutions to manage large infrastructures through Azure Automation, ARM templates, and more...
- Efficient and seamless handling of Azure components
- Design High availability and disaster recovery methodologies
- Handle advanced diagnostics to perform troubleshooting performance issues
- Understand advanced security in Azure SQL
- Learn analytics integration using Log Analytics and SQL Analytics
- Perform database-related integration using Azure Logic Apps

- Deep dive into administering relational database on Azure Cloud
- Explore the key concepts that you should consider when making a move to Azure SQL
- Recognize the essentials to become a Cloud DBA

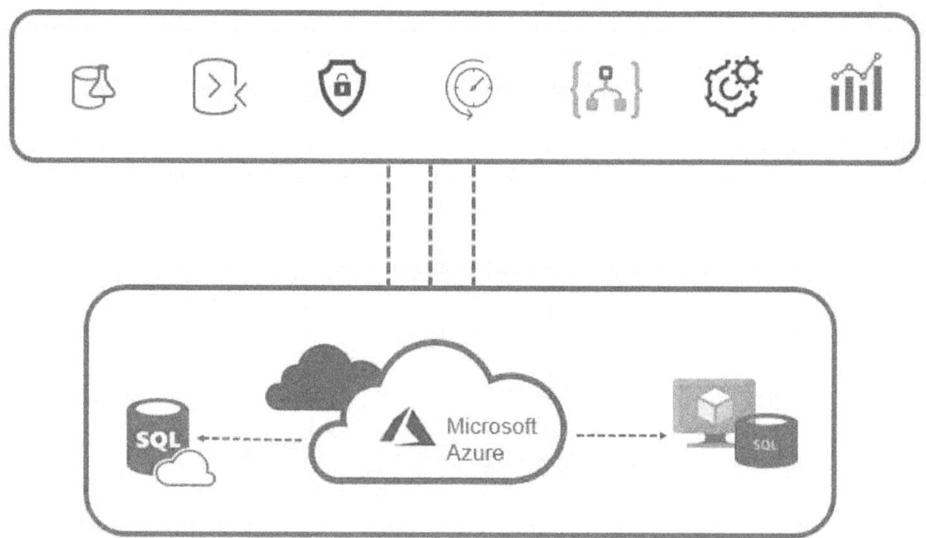

By the end of this book, you will learn the Azure SQL concepts and gain the required skill to perform the Azure SQL administration. The practice tests and tips help you pass the Exam DP-300: Administering Relational Databases on Microsoft Azure.

Why become Microsoft Certified

The Information technology field is not an easy one. You need to keep tracking all new technologies in order to reserve your seat in this market.

It is essential to know about the certification and become an expert. On the other hand, as an expert in your field, becoming a Microsoft Certified associate helps you verify your skills and makes it easier and faster for you to be noticed and recognized globally. In addition, it helps in unlocking new opportunities for you.

If you graduated recently and started your working journey, becoming a Microsoft certified associate helps you draw your career path, showing that you are growing faster and opening better opportunities for you.

If you like your current job and consider it as your dream job, being a Microsoft certified associate helps you get promotions and move in your career path faster.

The first step in specifying your certification plan is choosing the path that meets your current job role or the role you plan to achieve. You will see in the Microsoft Certifications site: https://docs.microsoft.com/en-us/learn/certifications/, that the certificates are categorized based on the job roles, as shown below:

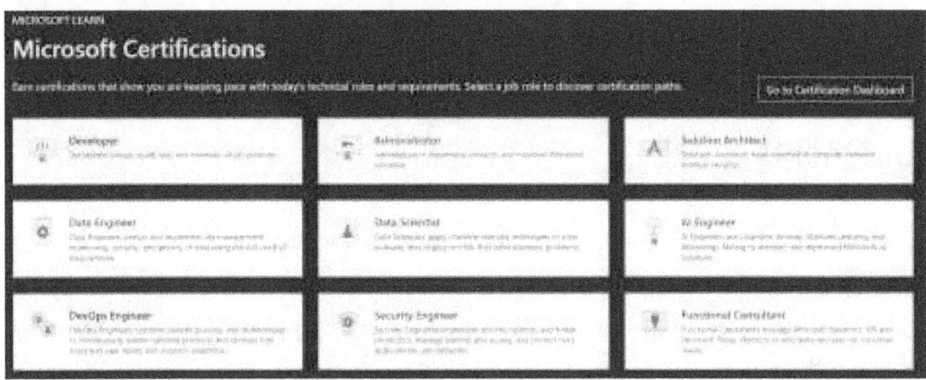

Clicking on your job role, you will see the list of required exams for that role's certifications. Under each certification path, you will find the Fundamentals certifications recommended for beginners in that technology. The Associate certifications require you to have a minimum of two years of practical experience in the certificate technology. The Expert certifications require you to have up to five years of in-depth practical experience in that technology.

Before you plan to prepare for a specific certification exam, visit the Microsoft certifications site and check the latest exam for the certificate you are planning to gain. Also, make sure that this certificate is not retired. For a complete list of all retired certificates, check this site: **https://www.microsoft.com/en-us/learning/retired-certifications.aspx**.

Hardware and software requirements

In general, the configuration is required as a minimum requirement to work with this book. Below is an overview of the minimum system requirements:

Hardware requirements

For the optimal learning experience, we recommend the following hardware configuration:

- Windows 10 or Linux system
- Processor: A minimum of Pentium 4 1.8 GHz or higher
- Memory: 4 GB RAM
- Hard disk: 20 GB free space
- An active internet connection

Software requirements

We also recommend that you have the following software configuration in advance

- **Azure subscription**:
    - Use your Azure subscription or sign in for a free Azure account.

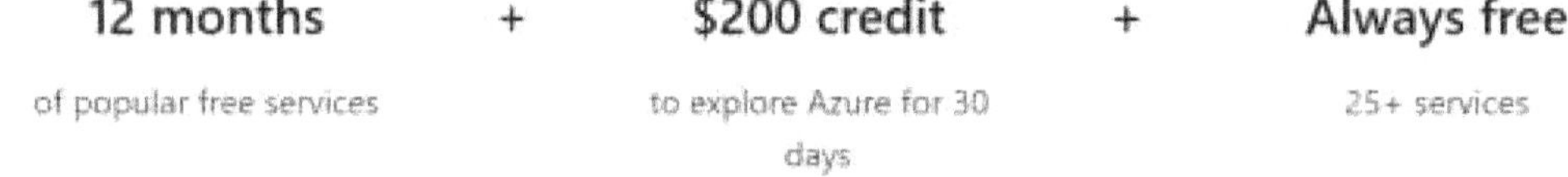

Reference URL: https://azure.microsoft.com/en-in/free/

- **The latest version of SQL Server Management Studio**:

https://docs.microsoft.com/sql/ssms/download-sql-server-management-studio-ssms?view=sql-server-ver15

- **Azure Data Studio:**

https://docs.microsoft.com/sql/azure-data-studio/_download-azure-data-studio?view=sql-server-ver15

- **Azure PowerShell module**:

https://docs.microsoft.com/en-us/powershell/azure/new-azureps-module-az?view=azps-5.5.0&viewFallbackFrom=azps-5.2.0

- **Install Azure CLI**

https://docs.microsoft.com/en-us/cli/azure/install-azure-cli

- **Azure Cloud Shell :**

You can use Azure PowerShell and Azure CLI using Cloud Shell.

  - Direct Link: https://shell.azure.com
  - Using Azure portal:

- **Visual Studio Code:**

https://code.visualstudio.com/

- **Visual Studio Code Azure extensions:**

https://code.visualstudio.com/docs/azure/extensions

- Power BI Desktop (optional):

https://www.microsoft.com/en-us/download/details.aspx?id=58494

Chapter 1 Azure Fundamentals and Concepts

In the last decade, Cloud has propelled every sector to its breath-and-depth because of several of its qualities such as flexibility, dynamism, remoting capabilities, services, cost, SLA's, ease of integration, faster migration, etc.

Synergy Research Group's detailed review of enterprise IT spending over the last ten years shows that annual spending on cloud infrastructure services has gone from virtually zero to almost $100 billion.

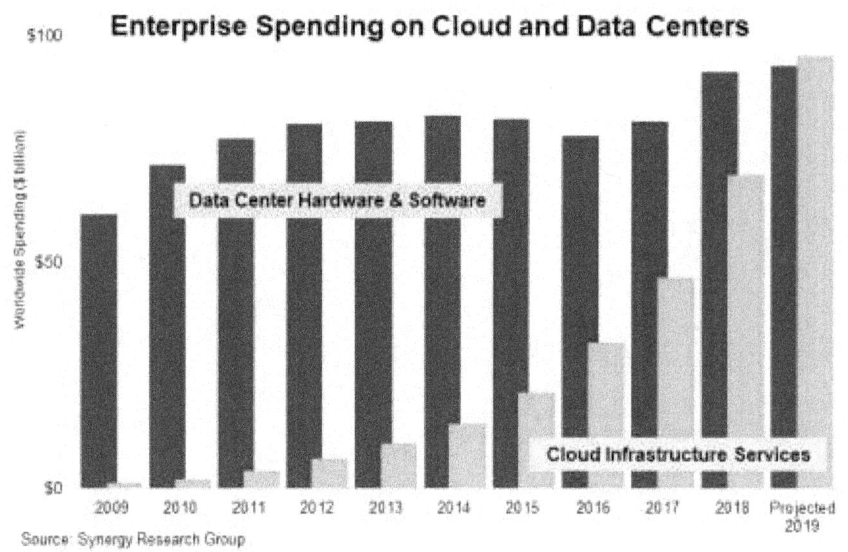

The emphasis on a Cloud DBA is prevalent nowadays. In addition, the importance of cloud certification has more emphasis in today's world and this has driven us to propose this book.

This book is ideal for IT professionals who have some experience with SQL Server or Database but are looking for a rich hands-on resource with guidance to explore each of the Azure SQL administrator concepts and the solutions the cloud provider offers.

"Azure SQL Database named among the top 3 databases of 2020 according to DB-Engines".

Azure SQL Database is primarily for SQL DBAs who are dipping their feet into the world of Cloud since Cloud services are becoming the de-facto platform for most of the agile development and implementation. Numerous companies worldwide are now drifting to cloud solutions, and Microsoft Azure is one of the prominent ones. The book is primarily designed for Cloud DBAs (with ample knowledge of SQL server) who are new to Azure and want to have a solid start and get an in-depth glimpse on advanced topics that will help them to solve day to day issues plus effectively support the Azure databases.

The emphasis on a Cloud DBA is very popular nowadays. In addition, the importance of cloud certification has more emphasis in today's world and that has driven us to propose this book.

In the last decade, Cloud has propelled every sector to its breath-and-depth because of several of its qualities such as flexibility, dynamism, remoting capabilities, services, cost, SLA's, ease of integration, faster migration, etc.

"The global public cloud infrastructure market will grow 35 percent to $120 billion in 2021, as the cloud continues to "take center stage" in the recovery from the pandemic, according to Forrester Research."

There is a saying, "It's never too late....." Why wait? Let us get started...

It is never too late to turn the corner from "On-premise DBA" to "Cloud DBA specialist". In most technical discussions, we see a vast gap in cloud adoption and the reality of absorption. There is always a need to learn the Next-Gen technology. In this book, you explore the importance of understanding and managing cloud databases and the skills, you must build around the cloud to face the cloud DBA certification. In addition, along the way, you will pick up great interesting insights, real-time scenarios and fundamentals, concepts of cloud, cloud management tools, test cases, and several practice solutions.

Cloud Computing Concepts

Cloud Computing is the process of delivering different types of computing services, such as storage services, networking services, database platform services, infrastructure services, and other analytics and machine learning services. These services are hosted in data centers managed by the cloud service provider, such as Microsoft Azure, Amazon Web Services or Google Cloud Platform, and accessed by the users over the internet.

Cloud computing provides you with the ability to focus on designing and implementing your systems instead of delaying the project's release while waiting for the execution environment installation or stop it entirely due to resource limitation. It gives flexibility in the resources scaling process when the business demands change, and the security and efficiency of the computing resources that are upgraded to the latest versions

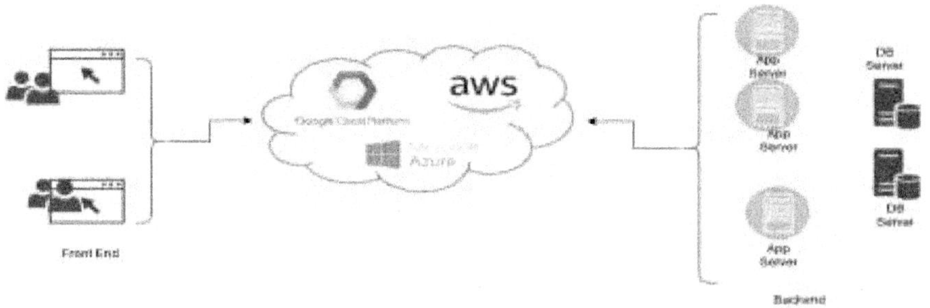

Cloud computing understands each business's different requirements and provides us with the number of services that help meet these requirements. The provided services include the Compute services, such as the Virtual Machines and the Web Applications, the Storage services, such as tables, files, queues and databases, Networking services, such as Virtual Networks, Express Routes and Azure Firewalls, Analytical and Machine Learning services, such as Power BI service and Cognitive services.

Cloud computing also requires a look from the financial side. It involves the following:

- The costs of buying the hardware and software requirements
- Maintain its reliability and availability requirements
- Human resources for installing and managing the environment
- Datacenter setup and maintenance costs

Instead, the cloud computing billing model is built on the fact that you will pay only for the cloud services you use, lowering your project's overall operating cost!

Cloud Computing Models

Cloud computing provides us with three types of models that can be used to deploy cloud services. It includes deploying the resources on a Public Cloud, Private Cloud, or Hybrid Cloud.

Public Cloud	**Private Cloud (internal or corporate cloud)**
Services are owned and operated by a third-party service provider such as Microsoft Azure, Amazon Web Services.	It provides a dedicated infrastructure to a single organization.
It supports connectivity over the internet.	It supports connectivity over the internet, fiber and private network.
The public Cloud is suitable for less confidential data.	It offers higher security, therefore suitable for secure, confidential data such as Financial, PII data.
It supports the Pay-as-you-Go model. Therefore, you get charged for resource usage.	It has a higher cost because the implementation, ownership and maintenance responsibility is with the organization.
Multi-Tenant implementation	Single-Tenant implementation
Lesser flexibility and control over the Infrastructure	It gives greater flexibility and control over the infrastructure.
Very high scalability	Limited scalability
Less reliability compared to private Cloud	Very high reliability

Hybrid Cloud: Hybrid cloud computing is a combination of both public and private cloud computing models. It allows the different applications and their related data to move between the public and private environments and run in the proper location, providing more hosting flexibility and security.

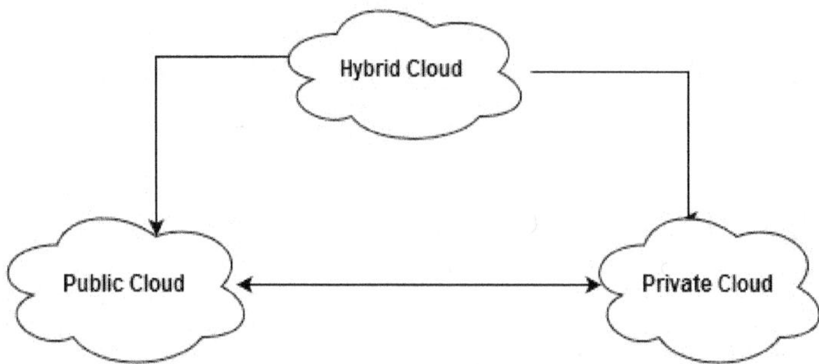
• Combination of both Public and Private cloud
• Greater flexibility
• Manageable security
• Helps maintain tighter control over sensitive data and processes
Hybrid Cloud
Public Cloud
Private Cloud

With Hybrid cloud computing, you can keep the sensitive customer or financial data in an on-premises private cloud with full control of these resources and the ability to apply any needed security or compliance requirements. In contrast, the less sensitive data will be stored in a public cloud, taking advantage of all the public cloud benefits.

On the other hand, with all the advantages that we can gain from the Hybrid cloud model, the overhead cost of buying and managing your resources and maintaining the movement between two different cloud models could be a clear drawback.

Before making the decision to use a specific cloud-computing model, we should understand the organization requirements, budget and the resources participate in the project. After that and based on the pros and cons for each model, we can specify the appropriate model that helps us in achieving these requirements with the best performance and the lowest operating cost.

Cloud Computing Services Types

Cloud computing services fall into one of the main three services categories based on the cloud provider's management responsibilities and users. The cloud services categories are Infrastructure as a Service (IaaS), Platform as a Service (PaaS) and Software as a Service (SaaS). You should note that the management responsibilities will always be shared between the cloud service provider and the users in these cloud services categories, but what the user and the cloud provider manage depend on the service category you use.

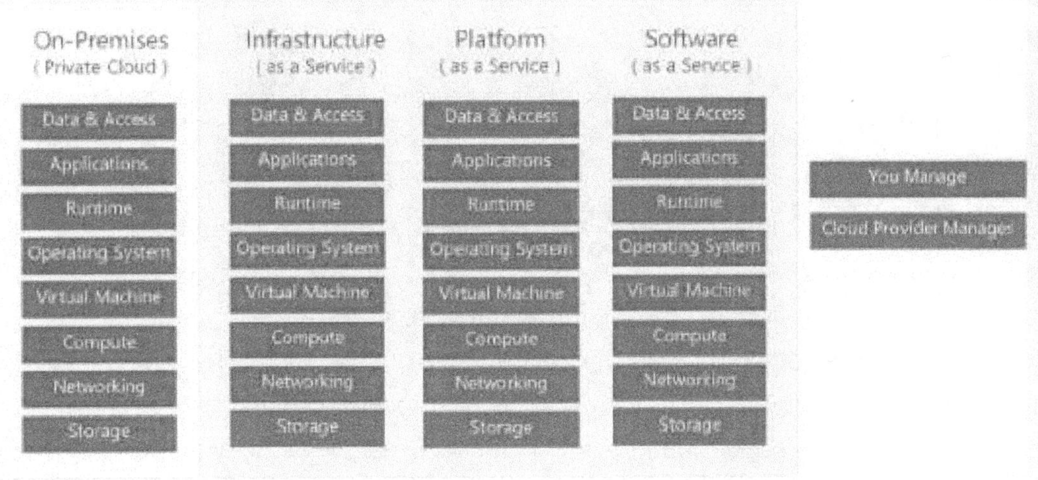

Infrastructure as a Service (IaaS)

Infrastructure as a Service (IaaS) is a cloud computing service, in which you provision infrastructure services, such as a virtual machine with the storage and network components and manage it over the internet, with the ability to scale it up and down based on the business requirement changing. You will pay only for what you use.

With Infrastructure as a Service (IaaS), you will avoid the need to buy and manage the servers in the organization datacenter and focus on managing the operating system that meets your project requirements and the applications deployed in these servers. No need to wait for buying additional hardware when you plan to scale up to meet the workload changes, wherein in a few minutes, you will be able to jump to the next tier and enjoy adding the extra resources. It can scale down resources when the workload goes back to normal. You cannot do that for on-premises hardware because it is to the server forever and cannot be detached easily.

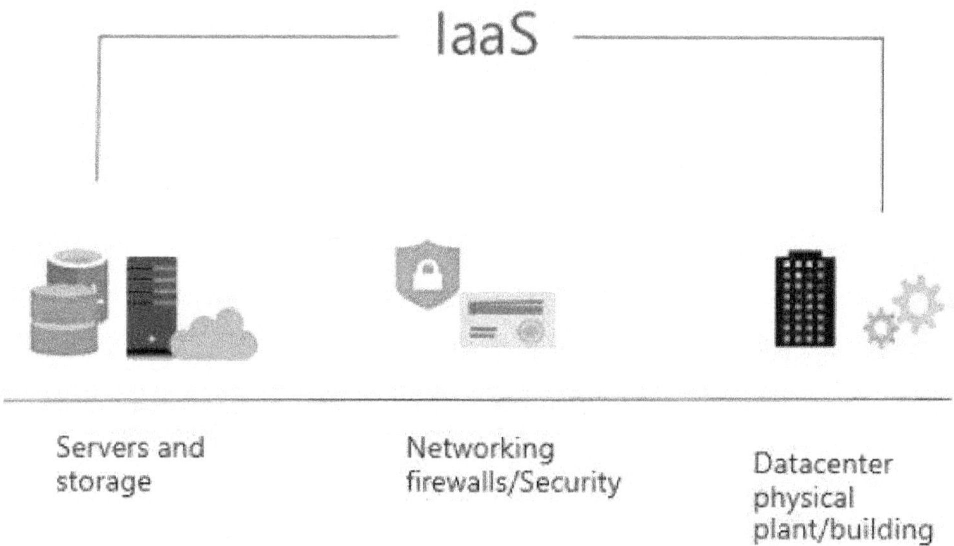

Designing and implementing high availability and disaster recovery solutions to maintain your system continuity is cheaper now with the different built-in choices provided by the IaaS cloud services. You are not required to upgrade or troubleshoot the hardware issues, as the cloud services provider will be responsible for making sure that the provided infrastructure is functioning well. With the shared responsibilities concept discussed earlier, the cloud users will be responsible for configuring and maintaining the availability and the functionality of the operating system and all applications installed in that infrastructure.

Platform as a Service (PaaS)

Platform as a Service (PaaS) is the cloud computing services that provide a complete environment for developing, testing, deploying, and managing software applications in the Cloud. Platform as a Service helps deliver the web applications or mobile applications quickly, without worrying about buying, setting up, managing, or maintaining the underlying infrastructure, such as the Hardware, the Operating System or the system and hardware updates.

Platform as a Service (PaaS) provides all resources required for the complete software application lifecycle, where you will be able to access it and manage it via a secure internet connection. You pay only for the resources that you use, avoiding the overhead of buying and managing the infrastructure components, the required software, and licenses.

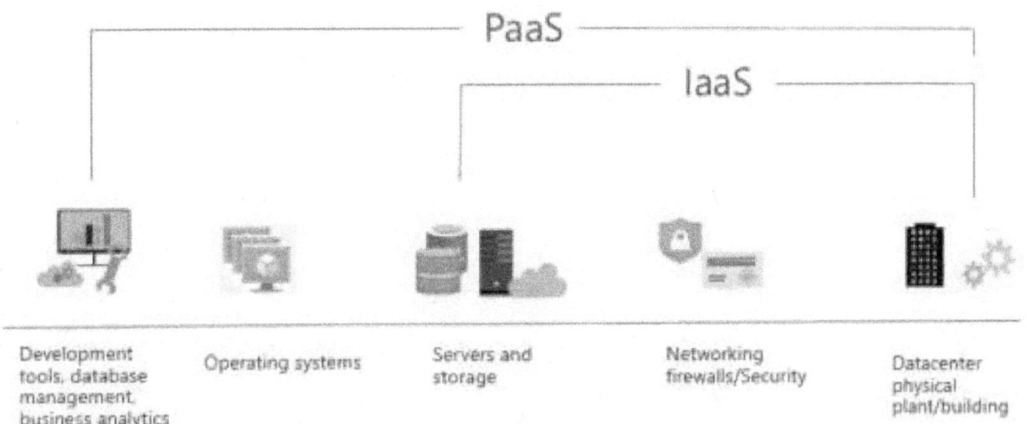

With Platform as a Service, you are leaving the infrastructure and operating system management to the cloud services provider, reducing the time required to develop and deploy a new application in multiple platforms within all supported regions. Visiting the shared responsibilities concept again, with Platform as a Service, you will be responsible for developing, deploying, and managing your software application.

The following image depicts Cloud computing growth predictions for cloud computing revenues to 2021 from 451 Research.

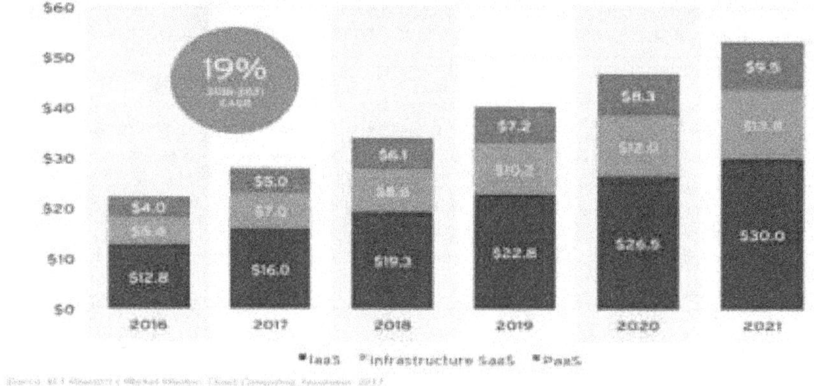

Serverless compute

It is a specific type of Platform-as-a-Service cloud computing model that allows developers to build software applications quickly. You do not require considering the infrastructure as a backbone of your application. The cloud service provider will be responsible for provisioning, managing, and maintaining the infrastructure needed to run the deployed code.

The Serverless model's infrastructure scaling is performed automatically and driven by the workload or when a specific event is fired. With the approach, the developers will focus on the business logic and deliver the application faster instead of wasting time in the infrastructure setup.

Software as a Service (SaaS)

Software as a Service (SaaS) is the cloud computing services that deliver a complete cloud-based software application, such as Office 365, to the users over a secure internet connection from their tablets, mobiles, personal computers, and pay only for what you use.

Software-as-a-Service is centrally hosted, managed and maintained by the cloud services providers, who are also responsible for the underlying infrastructure provisioning and management. It is suitable for applications with one version that can serve all customers. Before going with Platform as a Service, ensure that the PaaS software limitations are acceptable for your workload!

The decision of using IaaS, PaaS or SaaS in your organization depends

- Workload requirements
- Service Control level

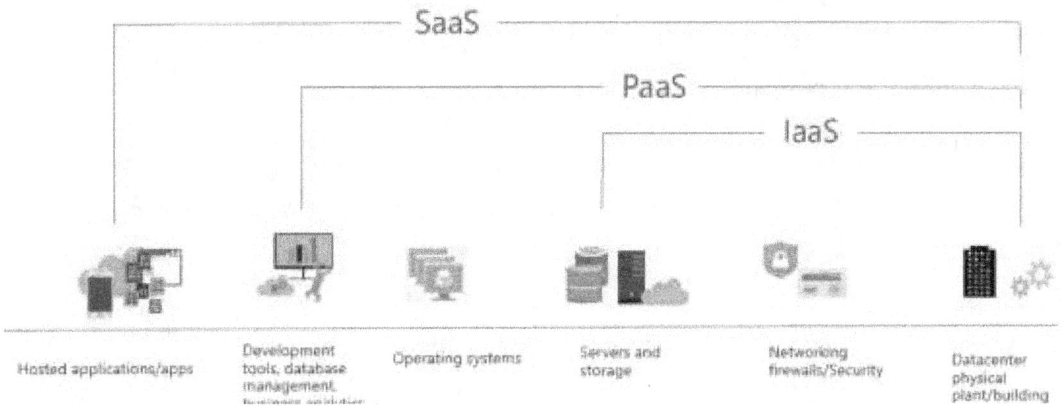

Azure architectural components

Before we dig deeper into the different IaaS, PaaS, and SaaS services provided by Microsoft Azure, it is essential to understand where these services are hosted and how the services hosting is organized.

- **Region**: Basically, Microsoft Azure consists of data centers located in different locations around the world. A group of nearby data centers organized and networked together to provide services for the users with the lowest possible latency and shape a geographical region is called an **Azure Region**.

Whenever you plan to create an Azure service, you will be asked to specify the region from the list of regions supporting the selected service, such as West Europe, Japan West, Australia East, or West US, where you want to deploy it. Azure will automatically assign resources for that service within the selected region and ensure its workload balance.

Note: Azure does not ask for a region for the Azure Active Directory, Microsoft Azure Traffic Manager, or Azure DNS.

Consolidating the data centers into regions provides us with flexibility and scalability to deploy our services in the closest geographical location to the service users, allowing them to access and use that service faster and more efficiently.

Geography: Microsoft Azure groups two or more regions that preserves the data residency and comply together in a Geography structure. It helps organizations with specific data compliance or residency requirements to host their data in the same boundary. The Microsoft Azure geographies include the Americas, Africa, Europe, the Middle East, and the Asia Pacific.

- **Paired region**: At the same geography, each region, except for Brazil South, will be **paired** with another region, with at least 300 miles distance between these two regions. In this way, it will replicate the resources between the regions and increase the availability, redundancy of these regions' services by performing a service failover from one region to another in case of an outage due to a natural disaster. It also helps minimize the downtime required for the planned maintenance by performing the maintenance sequentially on the first region and directing the workload to the second replica. Once finished, Microsoft Azure will perform the same maintenance on the second replica and direct the updated region's workload.
- **Availability Sets**: To maintain the application availability and make sure that the services remain online during the planned maintenances or in case of any failure, Microsoft Azure introduced the **Availability Sets** concept, that made up of:
    - The **Update Domains (UD)**, in which the data center is divided logically into domains. The performance and security updates are applied to the hosts sequentially to these domains, ensuring that the data center will not be completely unavailable during the update process.
    - The **Fault Domains (FD)**: The workload is physically distributed across different power, cooling and network hardware that supports the servers' data center racks. It ensures that only the failing rack will be unavailable during the outage, without affecting the overall data center, in case of any hardware failure.

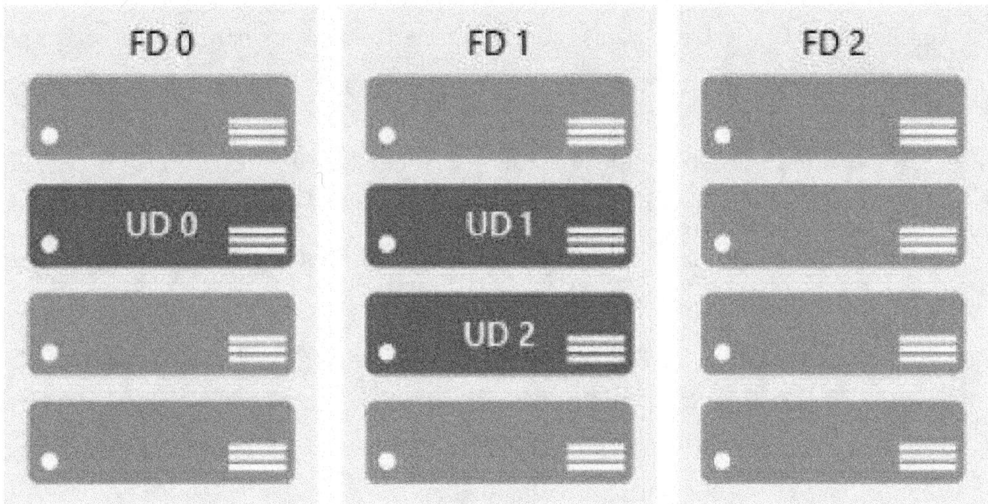

- **Availability Zones**: The Azure region is physically divided into separate data-centers. To increase the same region's availability, a minimum of three data centers connected via high-speed and private fiber-optic connections, with each data center having its power, cooling, and networking resources. These isolated data centers are called **Availability Zones**. If one of these availability zones goes down, the other availability zones will handle the workload, ensuring that the service will stay available.

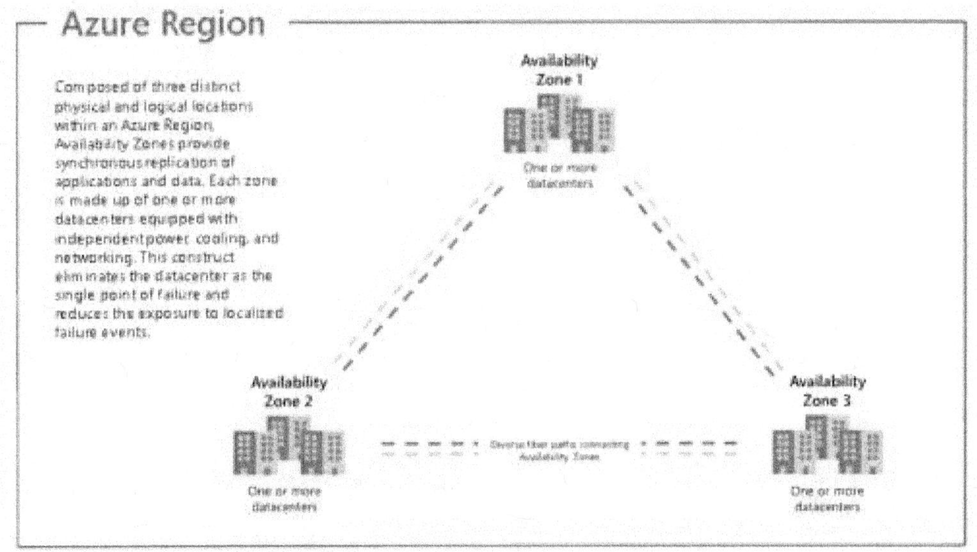

Availability zones are supported in specific regions and for specific Azure services. The Azure services that support the availability zones can be Zonal services, which require you to pin that service to a particular zone or Zone-redundant services replicated automatically to other zones.

- **Resource Group**: To make it easier to manage the different resources, Microsoft Azure defines the **Resource Group** as a management unit for your Azure resources. You can imagine it as a container, under which you can aggregate the different resources based on a specific aggregation criterion to serve your business, such as aggregating the resources based on the resource's lifecycle. In this way, you will make it easier to manage the resources billing, monitoring, altering, access control, policies and quota at the resource group level, which will be applied to all resources under that resource group, instead of using it to the individual resources.

Azure Compute Service

Azure compute service is the service that is used to run the cloud-based applications in Azure. It provides all computing resources, such as the storage disks, the memory, the processors, the networking and the operating system, that are required to run your software application in Azure, with the ability to provision or scale these resources with few clicks!

Azure Virtual Machine is an example of Microsoft Azure computing services. It allows us to create a virtual machine in Azure, categorized under the Infrastructure as a Service (IaaS) services category. As discussed earlier, it provides us with full control over the Operating system and all applications deployed on that virtual machine, eliminating the overhead of managing and maintaining the machine's hardware resources.

It includes Azure App services as a PaaS solution to quickly build, deploy, and scale different applications running on multiple platforms. The Azure Function allows you to provide your code logic and run it to respond to a specific event or timer without worrying about the underlying platform or infrastructure where this code will be running.

Azure Network Services

Microsoft Azure provides us with many network services that help us connect and manage the different resources hosted in Azure appropriately and securely, helping to achieve the organization's networking and security requirements.

For example, the **Azure Virtual Network** makes the communication between the Azure resources with each other, the Azure resources with the on-premises resources and the Azure resources the internet secure and isolated. Azure provides us with the ability to add the resources from the same region to a single virtual network, with the ability for the resources located in different virtual networks to communicate together using the virtual networks peering.

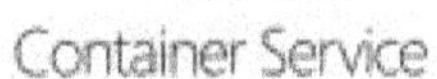

The **Azure Load Balancer** maintains your application's high availability by balancing the incoming internal requests, internet requests across the Azure services, or the outbound connections from the virtual machines within the same virtual network, handling that workload with the highest possible throughput and lowest latency.

Microsoft Azure also provides us with a particular type of load balancers that can be used to manage the traffic to the web applications called the Azure Application Gateway. This load balancer helps us route the incoming traffic based on the IP address and the port number of both the source and destination. It also helps in protecting the web application using the Web Application Firewall of that load balancer.

The **Virtual Private Network gateway (VPN)** provides a secure connection between the Azure Virtual Network and the on-premises network by encrypting the traffic flowing between the two sites.

Azure provides us with another useful networking service that helps cache and deliver the web content, such as multimedia content, to the users in their local regions or the nearest region. Azure **Content Delivery Network (CDN)** minimizes web page startup latency and provides the best performance to the web application.

Azure Storage Services

As all applications and services hosted in Azure interact with data in different shapes, Microsoft Azure introduces the Azure Storage services that help store all types of data required by or generated from the various Azure on-premises services. Microsoft Azure provides us with several storage services such as Disks, Files, Blobs, Queues and Tables.

The **Disk storage**, such as the virtual machines and applications disks, helps store and access the data permanently in a virtual hard disk, attached to the Azure resource, and managed by Azure. Microsoft Azure allows you to choose from different performance levels and sizes of the available disk storages, such as the SSD and HDD drives.

The **Azure Blob storage** stores unstructured data, such as images, video files, audio files, documents, text files, binary data, or backup files, with massive size, that can be accessed and processed quickly from any Azure or on-premises service.

The **Azure files** allow us to set up a network file share that is highly available and accessed easily, using the SMB protocol, for both read and write operations, from anywhere using the URL of that file.

The **Azure Queue** service allows us to store and retrieve millions of messages that will be processed asynchronously by different applications. Each application has its speed in processing the provided messages.

The **Azure Table storage** is used to store and query terabytes of structured but non-relational or NoSQL data that will be accessed and processed by Azure and on-premises services, with the ability to scale that table storage based on the workload expansion demands.

With the different types of storage services provided by Microsoft Azure, which can store any structured, unstructured, and semi-structured data, Azure storage services can be easily integrated with Azure or on-premises service to keep the generated data or to process the stored data. Choosing the storage service that fits your scenario depends highly on your storage requirements and each Azure storage service capability.

Summary

In this chapter, you learn various Azure fundamental concepts such as differences in Paas, IaaS and SaaS models. You also get a high-level overview of different Azure components, services for compute, network and storage.

Chapter 2 Explore Azure Data Platform roles

Overall, DBAs and their business units are already embracing the cloud journey in a big way. In this chapter, you will learn how to change the current on-premise DBA roles and aspire to become cloud DBA. Besides, you will see how seamlessly adapt to the growing importance of cloud-based data and databases. The DBAs are free from doing mundane, repetitive, day-to-day operational tasks—it is critical to climbing up the ladder to provide more incredible ways to manage data in the Cloud.

You are not alone in the Data world. In large and complex data projects, multiple people will be involved, and each one will play a specific role starting from the design phase until you all take it to the production phase. These roles are the Data Engineer, the Database Administrator, the Data Scientist, the Artificial Intelligence Engineer, and the Data Analyst. In this chapter, we will discuss these data-related roles in detail.

Azure Data Engineer

The Azure Data Engineer is responsible for designing, implementing, management, monitoring, securing, and maintaining data-related solutions.

In any data-related solution, the Azure Data Engineer will participate with the stakeholders in designing and architecting the data related solutions, then requested to provision and configure the data platform technologies required in that project. It includes relational databases, non-relational databases, data streams, and file stores hosted in the on-premises data-centers or the Cloud.

The Azure Data Engineer is involved with the data from the starting journey. He will be responsible for acquiring, ingesting, egressing, validating, transforming and cleaning up the data from the different types of sources using several Extract, Transform and Load (ETL) services and tools based on the business requirements.

Azure Database Administrator

The Azure Database Administrator is responsible for implementing, managing, troubleshooting and operating the data related solutions using the cloud-native and hybrid data platform solutions built on Microsoft Azure data services and Microsoft SQL Server such as Azure SQL Databases, Azure SQL Managed Instance, Azure SQL Data Warehouse, Azure Database for MySQL, Azure Database for PostgreSQL, Azure Database for MariaDB and SQL Server on Azure Virtual Machines.

The Azure Database Administrator ensures that the data stored in these relational database engines are always available for the database users and the applications. Also, he is responsible to make sure that the data is secured while being held in the database files and transiting between the different parties and accessible from anywhere efficiently with no connectivity or performance blockers.

Azure Data Analyst

The Azure Data Analyst helps in maximizing the value of the organizations' data assets. He is responsible for designing and building scalable data models by cleaning and transforming the data extracted from different data sources. He extracts data in a format that can be easily analyzed using advanced analytic capabilities. The Data Analyst is responsible for providing a meaningful business value for the numbers and characters stored in the data sources through easy-to-comprehend data visualizations so that the stakeholders can make a correct business decision.

The Data Analysts work closely with the stakeholders to clarify their requirements and questions and identify the necessary data and reporting requirements.

The Azure Data Analyst works closely with the Azure Data Engineer and the Azure Database Administrator to get the required permissions to the necessary data sources and understand the different data sources capabilities and connectivity mechanisms. He also works with the business analysts by providing them with the analysis outputs to translate it into business results.

Azure Data Scientist

The Azure Data Scientist is responsible for applying the data science and the different machine learning techniques in implementing and running machine learning workloads on Azure to solve business-related problems by training, evaluating, and deploying the machine learning models.

Azure Artificial Intelligence Engineer

The Azure AI Engineer is responsible for using the Cognitive Services, the Azure Machine Learning Service, and Knowledge Mining to architect and implement different types of Microsoft AI solutions. This also involves natural language processing, computer vision, bots, agents, and speech processing solutions.

The supported Cognitive Services includes Computer Vision, Text Analytics, Bing Search, and Language Understanding (LUIS), among others. The Azure AI Engineers will implement cognitive Service APIs' prebuilt capabilities and embed this intelligence within a new or existing application or, more recently, Bots, instead of creating models from scratch.

On-premise Database Administrator

Organizations worldwide work on retooling their entire IT infrastructure, services, and strategies to embrace the Cloud. This mighty change is pushing people to shift their knowledge from "traditional" to "cloud".

Once you've got the right people on the bus, it's time to get them in the right seats, and that means defining and understanding the key differences between the roles and their responsibilities is the key objective of this lesson.

The traditional Relational Database Management System (DBMS) is a software package that enables database administrators to create, maintain, and manage databases. The administrators must possess a deep understanding of the architecture of the database and the underlying operating system. There is strong integration between logical and physical entities of databases.

How to move to Azure Database Administrator role

The careers in the cloud space are more nowadays than in other areas—it is the fact that there are more jobs available than qualified people. Cloud computing, as part of the technology industry—is growing exponentially over the years, and it has been experiencing exponential growth. A recent report by Google cited that 94% of IT managers said it is challenging to find skilled cloud engineers. And as a software cloud architect,

Do you want to start a career in the DBA cloud but don't know where to begin? Whether you are a DBA, developer, IT administrator or IT professional or student, this book is definitely for you. We try to cover the concepts that range from Azure fundamental to Azure database administration, which will build your career path and certifications that you should consider if you are interested in transitioning into the DBA cloud. This book covers concepts, use-case study and scenarios-based question and career paths details, including Azure database administrator, Azure data engineer, Azure data scientist, Azure data analyst, and Azure architect roles.

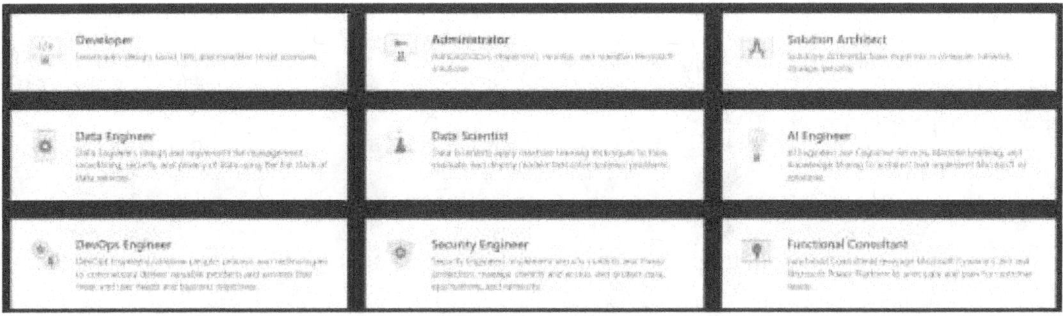

The niche cloud skill around the databases is deemed high in demand. It is exciting because it gives a virtualization platform to scale your services horizontal and vertical. The ability to scale the required hardware configuration with near-zero time helps the organization shift their trend to Cloud. With this enablement, management of most commonly faced on-premise incidents becomes seamless. The major cloud platforms—AWS, Microsoft Azure, Google, Oracle, Rackspace and Alibaba, give flexible offerings to meet all the requirements and objectives that one could expect to migrate the database into the cloud databases.

In the cloud ecosystem, the role that all the major vendors most highly value is cloud architect. Now, within cloud architect, there are different classification. Sometimes, they are addressed as solution architects, system architects, and you can even go more granular than that; database architects, security designs, machine-learning architects, so on and so forth. Besides, it depends on the size and scope of the project.

To become a database architect, you have to have all the database skills. In addition, this is one of the reasons that cloud architects are paid the most. It takes years to understand the variety of public cloud product offerings. If you are interested in becoming an architect, then this book is for you. As you begin to read and learn the skills, you will need to have a successful database career and work with the public Cloud, and we have several tips that you should keep in mind.

- Always go through **Vendor documentation**
- Explore the architectural diagrams and examples.
- Hands-on experience
- Participate in the tech forums
- Take benefits of the **free tier services.**
- Consider cost, performance optimization in mind before deploying a resource.
- Remove all resources (if not in use) to avoid recurring cost.

Migrate to the Cloud

Get an overview of cloud computing and the key concepts you should consider when moving to the Cloud. There are three types of cloud solutions: software as a service, infrastructure as a service, and platform as a service. There has been a notable trend of moving existing systems to the Cloud. It is easy to build new applications quickly using cloud services with agile methods. It will, in turn, affect the on-premises costs.

Now, shifting from the on-premise workload to Cloud needs good planning. You must understand how to set up the business for success:

Educate

Get educated about the data and list the applications that are best suited to the Cloud. Understand how best you can migrate the data and application. Moreover, figure out a way or alternate products that can be an option or solution for the system where it is not a suitable candidate for the migration.

It is essential to understand the service offerings, integration and deployment procedures before the migration. Identify the efficient cloud provider based on these constraints and then begin the plan.

Explore the cloud management and migration tools

Explore the day-to-day operations and tools needed for IT administrators to keep their cloud-based infrastructure up and running.

Start with a small chunk to understand the entire life cycle. Migrating to the Cloud requires careful preparation and planning if you want to get it done right and with as little hassle as possible, so let us explore a good road map for moving into the Cloud.

Start your analysis to define the baseline metrics

First, start your analysis, draw a baseline picture of your current infrastructure, and calculate the equivalent cost in the Cloud.

It is easy to get a reasonable general estimate of your cost savings by simply understanding the workload. The fundamental metrics such as CPU and memory footprint of your current infrastructure and current bandwidth usage, and then compare the offering with various cloud providers, such as Microsoft, Google, Oracle, and Amazon.

Build the confidence

Once you have found out the savings and internals of migration, it could lead you with the ammunition that you need to get that business shifted to Cloud.

Assess the security

Security is the key consideration. Assess the migration strategy either by considering a part of your application, typically database, must reside in-house or at a remote host. If your business has

HIPAA or PCI, or GDPR requirements—learn the impacts of moving them to the Cloud as well. It requires careful study, and you must think of undergoing data classification and other encryption techniques to meet the requirement. It is the most common scenario with every migration.

If your organization requires any HIPAA, PCI, GDPR, SOX, or SAS compliance or audits, make sure your legal and compliance teams are aware, and of course, they endorse your steps into the Cloud. You need a green light before you find a reliable way to handle security issues.

Prepare migration

Always take baby steps, aim at the small objective to ensure you are ready to handle the vast problems. We advise it to attempt a migration after you have several successes and lessons learnt under your belt. Next, do a series of test migrations to find and work out the kinks. Induce a workload to test internally to assess the performance. In some cases, it requires further investigation if it does not meet the performance expectation.

Prepare for a live cutover

A good thing to do would write a granular, systematic checklist of what you need to do for the cutover to live. Remember, prior planning prevents potential pitfalls. Always plan for database dumps and outages. You will need a snapshot of the user data at the very last second before you bring your site down to dump the database. So plan for disruptions, schedules, product availability around the days and hours that your migration will take place, and plan to have your team working in the middle of the night when the load is at its lowest.

Rollback strategy

You should also build a rollback strategy, do not assume that any part of the migration will go smoothly. Instead, ask and answer the question of what would happen if everything went wrong? It is almost a given that part of your cutover will not go as planned.

Perform continuous testing

Planning is so essential to a successful migration to the Cloud. In closing, here are some tips that every organization should consider when they create their plan for migrating to the Cloud.

Pick one application and use it as a test project for the Cloud. Migrate mission-critical applications slowly so that you do not harm those processes. Think about participation. The system is only successful if the staff use it.

Dig into all the costs associated with a cloud-based environment compared to your existing infrastructure. Remember that software-as-a-service is built on a pay-as-you-go basis. Besides, of course, you need to choose the right service provider.

Understand the TCO (Total Cost of Ownership) and ROI (Return on Investment)

In this section, we will understand the total-cost-of-ownership. In the real world, when we talk about Cloud, the first question from the business and all organizations urge getting an explanation for total-cost-of-ownership and return-on-investment, TCO, and ROI the case, it is directly proportional to the business outcome. All organizations are in the space of "Faster-time-to-market", and it is necessary to understand the importance of cloud-architects.

We need to prepare a solid business case before the migration can begin. Ultimately, we need to determine the business case to understand how technology will be applying. It is essential for you to provide leadership with baselines and key metrics, such as total-cost-of-ownership and return-on-investment, that you will see after the migration. If you estimate to say a 50% return-on-investment in the first three years after the migration into cloud computing, advise you to assess and understand the design implication.

During the cost calculation TCO, it is essential to understand the key metrics and implication that we run this thing in the first year, second, third, fourth or five years down the line.

The TCO makes up applications, databases, Cloud compute, network, security etc. It is essential to segregate the key difference between the Cloud and total-cost-of-ownership with the traditional on-premise setup. The other hidden key metrics are transitional cost or migration cost—in other words, what it takes to migrate the existing conventional systems to on-premise systems as we migrate into the Cloud.

So total cost of ownership or return on investment, we need to do the cost calculations pure TCO, the total cost of ownership.

- What will cost us to run this thing, the first year, the second year, the third year or five years down the line?
- What are the metrics as to the total cost of ownership for applications, databases, cloud instances?
- How does it differ from the total cost of ownership now, with our traditional on-premise systems, as we move into the Cloud?

We have to figure out transitional costs—what it costs to get us from the existing conventional methods on-premise into the public cloud-based system. In addition, we also need to understand the operational costs, the migration costs, the refactoring costs, security implication, and changes of governance model, performance management and operations. Ultimately, this list goes on-and-on. The other important consideration is to adopt the ability of the business to meet "Faster-time-to-market."

You need to have a clear vision to have a reason to move your application into the Cloud. Business always looks for the money that comes back over the period. It can take a year, two years, or ten years. Nevertheless, it is necessary to articulate the details that include the full program cost versus value realization. It need not be the case in all the scenarios.

Microsoft Azure provides a Total Cost of Ownership (TCO) calculator to estimate cost-saving by migrating your Azure workload.

Reference URL: https://azure.microsoft.com/en-in/pricing/tco/calculator/

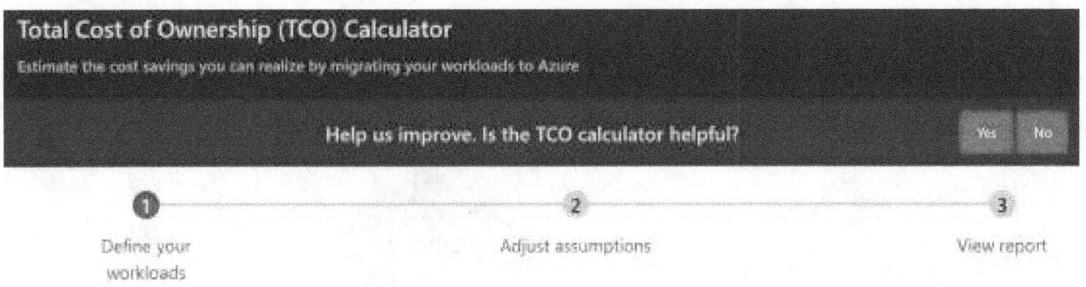

For a sample infrastructure workload, Azure TCO gives an estimated cost saving of approx. USD 1,33,32,410.

View report

Over 5 year(s) with Microsoft Azure, your estimated cost savings could be as much as US$1,33,32,410

The below figure compares the on-premise cost and Microsoft Azure cost over time.

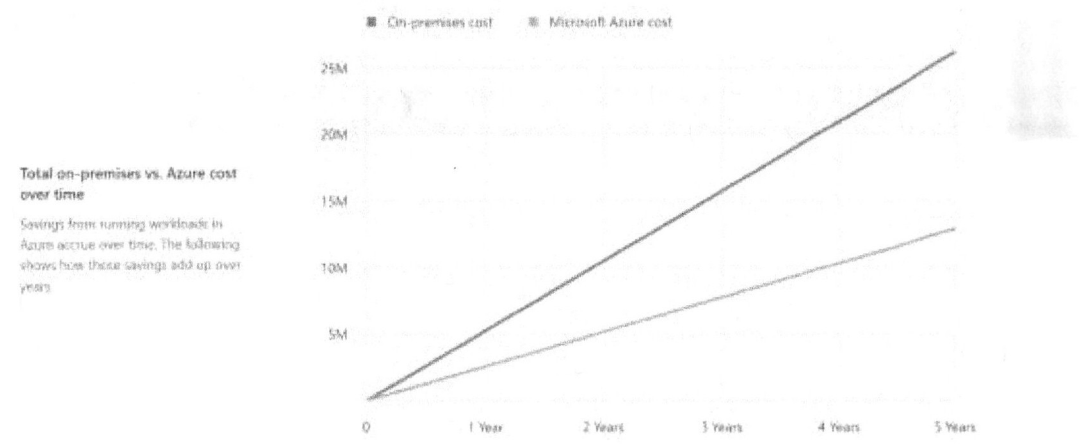

The following gives a breakdown of the total cost for on-premise and Azure infrastructure.

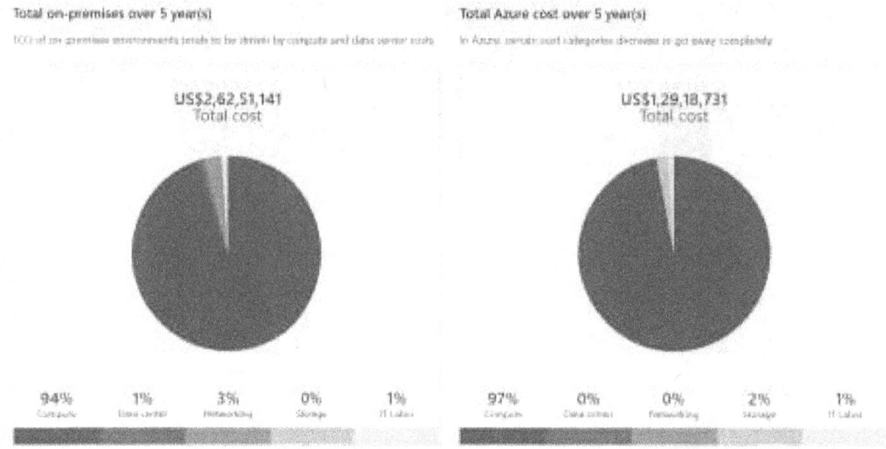

It considered the Compute, Datacenter, Networking, Storage, and IT labour cost to compare TCO.

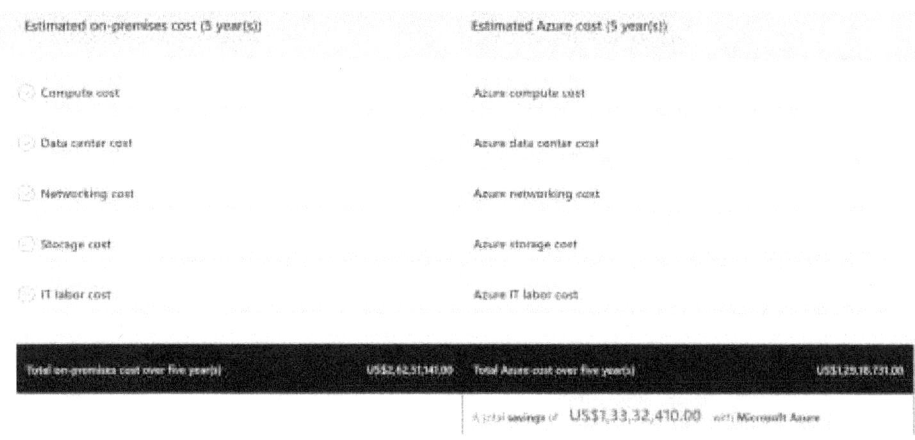

Summary

It is essential to understand different Azure Data platform roles and their responsibilities. Therefore, in this chapter, we explore different roles such as Azure Data Engineer, Azure Database administrator, Azure Data Analyst, Azure Data Scientist and Azure Artificial Intelligence Engineer.

Further, we explored the high-level steps for planning migrating your workload to Azure cloud keeping TCO and ROI in mind.

Chapter 3 Azure Database Platform choices in Azure

Software, services and offering for relational databases have been an integral part of the Microsoft product over the years. This chapter will learn about Azure SQL deployment options to bring value to add the business.

Azure data categories

In Microsoft Azure, the data can be categorized into structured, semi-structured, and unstructured data.

Structured data, also known as relational data, is the data that is stored in database tables, in the shape of rows and columns, and follows a specific schema, where all records will have the same attributes. The structured data depends on the keys that shape the relation between the tables.

A table row in a specific table with a corresponding row in another table can easily insert, modify, compare, and analyze the relational tables' data quickly. It follows the same schema, such as the Microsoft SQL Server database engine.

Semi-structured data, also known as non-relational or NoSQL data, is the data that does not follow a fixed schema and cannot be stored in a tabular structure of data models associated with relational databases shape of rows and columns. The semi-structured data contains tags to separate semantic elements and enforce hierarchies of records and fields within the data, such as HTML documents.

Unstructured data does not have a specified structure of the pre-defined model, allowing it to store any business data type. Unstructured data includes text files, flat files, images, PDF documents and video files.

Azure database services

Microsoft Azure provides a comprehensive range of relational and non-relational Platform as a Service (PaaS) database services that help us in focusing on the database design and performance aspects instead of spending a long time installing and managing the underlying infrastructure and allow us to scale the database resources up and down and tune the performance automatically in response to the workload changes.

Suppose you need more control on your database server or plan to migrate your databases directly from your on-premises database servers to Microsoft Azure without performing changes in your databases or applications. In that case, Microsoft Azure provides you with PaaS and IaaS choices that make the database migration process smooth.

Azure database services are divided mainly into two categories: Infrastructure as a Service offering (IaaS) database services, includes SQL on Azure Virtual Machine, and Platform as a Service (PaaS) database services, includes Azure Database Services, Azure SQL Managed Instance, Azure MySQL/MariaDB/PostgreSQL, Azure Synapse Service and Azure Cosmos DB.

As we will see later in the next chapter, the Azure database services can be provisioned using the Azure Portal or using the Azure Resource Manager Templates, also known as ARM templates, which is the best approach for large scale deployments.

The Azure Resource Manager is the management and deployment service in Azure. It allows us to deploy the different Azure resources using the Azure Portal. These resources will be translated internally to an ARM template. Azure allows you to provide a customized ARM template to deploy a set of related resources in a single template, with the ability to define dependencies between them and parameters to offer values during the deployment process.

The ARM template is a JSON document that describes the structure and the state of the resources deployed, different from the imperative language that uses procedural models to specify the deployment process, such as PowerShell, Azure CLI.

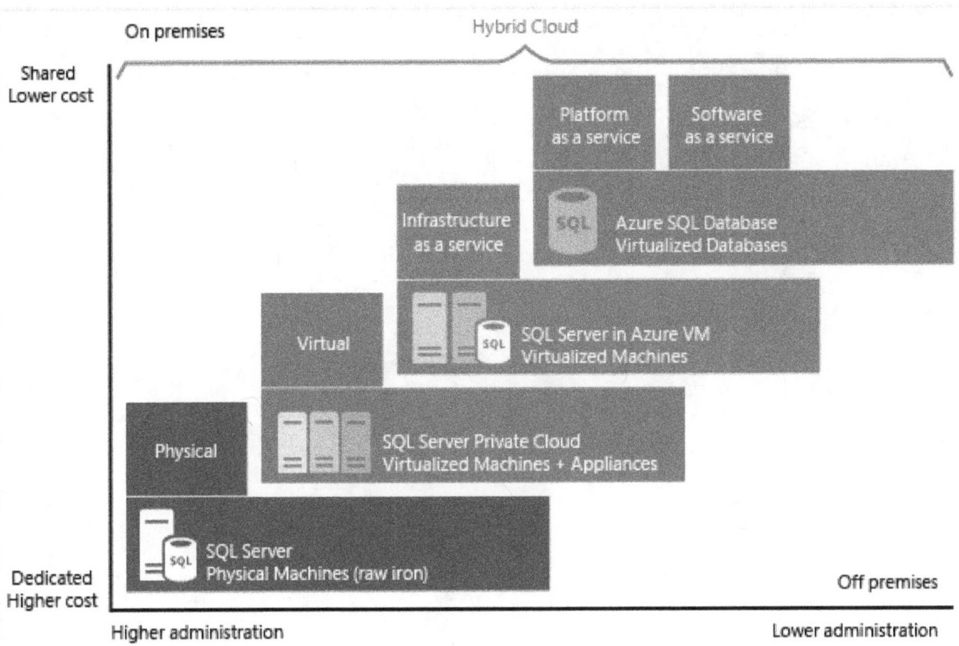

Let us go through these services in detail.

SQL Server in an Azure VM

When deciding whether to use SQL Server on Azure Virtual Machines, you require an answer to the following questions:

- Do your existing or new applications require large databases?
- Do your existing or new applications require access to all features in SQL Server or Windows/Linux?
- Do your existing applications have compatibility issues with the latest version of SQL Server?
- Do you want to avoid the time and expense of acquiring new on-premises hardware?
- Do you want to migrate existing on-premises applications and databases to Azure as-is?

SQL Server on Azure VM can be an excellent fit for the above requirements. As an Infrastructure as a Service (IaaS), SQL Server on Azure Virtual Machine provides you with additional control over the Operating System patching, the SQL Server patching, the networking and storage configurations on the Virtual Machine.

Azure provides us with several features that we will explore in the book.

- Availability sets
- Availability zones
- SQL Server failover cluster
- Always On Availability Groups
- Load balancing techniques

When talking about the storage model in Microsoft Azure, you will see fully redundant storage with four main storage types that can be used for the Azure VM hosting the SQL Server instance. It includes the Standard HDD and SSD Storage, Premium SSD storage, Ultra disk for different use cases.

Azure SQL Database

Azure SQL Database is Platform as a Service (PaaS) relational database service that makes it easier and more cost-effective to store the data processed by any new application deployment. It enables developers to focus on database design and performance optimization. You will not worry about spending your time and effort purchasing, installing, and implementing the infrastructure required to host the database, patching the operating system and SQL Server with the latest security updates.

With Azure SQL Database, Microsoft Azure will be responsible for managing and maintaining the underlying infrastructure, keeping the software requirements patched with the latest security updates, and managing all backup, restore, or retention policies. What is required from you is providing a name for your database and choosing a few options, then you will have your database up and running within a few minutes!

With the several pricing tiers provided by Azure SQL Database, you can quickly scale the resources up and down by tuning the performance tier on the fly to meet your current workload requirements and at your convenience.

Azure SQL Database supports the following resources charging models.

- Database Transaction Unit (DTU) model: In this model, you pay one fixed price for your compute (or IO/memory), as well as your data storage.
- vCore model: It allows you to have separate charges for your compute (what type of node or compute power you're using) and a separate charge for your storage, which provides more flexibility in managing your costs than with DTU.

Azure SQL Database has several deployment models.

- Single database
- Elastic pools
- Hyper-scale

The **Single Database** deployment is the simplest deployment model of Azure SQL Database. In this deployment, you will create a logical server, deploy your database to that server, and connect to that database directly. Each database created under that logical server will be managed and scaled individually, with its dedicated resources.

On the other hand, in the **Elastic Pools model**, a database will be deployed to an elastic pool and share the same resources with other databases deployed to the same pool. Multiple databases will share the same elastic pool's resources, reducing the overall cost of hosting these databases in Azure and allowing the scaling process to be performed at the elastic pool level. The elastic pools model fits the unstable workloads with non-concurrent or not-frequent spikes in the workload.

The **Azure SQL Database Hyperscale** model allows us to overcome the 4 TB storage limitation of the Azure SQL Database. It can expand 100 TB and beyond storage for each database using an advanced scaling technique by adding compute nodes as the data sizes grow, with the additional cost only per terabyte for the storage.

The last deployment model is the **Serverless model**. It can lower the costs of the development and testing environments, with the easy auto-scale and auto-close capabilities of the Azure SQL Database, where the database charging will pause after an hour of inactivity, but with higher per hour or vCore pricing cost than the other Azure SQL Database deployment models.

Azure SQL Database provides the automatic database tuning feature to help identify the expensive queries, automatically forcing the last good performing execution plan and adding and removing indexes based on the workload requirements, using built-in intelligence and advanced heuristics mechanisms.

Azure SQL Database guarantees 99.99% percent uptime. You never lose data due to a failure. Your database has no single point of failure, with the high availability and disaster recovery solutions that are built-in to that PaaS platform. In Azure SQL Database, the backup is fully managed by Microsoft Azure, where it takes weekly full backup, twice-daily differential backup, and log backups every 5-10 minutes.

Azure SQL Managed Instance

The preferred solution for migrating the databases from your on-premises environment to Microsoft Azure is deploying the database to a SQL Server instance hosted in an Azure Virtual machine, known as IaaS platform, supporting the same features and structure supported by the Microsoft SQL Server. But in this way, you will not take advantage of the additional security and performance features, the lower price and less administrative effort provided by the Azure SQL Database PaaS service.

Azure SQL Managed Instance is a particular type of Azure SQL Database service. It provides us with the ability to easily migrate your databases by taking a backup from the on-premises SQL Server, saving it in an Azure storage account, and restoring it to your Azure SQL Managed Instance.

On the other hand, and to overcome the cross-database querying limitation of the Azure SQL Database, Azure SQL Managed Instance allows us to host up to 100 databases in the same SQL Server instance. Besides, Azure SQL Managed Instance breaks other limitations in the Azure SQL Database. For example, it supports the common language runtime (CLR) feature, provides us with access to the system databases, allows the use of SQL Agent jobs, and provides us with the ability to take copy-only backups of the databases to Azure storage manually.

Azure SQL Managed Instance comes in two service tiers: The General Purpose and the Business-Critical tiers with the Business Critical supporting the In-Memory OLTP, readable secondary replicas, includes more memory per core, offers lower storage latency by using direct-attached storage.

With the Azure SQL Managed Instance, you can easily migrate your workload to Microsoft Azure PaaS database platforms, taking advantage of the low price and great features provided by the Azure SQL Database and overcome most of the limitations in Azure SQL Database!

The following figure summarizes the differences at a high-level for Azure SQL Database, Azure SQL Managed instance and SQL Server on Azure VM.

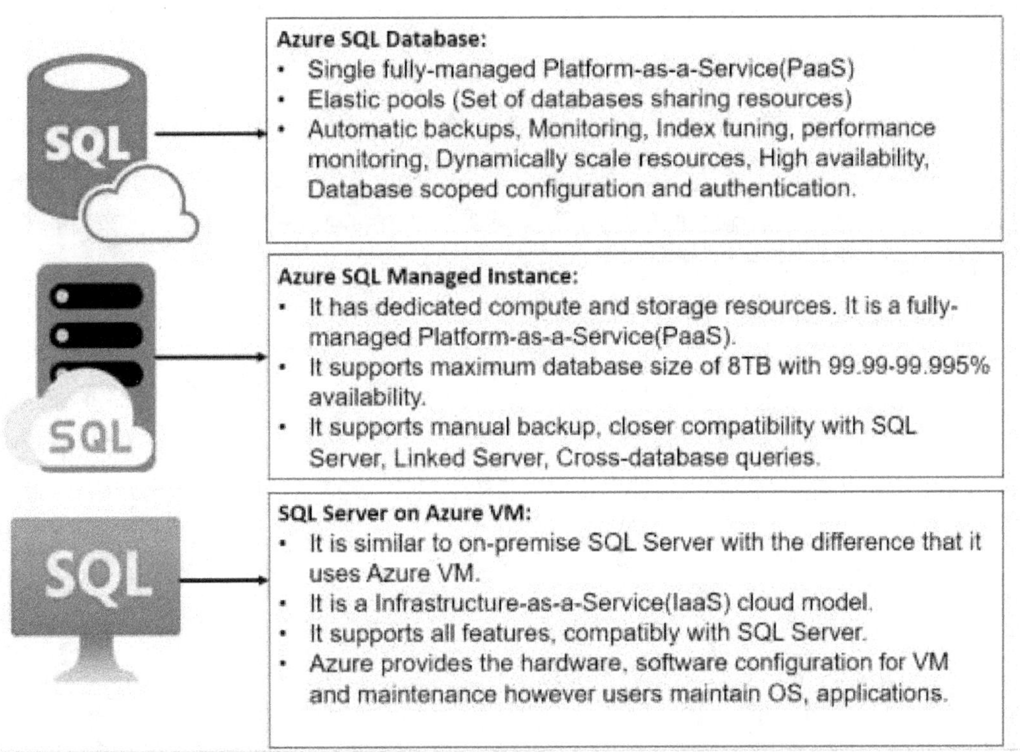

SQL
Azure SQL Database:
• Single fully-managed Platform-as-a-Service(PaaS)
• Elastic pools (Set of databases sharing resources)
• Automatic backups, Monitoring, Index tuning, performance monitoring, Dynamically scale resources, High availability, Database scoped configuration and authentication.
SQL
Azure SQL Managed Instance:
• It has dedicated compute and storage resources. It is a fully-managed Platform-as-a-Service(PaaS).
• It supports maximum database size of 8TB with 99.99-99.995% availability.
• It supports manual backup, closer compatibility with SQL Server, Linked Server, Cross-database queries.
SQL
SQL Server on Azure VM:
• It is similar to on-premise SQL Server with the difference that it uses Azure VM.
• It is a Infrastructure-as-a-Service(IaaS) cloud model.
• It supports all features, compatibly with SQL Server.
• Azure provides the hardware, software configuration for VM and maintenance however users maintain OS, applications.

Open-Source Databases on Azure SQL Platform

Microsoft supports several open-source database platforms, such as MySQL, MariaDB, and PostgreSQL on the Azure PaaS platform, running on different database engines but providing the same architecture and features as Azure SQL Database.

Azure Database for PostgreSQL is a fully managed, intelligent, and scalable PostgreSQL database with full compatibility with community PostgreSQL and support for several extensions, such as PLV8 and PostGIS, and popular frameworks and languages like Ruby on Rails, Python with Django, Java with Spring Boot, and Node.js. It allows you to scale quickly to hundreds of nodes, with no need to perform changes to your application, ensuring your data is always available with up to 99.99% SLA and zone redundant high availability.

Besides, the Azure Database for PostgreSQL supports the query store feature. The query store keeps track of both query execution runtime statistics and waits stats, but with a slight difference in the implementation from the one supported by the Azure SQL Database.

Azure Database for MySQL also provides us with an easy way to set up, manage, and scale the MySQL databases in Azure. It is built with the latest community edition of MySQL, including versions 5.6, 5.7, and 8.0, allowing us to use different management tools, such as MySQL Workbench, and programming languages, such as PHP, Java, Node.js, and. NET.

Azure Database for MariaDB combines the MariaDB Community edition's capabilities with the Azure SQL Database benefits by removing the overhead of managing that service to the Microsoft Azure and focusing on building the applications. It works with different open-source frameworks and languages and features tight integration with Azure Web Apps. It can be quickly provisioned in minutes, and then you can scale the compute and storage resources independently within a few seconds.

Azure Synapse Analytics

Azure Synapse Analytics is an integrated analytics service that allows us to implement data warehousing solutions using the standard T-SQL language. It provides a serverless resource model used with predictable performance and cost workloads and a dedicated resource model, used with unplanned or ad-hoc workloads, to handle the descriptive and diagnostic analytical options and accelerate the time to insight across data warehouses and big data systems.

Azure Synapse Analytics combines the following technologies in an integrated console.

- The benefits of the SQL technologies that are useful in the enterprise data warehousing,
- The Spark technologies used for big data solutions,
- The pipelines capabilities for ETL/ELT data operations,
- Azure services such as Power BI, Azure CosmosDB, Azure Machine Learning,
- Azure Data Catalog, Azure Data Lake Storage, Azure Databricks, Azure HDInsight,
- Azure Synapse supports different languages such as SQL, Python, .NET, Java, Scala, and R.

The Azure Synapse capabilities allow us to create data-driven workflows to orchestrate data movement and transform data at scale.

When the data is stored in the big data store, which is Azure Data Lake storage in this situation, Hadoop, Spark, and machine learning algorithms will be used to prepare and train that data.

It performs the complex analysis, and the Synapse dedicated SQL pool will use the PolyBase feature to query the big data stores. It uses the standard T-SQL queries, dedicated SQL pool relational tables, and columnar storage to reduce the cost of storing the huge data. It further improves data retrieval performance, allowing us to run a massive analytics scale that returns the results in a few seconds.

Azure Cosmos DB

Azure Cosmos DB is a Microsoft Platform as a Service (PaaS) non-relational and multi-model database service. In this service, data is distributed to other regions without affecting the data consistency across various areas where the data replicates. It improves the Cosmos DB account's availability. Azure Cosmos DB fits any web application, mobile application, gaming or IoT application that requires processing, reading, and writing a massive amount of data.

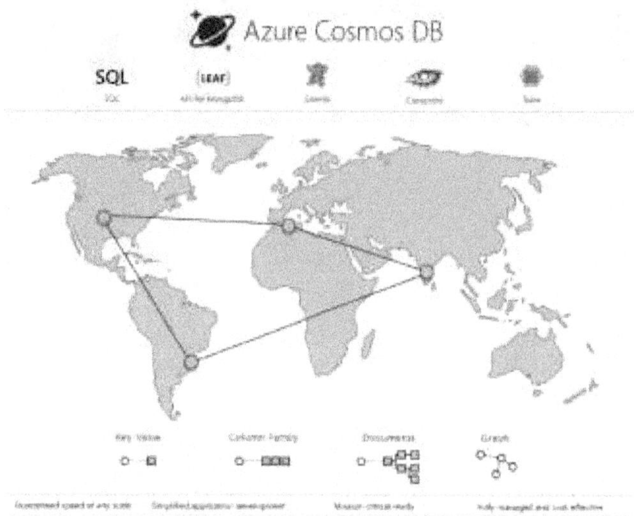

Azure Cosmos DB enables you to scale the throughput and the storage resources elastically and independently across any number of Azure regions and enjoy the fast, less than 10ms latency for both reads and writes workloads due to using local data caching and automatically indexes all incoming data.

Azure Cosmos DB can access the stored data using the API that fits your application requirements, from the supported SQL, MongoDB, Cassandra, Tables, or Gremlin, and the appropriate SDK from the .NET, Java, Node.js, Python, and Xamarin supported SDK. You can migrate the application to Cosmos DB without the need to perform significant changes.

Azure Cosmos DB provides us with five well-defined consistency options: Strong, bounded staleness, session, consistent prefix, and eventual that offers full flexibility and low cost-to-performance ratio.

To respond directly to any unexpected workload spikes, Azure Cosmos DB provides us with the ability to scale the read and write operations, also known as throughput, and add or remove any Azure regions to the Cosmos DB account.

The data stored in Azure Cosmos DB is always secured using data encryption at rest and in motion, in addition to the ability to configure the row-level authorization.

Summary

In this chapter, we explored various Azure database services at a high-level. These services include Azure SQL Database (Single, Elastic pools), Azure SQL Managed instance, SQL Server in Azure VM, Azure Synapse Analytics and Azure Cosmos DB.

Chapter 4 Plan and implement data platforms resources in Azure

This chapter introduces the readers to understand the several deployment features and choices that one could use to meet the end-user needs. Azure SQL cloud offers the flexibility to choose various deployment options. You will also learn some technical specifications for each of these options. Relational databases are always an excellent choice for working with data. Still, Microsoft Azure offers many features and additional options, each with its unique deployment options, pricing tiers, performance characteristics, HA features, migrate and upgrade capabilities. In this chapter, you will explore these options and understand how to get the most from your investment.

Explain IaaS options for deploying SQL Server in Azure

The key decision point for an organization planning for Azure infrastructure is to choose between the two deployment options.

- SQL Server on Azure VM
- Azure SQL Database or Azure SQL Managed instance

The Azure SQL deployment differs in the cost and granular control over the underlying platform. The following table highlights the key differences between SQL Server on Azure VM and Azure SQL Database.

Azure SQL Database vs SQL Server on Azure VMs	**Azure IaaS SQL Server**	**Azure SQL Database**
Database Features	It is similar to an on-premise SQL Server with all existing features.	It supports the majority of database features such as database auditing, T-SQL, database scoped configurations, TDE

Database size	The maximum database size is dependent on the VM type and storage disk. For example, we can use a 32TB database in the premium SSD on a single disk. VM size defines the maximum number of data disks. For example, a DS2_v2 can have eight data disks while DS13_2 supports 32 data disks	Azure SQL Database storage size depends on the service tier. 1. General Purpose and Business critical: 5 GB to 4 TB 2. Hyperscale: up to 100 TB 3. It allows a maximum of 5000 databases in a logical Azure SQL Server.
Filegroups	You can add file groups and place files in different directories as well. Multiple log files are supported	Primary filegroup only. Multiple log files are not supported
Compute resources	You can choose the appropriate VM size category for computing resources. Reference: https://docs.microsoft.com/en-us/azure/virtual-machines/windows/overview	Azure SQL Database provides a DTU and vCPU based computing model. Reference Link: https://dtucalculator.azurewebsites.net/
Availability	Azure Iaas VM provides 99.99% availability. Azure infrastructure provides fault-tolerance and high Availability for the VMs. You can configure WSFC or AG for HADR.	Azure SQL Databases are 99.995% available. It has in-built fault-tolerance and high Availability mechanism. It uses geo-redundant (RA-GRS) storage blobs that are replicated to a paired region. It also supports active geo-replication and failover groups for HADR.

Database Backup	You can manage VM level backup or native SQL backups (Backup To URL) for consistent database backups	Azure SQL Databases provides automatic backup functionality. The backup retention period is short-term (7 days to 35 days) and long term up to 10 years.
Database Patching	Manual, Similar to an on-premise SQL Server	Automatic
License	Azure Iaas VM gives the option to choose from the built-in SQL Server license as well as BYOL(Bring Your License) model	Azure SQL Databases has an in-built licensing model. The pricing depends on the service tier. You can also choose a serverless tier for the resume database if not in use.
SQL Agent, Linked server & DB Mail	It supports SQL Agent, Linked server & DB Mail, similar to an on-premise SQL Server.	No SQL agent or DB mail or Linked server
Business Intelligence Services	Power BI for SSRS (SQL Server Reporting Services) SSAS SSIS	Azure Data Factory for SSIS Azure Analysis Services for Tabular model
Recovery model	All supported recovery models	Only the Full Recovery model
Usage	It is suitable for database infrastructure where you require full control over SQL Server and requires all SQL Server features.	The built-in database features such as backups and HADR solutions. No manual infrastructure management. Automatic patching

The IaaS infrastructure gives granular access for SQL Server or any relational database compared to other solutions- SaaS and PaaS. In the following pyramid, we see the granularity control for SaaS, PaaS and IaaS.

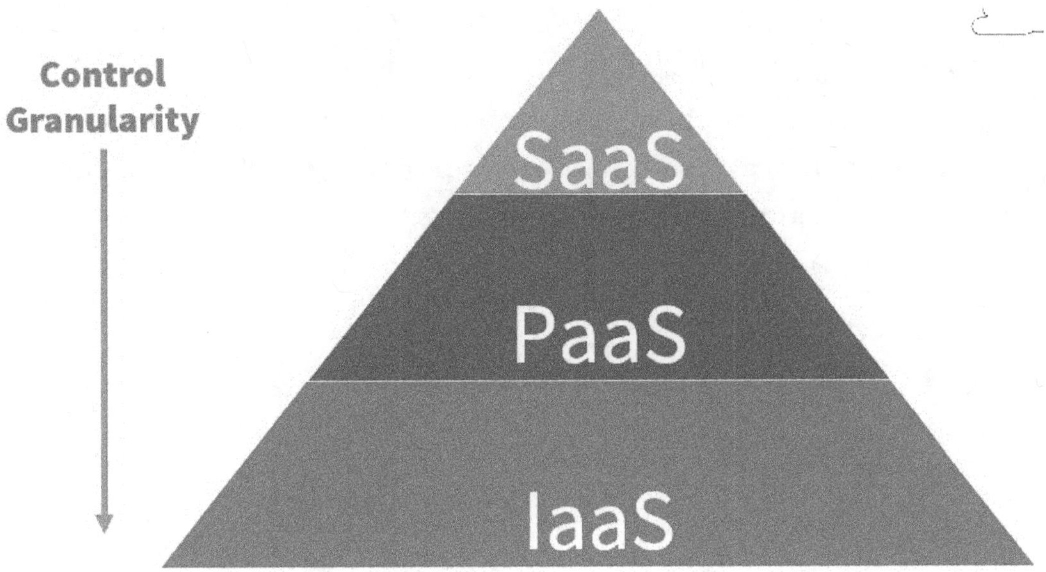

Therefore, many organizations want to move their application to SQL Server on Azure VM instead of the managed Azure SQL Databases. A few reasons for this can be:

- Use native SQL Server solutions such as SSAS, SSRS, SSIS. Machine-learning (R, Python)
- You have a legacy application running on older SQL Server versions.
- Application compatibility and feature restrictions
- Direct access to the OS

Deploy SQL Server on Azure VM

SQL Server on Azure VM allows database professionals to use the full SQL Server version in Azure infrastructure without managing the on-premise hardware. To deploy SQL Server on Azure VM, we need to look at the following components.

SQL Server licensing models

Azure provides the following licensing model for deploying SQL Server on Azure VMs.

- **Pay-As-You-Go:** You can choose a Pay-As-You-Go model for paying pay-per-minute for the use of SQL Server. The cost per minute includes the cost of the virtual machine. You can select an image from the Azure Market place and use a pre-configured

VM with SQL Server installed. You can use this method irrespective of whether you are participating in the Microsoft Software Assurance (SA) program or not.

- **BYOL:** In the Bring Your Own License, you require a valid SQL Server license and you can apply it to Azure VM. In this method, you can manually install and configure a SQL Server similar to the on-premise VM. In the Azure Marketplace, you can find BYOL images identical to the following.

- **Azure Hybrid Benefits:** You can also take advantage of Azure Hybrid Benefits (AHB) to significantly reduce the cost of running the Azure cloud. In this model, you can use an on-premise software assurance to activate SQL Server and Windows license on Azure cloud. It is applicable for RedHat and SUSE subscriptions as well. It applies SQL Server 1 to 4 vCPUs exchange.

The following figure highlights cost-saving between SQL VM on Azure VM with hybrid benefit.

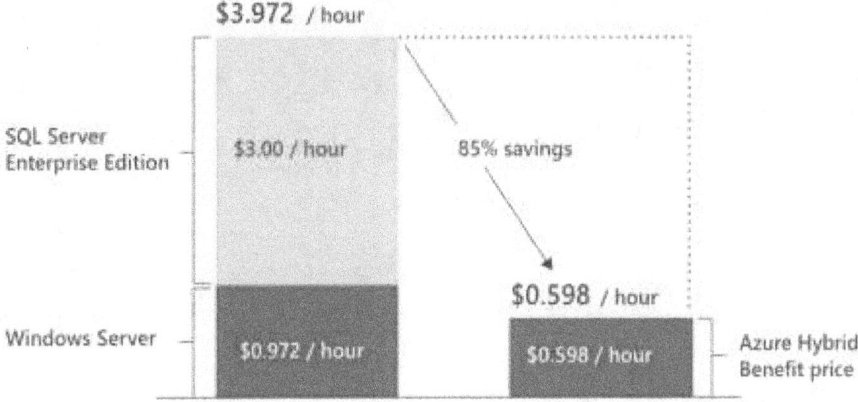

Refer to Azure Hybrid Benefit Savings Calculator (**https://azure.microsoft.com/en-in/pricing/hybrid-benefit/#calculator**) for cost saving analysis.

For example, the below figure estimates an annual saving of 85.4% for virtual machines deployment per month.

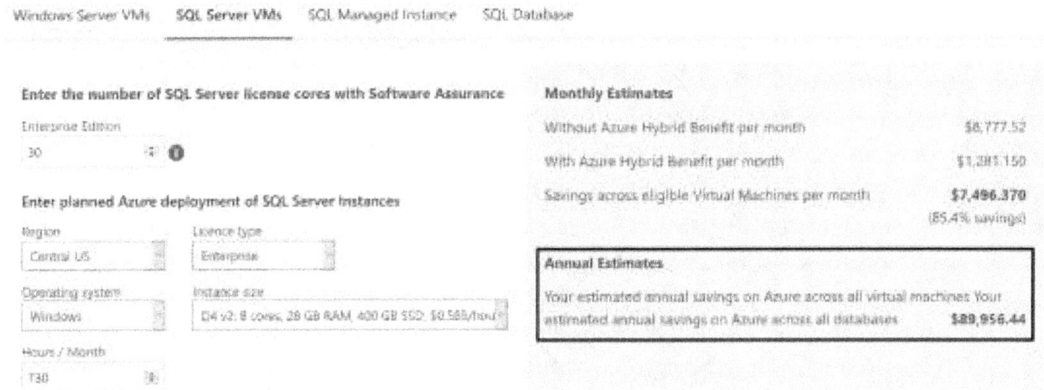

Virtual machine families

Azure Virtual Machine provides several VM familiar with the combination of Memory, CPU and Storage. It provides the following VM families.

- General-purpose
- Compute Optimized
- Memory-Optimized
- Storage Optimized
- GPU
- High performance compute.

Type	Sizes	Description
General purpose	B, Dsv3, Dv3, Dasv4, Dav4, DSv2, Dv2, Av2, DC, DCv2, Dv4, Dsv4, Ddv4, Ddsv4	Balanced CPU-to-memory ratio. Ideal for testing and development, small to medium databases, and low to medium traffic web servers.
Compute optimized	F, Fs, Fsv2	High CPU-to-memory ratio. Good for medium traffic web servers, network appliances, batch processes, and application servers.
Memory optimized	Esv3, Ev3, Easv4, Eav4, Ev4, Esv4, Edv4, Edsv4, Mv2, M, DSv2, Dv2	High memory-to-CPU ratio. Great for relational database servers, medium to large caches, and in-memory analytics.
Storage optimized	Lsv2	High disk throughput and IO ideal for Big Data, SQL, NoSQL databases, data warehousing and large transactional databases.
GPU	NC, NCv2, NCv3, NCasT4_v3 (Preview), ND, NDv2 (Preview), NV, NVv3, NVv4	Specialized virtual machines targeted for heavy graphic rendering and video editing, as well as model training and inferencing (ND) with deep learning. Available with single or multiple GPUs.
High performance compute	HB, HBv2, HC, H	Our fastest and most powerful CPU virtual machines with optional high-throughput network interfaces (RDMA).

You can compare the VM sizes during the VM configuration according to the vCPU, RAM(GiB), Data disks, Max IOPS, Premium disk support, and cost per month. It also shows the VM popular amount of Azure users for a quick review.

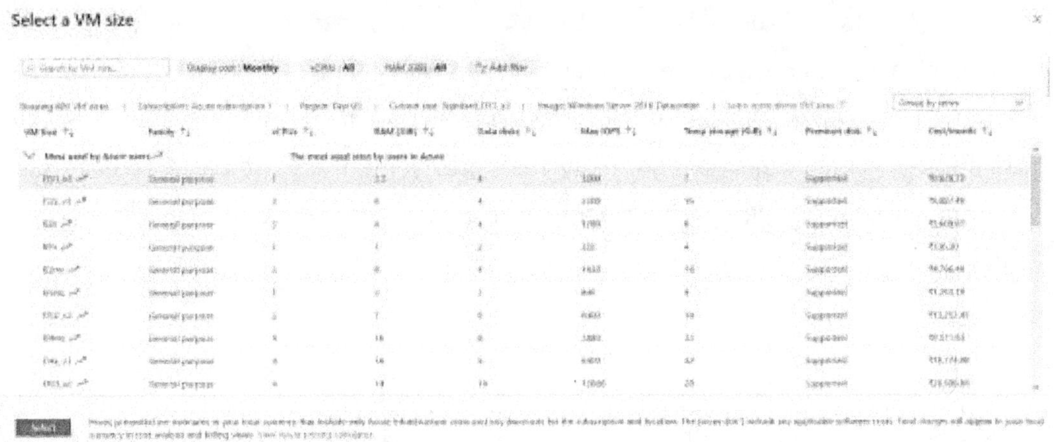

1.1.1 High availability

Azure VM provides 99.9% high availability with the Azure Managed storage. The three nine means that it guarantees a maximum downtime of 8.77 hours per year. Azure supports these SQL Server technologies for business continuity:

- ✓ Always On availability groups
- ✓ Always On failover cluster instances (FCIs)
- ✓ Log shipping
- ✓ SQL Server backup and restore with Azure Blob storage
- ✓ Azure Backup for SQL Server
- ✓ Azure Site Recovery

The Azure platform offers several options for providing higher levels of availability for VM and PaaS workload.

- ✓ Availability Zones
- ✓ Availability Sets
- ✓ Azure Region

You can refer to Chapter 10 for exploring the HADR solution in detail.

1.1.2 VM disks

The Azure VM is equipped with at least two disks.

✓ **Operating system disk**: The operating system disk contains the boot volume. By default, it gets a C drive letter in Windows OS or /dev/sda1 for Linux OS. Azure automatically installs OS on the Operating system disk.

✓ **Temporary disk**: The temporary disk is used for temporary storage. It is useful for data that does not require durability. For example, temp files, swap files, or page files. During the VM reboot, the data inside the disk is lost. The drive letter D in Windows and /dev/sdb1 on Linux OS is used for the temporary disk.

You must not use the temporary disk for storing database or transaction log files.

Create a virtual machine

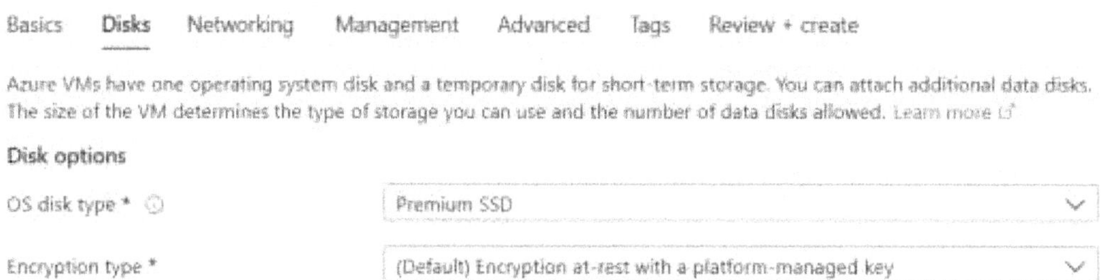

✓ **Data Disks**: Azure uses a managed disk for storing database files as per the configured IOPS and storage capacity.

Azure portal uses the term **data disks** for the managed disks.

In the following figure, you get a comparison between different managed disk types. The Ultra disk provides the maximum throughput, disk size and IOPS.

Detail	Ultra disk	Premium SSD	Standard SSD	Standard HDD
Disk type	SSD	SSD	SSD	HDD
Scenario	IO-intensive workloads such as SAP HANA, top tier databases (for example, SQL, Oracle), and other transaction-heavy workloads.	Production and performance sensitive workloads	Web servers, lightly used enterprise applications and dev/test	Backup, non-critical, infrequent access
Max disk size	65,536 gibibyte (GiB)	32,767 GiB	32,767 GiB	32,767 GiB
Max throughput	2,000 MB/s	900 MB/s	750 MB/s	500 MB/s
Max IOPS	160,000	20,000	6,000	2,000

Provision and deploy SQL Server to Azure virtual machines

Azure offers several methods for provisioning a SQL Server instance on the Azure VM. These options are as below.

- ✓ Azure Marketplace
- ✓ Azure PowerShell
- ✓ Azure CLI
- ✓ Azure Resource Manager templates

Deployment using the Azure Marketplace

The Azure Marketplace is a centralized location for deploying Azure resources with predefined templates. You can quickly deploy a SQL Server on Windows, Linux OS by providing necessary information such as VM name, storage configuration.

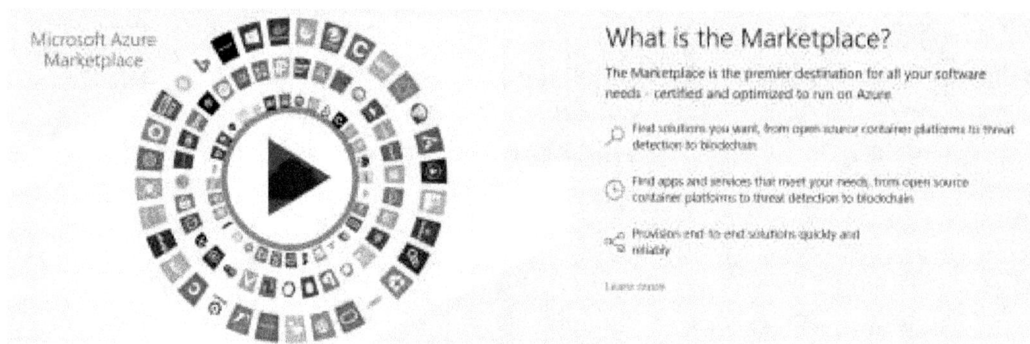

You can click for a specific Azure resource category or search for a particular image using the search box.

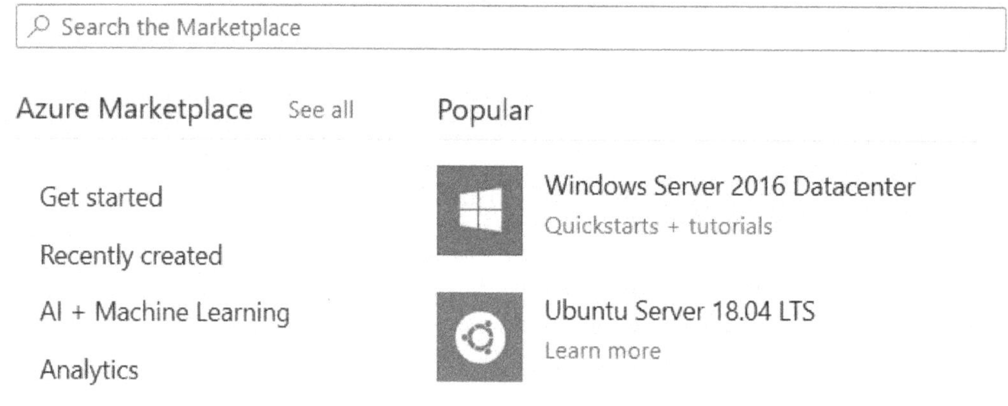

For example, lets search for SQL Server 2019, and you can choose an appropriate image from the marketplace.

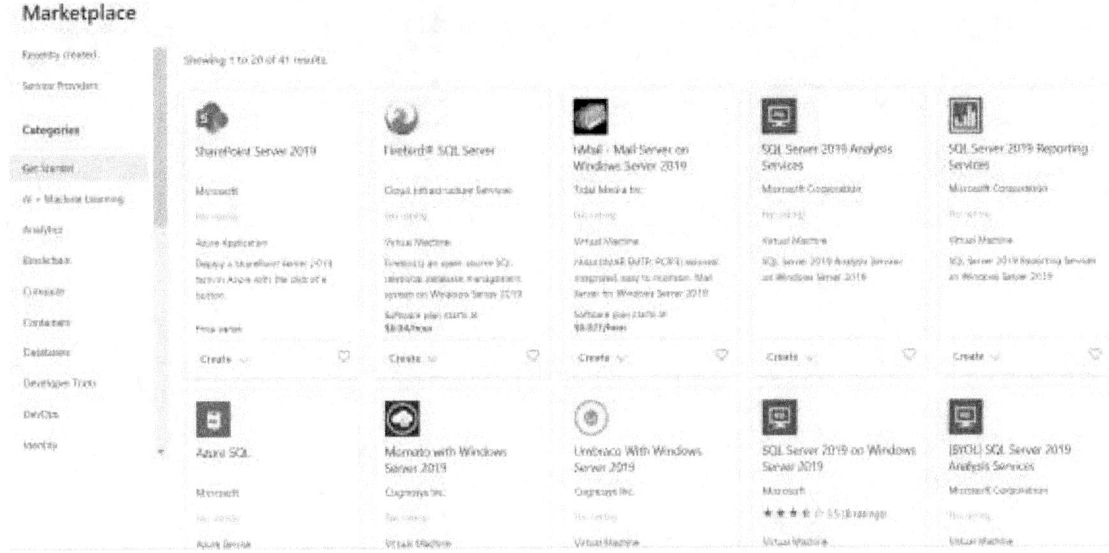

Suppose I choose the image - SQL Server 2017 on Windows Server 2019.

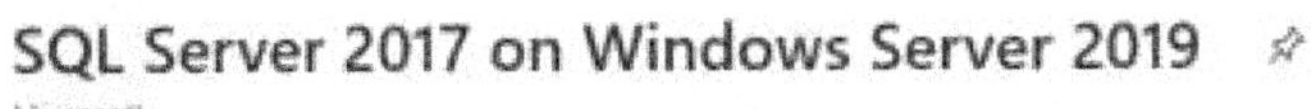

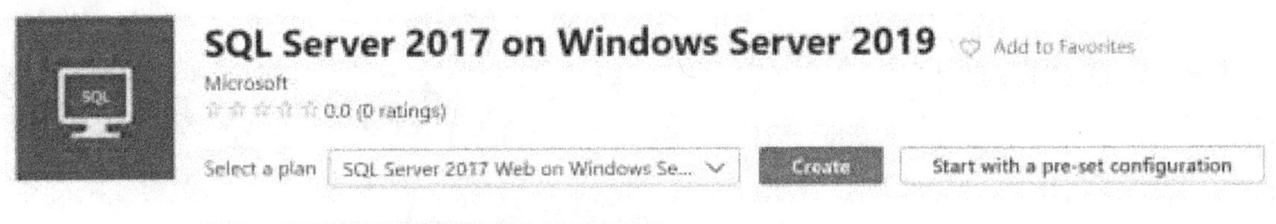

It gives the options

- Create it with your custom configuration
- Start with a pre-set configuration.

To quickly optimize the virtual machine, you are required to select the workload environment and workload type.

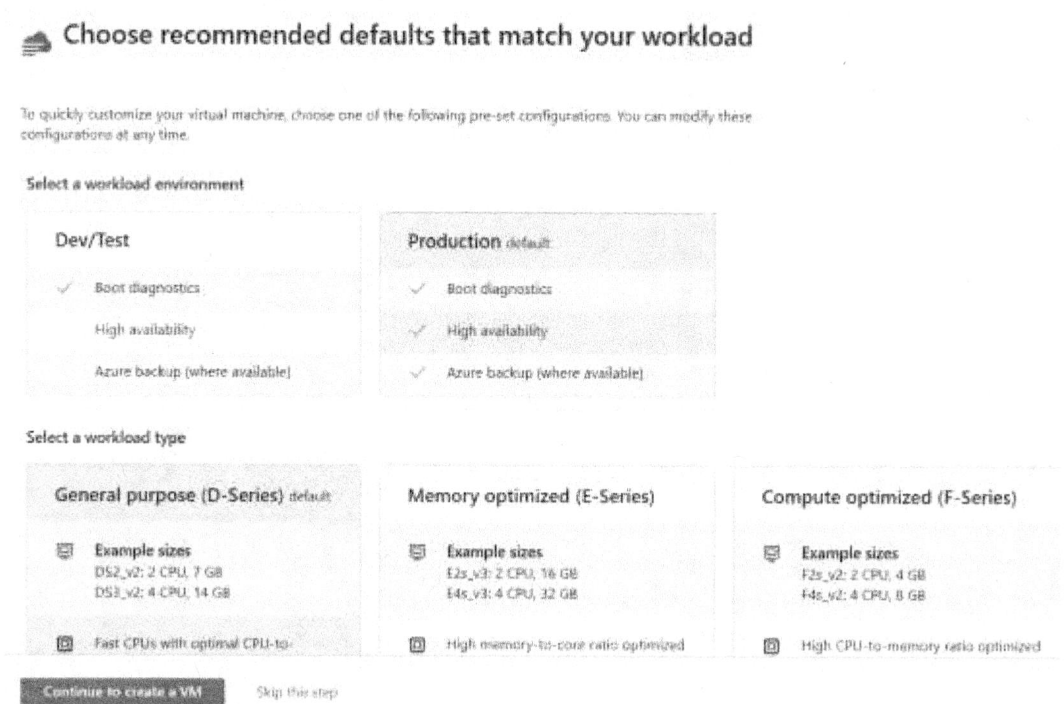

The disadvantage of deploying Azure resources using the Azure portal is repeatability. Suppose you require deploying multiple VMs with similar configuration. In the Azure portal, you need to repeat the process for each VM. Therefore, you can use other deployment options to deploy multiple Azure resources quickly.

Deploying via Azure PowerShell

The Azure PowerShell cmdlets can be used to deploy and manage Azure resources such as Azure VM. You can browse to the URL https://shell.azure.com/powershell and write your PowerShell code. It uses the following cmdlets.

- ✓ **New-AzResourceGroup**: To create a new Azure resource group.
- ✓ **New-AzVM**: This cmdlet creates a new virtual machine using the specified argument such as VM name, location, image name, virtual network name, subnet, public IP address, and credentials and ports to be opened for the firewall.

```
# Variables for common values
$resourceGroup = "myResourceGroup"
$location = "westeurope"
$vmName = "myVM"

# Create user object
$cred = Get-Credential -Message "Enter a username and password for the virtual machine."

# Create a resource group
New-AzResourceGroup -Name $resourceGroup -Location $location

# Create a virtual machine
New-AzVM `
  -ResourceGroupName $resourceGroup `
  -Name $vmName `
  -Location $location `
  -ImageName "Win2016Datacenter" `
  -VirtualNetworkName "myVnet" `
  -SubnetName "mySubnet" `
  -SecurityGroupName "myNetworkSecurityGroup" `
  -PublicIpAddressName "myPublicIp" `
  -Credential $cred `
  -OpenPorts 3389
```

Deploying via Azure CLI

You can deploy Azure resources using Azure command-line interfaces(CLI). The CLI script uses a fewer line of code and provides more flexibility than the PowerShell.

It uses the following CLI commands.

- ✓ az group create
- ✓ az vm create

```
az group create --name myResourceGroup --location eastus

az vm create \
    --resource-group myResourceGroup \
    --name myVM \
    --image win2016datacenter \
    --admin-username azureuser
```

s

Deploying using the Azure Resource Manager templates

Azure Resource Manager(ARM) templates provide resource deployment using the single declarative template. You can define the template and deploy it using the Azure DevOps pipeline or custom deployment blade using the Azure portal. It uses the configuration in a JSON document. You can create a standard template and use the parameters for providing runtime information.

```
{
  "$schema": "https://schema.management.azure.com/schemas/2019-04-01/deploymentTemplate.json#",
  "contentVersion": "1.0.0.0",
  "parameters": {
    "adminUsername": {
      "type": "string",
      "metadata": {
        "description": "Username for the Virtual Machine."
      }
    },
    "adminPassword": {
      "type": "securestring",
      "metadata": {
        "description": "Password for the Virtual Machine."
      }
    },
    "dnsLabelPrefix": {
      "type": "string",
      "metadata": {
        "description": "Unique DNS Name for the Public IP used to access the Virtual Machine."
      }
    },
    "windowsOSVersion": {
      "type": "string",
      "defaultValue": "2016-Datacenter",
      "allowedValues": [
        "2008-R2-SP1",
        "2012-Datacenter",
        "2012-R2-Datacenter",
        "2016-Nano-Server",
        "2016-Datacenter-with-Containers",
        "2016-Datacenter",
        "2019-Datacenter"
      ],
      "metadata": {
        "description": "The Windows version for the VM. This will pick a fully patched image of this given Windows version."
      }
```

You should refer to **https://docs.microsoft.com/en-us/azure/azure-sql/virtual-machines/windows/performance-guidelines-best-practices** for performance best practices using SQL Server on Azure VM.

Note: We cover Azure PowerShell or CLI in detail in chapter 9 - Perform automation of tasks.

Lab 1: Provision a SQL Server on an Azure virtual machine

Suppose you are a database administrator. You want to deploy SQL Server on Azure VM for development purposes.

Step 1: Browse to URL https://portal.azure.com/ and search for the Azure SQL.

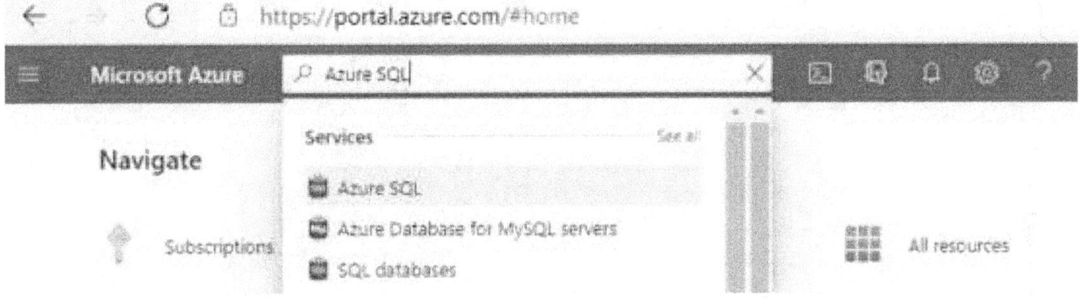

In the Azure SQL resource page, click on **Create Azure SQL resource.**

No Azure SQL resources to display

Try changing your filters if you don't see what you're looking for.

Learn more

Create Azure SQL resource

Step2: You get three SQL deployment options.

- ✓ SQL databases
- ✓ SQL Managed instances
- ✓ SQL virtual machines

In the SQL virtual machine, select the required image. Here, I choose **Free SQL Server License: SQL Server Developer on Windows Server 2019**.

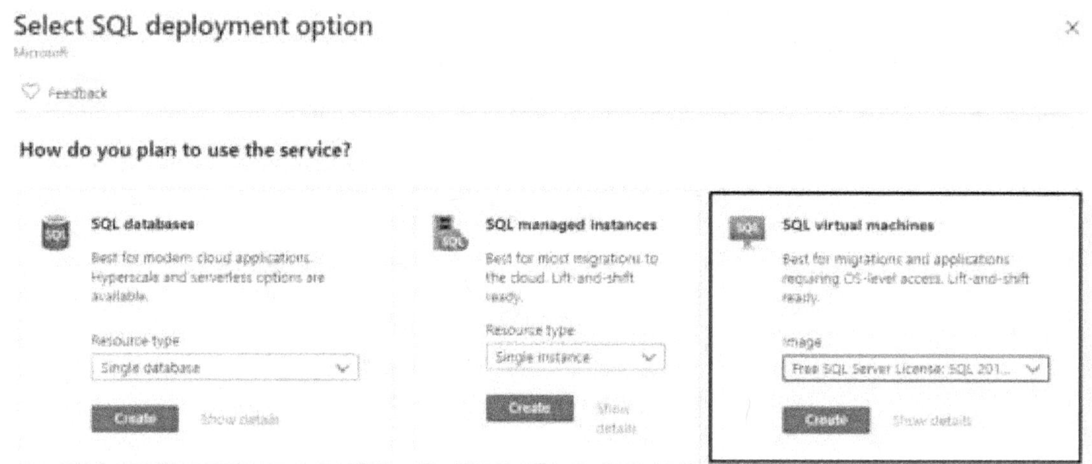

Click on Create. It opens a create virtual machine configuration. On this page, enter the following information.

- ✓ Resource group
- ✓ Virtual machine name
- ✓ Region
- ✓ VM size
- ✓ Administrator credentials

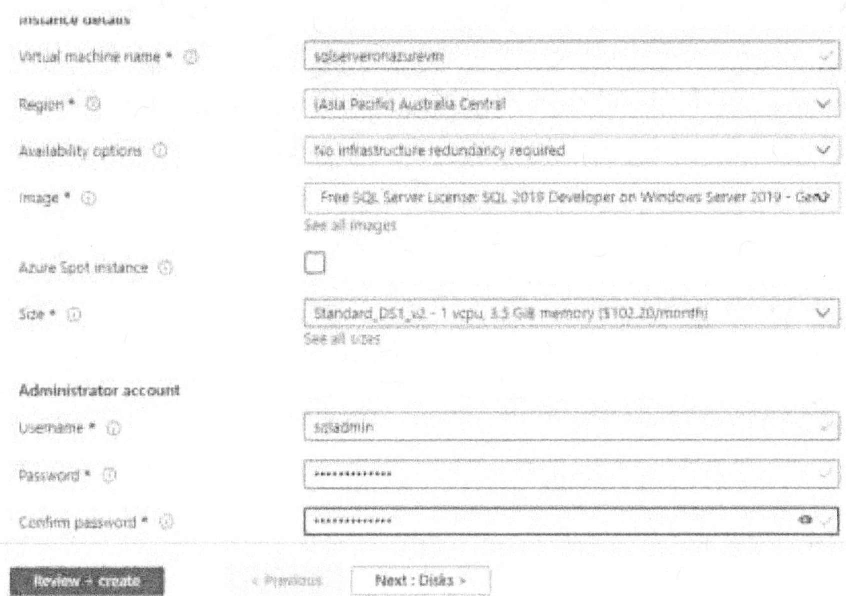

Scroll-down and specify the port that you wish to open from the firewall. Here, we use the RDP port 3389.

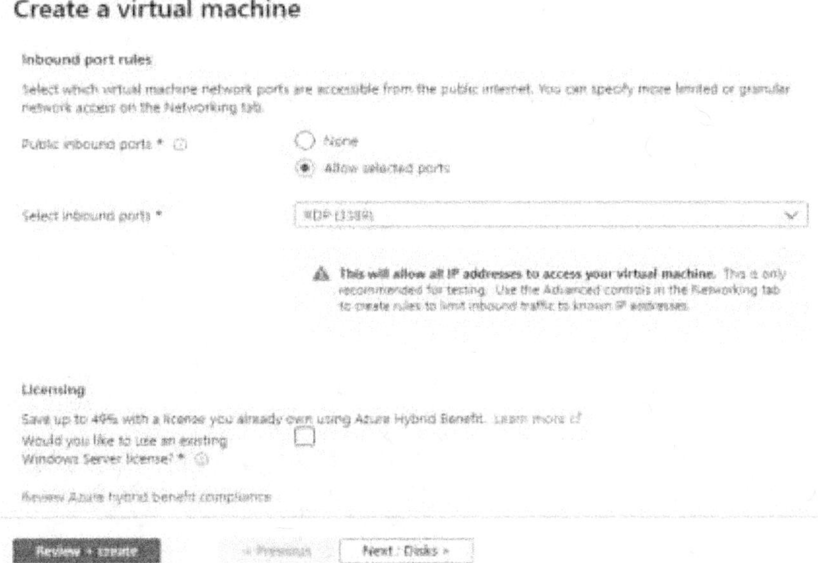

Click Next for the disk configuration. By default, it selects the **Premium SSD** for the OS disk.

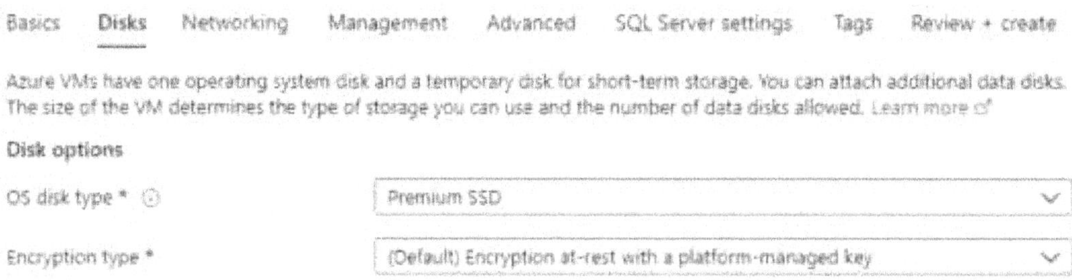

In the next step, select the network interface – Virtual network, Subnet, Public IP, Public Inbound ports.

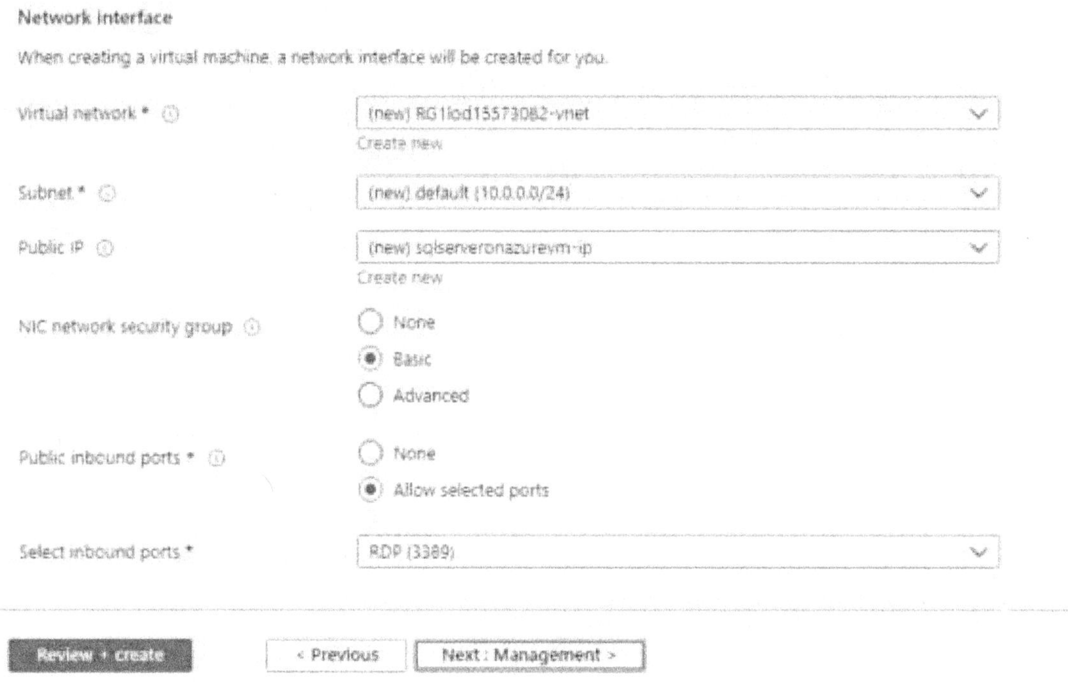

In the networking configuration, we will use a NIC network security group for restricting VM access to specific IP addresses.

Click on Advanced for NIC network security group. It gives another option – Configure network security group.

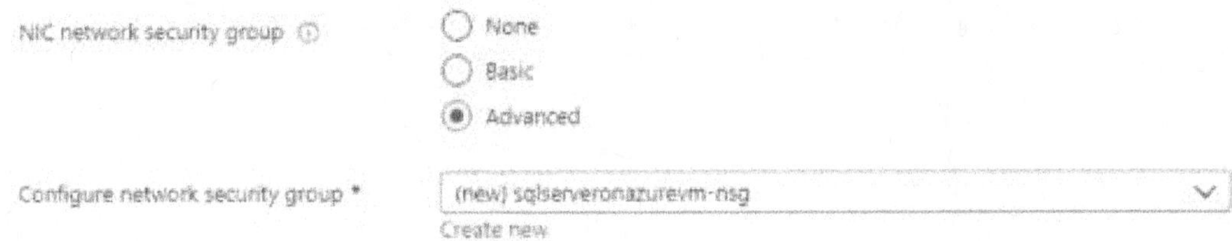

Click on create new on the configure network security group. Configure the Inbound and Outbound rules for VM connection.

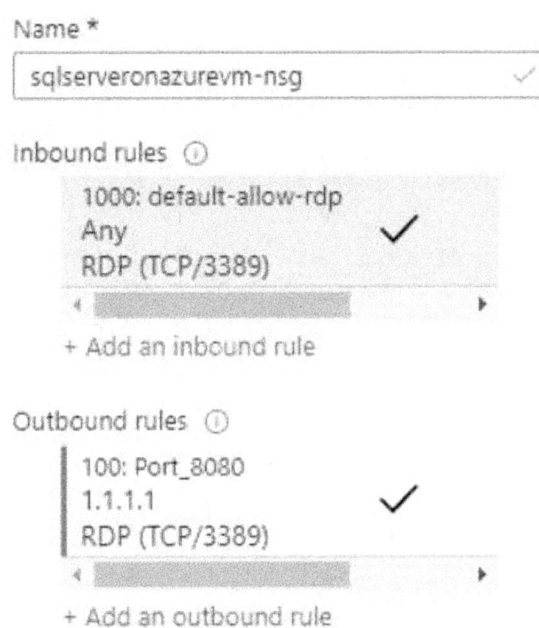

On the next page, review the management configuration. The VM is enabled with the managed storage account.

Basics Disks Networking **Management** Advanced SQL Server settings Tags Review + create

Configure monitoring and management options for your VM.

Azure Security Center

Azure Security Center provides unified security management and advanced threat protection across hybrid cloud workloads.
Learn more

Your subscription is protected by Azure Security Center basic plan.

Monitoring

Boot diagnostics: Enable with managed storage account (recommended) / Enable with custom storage account / Disable

Enable OS guest diagnostics

Identity

Review + create | < Previous | Next : Advanced >

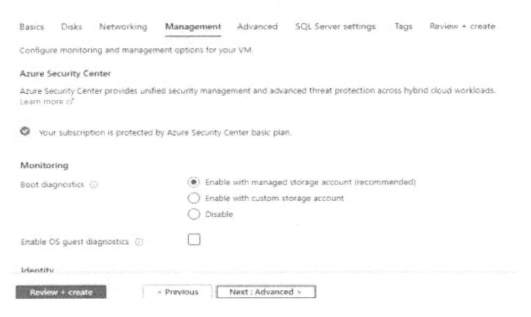

Navigate to the SQL Server setting tab. By default, SQL Server has the following default configurations.

- ✓ Port: 1433
- ✓ SQL authentication: Disable. If you want to use SQL authentication, click on enable. By default, it uses the credentials that we specified for VM authentication.
- ✓ Azure key-value integration: Disable

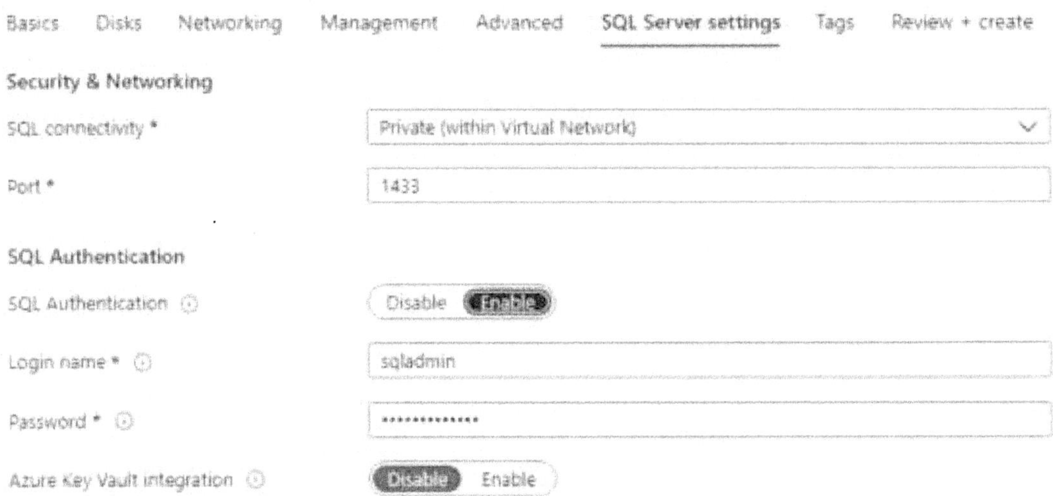

The default storage configuration for SQL Server on Azure VM has the following config.

- ✓ Storage optimization: Transactional processing
- ✓ SQL data: 1024 GiB, 5000 IOPS, 200 MB/s, read caching
- ✓ SQL Log: 1024 GiB, 5000 IOPS, 200 MB/s
- ✓ SQL TempDB: Use local SSD drive(D:\Windows)

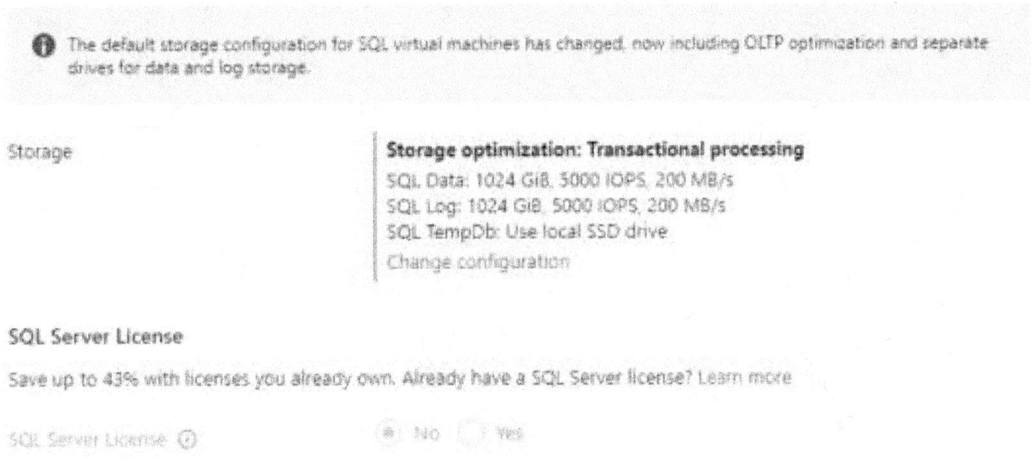

The default storage configuration for SQL virtual machines has changed, now including OLTP optimization and separate drives for data and log storage.

Storage

Storage optimization: Transactional processing
SQL Data: 1024 GiB, 5000 IOPS, 200 MB/s
SQL Log: 1024 GiB, 5000 IOPS, 200 MB/s
SQL TempDb: Use local SSD drive
Change configuration

SQL Server License

Save up to 43% with licenses you already own. Already have a SQL Server license? Learn more

SQL Server License ⓘ ◉ No ◯ Yes

On the next page, review your SQL Server on Azure VM configuration and click on Create.

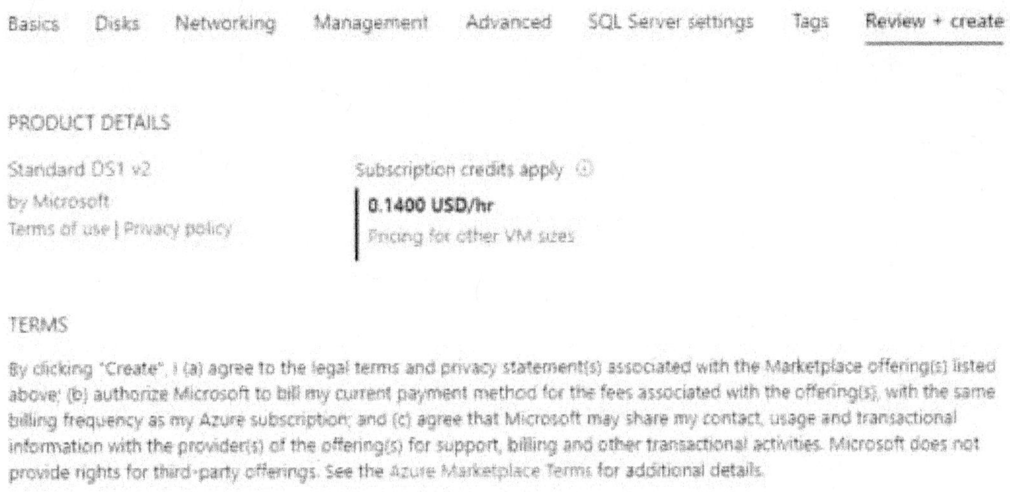

Basics Disks Networking Management Advanced SQL Server settings Tags Review + create

PRODUCT DETAILS

Standard DS1 v2
by Microsoft
Terms of use | Privacy policy

Subscription credits apply ⓘ
0.1400 USD/hr
Pricing for other VM sizes

TERMS

By clicking "Create", I (a) agree to the legal terms and privacy statement(s) associated with the Marketplace offering(s) listed above; (b) authorize Microsoft to bill my current payment method for the fees associated with the offering(s), with the same billing frequency as my Azure subscription; and (c) agree that Microsoft may share my contact, usage and transactional information with the provider(s) of the offering(s) for support, billing and other transactional activities. Microsoft does not provide rights for third-party offerings. See the Azure Marketplace Terms for additional details.

It deploys the necessary resources for the virtual machine. You can RDP by using the public IP address and access SQL Server.

SQL Server to SQL Server on Azure VMs migrations

This section understands the different migration strategies for migrating on-premises SQL Server to SQL Server on Azure VMs. You can also use the migration SQL Server from Amazon Web Service(AWS) EC2, AWS RDS or Google cloud platform (GCP).

At a high-level, the migration process involves Discover, Assess, Migrate, Cutover and Optimize.

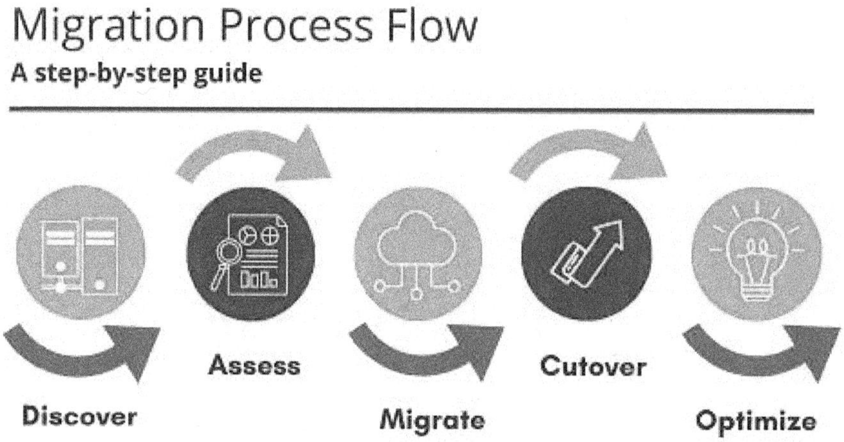

1.1.3 Discover:

It is a pre-migration phase in which you access the migration possibility of on-premise resource to the Azure cloud with cost estimates. For this phase, we can use the **Azure Migrate** tool. The Azure Migrate tool can access on-premise VM, Hyper VM and physical server for assessment in a centralized location.

It supports the following types of assessment types.

✓ **Azure VM:** It can assess on-premise VMware VM, Hyper VM and physical server migration to Azure virtual machine.

✓ **Azure VMware Solution (AVS):** It provides assessment to migrate on-premises VMware VMs to Azure VMware solution.

Assessment Overview

Azure uses the Azure Migrate tool as a central hub to discover, assess and migrate the on-premise application and workload. It requires to deploy a lightweight appliance deployed on a virtual or physical machine. It discovers the on-premise servers, and the appliance sends metadata, performance metric of each server to Azure Migrate.

The appliance collects the real-time sample point as below.

- **VMware VMs**: Every 20 seconds.
- **Hyper-V VMs**: Every 30 seconds.
- **Physical servers**: Every five minutes.

It collects the following performance metrics data as well.

- CPU utilization
- RAM utilization
- Disk IOPS (read and write)
- Disk throughput (read and write)
- Network throughput (in and out)

The Azure Migrate assigns a readiness category for each Server for migration using the server assessment reviews.

These categories are below.

- ✓ Read for Azure: The VM can be migrated to Azure without any changes.
- ✓ It is conditionally ready for Azure: This might be moved to Azure, but it might not have full Azure support. For example, an old Windows version server might fall into this category.
- ✓ Not ready for Azure: The machine is not compatible with Azure infrastructure.
- ✓ Readiness unknown: Due to insufficient data, Azure migrate cannot determine readiness.

Each Azure VM assessment also gets a confidence rating based on the reliability of Azure migrate size recommendations.

Availability of data points	Confidence rating
0-20%	1 star
21-40%	2 stars
41-60%	3 stars
61-80%	4 stars
81-100%	5 stars

Once Azure Migrate provides VM size recommendations, it also calculates the compute and store cost after migration to Azure cloud.

- ✓ Compute cost: It considers the OS, Software assurance, Reserved instance, VM up time, location and currency settings.
- ✓ Storage cost: It provides a monthly storage cost by aggregating all disks' monthly fee attached to the VM.

You can refer to **https://docs.microsoft.com/en-us/azure/migrate/concepts-assessment-calculation** for a detailed information on Azure Migrate assessment. Refer to **https://docs.microsoft.com/en-us/azure/migrate/best-practices-assessment** for the assessment best practices.

Assess

Azure Data Migration Assistant (DMA) is a comprehensive tool for assessing on-premise SQL Server for migrating to SQL Server on VM and identifying gaps between source and destination instances. You can use the tool to migrate between versions of SQL Server. For example, on-premise to Azure VM, Azure SQL Database or Azure SQL Managed Instance. The DMS can access queries from the extended event trace files as well as SQL queries.

DBA provides a list of the impacted object, resource, issues and recommendations for any breaking changes. It prevents upgrading the database compatibility until the deprecated items are resolved.

Note: If we are not upgrading the SQL Server version, skip the step and move to the Migrate section.

Migrate

Azure supports multiple migration approaches for migrating your SQL Server database to SQL Server on Azure VM.

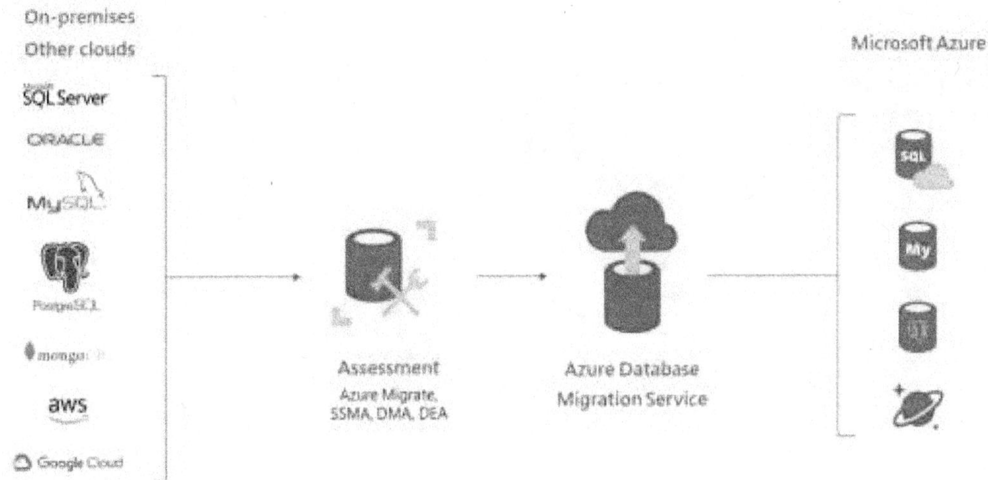

The available migration methods for migration are below.

Backup and restore method:

It is a standard migration using database backup and restores.

- Stop application for databases intended for migration
- Put the database in the single-user mode
- Perform full database backups to an on-premise location
- Copy the backup files to Azure VM using Azure Data explorer or AZ Azure CLI.
- Restore full backup on Azure VM.
- Minimum source version: SQL Server 2008 SP4
- Minimum target version: SQL Server 2008 SP3
- Source backup size constraint: Azure VM storage limit

Backup to URL

This method also uses the database backup and restore strategy. The difference is that you do not store backups to an -on-premise location. Instead, database backups are stored in the Azure blob storage container. You can configure the Backup to URL using a storage access key or shared access signature for secure access.

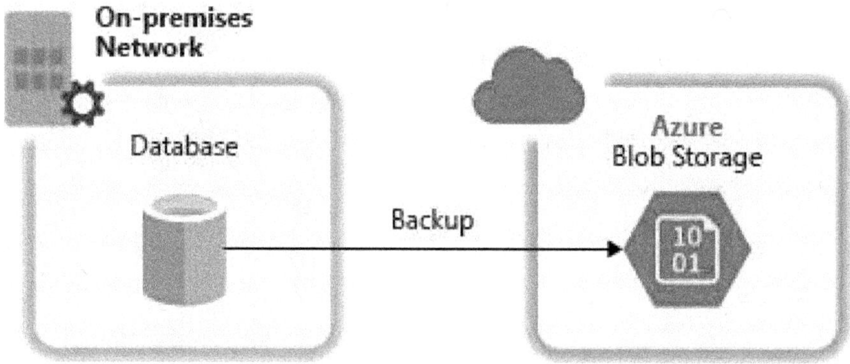

Note: You get more details on it in chapter 10.

- Minimum source version: SQL Server 2012 SP1 CU2
- Minimum target version: SQL Server 2012 SP1 CU2
- Source backup size constraint: 12.8 TB for SQL Server 2016, otherwise 1 TB

Detach and attach

In this migration approach, we use the following steps.

- We can detach the user database from the on-premise SQL Server instance.
- Copy the detached database files(data, log) into Azure Blob storage.
- Attach the database files to the Azure VM using the Azure URL.
- Minimum source version: SQL Server 2005
- Minimum target version: SQL Server 2005
- Source backup size constraint: Azure VM storage limit

Log shipping

This approach uses the log shipping configuration for migration databases to Azure VM.

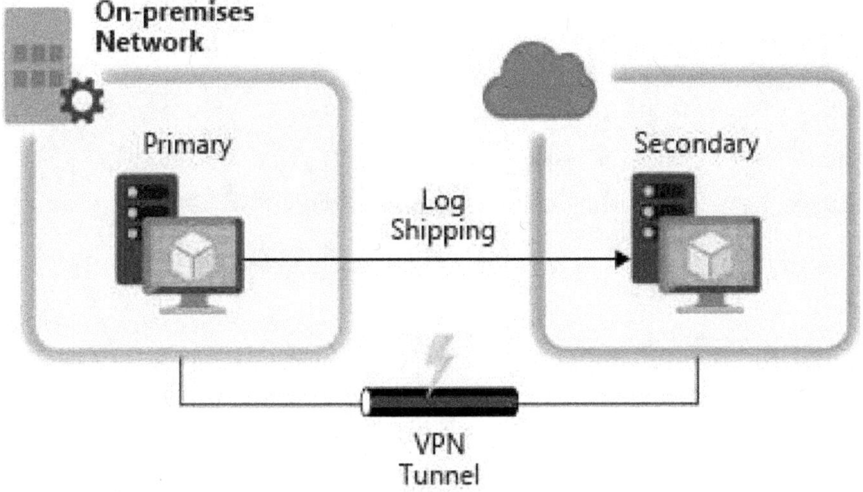

- The databases should be in full or bulk-logged recovery model.
- Take a full database backup to the on-premise location.
- Modify existing full backup database agent jobs to take COPY ONLY backup.
- Copy the backup files to Azure VM using Azure data explorer or AZCopy command line.
- Restore full database backup in NORECOVERY mode.
- Configure the log-shipping between the source on-premise SQL instance and destination SQL Server on Azure VM.

- During cut-over, make the following activities.
    - Stop applications
    - Take final database log backups using the log shipping backup job.
    - Disable the backup job.
    - Manually execute the copy and restore log shipping job.
    - Ensure the primary and secondary databases are in sync.
    - Perform a controlled log-shipping failover to SQL Server on Azure VM.
    - Minimum source version: SQL Server 2008 SP4
    - Minimum target version: SQL Server 2008 SP4
    - Source backup size constraint: Azure VM storage limit

Database Migration Assistant (DMA)

The Database Migration Assistant (DMA) can upgrade the database to a new SQL Server or Azure SQL Database version. It provides performance and reliability recommendations for the optimized database after migration.

- Minimum source version: SQL Server 2005
- Minimum target version: SQL Server 2008 SP4
- Source backup size constraint: Azure VM storage limit
- We cannot use DMA on Filestream-enabled user databases.

Distributed availability group

The distributed availability group is a particular type of availability group configuration that spans two separate availability groups in different WSFC. It provides cross-domain support as well. You can perform a failover from a WSFC (on-premise) to another WSFC (Azure VM). This method minimizes the downtime required for migration.

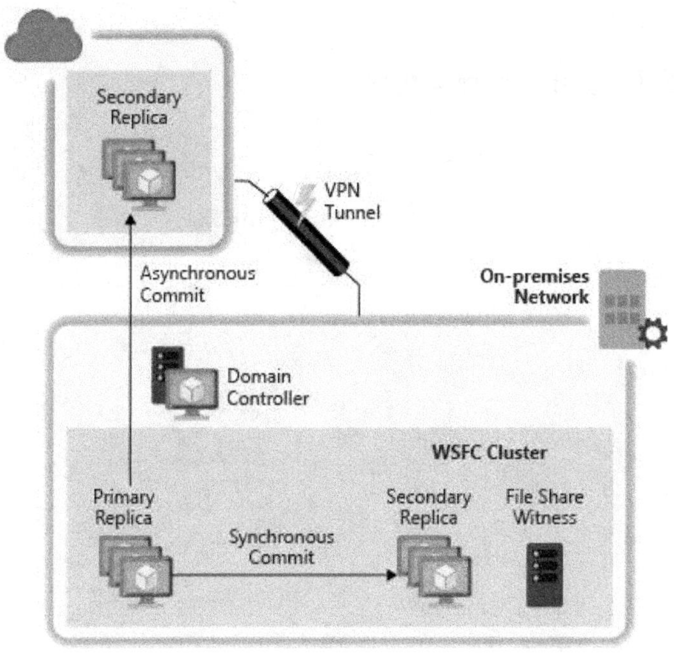

- Minimum source version: SQL Server 2016
- Minimum target version: SQL Server 2016
- Source backup size constraint: Azure VM storage limit

Post-migration

Once you have migrated On-premise SQL Server to SQL Server on Azure VM, you can do the validation test and perform post-migration steps.

- Perform validation tests
- Performance tests and compare metrics with the on-premise baselines.
- Perform post-migration steps such as backup configuration, applying default configuration, replication, audits etc.

Refer to **https://docs.microsoft.com/en-us/azure/azure-sql/migration-guides/virtual-machines/sql-server-to-sql-on-azure-vm-individual-databases-guide** for a detailed guide on database migration to Azure VM.

PaaS options for deploying SQL Server in Azure

The Platform-As-A-Service (PaaS) provides the solution for complete deployment in the Azure cloud. In the following figure, we can compare the SaaS, PaaS and IaaS solutions.

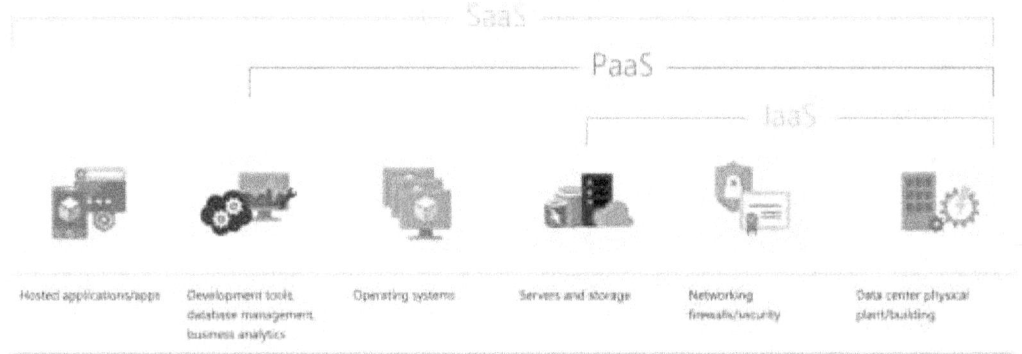

The PaaS platform uses Azure managed OS and management for your databases. It offers the following two deployments for Azure SQL.

- Azure SQL database: It supports a single database, elastic pools databases.
- Azure SQL Managed instance

To deploy an Azure PaaS solution, we need to select the purchasing model. Azure offers two purchasing models.

1. Provisioned model
    - Database Transaction Unit(DTU) model.
    - Virtual Core(vCores) based
2. Serverless model

Database Transaction Unit(DTU) model

This model bundles measures of compute, storage and IO resources. For a single database, these units are expressed in DTUs. It is suitable for customer required simple and predefined resource options.

Note: DTU model applies to both Azure SQL Database and Azure SQL Managed Instance.

In the DTU model, we can choose a service tier based on the uptime SLA, IO latency, CPU, IOPS and supported features.

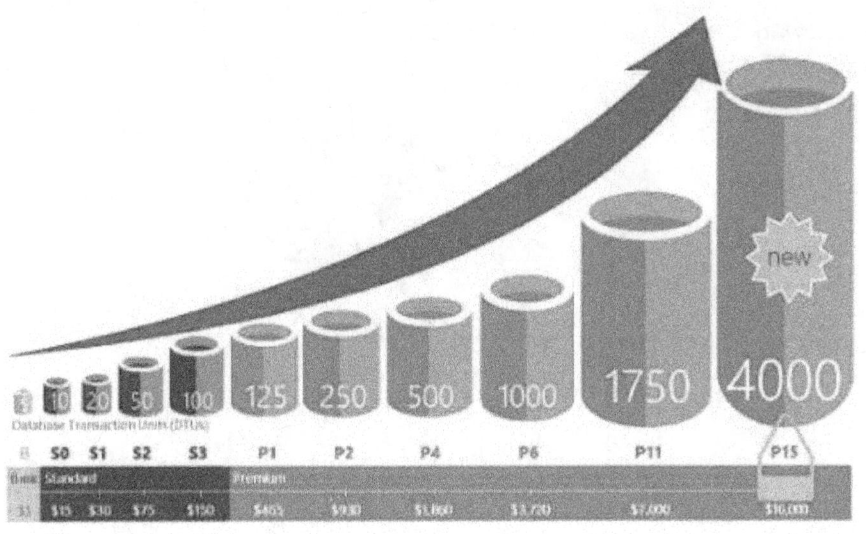

s

The following table shows the comparison between basic, standard and premium service tier.

	Basic	Standard	Premium
Target workload	Development and production	Development and production	Development and production
Uptime SLA	99.99%	99.99%	99.99%
Maximum backup retention	7 days	35 days	35 days
CPU	Low	Low, Medium, High	Medium, High
IOPS (approximate)*	1-4 IOPS per DTU	1-4 IOPS per DTU	25 IOPS per DTU
IO latency (approximate)	5 ms (read), 10 ms (write)	5 ms (read), 10 ms (write)	2 ms (read/write)
Columnstore indexing	N/A	S3 and above	Supported
In-memory OLTP	N/A	N/A	Supported

Azure guarantees a certain predictable level of performance based on the DTU allocated. It uses online transaction processing (OLTP) benchmark workload for real-time workloads. If the resources exceed the thresholds, it results in timeouts.

Database Transaction Unit – DTU

Bounding box

Monitoring database workload utilization within bounding box

- Represents the relative power (resources) assigned to the database
- Blended measure of CPU, memory, and read-write rates
- Compare the power across performance levels
- Simplifies talking about performance, think IOPS vs. %

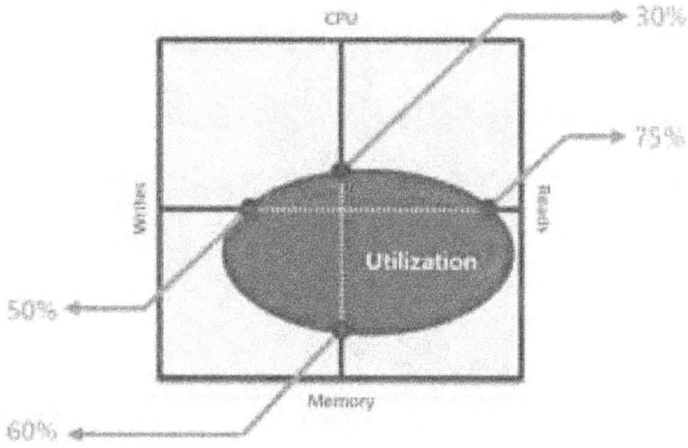

The single database has the following restrictions for database size and maximum DTUs.

	Basic	Standard	Premium
Maximum storage size	2 GB	1 TB	4 TB
Maximum DTUs	5	3000	4000

vCores-based purchasing model

In the vCores model, you can choose the compute and storage resources independently. You can also use the Azure Hybrid Licensing model for the vCores based purchasing model.

Note: The vCores purchasing model applies to both Azure SQL Database and Azure SQL Managed Instances.

The following table summarizes the differences between service tiers of the vCores model.

-	General Purpose	Business Critical	Hyperscale
Best for	Most business workloads. Offers budget-oriented, balanced, and scalable compute and storage options.	Offers business applications the highest resilience to failures by using several isolated replicas, and provides the highest I/O performance per database replica.	Most business workloads with highly scalable storage and read-scale requirements. Offers higher resilience to failures by allowing configuration of more than one isolated database replica.
Storage	Uses remote storage. **SQL Database provisioned compute:** 5 GB – 4 TB **Serverless compute:** 5 GB - 3 TB **SQL Managed Instance:** 32 GB - 8 TB	Uses local SSD storage. **SQL Database provisioned compute:** 5 GB – 4 TB **SQL Managed Instance:** 32 GB - 4 TB	Flexible autogrow of storage as needed. Supports up to 100 TB of storage. Uses local SSD storage for local buffer-pool cache and local data storage. Uses Azure remote storage as final long-term data store.
IOPS and throughput (approximate)	**SQL Database:** See resource limits for single databases and elastic pools. **SQL Managed Instance:** See Overview Azure SQL Managed Instance resource limits.	See resource limits for single databases and elastic pools.	Hyperscale is a multi-tiered architecture with caching at multiple levels. Effective IOPS and throughput will depend on the workload.
Availability	1 replica, no read-scale replicas	3 replicas, 1 read-scale replica, zone-redundant high availability (HA)	1 read-write replica, plus 0-4 read-scale replicas
Backups	Read-access geo-redundant storage (RA-GRS), 7-35 days (7 days by default)	RA-GRS, 7-35 days (7 days by default)	Snapshot-based backups in Azure remote storage. Restores use these snapshots for fast recovery. Backups are instantaneous and don't impact compute I/O performance. Restores are fast and aren't a size-of-data operation (taking minutes rather than hours or days).
In-memory	Not supported	Supported	Not supported

Hyperscale

- The Hyperscale service tier supports a database up to 100 TB.
- It provides nearly instantaneous database backups using the file snapshot stored in the Azure blob storage.
- It enables fast database restores.
- It has the highest performance due to its extended throughput and faster transaction commit.
- It can rapidly scale up and scale down.
- It is designed for an extensive database with fast vertical and horizontal compute scaling, high performance, fast database backup and restores.

You can refer **https://docs.microsoft.com/en-us/azure/azure-sql/database/service-tier-hyperscale** for more details on Hyperscale service tier.

Comparison between vCores and DTU based model

The following table summarizes the differences between vCores and DTU based models.

Feature	DTU	VCores
Feature	Blend of compute and storage resources	We can define compute and storage resources independently.
Scale	At DTU level	VCores, Storage
Geo-replication	Yes	Yes
SLA	99.99%	99.99%
Tiers	Basic, Standard and Premium	General purpose, Business-critical and Hyperscale
Max compute capacity	4000 DTU	80 vCores
Max Storage	4 TB	4 TB (Hyperscale can scale database beyond 4 TB limit)
Pricing	Price is at the DTU level	Price is separate for compute and storage.

The following figure compares the DTU and vCores model based on storage and compute resources scalability.

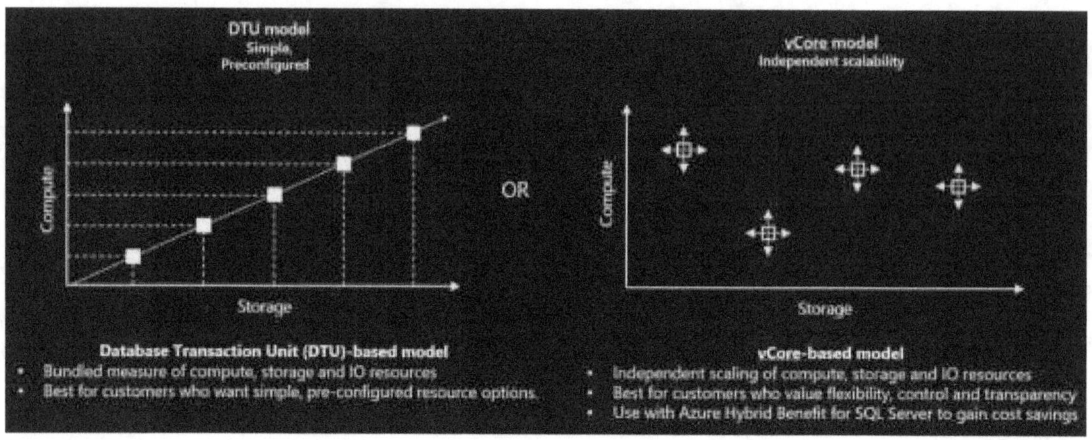

Azure SQL Database in Serverless configuration

Azure SQL Database serverless provides automatic scale up and down compute tier for a database based on the resource demand.

- You can specify minimum and maximum vCores in the Serverless model.
- The memory and IO resources are proportional to the specified range.
- You can use a minimum of 0.5 vCores and a maximum of 16 vCores.
- It automatically scales up and down resources based on the resource requirement.

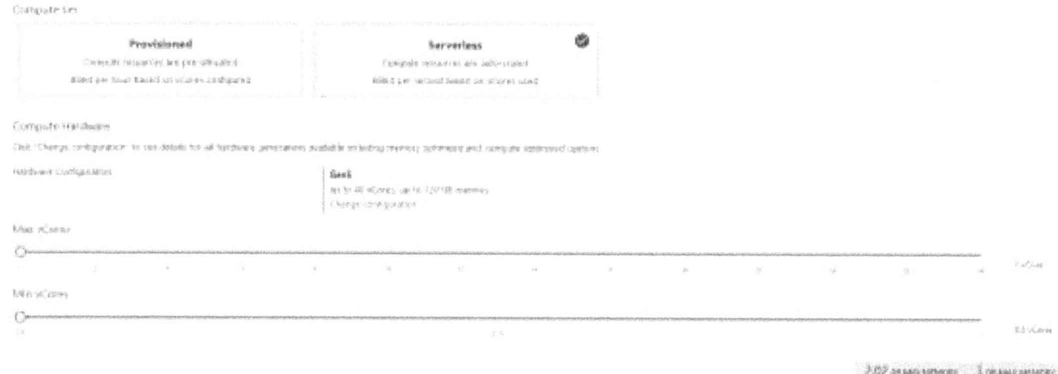

- You cannot pause or stop an Azure SQL Database in the provisioned tier. The serverless model allows you to specify an auto-pause delay. If the Azure database remains idle during the specified period, its status changes to Paused. During the paused state, Azure does not charge you for vCores. However, you get charged for storage cost.

○ Once the Azure database receives a connection attempt, the database resumes and is available for user transactions.

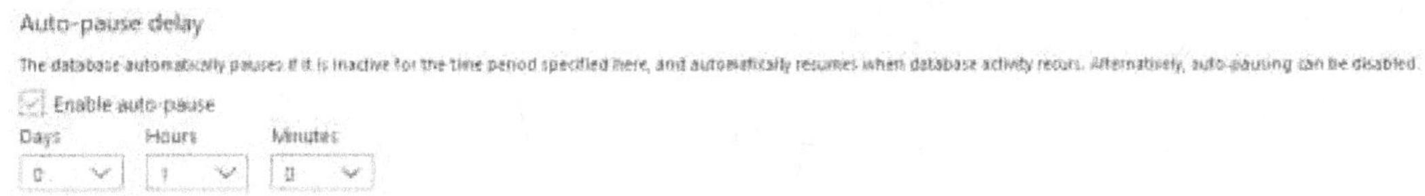

In the following figure, we can see the serverless database in the inactive and paused state. During the paused state, you do not get charged for vCores usage.

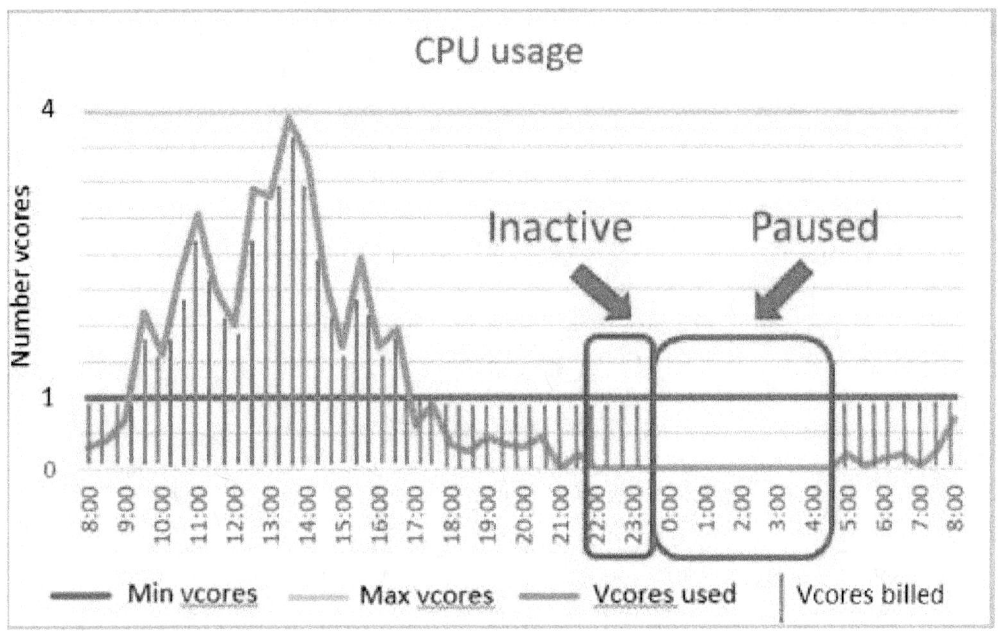

1.1.3.1 Restrictions of Serverless model

The Azure SQL Database serverless model has the following restrictions.

- No support for Geo-replication
- It does not support long-term backup retention.
- It does not support elastic jobs.
- SQL Database sync service is not supported.

Note: Currently, the Azure SQL Database serverless model is supported in the General purpose service tier with Gen5 hardware and vCPU purchase model.

Azure SQL Database in Serverless architecture is suitable for a single database with intermittent and unpredictable usage patterns

Comparison between Provisioned and Serverless compute tier

The following table summarizes the differences between provisioned compute and serverless compute.

	Serverless compute	Provisioned compute
Database usage pattern	Intermittent, unpredictable usage with lower average compute utilization over time.	More regular usage patterns with higher average compute utilization over time, or multiple databases using elastic pools.
Performance management effort	Lower	Higher
Compute scaling	Automatic	Manual
Compute responsiveness	Lower after inactive periods	Immediate
Billing granularity	Per second	Per hour

Refer to **https://docs.microsoft.com/en-us/azure/azure-sql/database/serverless-tier-overview** for more details on Serverless compute tier of Azure SQL Database.

Lab 2: Deploy a single SQL database

Suppose you are a database administrator and want to deploy an Azure SQL Database using the Azure Portal.

To create the Azure SQL Database, browse the Azure portal https://portal.azure.com and navigate SQL Databases in the portal.

Azure services

In the create SQL Database, give the following inputs.

- **Resource group**: Select an existing resource group or create a new resource group.
- **Database name**: Provide an Azure SQL Database name
- **Server**: Each Azure SQL Database must reside on a logical server. You can choose an existing server or click on Create new to deploy a new logical server. If you create a new logical server, it asks for the server name, server admin credentials and location.
- **Compute + Storage:** By default, Azure SQL Database uses Gen5, 2vCores, 32 GB storage.

To change the service model or tier, click on configure database. As shown below, the default tier is the general-purpose provisioned compute tier.

You can choose the Serverless to compute tier or change the provisioned tier based on DTU or vCPU model.

It gives you cost estimates for your configured option.

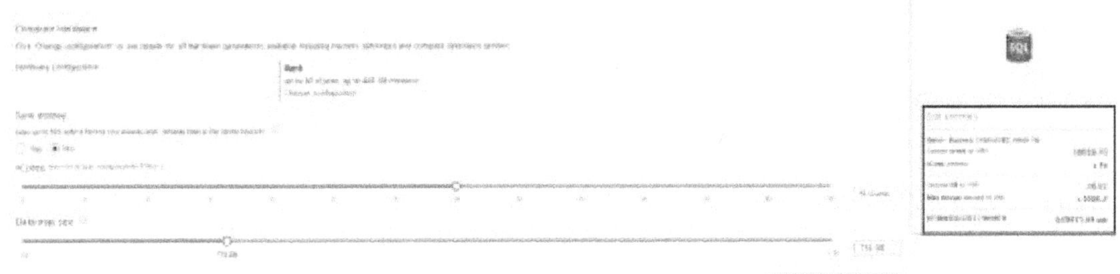

Lab 3: Deploying an Azure SQL Database via PowerShell/CLI

You can deploy the Azure SQL Database using PowerShell script as well. The below script does the following tasks

- Create a new resource group
- Define SQL administrator credentials
- Creates a new Azure logical server
- Create a new Azure SQL Database with an S0 performance level and sample AdventureWorksLT schema.
- Define firewall rules

Note

Copy script from
https://github.com/AzureDP300/AzureDP300/blob/main/Chapter4/Script1.ps1

Similarly, you can use Azure CLI script for Azure SQL Database deployment.

Note

Copy script from
https://github.com/AzureDP300/AzureDP300/blob/main/Chapter4/Script2.ps1

Lab 4: Deploying Azure SQL Database Using Azure Resource Manager templates

In this lab, we deploy the Azure SQL Database using the Azure Resource Manager(ARM) templates. You can use the GitHub repository "Azure-Quickstart-Templates" (https://github.com/Azure/azure-quickstart-templates) for ARM template reference.

Copy script from
https://github.com/AzureDP300/AzureDP300/blob/main/Chapter4/Script3.ps1

SQL elastic pools

Many times, organizations face issues due to unpredictable workloads on multiple databases having critical applications. If you use the high resources based on the peak usage, you need to invest a high amount. However, if you compromise with the lower resources, you do not get the desired performance.

Azure SQL database provides elastic pools as a cost-effective and straightforward solution for scaling multiple databases with unpredictable workloads. These databases are on a single logical server and share a set of resources at a set price. All databases share the same resource allocations (CPU, Memory, Worker thread, TempDB, Storage space). It assumes that only a subset of pool databases uses the compute resources at a given time. It enables developers to optimize database performance with a specified budget while delivering all Azure databases' performance elasticity.

- We can use either DTU based or vCore based purchasing models for elastic pool databases.
- It allows us to specify a minimum and maximum resources for an individual database in the pool.
- You can configure basic, standard and premium tier for the elastic database.

The following table highlights the differences between Basic, Standard and Premium tiers.

	Basic	Standard	Premium

Max. Size per database	2 GB	1 TB	1 TB
Max. storage size per pool	156 GB	4 TB	4 TB
Max. eDTU per database	5	3000	4000
Max eDTU per pool	1600	3000	4000
Max. number of the database in a pool	500	500	100

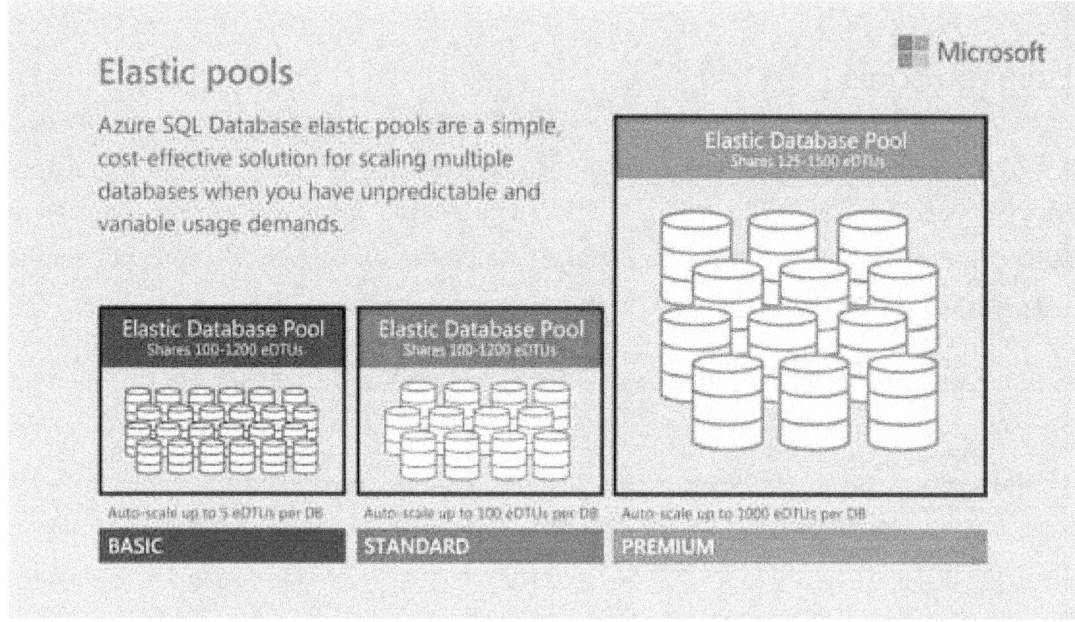

- **Basic elastic pool limits**

eDTUs per pool	50	100	200	300	400	800	1200	1600
Included storage per pool (GB)	5	10	20	29	39	78	117	156
Max storage per pool (GB)	5	10	20	29	39	78	117	156
Max In-Memory OLTP storage per pool (GB)	N/A	N/A	N/A	N/A	N/A	N/A	N/A	N/A
Max number DBs per pool [1]	100	200	500	500	500	500	500	500
Max concurrent workers (requests) per pool [2]	100	200	400	600	800	1600	2400	3200
Max concurrent sessions per pool [2]	30000	30000	30000	30000	30000	30000	30000	30000
Min DTU per database choices	0, 5	0, 5	0, 5	0, 5	0, 5	0, 5	0, 5	0, 5
Max DTU per database choices	5	5	5	5	5	5	5	5
Max storage per database (GB)	2	2	2	2	2	2	2	2

- **Standard elastic pool limits**

eDTUs per pool	50	100	200	300	400	800
Included storage per pool (GB) [1]	50	100	200	300	400	800
Max storage per pool (GB)	500	750	1024	1280	1536	2048
Max In-Memory OLTP storage per pool (GB)	N/A	N/A	N/A	N/A	N/A	N/A
Max number DBs per pool [2]	100	200	500	500	500	500
Max concurrent workers (requests) per pool [3]	100	200	400	600	800	1600
Max concurrent sessions per pool [3]	30000	30000	30000	30000	30000	30000
Min DTU per database choices	0, 10, 20, 50	0, 10, 20, 50, 100	0, 10, 20, 50, 100, 200	0, 10, 20, 50, 100, 200, 300	0, 10, 20, 50, 100, 200, 300, 400	0, 10, 20, 50, 100, 200, 300, 400, 800
Max DTU per database choices	10, 20, 50	10, 20, 50, 100	10, 20, 50, 100, 200	10, 20, 50, 100, 200, 300	10, 20, 50, 100, 200, 300, 400	10, 20, 50, 100, 200, 300, 400, 800
Max storage per database (GB)	500	750	1024	1024	1024	1024

- **Premium elastic pool limits**

eDTUs per pool	**125**	**250**	**500**	**1000**	**1500**
Included storage per pool (GB) [1]	250	500	750	1024	1536
Max storage per pool (GB)	1024	1024	1024	1024	1536
Max In-Memory OLTP storage per pool (GB)	1	2	4	10	12
Max number DBs per pool [2]	50	100	100	100	100
Max concurrent workers per pool (requests) [3]	200	400	800	1600	2400
Max concurrent sessions per pool [3]	30000	30000	30000	30000	30000
Min eDTUs per database	0, 25, 50, 75, 125	0, 25, 50, 75, 125, 250	0, 25, 50, 75, 125, 250, 500	0, 25, 50, 75, 125, 250, 500, 1000	0, 25, 50, 75, 125, 250, 500, 1000
Max eDTUs per database	25, 50, 75, 125	25, 50, 75, 125, 250	25, 50, 75, 125, 250, 500	25, 50, 75, 125, 250, 500, 1000	25, 50, 75, 125, 250, 500, 1000
Max storage per database (GB)	1024	1024	1024	1024	1024

You can refer **https://docs.microsoft.com/en-us/azure/azure-sql/database/resource-limits-vcore-elastic-pools** for Resource limits for elastic pools using the vCore purchasing model.

When should you consider a SQL Database elastic pool?

Suppose you have a single Azure SQL Database with the following resource utilization pattern. It shows the DTU usage between 12:10 resource utilization peaks at 90 DTU. Most of the time, resource utilization is normal.

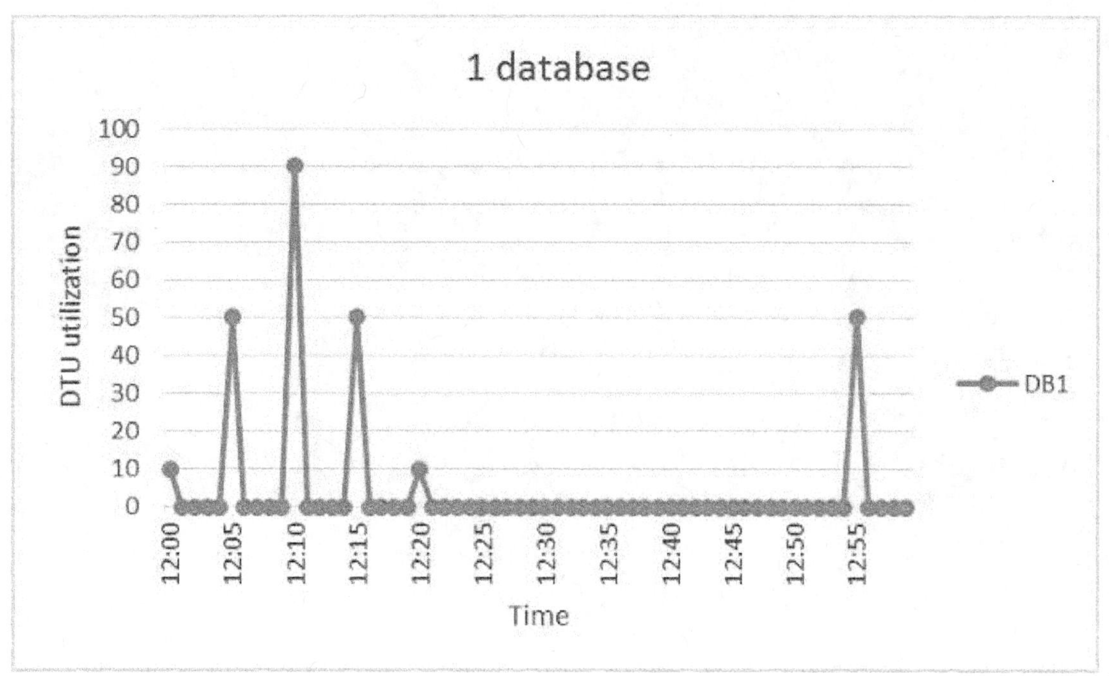

In the elastic pool, we can share the unused DTU across multiple databases. In this case, your overall cost remains controlled, and your database gets optimized resources.

Look at the resource utilization for 4 and 20 databases in a pool. It shows the maximum DTU utilization is 100 DTU for 20 databases. Therefore, you can configure 100 eDTU for the pool, and it shares the cost among all databases.

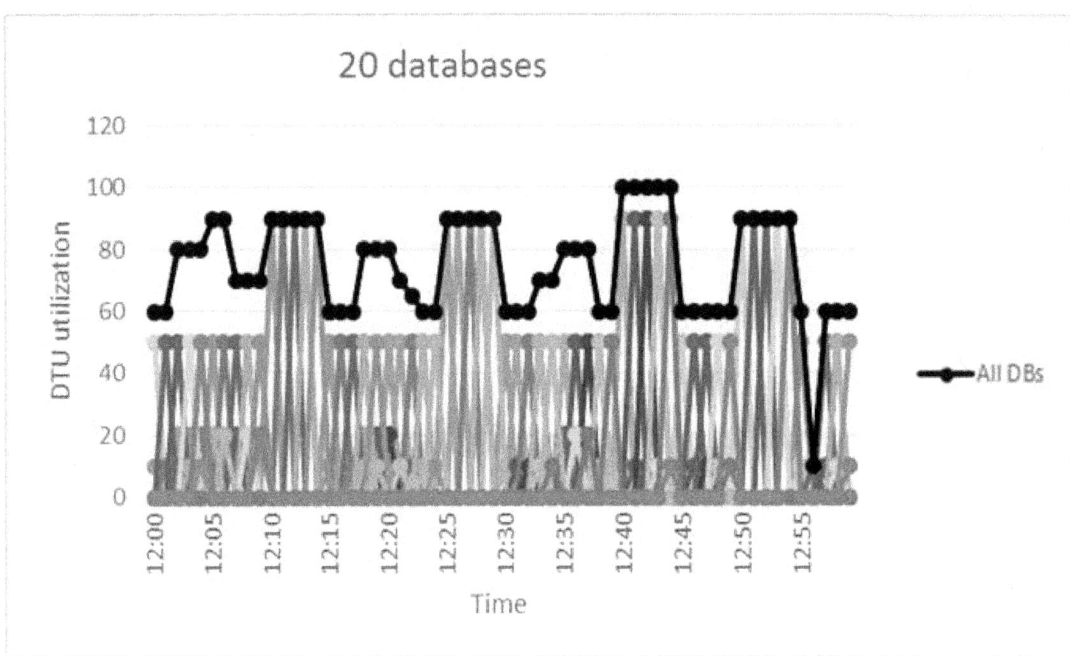

Lab 5: Deploy an elastic pool for Azure SQL Database

In this lab, we configure an elastic pool for Azure SQL Database and explore various configuration options.

In the Azure portal, navigate to the SQL database and click on Create new database. In the create SQL database page, it gives an option- want to use SQL elastic pool.

By default, you get a single Azure SQL Database.

Create SQL Database
Microsoft
provision with smart defaults, or visit each tab to customize. Learn more

Project details

Select the subscription to manage deployed resources and costs. Use resource groups like folders to organize and manage all your resources.

Subscription * Azure subscription 1

Resource group * MyAzureLabSQL
Create new

Database details

Enter required settings for this database, including picking a logical server and configuring the compute and storage resources

Database name * Enter database name

Server * azuredemosqldemo (Central India)
Create new

Want to use SQL elastic pool? * Yes No

Review + create Next : Networking >

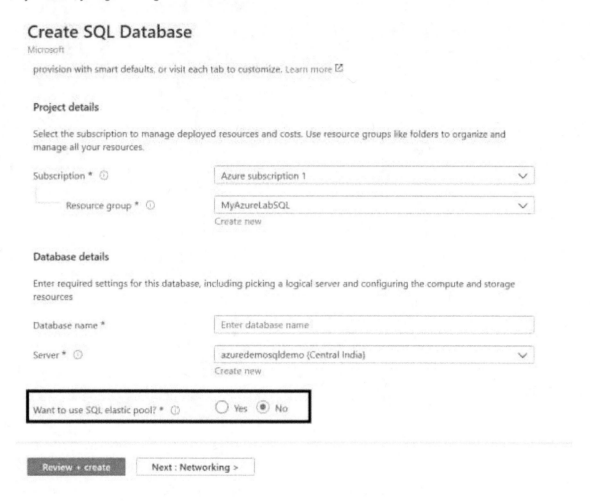

Therefore, click on Yes for SQL elastic pool and create a new elastic pool. By default, it uses Gen5, 2vCores, 32 GB and 0 databases.

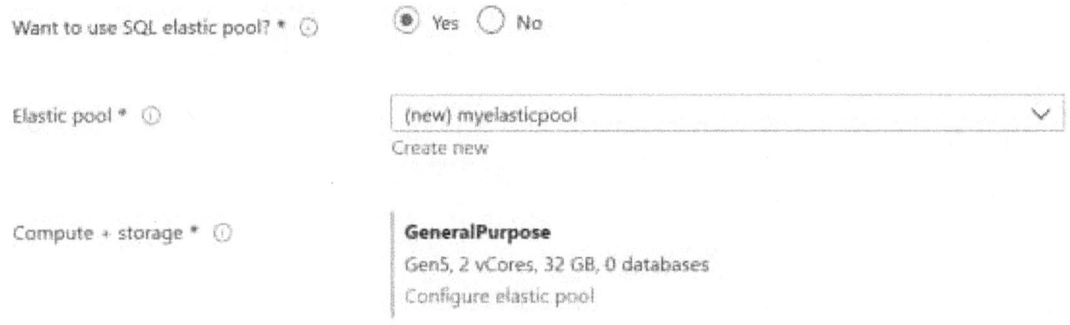

Click on Configure elastic pool. On the next page, you have two configurations.

- Pool settings
- Per database settings

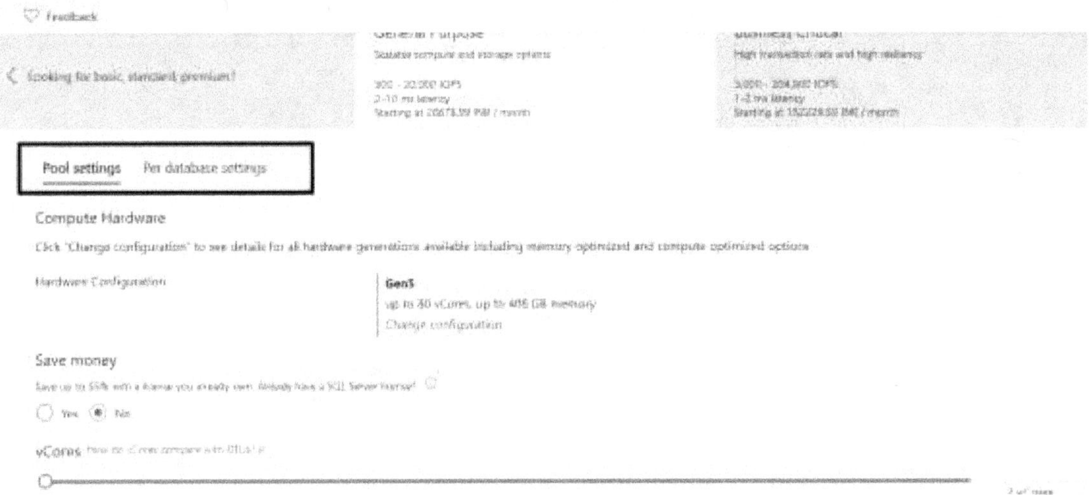

In the pool setting, you can configure the service tier, vCPU and max data size. For example, let's select the following for the demo elastic pool.

- vCores: 20 vCores
- Data max size: 1.5 TB

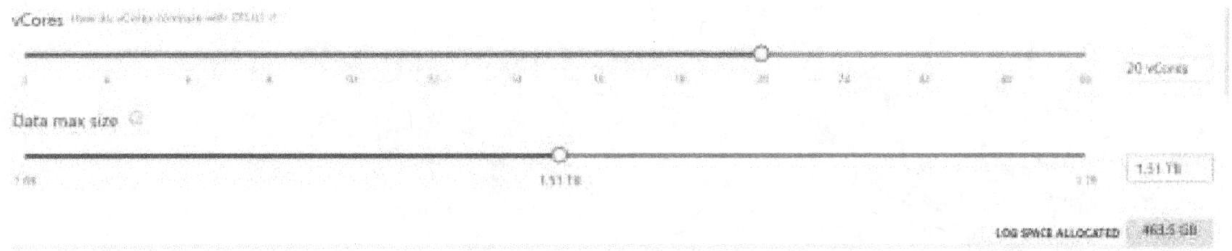

Now, click on per-database settings. Here, you can specify the maximum vCores per database in the pool. You can choose the maximum vCores as per your pool vCores configuration. For example, here, I specify a maximum of 4 vCores per database.

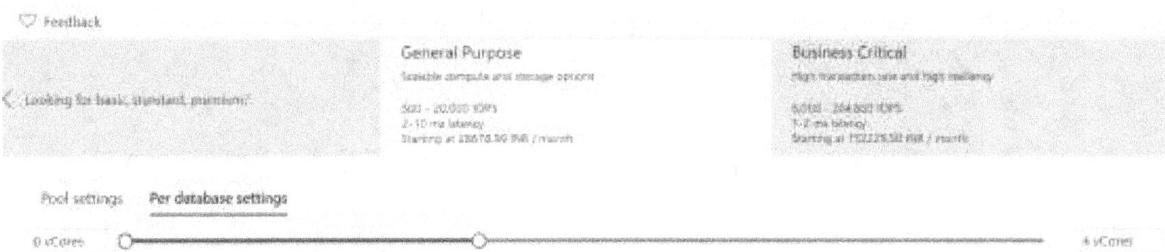

You can review the configuration and create an elastic pool, add databases into it.

Refer to **https://docs.microsoft.com/en-us/azure/azure-sql/database/elastic-pool-overview** for a detailed information on SQL elastic pools.

SQL managed instance

Azure SQL Managed Instance is a fully functional SQL Server instance. It provides almost 100% compatibility with the on-premise SQL Server with features such as SQL Server agent, TempDB access, cross-database queries, and common language runtime. It has all benefits of the PaaS service, and it uses the Azure SQL Database infrastructure.

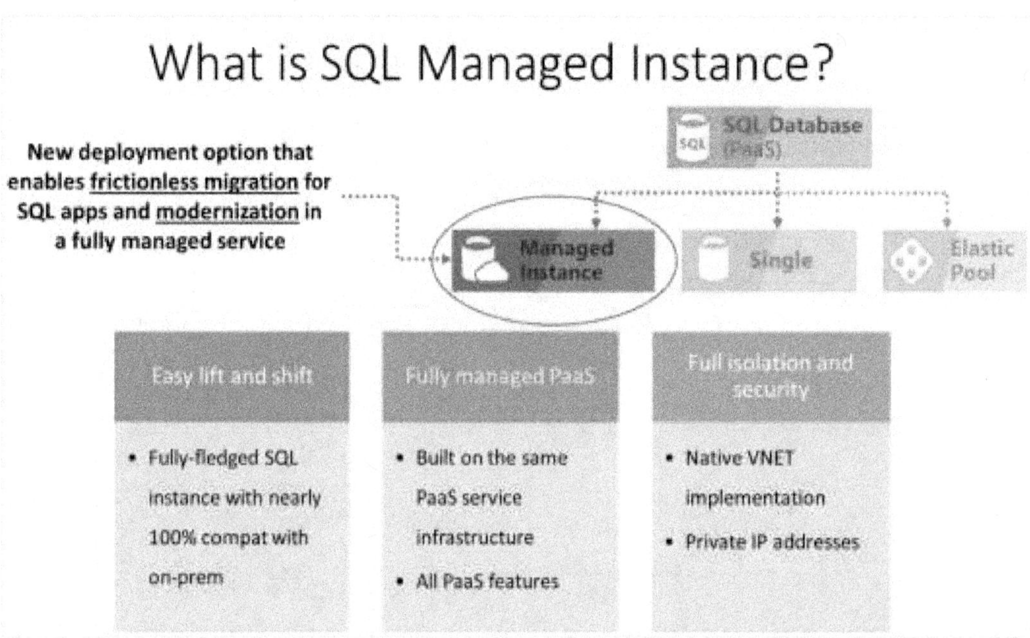

The following table highlights the differences between Azure SQL Database and Azure SQL Managed Instance.

Feature	Azure SQL Database	Azure SQL Managed Instance
Always Encrypted	Yes	Yes
Automatic tuning (plan forcing), Change tracking, Database collation, Contained databases, Contained users, Data compression, Database configuration settings, Online index operations, Partitioning, and Temporal tables	Yes	Yes
Application roles, Dynamic data masking (see getting started guide), Row Level Security	Yes	Yes
Graph processing, JSON data (see getting started	Yes	Yes

guide), OPENXML, Spatial, OPENJSON, and XML indexes.		
Availability	It offers 99.99-99.995% availability is guaranteed for every database	It offers 99.99.% availability is guaranteed for every database, and the user can't manage it.
Attach database	No	No
Auditing	Yes	Yes*
Azure Active Directory (Azure AD) authentication	Azure AD users only.	Yes. Including server-level Azure AD logins.
Native backups	No	Yes, user-initiated copy-only backups to Azure Blob storage (user can't initiate automatic system backups)
Built-in functions	Yes	Yes*
BULK INSERT statement	Yes	Yes*
Certificates and asymmetric keys	Yes	Yes, without access to file system for `BACKUP` and `CREATE` operations
Change data capture – CDC	No	Yes
Credentials	Yes, Database scoped credentials	Yes, but only **Azure Key Vault** and `SHARED ACCESS SIGNATURE` are supported
Cross-database/three-part name queries	No	Yes, with additional Elastic queries support.
Cross-database transactions	No	Yes* (Within the instance)
Database Mail	No	Yes
Database mirroring, Database snapshots	No	No
DBCC statements	Yes, Most of the DBCC statements work.	Yes*

DDL statements	Yes, Most of the DDL statements work.	Yes*
Distributed transactions - MS DTC	No	No
DML triggers	Yes, Most of the DDL statements work.	Yes
Event notifications	No	No
Expressions	Yes	Yes
Extended events (XEvent)	At database level	Yes*
Files and filegroups	Only the Primary file-group	Yes. File paths are automatically assigned, and the file location can't be specified in ALTER DATABASE ADD FILE statement.
Filestream	No	No
In-memory optimization	Yes	Yes
Linked servers	No	Yes. Only to SQL Server and SQL Database without distributed transactions.
Log shipping	No	Not available as a High availability solution
Recovery models	Only Full Recovery that guarantees high availability is supported. Simple and Bulk Logged recovery models are not available.	Only Full Recovery that guarantees high availability is supported. Simple and Bulk Logged recovery models are not available.
Restore the database from backup	From automated backups	From automated backups
Server configuration settings	Yes	Yes*
SQL Server Agent	No	Yes*

TempDB	Yes. 32-GB size per core for every database.	Yes. 24-GB size per vCore for entire GP tier and limited by instance size on BC tier
Time zone choice	No	Yes
Trace flags	No	Yes*
Transactional Replication	Yes (Transactional and Snapshot replication subscriber-only)	Yes (in public preview)
Windows authentication	No	No
WSFC	No	No

You can go through **https://docs.microsoft.com/en-us/azure/azure-sql/managed-instance/transact-sql-tsql-differences-sql-server#stored-procedures-functions-and-triggers** for exploring T-SQL differences between SQL Server & Azure SQL Managed Instance

Refer to **https://docs.microsoft.com/en-us/azure/azure-sql/managed-instance/sql-managed-instance-paas-overview** for a detailed information on Azure SQL Managed instances.

Deploy MariaDB, MySQL, and PostgreSQL on Azure

The Azure infrastructure allows you to deploy open-source databases such as MySQL, MariaDB and PostgreSQL. These database systems come as fully managed databases in the Azure cloud. Azure provides features such as high availability, automatic backups, automatic patching, and the highest security level for these database systems.

Azure Database for MySQL

Azure Database for MySQL offers relational database service in the Microsoft Azure cloud-based on the MySQL community edition. It provides the following features

- Built-in high availability
- Automatic backups
- Point-in-time restore up to 35 days
- Automatic hardware, OS and database engine maintenance
- Predictable performance
- Pay-As-You-Go price model
- Elastic scaling
- Cost optimization using the ability to stop and start-server
- Enterprise level security
- Encryption
- Monitoring and automation functionality for large scale deployments

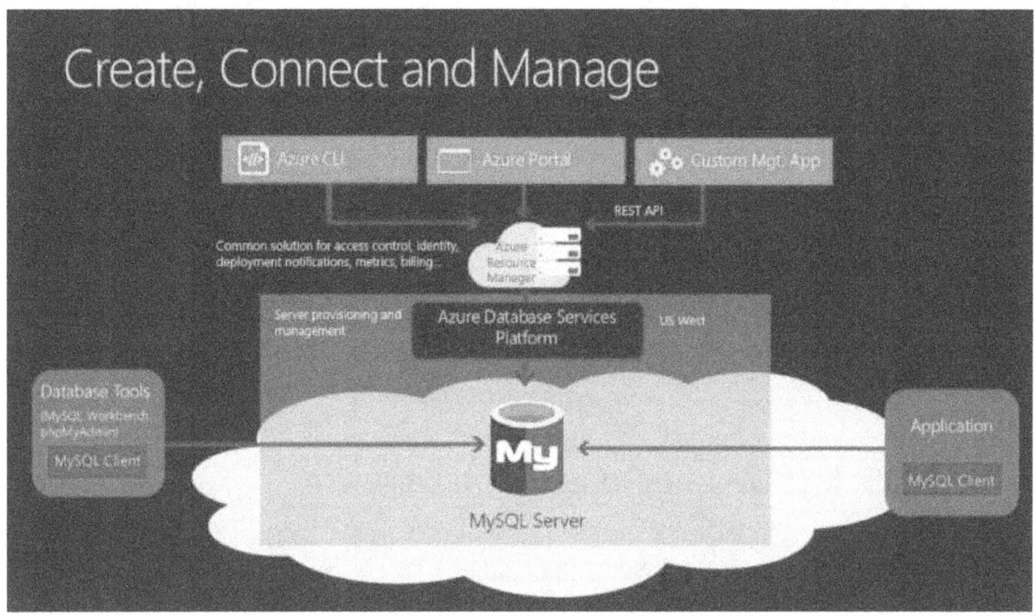

Azure Database for MySQL comes in the following deployment models.

Single Server

- Fully managed service
- automatic patching, backups, high availability, user management with minimal user configuration.
- It supports MySQL 5.6, 5.7 and 8.0 version

- You can configure Basic, General purpose and Memory optimized pricing tiers.
- It is suitable for cloud-native applications without the requirement of granular control on patching and custom MySQL configurator.

Azure Database for MySQL – Single Server

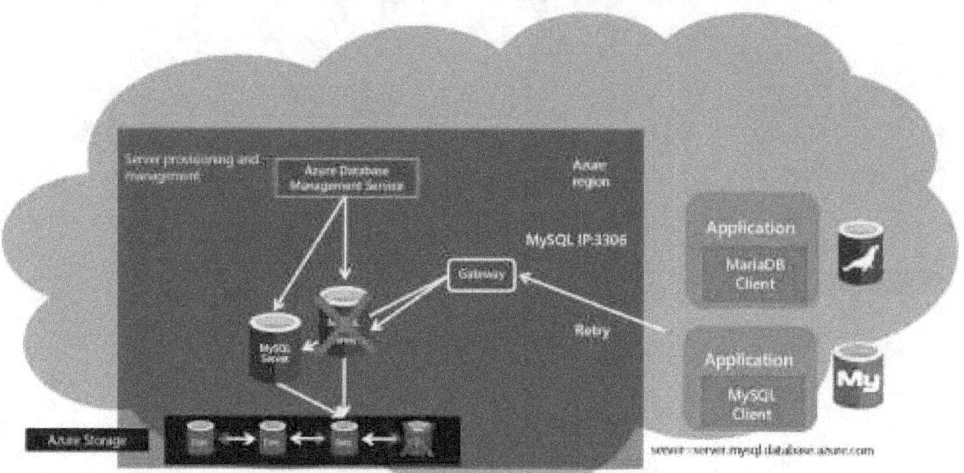

3 copies of data for data reliability Compute Redundancy

Refer to article **https://docs.microsoft.com/en-us/azure/mysql/single-server-overview** for detailed information on Azure MySQL single server.

Flexible server (preview)

Azure MySQL flexible server provides more granular control and flexibility over the database management and database configurations.

- It provides flexibility for users to opt for high availability within a single availability zone and across multiple availability zones.
- It provides cost optimization control using the start and stops server functionality.
- It supports MySQL 5.7 community edition.
- This server is in public preview.

- It is suitable for the application that requires granular control and customization, managed maintenance window and zone redundant high availability.

Azure Database for MySQL - Flexible Server

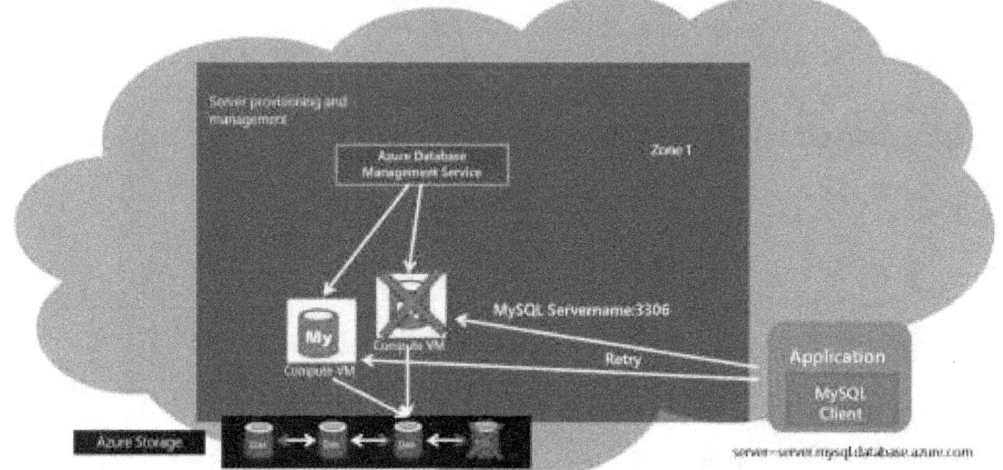

3 copies of data for data reliability Compute Redundancy

You can refer **https://docs.microsoft.com/en-us/azure/mysql/flexible-server/overview** for more details on Azure MySQL flexible server.

Azure Database for PostgreSQL

Azure Database for PostgreSQL is a relational database service in the Microsoft Azure cloud-based on the PostgreSQL community edition. It provides the following features

- Built-in high availability
- Automatic backups with point-in-time restore up to 35 days
- Automatic hardware, OS and database engine maintenance
- Predictable performance
- Pay-As-You-Go price model
- Elastic scaling within seconds
- Cost optimization using the ability to stop and start-server

- Enterprise level security
- Encryption, Monitoring and automation functionality for large scale deployments

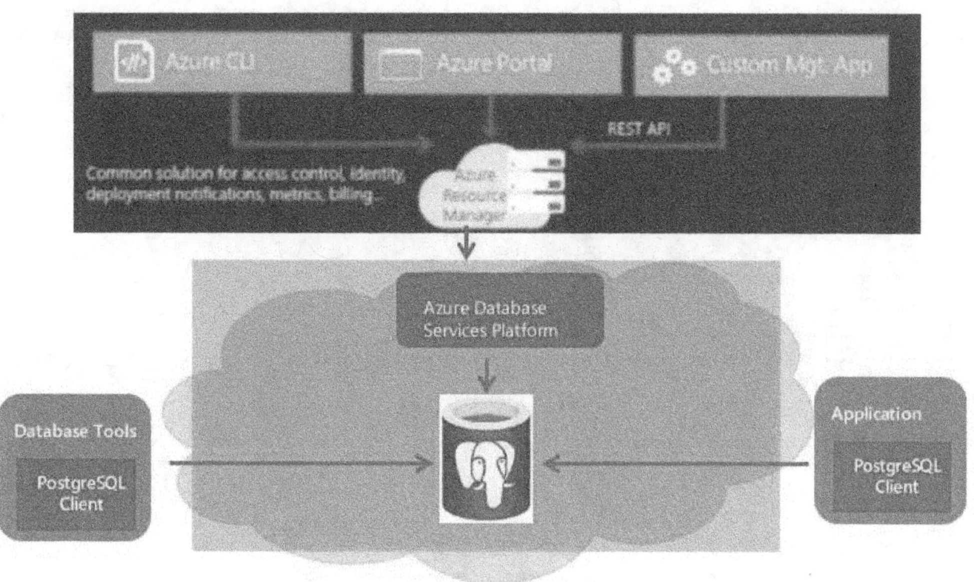

Azure Database for PostgreSQL provides the following deployment models.

- Single Server
- Flexible Server (Preview)
- Hyperscale (Citus)

Azure Database for PostgreSQL - Single Server

- Fully-managed database service with minimal customizations
- Supports database functions such as automatic patching, backups, high availability, security.
- It offers 99.99% availability with a single availability zone
- It supports PostgreSQL community version 9.5,9.6,10 and 11.
- It offers Basic General purpose and Memory-optimized development options.

The following image shows the high availability of PostgreSQL single server using the automated procedure.

1. Azure provisions a new compute container.
2. It maps the storage with data files to the new compute container.
3. The PostgreSQL database is brought online on the new container.
4. The gateway service ensures transparent failure with no application changes.

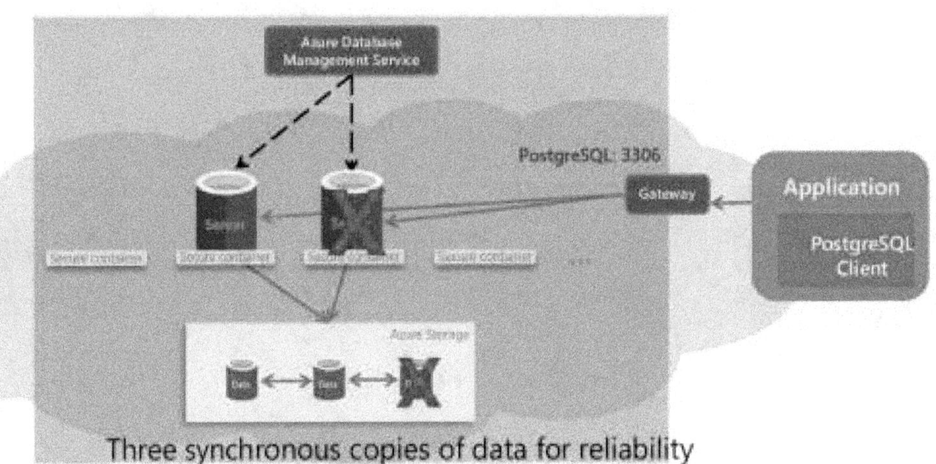

Three synchronous copies of data for reliability

Refer to **https://docs.microsoft.com/en-us/azure/postgresql/overview-single-server** for more details on Azure PostgreSQL Single server.

Azure Database for PostgreSQL - Flexible Server (Preview)

- It is a fully-managed database service with more granular control and flexibility over database functions and configurations.
- You can configure high availability within a single availability zone and across multiple availability zones.
- It allows users to the collate database engine with the client tier for low latency and high availability.
- It supports PostgreSQL community version 11 and 12.
- It is in the preview phase.

- You can stop and start Azure PostgreSQL for cost optimization.
- It is suitable for applying granular control, zone redundant high availability, and managed maintenance window.

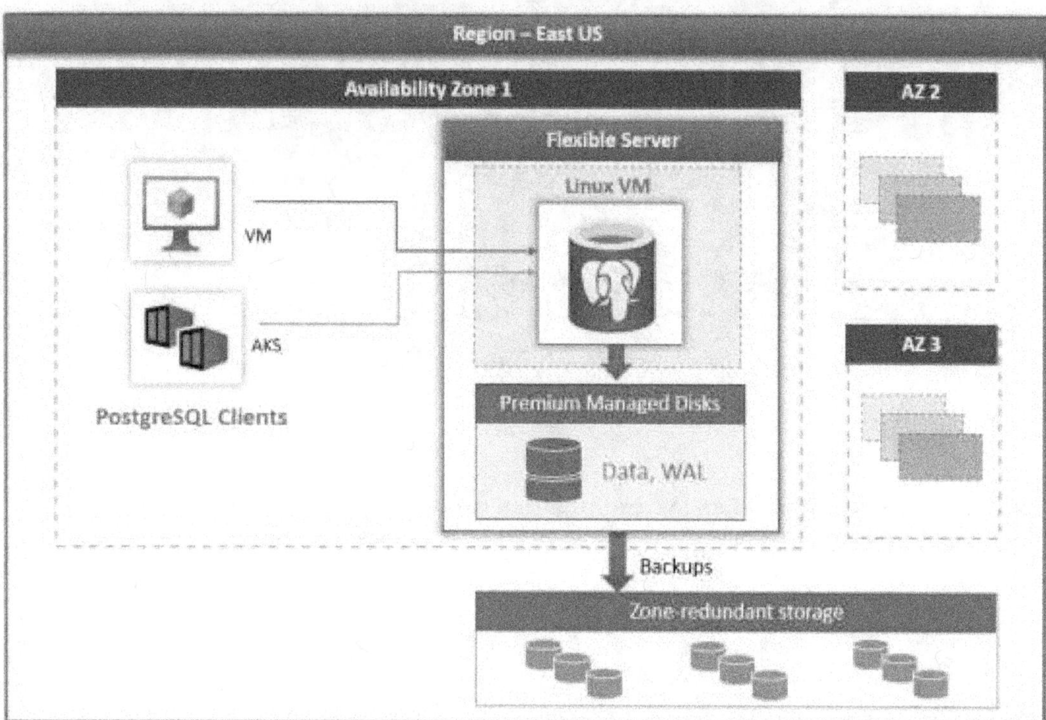

The following figure describes the high availability of the flexible server.

1. It provisions a new compute Linux VM.
2. Azure maps the storage with data files to the new VM
3. PostgreSQL database engine is brought online on the new VM.

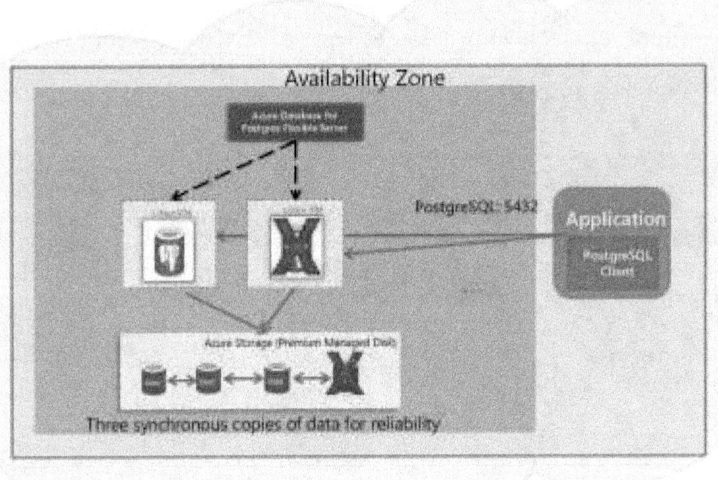

You can refer **https://docs.microsoft.com/en-us/azure/postgresql/flexible-server/overview** for detailed information on PostgreSQL flexible server.

Azure Database for PostgreSQL – Hyperscale (Citus)

The PostgreSQL hyperscale (Citus) uses sharding to scale queries horizontally. It uses a parallel query engine for faster query response on large databases. It provides high throughput transactional workloads, multi-tenant applications and real-time operational analytics.

Azure Database for MariaDB

Azure Database for MariaDB is a fully managed relational database service for the MariaDB community edition. It offers the following features.

- Built-in high availability
- Predictable performance
- Pay-as-you-go pricing
- It quickly scales the resources within seconds
- Encryption, automatic backups

- Enterprise-grade security, compliance

The following table summarizes the different service tiers for Azure MariaDB.

Resource	Basic	General Purpose	Memory Optimized
Compute generation	Gen 5	Gen 5	Gen 5
vCores	1, 2	2, 4, 8, 16, 32, 64	2, 4, 8, 16, 32
Memory per vCore	2 GB	5 GB	10 GB
Storage size	5 GB to 1 TB	5 GB to 4 TB	5 GB to 4 TB
Database backup retention period	7 to 35 days	7 to 35 days	7 to 35 days

Lab 6: Create an Azure Database for the MariaDB server by using the Azure portal

In this lab, we deploy an Azure Database for the MariaDB server using the Azure portal. In the Azure portal, search for Azure Database for MariaDB, and it gives the following result.

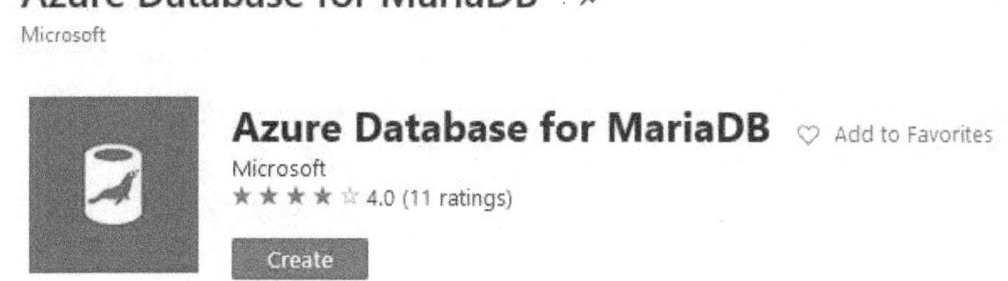

Click on Create. In the create MariaDB Server, enter the following details.

- Resource group
- Server details
    - Server name
    - Data source
    - Location

- version
- Pricing tier

By default, Azure uses the following pricing tier configurations.

- Compute Generation (Gen 5)
- vCore (4 vCores)
- Storage (100 GB)
- Backup Retention Period (7 days)

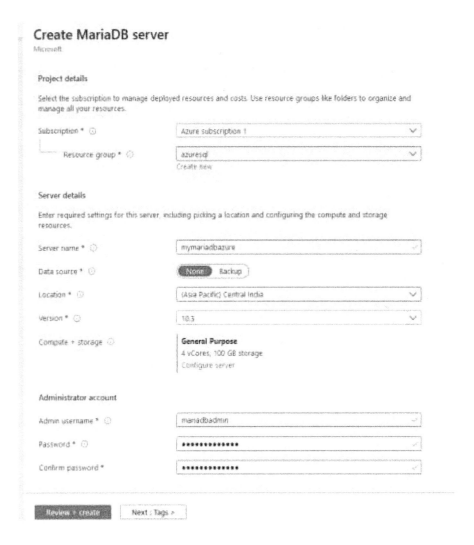

Create MariaDB server
Microsoft

Project details

Select the subscription to manage deployed resources and costs. Use resource groups like folders to organize and manage all your resources.

Subscription * Azure subscription 1

Resource group * azuresql
Create new

Server details

Enter required settings for this server, including picking a location and configuring the compute and storage resources.

Server name * mymariadbazure

Data source * None Backup

Location * (Asia Pacific) Central India

Version * 10.3

Compute + storage General Purpose
4 vCores, 100 GB storage
Configure server

Administrator account

Admin username * mariadbadmin

Password * ••••••••••••••

Confirm password * ••••••••••••••

Review + create Next : Tags >

Click on Configure server to specify the compute configurations. Here, you can do the following configurations.

- Compute tier: Choose Basic(1-2 vCores), General purpose (2-64 vCores) and Memory-optimized (2-32 vCores)
- vCores: Specify the vCores as per your selected compute tier
- Storage size in GB
- Storage auto-growth: Enabled
- Backup retention period
- Backup redundancy: Locally Redundant or Geo-Redundant.

Compute + storage

Compute resources are pre-allocated and billed per minute based on vCores configured.

Compute tier
Basic (1-2 vCores) - Best for workloads that require light compute and I/O performance
General Purpose (2-64 vCores) - Balanced configuration for most common workloads
Memory Optimized (2-32 vCores) - Best for workloads that require a high memory to CPU ratio

vCores 4
Memory 20 GB

Would you like to configure larger storage (Public Preview)? Learn More
Yes (5GB up to 16TB and 20000 IOPS)
No (5GB up to 4TB and 6000 IOPS)

Storage size (in GB) 100
100 GB

UP TO 300 AVAILABLE IOPS

Storage Auto-growth
Storage auto-growth enabled

Backup

Configure automatic server backups that can be used to restore your server to a point-in-time. Learn More

Backup Retention Period 7

Backup redundancy
Locally Redundant - Recover from data loss within region
Geo-Redundant - Recover from regional outage or disaster

Apply Cancel

General Purpose
Cost per vCore / month (in INR) 6614.38
vCores selected x 4

Cost per GB / month (in INR) 9.45
Storage selected (in GB) x 100

EST. MONTHLY COST 27402.04 INR

Additional charge per usage
See pricing details for more detail

Select **Review + create** to provision the server. By default, it creates the **information_schema**, **MySQL**, **performance_schema**, and **sys** databases in the Azure Database for MariaDB.

Lab 7: Deploy a PostgreSQL database server to Azure

In this lab exercise, we deploy an Azure Database for PostgreSQL using the single server deployment. In the Azure portal, search: Azure Database for PostgreSQL. It gives you the following deployment options.

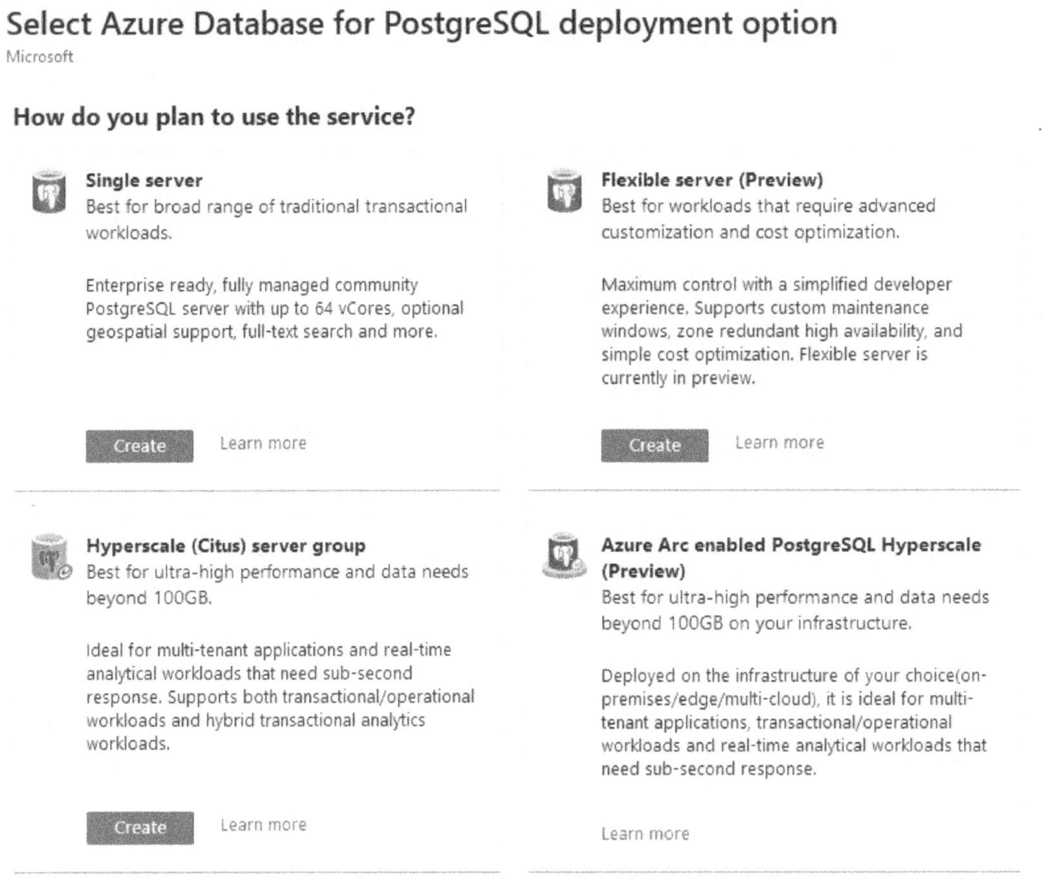

Select Azure Database for PostgreSQL deployment option
Microsoft

How do you plan to use the service?

Single server
Best for broad range of traditional transactional workloads.

Enterprise ready, fully managed community PostgreSQL server with up to 64 vCores, optional geospatial support, full-text search and more.

Create Learn more

Flexible server (Preview)
Best for workloads that require advanced customization and cost optimization.

Maximum control with a simplified developer experience. Supports custom maintenance windows, zone redundant high availability, and simple cost optimization. Flexible server is currently in preview.

Create Learn more

Hyperscale (Citus) server group
Best for ultra-high performance and data needs beyond 100GB.

Ideal for multi-tenant applications and real-time analytical workloads that need sub-second response. Supports both transactional/operational workloads and hybrid transactional analytics workloads.

Create Learn more

Azure Arc enabled PostgreSQL Hyperscale (Preview)
Best for ultra-high performance and data needs beyond 100GB on your infrastructure.

Deployed on the infrastructure of your choice(on-premises/edge/multi-cloud), it is ideal for multi-tenant applications, transactional/operational workloads and real-time analytical workloads that need sub-second response.

Learn more

Click on Create in the Single server and enter the following information.

- Resource group
- Server details
    - Server name
    - Data source

- Location
- version

By default, it uses 4vCores with 100 GB storage in the General purpose pricing tier.

Compute + storage ⓘ | **General Purpose**
4 vCores, 100 GB storage
Configure server

Click on Configure server. Select the pricing tier, vCores, Storage, backup retention period and backup redundancy.

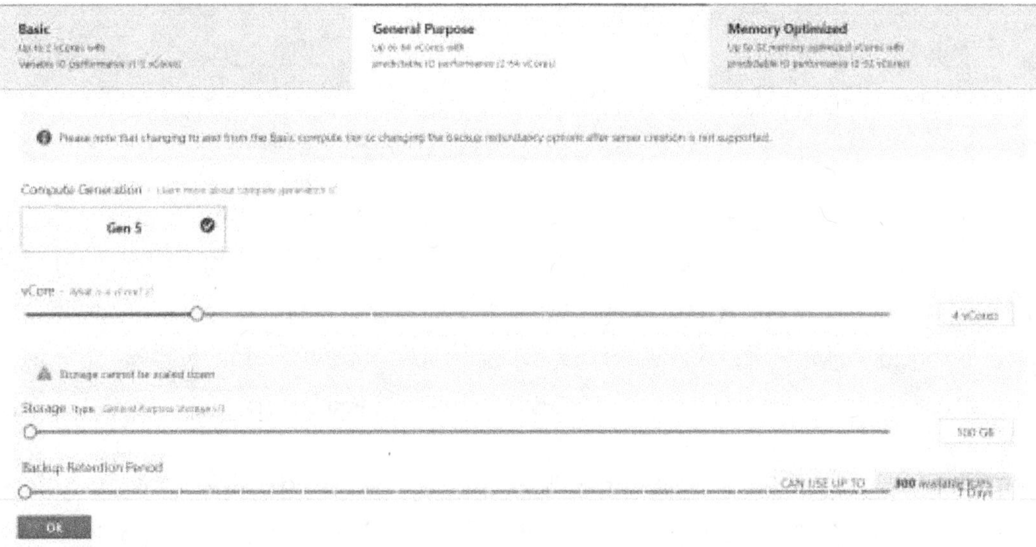

Click Ok, and it takes you to create a Single server page. You can review the configuration and click on Review + Create to deploy Azure Database for PostgreSQL.

Summary

In this chapter, we get hands-on experience in implementing Azure SQL in both Paas and Iaas platform. It also covers the DTU, vCPU model, their differences so that you can plan your Azure infrastructure resources accordingly. We also explored Azure web portal , Azure PowerShell and Azure CLI for implementing , configuring and maintaining these resources.

Chapter 5

Implement secure data platform environment in Azure.

Microsoft Azure offers several features for IT professionals to secure cloud services. In this chapter, you will learn to implement security controls using Azure AD, Azure Key Vault, data classification, threat protection, manage identity and access, protect data, applications, audits, vulnerability assessments, and networks in cloud and hybrid environments.

SQL Server Authentication Methods

Authentication is the process of ensuring that a principal is who, or what, they state they are so they can use the SQL Server resources.

SQL Server instance hosted on an on-premises server or an Azure Virtual machine supports two types of authentication, SQL Server Authentication and Windows Authentication.

Using the SQL Server authentication, the login name and the password information will be stored in the master system database on the hosting SQL Server instance or in the database itself in the case of the contained database. And to connect to that SQL Server using SQL Authentication, you will be requested to provide the username and the password that will be authenticated locally within that SQL Server instance and authorized based on the permissions granted to that SQL user.

Using the Windows Authentication, the user will connect to the SQL Server instance using the Active Directory account used to log into the current machine. It does not ask for the username and password. The authentication will be performed by connecting to the Active Directory service and the authorization based on the Windows user's permissions.

Authenticating the users using Active Directory is more secure than authenticating them using SQL Server Authentication. The authentication information will be encrypted while being transferred across the network, where it will be shown as plain text in the case of the SQL Server authentication. For example, suppose an employee leaves the organization. In that case, the database administrator needs to disable the windows account associated with that employee to prevent unsecured data access. The mission will not be easy for the database administrator to identify which SQL Server authentication user this employee uses.

Azure SQL Database and Azure SQL Managed Instance also support two authentication modes, SQL Server authentication, similar to the SQL Server authentication supported by the on-premises SQL Server that we discussed previously, as shown below:

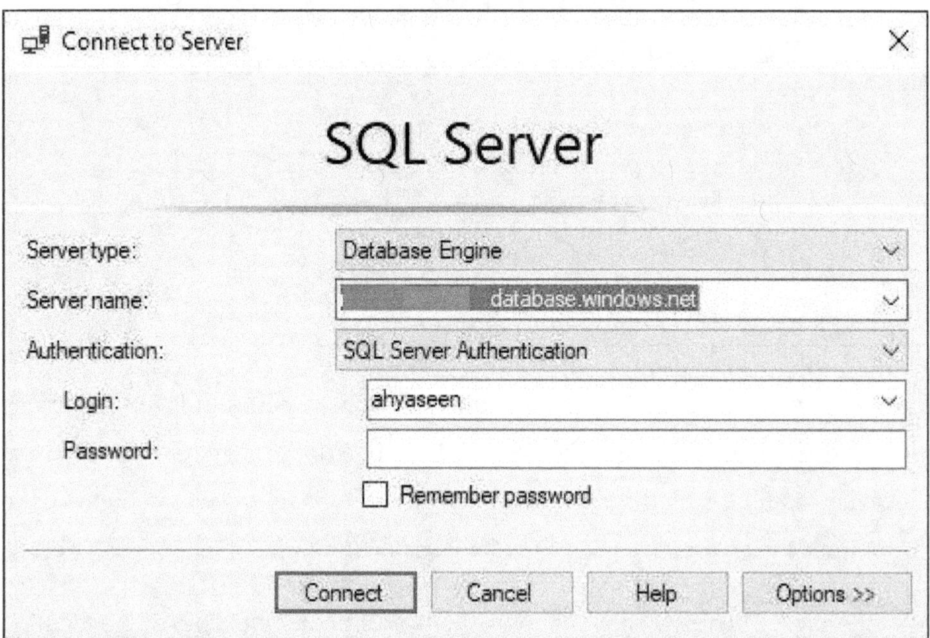

Azure database services also support Azure Active Directory authentication, which provides the users with the ability to use the same username and password that is used to access the Azure portal, Microsoft 365 or SQL Server Management Studio, as below:

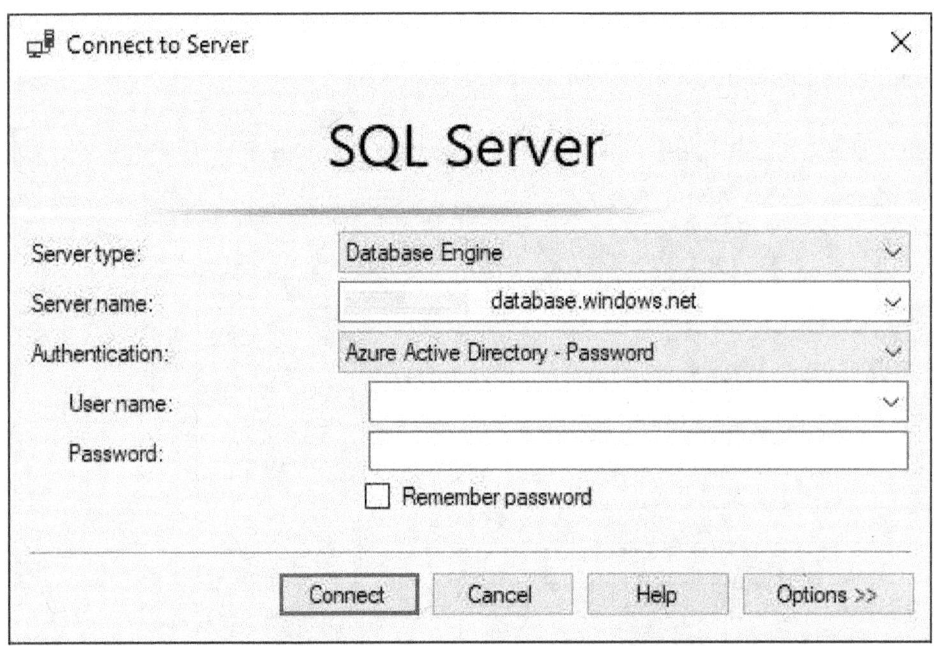

The main difference in the authentication and authorization processes between the on-premises SQL Server and the Azure relational database platforms is that the Windows authentication is not supported in these Azure database platforms as these Azure database services rely on Azure Active Directory. In contrast, the on-premises SQL Server relies on Windows Server Active Directory.

Although both Azure Active Directory and Windows Active Directory provide authentication services and identity management, they perform these services differently. Windows Server Active Directory uses Kerberos protocol to provide authentication using tickets and queried using the Lightweight Directory Access Protocol (LDAP).

On the other hand, Azure Active Directory provides a multi-tenant cloud identity platform. It uses HTTPS protocols, such as SAML and OpenID Connect for authentication, the OAuth protocol for authorization and Graph API for data access.

Microsoft Azure allows us to use the Azure Active Directory Connect tool to sync the Active Directory identities with Azure Active Directory, enabling the users to use the same usernames and passwords to access both the on-premises and Azure resources.

An additional security measure can be added by the Azure Active directory when connecting to an Azure relational database service using multi-factor authentication (MFA). When the MFA is enabled on a specific account, you can connect to that Azure database service by providing the username and password for that account. After that, you will be routed to the second level of authentication, such as using a Windows Authenticator application. It sends a push notification to your phone or sends a text message with an access code that should be provided when connecting to the Azure database service using the Azure Data Studio or the SQL Server Management Studio, as below:

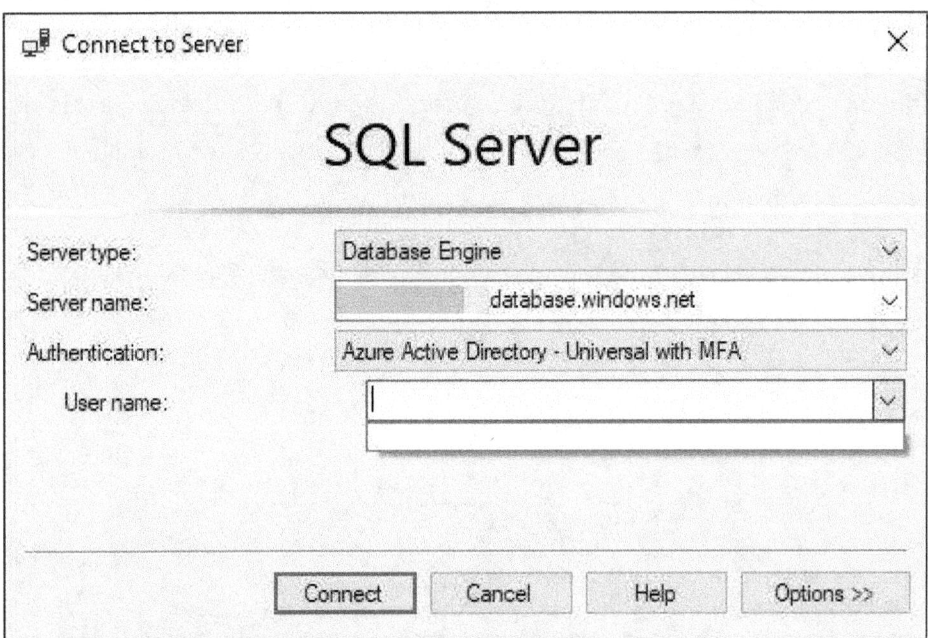

Configure Azure AD authentication

Each Azure database server starts with a single server administrator account defined when creating the logical database server. Azure SQL Database for SQL Server and Azure Database for PostgreSQL provides the ability to configure the logical server that hosts the database to use Azure Active Directory Authentication.

This user will be created as a contained database user in the master database of the logical database server, then as a member of the db_owner fixed database role in all databases hosted under that logical server.

This Azure Active Directory user helps access and administrate all the databases in that logical server using the same user. You can configure the Active Directory Admin of that Azure database service to be an Azure Active Directory group that contains all the database administrators, with sysadmin like permission, who are responsible for administering the databases hosted in that logical server.

As the admin account should be set at the logical server level and not at the database level, you need to use the Azure Portal, PowerShell, or CLI to configure the Active Directory admin.

To set an Active Directory admin using Azure Portal, connect to the Azure Portal in your internet browser (https://portal.azure.com/). Then click on your Azure SQL Database server that you plan to add the Active Directory admin to it.

From the Overview page of the logical SQL Server, click on the hyperlink beside the Active Directory Admin setting to configure a new Active Directory admin or change the current admin:

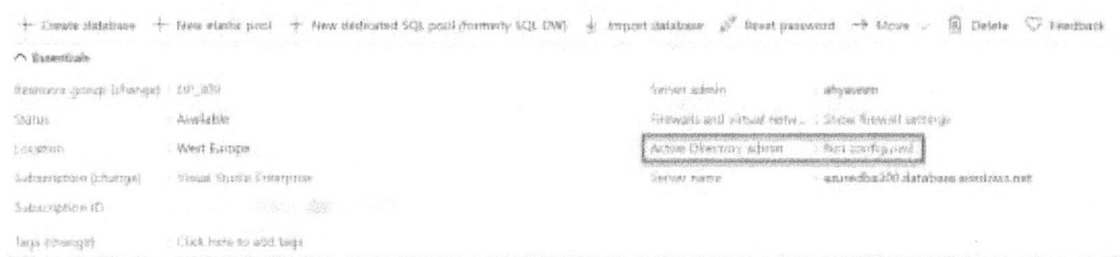

In the displayed Active Directory Admin page, select the Set Admin option:

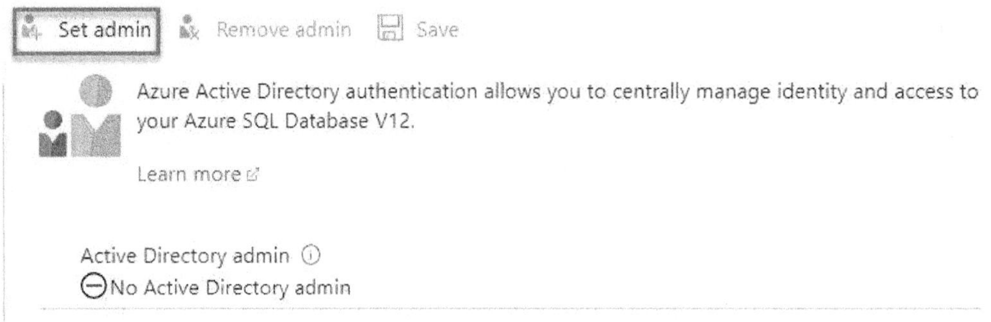

In the Add admin page, you need to search for the Active Directory user or group that you plan to set as an administrator, then click on the Select option:

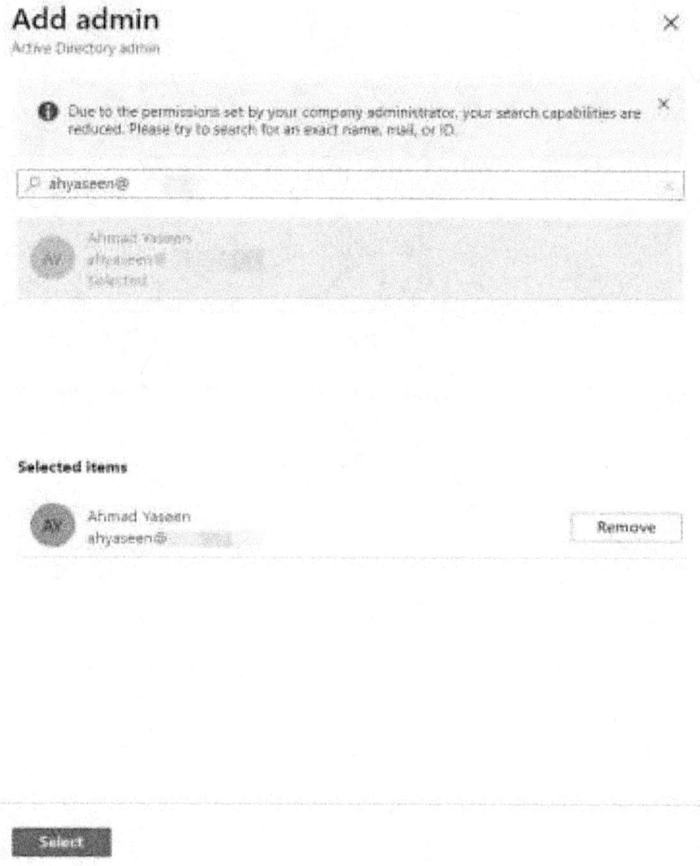

This will take you back to the Active Directory admin page with the selected Active Directory user. Click on the Save option to set the selected user as an admin to all databases hosted under that logical server.

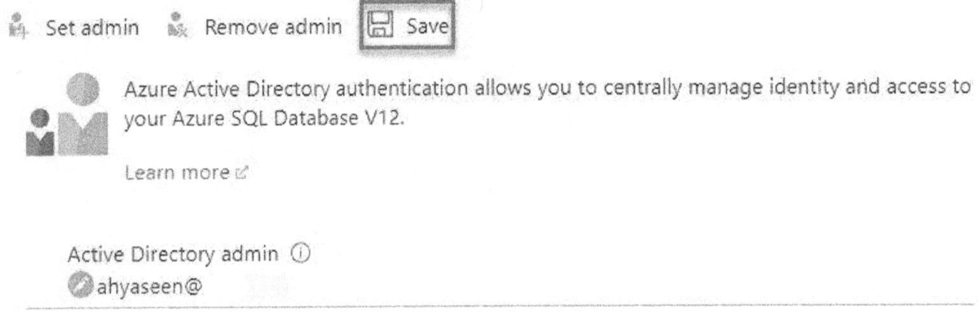

This process may take a few minutes to take effect and display the user to the Active Directory admin field of the SQL server properties:

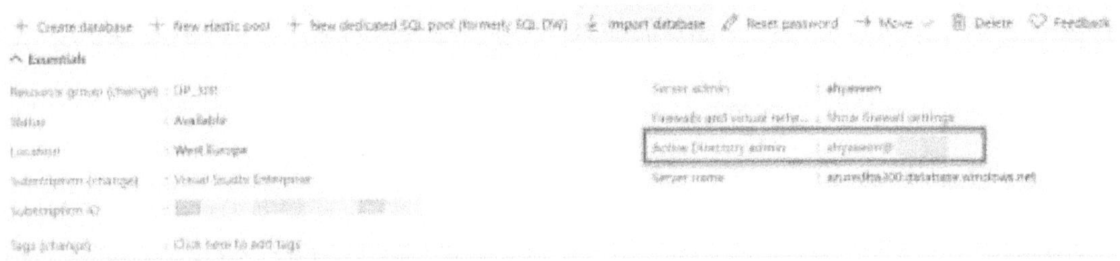

Configure Security Principals

In general, the security concept is related to the process of providing someone or something with the ability to access a specific resource and allow it to perform restricted actions on that resource. For example, an Azure administrator is requested to grant the users access to write to a specific shared folder. The security concept consists of three main components:

- Securable: The resource on which the action will be performed.
- Principal: Someone who needs to perform that action on the securable.
- Permission: The configuration used to allow the principal to act on the securable.

In the previous example, the shared folder is a securable, the organization users are the principals, and the Azure administrator will grant the organization users the "write" permission on that shared folder.

From the SQL Server security perspective, the security principal is the entity that requests to be granted permissions on a specific SQL Server securable or resource. These SQL Server security principals can be created at the SQL Server instance level and stored in the master database under that instance, such as a Server Login or Server Role. It can also be made at the SQL Server database level and held in that database, such as a Database User, Database Role or Application Role. The principal can be either an individual user/login or a group.

In the Active Directory Authentication method, a server login should be created for that user then mapped to a database user, that also should be created within that database, as the login itself cannot be directly granted permissions at the database level, as below:

```
USE [master]
GO
CREATE LOGIN [.....] FROM WINDOWS

GO
USE [UserDatabase]
GO
CREATE USER [.....] FOR LOGIN [.....]

GO
```

By default, the Azure SQL Database uses a contained database feature. The user will be created at the user database's scope and not in the master database. It has access to the database on which the user is set up.

To achieve that, execute the below query in the context of the user database, where the EXTERNAL PROVIDER indicates that this user is an Azure Active Directory user:

```
USE [UserDatabase]
GO
CREATE USER [...] FROM EXTERNAL PROVIDER;
GO
```

The Azure SQL Database securable is the database resources to grant permissions, such as a database table or column. And these securables can be at three levels or scopes, which makes it easier for us to manage the security principals' permissions. These scopes are the SQL server, the database, and the schema. The schema is a collection of database objects, such as tables, stored procedures or functions grouped as one security set, with dbo as the default schema.

Each user will have a default schema. It will be used as a starting schema for that user when creating a new database object or querying a database object without specifying the schema name. The SQL Server will create that database object or search for that object inside the user's default schema.

```
USE [ADS_Demo_Test]
GO
CREATE USER [.....] FOR LOGIN [.....] WITH DEFAULT_SCHEMA=[dbo]

GO
```

Suppose the user is trying to search for an object without specifying the schema name explicitly, and the SQL Server cannot find that object in the user's default schema. In that case, it will search for it in the dbo schema and return an error message if it is not found in these two schemas or the user does not have permission to the dbo schema.

```
SELECT * FROM Employees
```

Therefore, it is highly recommended to explicitly mention the schema's name when creating or querying a database object to eliminate the overhead of checking other schemas.

The permissions that can be granted at the server level are mainly related to administrative actions, such as creating logins, databases, configuring database mirroring, etc. These permissions are organized as a hierarchy, where granting server-level permission to a server principal will implicitly grant all child permissions to that principal, with the CONTROL SERVER permission is the topmost node in that hierarchy.

On the other hand, the permissions at the database level are mainly related to the database objects administrative actions, such as database objects creation, alter or backup, or user actions, such as SELECT, UPDATE or DELETE permissions. Similarly, the database permissions are also organized in a hierarchy, where granting database-level permission to a database user will implicitly grant all child permissions to that user, except for CREATE DATABASE permission that has no children, with the CONTROL permission is the topmost node in that hierarchy.

The SQL Server security management, especially with many users requesting permissions to the SQL Server resources, can be simplified by using role-based security. You can imagine these roles as security groups that share the same set of permissions. In other words, we are combining the standard permissions required by a number of users into a single role, and then the users will be assigned to those roles and granted the permissions set that are defined in that security role.

SQL Server includes built-in roles and custom roles. These roles can grant a set of permissions at the SQL Server level and the database levels. The server roles are available in Microsoft SQL Server and Azure SQL Managed Instance but not supported in Azure SQL Database.

The fixed or built-in server roles help grant all the permissions required to perform a specific SQL Server administration task, considering that the fixed server roles' permissions cannot be altered.

The following table from Microsoft documentation shows a list of all the SQL Server fixed server-level roles with a description of the permissions granted to each role members:

Fixed Server-Level Role	**Description**
sysadmin	This role grants permissions to perform any action on the server. You should limit membership in this role as far as possible.
serveradmin	This role grants permissions to configure server-wide settings and to shut down the server.
securityadmin	This role grants permissions to manage logins. It includes the ability to create and drop logins and the ability to assign permissions to logins. Members of this role can grant and deny server-level permissions to other users and grant and deny database-level permissions to other users on any database to which they have access. The Membership of this role should be limited as much as possible. It should be treated as equivalent to sysadmin.
processadmin	This role grants permissions to terminate sessions running on the SQL Server instance.
setupadmin	This role grants permissions to manage linked servers.

bulkadmin	This role grants permissions to execute the BULK INSERT statement.
diskadmin	This role grants permissions to manage disk files.
dbcreator	This role grants permissions to manage databases.
public	Every user is a member of the public, and this cannot be changed. This role does not initially grant any administrative permissions. Though you can add permissions to this role, this is not advisable because the permissions would be granted to every user. All logins are automatically a member of the public server-level role, which is a unique role that represents all server-level principals. The public role membership cannot be altered, and the public role cannot be removed.

Each one of these fixed-server roles consolidates one or more lower-level server permissions, as shown in the figure below:

SERVER LEVEL ROLES AND PERMISSIONS: 9 fixed server roles, 34 server permissions

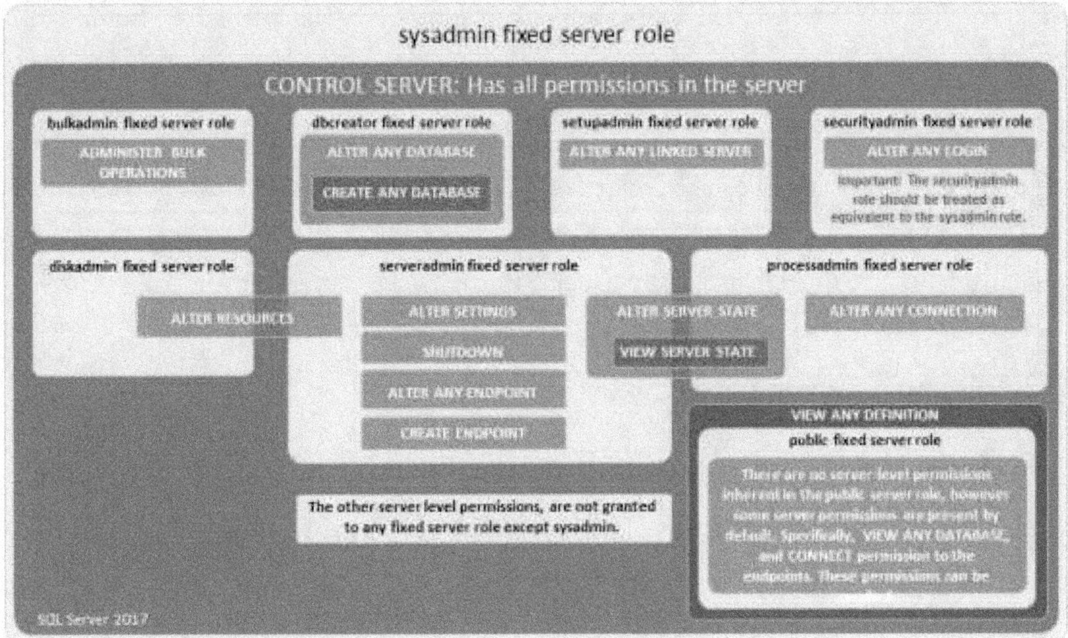

You can easily add an existing server login to these fixed-server roles and grant the login the role's permissions, using the ALTER SERVER ROLE T-SQL command, as in this script:

```
USE master
GO
ALTER SERVER ROLE [sysadmin] ADD MEMBER [.....]

GO
```

Azure SQL Database has another two built-in roles that are defined in the master database of the Azure SQL server.

- The dbmanager role that allows the server logins to create additional databases within the Azure SQL Database environment, which is equivalent to the dbcreator fixed server role in the on-premises SQL Server,
- The loginmanager role that allows the server logins to create additional logins at the server level, which is equivalent to the securityadmin fixed server role in the on-premises SQL Server.

Suppose you need to grant customized server-level permission to a large number of server logins, but you cannot find any built-in server-level role that meets your requirements. In that case, SQL Server allows you to create a user-defined server role, grant the required permissions to that role then add the logins as members of that role.

A user-defined server-level role can be created using the SQL Server Management Studio or using the CREATE SERVER ROLE Transact-SQL command. The T-SQL script below is used to create a user-defined role server-level that allows the logins to run Dynamic Management Objects to check the server state then add an existing server login as a member of that role:

```
USE [master]
GO
CREATE SERVER ROLE [CustomServerRole]
GO
GRANT VIEW SERVER STATE TO [CustomServerRole]
GO
ALTER SERVER ROLE [CustomServerRole] ADD MEMBER [.....]
```

SQL Server provides us with a number of built-in database-level roles at the database level. These fixed roles help us grant a set of common permissions to the database users instead of granting the users low level and detailed permissions for each functionality, making it easier to administer the database-level security. The following table, from Microsoft documentation, lists all the built-in fixed database-level roles that are available in both SQL Server and Azure SQL Database, with a description for each:

Fixed-Database role name	**Description**
db_owner	Members of the db_owner fixed database role can perform all configuration and maintenance activities on the database and drop the SQL Server database. (In SQL Database and Azure Synapse, some maintenance activities require server-level permissions and cannot be performed by db_owners.)
db_securityadmin	Members of the db_securityadmin fixed database role can modify role membership for custom roles only and manage permissions. Members of this role can potentially elevate their privileges, and their actions should be monitored.
db_accessadmin	Members of the db_accessadmin fixed database role can add or remove access to the database for Windows logins, Windows groups, and SQL Server logins.

db_backupoperator	Members of the db_backupoperator fixed database role can back up the database.
db_ddladmin	Members of the db_ddladmin fixed database role can run any Data Definition Language (DDL) command in a database.
db_datawriter	Members of the db_datawriter fixed database role can add, delete, or change data in all user tables.
db_datareader	Members of the db_datareader fixed database role can read all data from all user tables.
db_denydatawriter	Members of the db_denydatawriter fixed database role cannot add, modify, or delete any data in a database's user tables.
db_denydatareader	Members of the db_denydatareader fixed database role cannot read any data in the user tables within a database.

Each one of these fixed-database roles consolidates one or more lower-level database permissions, as shown in the figure below:

DATABASE LEVEL ROLES AND PERMISSIONS: 11 fixed database roles, 77 database permissions

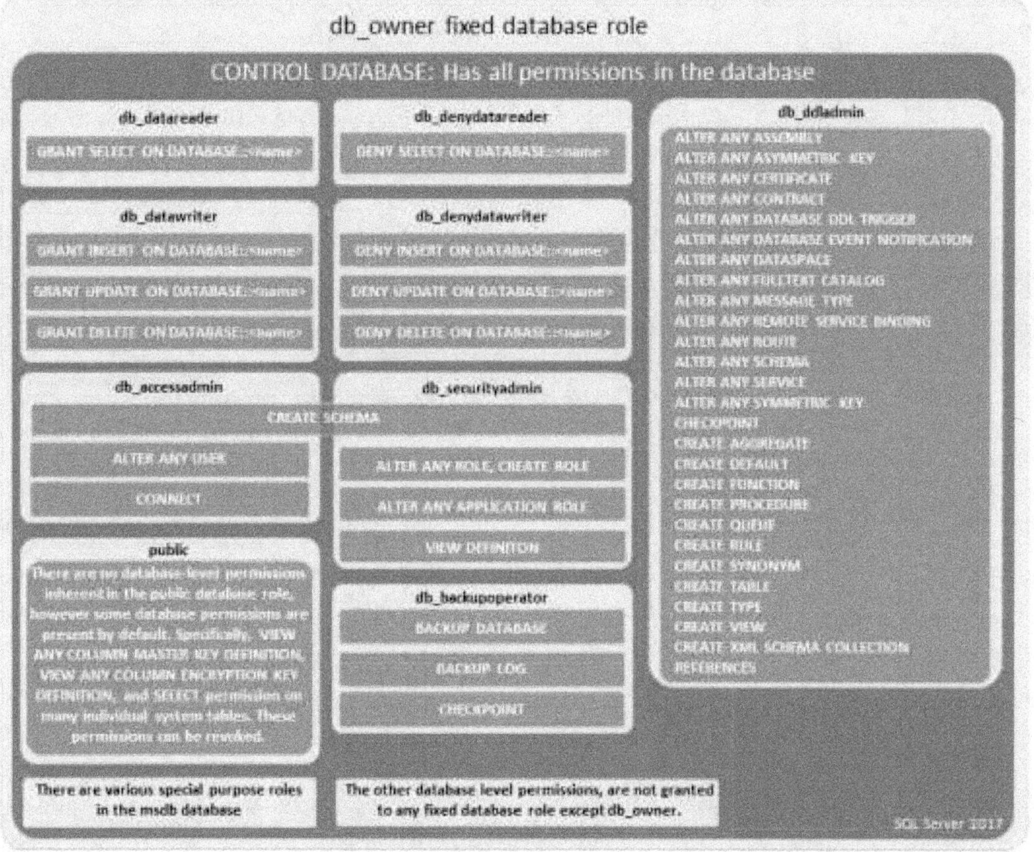

The msdb system database provides us with additional special-purpose built-in database roles that help in granting permissions to the different operations supported by that system database. The following table from Microsoft documentation lists the additional database-level roles that you can add members to, within the msdb database:

msdb role name	Description
db_ssisadmin db_ssisoperator db_ssisltduser	Members of these database roles can administer and use SSIS. Instances of SQL Server upgraded from an earlier version might contain an older version of the role named using Data Transformation Services (DTS) instead of SSIS.
dc_admin dc_operator dc_proxy	Members of these database roles can administer and use the data collector.
PolicyAdministratorRole	Members of the db_ PolicyAdministratorRole database role can perform all configuration and maintenance activities on Policy-Based Management policies and conditions.
ServerGroupAdministratorRole ServerGroupReaderRole	Members of these database roles can administer and use registered server groups.
dbm_monitor	Created in the msdb database when the first database is registered in the Database Mirroring Monitor. The dbm_monitor role has no members until a system administrator assigns users to the role.

A database user can be added as a member of a fixed database-level role and granted the database permissions assigned to that role using the ALTER ROLE T-SQL command, as below:

```
USE [AdventureWorks2016]
GO
ALTER ROLE [db_datareader] ADD MEMBER [.....]
GO
```

Suppose you are not able to find any database-level built-in role that meets your security requirements. In that case, SQL Server allows you to create a user-defined database role, grant the required permissions to that role then add the database users as members of that role. The user-defined database-level role can be created using the SQL Server Management Studio or using the CREATE ROLE Transact-SQL command.

The T-SQL script below is used to create a user-defined database-level role that allows the database users to run Dynamic Management Objects to check the database state then add an existing database user as a member to that role:

```
USE [AdventureWorks2016]
GO
CREATE ROLE [DMOAdmin]
GO
GRANT VIEW DATABASE STATE TO [DMOAdmin]
GO
ALTER ROLE [DMOAdmin] ADD MEMBER [.....]
```

Another type of database-level roles supported by SQL Server, and Azure SQL Database is the Application role. Application role allows us to assign the set of permissions required by a specific application to the application role and secure that application role using a password without adding members to that database role.

To use the application role to connect to the database, the application role should be activated by the user, using the sp_setapprole system stored procedure, by providing the application role's password, where the security context of the connected session will be switched from the current user's session to the application role. Then the application role's session can be deactivated by using the sp_unsetapprole system stored procedure.

An application role can be created using the SQL Server Management Studio or by using the CREATE APPLICATION ROLE Transact-SQL command. The T-SQL script below is used to create an application role that allows executing all stored procedures and scalar functions under the dbo schema, then activate that application role in order to connect to the database using its context:

```
USE [AdventureWorks2016]
GO
CREATE APPLICATION ROLE dp_300_AppRole WITH PASSWORD = N'*****'
GO
```

```
GRANT EXECUTE ON schema::dbo to dp_300_AppRole
GO
EXEC sp_setapprole @rolename = N'dp_300_AppRole', @password = N'*****'
GO
```

Configure database authorization

In SQL Server, authorization determines which securable resources a principal can access and which operations are allowed for those resources.

The permissions granted to the server logins or database users can be managed by using the GRANT, DENY, and REVOKE T-SQL statements. Most of these permissions can be managed by the SQL Server Management Studio.

By default, the principal has no permission to perform any action unless permission is granted to it. The GRANT T-SQL statement is used to grant permissions to the principals on a specific SQL Server resource. On the other hand, the REVOKE T-SQL statement can be used to remove the principals' permissions.

Since a windows authentication user can be granted permissions by inheriting these permissions from being a group member, we may still need to remove these permissions from a specific member without affecting the whole group or remove the user from that group. To achieve that, SQL Server supports using the DENY T-SQL statement, which can be used to explicitly remove a user's permission that is inherited from being a member of a group or role.

Configure database and object-level permissions

In Microsoft SQL Server, also applied to Azure Database for MySQL and Azure Database for PostgreSQL, the data manipulation language (DML) operations on tables and views are controlled by the SELECT, INSERT, UPDATE, and DELETE permissions.

- The SELECT permission allows the database users to view the data within the table or view.
- The INSERT permission allows the database users to insert data into the object.
- The UPDATE permission allows the database users to modify data within the object
- The DELETE permission allows the database users to delete data within the object.

- Other permissions that can be granted on the database tables include:

- The REFERENCES permission that grants the database user permissions to view the foreign keys on the object.
- The TAKE OWNERSHIP permission that grants the database user permissions to take ownership of the object.
- The VIEW CHANGE TRACKING permission that grants the database user permissions to view the object's change tracking setting.
- The VIEW DEFINITION permission that allows the database user permissions to view the definition of the object.

These permissions can be granted to a database user on a specific table or view by providing (optionally) the **OBJECT::** prefix before the name of the database object on which the permissions will be granted. It is recommended to specify the schema for the table or view on which the permission will be granted. It ensures that permission is given on the correct object. If the schema name is not provided, the SQL Server will search for the database object in the user's default schema then in the dbo schema if the object is not found in the user default schema. In the T-SQL commands below, both commands will work in the same way and grant permission for the database user on the provided database object:

```
USE [AdventureWorks2016]
GO
GRANT SELECT ON OBJECT::[HumanResources].[Department] TO [.....]
GO
GRANT SELECT ON [HumanResources].[Department] TO [.....]
GO
```

In addition to granting permissions at the server level, database level and database object level, permissions can also be granted to the database users at the columns-level by providing the list of columns in the GRANT or DENY statement. For example, the command below is used to grant the database user SELECT permissions on specific columns in the target table:

```
USE [AdventureWorks2016]
GO
GRANT SELECT ON [HumanResources].[Department] ([DepartmentID], [Name]) TO [.....]
```

```
GO
```

Suppose we grant a database user-specific permission on a database object and allow that user to grant the same permissions to the other database users, using the WITH GRANT OPTION clause. In that case, the real challenge here comes when you need to REVOKE or DENY the granted permissions from that user. It is since we don't know the users that also granted permissions by that user.

To overcome that issue, the CASCADE clause can be used in the revoke or deny statement to remove the permissions from all the users for who the mentioned database user had granted permissions.

In the below T-SQL command, we grant SELECT permission to a database user permission on a specific database table, allowing him to grant that permission to other database users. After that, we revoke the permissions from that user and all users granted permissions by that user:

```
USE [AdventureWorks2016]
GO
GRANT SELECT ON [HumanResources].[Department] TO [.....] WITH GRANT OPTION
GO
REVOKE SELECT ON [HumanResources].[Department] FROM [.....] CASCADE
GO
```

The database users can be granted also permissions at functions and stored procedures. It includes the ALTER permission that grants the database user permissions to change the object's definition and the EXECUTE permission that grants the database user permissions to execute the database object.

The below T-SQL command is used to grant a database user the permission to execute a specific stored procedure:

```
USE [AdventureWorks2016]
GO
GRANT EXECUTE ON [dbo].[uspSearchCandidateResumes] TO [.....]
GO
```

Ownership chaining

By default, any new database object will be owned by the owner of a schema under which the object is created. If a database object such as a view, functions or stored procedures reference another object, an ownership chain will be established. As a result, the users will inherit permissions from other database objects during the execution of the view, function or stored procedure, and only within the context of the view, function or stored procedures execution.

If the view, function or stored procedure has the same owner as the reference database object, the view, function, or stored procedure will be able to access the table, even though the database user does not have permissions to access the table directly.

In the first scenario presented in the image below:

- User2 is the owner of Table 1 and the view that is reading from that table.
- User1 has permission to select from the view granted by User2
- User1 is able to read from that view and the underlying table under the execution context of that view.
- As a result, the ownership chaining is not broken here.

In the second scenario presented in the same image :

- User3 is the owner of Table 2.
- User2 is the owner of the view that is reading from Table 2.
- User 1 has permission to use the view granted by User2.
- User1 will not be able to access the underlying table as the owner of Table2 is different from the owner of the view that is reading from that table.
- User1 ownership chain is broken.

This issue can be fixed by granting user 1 permissions on the underlying table directly by user 3, the owner of table 2.

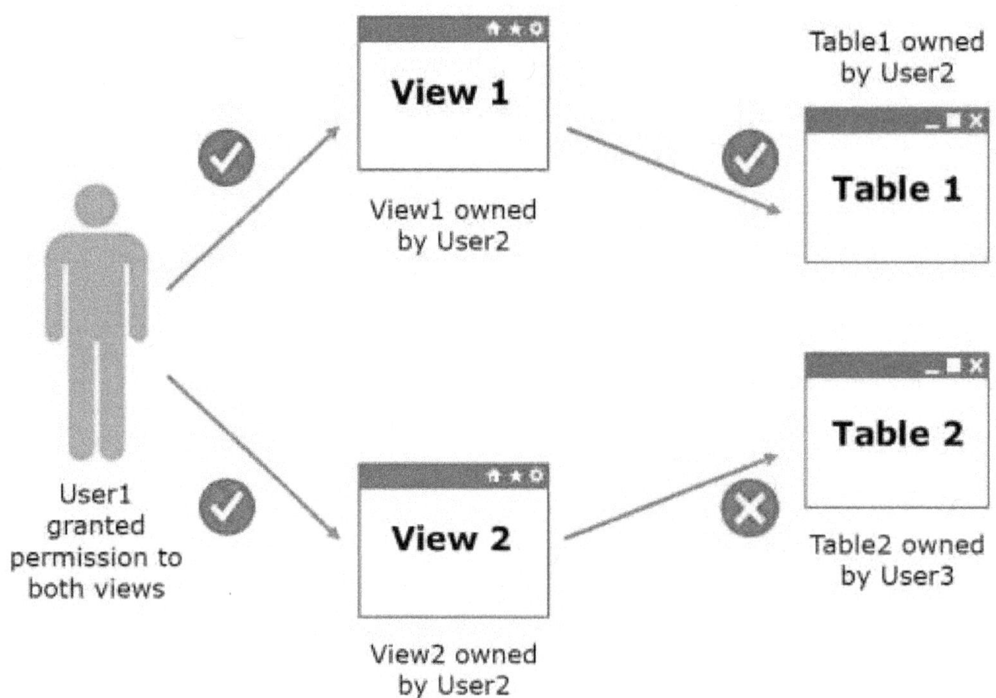

Switch the Execution Context

Suppose we want to fix the broken ownership chain caused by different object owners. In that case, we can execute the code by using other user's permissions to validate permissions on all of the accessed objects, which is called the execution context switch. It allows us to execute the required code, such as user-defined functions, stored procedures, and triggers, and still take advantage of SQL Server's granular permissions by keeping tight control over the permissions to underlying database objects.

The execution security context of a query can be changed by using the EXECUTE AS [user] or EXECUTE AS [login] commands as part of the object's definition. It ensures that the code should be running under the security context of the specified user. In this case, all subsequent queries and statements will be executed using the new context with the permissions granted to that context.

In the script below, the SELECT statement provided in the stored procedure will be executed under the security context of the mentioned "TestUser", regardless of the user who is executing the stored procedure:

```
USE [AdventureWorks2016]
GO
CREATE PROCEDURE SwitchContext
WITH EXECUTE AS 'TestUser'
AS
SELECT * FROM [AdventureWorks2016].[HumanResources].[Employee]
WHERE BusinessEntityID >280
```

Apply the principle of least privilege for all securable

The least privilege approach is an important security concept that should be considered when granting permissions to a database user. We are granting the minimum permissions required for the user or the role to perform a specific task.

For example, suppose the database user can read/delete from and write to a specific database table. In that case, this user should be granted the SELECT, UPDATE, and DELETE permissions at the table level instead of granting these permissions at the database level. In this way, the user will perform the required tasks using that "least" permission without granting it excessive permissions.

You may find it easier to create a database user and grant it higher general permissions at the database or server level. This is due to the extra overhead, the testing and applying the least privilege approach adds to the SQL Server security management. On the other hand, granting excessive permissions to the users can leave the application vulnerable to attack and unpleasant surprises.

Implement security for data at rest

Protecting the data at rest is considered one of the most important security compliance policies that helps mitigate any risk of the physical theft of the different types of data storage media, such as the data disks and backup media.

Encryption at rest by itself will not encrypt data at the table or column level. It will not prevent anyone with the appropriate permissions from reading the data from the underlying tables or share it with other users. It protects restoring the database backup files or attaching the database files to any unsecured server.

Microsoft SQL Server, Azure SQL Database, Azure SQL Managed Instance, and Azure Synapse Analytics support a method for protecting the data against the threat of malicious offline activity by encrypting data at rest, which is called Transparent Data Encryption (TDE). The TDE encrypts all the data in your database at the page level.

TDE performs real-time encryption and decryption of the database data files, associated backups, and transaction log files at rest without performing any changes to the application. The data within the database will be encrypted when written to the data page on the underlying disk and decrypted automatically when the data page is read into the memory. The database backup files will also be encrypted, as the backup operation will copy the data pages from the database file to the backup media.

Enabling TDE in Azure SQL Database is a simple task that requires switching on that feature in a single click from the "Transparent Data Encryption" pane within the Azure portal.

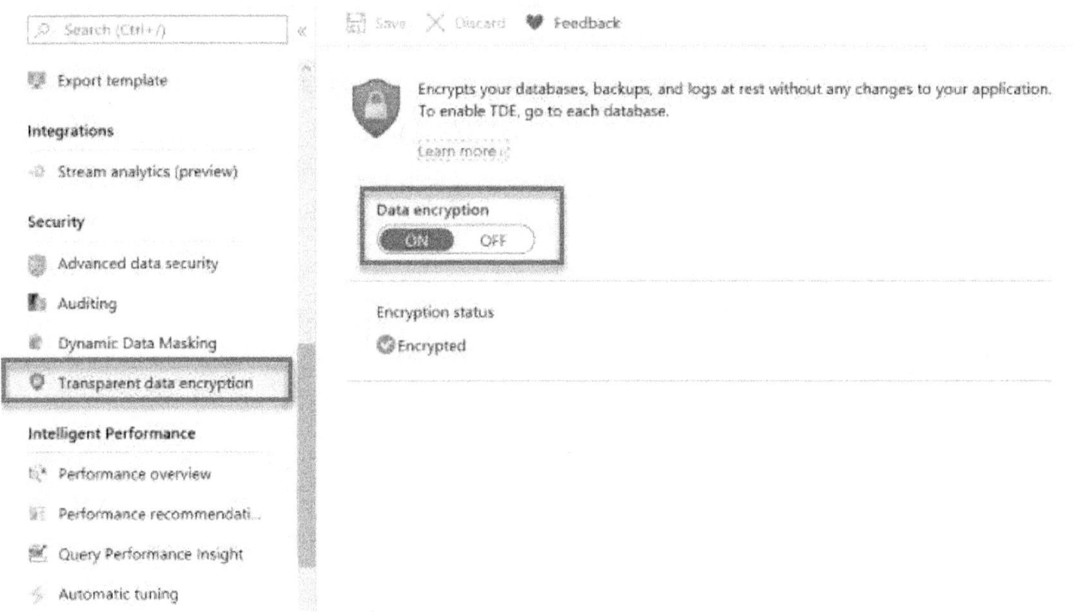

All Azure SQL Databases that were created in May 2017 and later will have the TDE feature enabled automatically. Also, all Azure SQL Managed Instance databases that were created after February

2019 will have the TDE feature enabled automatically. TDE must be manually enabled for Azure Synapse Analytics.

In the Azure SQL Database platform, the database will be encrypted using a Microsoft provided certificate, with the ability to use a certificate that was created by your company and uploaded to Azure using Bring Your Own Key option. The only risk of using your own certificate is that, if the certificate is removed from Azure, no access to the database will be allowed, and the current database connections will be closed.

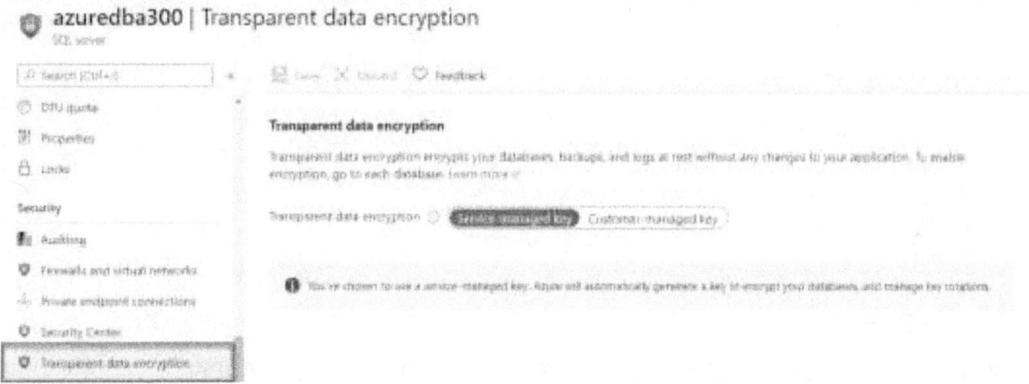

Landing from the cloud to the earth, enabling the TDE feature within a Microsoft SQL Server Database and encrypting your database at rest requires running few T-SQL commands. It includes:

- Setting a database master key within the master database using the CREATE MASTER KEY ENCRYPTION command, where this key will be encrypted using the service master key, that is created at the time of the SQL Server installation, and a password.
- Creating a certificate in the master database, using the CREATE CERTIFICATE command, that is encrypted by the database master key created in the previous step and used to encrypt the database encryption key.
- Creating a database encryption key within the database, using the CREATE DATABASE ENCRYPTION KEY command. It is encrypted by the certificate and allows us to enable the TDE feature in the database.
- Enable the TDE feature in the database using the ALTER DATABASE command.

The encryption process is a background process that will run at a low priority without overloading the server resources. It will take some time to encrypt the database pages based on the database's size to be encrypted.

The below script shows all the commands that are required to configure the TDE feature in your database:

```
USE master;
GO
CREATE MASTER KEY ENCRYPTION BY PASSWORD = '*****';
GO
CREATE CERTIFICATE DB300Cert
WITH SUBJECT = 'DB300Cert';
GO
USE AdventureWorks2016;
GO
CREATE DATABASE ENCRYPTION KEY
WITH ALGORITHM = AES_256 ENCRYPTION BY SERVER CERTIFICATE DB300Cert;
GO
ALTER DATABASE AdventureWorks2016 SET ENCRYPTION ON;
GO
```

Once created, the TDE certificate should be manually backed up and stored in a safe place. It is because if the certificate is lost, the database cannot be restored from a backup or attached from the database files to another server. The T-SQL script below is used to generate a backup from the TDE certificate that is used to encrypt the source database:

```
BACKUP CERTIFICATE DB300Cert
TO FILE = 'DB300Cert'
WITH PRIVATE KEY
(
  FILE = 'DB300CertPrivate',
  ENCRYPTION BY PASSWORD = '****'
);
GO
```

If you plan to move an encrypted database to another server, you should also move the associated keys and certificates that are used to encrypt that database. This includes creating a service master key in the master database on the destination server, generating a server certificate on the destination server from the backup of the original server certificate and its private key, then restoring the backup file or attaching the database files to that destination server.

```
CREATE CERTIFICATE DB300Cert
FROM FILE = 'DB300Cert'
WITH PRIVATE KEY (FILE = 'DB300CertPrivate',
DECRYPTION BY PASSWORD = '****');
GO
```

To use the TDE feature with databases in an Always-on Availability Group, the certificate that is used to encrypt the database should be restored to all the Availability Group replicas that will be hosting copies of the TDE encrypted database.

Azure SQL Database for MySQL and Azure SQL Database for PostgreSQL don't support the TDE feature. Instead, the database will be encrypted using the Microsoft Azure disk encryption method, which encrypts the databases stored on the encrypted disk and protects them from any physical theft. Azure disk encryption Allows you to use a certificate managed by Azure or to Bring Your Own Key and use it for the encryption.

Azure disk encryption can be used in Azure VMs that host the SQL Server instances to encrypt your databases that are stored in the encrypted disk. You can use the Azure disk encryption with TDE to protect your databases by multiple layers of encryption, the Azure disk encryption layer and the TDE layer for encrypting the SQL Server database files and backup files.

For more information how to perform Azure Disk Encryption, check this Microsoft documentation: **https://docs.microsoft.com/en-us/azure/virtual-machines/windows/disk-encryption-portal-quickstart**

Managing encryption keys and certificates at the individual database server level is not the best practice. It is recommended to have a solution that can manage encryption keys and certificates and store it securely. Extensible Key Management (EKM) makes it possible to register modules from third-party vendors in SQL Server and SQL Server on Azure VM, enabling SQL Server to use the encryption keys stored on them.

Azure Key Vault is an example of an EKM provider that can be used for SQL Server instances running on-premises or on Azure virtual machines, for features such as Transparent Data Encryption, Backup Encryption, or Always Encrypted.

Azure Key Vault is a Microsoft Azure service that can be used as a secure area for storing and accessing secrets, such as passwords, certificates, or keys, to be accessed securely. Azure Key Vault can be integrated with SQL Server by setting the Key Vault URL, the Principal name, the Principal secret, and the credential's name.

To allow the SQL Server to connect to Azure Key Vault, we need to create a SQL Server Login, and a Credential mapped to the created login, with the key vault's name as the identity of the credential, and the application ID as the secret of that credential.

After creating the credential, you can easily:

- Create an asymmetric key within the Azure Key Vault,
- Create an asymmetric key within the SQL Server database,
- Map that key to the Azure Key Vault asymmetric key using the CREATE ASYMMETRIC KEY command with the FROM PROVIDER syntax,
- Then use that key for TDE, or Backup Encryption or Always Encrypted.

For more information about using Azure Key Vault with TDE, refer to **https://docs.microsoft.com/en-us/sql/relational-databases/security/encryption/setup-steps-for-extensible-key-management-**

Implement object-level encryption

Always Encrypted is a data protection feature that helps in transparently encrypting the sensitive data stored in a specific column, at rest on the server, during the movement between client and server, and while the data is in use, using a special database driver.

Always Encrypted ensures that the sensitive data will not appear as plain-text inside the database system. It means that the data will not be accessible by the SQL Server administrators, where both the encryption and decryption will be performed at the client application side. This means that only the client applications or app servers that have access to the encryption keys can access the plain-text data.

Always Encrypted supports two types of encryption:

- Deterministic encryption, in which a given plain-text value will always give the same cypher-text value. The deterministic encryption allows the use of filtering and grouping by ranges of encrypted values. This type of encryption is less secure as it allows the attackers to guess the plain-text column values by analyzing the encryption patterns of the encrypted values.

- Randomized encryption, in which the cypher-text value cannot be predicted based on the plain-text value and the same value is not always encrypted the same way. Although this encryption type is more secure, it is more limited. The column value cannot be used in the filters or grouping expressions and cannot be indexed.

Starting from SQL Server 2019, Microsoft introduced the Always Encrypted with secure enclaves that overcome these limitations by enabling pattern matching, comparison operations, and indexing on encrypted columns using randomized encryption. A secure enclave provides a secured region of memory within the SQL Server, which acts as a trusted execution environment for processing encrypted data without being able to view any data inside that region of the memory.

Always Encrypted works based on two types of encryption keys:

- Column master key, that is used to create and encrypt the column encryption keys. Make sure to store the master key in a trusted key store.
- Column encryption keys, that is used to encrypt data inside the column. This key will be securely stored in the database.

When a column that is encrypted using the Always Encrypted feature is called in your query, the Always Encrypted driver should decrypt the data. To achieve that, it will perform the following:

- Retrieve the column encryption key from the database and the column master key from the trusted key store.
- Use the column master key to decrypt the retrieved column encryption key.
- Use the decrypted column encryption key to decrypt the column data and display the data in plain text.

Always Encrypted can be used to encrypt a specific column using SQL Server Management Studio by right-clicking on the table and choose the Encrypt Column option, as shown below:

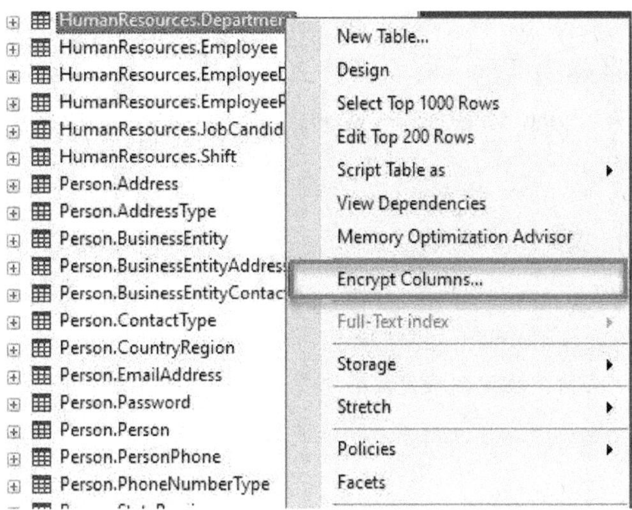

From the displayed Always Encrypted wizard, check the Introduction page that describes the Always Encrypted feature, then click Next.

In the Column Selection page, select the columns to be encrypted, the type of encryption Randomized or Deterministic, based on your querying requirements, and the column encryption key that will be used:

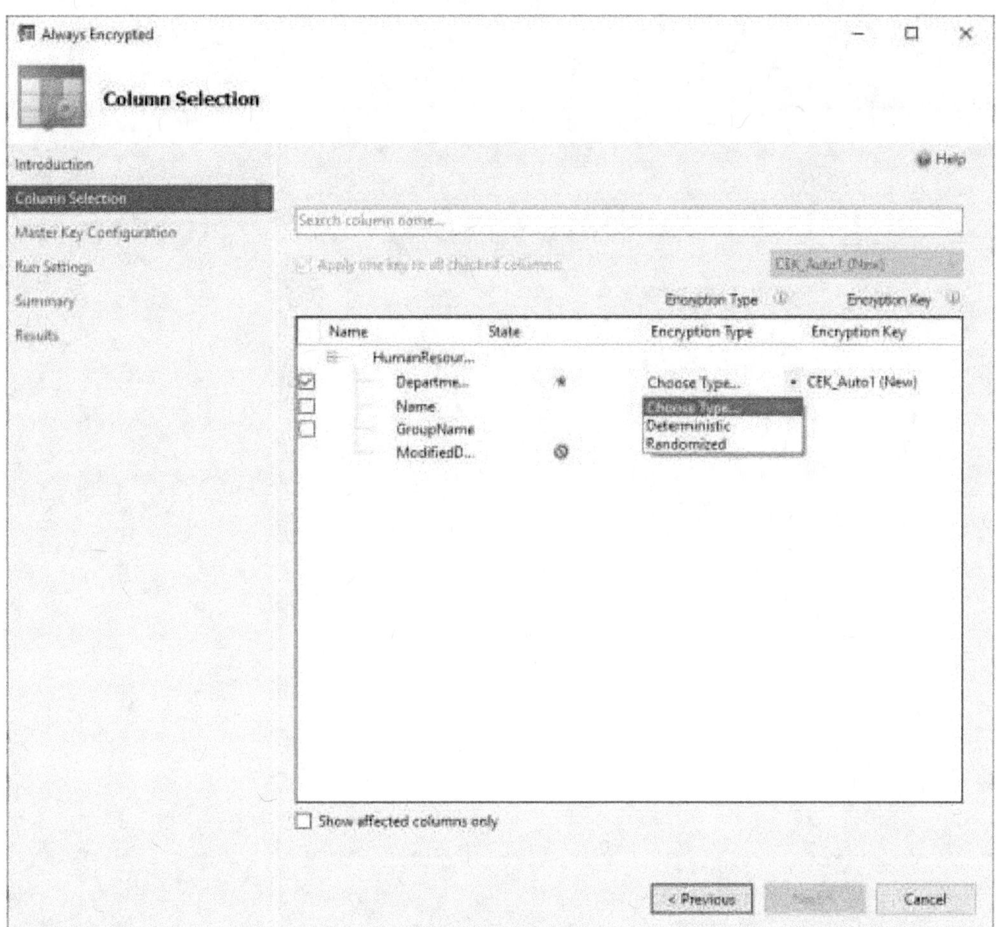

In the Master Key Configuration page, we need to set up the column master key and select the trusted key store where this key will be stored. Always Encrypted allows us to store the column master key in the Windows certificate store, Azure Key Vault, or a hardware security module:

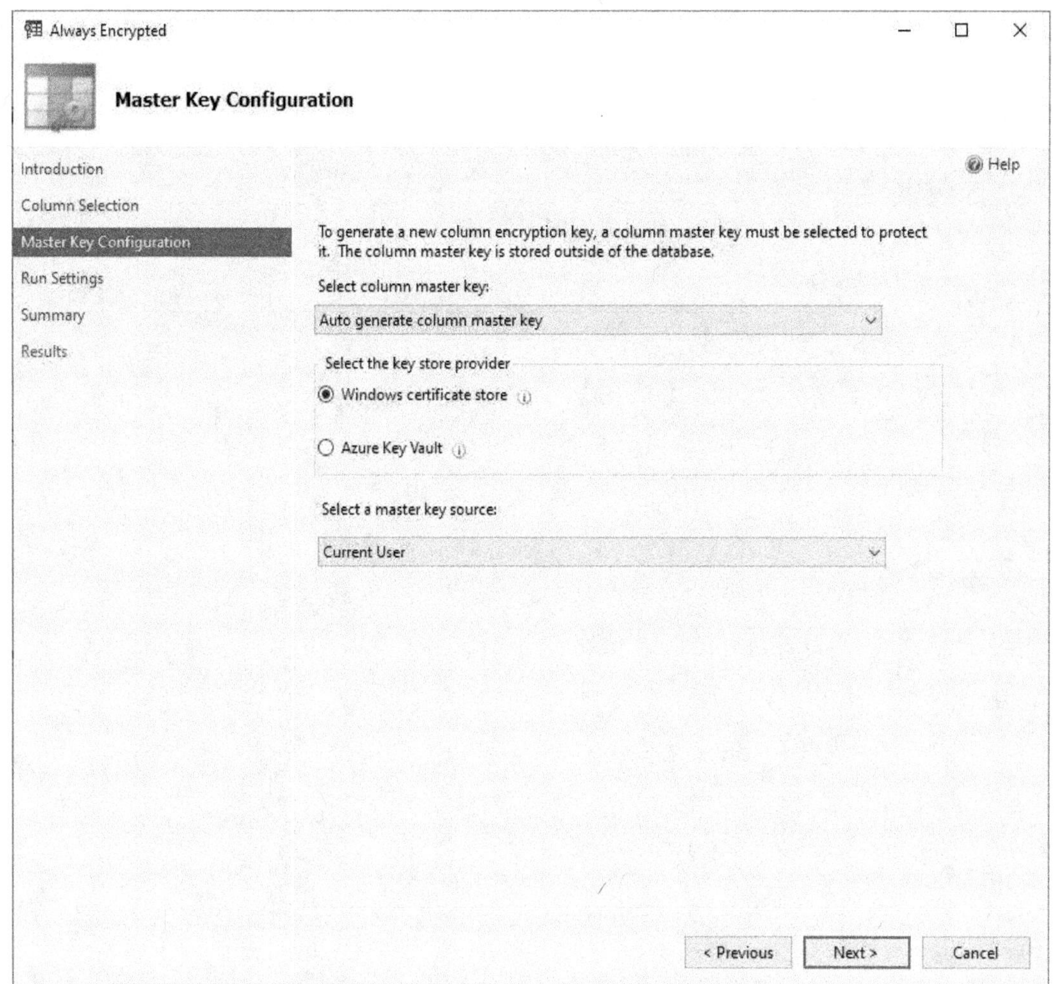

The validation page allows you to encrypt the columns now or save a PowerShell script to run it later. Review all your settings from the Summary page, then click Finish to proceed with the column encryption.

Once the column is encrypted using the Always Encrypted feature, the plain text values cannot be displayed directly from the database. If you try to query the column values using SSMS, the values will be displayed as random values. The real values of that encrypted column can be displayed only using a trusted application client. The image below shows how the SQL Server database administrator will see the encrypted columns, considering that we encrypted both the NationalIDNumber and BirthDate columns from that table:

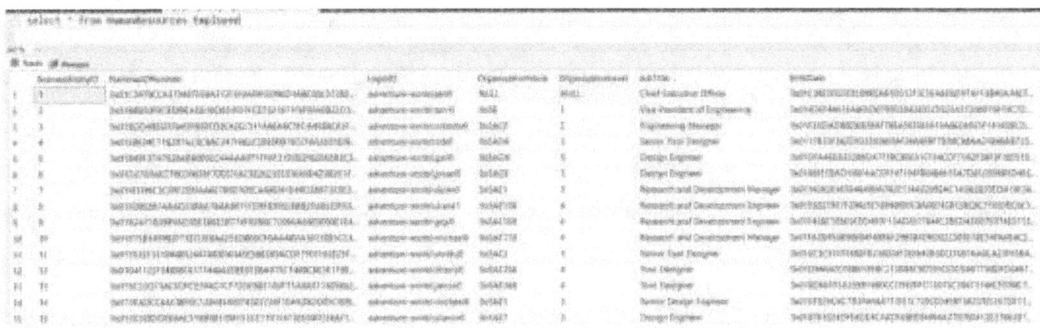

Implement Dynamic Data Masking

Dynamic Data Masking, also known as DDM, is a security feature that limits unauthorized users' access to sensitive data at the database layer. It allows you to mask your "sensitive" data, by configuring the suitable built-in or customized masking function. DDM masks the sensitive data "on the fly" to protect sensitive data from non-privileged users without preventing them from retrieving the unmasked data.

A useful scenario for using the Dynamic Data Masking when you need to allow the call center employee to access the customer's information to mitigate his issue, without allowing that employee to view any critical financial data, such as the bank account number or the credit card full number.

Dynamic Data Masking supports several masking functions that can be used to mask your data. This includes:

- The default masking function that fully masks the data in the column without exposing any part of the values to the user, where it will mask the string values with XXXX, the numbers with 0, and the date values with 01.01.1900.
- The Credit Card masking function, that masks all the values except for the final four characters, where the data will be shown in the usual format of a credit card number XXXX-XXXX-XXXX-1234.

- The Social Security Number function, that masks all the values except for the final four characters, with the masked data displayed as the United States Social Security Number in the format of XXX-XX-1234.
- The Random Number masking function that is used with the numeric columns. It masks the column values with a random number between two values.
- The Custom Text masking function allows you to specify any rules that fit your requirements. For example, you can display a custom number of characters at either end of the masked value. If the length of the column value that is masked is equal to or less than the number of characters that the mask specifies to be displayed, then only the masked characters will be displayed.

Dynamic Data Masking can be implemented in the Azure portal or using T-SQL. To configure the Dynamic Data Masking to mask specific columns, using Azure Portal, click on the Dynamic Data Masking blade under the Security section of the database, where you will see the columns that are flagged for masking by the recommendation engine.

You can click on Add Mask option to accept the provided recommendation and add a mask on that column, where the mask will be created using the default masking function, with the ability to change the masking function to fit your requirements:

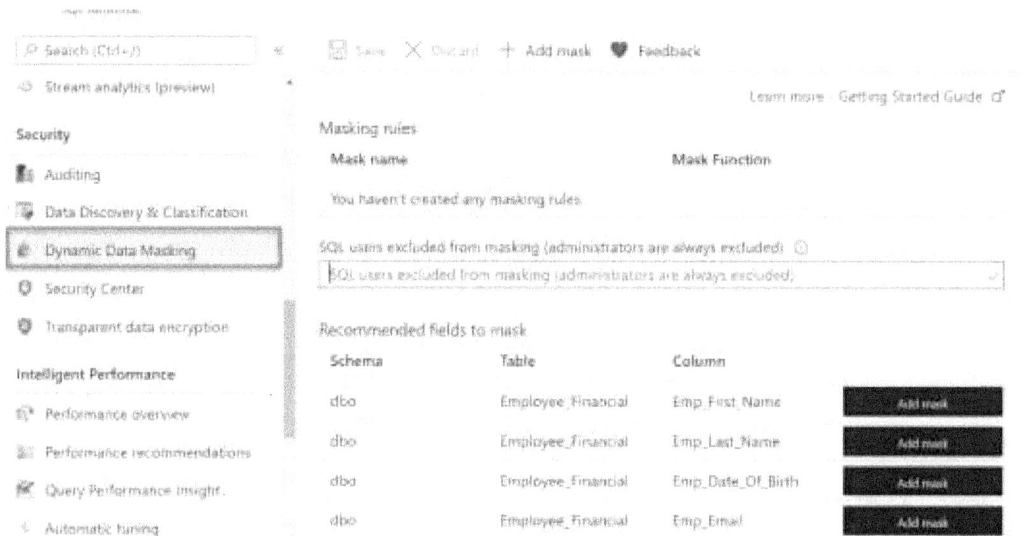

You can also configure the Dynamic Data Masking by adding a mask on any other column from the database tables. Click on the Add Mask option at the top of the page, choose the column you plan to add the mask on, and then configure the masking function used to mask that column. Click Save to apply that masking function.

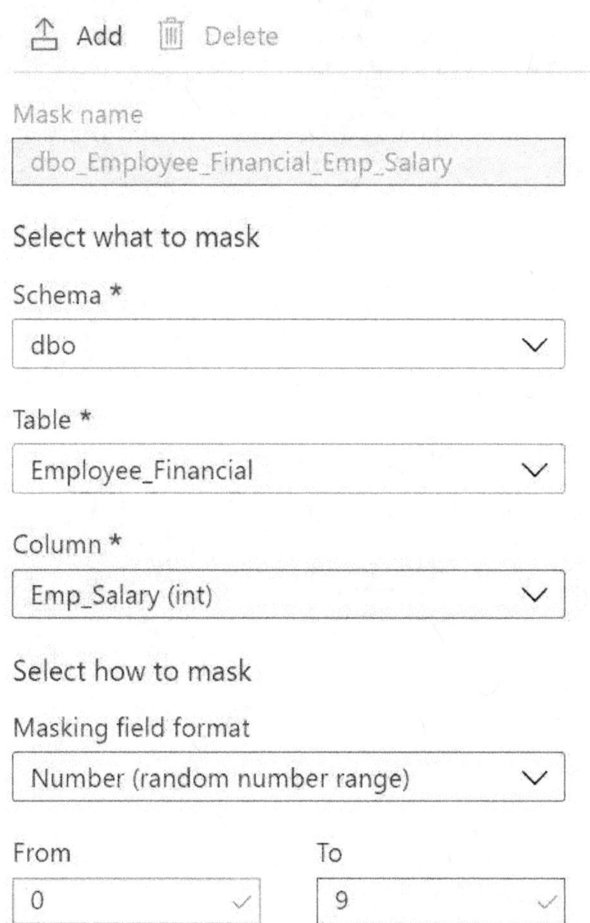

In the previous image, we are masking the Salar column using the random masking function. This masking function will mask the column values using random numbers between 0 and 9. If you try to read the data from that table using a user who has read-only permission on that table, you will see that the user will not be able to see the real values. Instead, you will see only the masked values.

Trying the same using an admin user, you will see that the real column values will be displayed, indicating that the data will be masked and not changed:

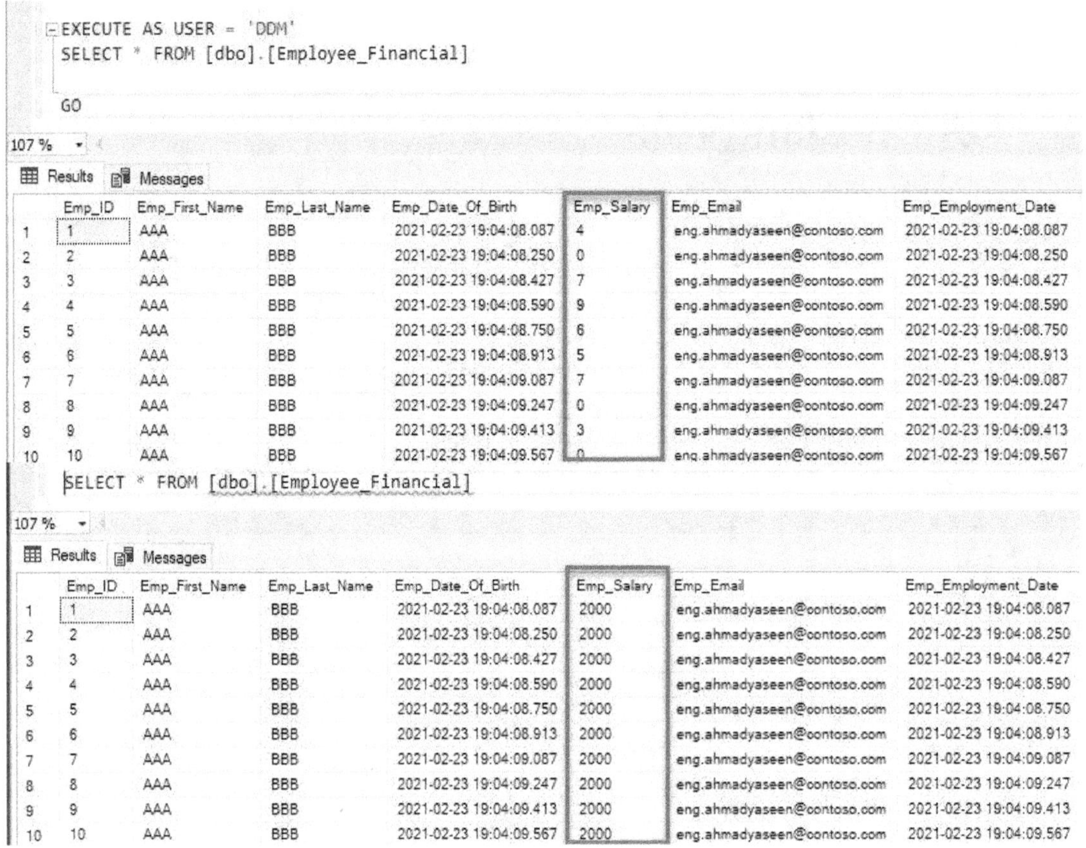

```
EXECUTE AS USER = 'DDM'
SELECT * FROM [dbo].[Employee_Financial]

GO
```

	Emp_ID	Emp_First_Name	Emp_Last_Name	Emp_Date_Of_Birth	Emp_Salary	Emp_Email	Emp_Employment_Date
1	1	AAA	BBB	2021-02-23 19:04:08.087	4	eng.ahmadyaseen@contoso.com	2021-02-23 19:04:08.087
2	2	AAA	BBB	2021-02-23 19:04:08.250	0	eng.ahmadyaseen@contoso.com	2021-02-23 19:04:08.250
3	3	AAA	BBB	2021-02-23 19:04:08.427	7	eng.ahmadyaseen@contoso.com	2021-02-23 19:04:08.427
4	4	AAA	BBB	2021-02-23 19:04:08.590	9	eng.ahmadyaseen@contoso.com	2021-02-23 19:04:08.590
5	5	AAA	BBB	2021-02-23 19:04:08.750	6	eng.ahmadyaseen@contoso.com	2021-02-23 19:04:08.750
6	6	AAA	BBB	2021-02-23 19:04:08.913	5	eng.ahmadyaseen@contoso.com	2021-02-23 19:04:08.913
7	7	AAA	BBB	2021-02-23 19:04:09.087	7	eng.ahmadyaseen@contoso.com	2021-02-23 19:04:09.087
8	8	AAA	BBB	2021-02-23 19:04:09.247	0	eng.ahmadyaseen@contoso.com	2021-02-23 19:04:09.247
9	9	AAA	BBB	2021-02-23 19:04:09.413	3	eng.ahmadyaseen@contoso.com	2021-02-23 19:04:09.413
10	10	AAA	BBB	2021-02-23 19:04:09.567	0	eng.ahmadyaseen@contoso.com	2021-02-23 19:04:09.567

```
SELECT * FROM [dbo].[Employee_Financial]
```

	Emp_ID	Emp_First_Name	Emp_Last_Name	Emp_Date_Of_Birth	Emp_Salary	Emp_Email	Emp_Employment_Date
1	1	AAA	BBB	2021-02-23 19:04:08.087	2000	eng.ahmadyaseen@contoso.com	2021-02-23 19:04:08.087
2	2	AAA	BBB	2021-02-23 19:04:08.250	2000	eng.ahmadyaseen@contoso.com	2021-02-23 19:04:08.250
3	3	AAA	BBB	2021-02-23 19:04:08.427	2000	eng.ahmadyaseen@contoso.com	2021-02-23 19:04:08.427
4	4	AAA	BBB	2021-02-23 19:04:08.590	2000	eng.ahmadyaseen@contoso.com	2021-02-23 19:04:08.590
5	5	AAA	BBB	2021-02-23 19:04:08.750	2000	eng.ahmadyaseen@contoso.com	2021-02-23 19:04:08.750
6	6	AAA	BBB	2021-02-23 19:04:08.913	2000	eng.ahmadyaseen@contoso.com	2021-02-23 19:04:08.913
7	7	AAA	BBB	2021-02-23 19:04:09.087	2000	eng.ahmadyaseen@contoso.com	2021-02-23 19:04:09.087
8	8	AAA	BBB	2021-02-23 19:04:09.247	2000	eng.ahmadyaseen@contoso.com	2021-02-23 19:04:09.247
9	9	AAA	BBB	2021-02-23 19:04:09.413	2000	eng.ahmadyaseen@contoso.com	2021-02-23 19:04:09.413
10	10	AAA	BBB	2021-02-23 19:04:09.567	2000	eng.ahmadyaseen@contoso.com	2021-02-23 19:04:09.567

You can also mask the column using SSMS by altering the column definition and add the mask function as in the T-SQL script below:

ALTER TABLE Employee_Financial

ALTER COLUMN EMP_Salary int MASKED WITH (FUNCTION='random(0,9)');

Take into consideration that granting the user UNMASK permissions will allow him to display the data's real values without applying the masking functions.

Configure server and database-level firewall rules

In Azure SQL Database, the databases are protected by firewalls. All connections to the server and database are rejected by default, allowing you to manually add the IP addresses or IP ranges that are authorized to access the SQL databases. In this way, we are preventing any unauthorized user from accessing the SQL databases.

Azure SQL Database provides us with two sets of firewall rules, the server-level firewall rules and database-level firewall rules. Both the server and the database-level-firewalls control the access to the SQL databases using IP Address rules. In this way, you can add the public outbound IP address for all users who are authorized to access a specific database, instead of explicitly allowing the access by adding logins, as in the on-premises SQL Server.

The server-level firewall rules control the access to the master database and all databases hosted on the same logical server. Whereas the database-level firewall rules control the access on a specific database only.

When you connect to an Azure SQL Database, the following will be performed:

- The connected public IP address will be checked first for any matching server-level firewall rule in the master database. If any matching rule is found, then the connection process will complete.
- If no matching server-level firewall rule is found, and the database name is provided in the connection string, then the IP address will be checked for any matching database-level firewall rule. If any matching database rule is found, then the connection process will complete.
- Suppose you connect via SQL Server Management Studio or Azure Data Studio, and no matching server level or database level firewall rule is found. In that case, a message will be displayed asking to create a new firewall rule for the connecting IP address.

You can configure the server-level firewall rules using the Azure portal or using the sp_set_firewall_rule T-SQL command within the master database. On the other hand, the database-level firewall rules can be configured using the sp_set_database_firewall_rule T-SQL command only within the user database.

The first firewall rule that should be created when provisioning an Azure SQL Database is a server-level firewall rule. This rule can be created using the Azure Portal by adding the client who provisioned the Azure SQL Database. Then you can add the IP address or IP range for the users who need to access all databases created under that logical server. They will be able to connect to that database from outside the Azure Portal and perform their tasks. This includes administering the service and creating additional server-level and database-level firewall rules using the T-SQL commands.

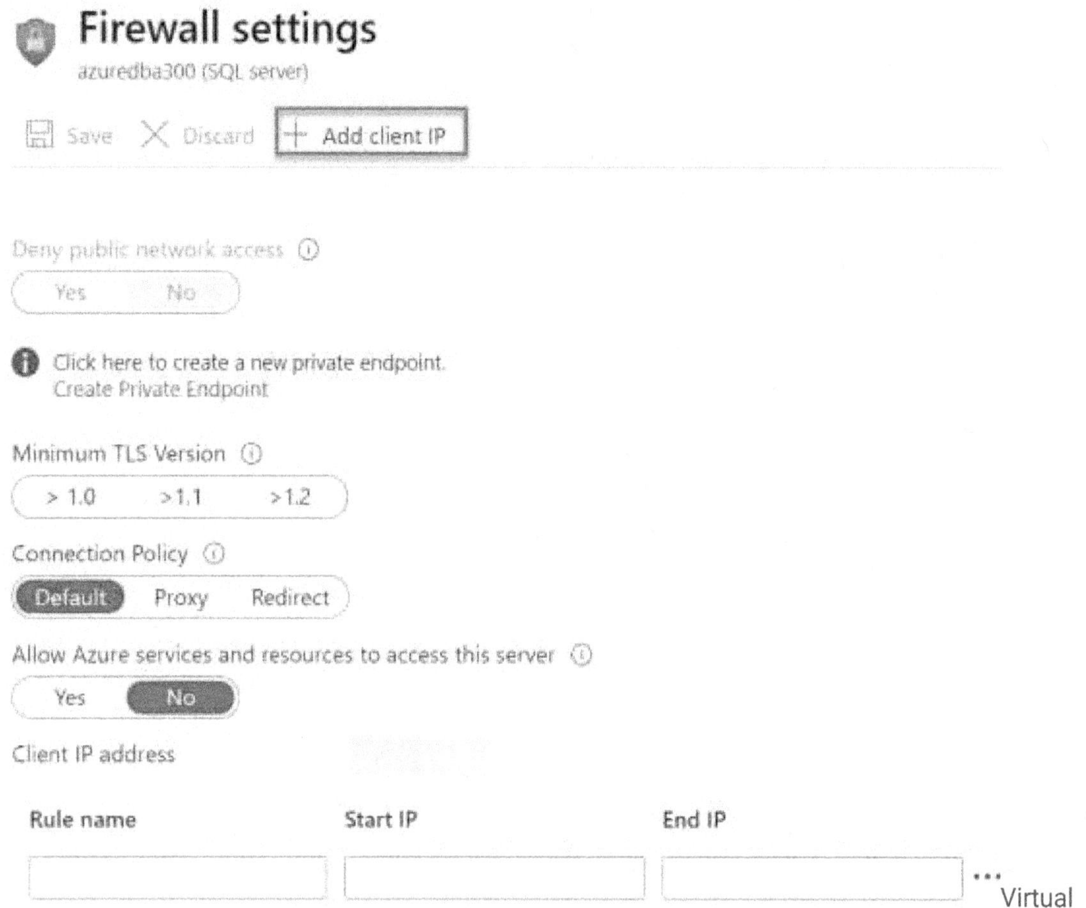

Virtual network firewall rules can be added also to control the subnets and virtual networks that are allowed to connect to that Azure SQL logical server. This rule will be applied to all databases hosted in that logical server and not at the database level. To create a virtual network rule, a virtual network endpoint should be available to act as a reference for that rule, with each virtual network endpoint applied only to one Azure region, which is the underlying endpoint's region.

The Virtual Network firewall role can be added by providing an existing virtual network or create a new virtual network, as below:

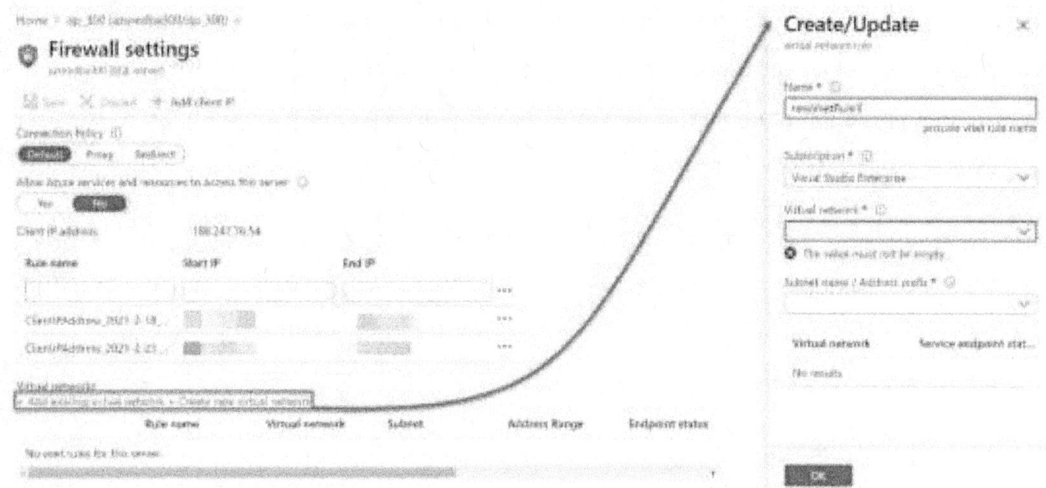

Another feature provided by Microsoft Azure that is used to secure the connection to an Azure SQL Database using a private endpoint is the Private Link feature. When connecting to the Azure SQL Database using a private endpoint, this connection will be routed over the Azure backbone network instead of going over the public internet.

The Private Link allows us to enable cross-premises access to the private endpoint using ExpressRoute, private peering, or VPN tunnelling, allowing us to disable any access via the public endpoint and stop using the IP-based firewall rules.

Row-Level Security

In addition to the security features discussed previously that are used to secure the data at the column level or at rest, Microsoft provides us with another security feature that can be used to control the access at the row level. This feature is supported by Microsoft SQL Server, Azure SQL Database, Azure SQL Managed Instance and Azure Synapse Analytics.

Row Level Security, also known as RLS, is a data security feature that is used to control the access to the rows in the database tables using the query execution context. In other words, it allows the users to work only on the rows that they have access to. For example, the salesperson is allowed to view and update his customer's data rows only, without being able to access other salesperson's customer's data.

Row Level Security simplifies the database security design and makes it more reliable. With RLS, the access restriction logic will be performed in the database tier without performing any change at the application tier. Each time data access is attempted from any tier, the database system will apply the defined access restrictions.

Row Level Security can be performed by creating a security policy and predicates that are created as inline table-valued functions and invoked and enforced by a security policy. This security policy will work as a predicates container. SQL Server allows you to define multiple active security policies but without overlapping the predicate.

RLS supports two types of security predicates:

- The filter predicate that filters rows silently for read operations. It includes the SELECT, UPDATE and DELETE statements. In other words, the application will not be aware that the data is filtered, and no error message will be raised in case that all the rows are filtered. Instead, It will return null values.
- The Block predicate that prevents the write operation that violates the defined predicate. It will return an error message because of the block.

RLS supports the following blocking types:

- AFTER INSERT and AFTER UPDATE predicates that will prevent the users from updating the rows to values that will violate the predicate.
- BEFORE UPDATE predicates that will prevent the users from updating the rows that are violating the predicate currently.
- BEFORE DELETE predicates, that will prevent the users from deleting the rows.

Row-Level Security has several limitations when combined with other SQL Server features. For example, RLS is incompatible with Filestream and the Partitioned Views and may have some restrictions working with different features. For a complete list of these restrictions, and other detailed information about RLS in general, check this document: https://docs.microsoft.com/en-us/sql/relational-databases/security/row-level-security.

To understand practically how the Row Level Security feature works, we will imagine the scenario below:

- We have three couriers who are responsible for delivering shipments to different locations.
- Each courier is allowed to view the shipments that he should deliver and based on the courier name.
- The manager is responsible for monitoring the shipment's details for all couriers.

First of all, we will create the Manager and the three couriers' users in the database:

```
CREATE USER Manager WITHOUT LOGIN;

CREATE USER Courier1 WITHOUT LOGIN;

CREATE USER Courier2 WITHOUT LOGIN;

CREATE USER Courier3 WITHOUT LOGIN;
```

After that, we will create a table that will host the couriers' shipments information:

```
CREATE TABLE [dbo].[Shipments_Info]

(

    [Shipment_ID] int IDENTITY(1,1) PRIMARY KEY,

    [CourierName] varchar(10) NULL,

    [Package_Receive_DateTime] datetime NULL,

    [PackageCostOnDelivery] decimal(6,2) NULL,

    [Package_Address_City] varchar(10) NULL

)
```

Now, we will insert two records for each courier in the created table:

```
INSERT INTO [dbo].[Shipments_Info] VALUES ('Courier1',GETDATE(), 20.35, 'AMM')

GO
```

```
INSERT INTO [dbo].[Shipments_Info] VALUES ('Courier1',GETDATE(), 18.12, 'Zar')

GO

INSERT INTO [dbo].[Shipments_Info] VALUES ('Courier2',GETDATE(), 74.11, 'Rus')

GO

INSERT INTO [dbo].[Shipments_Info] VALUES ('Courier2',GETDATE(), 14.28, 'Mar')

GO

INSERT INTO [dbo].[Shipments_Info] VALUES ('Courier3',GETDATE(), 36.17, 'Abd')

GO

INSERT INTO [dbo].[Shipments_Info] VALUES ('Courier3',GETDATE(), 104.29, 'Swif')

GO
```

After that, we will grant permissions to the manager and the couriers to view the data in that table:

```
GRANT SELECT ON [Shipments_Info] TO Manager

GO

GRANT SELECT ON [Shipments_Info] TO Courier1

GO

GRANT SELECT ON [Shipments_Info] TO Courier2

GO

GRANT SELECT ON [Shipments_Info] TO Courier3

GO
```

In order to create the Row-Level Security objects, it is recommended to create a separate schema to host these objects:

```
CREATE SCHEMA RLS_Sch;

GO
```

We will create a predicate inline table-valued function that returns 1 when a row in the CourierName column is the same as the user who executes the query. It will return 1 also if the query is executed using the manager's security context:

```
CREATE FUNCTION RLS_Sch.fn_securitypredicateCouriers(@CourierName AS sysname)

   RETURNS TABLE

WITH SCHEMABINDING

AS

    RETURN SELECT 1 AS 'AllowedCourierShipments'

WHERE @CourierName = USER_NAME() OR USER_NAME() = 'Manager';
```

After that, we will create a Security Policy on the same table using the created predicate function then enable that policy:

```
CREATE SECURITY POLICY CouriersFilter

ADD FILTER PREDICATE RLS_Sch.fn_securitypredicateCouriers(CourierName)

ON dbo.Shipments_Info

WITH (STATE = ON);
```

Now, the Row-Level Security is configured entirely and ready to start filtering all new data access on that table.

Let us try to execute the same SELECT statement from that table, but under the four users' execution contexts and compare the returned result:

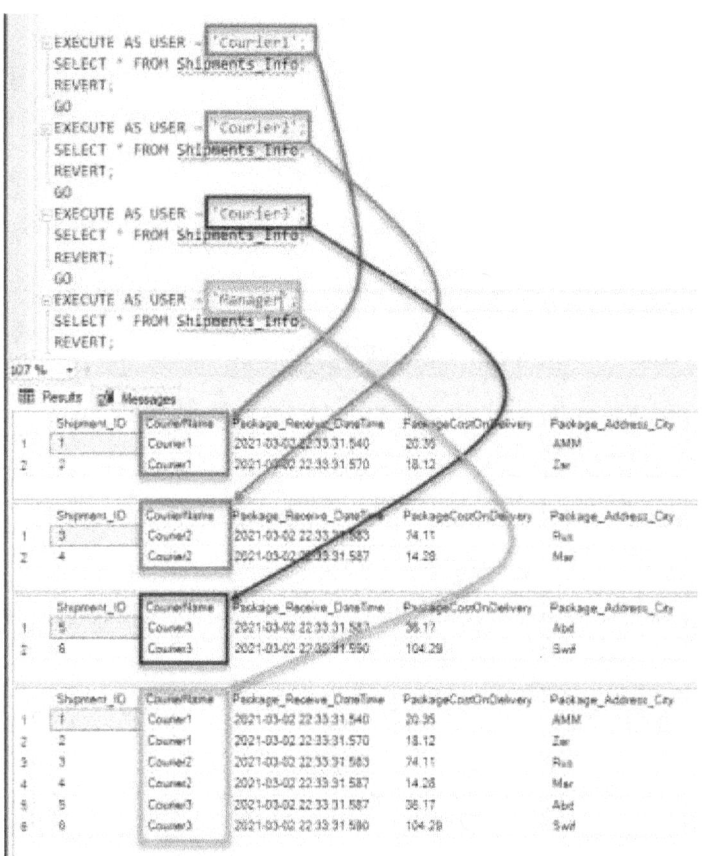

It is clear from the previous result that when the query is executed under each courier's context, he will be able to retrieve the records for the shipments he is responsible for delivering. Executing the SELECT query using the Manager's user context returns all shipments' records without any restriction.

Apply a data classification strategy

Azure SQL Database, Azure SQL Managed Instance, and Azure Synapse Analytics provides us with the ability to discover, classify, label, and report sensitive and confidential data in your databases. Examples of sensitive data include business, financial, healthcare, or personal information., This Azure database built-in feature is called Data Discovery and Classification.

Discovering and classifying sensitive data helps in meeting data privacy and regulatory compliance requirements. It also helps in managing access to that sensitive data properly.

With the Data Discovery and Classification, the classification engine will scan the database to identify all columns containing the sensitive data, based on the name of the column. After that, it will allow you to apply the recommended classification.

It provides you also with the following:

- The ability to apply the sensitivity-classification labels to the classified columns using the metadata attributes,
- Calculate the sensitivity of a query result set in real-time,
- View the database-classification state in a detailed dashboard within the Azure portal.

Those are helpful for data protection and auditing purposes.

The data classification is performed on a column-by-column basis within the database. You can find a column classified as public, another one classified as confidential and one column classified as highly confidential in the same table.

Azure portal and SQL Server Management Studio can be used to classify your data. To classify your data using the Azure portal, perform the following:

- Click on the Data Discovery and Classification pane under the Security section under the Azure SQL Database's main blade.
- Review the Overview tab. This tab provides you with a summary of the current classification state of the connected database. It includes a list of all classified columns, with the ability to filter the result based on different criteria.
- If no classification is performed yet, move to the Classification page. On this page, the classification engine will scan the database for all columns that contain sensitive data and provide a list of all recommended classifications.

After reviewing the recommended classifications, you can select the recommended classifications that you plan to apply the classification then click on the Accept Selected Recommendation to apply these classifications, and Save to confirm the classifications:

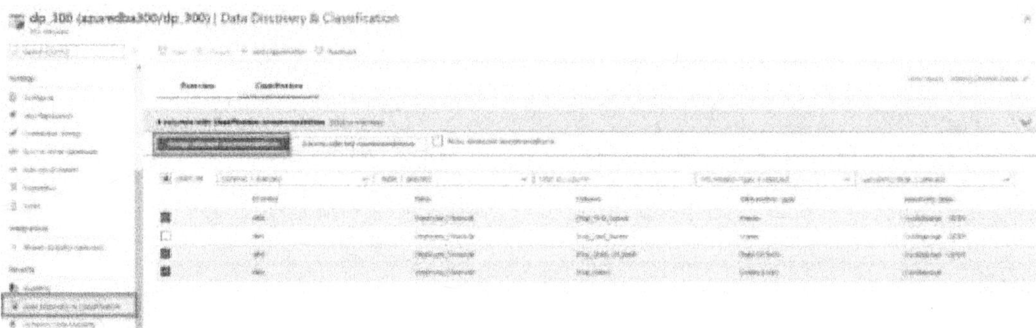

You can also classify the columns that contain sensitive data but not provided in the classification engine recommendations by clicking on the Add Classification option. In the Add Classification page, provide the following:

- The schema, table, and column to be classified manually,
- The type of data stored in that column,
- The confidentiality level of the data stored in that column.

Click Add Classification, then Save to apply the classification on that column:

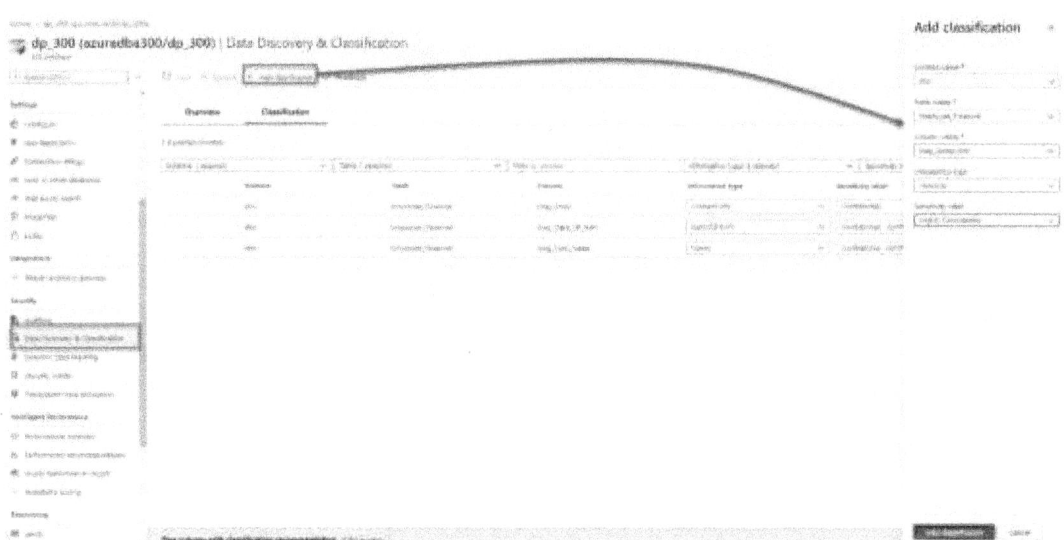

Returning back to the Overview page after classifying the database columns, you will see a summary for the data classifications that are applied to the database columns, with the ability to export the classification report:

Advanced Threat Protection

As a part of the Azure Defender for SQL offering, Microsoft Azure databases, such as Azure SQL Database, Azure SQL Managed Instance and Azure Synapse Analytics, supports the Advanced Threat Protection (ATP) feature.

ATP is used to monitor the connections to the Azure databases and the queries that are executed against these databases and detect any abnormal activities that indicate potentially harmful attempts to access or exploit the Azure databases.

Advanced Threat Protection helps in sending alerts in response to many threats, such as:

- Vulnerability to SQL injection. This alert looks for T-SQL code that may be vulnerable to SQL injection attacks. In the SQL Injection, the attacker will append the SQL command that is dynamically generated within the client application to the back end of a form field in the application and execute the injected SQL script into the form field.
    - For example, if this query is expecting the ID to be provided in the ID field in the form:
    - SELECT * FROM Orders WHERE OrderId=@ID
    - but the attacker inserts:
    - "25; DELETE FROM Orders;"
    - The query will become:

- SELECT * FROM Orders WHERE OrderID=25; delete from Orders; DELETE FROM Orders;
- And truncate all table's data!
- Although fixing the application code is the starting point to fix that issue, it will not be applicable in some cases. Having Advanced Threat Protection will provide an additional layer of protection for the sensitive data stored in the database.

- Potential SQL injection, that is raised when an attacker is trying to execute a SQL injection attack.
- Access from an unusual location, that is raised when a user logs in from an unusual geographic location.
- Access from an unusual Azure data center, that looks for attacks caused by users log in from an unusual Azure data center.
- Access from an unfamiliar principal. This alert is raised when a login attempts from an unusual user or application to a database.
- Access from a potentially harmful application that detects the common tools that are used to attack the databases.
- Brute force SQL credentials. Thus alert is raised when there are a high number of login failures with different credentials.

The Azure Threat Protection can be activated by enabling the Azure Defender for SQL from the Azure Security Center pane of the Azure SQL Database, where the alerts will be integrated with Azure security center that allows you to review these alerts, as below:

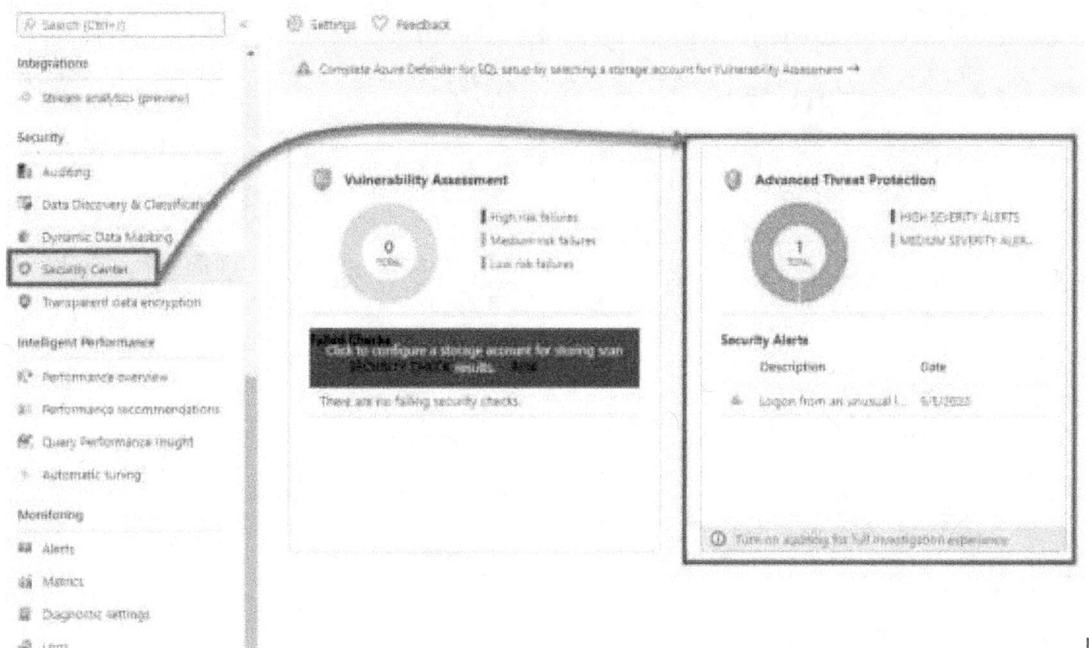

It is highly recommended to enable the auditing feature on the Azure SQL databases, in addition to the Advanced Threat Protection, in order to perform an in-depth investigation into the source of the detected problem.

If the Azure Threat Protection detects any anomalous activity, an email with information about the detected event will be received. This email includes:

- The nature of the activity,
- The database and the server name,
- The event time,
- Possible causes,
- The recommended actions to investigate and mitigate the potential threat.
- An Azure SQL Auditing Log link can be used to show the relevant auditing records for the event's time.

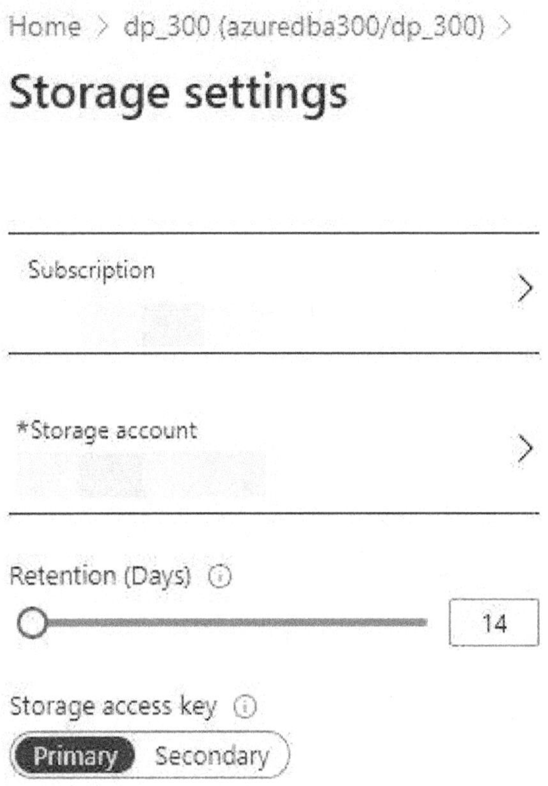

Home > dp_300 (azuredba300/dp_300) >

Storage settings

Subscription

*Storage account

Retention (Days)

14

Storage access key

Primary Secondary

Configure server and database audits

SQL Server Database auditing is considered one of the most important parts of the IT auditing process. It helps ensure that the company's data is secured, starting from evaluating the infrastructure where these data is stored and used, examining the business operations that are processing the data and finishing with the backup solutions that are used to keep these data.

SQL Server Database auditing is the process of tracking and logging all events occurring on that SQL instance. It requires specifying what to audit, how to audit, who should perform the audit, whom to audit and the acceptable auditing result.

A database audit is essential for the organization decision-makers as it potentially affects business continuity and will help build the trust bridge between customers and the organization. The customer will be more amenable to dealing with an organization that keeps sensitive data secured and always available.

For most SQL Server audit strategies, there are several common and critical events that you should keep an eye on as a minimum requirement for an audit. These events include Failed Logins that track the users who tried to connect to the SQL Server instance but failed. The importance of keeping an eye on such an event is that an excessive number of incidences of this event could indicate an attack on that SQL Server.

Another important action that should be monitored is the SQL Server Login Changes. It includes adding new login to the SQL Server instance, dropping a login, or changing the SQL Server instance's login privileges. This action is acceptable if the authorized person performs it and logged adequately in the changes log. Otherwise, it is maybe a fake key that will be used to hack the SQL Server.

A rule of thumb also here for the SQL Server logins is having the Password Policy Enforced. In this case, you will guarantee that the password for any new SQL user or the new password for an existing user is following the Operating System password policy, such as the password complexity and expiration, configured in the Active Directory.

Tracking the database successful and unsuccessful Users Changes is a significant event that should be considered in any SQL Server auditing strategy. It includes creating or dropping a database user or changing the permission granted to that database user. Successful changes should be performed by an authorized person and logged properly in the changes log. Otherwise, it is an alarm for an attack on the SQL Server instance.

When the previous SQL Server audit base is specified, you can now go deeper based on your organization's requirement. Tracking Schema Changes, such as creating a new database object, dropping an existing one or changing its structure, is also important and should be monitored. It helps catch any illegal schema changes, as all official schema changes should be appropriately logged.

To have a strong SQL Server auditing strategy, you shouldn't leave any key under the carpet for the hackers. Tracking the Audit Changes, such as disabling the audit solution, dropping or altering the tracking events or performing changes on the audit result destination, will protect you from the hidden actions or actions performed under the absence of the auditing strategy. Hackers are malevolent but also clever. To be cleverer than them, we should track and consider any illegal change performed on the SQL audit solution that is not logged in the changes log.

Auditing your SQL Server instance works fine only if it is done regularly, without long gaps between the audits. In this way, the audit process will be less complex, resulting in a meaningful report and achieving its goal. In addition, you should compare the result of the current audit against the previous audit results. In this way, you can identify the normal actions from the critical ones.

The scope of the SQL audit should be specified correctly. You will be happy with the visibility into all corners of your SQL Server instance and Operating System. Still, you may not be happy when you start suffering from your SQL audit solution's performance impact, such as increasing memory, CPU and I/O utilization.

For this reason, it is recommended to start with a narrow audit scope, then tune it to a broader scope that covers what you want to audit. And this should be performed on your development environment first then replicated to the production once tuned and tested correctly.

A SQL Server audit can be performed using a various number of methods. It includes using the built-in SQL Server Audit feature, using third-party tools from the SQL Server market or simply performs the audit task using the legacy methods manually.

The Manual SQL Server auditing methods include:

- Read the logs written to the SQL Error Logs, the C2 trace files, the system tables and views.
- Use the SQL profiler, SQL Trace, Extended Events, SQL Server Triggers, Change Data Capture, Change Tracking or System-versioned Temporal Table to collect additional logs.

Note For more information about manual SQL Server audit methods refer to **https://github.com/AzureDP300/AzureDP300/edit/main/Chapter5/RefLinks.html**

Starting from SQL Server 2008, Microsoft introduced the SQL Server Audit feature. This feature is built using the SQL Server Extended Events and used as a complete, secure and easy to manage auditing solution. SQL Server Audit is used to track the changes performed at both the SQL Server instance and database levels, with the minimal performance impact on the audited server.

The SQL Server Audit feature consists of three main components that combine together to produce a complete SQL Server Audit solution. These components are:

- The SQL Server Audit feature.
- The Database Audit Specification.
- The Server Audit Specification.

The SQL Server Audit is the parent component of the SQL Server Audit feature that contains both the Server Audit Specifications and the Database Audit Specifications. It is used to define where the audit information will be stored in the audit, if it will be performed in synchronous or asynchronous mode, how to handle the audit file rollover, and what action will be performed in case of audit failure. All this information will reside in the master system database.

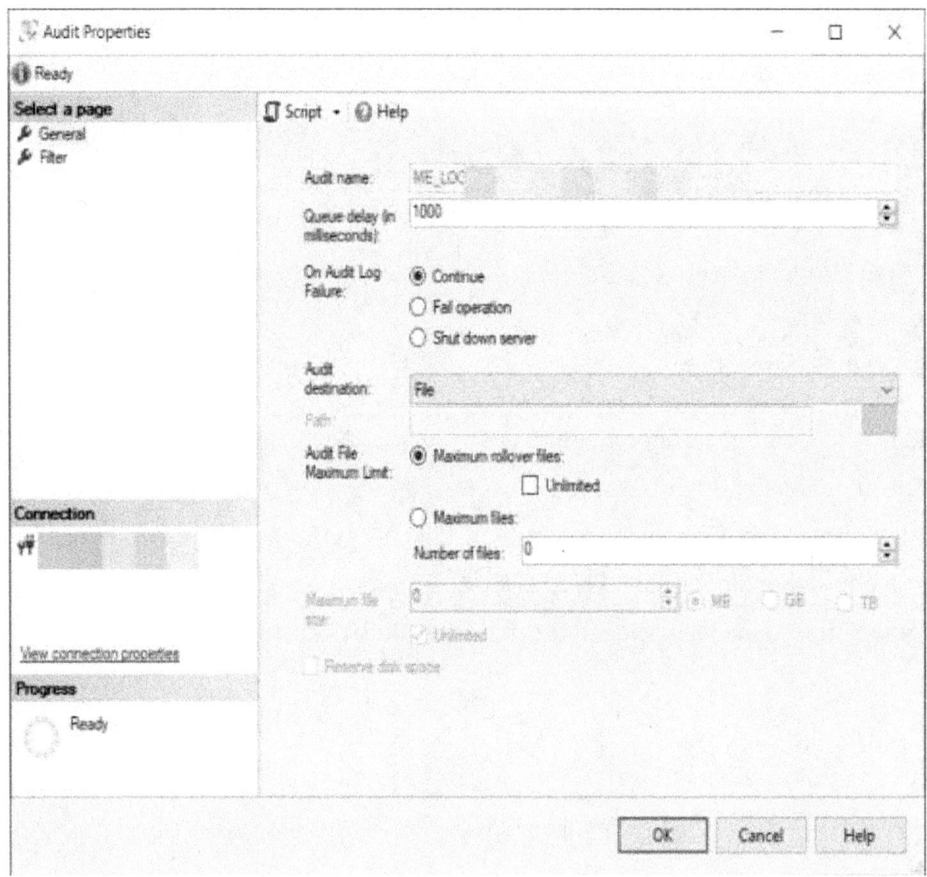

The Server Audit Specifications is used to track and collect different types of changes that are performed at the SQL Server instance level and raised by the Extended Events feature. These server-level actions are grouped together in the shape of predefined groups of actions that are called Audit Action Groups. These action groups include creating or modifying a server login, successful or failed login attempt, DBCC actions and so on.

To create a Server Audit Specifications, a SQL Server Audit should be created on the SQL Server instance. SQL Server allows you to create only one Server Audit Specification per each SQL Server

Audit, as both will be created at the SQL Server instance level.

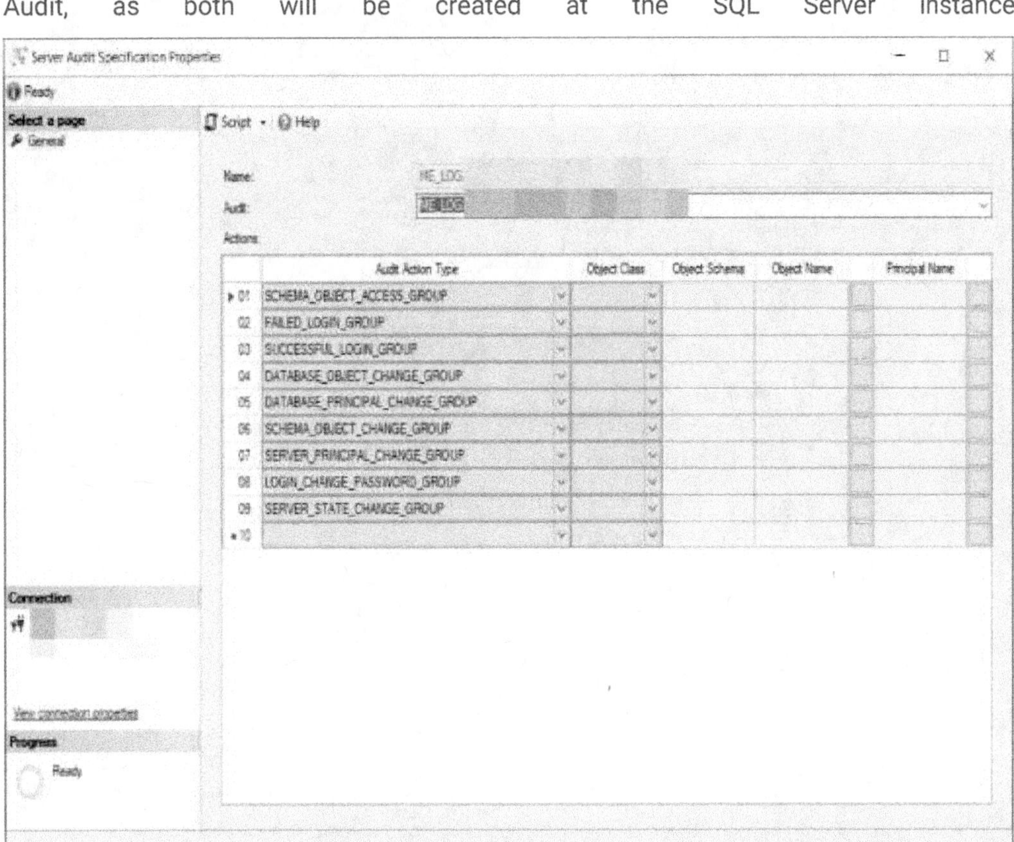

The Database Audit Specification is an auditing feature that can be used to collect different actions performed at the database level and raised by the Extended Events feature. The tracked database level events can be included as single audit events or in the shape of predefined audit action groups.

To create a Database Audit Specification, a SQL Server Audit should be created on the SQL Server instance. You can create only one Database Audit Specification per each SQL Server database SQL Server Audit.

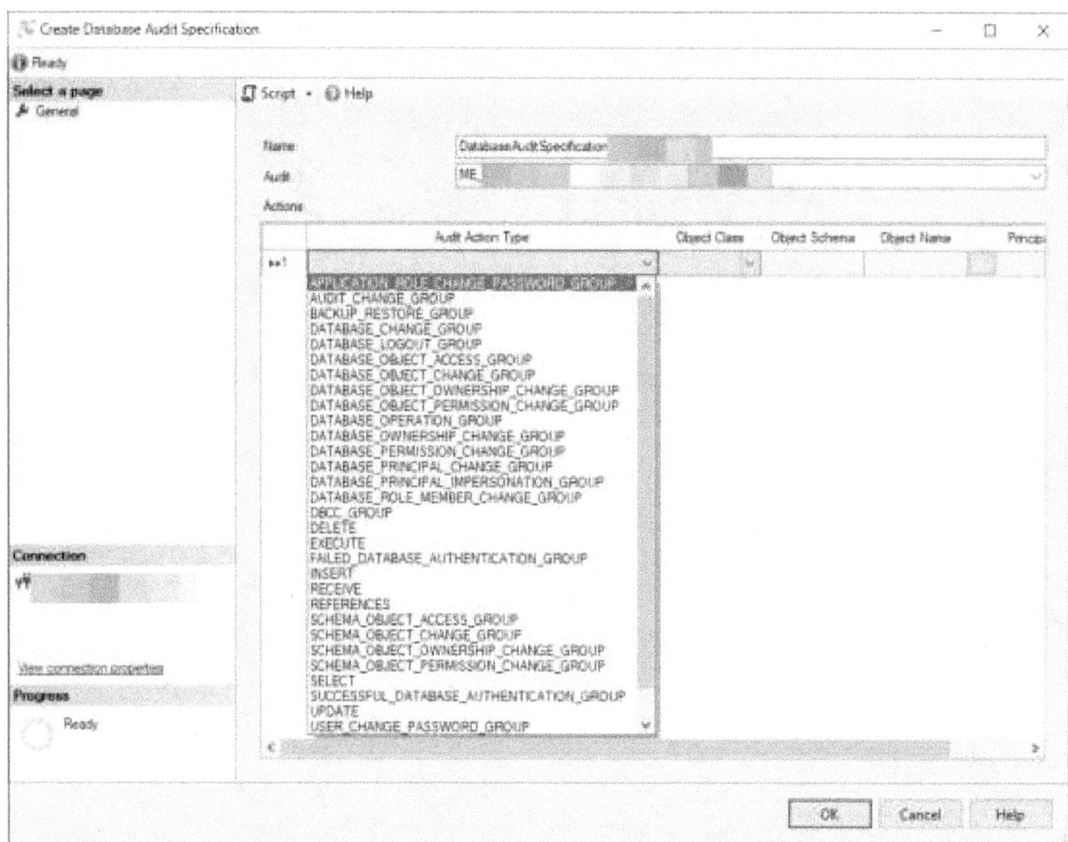

For more information about manual SQL Server audit methods refer to **https://github.com/AzureDP300/AzureDP300/blob/main/Chapter5/RefLinks.html**

In Azure SQL Database and Azure Synapse Analytics, auditing is used to track the different types of database events and log these events to an audit log in your Azure storage account, Log Analytics workspace, or Event Hubs.

Auditing your Azure databases helps meet the compliance requirements, understand the database activities, and identify the actions that may cause business concerns or security violations.

Auditing is disabled by default in the Azure database services and can be enabled using the Azure Portal by clicking on the Auditing panel under the Security Section. Under the Azure SQL Auditing, turn ON the Enable Azure SQL Auditing option, then select whether to save the Audit logs in an Azure Storage Account, Log Analytics Workspace or Event Hubs. In this example, we will choose the Azure Storage Account as an Audit Log Destination, with the ability to store the audit logs in multiple destinations at the same time:

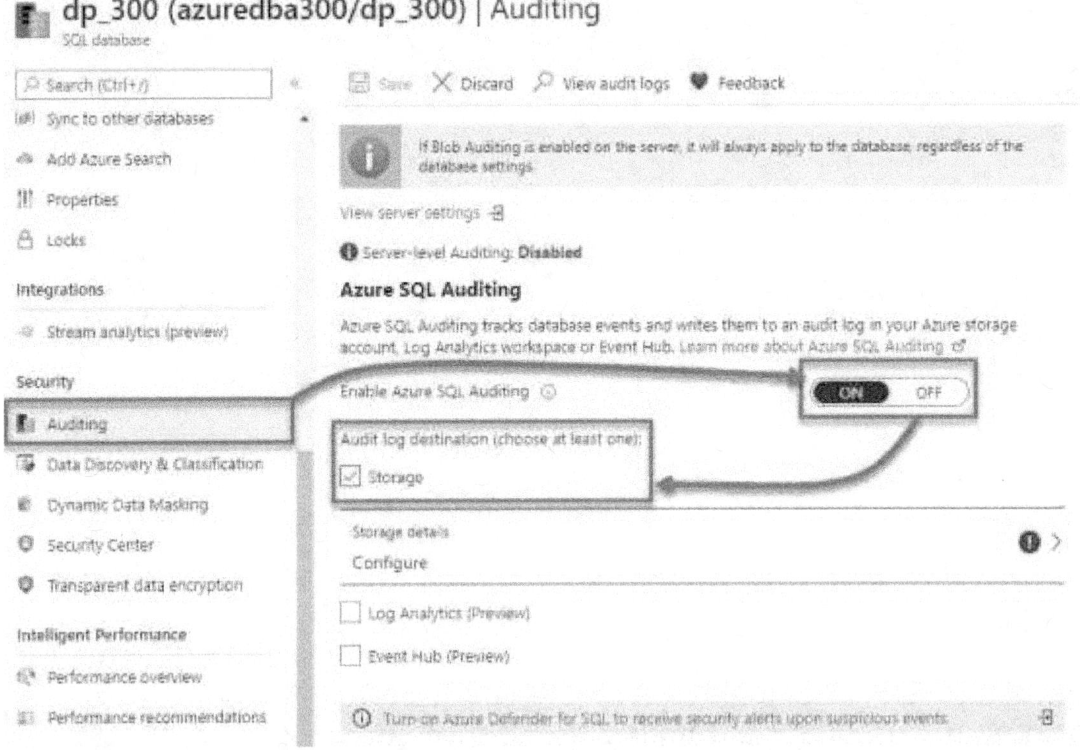

After selecting the Azure Storage Account as a destination, click Configure to set the storage account information, where you will be asked to provide:

- The subscription that hosts the Azure storage account,
- The storage account name,
- How long the log files will be kept in that storage
- The access key that the Azure SQL database will use to connect to the storage account:

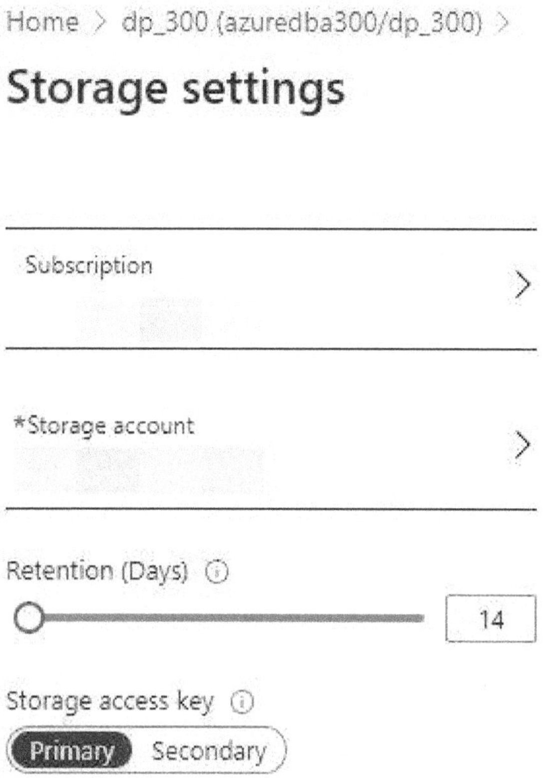

Home > dp_300 (azuredba300/dp_300) >

Storage settings

Subscription

*Storage account

Retention (Days)

14

Storage access key

Primary Secondary

Implement data change tracking

Change Data Capture, also known as CDC, is used to track the changes performed on the Microsoft SQL Server or Azure SQL Managed Instance database tables without performing any additional programming efforts.

CDC captures all INSERT, UPDATE and DELETE commands executed on a specific database table, using an asynchronous process. It reads the transaction log without impacting the system. It writes historical and detailed information about the performed changes in another table, which has the same columns schema as the source tables.

CDC adds several columns that will record these actions. It allows us to monitor the database changes for auditing purposes and incrementally load the OLTP data source's database changes to the target OLAP data warehouse using T-SQL command or ETL packages.

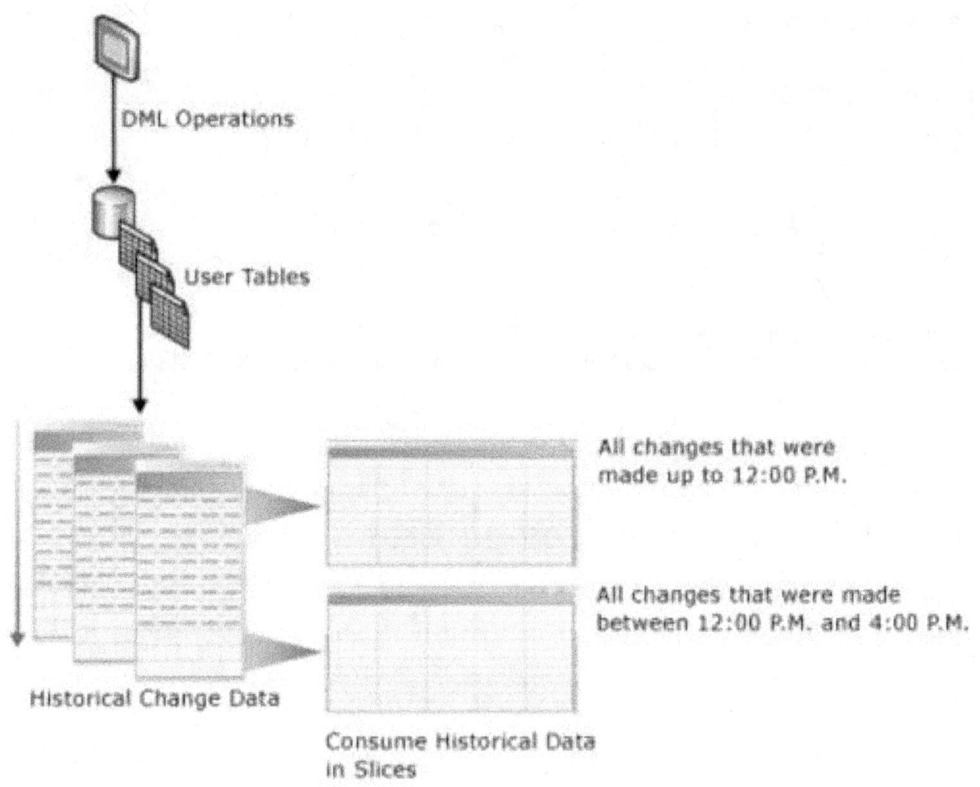

Change Data Capture can be enabled, in Microsoft SQL Server or Azure SQL Managed Instance, at the database level first using the sys.sp_cdc_enable_db system stored procedure then at the table level using the sys.sp_cdc_enable_table system stored procedure, as in the script below:

```
USE [AdventureWorks2016]

GO

EXEC sys.sp_cdc_disable_db

GO

EXEC sys.sp_cdc_enable_table

@source_schema = N'dbo',

@source_name   = N'Table_Name',
```

```
@role_name     = N'Role_Name',

@filegroup_name = N'DB_CT_Name',

@supports_net_changes = 1

GO
```

For more information about Change Data Capture, check: **https://github.com/AzureDP300/AzureDP300/blob/main/Chapter5/RefLinks.html**

On the other hand, Change Tracking, also known as CT, is a lightweight and synchronous tracking mechanism that helps in tracking the DML changes that are performed in a Microsoft SQL Server or Azure SQL database tables. These changes will be available directly once the DML change is committed, without the need to wait for the log reader agent to read the logs from the Transaction Log file, as in the case of the Change Data Capture.

Change Tracking captures the table rows that are changed without capturing the modified data or keeping historical data about the record changes.

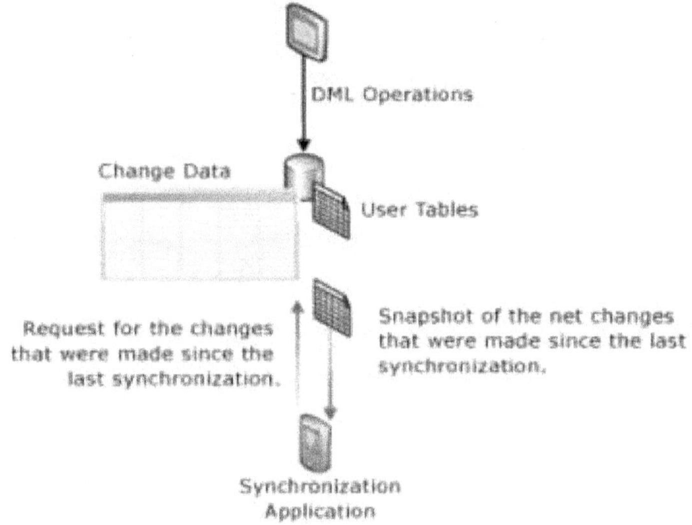

Change Tracking should be enabled, in Microsoft SQL Server or Azure SQL Database, at the database level first. It can be performed by enabling the Change_Tracking flag, providing the retention period and specifying whether to enable the automatic cleanup or not. After that, you need to enable it at the table level, using the ALTER TABLE...ENABLE_CHANGE_TRACKING command, as in the script below:

```
ALTER DATABASE [AdventureWorks2016]

SET CHANGE_TRACKING = ON

(CHANGE_RETENTION = 2 DAYS, AUTO_CLEANUP = ON)

GO

USE [AdventureWorks2016]

GO

ALTER TABLE Table_Name

ENABLE CHANGE_TRACKING

WITH (TRACK_COLUMNS_UPDATED = ON)
```

For more information about Change Tracking, check:
https://github.com/AzureDP300/AzureDP300/edit/main/Chapter5/RefLinks.html

Perform a vulnerability assessment

As a part of the Azure Defender for SQL offering, the Azure SQL vulnerability assessment is a built-in scanning service that is used to proactively improve database security and resolve security issues by discovering, tracking, and eliminating database vulnerabilities. Vulnerability assessment is supported for Azure SQL Database, Azure SQL Managed Instance, and Azure Synapse Analytics.

Vulnerability assessment can be easily used to:

- Monitor the Azure databases,

- Employ a knowledge base of rules to capture the security vulnerabilities at both database-level and server-level. It includes misconfigurations, excessive permissions, and unprotected sensitive data.
- Provide you with the actional steps that can be followed to mitigate each security issue to improve the overall SQL security.

The Vulnerability assessment can be configured using Azure Portal by connecting to the Azure database service and clicking on the Security Center pane under the Security section.

From the Security Center page, click on the Enable Azure Defender for SQL option to enable the Azure Defender feature:

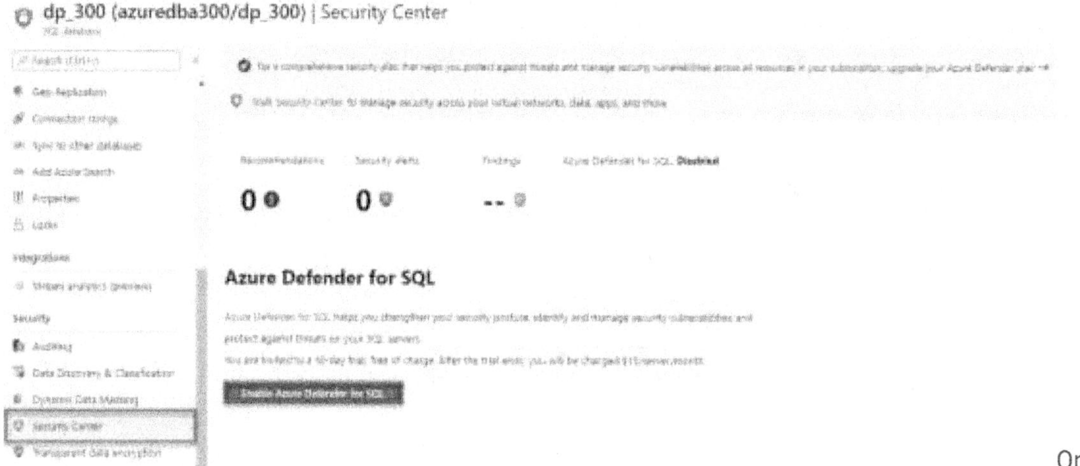

Once enabled, click on the Configure option to open the Azure Defender for SQL setting page and configure the vulnerability assessment feature, in which you will be requested to provide:

- The Azure subscription where this feature will be configured,
- The storage account where the scan result for all databases will be stored,
- If the vulnerability assessments scan should run on a weekly basis to detect security misconfigurations.
- The email address to which the scan result will be sent
- And whether to send a notification to admins and subscription owners or not:

Home > dp_300 (azuredba300/dp_300) >

Server settings

azuredba300

Save Discard Feedback

AZURE DEFENDER FOR SQL

ON OFF

Azure Defender for SQL costs 15 USD/server/month. It includes Vulnerability Assessment and Advanced Threat Protection. We invite you to a trial period for the first 30 days, without charge.

VULNERABILITY ASSESSMENT SETTINGS

Subscription

Storage account

Periodic recurring scans

ON OFF

Scans will be triggered automatically once a week. In most cases, it will be on the day Vulnerability Assessment has been enabled and saved. A scan result summary will be sent to the email addresses you provide.

Send scan reports to

Email addresses

☑ Also send email notification to admins and subscription owners

ADVANCED THREAT PROTECTION SETTINGS

Send alerts to

Email addresses

☐ Also send email notification to admins and subscription owners

Advanced Threat Protection types

All

Enable Auditing for better threats investigation experience

Once enabled, you can review the vulnerability assessment findings on the Security Center page or click on the View additional findings in Vulnerability Assessment to access the scan results from previous scans option to open the previous scan result:

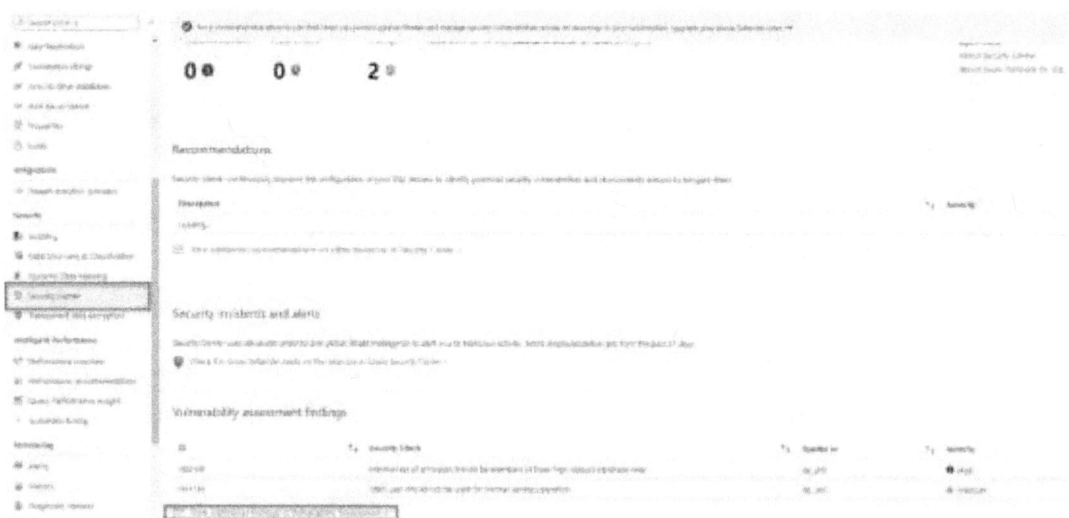

From the vulnerability assessment page, you can review the complete result of the previous scan, which contains:

- An overview of the security state,
- The number of issues found,
- A summary by the severity of the detected risks,
- A list of the findings for further investigations
- And the recommended actions that should be followed to mitigate the true vulnerability issues.

From the same page, you can review the scans history, export the current scan result, or start a new vulnerability assessment scan:

To remediate a vulnerability, click on that vulnerability from the vulnerability assessment page. Then review all information provided about that vulnerability and click on the Approve as Baseline option, to mark that vulnerability as an acceptable baseline in your Azure database environment and consider it as passes in the next scans:

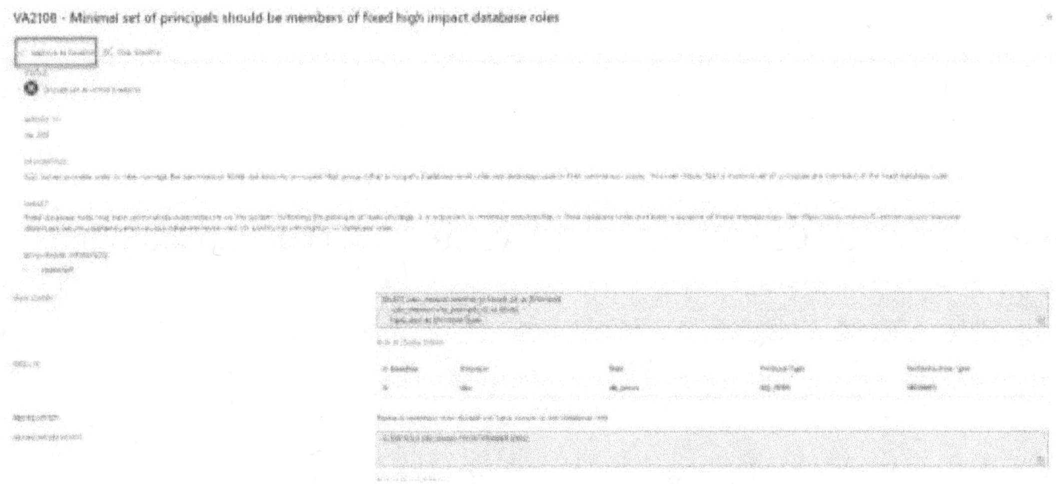

Summary

In this chapter, we explored various security controls in Azure infrastructure using the Azure Active Directory, Azure Key vault. We also configured the data classification, threat protections , vulnerability assessments, audits, change tracking , Row-level security, object level encryption. These security mechanisms are essential to safeguard your database solutions from the threats.

Chapter 6 Monitor and optimize Azure Data Platform resources

This chapter describes how to monitor different applications and services using Azure Monitor. Azure Monitor provides a common platform to monitor events that includes Logs and Metrics. Data collection provides flexibility to analyze the logs and metrics together using Azure Monitor. Analyzing the logs and improving services' performance has got the common aim to deep dive into the data platform and understand the significant differences in the abstraction layers and cloud services.

By the end of this chapter, you would be familiar with the following topics.

- View Azure SQL Database and Managed instance database resource utilization
- Diagnostic settings
- Query performance insights
- Azure Monitor
- Extended events
- Optimize Azure SQL Server on VM (IaaS)

Monitoring Azure SQL Database and Azure SQL Managed instances

Azure provides various tools for monitoring your Azure resources, creating baselines and troubleshooting resource consumption, performance issues. In this section, we explore the Azure portal for monitoring Azure SQL Database and Managed instances.

View Database data storage for Azure SQL Database

Once we deploy an Azure SQL Database, we specify the service tier and configure DTU, VCPU or max data storage. In the basic service tier, you have a maximum 2 GB database size. Similarly, you can configure a maximum of 1024 GB storage in the S3 service level in the standard service tier.

Standard service tier

Compute size	S0	S1	S2	S3
Max DTUs	10	20	50	100
Included storage (GB) [1]	250	250	250	250
Max storage (GB)	250	250	250	1024
Max in-memory OLTP storage (GB)	N/A	N/A	N/A	N/A
Max concurrent workers (requests)	60	90	120	200
Max concurrent sessions	600	900	1200	2400

Your database continues to grow due to transactions. Therefore, it is necessary to monitor the available free space in the database. In the Azure portal, to monitor the database usage and free space, go to your Azure SQL Database and Overview section.

Here, you get database data storage in a chart format.This includes:

- Used Space
- Allocated space
- Maximum storage size

Compute utilization *and ch*art formats

We get the compute utilization from the Azure SQL Database dashboard page as well. This overview page gives you a limited option to show data for the last 1 hour, 24 hours, and 7 days.

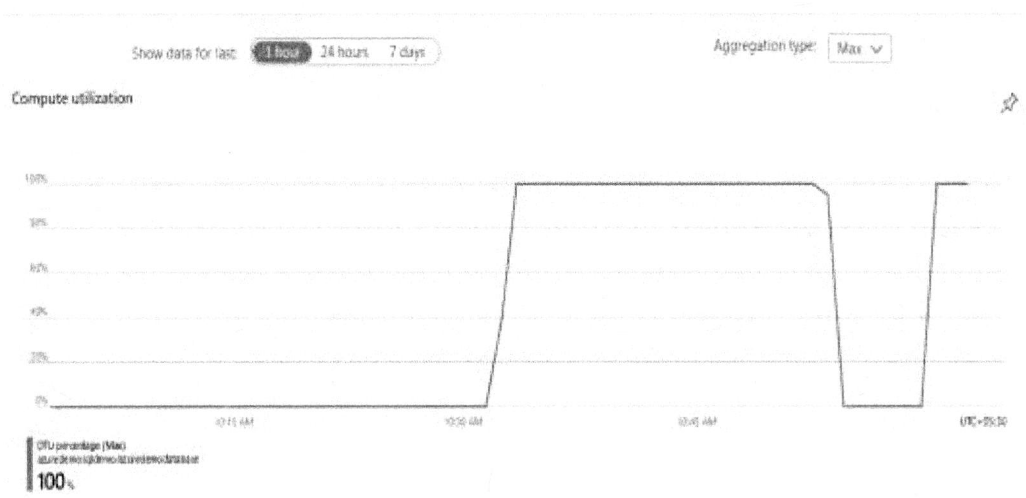

Click on the chart, and it opens a new window with the Azure Monitoring metrics page. By default, you get a line chart; however, you can modify it to Area chart, Bar chart, Scatter chart and Grid.

- Line chart:

- Area chart:

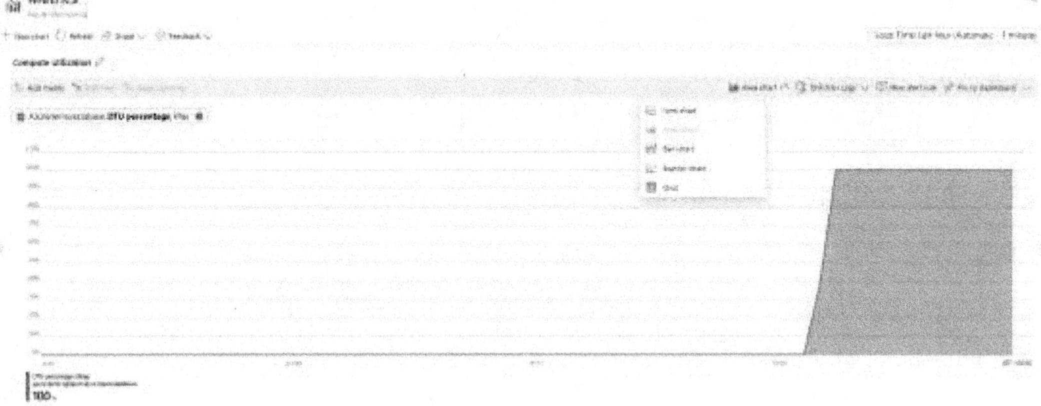

- Bar Chart:

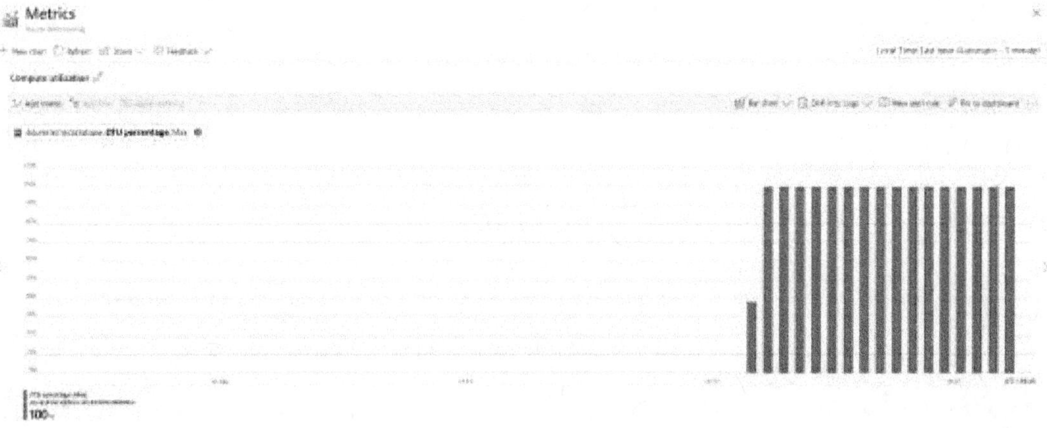

- Scatter chart:

- Grid:

Chart timeline

By default, it gives last hour data (automatic – 1 minute) in the dashboard. You get multiple options to configure the time range.

Azure Monitor Metrics data is retained for 93 days. However, if required, we can archive them to Azure Storage.

For example, if I want the last 30 minutes monitoring data, click on Last 30 minutes and click Apply.

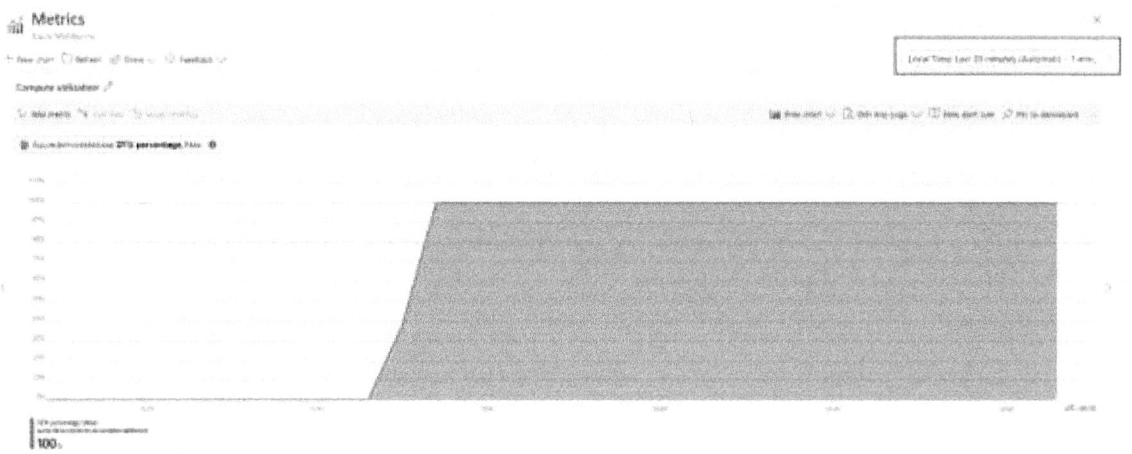

Chart Metrics

By default, the chart uses the metric – DTU percentage with Max aggregation.

Suppose we want to compute utilization based on the DTU used instead of the default DTU percentage. Select the required metric from the drop-down, and it updates the chart as shown below.

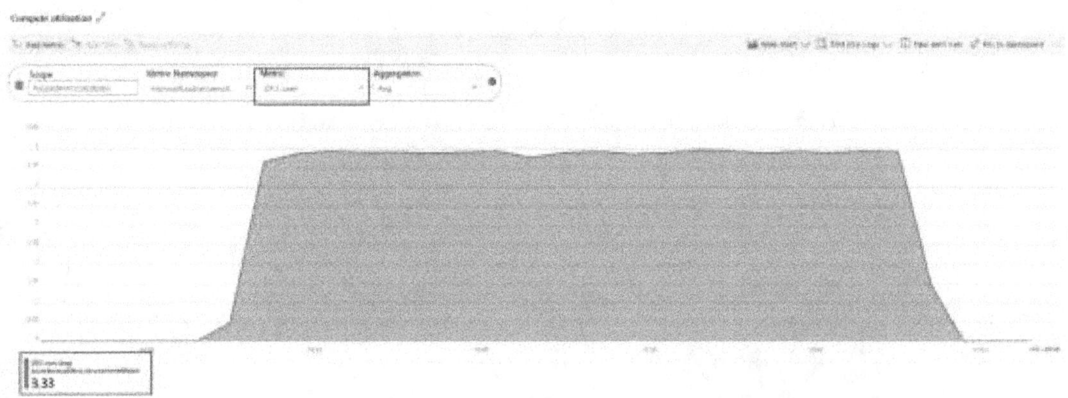

You can create your own monitoring dashboard using the customize metric. Click on Pin to dashboard.

Alert rules

In this section, we can configure custom metric alerts using the Azure portal. Search for Alerts in Azure SQL Database dashboard.

It starts with a nice tagline – Pay attention to what matters. I do not have any existing alert configured. Therefore, you get the message – You have not configured any alert rules.

Pay attention to what matters.

You have not configured any alert rules.

Configure alert rules and attend to fired alerts to efficiently monitor your Azure resources. Learn more

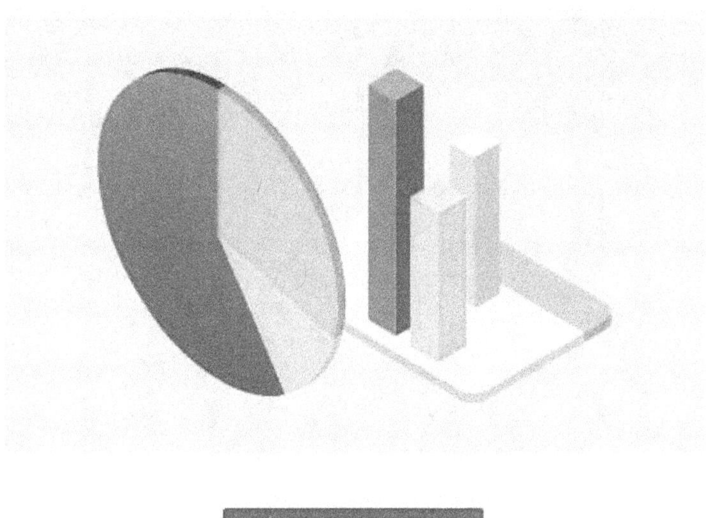

+ New Alert Rule

Click on New Alert Rule. The create new alert page displays the following sections.

- Scope: In the scope, Azure automatically displays your Azure SQL Database as a target resource for monitoring.
- Condition: Here, configure the condition that the alert will monitor.

- Action: Here, define the action based on the condition outcome.

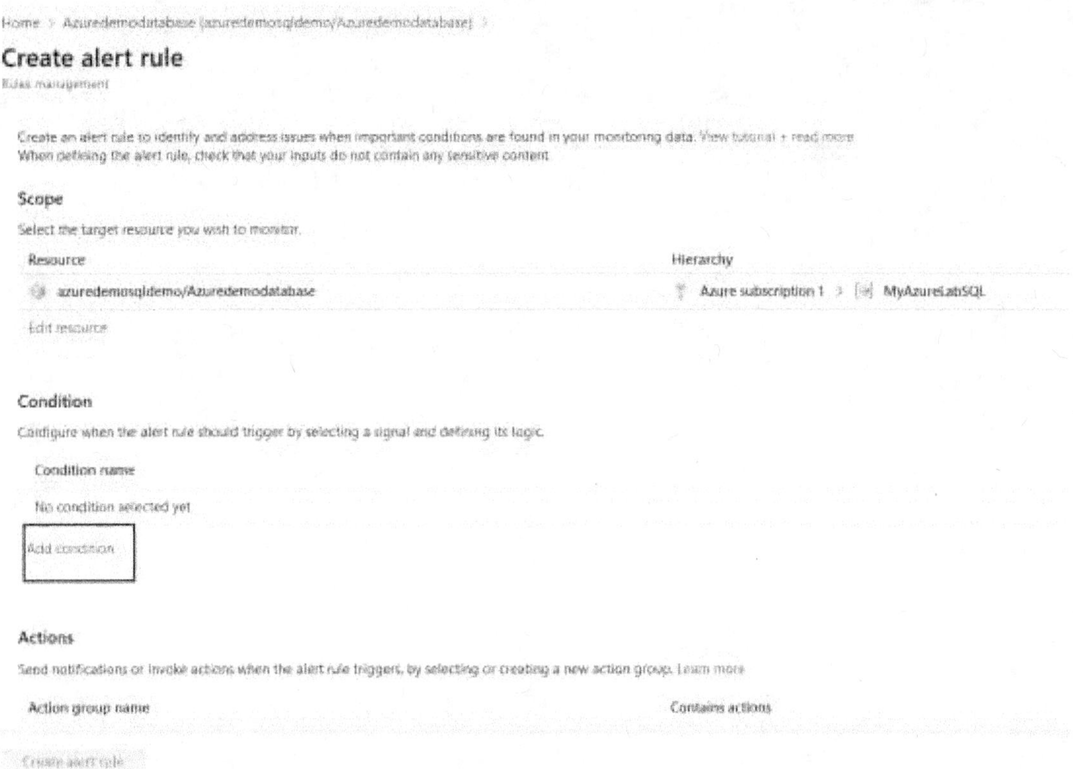

Click on Add Condition, and it opens another page for Configure signal logic with available configuration options.

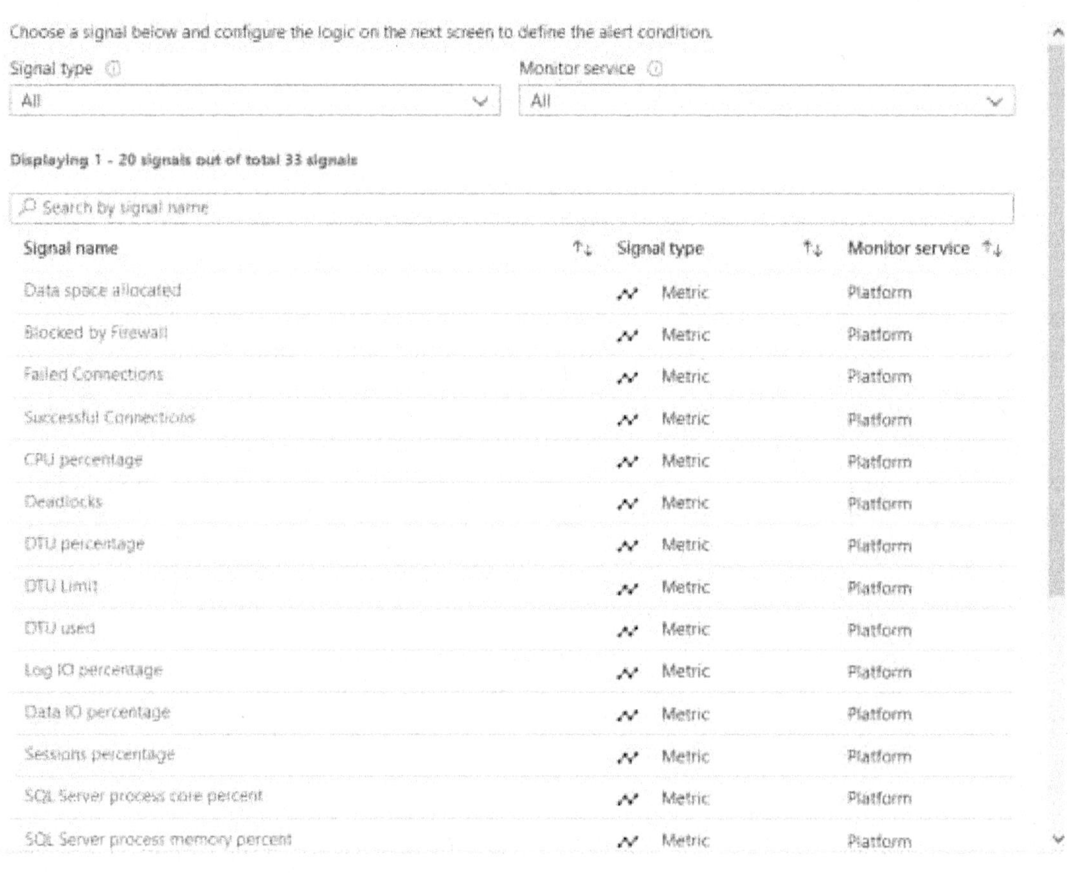

Suppose we want to configure the alert for DTU used. Select DTU used signal name. It gives a window for configuring signal logic. In this window, you have the following configurations.

- Chart period: By default, it shows chart data for over the last 6 hours. Select your required chart period from the drop-down menu.

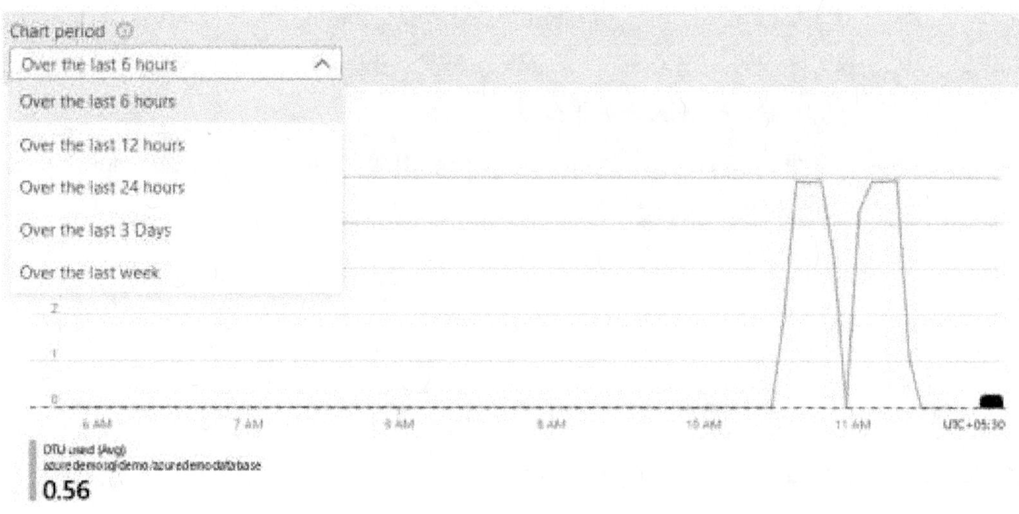

Static vs Dynamic threshold

In the alert logic, you get two ways of setting up the threshold.

- Static: The static threshold uses a specific threshold value. For example, 50%. Therefore, if the alert metric crosses the threshold, it raises an alert.

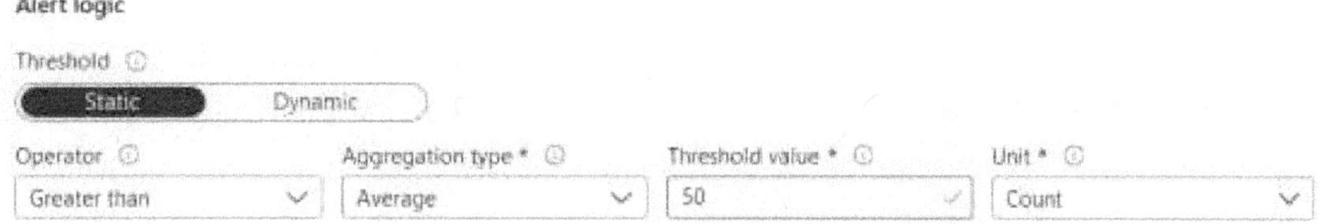

- Dynamic: The dynamic threshold detection uses machine learning algorithms for metric historical behavior, pattern identification, and anomalies for any possible issues. It continuously uses the metric series data and detects Patten based on frequency (hourly, daily, weekly). It requires the threshold sensitivity configuration. The threshold sensitivity defines the amount of deviation from the metric.
    - High: In the high sensitivity configuration, it follows a tight threshold. It raises an alert on a small deviation.

- Medium: In the medium sensitivity configuration, it uses a balanced threshold. It raised a few alerts compared to the high sensitivity. It is the default configuration for a dynamic threshold.
- Low: It raises alerts on a large deviation only. It is not recommended for a critical production workload.

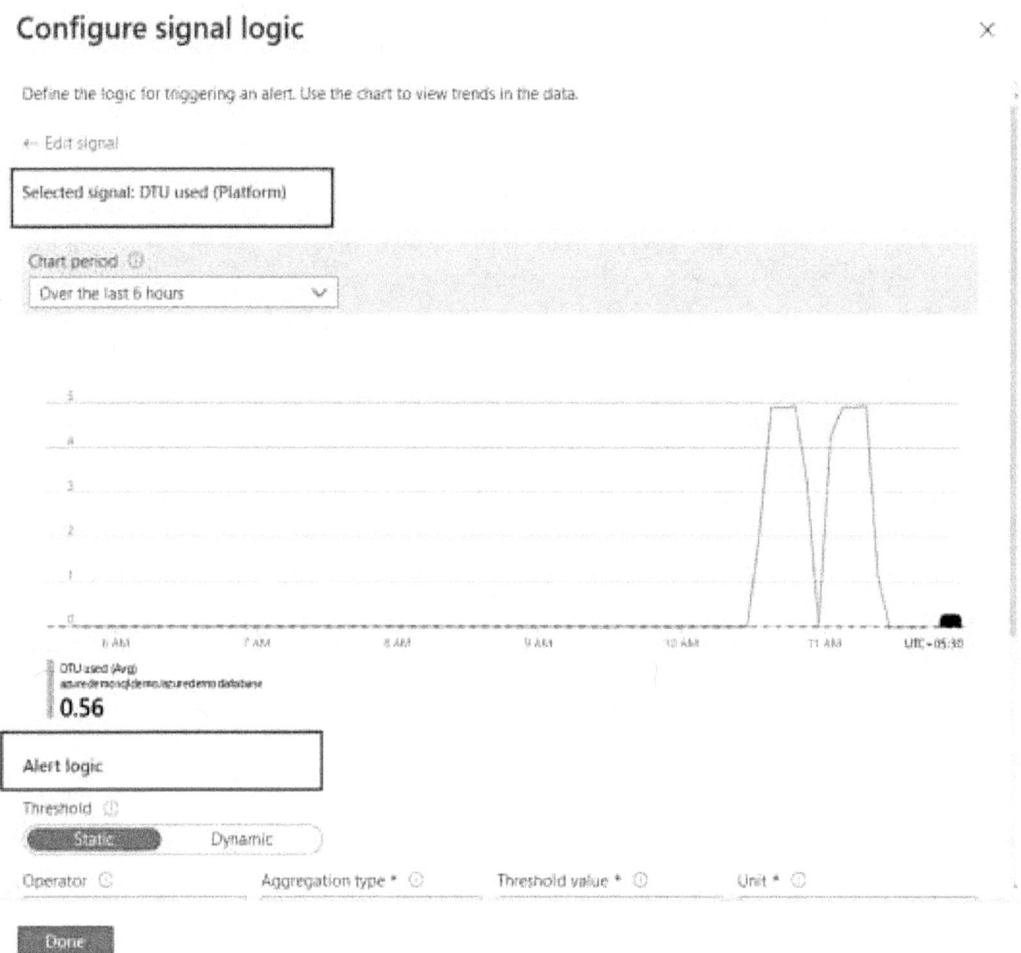

If you select a dynamic threshold, it changes the chart with data points, as shown below.

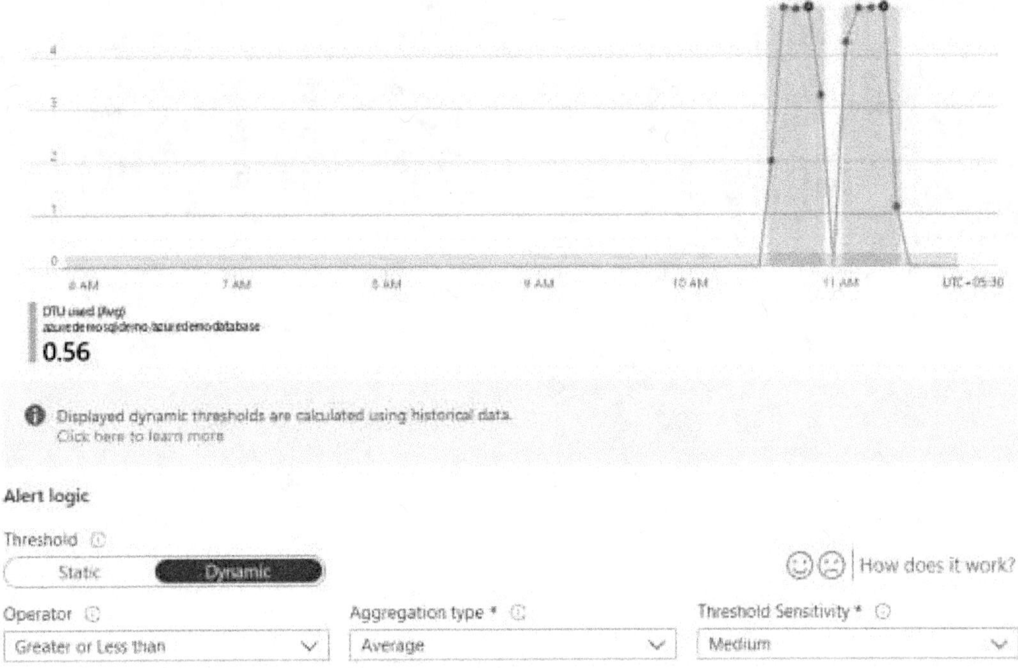

It also provides a few advanced settings.

- The number of violations to trigger the alert
  - Specify the number of violation(default: 4)
  - Evaluation period (default 20 minutes)
- You can also set an option – Ignore data before. It sets a date before which the machine learning historical data is ignored.

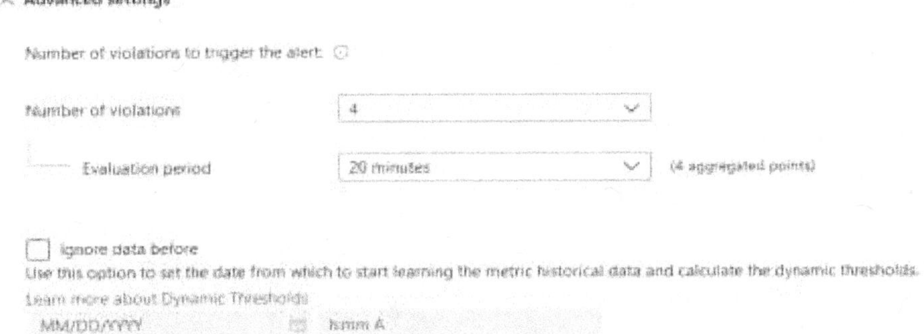

In the below image, we can view a chart having a metric with dynamic threshold limits.

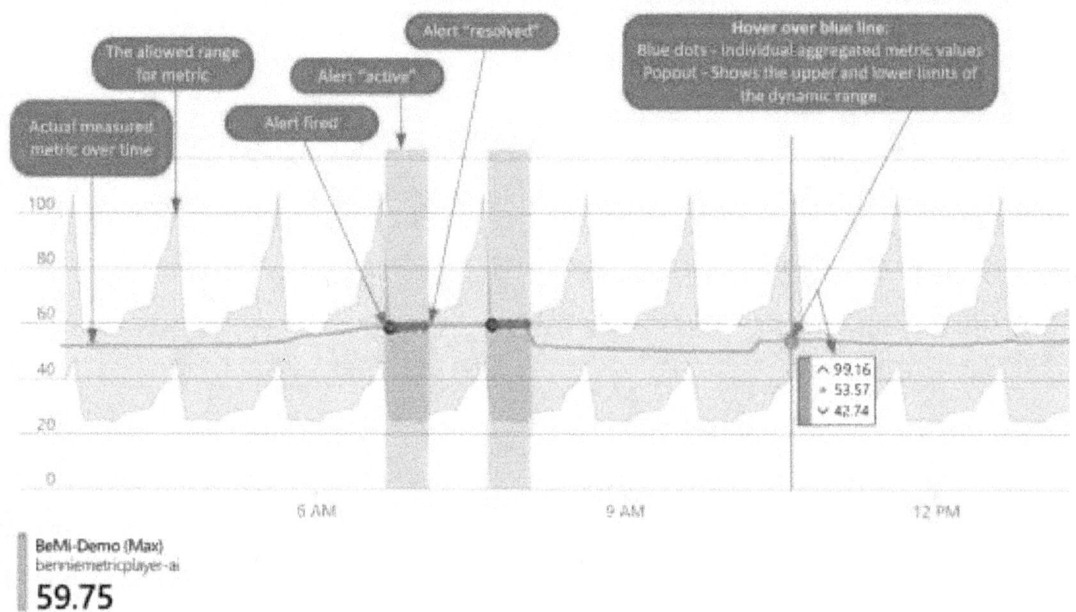

You can refer article **https://docs.microsoft.com/en-us/azure/azure-monitor/platform/alerts-dynamic-thresholds for a detailed information on dynamic threshold.**

For the demonstration purpose, I configure a static threshold with the following configuration.

- ✓ Alert logic: Whenever the average DTU used is greater than 0.5
- ✓ Evaluation criteria: Aggregation period: 1 minute
- ✓ Frequency of evaluation: 1 minute

In the chart, it marks a dotted line for the alert logic condition.

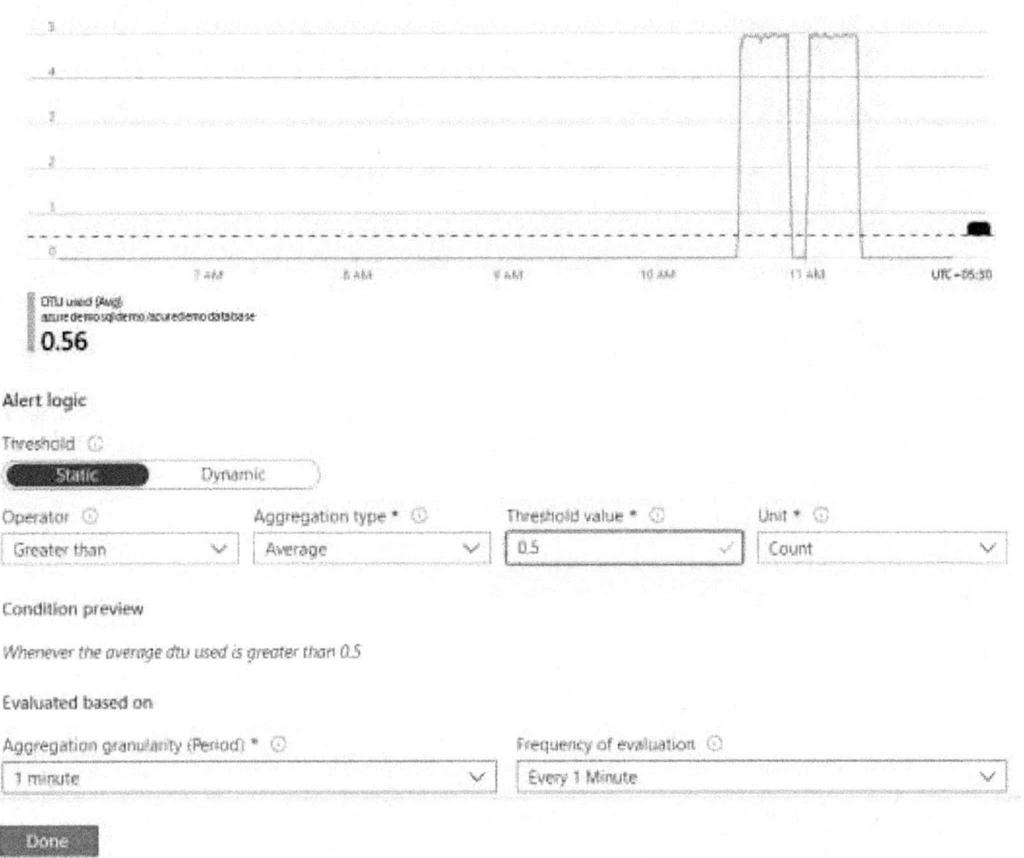

Click Done, and it displays the condition with an estimated monthly cost in USD.

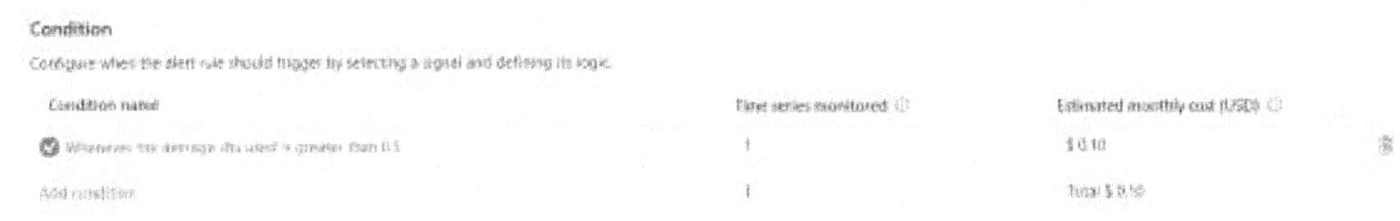

Actions groups

Once we have defined a condition, you need to specify the actions.

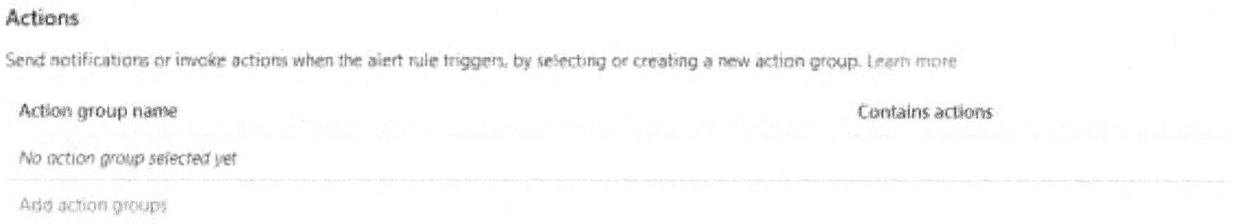

Actions

Send notifications or invoke actions when the alert rule triggers, by selecting or creating a new action group. Learn more

Action group name	Contains actions
No action group selected yet	

Add action groups

The action group defines a notification preference collection defined for an Azure subscription. The Azure monitor uses the action groups to notify the users once an alert is triggered. In the action group, we describe the following properties.

- Type: It defines the type of notification or actions. For example, you can add an email, SMS, voice call notification.
- Name: It is the name of the action group.
- Details: It specifies the details for the type specified.

Click on Add action groups and create an action group.

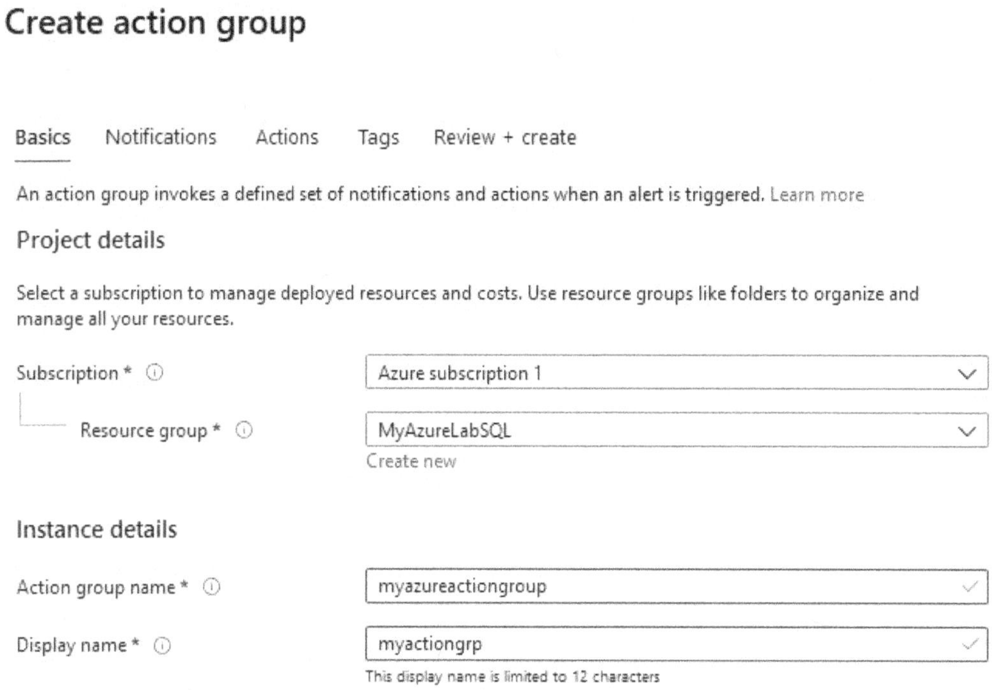

Create action group

Basics Notifications Actions Tags Review + create

An action group invokes a defined set of notifications and actions when an alert is triggered. Learn more

Project details

Select a subscription to manage deployed resources and costs. Use resource groups like folders to organize and manage all your resources.

Subscription * : Azure subscription 1

Resource group * : MyAzureLabSQL

Create new

Instance details

Action group name * : myazureactiongroup

Display name * : myactiongrp

This display name is limited to 12 characters

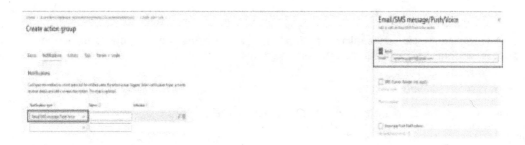

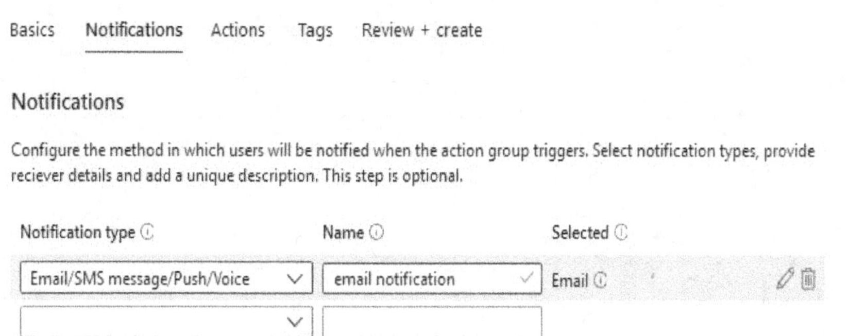

Email/SMS message/Push/Voice

Actions
Configure the method in which users will be notified when the action group triggers. Select notification types, provide reciever details and add a unique description. This step is optional.
Configure the method in which actions are performed when the action group triggers. Select action types, fill out associated details, and add a unique description. This step is optional.
Action type

In the actions type, select from Automation Runbook, Azure Function, ITSM, Logic app, Secure Webhook and Webhook.

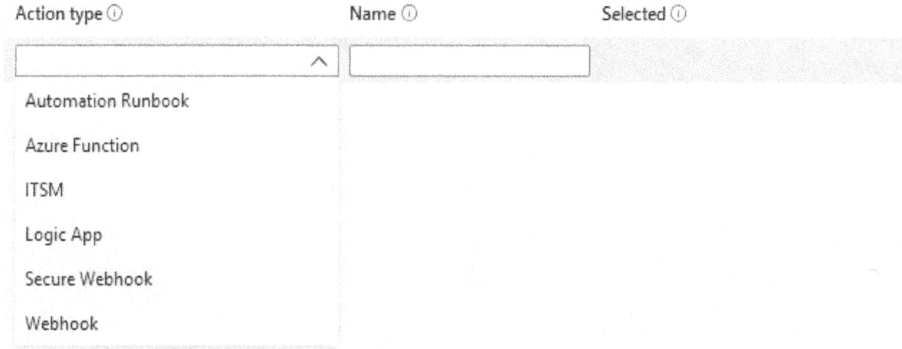

You can refer **https://docs.microsoft.com/en-us/azure/azure-monitor/platform/action-groups** for detailed information on the action groups.

Once you have defined the alert condition, actions, specify the alert rule name with an optional description.

Alert rule details

Provide details on your alert rule so that you can identify and manage it later.

Alert rule name *	AzureSQLDatabaseDTUAlert
Description	This is a sample alert for DTU usage in Azure SQL Database.
Enable alert rule upon creation	☑

Once the alert crosses the alert metric threshold, it takes action based on the action group configuration.

Diagnostic settings

Azure SQL Database provides diagnostic setting configuration for streaming export of logs and metrics for the specified resource into your configured destination. You can use the following destination.

- Azure log analytics workspace
- Event hubs
- Azure storage account

In the Azure SQL Database, search for the Diagnostics settings.

Click on the Diagnostics setting, and you get its dashboard page.

In the Azure SQL Diagnostics setting, we can configure the following collections.

Diagnostic telemetry for databases	Azure SQL Database support	Azure SQL Managed Instance support
Basic metrics: Contains DTU/CPU percentage, DTU/CPU limit, physical data read percentage, log write percentage, Successful/Failed/Blocked by firewall connections, sessions percentage, workers percentage, storage, storage percentage, and XTP storage percentage.	Yes	No
Instance and App Advanced: Contains tempdb system database data and log file size and tempdb percent log file used.	Yes	No
QueryStoreRuntimeStatistics: Contains information about the query runtime statistics such as CPU usage and query duration statistics.	Yes	Yes
QueryStoreWaitStatistics: Contains information about the query wait statistics (what your queries waited on) such are CPU, LOG, and LOCKING.	Yes	Yes
Errors: Contains information about SQL errors on a database.	Yes	Yes
DatabaseWaitStatistics: Contains information about how much time a database spent waiting on different wait types.	Yes	No
Timeouts: Contains information about timeouts on a database.	Yes	No
Blocks: Contains information about blocking events on a database.	Yes	No
Deadlocks: Contains information about deadlock events on a database.	Yes	No
AutomaticTuning: Contains information about automatic tuning recommendations for a database.	Yes	No
SQLInsights: Contains Intelligent Insights into performance for a database. To learn more, see Intelligent Insights.	Yes	Yes

Click on Add Diagnostics setting and specify a Diagnostics setting name.

Diagnostic setting

Save Discard Delete Feedback

A diagnostic setting specifies a list of categories of platform logs and/or metrics that you want to collect from a resource, and one or more destinations that you would stream them to. Normal usage charges for the destination will occur. Learn more about the different log categories and contents of those logs

Diagnostic setting name *

Category details

log

- [ ] SQLInsights
- [ ] AutomaticTuning
- [ ] QueryStoreRuntimeStatistics
- [ ] QueryStoreWaitStatistics
- [ ] Errors
- [ ] DatabaseWaitStatistics
- [ ] Timeouts
- [ ] Blocks
- [ ] Deadlocks

metric

- [ ] Basic
- [ ] InstanceAndAppAdvanced
- [ ] WorkloadManagement

Destination details

- [ ] Send to Log Analytics workspace
- [ ] Archive to a storage account
- [ ] Stream to an event hub

In the destination, you get three options.

- Send to Log Analytics workspace
- Archive to a storage account
- Stream to an event hub

The diagnostic telemetry streams data to any of the configured destinations, and It is useful for viewing resource utilization and query execution statistics monitoring.

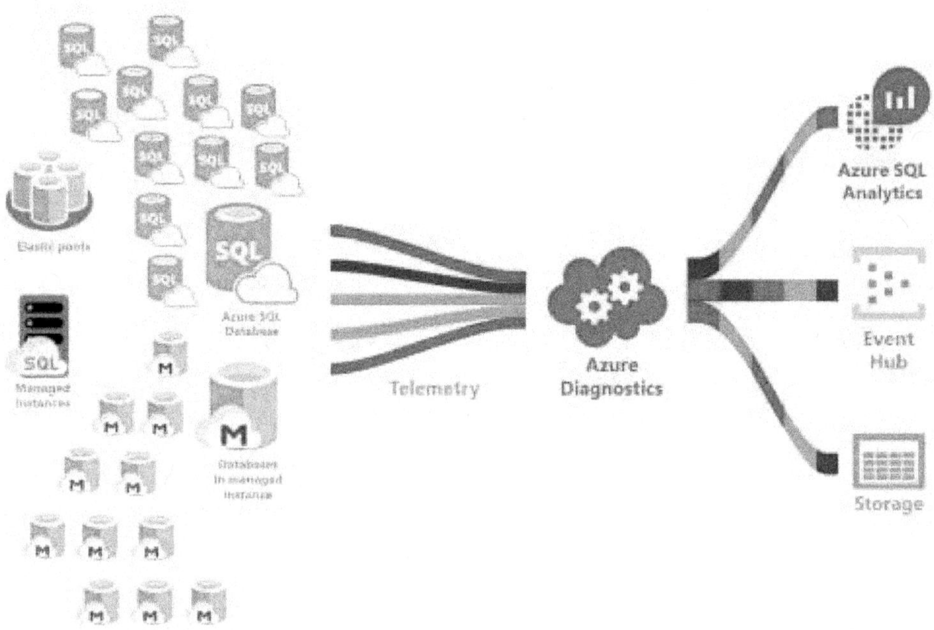

For the demonstration, Here, we select Errors, Blocks, Deadlocks and Basic metric. For the destination, we use the option – Send to Log Analytics workspace.

Note: If you do not already have a log analytics workspace, create it using the Azure portal, Log analytics workspace and create a new log analytics workspace.

The following screenshot automatically displays the log analytics workspace configured in my Azure subscription.

Diagnostic setting

Save | Discard | Delete | Feedback

A diagnostic setting specifies a list of categories of platform logs and/or metrics that you want to collect from a resource, and one or more destinations that you would stream them to. Normal usage charges for the destination will occur. Learn more about the different log categories and contents of those logs

Diagnostic setting name * azuresqldiagnostics

Category details

log

- [ ] SQLInsights
- [ ] AutomaticTuning
- [ ] QueryStoreRuntimeStatistics
- [ ] QueryStoreWaitStatistics
- [x] Errors
- [ ] DatabaseWaitStatistics
- [ ] Timeouts
- [x] Blocks
- [x] Deadlocks

metric

- [x] Basic
- [ ] InstanceAndAppAdvanced
- [ ] WorkloadManagement

Destination details

- [x] Send to Log Analytics workspace

Subscription: Azure subscription 1

Log Analytics workspace: azureloganalyticsdemo1 (centralindia)

- [ ] Archive to a storage account
- [ ] Stream to an event hub

Click on Save, and you get the following notification.

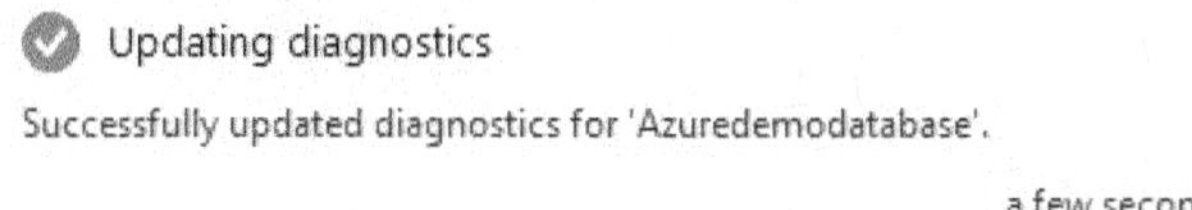
Updating diagnostics
Successfully updated diagnostics for 'Azuredemodatabase'.

a few seconds ago

In the Azure SQL Database dashboard, click on Logs in the monitoring group. It gives you pre-defined templates for query data using the Kusto query language (KQL)

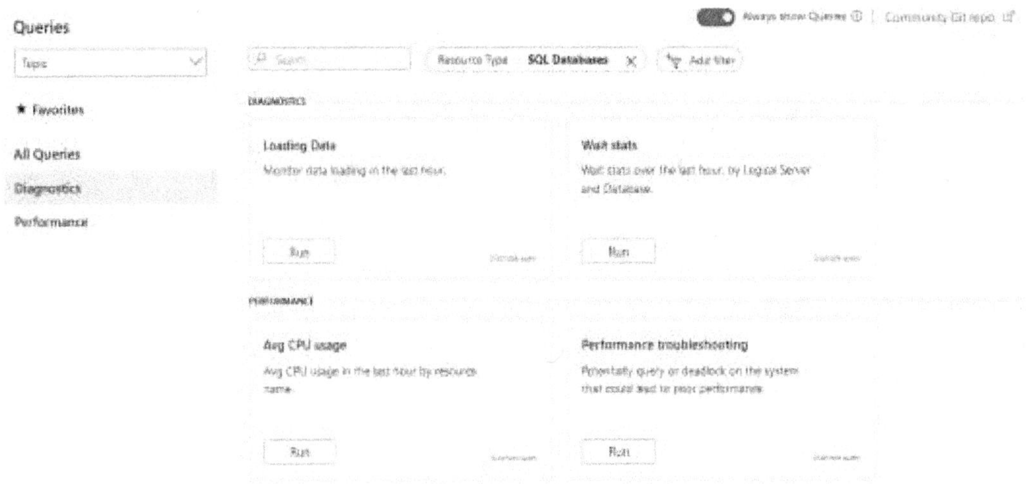

Avg CPU utilization:

Click on the Avg CPU utilization, and it gives you the following KQL query with the CPU usage output for Azure SQL Database.

```
AzureMetrics

| where ResourceProvider == "MICROSOFT.SQL" // /DATABASES

| where TimeGenerated >= ago(60min)

| where MetricName in ('cpu_percent')

| parse _ResourceId with * "/microsoft.sql/servers/" Resource  // subtract Resource name for _ResourceId

| summarize CPU_Maximum_last15mins = max(Maximum), CPU_Minimum_last15mins = min(Minimum), CPU_Average_last15mins = avg(Average) by Resource , MetricName
```

Log write percentage:

Suppose you want to monitor the transaction log write percentage in the last 60 minute for the Azure database. The below KQL script fetches data for the Azure SQL Database of the previous 60 minutes.

```
AzureMetrics

| where ResourceProvider == "MICROSOFT.SQL"

| where TimeGenerated >= ago(60min)

| where MetricName in ('log_write_percent')

| parse _ResourceId with * "/microsoft.sql/servers/" Resource// subtract Resource name for _ResourceId

| summarize Log_Maximum_last60mins = max(Maximum), Log_Minimum_last60mins = min(Minimum), Log_Average_last60mins = avg(Average) by Resource, MetricName
```

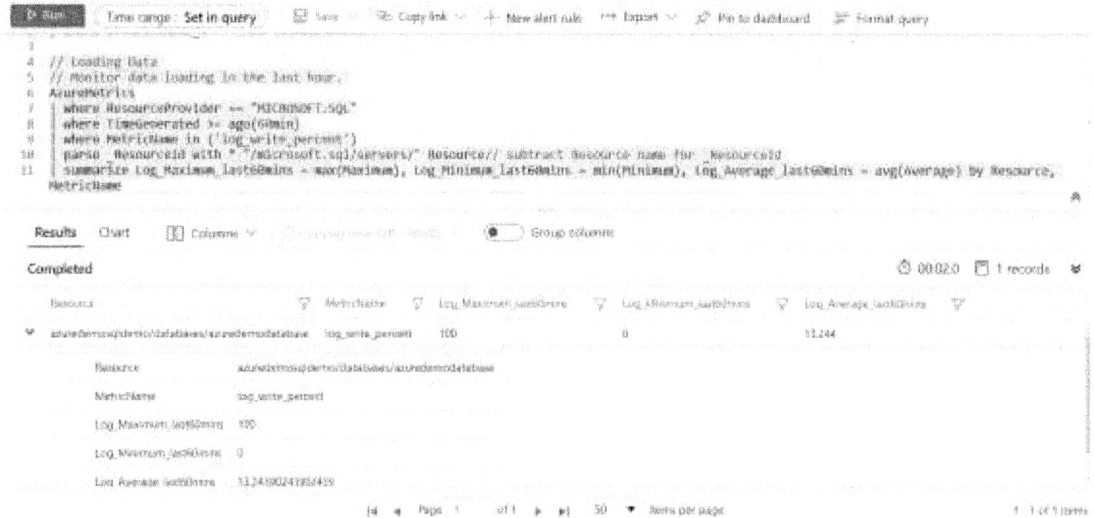

Deadlocks

We can monitor the deadlock as well as using the KQL. Click on Performance troubleshooting to populate a script for Deadlock occurred in the last 60 minute. As shown in the output, our sample database has one deadlock during the previous 60 minutes.

AzureMetrics

| where ResourceProvider == "MICROSOFT.SQL"

| where TimeGenerated >=ago(60min)

| where MetricName in ('deadlock')

| parse _ResourceId with * "/microsoft.sql/servers/" Resource // subtract Resource name for _ResourceId

| summarize Deadlock_max_60Mins = max(Maximum) by Resource, MetricName

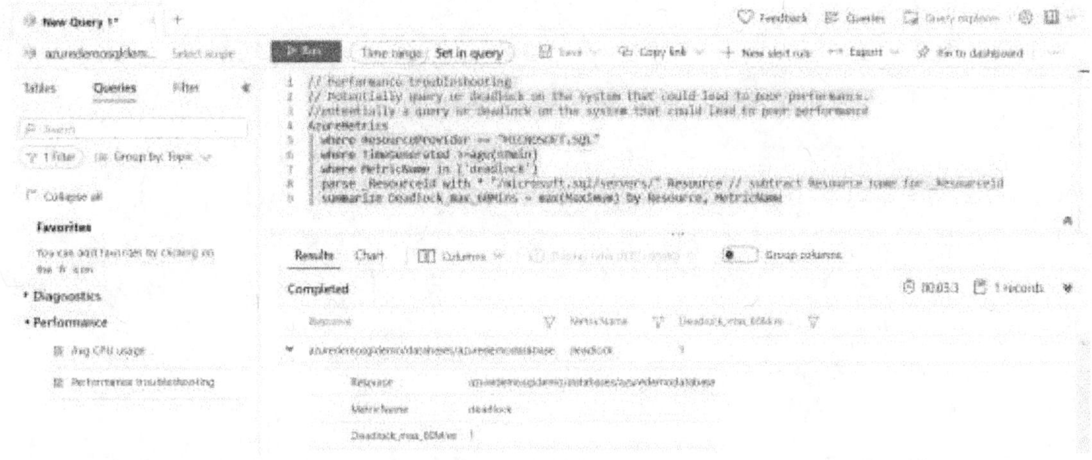

Filter diagnostics data for an Azure SQL Database

Suppose you want to view all diagnostic data filtered for a specific Azure SQL Database. You can use the following KQL and retrieve the result set.

AzureDiagnostics

| where DatabaseName_s == "Azuredemodatabase"

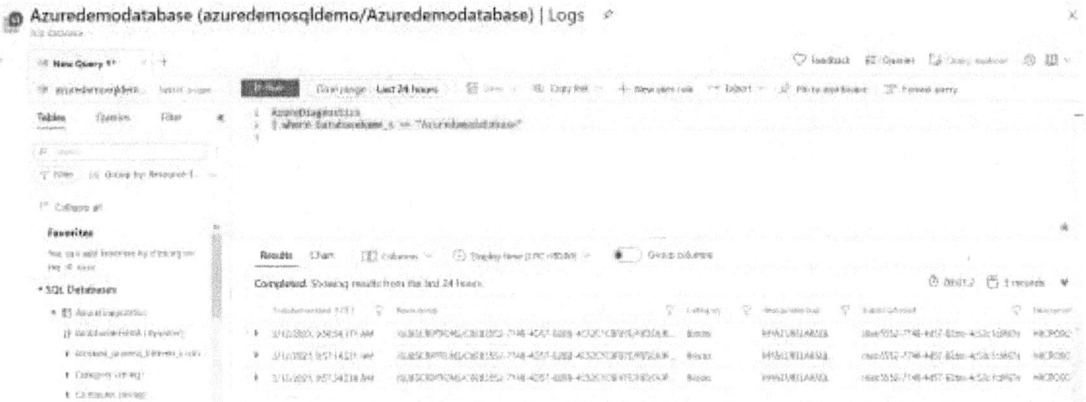

Script for failed logins

```
AzureDiagnostics

| where TimeGenerated >= ago(5d) //Events on last 5 days

| where action_name_s == "DATABASE AUTHENTICATION FAILED"

| extend additional_information_xml=parse_xml(additional_information_s)

| extend Error_Code=additional_information_xml.login_information.error_code

| extend Error_State=additional_information_xml.login_information.error_state

| project

    TimeGenerated, event_time_t,

    ResourceGroup, LogicalServerName_s, database_name_s,

    session_id_d, client_ip_s, application_name_s, session_server_principal_name_s,

    Error_Code, Error_State

| order by TimeGenerated desc
```

1.1.4 KQL to filter data for error id 8134 for Azure SQL database occurred in last 30 days

```
AzureDiagnostics

| where TimeGenerated >= ago(30d) // Last 30 days

| where Category =~ "Errors"
```

```
| where error_number_d == 8134 //Divide by zero error encountered.
| project
    TimeGenerated,
    ResourceGroup,
    LogicalServerName_s,
    DatabaseName_s,
    Message,
    error_number_d,
    Severity,
    state_d
| order by TimeGenerated desc
```

Similarly, you can write KQL script and fetch diagnostic, monitor data for Azure SQL Database.

You can refer to **https://docs.microsoft.com/en-us/azure/azure-monitor/insights/azure-sql** for more details on diagnostics log.

Refer to **https://docs.microsoft.com/en-us/sharepoint/dev/general-development/keyword-query-language-kql-syntax-reference** for learning KQL language.

Query Performance Insight

The Query performance insight enables database administrators with intelligent query analysis. You can identify top resource consuming query, long-tuning queries, workload performance. It is based on the Query Store. You can also view query plans for workload and force an optimized plan if required. It automatically gathers the query performance insights, query runtime statistics and query execution plans.

Note: By default, the Query Store is enabled for an Azure SQL Database.

To launch the query performance insight, search for it in the Azure SQL Database dashboard search box.

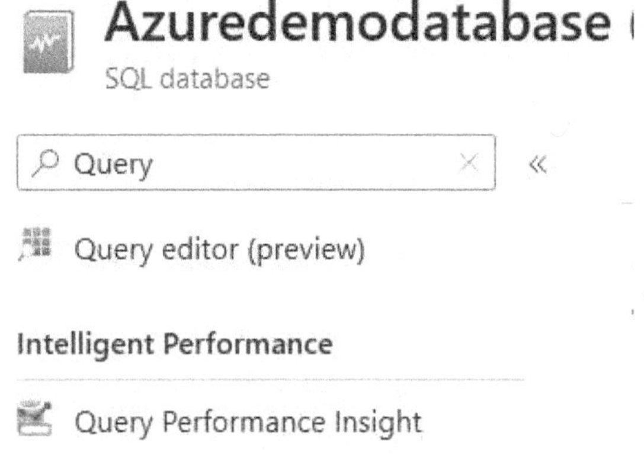

It launches the following query performance insight dashboard

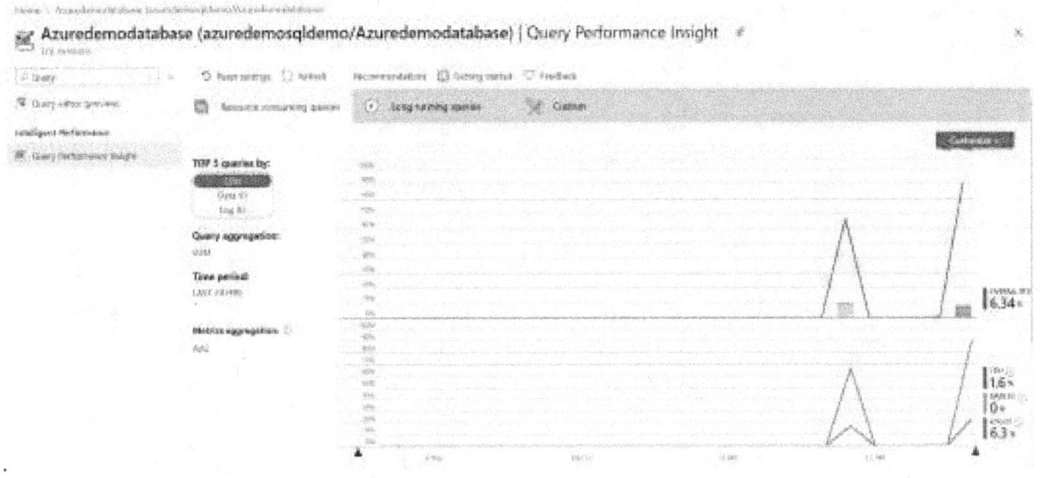

This dashboard has the following sections.

- ✓ Resource consuming queries
- ✓ Long-running queries
- ✓ Custom

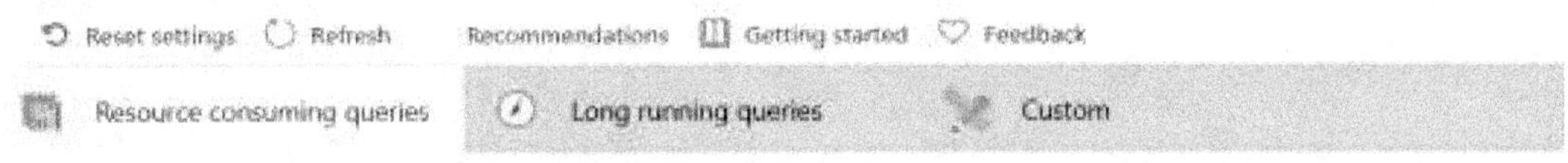

Resource Consuming Queries

The resource-consuming queries give you top queries based on the CPU, Data IO, and Log IO utilization.

Top 5 queries by CPU. Data IO and Log IO

By CPU:

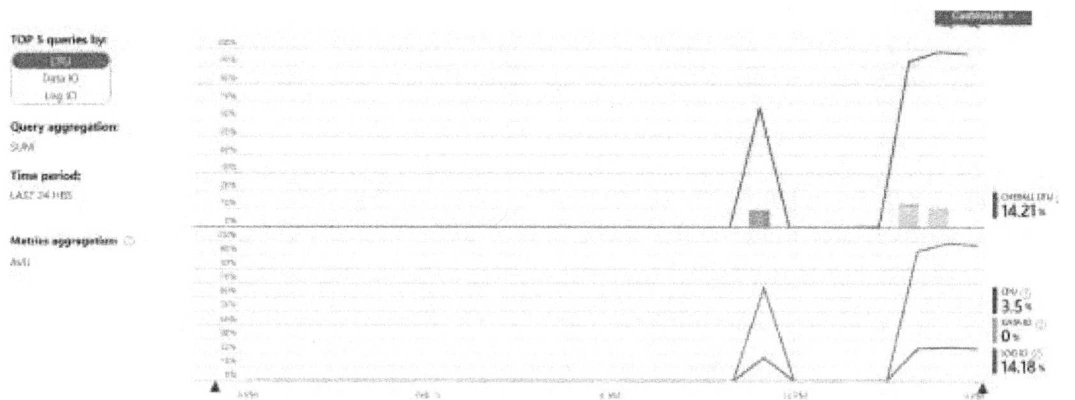

By Data IO:

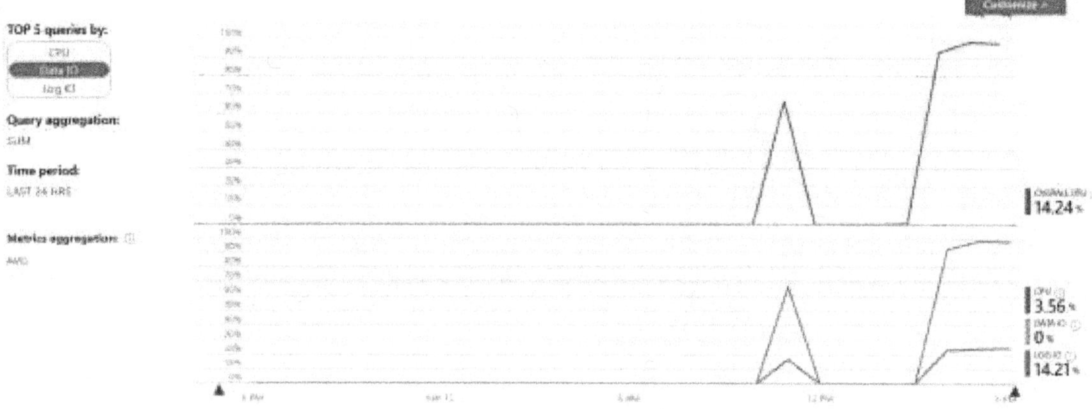

By Log IO:

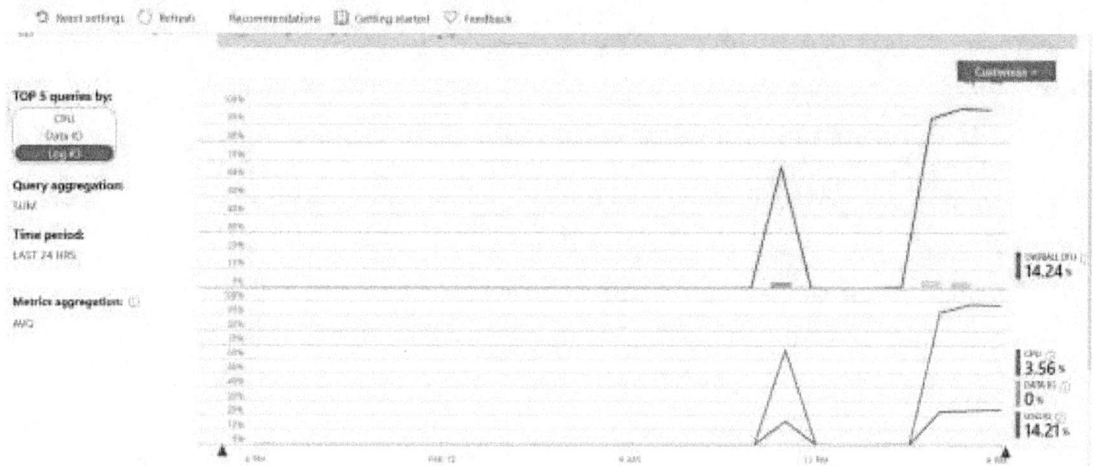

Lists the top queries by their %CPU, Data IO (%), Log IO (%), Duration and execution count.

In this section, you get query ID based on the CPU, Data IO, Log IO, duration and execution count. Each row has a unique color, and it matches with the line color in the bar graph.

Click on a row below to get the details for the selected query.

QUERY ID	CPU[%]	DATA IO[%]	LOG IO[%]	DURATION[hh:mm:ss]	EXECUTIONS COUNT	#
[illegible]	0.95	0	0.31	00:46:05.130	338443	
[illegible]	0.36	0	0.11	00:19:10.660	199971	
[illegible]	0	0	0	00:00:00.730	1	
[illegible]	0	0	0	00:00:00.240	1	
[illegible]	0	0	0	00:00:00.100	108	

Click on a specific query to get detailed information.

It gives granular details as well. For example, you see several executions and their CPU, Data IO and Log IO usage in a time interval.

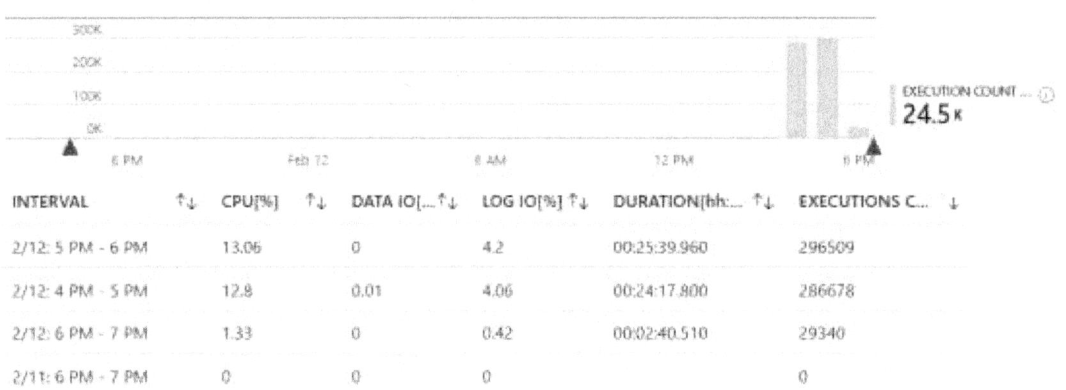

INTERVAL	CPU[%]	DATA IO[...	LOG IO[%]	DURATION[hh:...	EXECUTIONS C...
2/12: 5 PM - 6 PM	13.06	0	4.2	00:25:39.960	296509
2/12: 4 PM - 5 PM	12.8	0.01	4.06	00:24:17.800	286678
2/12: 6 PM - 7 PM	1.33	0	0.42	00:02:40.510	29340
2/11: 6 PM - 7 PM	0	0	0		0

Recommendations:

For a query level performance recommendation, click on the Recommendations tab. These recommendations can be of the following categories.

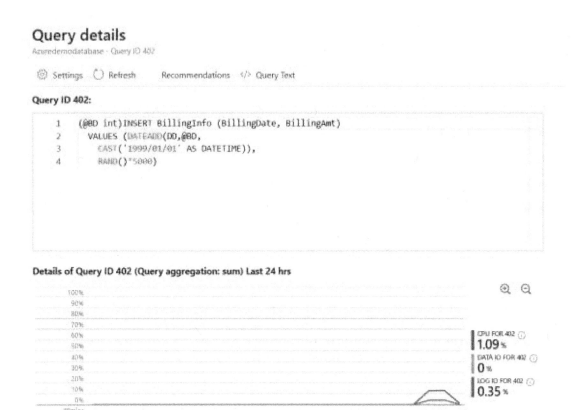

✓ Create an index
✓ Drop index
✓ parameterized queries recommendations

Query details

Azuredemodatabase - Query ID 402

Settings   Refresh   Recommendations   </> Query Text

Long-running queries

In the long-running queries section, you get tip queries by duration. Similar to the resource-consuming queries section, you get individual query details along with recommendations if any.

Custom dashboard

In the custom section, you can choose your metric, time period, number of queries, query aggregation type and metric aggregation, as shown below.

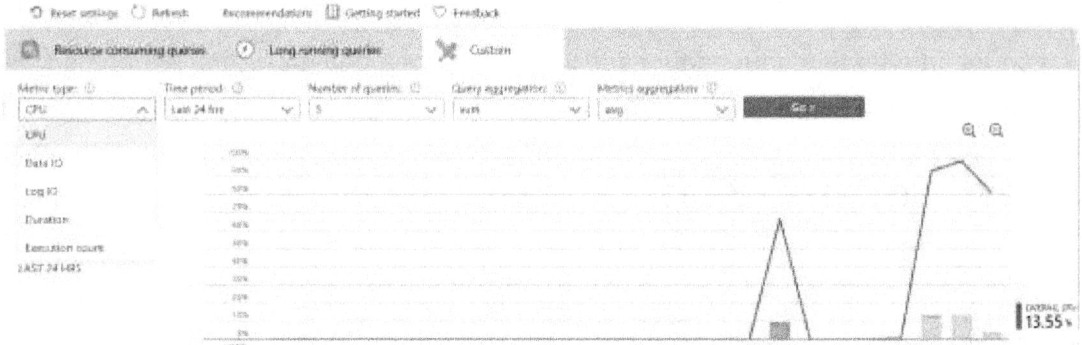

Review top queries per duration

The long-running queries are not suitable for your database performance. It holds resource locks, blocks other users and limits scalability. Therefore, you can customize the performance insight dashboard using the duration to view top queries per duration.

In the custom dashboard, do the following changes.

- ✓ Metrics: duration
- ✓ Time period: 24 hrs.
- ✓ Number of queries: 10
- ✓ Query aggregation and Metrics aggregation: Max

Here the Max aggregation, find queries with maximum execution time during the specified interval. Alternatively, you can specify the Sum and Avg aggregation types.

Click on Go, and it shows a custom dashboard like below.

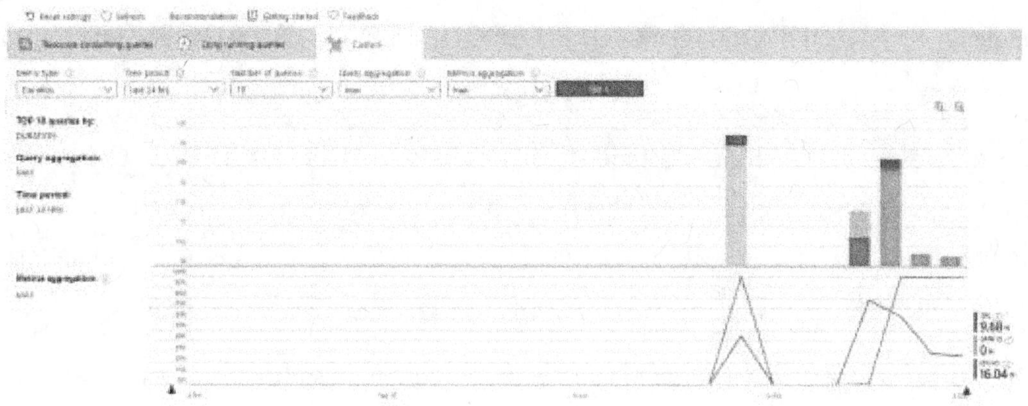

Review top queries per execution count

Suppose you want to review top queries based on the execution count. These queries might help to diagnose network traffic, processing workload.

For this requirement, do the following changes in the custom dashboard.

- ✓ Metric: execution count
- ✓ Number of queries: 10
- ✓ Metrics aggregation: Avg

Chapter 7 Monitoring Azure resources using the Azure Monitor

Azure Monitor is a comprehensive tool for monitoring one or more Azure SQL Database, Managed instances, VM by collecting, analyzing and identifying the issues. It helps you monitor applications, infrastructures, and multiple resources. Suppose you maintain a large Azure database environment. You can configure the Azure monitor for monitoring all together at a single console.

- It can detect and diagnose issues with infrastructure, and the application using the application insights.
- It can correlate multiple infrastructure issues for Azure monitor for VM and containers.
- It can utilize log analytic data for troubleshooting and diagnostics.
- You can create rich visualizations, dashboards using Azure monitors.

The following diagram gives a high-level overview of Azure Monitor.

- It has multiple sources of monitoring data, such as Azure metrics, logs.
- It displays multiple functions that the Azure monitor can perform with the collected data.
    - Insights
    - Visualize
    - Analyze
    - Respond
    - Integrate

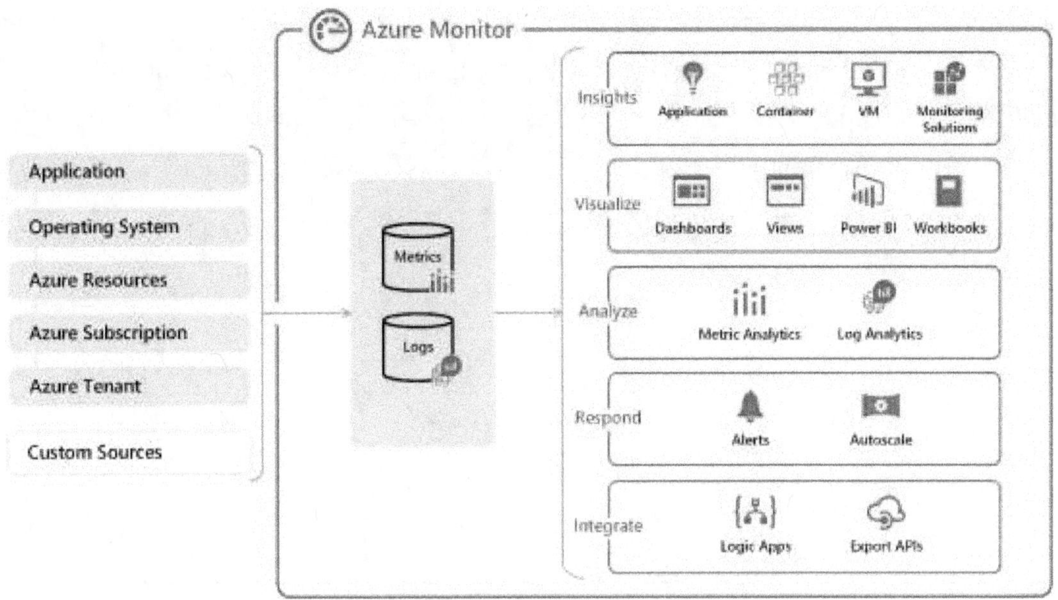

Azure Monitor uses the Kusto Query Language for queries data using advanced functionality including aggregations, joins, smart analytics.

Refer to article **https://docs.microsoft.com/en-us/azure/azure-monitor/log-query/get-started-queries** to be familiar with KQL language and its components.

Monitor Azure SQL Database using Azure Monitor

To configure Azure Monitor, search for Monitor in the Azure portal and open its launching page.

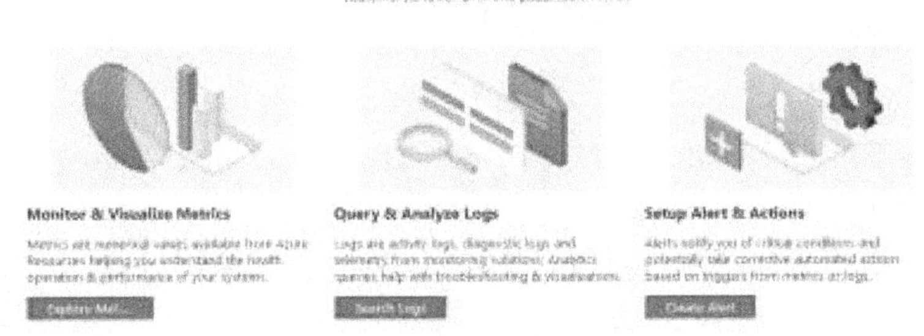

Suppose we want to monitor and visualize database metrics. Click on Explore more under the Monitor and Visualize Metrics. For the demonstration, I select the Azure SQL Database in my resource group. You can choose multiple similar resource types and locations.

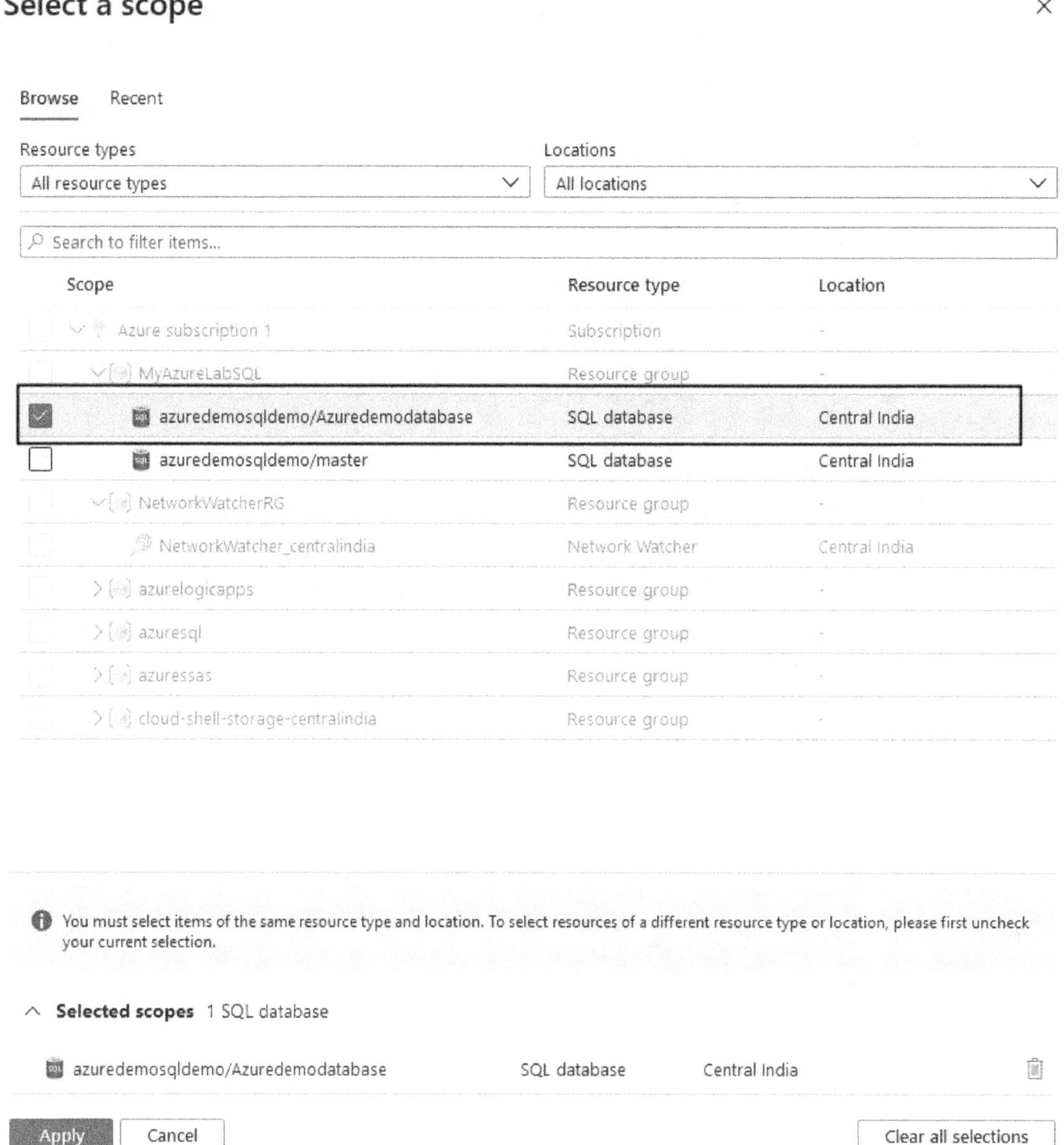

Click on Apply. It opens a blank chart with configuration options.

- Scope: It is the scope that we configured earlier.

- Metric Namespace: It loads different available metrics as per your scope selection.
- Metric: Select the metric that we want to view
- Aggregation: Aggregation available depending on the selected metric.

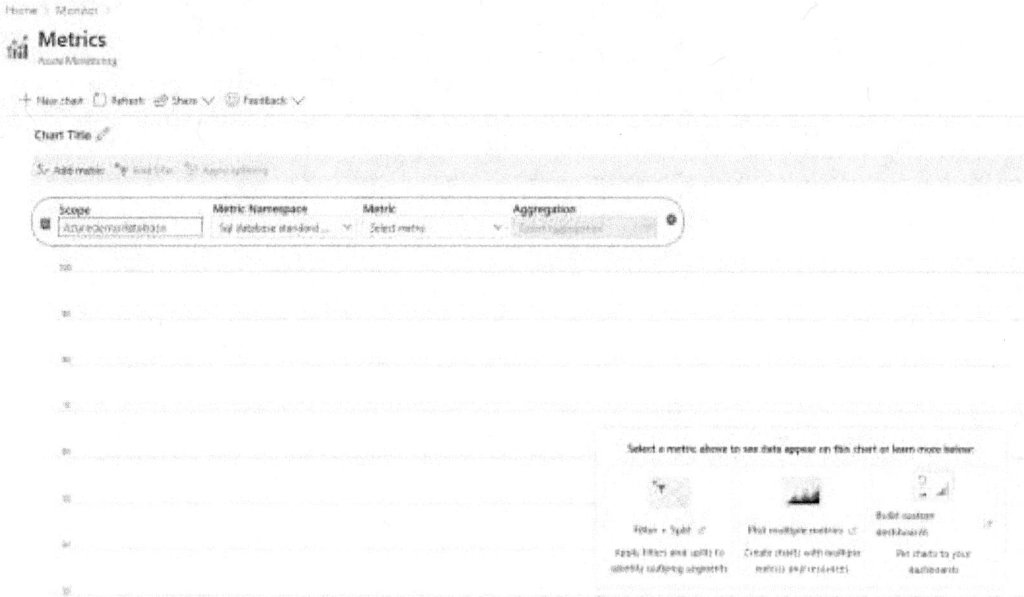

You can select the metric as per your requirement.

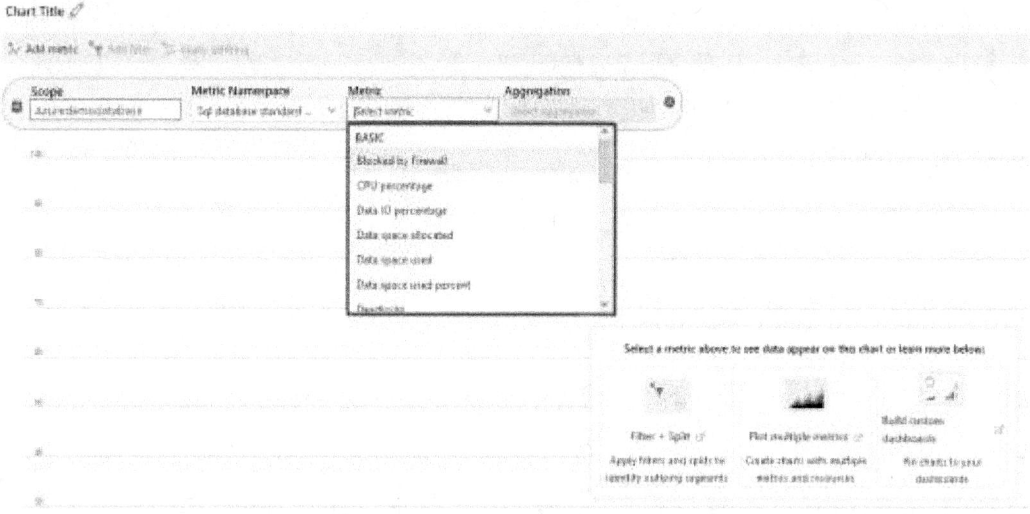

For example, let's select a few metrics and view the charts.

- CPU percentage:
  - Metric: CPU percentage
  - Aggregation: Avg

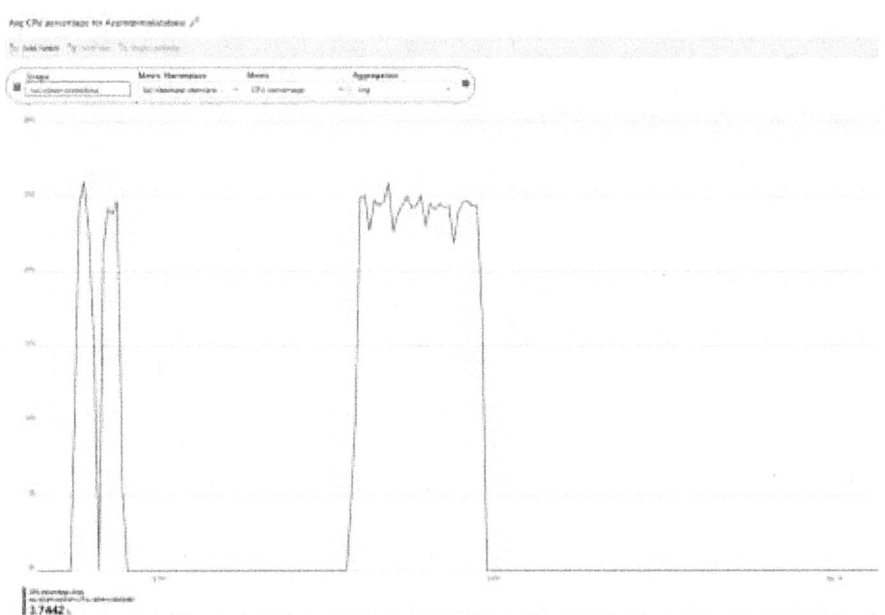

- Data Space used
  - Metric: Data space used
  - Aggregation: Max

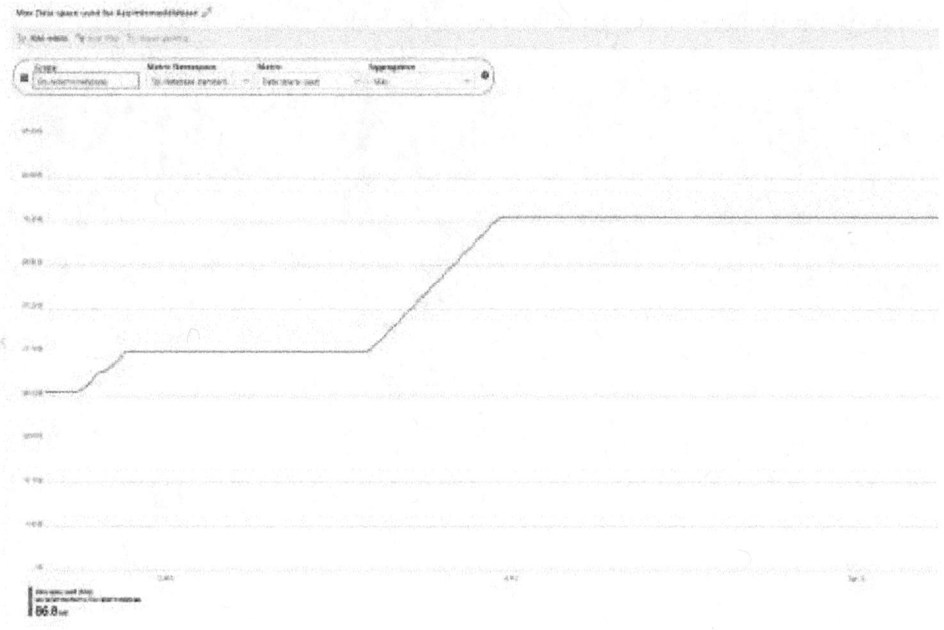

- Deadlocks
  - Metric: Deadlocks
  - Aggregation: Sum

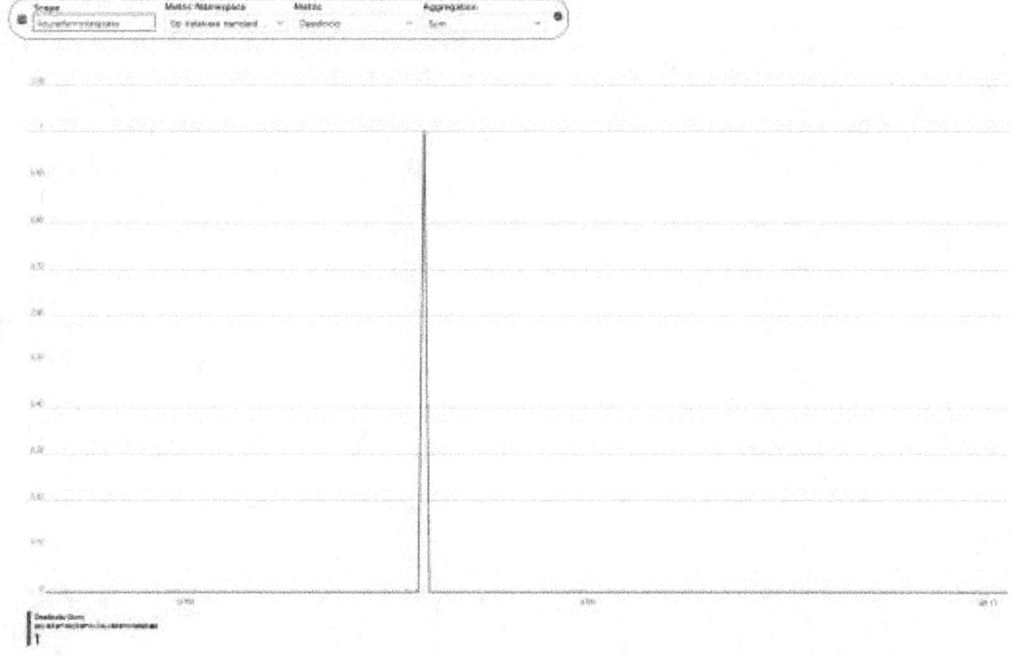

You can add multiple metrics as well on a single chart. For example, here, I add the following metrics together.

- Deadlocks
- CPU percentage
- Log IO percentage
- Worker percentage

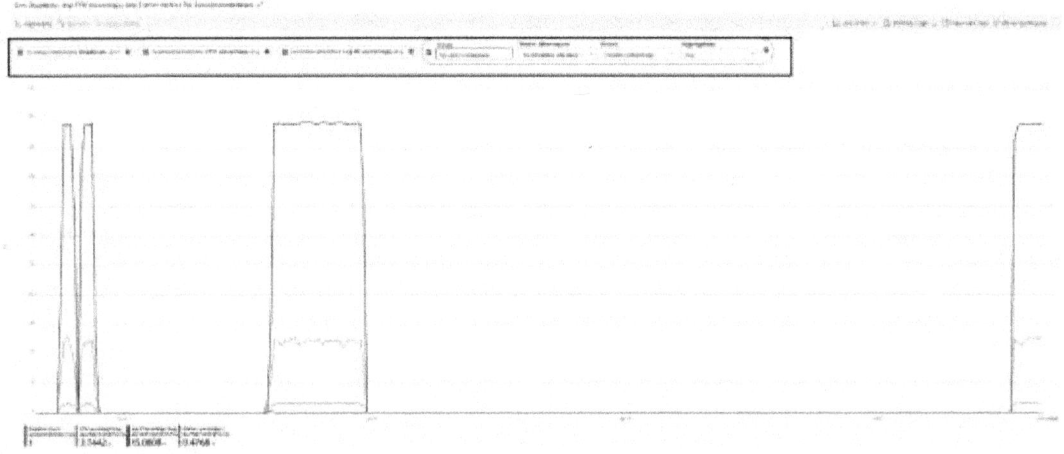

You can modify chart types from Area, Bar, Scatter and Grid format.

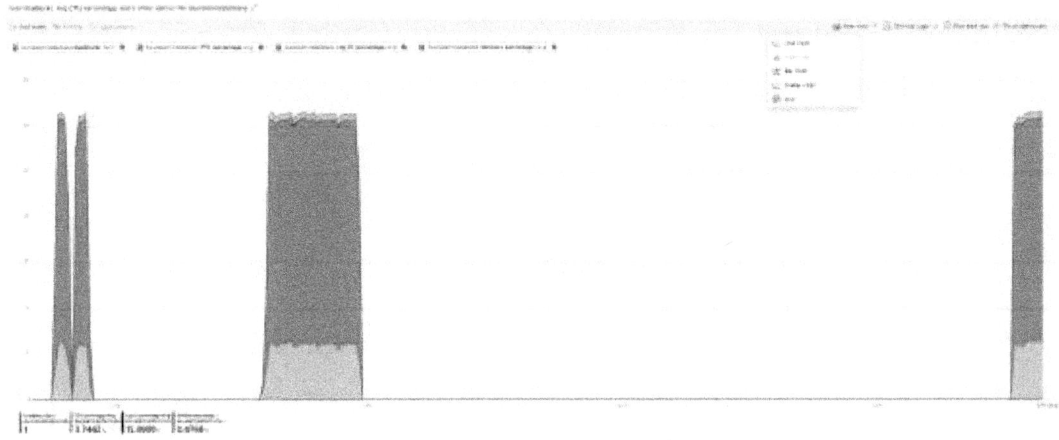

Azure SQL Analytics

Azure SQL Analytics (Preview) provides the ability to monitor performance metrics of all your Azure SQL Database, Azure elastic pools, and Azure SQL Managed instances in a single view. It collects, visualizes key performance metrics for performance troubleshooting using the built-in-intelligence. We can define custom monitoring rules, alerts. It uses the Azure Diagnostic metrics (Refer section 1.4) and Azure Monitor (Section 1.8) for a single log analytics workspace.

Note:

1. This preview solution supports up to 150,000 Azure SQL Databases and 5,000 SQL Elastic Pools.
2. Azure SQL Analytics does not use agents to connect to Azure Monitor. Therefore, it does not support monitoring of SQL Server hosted on-premises or in virtual machines.

Connected Source	Supported	Description
Diagnostics settings	Yes	Azure directly sends Azure metric and log data to Azure Monitor Logs.
• Azure storage account • Windows agents • Linux agents • System Center Operations Manager management group	No	Azure Monitor does not read data from the Azure Storage account, Direct Windows agents, Linux agents, System Center Operations Manager management group.

The below table highlights the supported features on Azure SQL Database and Azure SQL Managed Instance databases using Azure SQL Analytics dashboard.

Azure SQL Analytics option	Azure SQL Database support	Azure SQL Managed Instance support	Description
Resource by type	Yes	Yes	The perspective that counts all the resources monitored.

Insights	Yes	Yes	Hierarchical drill-down into Intelligent Insights into performance.
Errors	Yes	Yes	Hierarchical drill-down into SQL errors
Timeouts	Yes	No	Hierarchical drill-down SQL Timeouts
Blockings	Yes	No	Hierarchical drill-down SQL blockings
Database waits	Yes	No	Hierarchical drill-down SQL wait statistics on the database level.
Query duration	Yes	Yes	Hierarchical drill-down on query execution statistics such as query duration, CPU usage, Data IO usage, Log IO usage.
Query waits	Yes	Yes	Hierarchical drill-down on query wait statistics by wait category.

Note: You must enable diagnostic settings(section 1.4) with Azure SQL Analytics (Preview) to your Log Analytics workspace.

In the Azure portal, search for Log Analytic Workspaces.

Create a new log analytics workspace. Enter the Azure SQL Analytics name, subscription, resource group, location, and pricing tier.

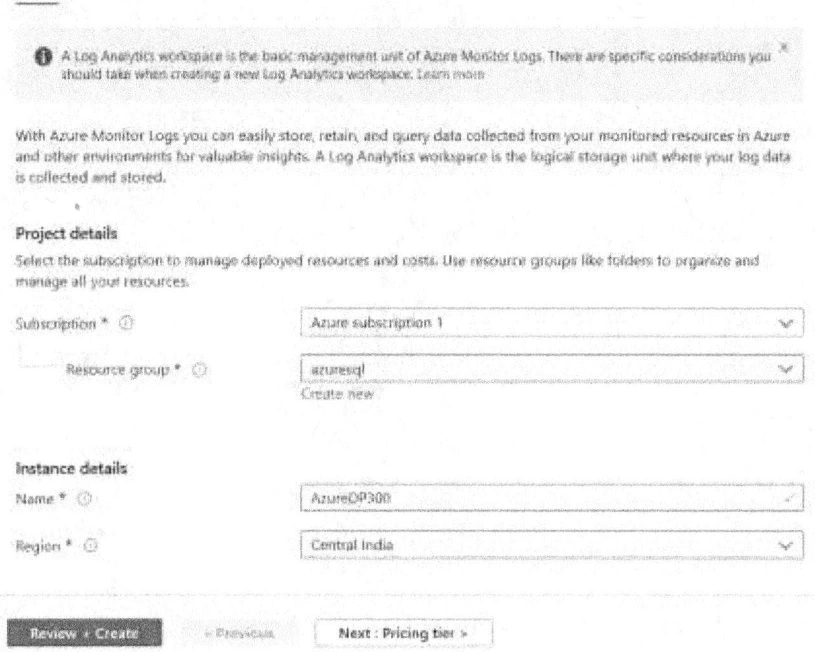

Choose the pricing tier as Pay-as-you-go

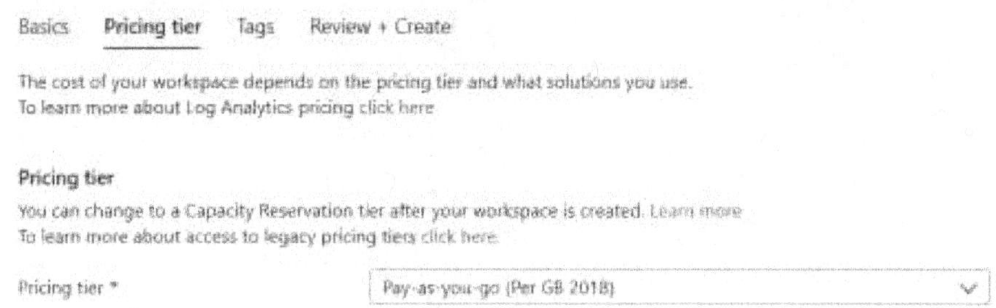

Deploy the analytics workspace, and it got the following dashboard.

In the log analytics workspace, navigate to General and Workspace summary.

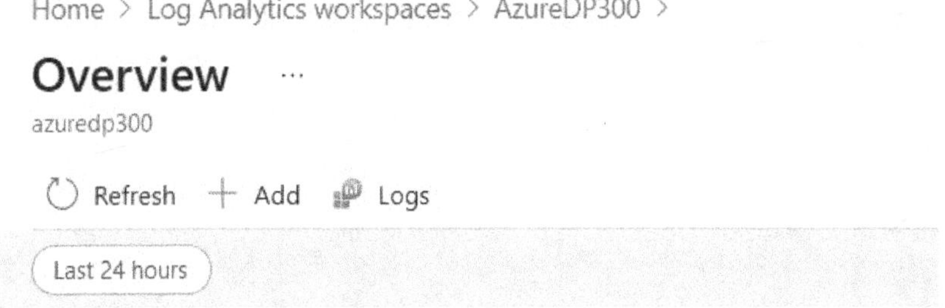

Click on +Add and search for Azure SQL Analytics(preview), and it lists the existing log analytics workspace.

Home > Log Analytics workspaces > AzureDP300 > Overview > Marketplace >

Azure SQL Analytics (Preview) ...

Create new Solution

*Log Analytics Workspace

AzureDP300

Deploy the resource, and it gives you a summary option for Azure SQL Analytics.

Click on View Summary. Here, it gives the following information for the monitored databases and instances.

- Azure SQL Database: The number of databases and elastic pools
- Azure database Managed instance count and database name.

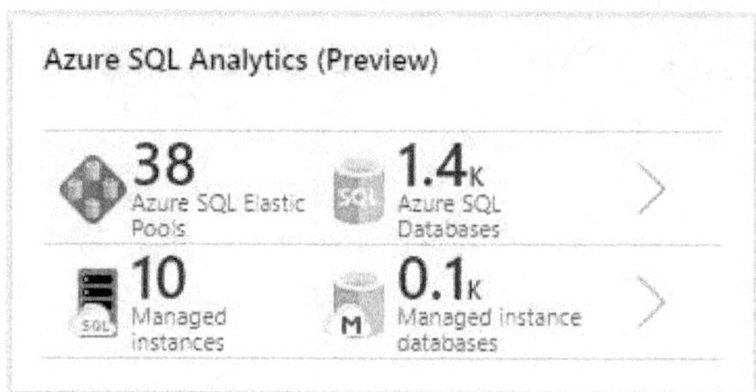

It has two separate views for Azure SQL Database and Azure SQL Managed Instances.

SQL Database view

Select the Azure SQL Database, and it loads the monitoring dashboard with relevant data.

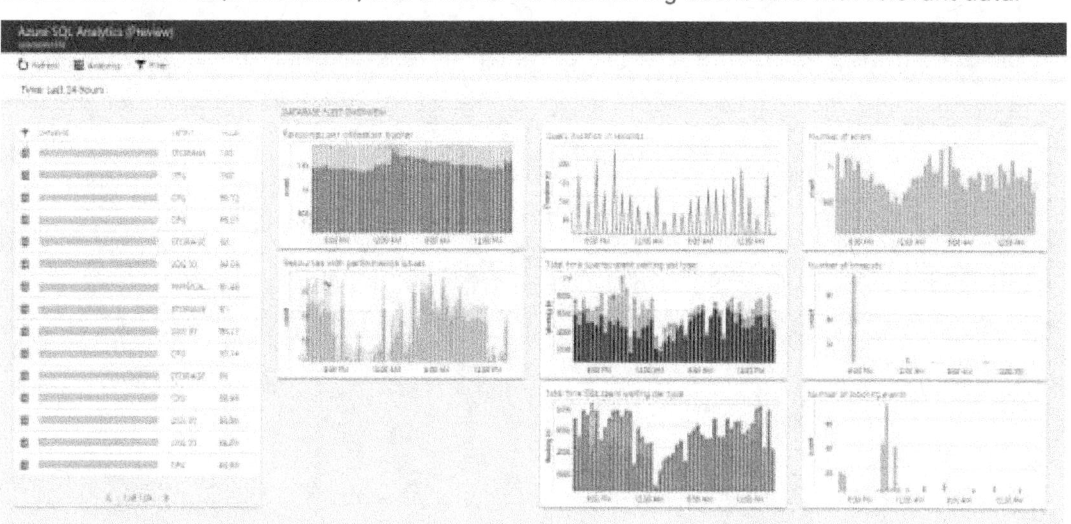

Click on any tile to get a hierarchical drill-down report.

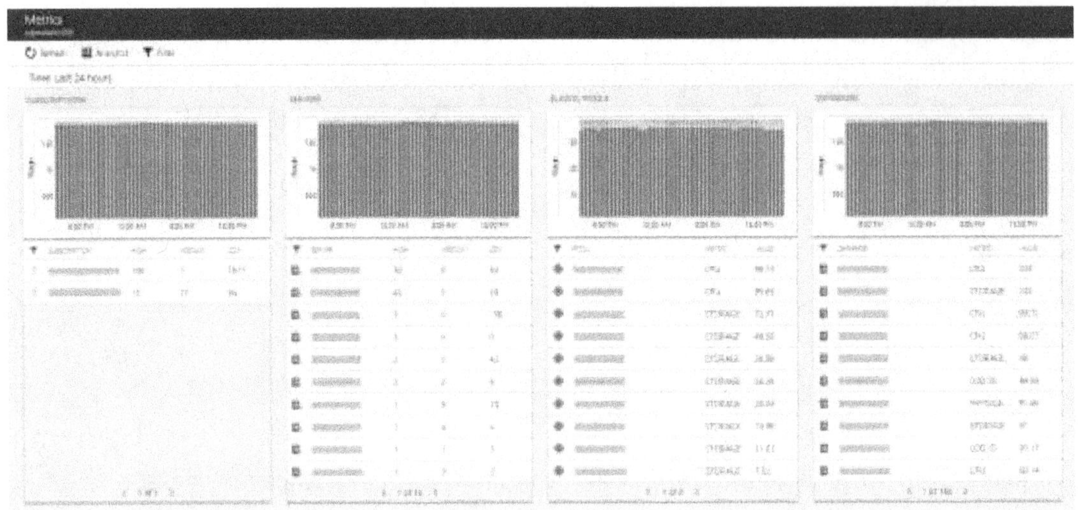

SQL Managed Instance view

Azure SQL Analytics dashboard for SQL managed instances looks like below.

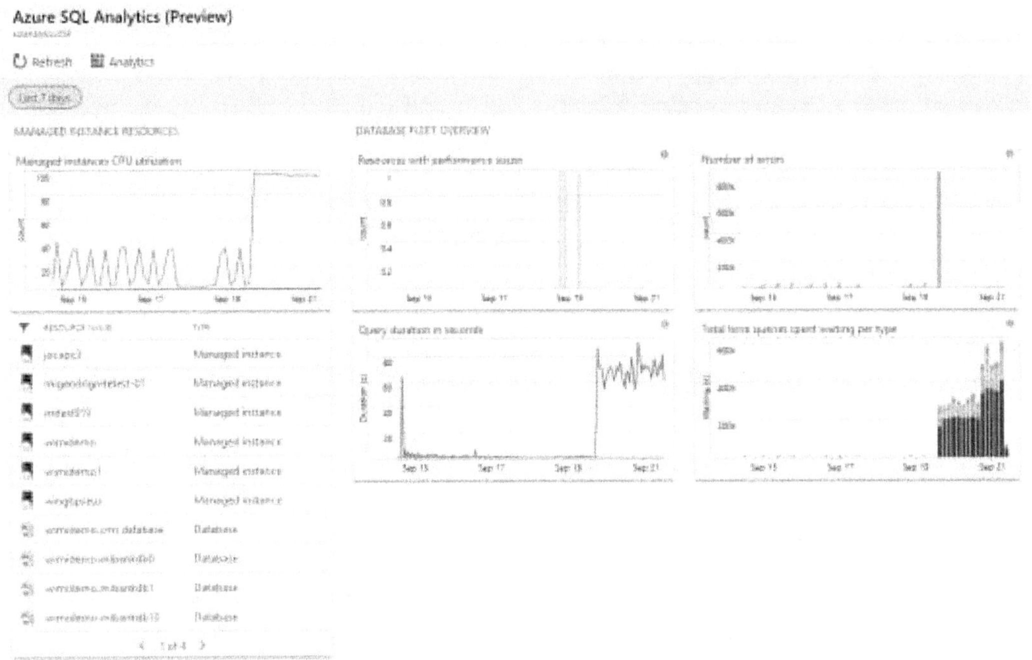

It gives the instance utilization, instance databases, telemetry on managed instance executed query in the SQL Managed instance view.

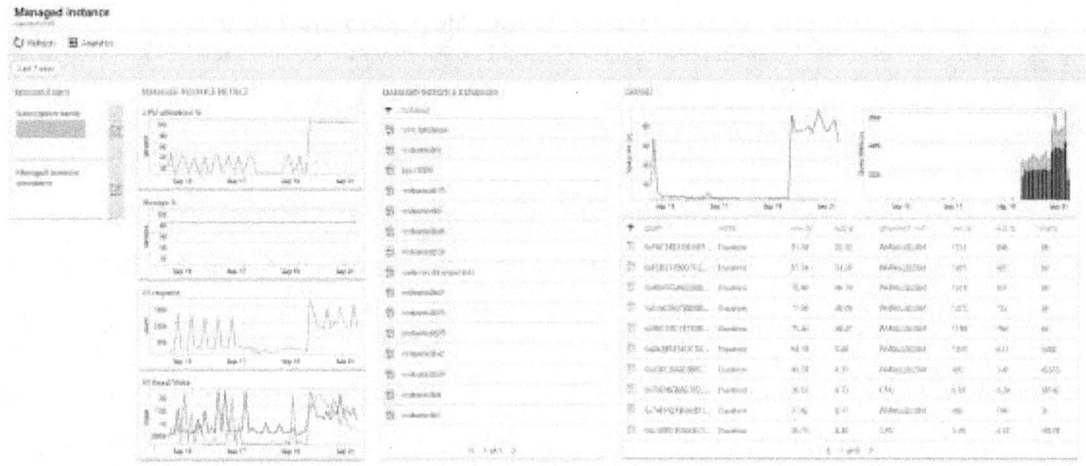

Intelligent Insights report

Azure SQL Database Intelligent insight reports help to identify the performance of all Azure SQL Databases. It has the following features.

- Proactive monitoring
- Custom performance insights
- Early detection of database performance degradation
- Root cause analysis of issues detected
- Performance improvement recommendations
- Scale-out capability on hundreds of thousands of databases
- The positive impact on DevOps resources and the total cost of ownership

It uses the following detection models to generate Intelligent Insights for monitoring:

- Query duration
- Timeout requests
- Excessive wait time
- Errored out requests

You can refer Microsoft documentation (**https://docs.microsoft.com/en-us/azure/azure-sql/database/intelligent-insights-overview#detection-metrics**) for a detailed information on detection models.

The intelligent insights compare database workload performance from the last hour with the past seven-day baseline workload. It uses data points for costly queries, extensive and repeated queries.

It also monitors operational threshold, excessive waits, critical exceptions, query parameterization issues. Once it detects a performance degradation using the AI-based analysis, it generates a diagnostics alert with intelligent insight information. It makes it easy to track performance issues until it is resolved.

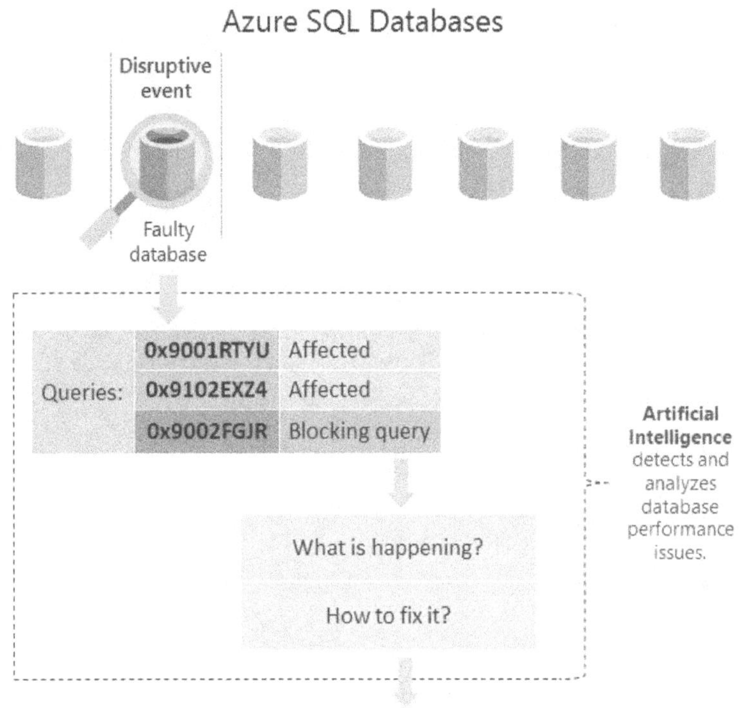

Here, you get a sample intelligent insights dashboard.

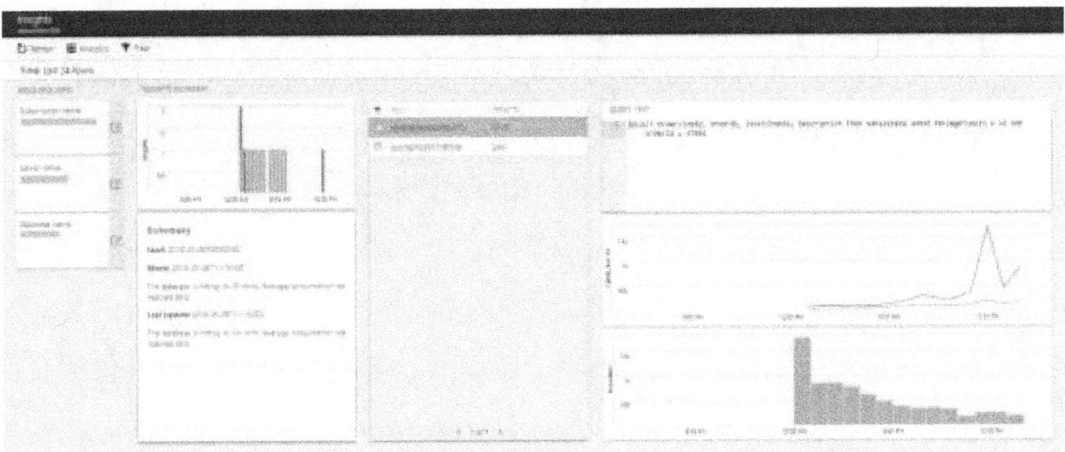

Elastic pools and database reports

Azure SQL elastic pools and databases have a separate report to display data collected in the specified time.

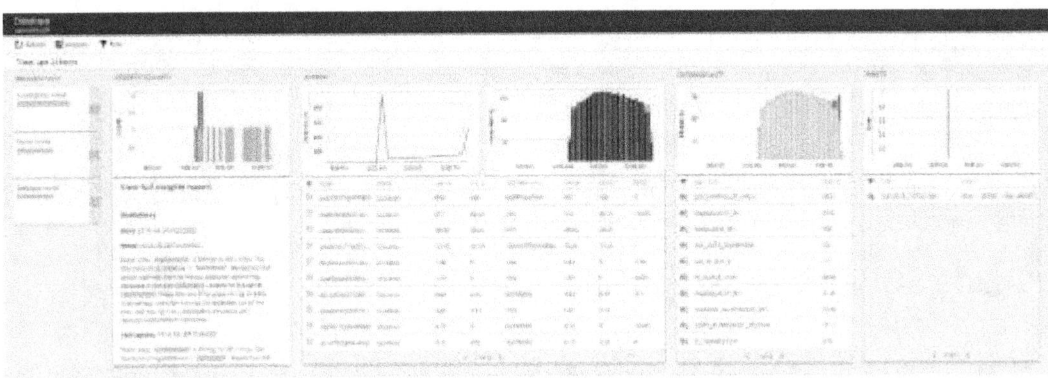

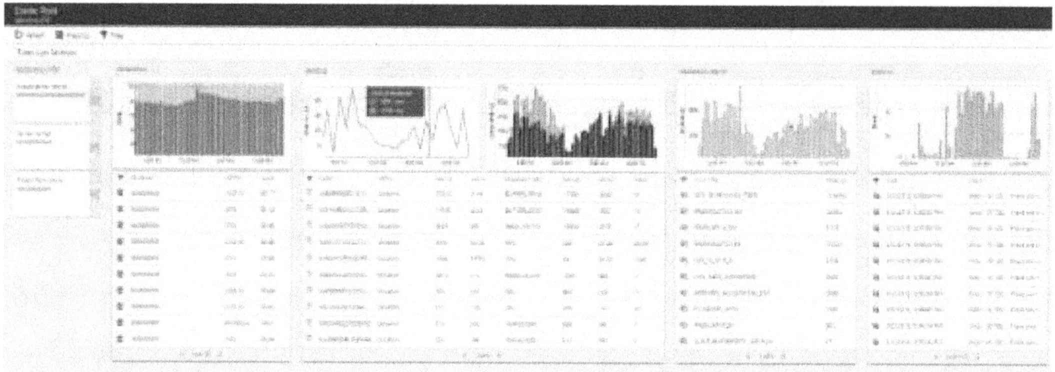

Query reports

The query report compares query performance across different databases. It makes it quick for DBA to pinpoint databases that perform the select query well versus slow ones.

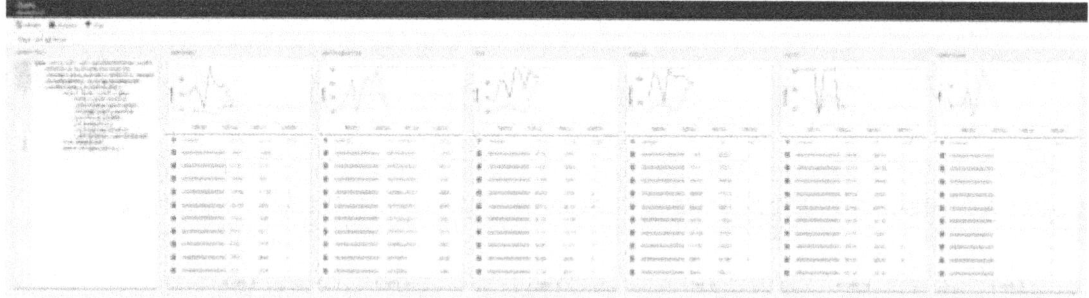

Similarly, you add multiple Azure SQL Databases, Managed instances together in a single workspace, and view their monitoring and performance data.

View Azure SQL Database Log analytics data using Power BI

Power BI dashboard provides a rich set of visuals for creating a dashboard with different sources of data. Suppose you fetch Avg CPU utilization using the following KQL script.

```
AzureMetrics

| where ResourceProvider == "MICROSOFT.SQL"

| where TimeGenerated >= ago(60min)

| where MetricName in ('cpu_percent')
```

```
| parse _ResourceId with * "/microsoft.sql/servers/"
```

You get the output in a tabular format with multiple columns. You can choose the required column in KQL output using the columns sections.

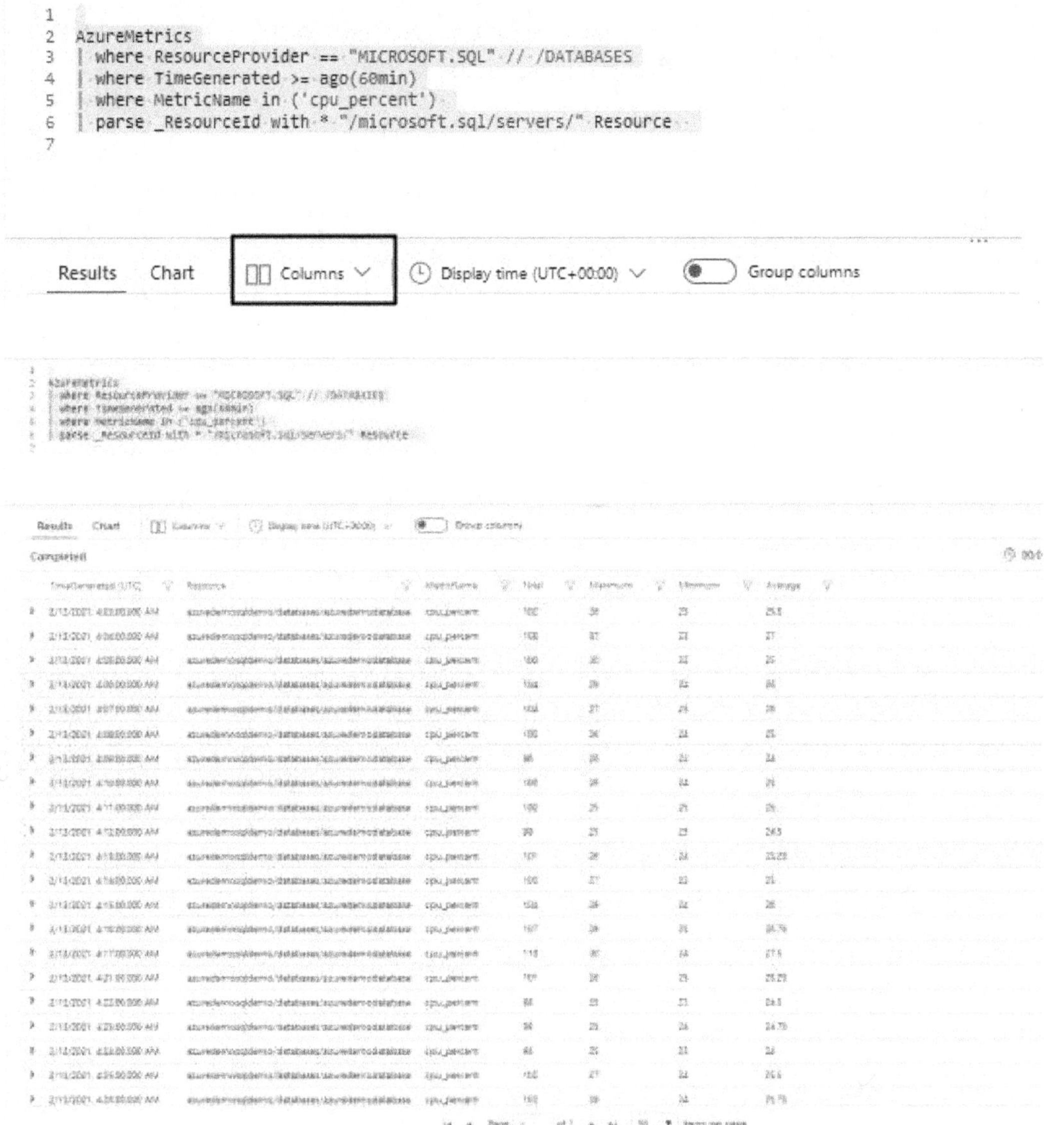
AzureMetrics
| where ResourceProvider == "MICROSOFT.SQL" // /DATABASES
| where TimeGenerated >= ago(60min)
| where MetricName in ('cpu_percent')
| parse _ResourceId with * "/microsoft.sql/servers/" Resource
Results
Chart
Columns
Display time (UTC+00:00)
Group columns

Once KQL returns relevant data, click on Export and Export to Power BI (M query).

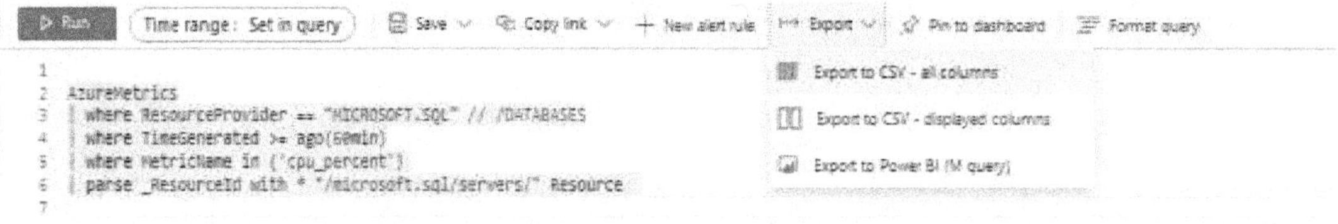

You get an option to save the PowerBUQuery.txt.

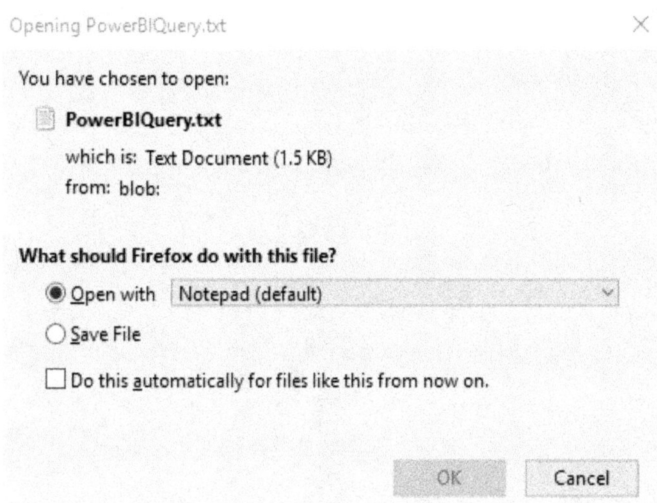

Open the file in Notepad or Visual Studio Code. It has the M language query with the script, instructions.

```
/*
The exported Power Query Formula Language (M Language ) can be used with Power Query in Excel
and Power BI Desktop.
For Power BI Desktop follow the instructions below:
1) Download Power BI Desktop from https://powerbi.microsoft.com/desktop/
2) In Power BI Desktop select: 'Get Data' -> 'Blank Query'->'Advanced Query Editor'
3) Paste the M Language script into the Advanced Query Editor and select 'Done'
*/


let AnalyticsQuery =
let Source = Json.Document(Web.Contents("https://api.loganalytics.io/v1/workspaces/331c8dcc-13f8-4445-b50b-0e025fec1ebf/query",
[Query=[#"query"="AzureMetrics
| where ResourceProvider == ""MICROSOFT.SQL""
| where TimeGenerated >= ago(60min)
| where MetricName in ('cpu_percent')
| parse _ResourceId with * ""/microsoft.sql/servers/"" Resource

",#"x-ms-app"="OmsAnalyticsPBI",#"prefer"="ai.response-thinning=true"],Timeout=#duration(0,0,4,0)])),
TypeMap = #table(
{ "AnalyticsTypes", "Type" },
{
{ "string",   Text.Type },
{ "int",      Int32.Type },
{ "long",     Int64.Type },
{ "real",     Double.Type },
{ "timespan", Duration.Type },
{ "datetime", DateTimeZone.Type },
{ "bool",     Logical.Type },
{ "guid",     Text.Type },
{ "dynamic",  Text.Type }
```

You require Power BI Desktop for this section. You can download it from the **https://www.microsoft.com/en-us/download/details.aspx?id=58494**

Microsoft Power BI Desktop

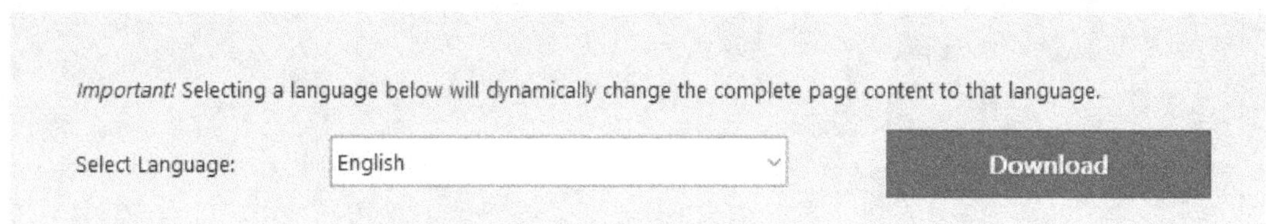

Launch Power BI Desktop and click on Get Data and Blank query from the home tab. It opens a Power Query Editor. Right-click on Query1 and select Advanced Editor.

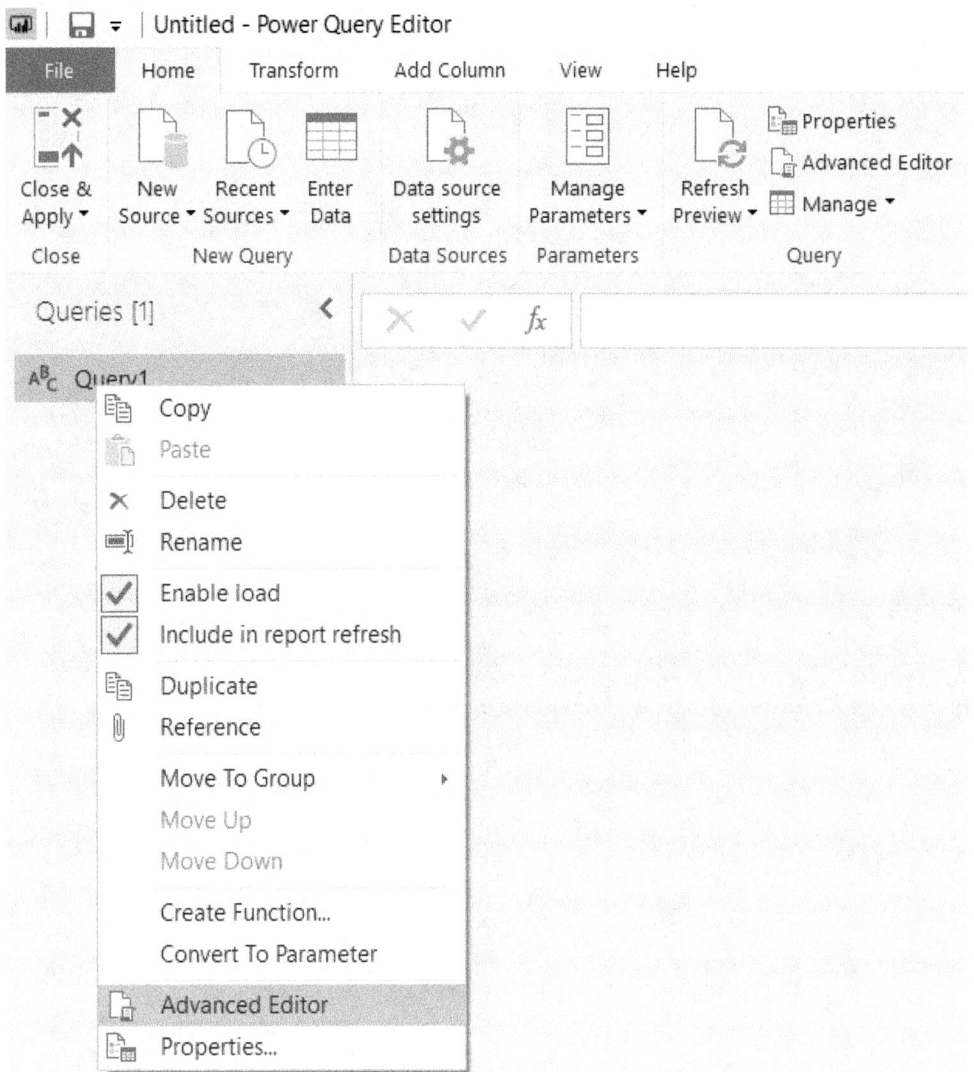

In the editor, paste the M language query that we exported from the KQL.

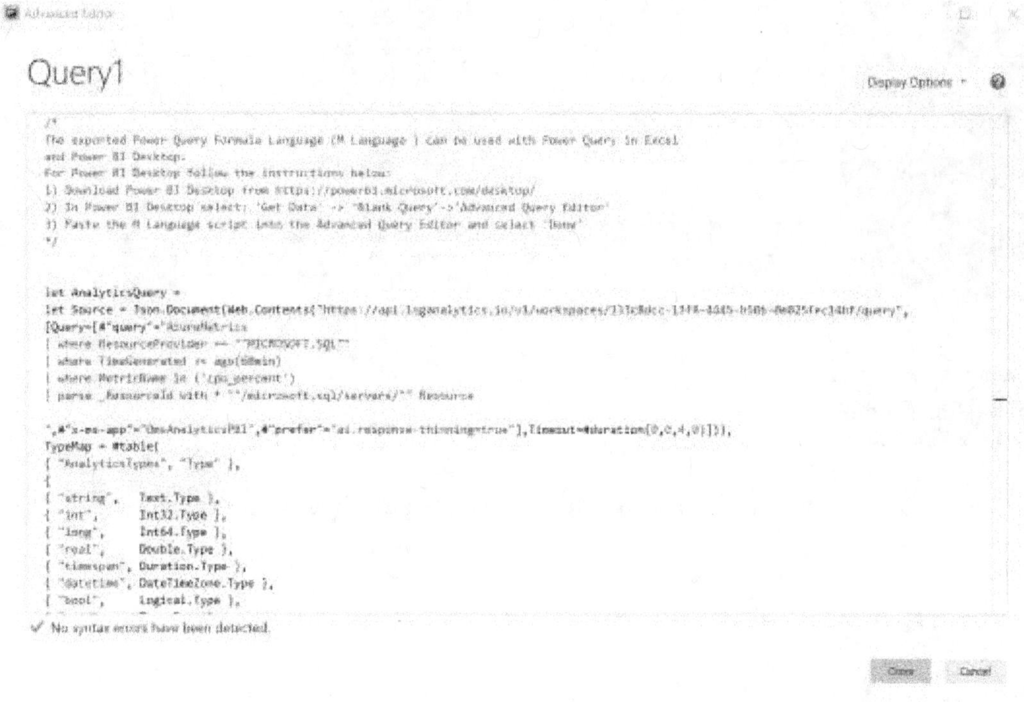

The next step asks for the Credentials so that Power BI can connect to the Log Analytics workspace.

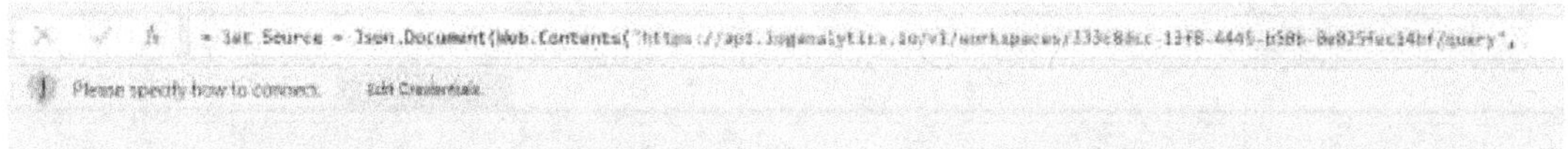

Click on **Edit Credentials**. In the access web content, select the organization account.

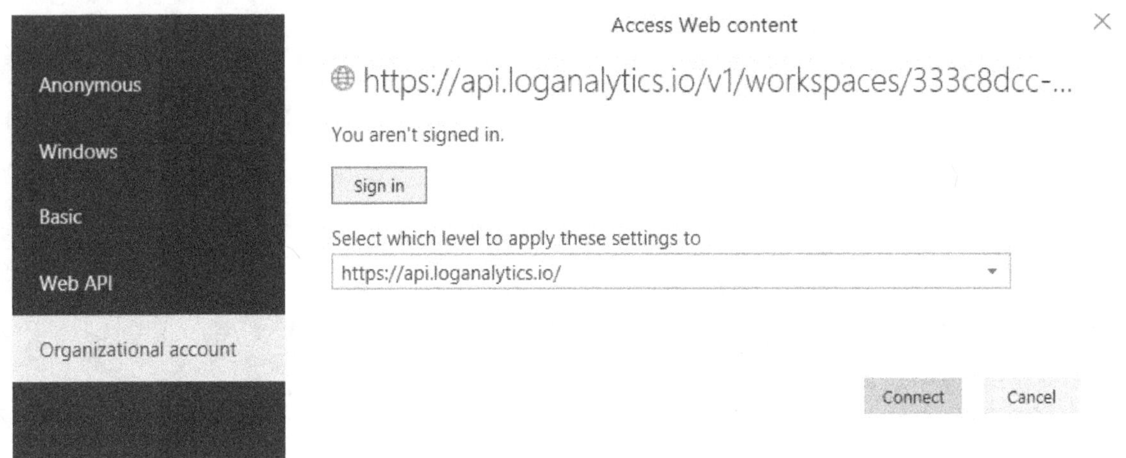

Click on Sign In. Provide your credentials, and it changes the status as – You are currently signed in.

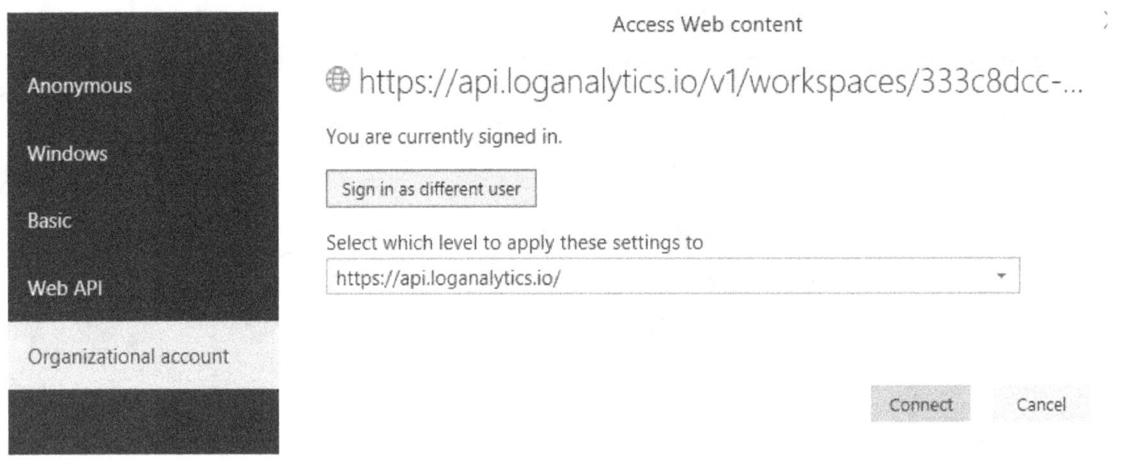

Click Connect. Power BI retrieves data from log analytics. It returns all columns that we receive in the query output.

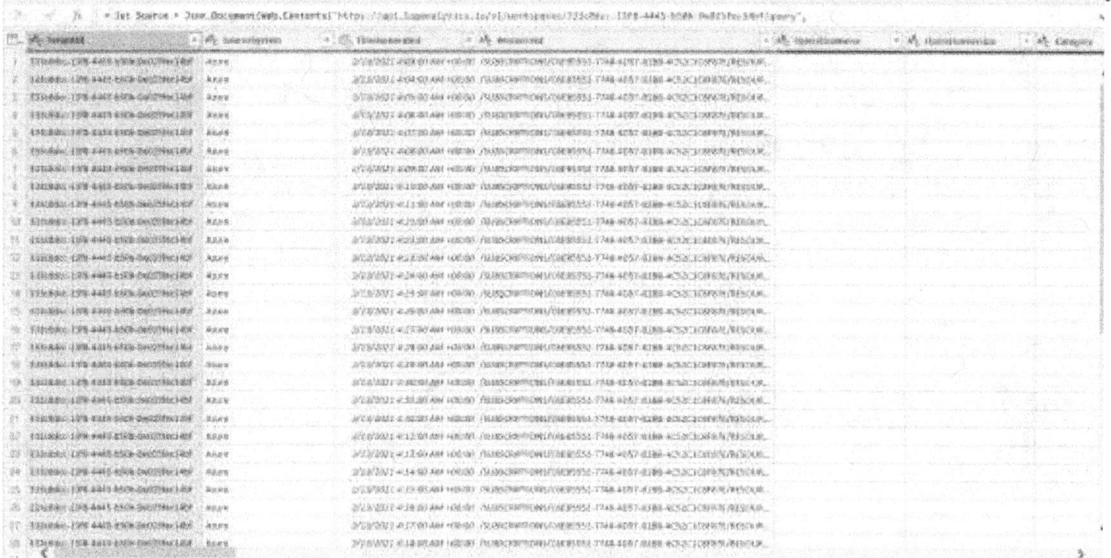

Select the undesired columns and remove them.

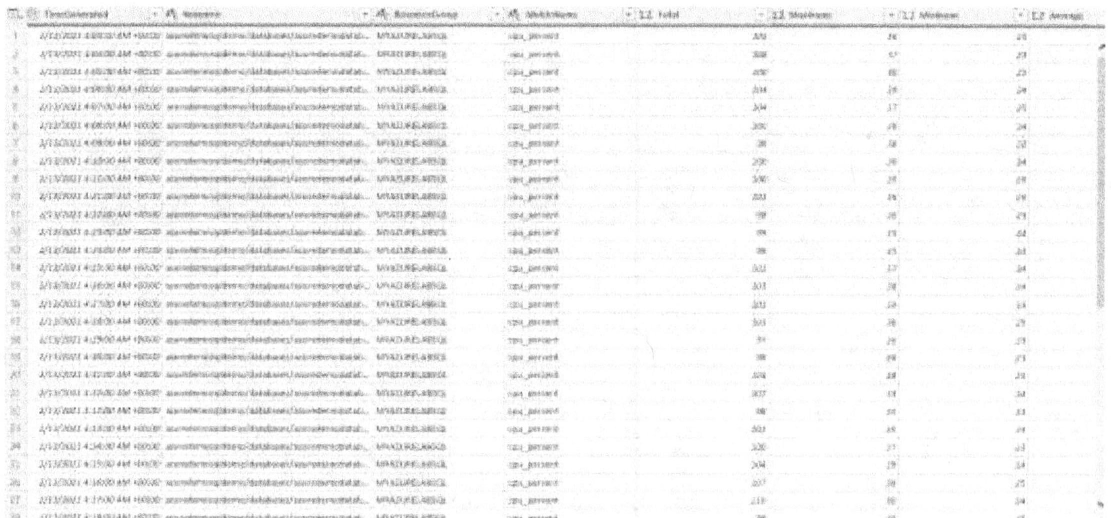

You can do additional formatting, such as creating a calculated column, measure, split columns. For example, I split the timestamp and have a column with time only. For this purpose, you can choose the split column by delimiter from the home tab. You can create the visualization as per your requirement. I created a sample line chart for demonstration.

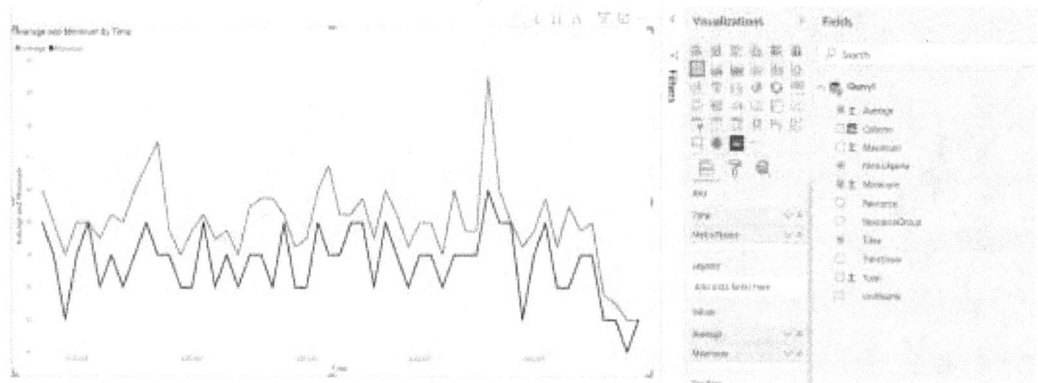

To learn more about Power BI , refer to Microsoft docs (**https://docs.microsoft.com/en-us/power-bi/**).

Extended Events in Azure SQL Database

The Extended events capture diagnostic information for SQL Server. It is similar to using a SQL profiler; however, they are lightweight, scalable. It uses minimal resources for capturing data. Therefore it does not cause performance issues while it is running.

The few essential terms for using the extended events are as below.

- Session: All extended events are captured in a specific configured extended event session. For the on-premise SQL Server, by default, it runs system_health extended session.
- Event: Data is stored in the target system for these actions. For example, we can use sql_statement_completed for capturing queries once a statement completes.
- Event fields: These are the columns related to a particular event.
- Global fields: By default, an extended event captures few data points irrespective of a specific event field.
- Target: The target specifies where the extended event session stores data.
    - Ring buffer target: In this data is stored in memory for a short interval.
    - Event file target: It is a file on your local storage.

In an on-premise instance, extended events are an instance-level configuration. However, the Azure SQL Database configures it at the database level. You can find it under your Azure SQL database and extended event folder.

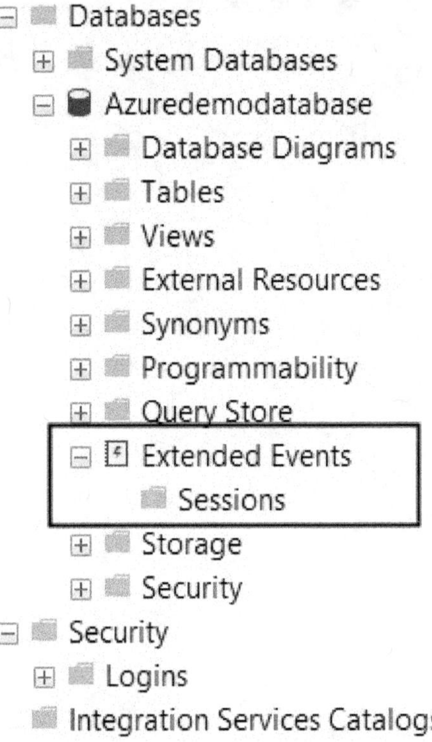

You can configure the database level extended event session using SSMS Extended event session wizard. You can set up ring_buffer_target as well as Microsoft Azure Storage for later analysis.

Azure SQL Database does not support all extended events similar to the on-premise or managed instance. To get a list of supported events, run the following query.

```
SELECT
        o.object_type,
        p.name          AS [package_name],
        o.name          AS [db_object_name],
        o.description  AS [db_obj_description]
```

```
FROM
        sys.dm_xe_objects  AS o
INNER JOIN sys.dm_xe_packages AS p  ON p.guid = o.package_guid
WHERE
o.object_type in
(
'action',  'event',  'target'
)
ORDER BY
o.object_type,
p.name,
o.name;
```

It gives a list of 456 extended events with their description.

	object_type	package_name	db_object_name	db_obj_description
1	action	rodmtargetpkg	mdmget_TimeStampUTC	Get time stmap UTC
2	action	package0	event_sequence	Collect event sequence number
3	action	sqlserver	client_app_name	Collect client application name
4	action	sqlserver	client_connection_id	Collects the optional identifier provided at connection...
5	action	sqlserver	client_hostname	Collect client hostname
6	action	sqlserver	client_pid	Collect client process ID
7	action	sqlserver	compile_plan_guid	Collect compiled plan guid. Use this to uniquely iden...
8	action	sqlserver	context_info	Collect the same value as the CONTEXT_INFO() fun...
9	action	sqlserver	database_id	Collect database ID
10	action	sqlserver	database_name	Collect current database name

system_health extended event session in Azure SQL Database

You can create the system_health extended event session in the Azure SQL Database using the following script and uses the ring_buffer target.

Note: It uses ON DATABASE clause for Azure SQL Database instead of ON SERVER clause for On-premise SQL Server or Azure SQL Managed Instance.

Download script from
https://github.com/AzureDP300/AzureDP300/blob/main/Chapter7/Script1.sql

Refresh the extended event folder for Azure SQL Database, and the system_health event is in running state.

- Databases
  - System Databases
  - Azuredemodatabase
    - Database Diagrams
    - Tables
    - Views
    - External Resources
    - Synonyms
    - Programmability
    - Query Store
    - Extended Events
      - Sessions
        - system_health
    - Storage
    - Security

You can query system_health extended events similar to the Azure Managed instance or on-premise SQL Server. The difference is that you need to use **sys.dm_xe_database_session_targets** DMV instead of the **sys,dm_xe_session_targets**.

Create an extended event to capture update statement

Suppose we have an important table, and you require an extended event session for capturing the sqlserver.sql_statement_starting event and filter it for the **UPDATE** statement. In this section, we create the following things.

- Create a table [tabEmployee] in the Azure SQL Database.

```
CREATE TABLE tabEmployee

(

    EmployeeGuid   uniqueIdentifier   not null  default newid()  primary key,

    EmployeeId       int                         not null  identity(1,1),

    EmployeeKudosCount   int                       , not null  default 0,

    EmployeeDescr  nvarchar(256)              null

);

GO
```

- Insert data into the [tabEmployee] table.

```
INSERT INTO tabEmployee ( EmployeeDescr )

    VALUES ( 'Rajendra Gupta' );

GO
```

- Create an extended event with **sqlserver.sql_statement_starting** event.
- Filter extended event session for the UPDATE statement on the [tabEmployee] table.

```
CREATE EVENT SESSION eventsession_gm_azuresqldb51
    ON DATABASE
    ADD EVENT
    sqlserver.sql_statement_starting
    (
    ACTION (sqlserver.sql_text)
    WHERE statement LIKE '%UPDATE tabEmployee%'
    )
    ADD TARGET
```

```
        package0.ring_buffer
        (SET
        max_memory = 500   -- Units of KB.
        );
GO
```

- Start the extended event session.

```
ALTER EVENT SESSION eventsession_gm_azuresqldb51
        ON DATABASE
        STATE = START;
GO
```

- Execute an UPDATE statement to trigger the extended event.

```
SELECT 'BEFORE_Updates', EmployeeKudosCount, * FROM tabEmployee;
 UPDATE tabEmployee
        SET EmployeeKudosCount = EmployeeKudosCount + 102;
 UPDATE tabEmployee
        SET EmployeeKudosCount = EmployeeKudosCount + 1015;
 SELECT 'AFTER__Updates', EmployeeKudosCount, * FROM tabEmployee;
GO
```

- View the extended event

Download script from
https://github.com/AzureDP300/AzureDP300/blob/main/Chapter7/Script2.sql

```
SELECT
    se.name                         AS [session-name],
    ev.event_name,
    ac.action_name,
    st.target_name,
    se.session_source,
    st.target_data,
    CAST(st.target_data AS XML)  AS [target_data_XML]
FROM
            sys.dm_xe_database_session_event_actions  AS ac

    INNER JOIN sys.dm_xe_database_session_events         AS ev  ON ev.event_name = ac.event_name
        AND CAST(ev.event_session_address AS BINARY(8)) = CAST(ac.event_session_address AS BINARY(8))

    INNER JOIN sys.dm_xe_database_session_object_columns AS oc
         ON CAST(oc.event_session_address AS BINARY(8)) = CAST(ac.event_session_address AS BINARY(8))
```

	session-name	event_name	action_name	target_name	session_source	target_data	target_data_X
1	eventsession_gm_azuresqldb51	sql_statement_starting	sql_text	ring_buffer	Azuredemodatabase	<RingBufferTarget truncated="0" processingTime="	<RingBufferT

Click on the target_data_XML and view the SQL statement captured using the XEvent session

```
        <value>438</value>
      </data>
      <data name="statement">
        <type name="unicode_string" package="package0" />
        <value>UPDATE tabEmployee
      SET EmployeeKudosCount = EmployeeKudosCount + 1015</value>
      </data>
      <action name="sql_text" package="sqlserver">
        <type name="unicode_string" package="package0" />
        <value>SELECT 'BEFORE_Updates', EmployeeKudosCount, * FROM tabEmployee;

UPDATE tabEmployee
    SET EmployeeKudosCount = EmployeeKudosCount + 102;

UPDATE tabEmployee
    SET EmployeeKudosCount = EmployeeKudosCount + 1015;

SELECT 'AFTER__Updates', EmployeeKudosCount, * FROM tabEmployee;
</value>
    </action>
  </event>
</RingBufferTarget>
```

Capture Deadlock information using the extended event

SQL Server uses locks for maintaining the ACID model. The ACID model uses the following properties.

- Atomicity
- Consistency

- Isolation
- Durability

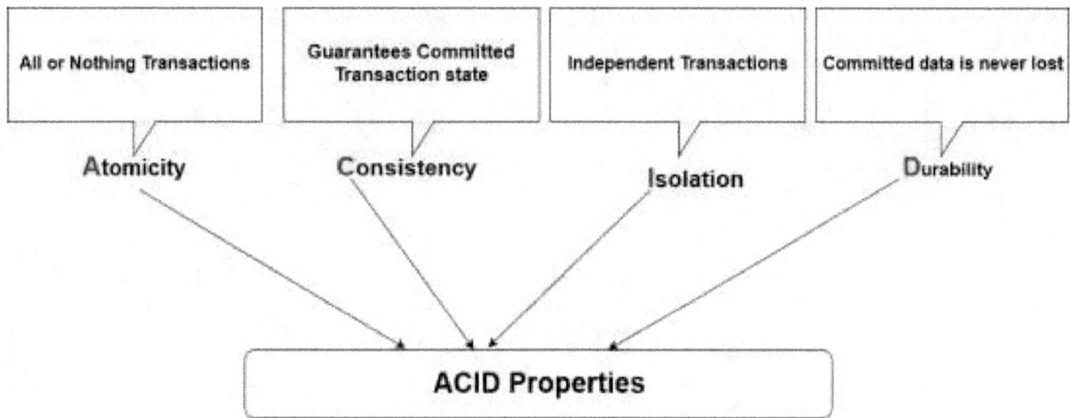

Therefore, SQL Server block actions can violate the data consistency and isolate the writes to the database. During a transaction, SQL Server locks a specific object (row, page, table, database) for a short period and releases the lock once the transaction finishes.

Suppose two users started transactions simultaneously.

- User A starts a process that acquires a lock on Resource A.
- User B starts a process that acquires a lock on the Resource B

Both the transactions require a lock on each other's resources so that the transactions can finish.

- Process A requires a lock on Resource B.
- Process B requires a lock on Resource A.

In that case, SQL Server decides to choose a process as a deadlock victim and kills the process so that another transaction can finish.

```
Transaction
(Process ID 82) was deadlocked on lock resources with another process
and has been chosen as the deadlock victim. Rerun the transaction.
```

Note: By default, SQL Server chooses the least expensive transaction to rollback as a deadlock victim.

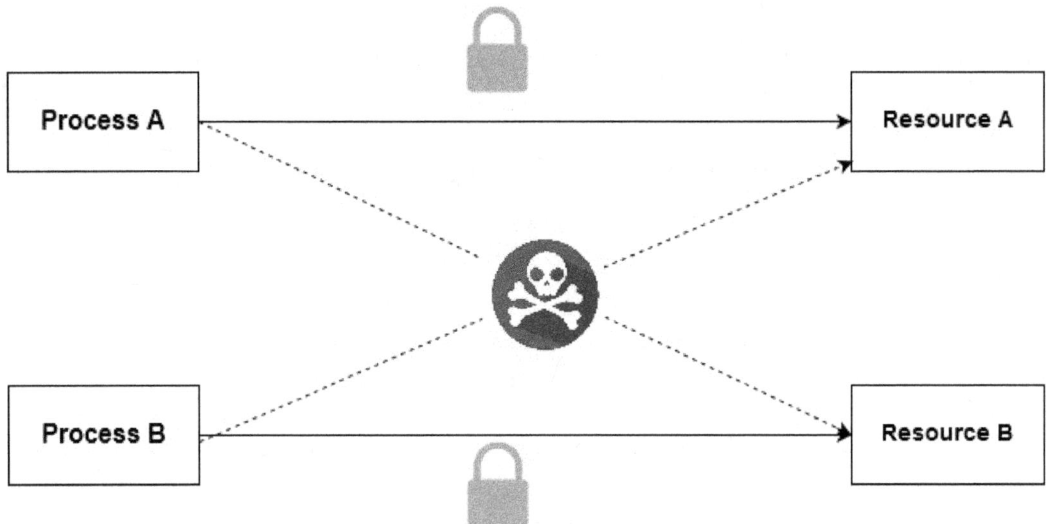

To simulate the deadlock, create the table with sample data.

```
CREATE TABLE Teacher

(

        id INT IDENTITY PRIMARY KEY,

        [name] NVARCHAR(50)

)

INSERT INTO Teacher values ('Raj')

INSERT INTO Teacher values ('John')

INSERT INTO Teacher values ('Joy')

 CREATE TABLE Student

(
```

id INT IDENTITY PRIMARY KEY,

[name] NVARCHAR(50)

)

INSERT INTO Student values ('Mark')

INSERT INTO Student values ('Rick')

INSERT INTO table2 values ('Arvind')

User A and B start two transactions, and SQL Server decides to kill a transaction due to a deadlock scenario.

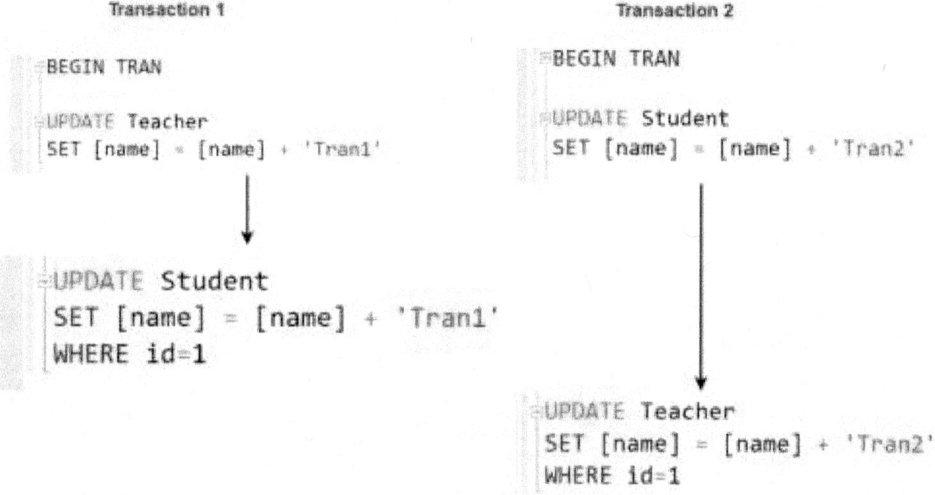


```
Msg 1205, Level 13, State 51, Line 7
Transaction (Process ID 74) was deadlocked on lock resources with another
 process and has been chosen as the deadlock victim. Rerun the transaction.
```

You can retrieve deadlock information for an Azure SQL Database using the system_health extended event session, a custom XEvent session, Azure diagnostic configuration (section 1.4).

Note: Execute the following T-SQL in the Master database of Azure SQL Database.

WITH Deadlock

```
AS (SELECT Cast(event_data AS XML) AS [target_data_XML]

FROM   sys.Fn_xe_telemetry_blob_target_read_file('dl', NULL, NULL, NULL

))

SELECT

target_data_xml.value('(/event/@timestamp)[1]', 'DateTime2')

AS Timestamp,

target_data_xml.query('/event/data[@name="xml_report"]/value/deadlock')

AS deadlock_xml,

target_data_xml.query('/event/data[@name="database_name"]/value').value('(/value)[1]', 'nvarchar(100)') AS [database]

FROM   Deadlock
```

It returns the deadlock information in the XML format.

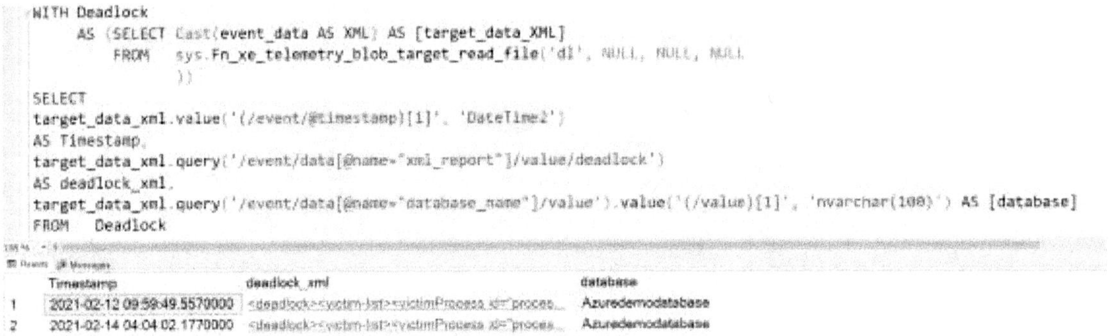

```
WITH Deadlock
     AS (SELECT Cast(event_data AS XML) AS [target_data_XML]
         FROM   sys.Fn_xe_telemetry_blob_target_read_file('dl', NULL, NULL, NULL
                ))
SELECT
target_data_xml.value('(/event/@timestamp)[1]', 'DateTime2')
AS Timestamp,
target_data_xml.query('/event/data[@name="xml_report"]/value/deadlock')
AS deadlock_xml,
target_data_xml.query('/event/data[@name="database_name"]/value').value('(/value)[1]', 'nvarchar(100)') AS [database]
FROM   Deadlock
```

	Timestamp	deadlock_xml	database
1	2021-02-12 09:59:49.5570000	<deadlock><victim-list><victimProcess id="proces...	Azuredemodatabase
2	2021-02-14 04:04:02.1770000	<deadlock><victim-list><victimProcess id="proces...	Azuredemodatabase

Click on the hyperlink and it gives you detailed information for deadlock.

```
<deadlock>
  <victim-list>
    <victimProcess id="process216e3d284e8" />
  </victim-list>
  <process-list>
    <process id="process216e3d284e8" taskpriority="0" logused="652" waitresource="KEY: 5:72057594048086016 (8194443284a0)" waittime="3130" ownerId="7078
      <executionStack>
        <frame procname="unknown" queryhash="0xa5e35d3992cd6b87" queryplanhash="0x0f8fd4febf779bc7" line="1" stmtstart="58" stmtend="164" sqlhandle="0x0
unknown    </frame>
        <frame procname="unknown" queryhash="0xa5e35d3991cd6b87" queryplanhash="0x0f8fd4febf779bc7" line="1" stmtend="112" sqlhandle="0x02000000cf60fd1f
unknown    </frame>
      </executionStack>
      <inputbuf>
UPDATE Teacher
SET [name] = [name] + 'Tran2'
WHERE id=1   </inputbuf>
    </process>
    <process id="process216e02f0108" taskpriority="0" logused="844" waitresource="KEY: 5:72057594048151552 (8194443284a0)" waittime="18892" ownerId="70?
      <executionStack>
        <frame procname="unknown" queryhash="0x7e6c6c4ff628285a" queryplanhash="0x0e8112f148cd8670" line="1" stmtstart="58" stmtend="164" sqlhandle="0x0
unknown    </frame>
        <frame procname="unknown" queryhash="0x7e6c6c4ff628285e" queryplanhash="0x0e8112f148cd8670" line="1" stmtend="112" sqlhandle="0x0200000054f68638
unknown    </frame>
      </executionStack>
      <inputbuf>
UPDATE Student
SET [name] = [name] + 'Tran1'
WHERE id=1   </inputbuf>
    </process>
  </process-list>
```

Save the file with the XDL extension and open it in SSMS to view the deadlock graph. In the graph, you get one eclipse with a cross mark, and it is the deadlock victim.

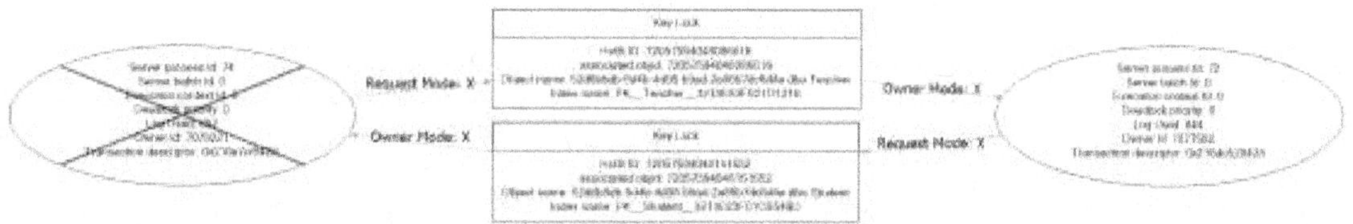

Note: You can refer to https://docs.microsoft.com/en-us/azure/azure-sql/database/xevent-db-diff-from-svr for extended events (XEvents) for Azure SQL Database.

Describe automatic tuning

Azure SQL Database and Azure SQL Managed instances provide automatic tuning features for delivering optimized performance using continuous performance tuning. It uses artificial intelligence (AI) and Machine Learning (ML) for automatic tuning. Automatic tuning is a fully managed Azure service for improving database performance automatically. It can provide the following benefits.

- Automatic performance tuning of databases.
- Capturing baseline and verification of performance gains.
- Automatic rollback and self -correction.
- Captures performance tuning history
- Proactive monitoring and tuning
- Scale-out resources
- It is a Safe, Reliable, and tested method on millions of Azure databases.
- It is designed in a way to not interfere with the user workload. Azure applies automatic recommendations during low utilization times.

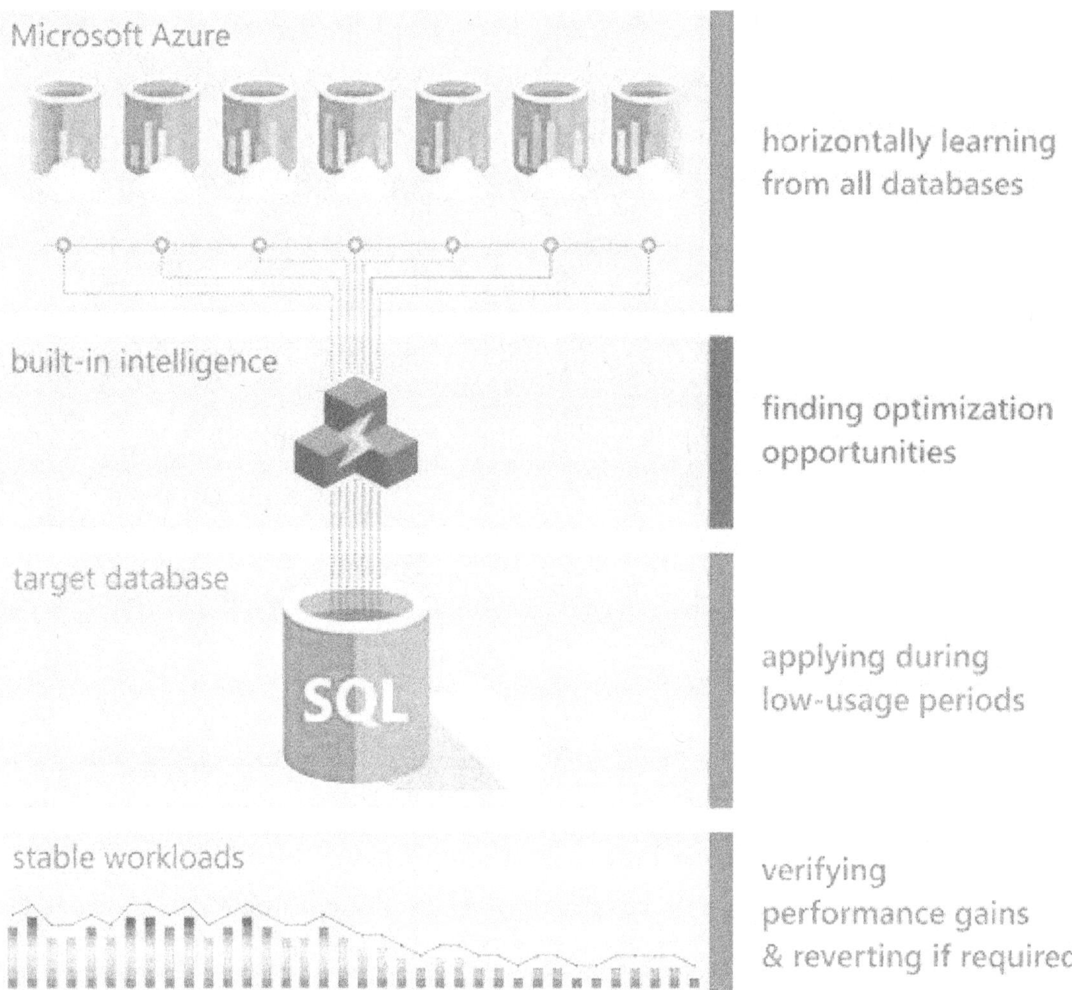

By default, the automatic tuning feature is configured for Azure SQL Database at the Azure server level. To view the current status, navigate to database features on the Azure SQL Server dashboard page.

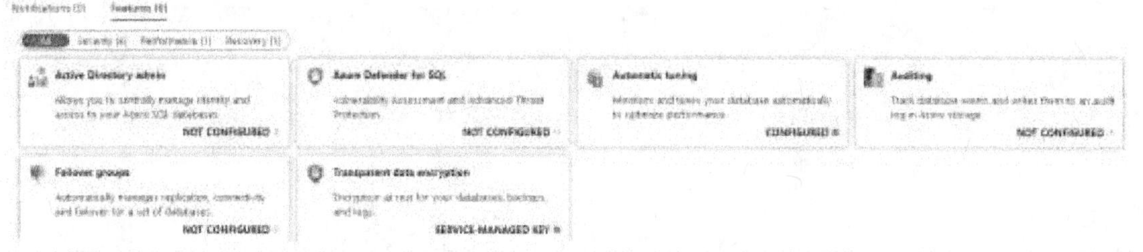

Click on Automatic tuning. It has the following options.

- Force plan
- Create an index
- Drop index

Note: You can configure the automatic tuning feature at the Azure Database level as well. In this case, you override the automatic tuning options configured at the server level. In the current state, it specifies inherited from the Azure defaults.

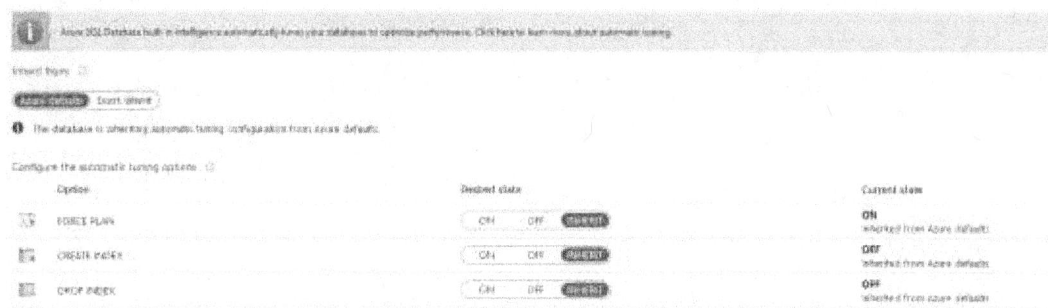

Note:

Azure changes the Azure defaults configuration from March 2020. It has the following configurations applicable for Automatic tuning.

- Force plan: Enabled
- Create Index: Disabled

- Drop Index: Disabled.

Automatic plan correction

By default, Azure SQL Database is configured with the query store for capturing query executing plans regressed in their performance. We can visualize multiple execution plans for a query and force a good plan if required. Azure SQL queries use the last known good plan instead of regressed plan using the automatic plan correction.

Note: This feature is available for both Azure SQL Database and Azure SQL Managed Instance.

Create Index

Azure SQL Server automatically identifies an index that may improve query performance. Once the index is deployed, Azure automatically verifies the query performance after the index.

Note: This feature is available only for Azure SQL Database.

Drop Index

Azure SQL Server identifies the redundant and duplicate index daily except for the unique indexes and indexes that were not used for more than 90 days.

Note:

1 The dropping index is not supported on the premium and business-critical service tier.
2 This feature is available only for Azure SQL Database.
3 The drop index is not compatible with the application using partition switching and index hints.

You can modify the Azure defaults and set the desired state as ON to use all automatic tuning features

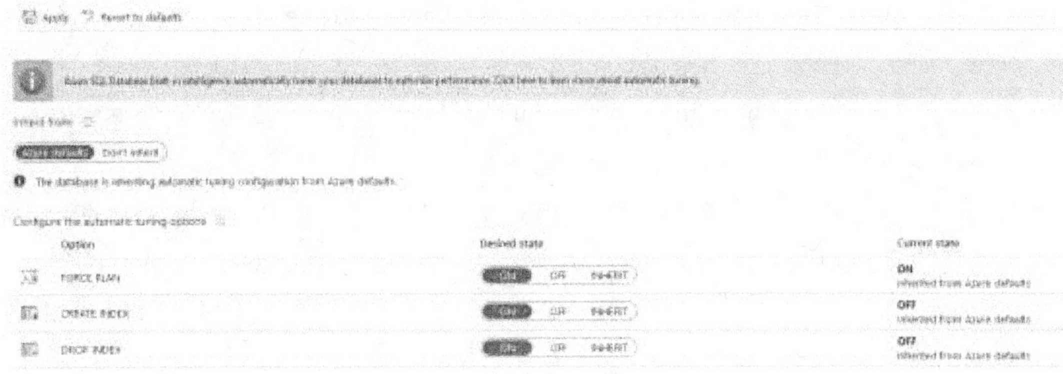

Click Ok.

Do you want to continue?

Please note that the Drop index option is currently not compatible with applications using partition switching and index hints. Do you want to continue?

OK Cancel

The following figure shows current status changes to On (Forced by user).

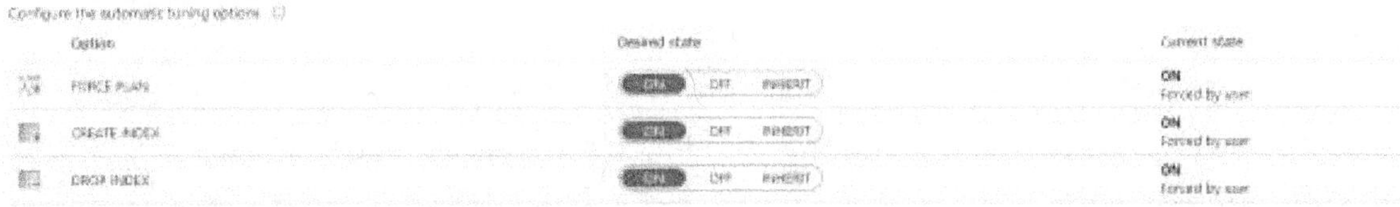

Alternatively, you can use T-SQL to enable the automatic tuning feature using the T-SQL.

ALTER DATABASE current SET AUTOMATIC_TUNING = AUTO | INHERIT | CUSTOM

ALTER DATABASE current SET AUTOMATIC_TUNING (FORCE_LAST_GOOD_PLAN = ON, CREATE_INDEX = DEFAULT, DROP_INDEX = OFF)

View performance recommendations for Azure SQL Database

You can view the performance recommendation for Azure SQL Database using the performance recommendations section.

In the following figure, we view high impact performance recommendations.

- High: The high impact recommendations provide the most significant performance impact.
- Medium: The medium-impact recommendation might improve performance but not substantially.
- Low: The low impact performance recommendation might not improve performance significantly.

Recommendations

ACTION	RECOMMENDATION DESCRIPTION		IMPACT
CREATE INDEX	Table: Indexed columns:	[test_table_0.430709] [index_1],[index_2],[index_3]	HIGH IMPACT
CREATE INDEX	Table: Indexed columns:	[test_table_0.914675] [index_1],[index_2],[index_3]	HIGH IMPACT
DROP INDEX (PREVIEW)	Index name: Reason:	IR_[test_schema]_[test_table_0.112348]_CD2E5085881888FC9A4 Duplicate index	HIGH IMPACT
DROP INDEX (PREVIEW)	Index name: Reason:	IR_[test_schema]_[test_table_0.950691]_9A67D9E88A31B315D14 Duplicate index	HIGH IMPACT
FIX SCHEMA ISSUES (PREVIEW)	Error code: Error message:	208 Invalid object name 'dbo.Companies'.	HIGH IMPACT

Note: You might not get performance immediately after configuring the automatic tuning. The Azure database should run at least for one day with your database workload.

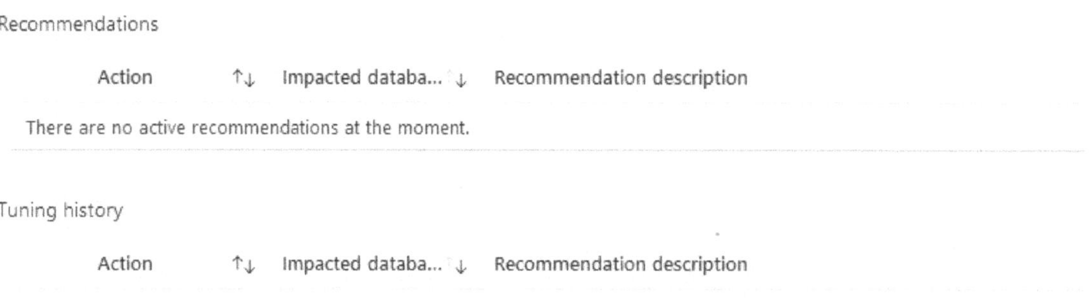

You can refer article **https://docs.microsoft.com/en-us/azure/azure-sql/database/database-advisor-find-recommendations-portal** for a detailed information on automatic tuning feature.

Optimize Azure SQL Server on VM

The IaaS Azure SQL Server on VM is similar to an on-premise SQL Server with a difference. In this, you store your database infrastructure utilizing Azure resources. Storage is a critical resource for a heavy IO using a resource such as SQL Server. Azure provides a highly scalable and secure storage platform for your workload. These storage types are as below.

- Blob storage: Blob storage is object-based storage. It provides several storage tiers based on their performance and costs. Usually, in a SQL Server environment, blob storage is used to store database backups using the backup to URL functionality.
- File storage: File storage is useful for a file share in a virtual machine. For example, we can use it for the WSFC quorum disk.
- Disk Storage: The Azure disk storage is similar to a physical disk for an on-premise SQL Server. Azure provides several performance tiers for these managed disks for storing your database data files and log files.

Virtual machines types

Azure Virtual Machine provides various options for deploying your application, database infrastructure. In the Azure VM configuration, it asks you to specify the VM size.

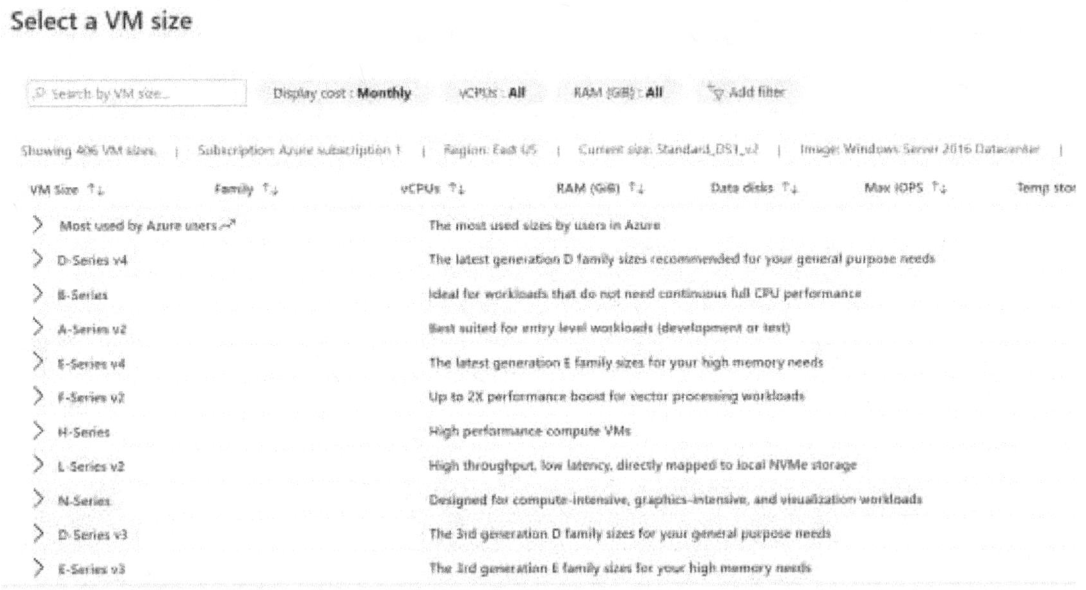

Select a VM size

Search by VM size... | Display cost : **Monthly** | vCPUs : **All** | RAM (GiB) : **All** | Add filter

Showing 406 VM sizes. | Subscription: Azure subscription 1 | Region: East US | Current size: Standard_DS1_v2 | Image: Windows Server 2016 Datacenter |

VM Size ↑↓	Family ↑↓	vCPUs ↑↓	RAM (GiB) ↑↓	Data disks ↑↓	Max IOPS ↑↓	Temp stor
> Most used by Azure users		The most used sizes by users in Azure				
> D-Series v4		The latest generation D family sizes recommended for your general purpose needs				
> B-Series		Ideal for workloads that do not need continuous full CPU performance				
> A-Series v2		Best suited for entry level workloads (development or test)				
> E-Series v4		The latest generation E family sizes for your high memory needs				
> F-Series v2		Up to 2X performance boost for vector processing workloads				
> H-Series		High performance compute VMs				
> L-Series v2		High throughput, low latency, directly mapped to local NVMe storage				
> N-Series		Designed for compute-intensive, graphics-intensive, and visualization workloads				
> D-Series v3		The 3rd generation D family sizes for your general purpose needs				
> E-Series v3		The 3rd generation E family sizes for your high memory needs				

It gives you the option to choose the following VM types.

- General-purpose
- Compute-optimized
- Memory-optimized
- Storage optimized
- GPU
- High performance

In the following table, you get a high-level comparison of different VM types.

Type	Sizes	Description
General purpose	B, Dsv3, Dv3, Dasv4, Dav4, DSv2, Dv2, Av2, DC, DCv2, Dv4, Dsv4, Ddv4, Ddsv4	Balanced CPU-to-memory ratio. Ideal for testing and development, small to medium databases, and low to medium traffic web servers.
Compute optimized	F, Fs, Fsv2	High CPU-to-memory ratio. Good for medium traffic web servers, network appliances, batch processes, and application servers.
Memory optimized	Esv3, Ev3, Easv4, Eav4, Ev4, Esv4, Edv4, Edsv4, Mv2, M, DSv2, Dv2	High memory-to-CPU ratio. Great for relational database servers, medium to large caches, and in-memory analytics.
Storage optimized	Lsv2	High disk throughput and IO ideal for Big Data, SQL, NoSQL databases, data warehousing and large transactional databases.
GPU	NC, NCv2, NCv3, NCasT4_v3 (Preview), ND, NDv2 (Preview), NV, NVv3, NVv4	Specialized virtual machines targeted for heavy graphic rendering and video editing, as well as model training and inferencing (ND) with deep learning. Available with single or multiple GPUs.
High performance compute	HB, HBv2, HC, H	Our fastest and most powerful CPU virtual machines with optional high-throughput network interfaces (RDMA).

Azure managed disks

Azure managed disk uses blob level storage volumes for storing your database files in an Azure VM. This disk provides the following benefits.

- Highly durable and available: This managed disk provides 99.999% availability with three highly durable data replicas.
- Scalable and straightforward VM deployment: Azure allows configuring up to 5000 VM disks in a subscription per region. Therefore, you can deploy thousands of VM in a single subscription.
- Availability set integration: The managed disks are integrated with the availability sets for ensuring safety from a single point of failures. These disks are automatically placed in the different storage scale units known as stamps. In case of failure of a stamp, only the VM with the disk on those VM fails.
- Availability Zones integration: Azure managed disk also integrates with the Availability Zones for providing a high-availability from datacenter failures. The availability zones provide 99.99% VM uptime SLA.
- Azure Disk Backup: Azure disk backup provides the cloud-based backup solution for protecting data stored in the managed disk. It is a secure, cost-effective and straightforward solution. It is in the preview phase.
- Direct upload: Azure managed disk provides flexibility to upload the VHD to the Azure managed disk in fewer steps. It allows uploading VHD up to 32TiB in size.
- Encryption: Azure Managed disk has server-side encryption (SSE) and Azure Disk encryption(ADE) for securing OS and data disk in the VM.
- Private link: You can use the private link that uses the timebound Shared Access Signature (SAS) URI for secure access to the managed disk. It is useful for import and export data in the managed disk.
- Managed disk snapshots: Azure provides managed disk snapshot that is a read-only and crash-consistent copy of a managed disk. You can use this disk snapshot for creating a new managed disk.

Azure provides the following managed disks.

- Ultra-disk: It is best for a high IO workload. For example, a critical production database with low latency.
- Premium SSD: It provides high throughput and low latency. It can satisfy the requirement for most of your database workload.
- Standard SSD: It is designed for use with a dev-test workload that requires less predictable latency.
- Standard HDD: It is suitable for backups. It provides a low throughput and IOPS.

In the following table, you compare these disk performance, max size, throughput and IOPS.

Detail	**Ultra disk**	**Premium SSD**	**Standard SSD**	**Standard HDD**
Disk type	SSD	SSD	SSD	HDD
Scenario	IO-intensive workloads such as SAP HANA, top tier databases (for example, SQL, Oracle), and other transaction-heavy workloads.	Production and performance sensitive workloads	Web servers, lightly used enterprise applications and dev/test	Backup, non-critical, infrequent access
Max disk size	65,536 gibibyte (GiB)	32,767 GiB	32,767 GiB	32,767 GiB
Max throughput	2,000 MB/s	900 MB/s	750 MB/s	500 MB/s
Max IOPS	160,000	20,000	6,000	2,000

You can refer **https://docs.microsoft.com/en-us/azure/virtual-machines/disks-types** for more details on IaaS VMs disk type.

SQL Server storage configuration best practices

For a SQL Server on Azure VM, Microsoft recommends the following best practices.

- You should create separate volumes for data files and transaction log files.

- Enable read caching for data file volume.
- Do not enable caching on the drive having transaction log files.
- You should plan disk type according to your workload IOPS. It is recommended to take additional provision while planning for disk storage.
- For the TempDB database, use the locally attached SSD.
- Use instance file initialization for reducing the file growth issues.
- Use a proportional fill mechanism for distributing data in multiple data files. In this mechanism, we specify the same initial size and auto-growth for data files. For example, suppose you have two data files with equal initial size and auto-growth. In this case, SQL Server evenly distributes data into both the files.
- Use TempDB best-practice configurations.
    - Create multiple TempDB data files. The thumb rule uses a single data file per core with a max of 8 data files. If TempDB still has contention issues, you can increase it by 4.
    - All Data files must have the same initial size and auto-growth.
    - You should pre-allocate space for TempDB files by setting the file size to a value large enough to accommodate your workload.

In the IaaS virtual machine configuration, you can use SQL Server templates for deploying VM with SQL Server. In the configuration, navigate to SQL Server Settings and Storage configuration. In the configure storage page, you get an option to choose storage optimization.

- General
- Transactional processing
- Data warehousing

You can configure the required disk type, IOPS as needed.

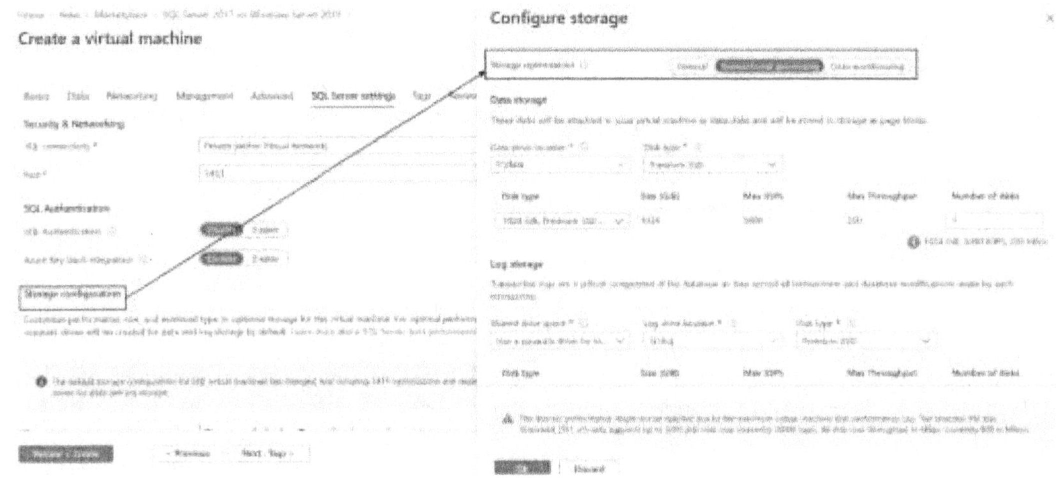

It stores the TempDB into the local SSD drive as per the best practice shared.

TempDb storage

The tempDb system database is a global resource that is available to all users connected to the instance of SQL Server. It is used to store temporary user objects and internal objects created by the database engine.

Shared drive space * ⓘ — Use local SSD drive

TempDb drive location * ⓘ — D:\tempDb

Refer to Performance guidelines for SQL Server on Azure Virtual Machines (**https://docs.microsoft.com/en-us/azure/azure-sql/virtual-machines/windows/performance-guidelines-best-practices**) for optimizing SQL Server performance in Azure VM.

SQL Server 2019 Memory-Optimized TempDB Metadata

SQL Server 2019 introduces a new memory-optimized TempDB metadata for resolving the commonly faced performance issues due to TempDB contention. It is launched under the In-Memory optimized Database feature category of SQL Server.

Note: This feature requires SQL Service restart to take effect.

You can enable the Memory-Optimized TempDB Metadata using the following query.

```
ALTER SERVER CONFIGURATION SET MEMORY_OPTIMIZED TEMPDB_METADATA = ON;
```

You can refer to **https://docs.microsoft.com/en-us/sql/relational-databases/databases/tempdb-database?view=sql-server-ver15** for detailed information on SQL Server 2019 Memory-Optimized TempDB Metadata.

Summary

Azure PaaS and Iaas database solution has in-built monitoring solutions to track database performance, resource usage, intelligent insight reports, query reports, extended events, automatic tuning, diagnostic settings, query performance insights. These solutions help you to monitor and optimize Azure Data platform solutions.

Chapter 8 Optimize query performance in SQL Server

Database performance depends on the various factors such as optimal resources- Compute, Storage, Memory, network bandwidth, database configuration, and optimized query. The optimal query defines an acceptable query performance with appropriate resources. Indeed, we do not want to merely increase compute resources and increase the cost of handling a database instead of focusing on query performance tuning.

You should evaluate the following fundamental questions before starting query development.

- How big is the query result set?
    - The query returns a few rows, a million rows, a billion rows or more than that.
- Does the query use static or dynamic parameters?
- Does the query handle NULL or invalid inputs?
- What is the frequency of query execution?
    - The possible values can be daily, weekly, monthly, yearly, or recurring – every second, minute, hour, or one.
- What is an acceptable query performance level?
    - You should be aware of the expected query performance level and the baseline of query execution duration. Sometimes, a query execution within a few seconds is an acceptable baseline; however, we often require less than a second.
- Do you require sorted data?
    - Many times, we don't require sort data based on a specific column or condition.
- Handling NULL values

The query performance optimization is independent of the database platform, whether on-premise SQL Server, SQL Server on Azure VM, Azure SQL database, or Azure SQL Managed Instance.

This chapter will get insights into useful ways to optimise a query performance with the following topics.

- Overview of the SQL Server execution plan and its different forms
- Lightweight query profiling

- An identifying problem in the execution plans
- SARGability
- Parameter sniffing
- Columnstore Index and In-memory OLTP
- Dynamic management views
- TempDB configuration for Azure SQL Database and Managed instance
- Query store

Execution Plans

In layman terms, users submit the T-SQL query and wait for the SQL Server engine to retrieve the required output. However, the query has to go through many phases between the user's query submission and getting a query output.

Query lifecycle

Once you submit the query to SQL Server, it goes through the following stages.

- **Parsing**:

In this first stage of query processing, SQL Server performs the following tasks.

  - It validates T-SQL statement syntax.
  - It breaks a T-SQL statement into smaller logical units such as expressions, keywords, operators, identifiers.
  - It returns a parsing tree that is an internal representation of the query steps.

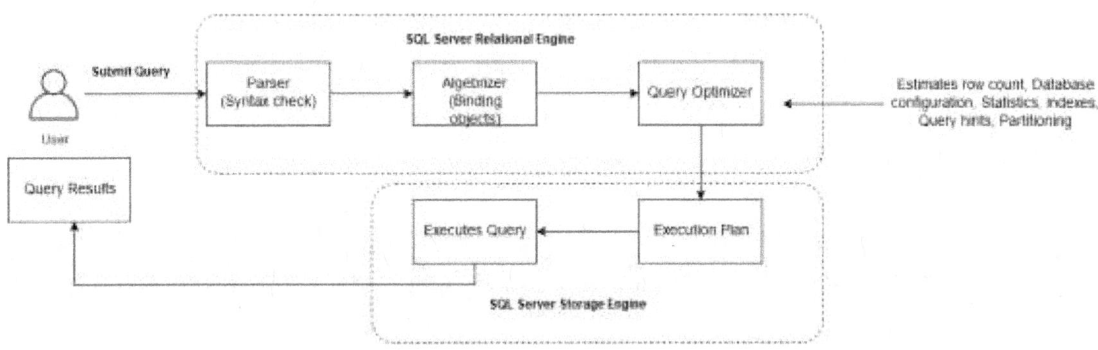

- **Algebrizer:**

The algebrizer receives the parse tree and performs the following operations.

  - It verifies objects, column names the existence of the objects in the target database. In case the object does not exist in the specified database, and it returns an error.
  - It validates all data types used in the T-SQL statement.
  - It validates the user permissions to execute the corresponding statement.

- **Query Optimizer:**

The Query optimizer receives the query processor tree as an input, and it creates the cost-optimized execution plan. To prepare the cost-optimized execution plan, SQL Server considers different execution methods based on indexes, statistics, resource consumption, estimated rows, configuration parameters such as MAXDOP, query hints. It assigns a cost to each operator and sums all operators together for an optimized query plan.

The query optimizer process is expensive; therefore, SQL Server stores these execution plans in the plan cache memory storage for future query references. Once a user submits the query, SQL Server first looks in the plan cache for an existing query plan. If it does not find any suitable plan, it starts the query optimizer process for a new execution plan.

- **Execution**

In this step, SQL Server follows the execution plan and coordinates with different operators, and with the storage engine for data retrieval.

Different format and types of the query execution plan

We can view a query execution plan in different formats.

Graphical execution plan

By default, SQL Server generates a graphical execution plan. It is a common, friendly and default format for viewing execution plans. Usually, DBA prefers the graphical plan because it represents all query operators, data flow in a friendly way. It gives more information for a specific operator if you hover the mouse over it.

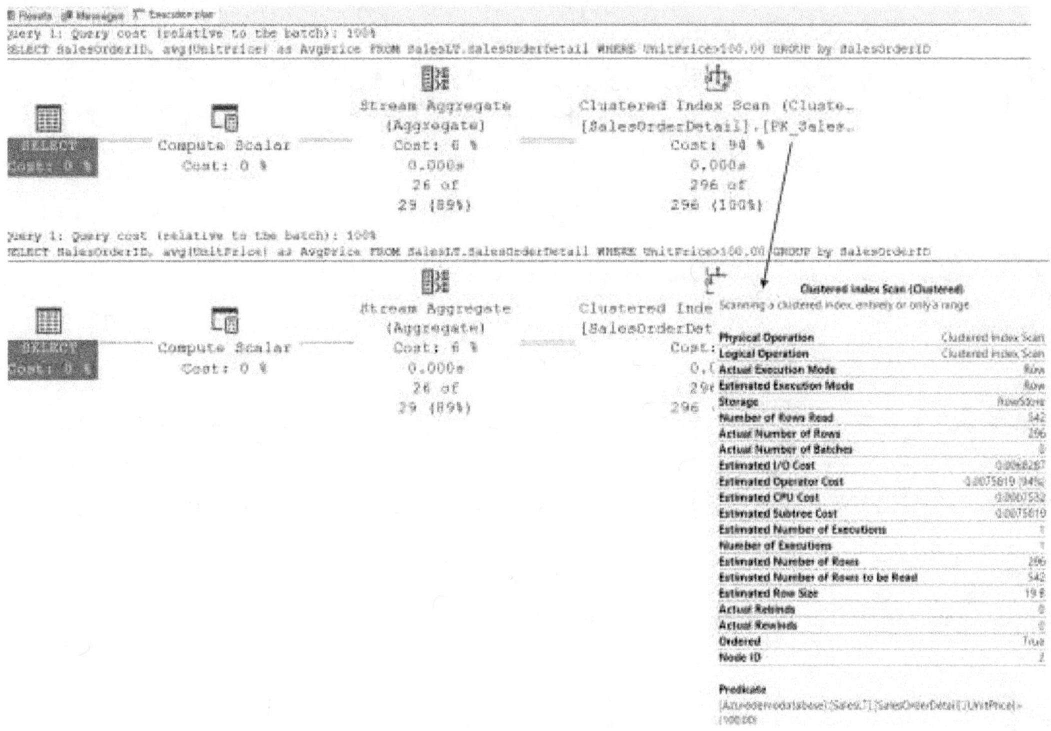

The thickness of the connecting line between operators gives the amount of data flow. The thicker line represents more data flow, while a thin line has a smaller number of rows shown in the execution plan.

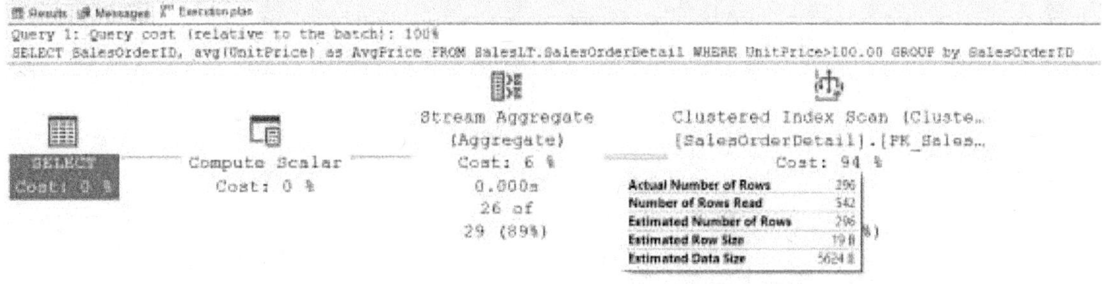

1.1.5 Text Format

The query text plan format gives information in a text format for all operators and their properties. It is difficult to understand these execution plans. Usually, DBA does not prefer it. To generate the execution plan in a text format, you can use the following statements.

- **SHOWPLAN_ALL**: It generates the estimated execution plan with full details.

```
SET SHOWPLAN_ALL ON
Go
SELECT SalesOrderID, avg(UnitPrice) as AvgPrice FROM SalesLT.SalesOrderDetail
WHERE UnitPrice>100.00
GROUP by SalesOrderID
```

	StmtText	StmtId	NodeId	Parent	PhysicalOp	LogicalOp	Argument
1	SELECT SalesOrderID, avg(UnitPrice) as AvgPrice FR...	1	1	0	NULL	NULL	1
2	|--Compute Scalar(DEFINE:([Expr1002]=CASE WHE...	1	2	1	Compute Scalar	Compute Scalar	DEFINE:([Expr1002]=CASE WHEN [Expr1007]
3	|--Stream Aggregate(GROUP BY:([Azuredemodata...	1	3	2	Stream Aggregate	Aggregate	GROUP BY:([Azuredemodatabase].[SalesLT].[
4	|--Clustered Index Scan(OBJECT:([Azuredemod...	1	4	3	Clustered Index Scan	Clustered Index Scan	OBJECT:([Azuredemodatabase].[SalesLT].[Sal

- **SHOWPLAN_TEXT**: It generates the estimated execution plan with limited details.

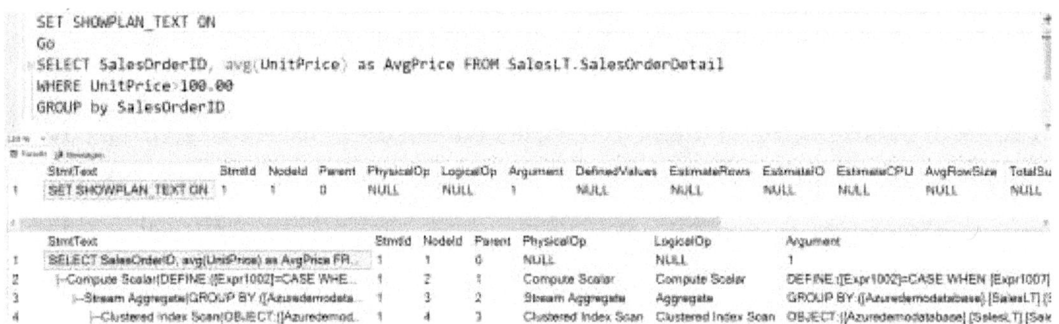

```
SET SHOWPLAN_TEXT ON
Go
SELECT SalesOrderID, avg(UnitPrice) as AvgPrice FROM SalesLT.SalesOrderDetail
WHERE UnitPrice>100.00
GROUP by SalesOrderID
```

	StmtText	StmtId	NodeId	Parent	PhysicalOp	LogicalOp	Argument	DefinedValues	EstimateRows	EstimateIO	EstimateCPU	AvgRowSize	TotalSu
1	SET SHOWPLAN_TEXT ON	1	1	0	NULL	NULL	1	NULL	NULL	NULL	NULL	NULL	NULL

	StmtText	StmtId	NodeId	Parent	PhysicalOp	LogicalOp	Argument
1	SELECT SalesOrderID, avg(UnitPrice) as AvgPrice FR...	1	1	0	NULL	NULL	1
2	|--Compute Scalar(DEFINE:([Expr1002]=CASE WHE...	1	2	1	Compute Scalar	Compute Scalar	DEFINE:([Expr1002]=CASE WHEN [Expr1007]
3	|--Stream Aggregate(GROUP BY:([Azuredemodata...	1	3	2	Stream Aggregate	Aggregate	GROUP BY:([Azuredemodatabase].[SalesLT].[
4	|--Clustered Index Scan(OBJECT:([Azuredemod...	1	4	3	Clustered Index Scan	Clustered Index Scan	OBJECT:([Azuredemodatabase].[SalesLT].[Sal

- **STATISTICS PROFILE**: It generates an actual query execution plan with complete details of execution.

```
SET SHOWPLAN_TEXT ON
Go
SELECT SalesOrderID, avg(UnitPrice) as AvgPrice FROM SalesLT.SalesOrderDetail
WHERE UnitPrice>100.00
GROUP by SalesOrderID
```

	StmtText	StmtId	NodeId	Parent	PhysicalOp	LogicalOp	Argument	DefinedValues	EstimateRows	EstimateIO	EstimateCPU	AvgRowSize	TotalSu
1	SET SHOWPLAN_TEXT ON	1	1	0	NULL	NULL	1	NULL	NULL	NULL	NULL	NULL	NULL

	StmtText	StmtId	NodeId	Parent	PhysicalOp	LogicalOp	Argument
1	SELECT SalesOrderID, avg(UnitPrice) as AvgPrice FR...	1	1	0	NULL	NULL	1
2	|--Compute Scalar(DEFINE:([Expr1002]=CASE WHE...	1	2	1	Compute Scalar	Compute Scalar	DEFINE:([Expr1002]=CASE WHEN [Expr1007]
3	|--Stream Aggregate(GROUP BY:([Azuredemodata...	1	3	2	Stream Aggregate	Aggregate	GROUP BY:([Azuredemodatabase].[SalesLT].[
4	|--Clustered Index Scan(OBJECT:([Azuredemod...	1	4	3	Clustered Index Scan	Clustered Index Scan	OBJECT:([Azuredemodatabase].[SalesLT].[Sal

1.1.5.1 XML Format

SQL Server generates an XML structure query execution plan. It provides all detailed information and is used by experienced DBA for troubleshooting purposes. Similar to the text format, we have the following options for an XML based execution plan.

- SHOWPLAN_XML: It displays an estimated execution plan in an XML format.

- STATISTICS XML: It displays an actual execution plan in an XML format

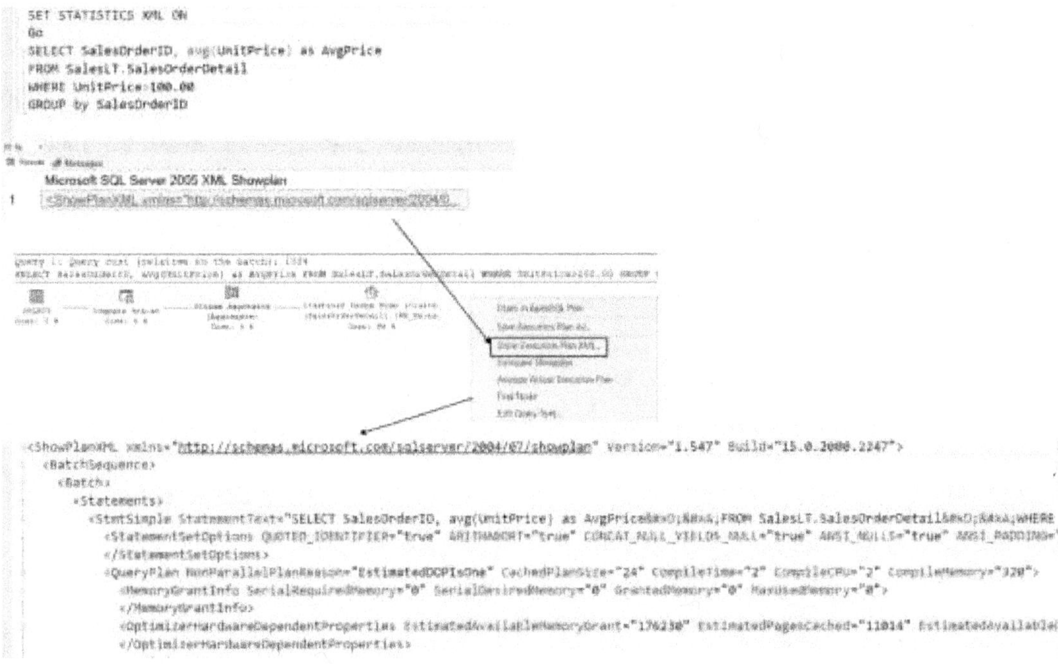

1.1.6 Types of an execution plan

SQL Server provides types of the query execution plan for investigating performance issues. These options are as below:

- Estimated execution plan
- Actual execution plan
- Live query statistics

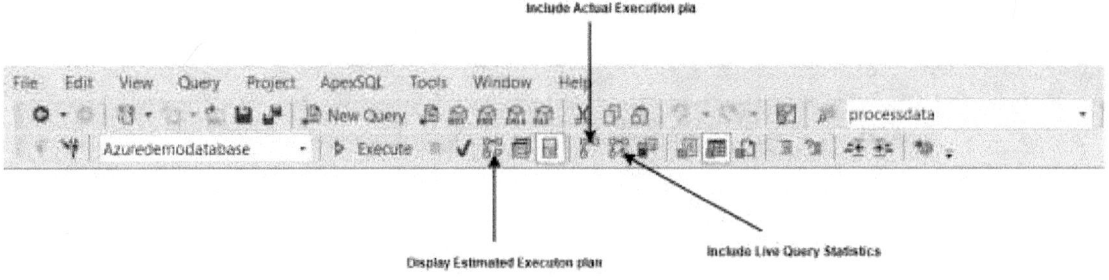

Estimated execution plan

In the estimated execution plan, SQL Server does not execute the T-SQL script. It generates an execution plan based on the available statistics during query compilation.

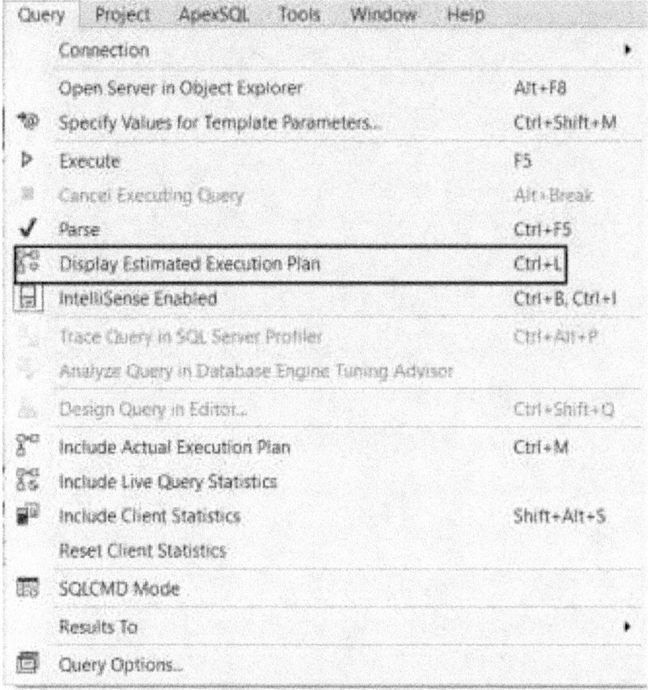

Note:

- You can also use Keyboard shortcut CTRL + L for generating an estimated execution plan.
- It generates a query plan immediately without query execution.

Actual execution plan

In the actual execution plan, SQL Server executes the query, and you get an actual plan used to run the query and fetch results. It is a preferred method for troubleshooting any performance issues. In most cases, the estimated and actual plan looks similar. However, it might generate a different actual execution plan based on actual table data, statistics, data modification.

Note:

- You can also use Keyboard shortcut CTRL + M for generating an estimated execution plan.
- It is a toggle that enables actual execution plan configuration. It does not display the execution plan until you execute the query.

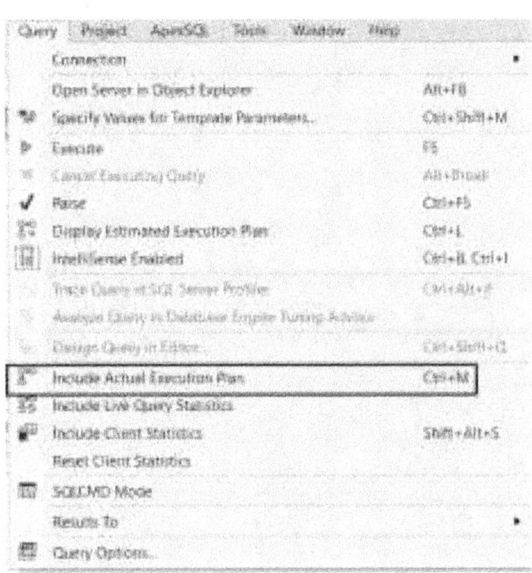

Live Query Statistics

The Live query statistics combine both estimated and actual execution plans. It displays an animated execution plan and shows query execution progress through different operators in the plan. SQL Server refreshes the live query statistics every second and displays them in an animated graphical format. In a long-running query, DBA waits for the query to finish and get an actual execution plan. Therefore, you can leverage live query statistics and monitor the query progress while it is still running.

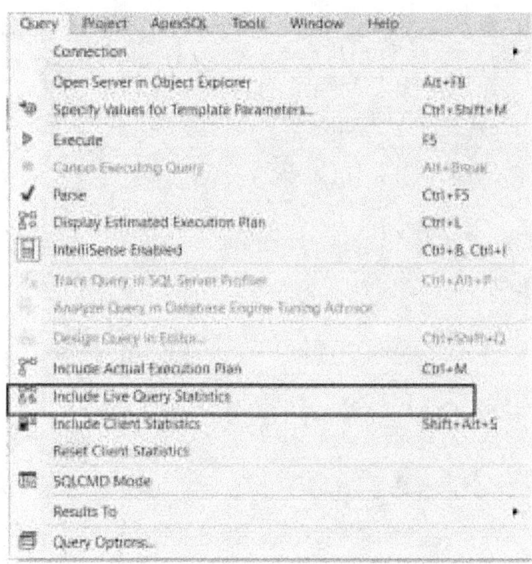

Note: You can view live query statistics only in graphical format.

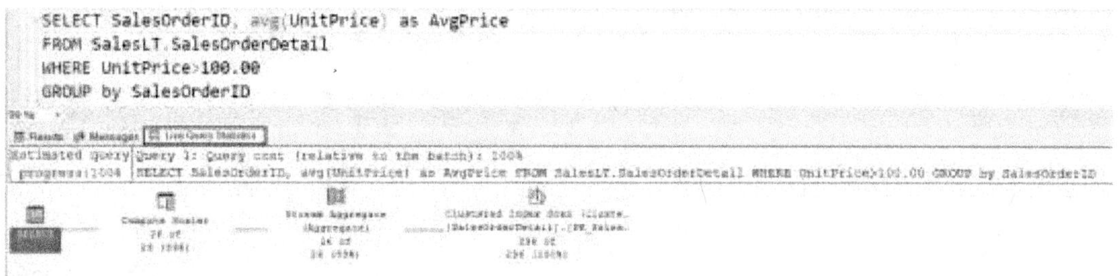

Read a graphical query execution plan

In this section, we start reading a graphical query execution plan. The query plan has the following sections.

1. In the upper section, it gives the cost of the query relatively to the overall batch.
2. It states the submitted query.

3. In case of the long question, you can click on a dotted square, and it gives the complete query as shown below.

```
/*
This query text was retrieved from showplan XML, and may be truncated.
*/

SELECT SalesOrderID, avg(UnitPrice) as AvgPrice
FROM SalesLT.SalesOrderDetail
WHERE UnitPrice>100.00
GROUP by SalesOrderID
```

4. The arrow represents the data flow between the operators. You get the actual and estimated number of rows by pointing the mouse over the arrow.

   a. In the below image, the thick line shows 296 rows while the thin row represents 26 rows.

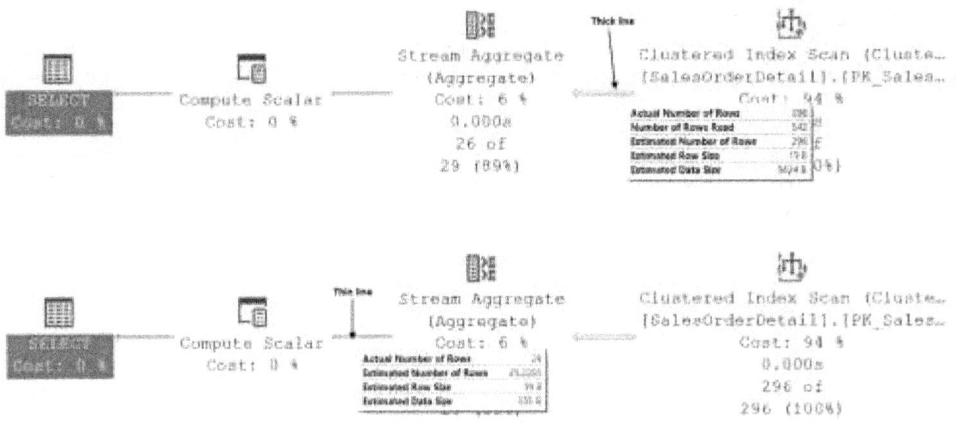

5. The graphical execution plan gives the percentage cost of each operator relative to the overall cost. For example, in the below image, the clustered scan index has 94% of comparative cost.

6. At a high-level, a graphical plan shows operator percentage cost, number of affected rows. To get more details, hover the mouse pointer over a specific operator. For example, it gives CPU cost, number of executions, IO cost, execution mode, physical and logical operation.

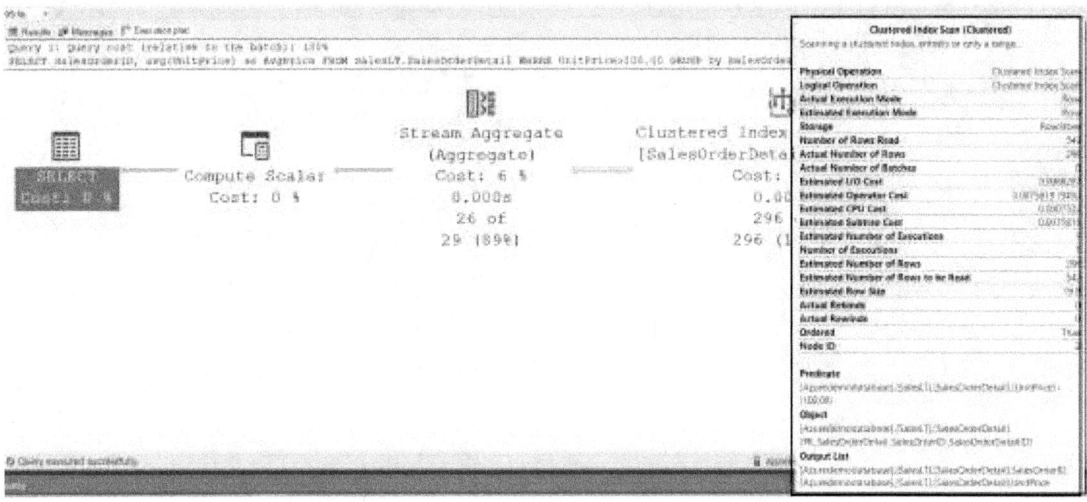

7. There is a difference in the information logged in the actual and estimated execution plan.

a. The actual execution plan gives both actual and estimated statistics information.

b. The estimated execution plan shows only the estimated stats.

c. If there is a difference between the estimated and actual statistics, you should review and update your index statistics.

Clustered Index Scan (Clustered)

Scanning a clustered index, entirely or only a range.

Physical Operation	Clustered Index Scan
Logical Operation	Clustered Index Scan
Estimated Execution Mode	Row
Storage	RowStore
Estimated Operator Cost	0.0075819 (94%)
Estimated I/O Cost	0.0068287
Estimated Subtree Cost	0.0075819
Estimated CPU Cost	0.0007532
Estimated Number of Executions	1
Estimated Number of Rows	296
Estimated Number of Rows to be Read	542
Estimated Row Size	19 B
Ordered	True
Node ID	2

Predicate
[Azuredemodatabase].[SalesLT].[SalesOrderDetail].[UnitPrice]>(100.00)
Object
[Azuredemodatabase].[SalesLT].[SalesOrderDetail].[PK_SalesOrderDetail_SalesOrderID_SalesOrderDetailID]
Output List
[Azuredemodatabase].[SalesLT].[SalesOrderDetail].SalesOrderID, [Azuredemodatabase].[SalesLT].[SalesOrderDetail].UnitPrice

Estimated execution plan

Clustered Index Scan (Clustered)

Scanning a clustered index, entirely or only a range.

Physical Operation	Clustered Index Scan
Logical Operation	Clustered Index Scan
Actual Execution Mode	Row
Estimated Execution Mode	Row
Storage	RowStore
Number of Rows Read	542
Actual Number of Rows	296
Actual Number of Batches	0
Estimated I/O Cost	0.0068287
Estimated Operator Cost	0.0075819 (94%)
Estimated CPU Cost	0.0007532
Estimated Subtree Cost	0.0075819
Estimated Number of Executions	1
Number of Executions	1
Estimated Number of Rows	296
Estimated Number of Rows to be Read	542
Estimated Row Size	19 B
Actual Rebinds	0
Actual Rewinds	0
Ordered	True
Node ID	2

Predicate
[Azuredemodatabase].[SalesLT].[SalesOrderDetail].[UnitPrice]>(100.00)
Object
[Azuredemodatabase].[SalesLT].[SalesOrderDetail].[PK_SalesOrderDetail_SalesOrderID_SalesOrderDetailID]
Output List
[Azuredemodatabase].[SalesLT].[SalesOrderDetail].SalesOrderID, [Azuredemodatabase].[SalesLT].[SalesOrderDetail].UnitPrice

Actual execution plan

8. You can still get more information from the operator properties page. Right-click on the operator and choose properties. You can also use shortcut key F4, and it displays the operator property. There is some expandable property (with + sign). You can expand it to get extra information.

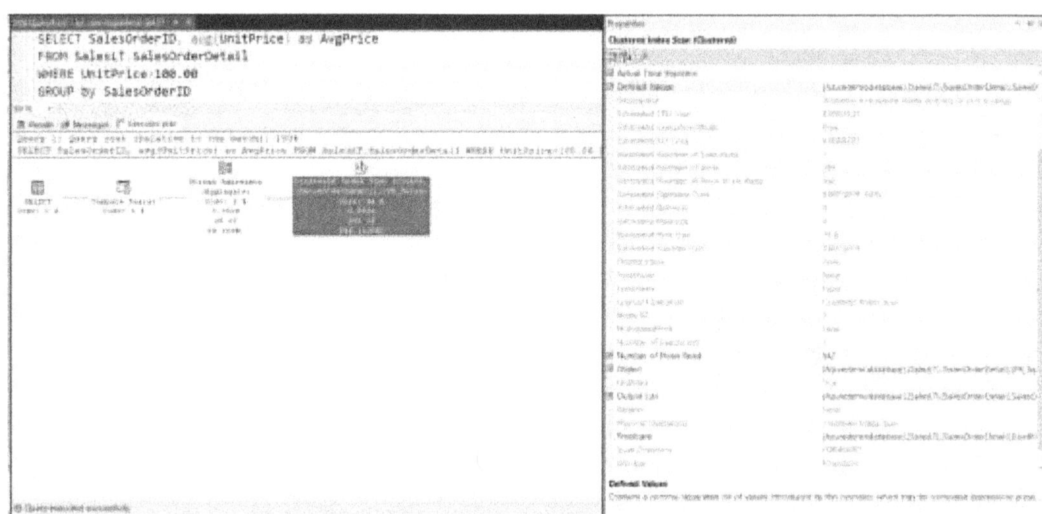

You can refer to Showplan Logical and Physical Operators (**https://docs.microsoft.com/en-us/sql/relational-databases/showplan-logical-and-physical-operators-reference?view=sql-server-ver15**) Reference for details on execution plan operators.

Lightweight query profiling

SQL Server enables DBAs to get query runtime information on the execution plan. As per the best practice, you should use the actual query plan for troubleshooting a performance issue. The live query statistics give real-time insights into the query progress using the run-time statistics such as the number of affected rows, elapsed time, and data flow from one operator to another. These live query statistics are useful for long-running transactions troubleshooting. The live resource monitoring might impact SQL Server resource utilization and introduce issues such as high CPU. It is not a desirable thing, especially if you are already investigating a performance issue.

Microsoft introduced a lightweight query execution statistics-profiling infrastructure that improves live statistics monitoring with minimal impact on SQL Server resources.

lightweight query execution statistics profiling infrastructure – V1

In this lightweight query execution, SQL Server collects the row count and IO usage information. The IO usage refers to the logical and physical read-writes performed by the database engine. It has an additional extended event query_thread_profile, and it gives execution statistics insights for each node and thread.

Note: This method was supported on SQL Server 2014 SP2 to SQL Server 2016.

Lightweight query execution statistics profiling infrastructure – V2

In the SQL Server 2016 SP1, Microsoft revised the lightweight query execution statistics for providing minimal overhead. It requires the global trace flag 7412 or query hint QUERY_PLAN_PROFILE to enable a lightweight profile at a query level.

Note: This method was supported on SQL Server 2016 SP1 to SQL Server 2017.

Lightweight query execution statistics profiling infrastructure – V3

In this revised V3 version of lightweight profiling, SQL Server collects row count data for all executions. It also has a new DMF sys.dm_exec_query_plan that returns the last query plan statistics (actual execution plan).

Note:

The SQL Server 2019, Azure SQL database and Azure SQL Managed Instance:

- It supports lightweight profiling V3.
- By default, lightweight profiling is enabled.
- You can disable lightweight profiling at a database level using the database scoped configuration.

To check the existing configuration for lightweight profiling, use the following query.

SELECT Name, is_value_default, value FROM sys.database_scoped_configurations

WHERE name='LIGHTWEIGHT_QUERY_PROFILING';

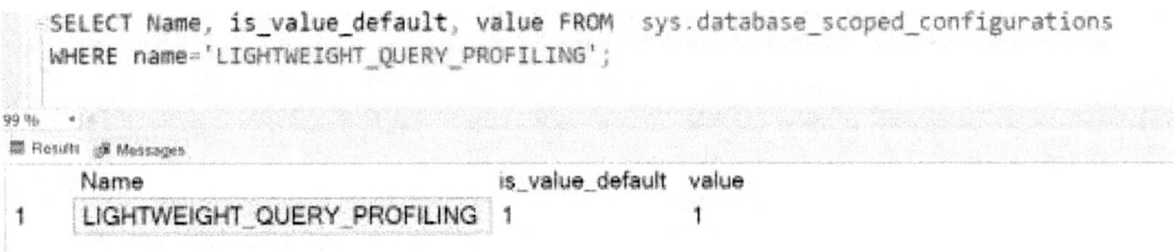

```
SELECT Name, is_value_default, value FROM  sys.database_scoped_configurations
WHERE name='LIGHTWEIGHT_QUERY_PROFILING';
```

99 %

Results Messages

	Name	is_value_default	value
1	LIGHTWEIGHT_QUERY_PROFILING	1	1

You can use the ALTER DATABASE statement to disable lightweight query profiling at the database level.

ALTER DATABASE SCOPED CONFIGURATION SET LIGHTWEIGHT_QUERY_PROFILING = OFF;

Go

SELECT Name, is_value_default, value FROM sys.database_scoped_configurations

WHERE name='LIGHTWEIGHT_QUERY_PROFILING';

```
ALTER DATABASE SCOPED CONFIGURATION SET LIGHTWEIGHT_QUERY_PROFILING = OFF;
Go
SELECT Name, is_value_default, value FROM  sys.database_scoped_configurations
WHERE name='LIGHTWEIGHT_QUERY_PROFILING';
```

	Name	is_value_default	value
1	LIGHTWEIGHT_QUERY_PROFILING	0	0

If the lightweight query profiling is disabled, you can leverage query hint QUERY_PLAN_PROFILE for enabling it at the query level.

Select SalesOrderID, avg(UnitPrice) as AvgPrice

FROM SalesLT.SalesOrderDetail

Where UnitPrice>100.0

GROUP BY SalesOrderID

OPTION(USE HINT ('QUERY_PLAN_PROFILE'))

The last query plans stats

SQL Server 2019 and Azure databases have a new DMF sys.dm_exec_query_plan_stats. It returns the last actual query execution plan.

To use this DMF, you need to enable trace flag 2451 at the instance level. It works with the on-premise SQL Server, and Azure managed instances. However, you cannot enable the trace flag at the server level in Azure SQL Database. Therefore, you can utilize a database scoped configuration.

In the below T-SQL, we do the following tasks.

- Enable LAST_QUERY_PLAN_STATS database scoped configuration for Azure SQL database.
- Execute a select statement
- Retrieve the last known actual execution plan using the DMF sys.dm_exec_query_plan_stats.

ALTER DATABASE SCOPED CONFIGURATION SET LAST_QUERY_PLAN_STATS = ON;

Go

Select SalesOrderID, avg(UnitPrice) as AvgPrice

FROM SalesLT.SalesOrderDetail

Where UnitPrice>100.0

GROUP BY SalesOrderID

Go

SELECT text, query_plan

FROM sys.dm_exec_cached_plans AS cp

CROSS APPLY sys.dm_exec_sql_text(plan_handle) AS st

CROSS APPLY sys.dm_exec_query_plan_stats(plan_handle) AS qps

where st.text like 'Select Sales%'

It returns an XML format execution plan.

```
ALTER DATABASE SCOPED CONFIGURATION SET LAST_QUERY_PLAN_STATS = ON;
Go
Select SalesOrderID, avg(UnitPrice) as AvgPrice
FROM SalesLT.SalesOrderDetail
Where UnitPrice>100.0
GROUP BY SalesOrderID
Go
SELECT text, query_plan
FROM sys.dm_exec_cached_plans AS cp
CROSS APPLY sys.dm_exec_sql_text(plan_handle) AS st
CROSS APPLY sys.dm_exec_query_plan_stats(plan_handle) AS qps
where st.text like 'Select Sales%'
```

	SalesOrderID	AvgPrice
1	71774	356.898
2	71780	455.5052

	text	query_plan
1	Select SalesOrderID, avg(UnitPrice) as AvgPrice ...	<ShowPlanXML xmlns="http://schemas.microsoft.com/sqlserver/2004/07/showplan" Version="1.547" Build...

Click on the hyperlink, and you get a graphical execution plan, as shown below.

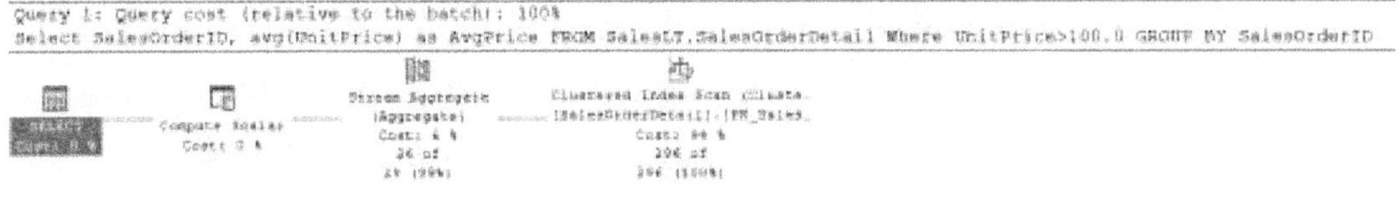

Identify problem areas in execution plans

There is not a direct way of identifying issues using the SQL Server execution plans. However, it has few general signs in the SQL Execution Plan that could indicate potentially harmful performance spots for executed T-SQL statements.

Table scan Vs Index scan Vs Index seek

The table scan refers to the heap tables. A heap table does not have any clustered index. In SQL Server, the clustered index sorts data physically using the cluster key. It is recommended to have a clustered index defined on each table.

For example, suppose you have a large table with million rows in it. The table scan operator needs to go through all rows physically. It might consume many SQL resources and give performance issues such as high CPU, memory, and blocking.

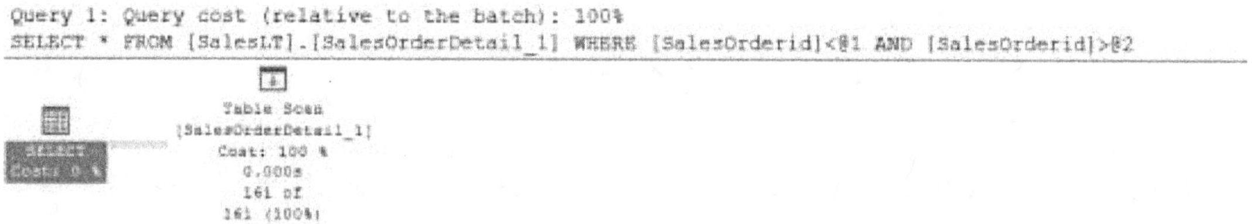

Once you define a clustered index on the table, it uses the clustered index scan instead of a table scan. In the clustered index scan, SQL Server retrieves data using the clustered index key.

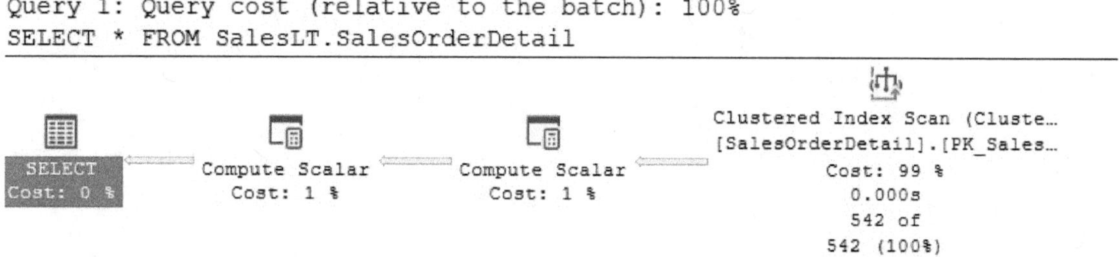

Suppose you want to retrieve specific rows from the table from a table with million rows. It is not an excellent idea to read all pages and then get a particular row from the table. Therefore, the clustered index seek is considered a useful performance indicator. It looks for corresponding pages satisfying the query and returns results to the user.

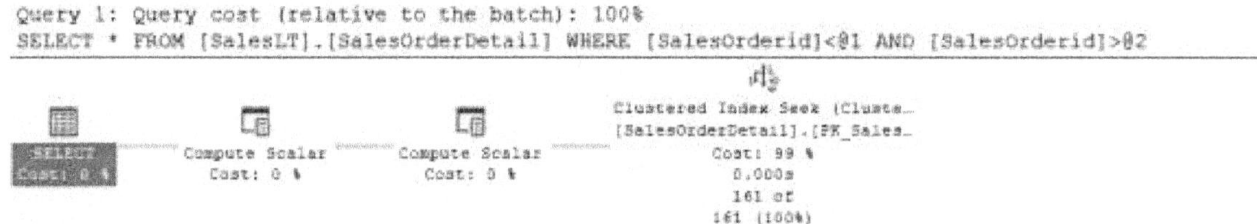

Note: Avoid using Select (*) in a query and use specific column names for data retrieval.

RID Lookup and Key Lookup

You should also look for the RID look and Key lookup in the execution plan for troubleshooting performance issues. This lookup occurs when the index doesn't satisfy query requirements, and it uses the clustered index or heap for fetching additional data.

- RID lookup: RID lookup occurs if the underlying table does not have a clustered index. You can eliminate this lookup by defining a clustered index on an appropriate column as the clustered index key.
- Key lookup: The key lookup uses the clustered index key for data retrieval. You can look for a non-clustered index for removing the key lookup.

Note: Key lookup does not always indicate performance issues. You can review your existing non-clustered index and consider adding a column in it or create a new non-clustered index if required.

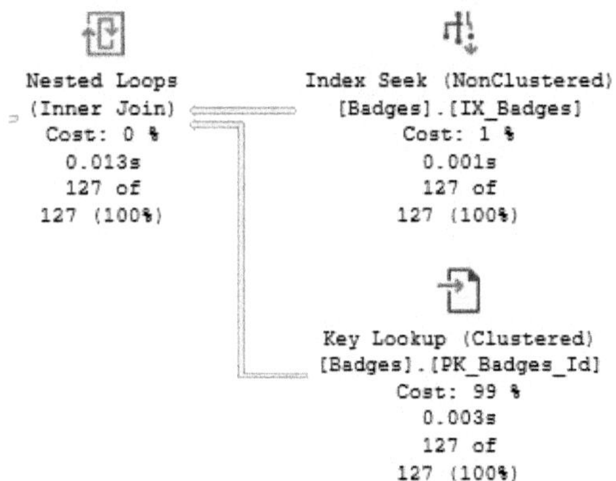

Sort operator

The sort operator put data in a specific descending or ascending order that might be a performance indicator. For example, in the following execution plan, the sort operator cost is 76% in the overall batch.

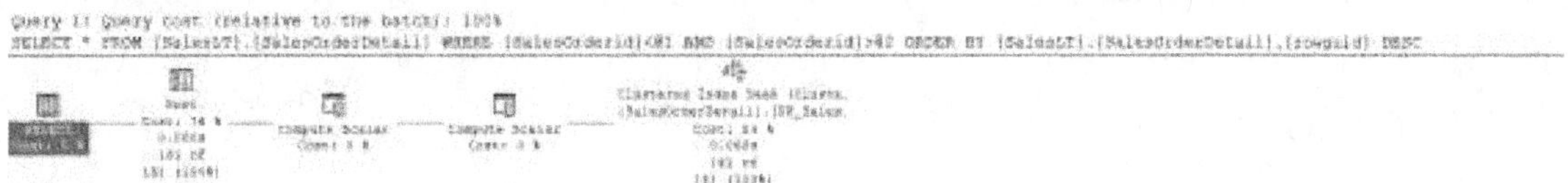

Sometimes, you also get a warning message in the sort operator – it needs to write data in TempDB for the complex queries.

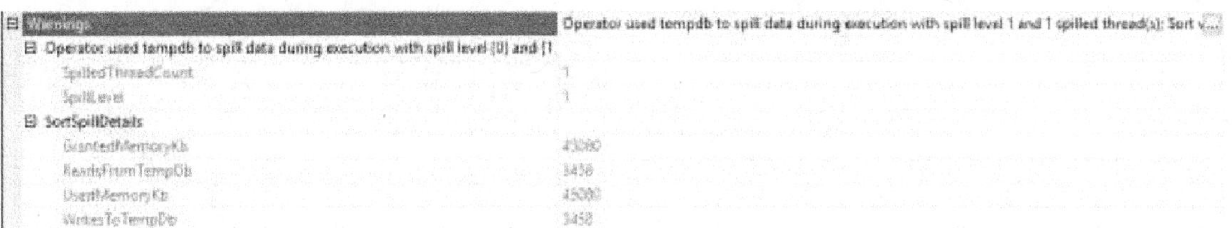

Therefore, as per best practice, if you require data sorted in a specific way, write the T-SQL in such a way that it performs the sort on the least number of rows.

Azure SQL Database and Azure SQL managed instance supports intelligent query processing for effective feedback from the last query executions. We already covered this in Chapter 7.

Parallelism

SQL Server uses parallelism for processing queries asynchronously on multiple CPUs. Usually, it is an excellent way to use all your compute resources. However, it might cause an issue if all queries start utilizing parallelism. In that case, your queries might need to wait for CPU, or it can cause worker thread exhaustion. It also puts an overhead where SQL Server has to divide chunks and rejoin them from the multiple CPU threads.

You should consider reviewing the cost threshold for parallelism and max degree of parallelism for tuning parallelism.

Note: Do not play with these configurations in a production instance. You need to review, test and change configuration accordingly.

Warnings

You should not ignore the warning in the execution plan. Query optimizer gives a warning (yellow exclamation mark) for the operators. For example, warnings related to implicit conversion, TempDB spill to disk, Memory grant warnings.

Inaccurate Row Estimates

Usually, the estimated and actual number of rows should be similar. It highlights that the statistics are up-to-date, and the query optimizer could use the cost-optimized execution plan. If these vary with a large number, you should review index statistics or review parameter sniffing where a procedure works fine for a specific value but runs longer for another parameter.

Missing Index

Sometimes, SQL Server suggests an index that might improve query performance. These suggestions are known as the Missing index.

Do not blindly follow the missing index recommendation. It is based on query execution at a specific point in time. It does not consider existing indexes, or current workload. Therefore, always take it as a suggestion only. Review the indexing requirement for your overall workload, not for a specific query. If you create the missing index blindly, it might improve individual query performance, but it can have a negative impact on remaining query workloads.

SARGAbility

The sargable word concatenates – Search, Argument and able. It refers to the where clause predicate that can utilize query performance using an index. If the predicate is in the correct format, it is known as 'SARGs or Search Arguments. A non-sargable query might have a negative impact on query performance. The non-sargable query works similar to a table without any index. For a SARG query, the query optimizer evaluates a non-clustered index on the column that references the SEEK operation.

For example, in the below query, we want records from the customer table, whose name starts with the letter R.

The query optimizer decides to use an index scan for returning the matching data.

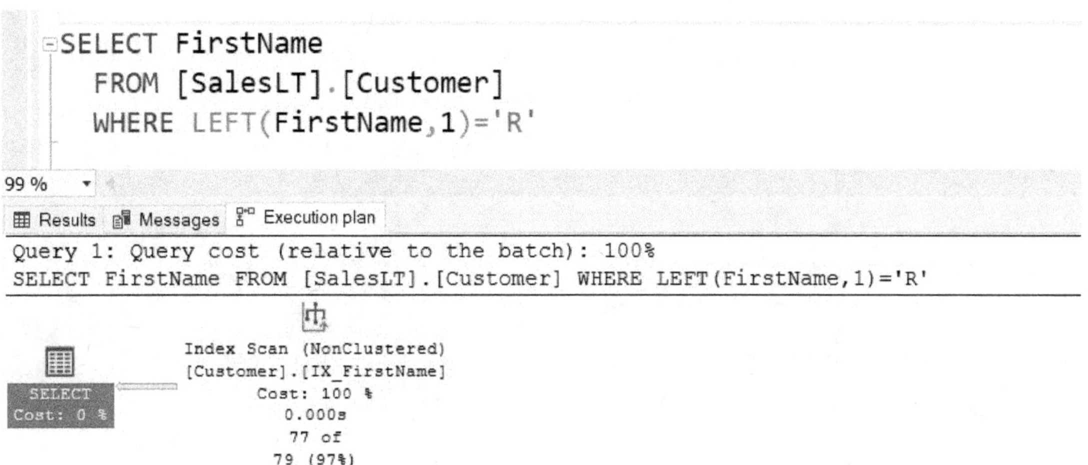

In the index scan property, look at the following values.

- Estimated number of rows to be read: 847
- Estimated number of rows: 79

Let’s modify the query. It uses an index seek instead of an index scan for a similar result set.

In the index seek property, look at the following values.

- Estimated number of rows to be read: 48
- Estimated number of rows: 48

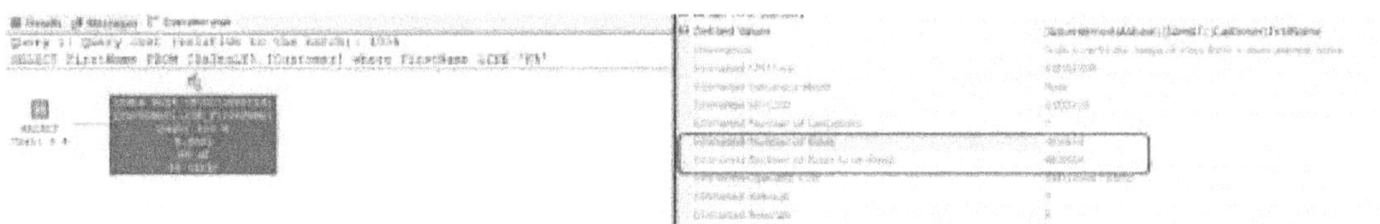

Similarly, look at the following non-sargable and sargable queries and compare their execution plans.

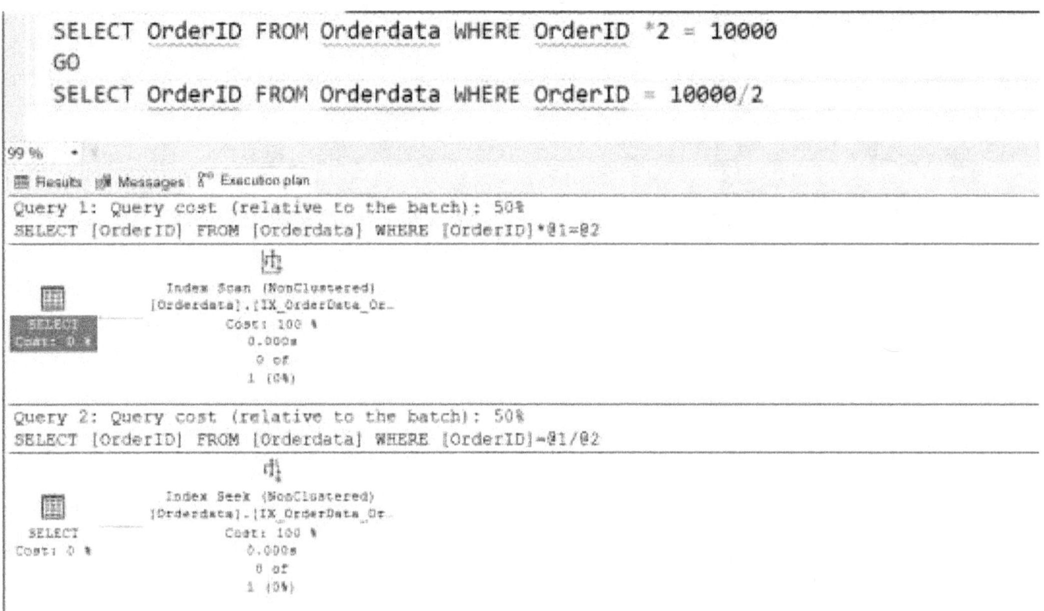

Let's look at an additional example of a sargable and non-sargable query with the data column. If we use a year() function, it ignores the non-clustered index; however, if we use a date filtering in where clause, it uses an index seek.

```
SELECT [Date] FROM Orderdata WHERE Year([Date]) = 2021

SELECT [Date] FROM Orderdata WHERE [Date] >= '01-01-2021' AND [Date] < '03-03-2021'
```

```
Query 1: Query cost (relative to the batch): 50%
SELECT [Date] FROM Orderdata WHERE Year([Date]) = 2021
```

```
Query 2: Query cost (relative to the batch): 50%
SELECT [Date] FROM [Orderdata] WHERE [Date]>=@1 AND [Date]<@2
```

Missing and out-of-date statistics

Statistics plays a vital role in preparing an optimized execution plan for all versions of SQL Server. By default, on-premise SQL Server, Azure SQL Database, and Azure SQL Managed Instances have enabled auto-update statistics.

The below screenshot shows the Azure SQL Database property for statistics.

- Auto-create statistics: True
- Auto-update statistics: True

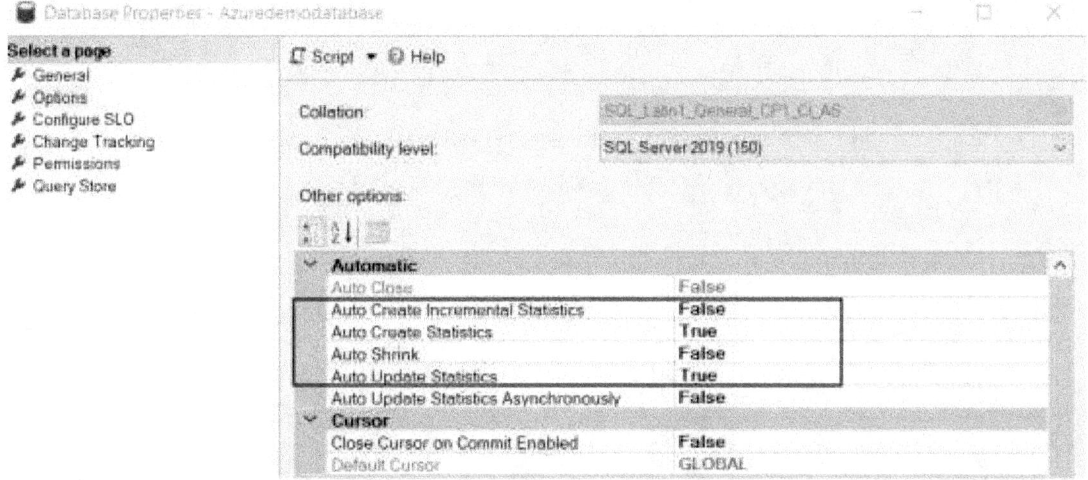

Parameter sniffing

Many times, DBA heard a complaint – My query was running fine, but suddenly it is running slow. One of the common reasons for it is parameter sniffing. In SQL Server, when we execute a parameterized query first time, SQL Server prepares a cost-optimized execution plan based on provided parameters. SQL Server stores the execution plan in cache and next time reuse it for further executions.

For example, we get two different execution plans for a stored procedure with a different parameter set. We get an index scan operator with a key lookup in the first execution plan, whereas the second execution plan uses the clustered index scan.

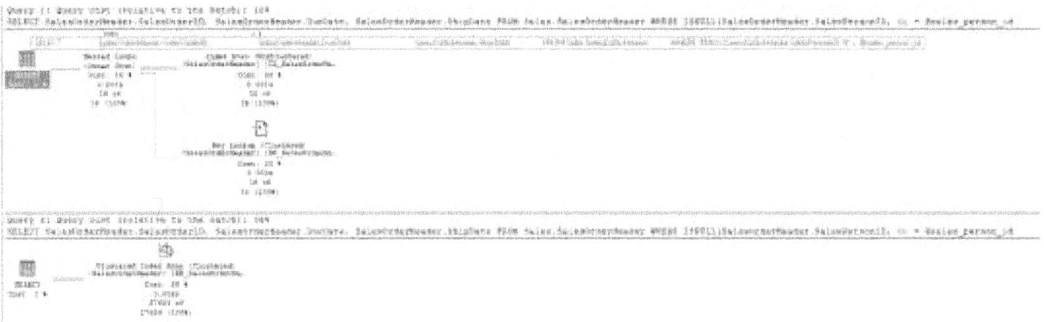

We can use the following options for parameter sniffing.

- OPTION(RECOMPILE)
- Dynamic SQL
- OPTIMIZE FOR UNKNOWN
- Disable Parameter Sniffing (Trace Flag 4136)
- Rewrite the stored procedure with improved business Logic

For an Azure SQL Database, you can use database scoped configuration for checking parameter sniffing configuration.

SELECT name, value FROM sys.database_scoped_configurations

where name= 'PARAMETER_SNIFFING'

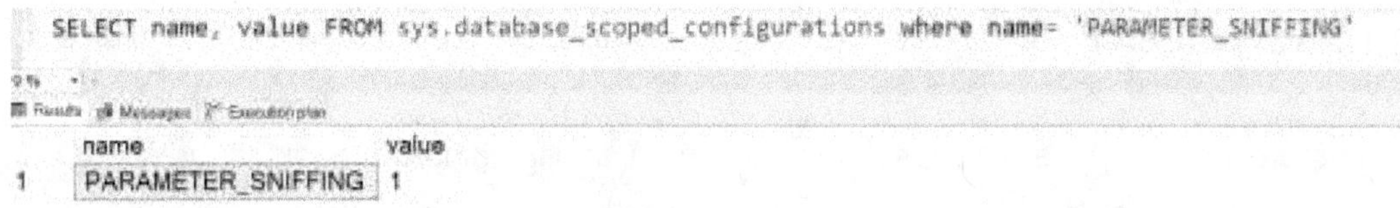

You can also check Azure database properties for parameter sniffing configuration at the database level.

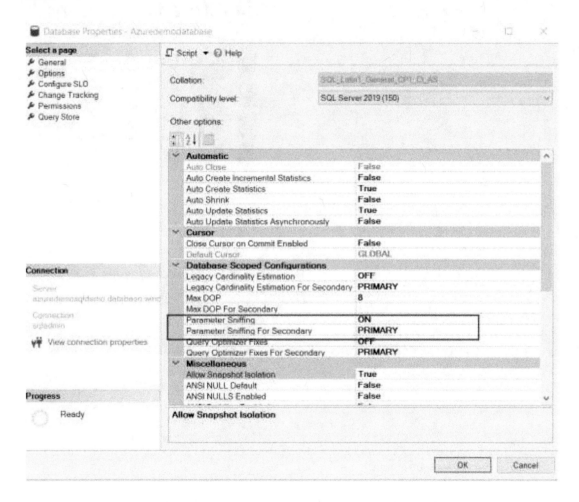

You can disable parameter sniffing configuring using the ALTER DATABASE statement.

ALTER DATABASE SCOPED CONFIGURATION SET PARAMETER_SNIFFING = OFF;

Note: You should not turn off parameter sniffing configuration blindly. It should be used by experienced DBA only.

Columnstore Index

The Columnstore index physically stores data in a column, and it logically organized them into row and column. By default, SQL Server stored data in a row store method. The column store is suitable for increasing the performance of analytical queries having massive row counts.

Data stored as rows

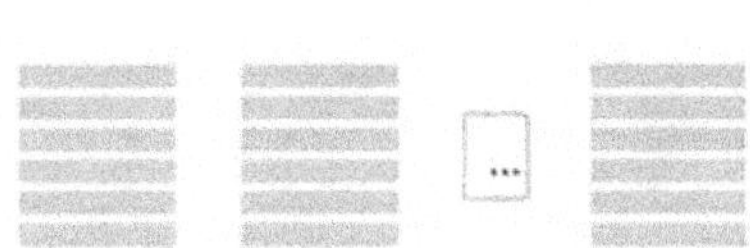

Data stored as columns

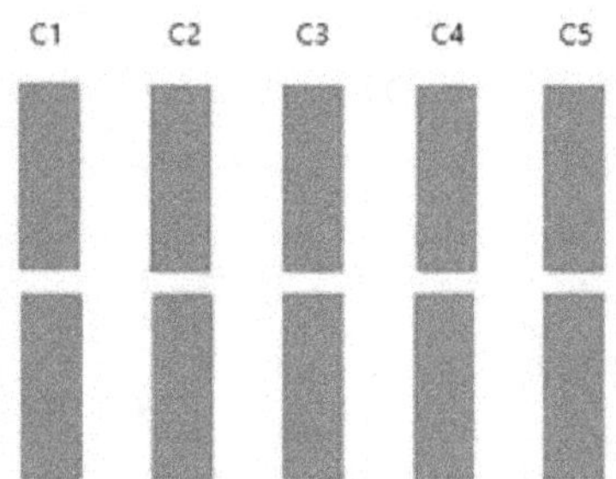

Note: The Columnstore index functionality is available for a premium service tier.

✓ **Query Performance:** According to the Microsoft documentation, the following table highlights performance differences in Rowstore and Columnstore index with different service tier.

Pricing Tier	With Rowstore	With Columnstore	Performance Gains
P1	30.6 secs	4.2 secs	14x
P15	19.5 secs	0.319 secs	60x

✓ **Storage requirement:**

Columnstore index requires less storage in comparison to the Rowstore index.

Number of Rows	Size Rowstore (MB)	Size columnstore (MB)	Savings
3626191	212 (PAGE compression)	120	1.8x
3626191	756 (NONE compression)	120MB	6.2x

✓ **Reduced IO:** Columnstore stores compressed data in the individual column. Usually, it provides compression around 10x. Therefore, it reduces the IO cost for your database significantly.

The Columnstore indexes are useful for large dimensional and fact tables in the data warehousing workloads. You can use a non-clustered Columnstore index on an OLTP workload.

You can follow **https://docs.microsoft.com/en-us/sql/relational-databases/indexes/columnstore-indexes-overview?view=sql-server-ver15** for a detailed information on Columnstore indexes.

Table Partitioning

The table partitioning uses a different partition scheme and functions to distribute data across multiple partitions in different filegroups. We can create multiple filegroups for on-premise SQL Server as well as Azure SQL Managed Instance. However, the Azure SQL database has a single primary filegroup. Therefore, all partitions get created in this primary filegroup.

The table partitioning can improve data loading, data archival, query performance, maintenance for a large table because SQL Server needs to process an individual partition instead of whole table data.

You can refer **https://docs.microsoft.com/en-us/sql/relational-databases/partitions/partitioned-tables-and-indexes?view=sql-server-ver15** for learning partition concepts.

In-Memory OLTP in Azure SQL Database and Managed instances

The memory-optimized table stores data in the cache(memory). These In-Memory OLTP provides excellent performance benefits for heavy transaction processing, data ingestion and transient data scenarios. It improves transaction throughput as well without the requirement to increase your pricing tier.

- High throughput and low latency

- High performance
- Zero or no lock escalation management is through an optimistic concurrency model, better concurrency management

Azure SQL Database and Managed instance support In-Memory OLTP

According to the Azure documentation, Azure SQL Database provided 75k transactions per seconds in a single database with 11x performance improvement over traditional tables with In-memory OLTP.

Pricing tier	TPS for In-Memory OLTP	TPS for traditional tables	Performance gain
P15	75,000	6,800	11X
P2	8,900	1,000	9X

All transactions are durable similar to a traditional database table. We can use the following objects for In-memory OLTP.

You can refer to **https://azure.microsoft.com/en-in/blog/in-memory-oltp-in-azure-sql-database/** for In--memory in Azure SQL Database.

You can refer to **https://docs.microsoft.com/en-us/sql/relational-databases/in-memory-oltp/in-memory-oltp-in-memory-optimization?view=sql-server-ver15** for a detailed explanation on In-Memory OLTP

Lab 9: Identify issues with a database design

In this lab session, DBA investigating the performance issue happening when users execute a query in the Azure database.

Execute the following T-SQL in the sample AdventureWorks2017 database and view the actual execution plan.

```
USE AdventureWorks2017;

SELECT BusinessEntityID, NationalIDNumber, LoginID, HireDate, JobTitle

FROM HumanResources.Employee

WHERE NationalIDNumber = 14417807;
```

In the select statement, you get a warning symbol. Hover the mouse pointer over the select operator, and it gives an implicit type conversion error.

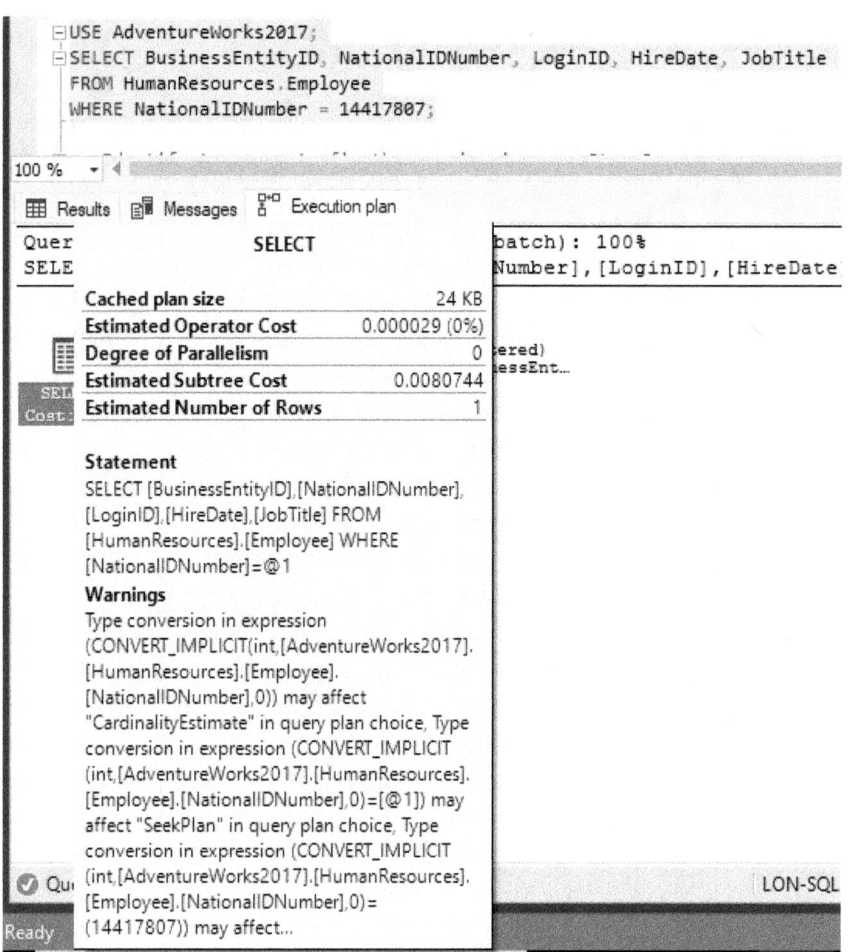

USE AdventureWorks2017;
SELECT BusinessEntityID, NationalIDNumber, LoginID, HireDate, JobTitle
FROM HumanResources.Employee
WHERE NationalIDNumber = 14417807;
100 %
Results
Messages
Execution plan
SELECT
Cached plan size 24 KB
Estimated Operator Cost 0.000029 (0%)
Degree of Parallelism 0
Estimated Subtree Cost 0.0080744
Estimated Number of Rows 1
Statement
SELECT [BusinessEntityID],[NationalIDNumber],[LoginID],[HireDate],[JobTitle] FROM [HumanResources].[Employee] WHERE [NationalIDNumber]=@1
Warnings
Type conversion in expression (CONVERT_IMPLICIT(int,[AdventureWorks2017].[HumanResources].[Employee].[NationalIDNumber],0)) may affect "CardinalityEstimate" in query plan choice, Type conversion in expression (CONVERT_IMPLICIT(int,[AdventureWorks2017].[HumanResources].[Employee].[NationalIDNumber],0)=[@1]) may affect "SeekPlan" in query plan choice, Type conversion in expression (CONVERT_IMPLICIT(int,[AdventureWorks2017].[HumanResources].[Employee].[NationalIDNumber],0)=(14417807)) may affect...
batch): 100%
Number],[LoginID],[HireDate
LON-SQL
Ready

As per the warning message, it is complaining about the data type for [NationalIDNumber] column. In the table design view, we can verify the data type is NVARCHAR(15). Notice that the [NationalIDNumber] column is compared to a number, but we are using a NVARCHAR data type.

Column Name	Data Type	Allow Nulls
BusinessEntityID	int	☐
NationalIDNumber	nvarchar(15)	☐
LoginID	nvarchar(256)	☐
OrganizationNode	hierarchyid	☑

- **Solution 1:** Change T-SQL to eliminate the implicit conversion

In the first solution, we use the value for the NationalIDNumber column in the single quote. It changes the value from a number to a character.

```
USE AdventureWorks2017;

SELECT BusinessEntityID, NationalIDNumber, LoginID, HireDate, JobTitle

FROM HumanResources.Employee

WHERE NationalIDNumber = '14417807';
```

As shown below, it does not have a warning symbol, and you get a different execution plan.

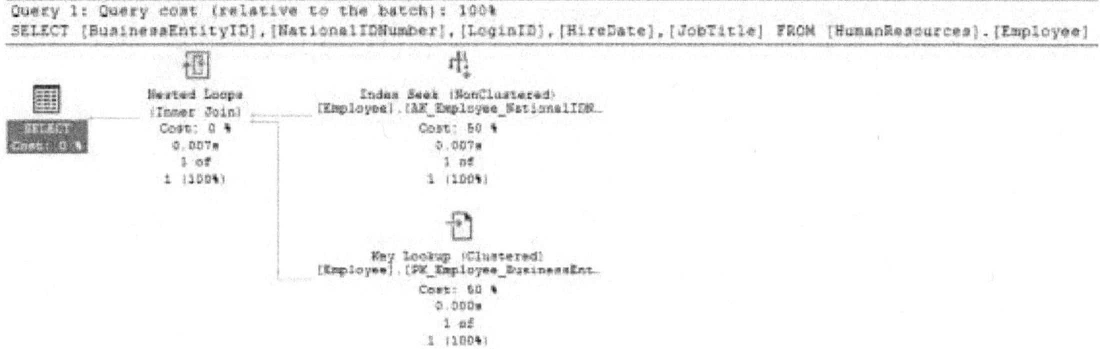

- **Solution 2:** Modify column data type

We can resolve the implicit conversion issue permanently by modifying the column data type. To change a column data type, remove its dependencies such as indexes, modify column data type, and create index again.

```
USE AdventureWorks2017

GO

DROP INDEX [AK_Employee_NationalIDNumber] ON [HumanResources].[Employee]

GO
```

ALTER TABLE [HumanResources].[Employee] ALTER COLUMN [NationalIDNumber]

INT NOT NULL;

GO

CREATE UNIQUE NONCLUSTERED INDEX [AK_Employee_NationalIDNumber]

ON [HumanResources].[Employee]([NationalIDNumber] ASC);

GO

Rerun the select statement, and it does not have an implicit warning.

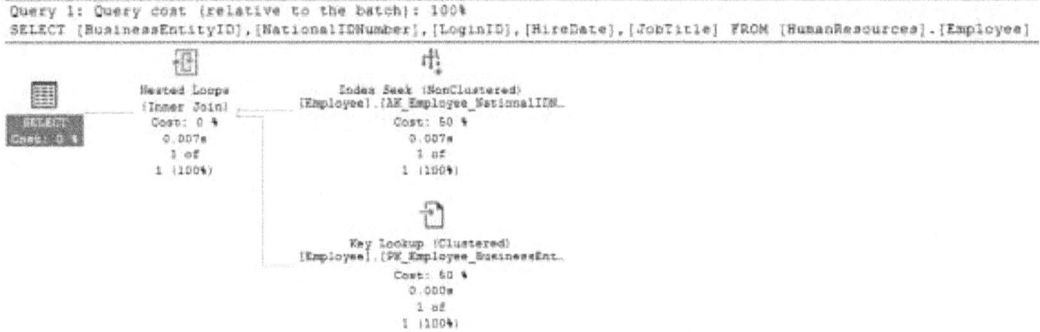

Dynamic management views and functions for performance monitoring

SQL Server provides dynamic management objects for DBAs to monitor instance health, diagnose issues and tune queries.

- Dynamic Management Views – DMV
- Dynamic Management functions – DMF

These dynamic management objects can refer to server scoped or database scoped. Broadly, we can divide them into the following categories.

- Database-related dynamic management objects
- Query execution-related dynamic management objects
- Transaction related dynamic management objects

Note:

- Azure SQL Database user requires VIEW DATABASE STATE permissions for DMVs.
- Azure SQL managed instance users required VIEW SERVER STATE permissions.
- You can view activity regarding the current database only in the Azure SQL Database.

Dynamic Management Queries

You can download all queries from this chapter using the link
https://github.com/AzureDP300/AzureDP300/tree/main/Chapter8

For individual scripts, refer to the following table.

Script Description	Link
Top 10 Active CPU Consuming Queries	https://github.com/AzureDP300/AzureDP300/blob/main/Chapter8/Script1.sql
Top 10 Active CPU Consuming Queries by sessions	https://github.com/AzureDP300/AzureDP300/blob/main/Chapter8/Script2.sql
Long-running queries that consume CPU are still running	https://github.com/AzureDP300/AzureDP300/blob/main/Chapter8/Script3.sql
The CPU issue occurred in the past	https://github.com/AzureDP300/AzureDP300/blob/main/Chapter8/Script4.sql
Identify data and log IO usage	https://github.com/AzureDP300/AzureDP300/blob/main/Chapter8/Script5.sql
View buffer-related IO using the Query Store	https://github.com/AzureDP300/AzureDP300/blob/main/Chapter8/Script6.sql

View total log IO for WRITELOG waits	https://github.com/AzureDP300/AzureDP300/blob/main/Chapter8/Script7.sql
Top queries that use table variables and temporary tables	https://github.com/AzureDP300/AzureDP300/blob/main/Chapter8/Script8.sql
Identify long-running transactions	https://github.com/AzureDP300/AzureDP300/blob/main/Chapter8/Script9.sql
Determine if a RESOURCE_SEMAHPORE wait is a top wait	https://github.com/AzureDP300/AzureDP300/blob/main/Chapter8/Script10.sql
Identify high memory-consuming statements	https://github.com/AzureDP300/AzureDP300/blob/main/Chapter8/Script11.sql
Identify the top 10 active memory grants	https://github.com/AzureDP300/AzureDP300/blob/main/Chapter8/Script12.sql
Calculates the size of the database	https://github.com/AzureDP300/AzureDP300/blob/main/Chapter8/Script13.sql
size of individual objects (in megabytes)	https://github.com/AzureDP300/AzureDP300/blob/main/Chapter8/Script14.sql
Retrieves information on the current connection	https://github.com/AzureDP300/AzureDP300/blob/main/Chapter8/Script15.sql
Azure SQL Database resource usage	https://github.com/AzureDP300/AzureDP300/blob/main/Chapter8/Script16.sql
Azure SQL Managed Instance resource usage	https://github.com/AzureDP300/AzureDP300/blob/main/Chapter8/Script17.sql
Maximum concurrent requests	https://github.com/AzureDP300/AzureDP300/blob/main/Chapter8/Script18.sql
Maximum sessions	https://github.com/AzureDP300/AzureDP300/blob/main/Chapter8/Script19.sql
Finding top N queries ranked by average CPU time.	https://github.com/AzureDP300/AzureDP300/blob/main/Chapter8/Script20.sql
query to find the actively executing queries and their current SQL batch text or input buffer text	https://github.com/AzureDP300/AzureDP300/blob/main/Chapter8/Script21.sql
currently blocked requests, their wait status, and their locks	https://github.com/AzureDP300/AzureDP300/blob/main/Chapter8/Script22.sql
query to return information on open transactions	https://github.com/AzureDP300/AzureDP300/blob/main/Chapter8/Script23.sql
Monitoring query plans	https://github.com/AzureDP300/AzureDP300/blob/main/Chapter8/Script24.sql
Azure SQL Database and Azure SQL Managed Instance CPU usage and storage data	https://github.com/AzureDP300/AzureDP300/blob/main/Chapter8/Script25.sql

Wait statistics

SQL Server uses waits for monitoring and tracking the threads and logs for which query resource is waiting. For example, if a query is waiting for CPU thread or memory grants, it won't finish in time even if you have tuned the query or your resources are in an optimal state. These wait statistics help the DBA to investigate the bottleneck for SQL Server.

We can divide the wait statistics into three parts.

- Resource waits: It occurs when the SQL Server worker thread waits for a resource used by another thread. For example, locks, disk IO waits, latches.
- Query waits: Query waits occur if the worker thread is idle and waiting for the work—for example, deadlock monitoring, ghost records cleanup.
- External waits: If SQL Server is waiting for an external process such as a linked server query, you get an external wait.

We can use DMV sys.dm_os_wait_stats to view the aggregated data for the wait statistics. For the Azure SQL Database, we can use the DMV sys,dm_db_wait_stats and it tracks wait encountered by threads during query execution.

```
SELECT * FROM sys.dm_db_wait_stats
```

	wait_type	waiting_tasks_count	wait_time_ms	max_wait_time_ms	signal_wait_time_ms
3	PAGELATCH_SH	32	58	57	58
4	PAGELATCH_EX	18	59	59	59
5	PAGEIOLATCH_SH	125	9417	201	7131
6	PAGEIOLATCH_UP	1	9	9	0
7	SLEEP_TASK	1	14	14	0
8	SOS_SCHEDULER_YIELD	3731	263808	1283	263807
9	MEMORY_ALLOCATION_EXT	214422	322	15	0
10	RESERVED_MEMORY_ALLOCATION_EXT	20312	15	0	0
11	IO_COMPLETION	1100	59786	104	3410
12	ASYNC_NETWORK_IO	202	4001	2016	145
13	WRITELOG	4989	34418	189	1963
14	PREEMPTIVE_OS_CRYPTOPS	12	31	5	0
15	PREEMPTIVE_OS_CRYPTACQUIRECONTEXT	46	66	48	0
16	PREEMPTIVE_OS_FILEOPS	1	0	0	0
17	PREEMPTIVE_OS_GETDISKFREESPACE	2	74	74	0
18	PREEMPTIVE_OS_WRITEFILEGATHER	1	497	497	0
19	PREEMPTIVE_HTTP_REQUEST	12	1	0	0
20	WRITE_COMPLETION	8	215	63	0
21	PREEMPTIVE_XHTTP	18	267	49	0
22	WAIT_ON_SYNC_STATISTICS_REFRESH	9	494	120	0

Few common waits types might indicate performance issues.

- **RESOURCE_SEMAPHORE**: It indicates query waiting for memory grants. You should review indexing, transaction management or changing the READ COMMITTED SNAPSHOT isolation level.
- **LCK**_M_X: This wait type indicates the blocking issues. You can tune your queries, transactions or isolation level to reduce the wait time.
- **PAGEIOLATCH_SH waits**: This wait can indicate the lack of indexes or improper indexes due to which SQL Server has to do a lot of page scans. It can also reflect a storage performance issue if the wait time is too high.
- **SOS_SCHEDULER_YIELD**: If your SQL Server runs under CPU pressure, you might get a high wait time on SOS_SCHEDULER_YIELD.
- **CXPACKET**: This wait type is due to parallelism. You can review MAXDOP and Cost Degree of Parallelism for this wait type along with the index tuning.
- **PAGEIOLATCH_UP**: We get this type as part of TempDB contention on the PFS (page free space) data pages. Usually, we can reduce the wait type by configuring the TempDB file by following TempDB best practices.
    - TempDB - One file per CPU core up to eight files.
    - The identical auto-growth setting for all data files

We cannot modify the number of TempDB files in Azure SQL Database and Managed instances.

Refer to Microsoft docs (**https://docs.microsoft.com/en-us/sql/relational-databases/system-dynamic-management-views/sys-dm-db-wait-stats-azure-sql-database?view=azuresqldb-current**) for a detailed list of wait types and their description.

Azure SQL Indexes and Statistics maintenance

Index fragmentation occurs if the logical page order does not match with the physical or index page allocation. We perform frequent insert, updates, delete data from tables in the OLTP environment. For example, SQL Server might split pages to insert new key values due to a large insert activity. Over time these modifications cause index fragmentation. The index fragmentation may degrade performance because it requires additional IO for locating data to which index points.

Note: The index fragmentation is applicable for all SQL Server versions, including Azure SQL Database and Azure SQL Managed Instance.

Usually, people think that Azure SQL Database is a managed database service, and we do not require managing indexes fragmentation, statistics. No, It is the DBA responsibility to monitor the index fragmentation and do index maintenance.

Index REBUILD	INDEX ORGANIZE
It drops and creates the index to remove fragmentation.	It physically reorders the leaf level pages on an index to match the leaf nodes' logical order.
It has options for online and offline index rebuild.	It is an online operation.
Recommended: If avg_fragmentation_in_percent value> 30% (ONLINE ON)	Recommended: If avg_fragmentation_in_percent value > 15% and < = 30%
You can specify FILLFACTOR while rebuilding an index.	It does not allow FILLFACTOR configuration.

It can use multiple CPUs	It is a single-threaded operation.

Detecting fragmentation

We use sys.dm_db_index_physical_stats to detect fragmentation for an index of a table or all indexes in a database. It returns the following useful columns output.

- avg_fragmentation_in_percent: It represents logical fragmentation **(out-of-order pages in the index).**percentage.
- fragment_count: It is the number of fragments in the index.
- avg_fragment_size_in_pages: It is the average number of pages in one fragment of the index.

The following query reruns the fragmentation for all tables in a SQL database along with the page counts. It is applicable for on-premise as well as Azure databases.

https://github.com/AzureDP300/AzureDP300/blob/main/Chapter8/Script26.sql

```
SELECT S.name as 'Schema',
T.name as 'Table',
I.name as 'Index',
DDIPS.avg_fragmentation_in_percent,
DDIPS.page_count
FROM sys.dm_db_index_physical_stats (DB_ID(), NULL, NULL, NULL, NULL) AS DDIPS
INNER JOIN sys.tables T on T.object_id = DDIPS.object_id
INNER JOIN sys.schemas S on T.schema_id = S.schema_id
INNER JOIN sys.indexes I ON I.object_id = DDIPS.object_id
AND DDIPS.index_id = I.index_id
WHERE DDIPS.database_id = DB_ID()
and I.name is not null
AND DDIPS.avg_fragmentation_in_percent > 0
ORDER BY DDIPS.avg_fragmentation_in_percent desc
```

	Schema	Table	Index	avg_fragmentation_in_percent	page_count
1	SalesLT	Product	AK_Product_ProductNumber	50	2
2	SalesLT	Address	AK_Address_rowguid	50	2
3	SalesLT	Address	IX_Address_StateProvince	50	2
4	SalesLT	CustomerAddress	AK_CustomerAddress_rowguid	50	2
5	SalesLT	SalesOrderDetail	IX_SalesOrderDetail_ProductID	50	2
6	SalesLT	Product	AK_Product_Name	33.3333333333333	3
7	SalesLT	SalesOrderDetail	AK_SalesOrderDetail_rowguid	33.3333333333333	3
8	SalesLT	Customer	AK_Customer_rowguid	33.3333333333333	3

AzureSQLMaintenance stored procedure

To perform index maintenance, we use the ALTER INDEX statement with the REBUILD OR REORGANIZE argument.

REBUILD:

ALTER INDEX Index_Name ON Table_Name REBUILD

--REBUILD Index with ONLINE OPTION

ALTER INDEX Index_Name ON Table_Name REBUILD WITH(ONLINE=ON) | WITH(ONLINE=ON)

REORGANIZE:

ALTER INDEX Index_Name ON Table_Name REORGANIZE

Alternatively, you can use AzureSQLMaintenance stored procedure(written by Yochanan Rachamim) compatible with the Azure SQL Database. The Ola Hallengren, index maintenance script, inspires this stored procedure.

1. Copy the stored procedure script from GitHub(https://raw.githubusercontent.com/yochananrachamim/AzureSQL/master/AzureSQLMaintenance.txt)
2. Create procedure AzureSQLMaintenance for Azure SQL Database.

This stored procedure has the following arguments.

- **@Operation:** We can specify the values index, statistics or all.
- **@Mode:** Smart(default) or dummy
    - **smart**: In the smart mode, the procedure checks only modified statistics and performs index maintenance by % of fragmentation.
    - **dummy**: *It checks all statistics or indexes.*
- ***@logtotable:***
    - *Value1 :* It logs stored procedure output in a [AzureSQLMaintenanceLog] table (auto-created).
    - *0: It disables logging for stored procedure output.*

Note: This stored procedure supports resume index functionality, resumable index rebuild, fix forwarded records in heaps.

You can execute this stored procedure, and it logs status in the message tab.

```
exec AzureSQLMaintenance 'all'
```

```
Messages
set ResumableIndexRebuild = 0
set RebuildHeaps = 0
set LogToTable = 0
----------------------------
Get index information...(wait)
------------------------------------------
Index Information:
------------------------------------------
Total Indexes: 44
Average Fragmentation: 37.7592
Fragmented Indexes: 1
------------------------------------------
Get statistics information...
------------------------------------------
Statistics Information:
------------------------------------------
Total Modifications: 259
Modified Statistics: 2
------------------------------------------
Start executing commands...
ALTER INDEX [IX_vProductAndDescription] ON [SalesLT].[vProductAndDescription] REBUILD WITH(ONLINE=ON,MAXDOP=1);
UPDATE STATISTICS [SalesLT].[ProductDescription] ([PK_ProductDescription_ProductDescriptionID]) WITH FULLSCAN;
UPDATE STATISTICS [SalesLT].[Product] ([_WA_Sys_0000000A_656C112C]) WITH FULLSCAN;
```

Monitoring performance by using the Query Store

The query store enables DBA to troubleshoot the performance impact of a query due to query plan changes. It automatically captures the query histories, their plans, runtime statistics. You can view different execution plans of a query in a time window.

By default, Azure SQL Database has a query stored configured. You can view database properties and Query store to view its configuration in the Azure SQL database.

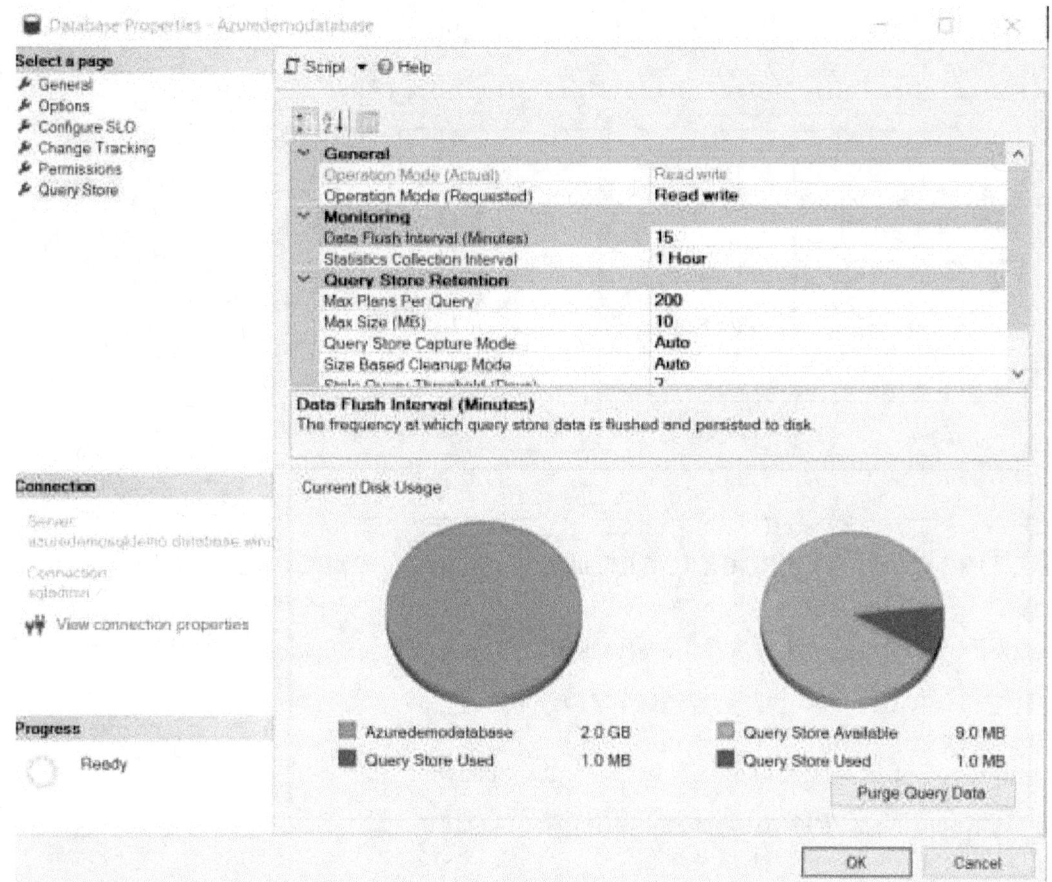

The query store can help to troubleshoot the following issues.

- It enables DBA to identify query execution plan changes quickly. You can compare existing and previous plans.
- You can identify top queries based on the execution time, memory consumption, CPU.
- You can audit the query plan history.
- You can force an optimized query plan for a specific query.
- It helps you to analyse wait stats for a particular query.
- It gives you a plan store, runtime state store and wait state store for execution plan and wait statistics information.

The below diagram gives a high-level architecture of the Query Store.

- Query plan and Query text are written directly to the disk using the ASYNC writer.

- It sends the query statistics every 15 minutes, by default. This period is known as the data flush interval.

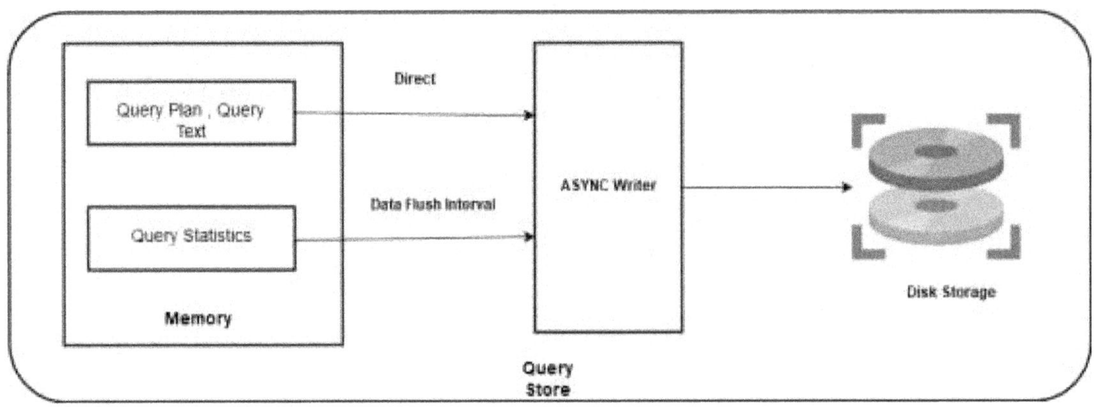

Lab 10: Use covering index for improving query execution plan

In this lab, we investigate a query performance issue using the actual execution plan, and Later, we add a covering index to improve the query performance.

Connect to Azure SQL Database and execute the following query in [AdventureWorks2017] database. Press CTRL + M to enable the Actual execution plan.

SET STATISTICS IO, TIME ON;

SELECT [SalesOrderID] ,[CarrierTrackingNumber] ,[OrderQty] ,[ProductID], [UnitPrice] ,[LineTotal],[ModifiedDate]

FROM [AdventureWorks2017].[Sales].[SalesOrderDetail]

WHERE [ModifiedDate] > '2012/01/01' AND [ProductID] = 772;

The key loop is the costly operator in the actual execution plan, and it takes 99% cost in the overall batch.

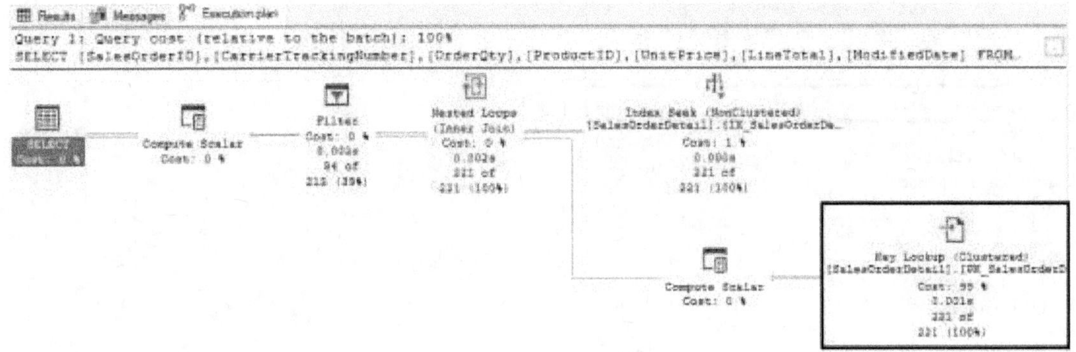

The query uses STATISTICS IO and TIME ON to capture statistics information in the message tab. As shown below, the above query has 687 logical reads, and it took 296ms for its execution.

```
SQL Server parse and compile time:
   CPU time = 0 ms, elapsed time = 0 ms.

(84 rows affected)
Table 'SalesOrderDetail'. Scan count 1, logical reads 687, physical reads 0,
page server reads 0, read-ahead reads 0, page server read-ahead reads 0,
lob logical reads 0, lob physical reads 0, lob page server reads 0,
lob read-ahead reads 0, lob page server read-ahead reads 0.

(1 row affected)

 SQL Server Execution Times:
   CPU time = 15 ms,  elapsed time = 296 ms.
SQL Server parse and compile time:
```

Take your mouse pointer over the key lookup and view its properties.

Key Lookup (Clustered)

Uses a supplied clustering key to lookup on a table that has a clustered index.

Physical Operation	Key Lookup
Logical Operation	Key Lookup
Actual Execution Mode	Row
Estimated Execution Mode	Row
Storage	RowStore
Number of Rows Read	221
Actual Number of Rows	221
Actual Number of Batches	0
Estimated Operator Cost	0.665093 (99%)
Estimated I/O Cost	0.003125
Estimated CPU Cost	0.0001581
Estimated Subtree Cost	0.665093
Number of Executions	221
Estimated Number of Executions	221
Estimated Number of Rows	1
Estimated Row Size	62 B
Actual Rebinds	0
Actual Rewinds	0
Ordered	True
Node ID	7

Object

[AdventureWorks2017].[Sales].[SalesOrderDetail].[PK_SalesOrderDetail_SalesOrderID_SalesOrderDetailID]

Output List

[AdventureWorks2017].[Sales].[SalesOrderDetail].CarrierTrackingNumber, [AdventureWorks2017].[Sales].[SalesOrderDetail].OrderQty, [AdventureWorks2017].[Sales].[SalesOrderDetail].UnitPrice, [AdventureWorks2017].[Sales].[SalesOrderDetail].UnitPriceDiscount, [AdventureWorks2017].[Sales].[SalesOrderDetail].ModifiedDate

Seek Predicates

Seek Keys[1]: Prefix: [AdventureWorks2017].[Sales].[SalesOrderDetail].SalesOrderID, [AdventureWorks2017].[Sales].[SalesOrderDetail].SalesOrderDetailID = Scalar Operator([AdventureWorks2017].[Sales].[SalesOrderDetail].[SalesOrderID]), Scalar Operator([AdventureWorks2017].[Sales].[SalesOrderDetail].[SalesOrderDetailID])

We can use a covering non-clustered index for removing the key lookup. To create the covering index, view the index seek properties and view the search condition. Here, it searches based on the [ProductID] column.

Index Seek (NonClustered)

Scan a particular range of rows from a nonclustered index.

Physical Operation	Index Seek
Logical Operation	Index Seek
Actual Execution Mode	Row
Estimated Execution Mode	Row
Storage	RowStore
Number of Rows Read	221
Actual Number of Rows	221
Actual Number of Batches	0
Estimated I/O Cost	0.003125
Estimated Operator Cost	0.0035251 (1%)
Estimated CPU Cost	0.0004001
Estimated Subtree Cost	0.0035251
Estimated Number of Executions	1
Number of Executions	1
Estimated Number of Rows	221
Estimated Number of Rows to be Read	221
Estimated Row Size	19 B
Actual Rebinds	0
Actual Rewinds	0
Ordered	True
Node ID	4

Object

[AdventureWorks2017].[Sales].[SalesOrderDetail].
[IX_SalesOrderDetail_ProductID]

Output List

[AdventureWorks2017].[Sales].
[SalesOrderDetail].SalesOrderID, [AdventureWorks2017].
[Sales].[SalesOrderDetail].SalesOrderDetailID,
[AdventureWorks2017].[Sales].[SalesOrderDetail].ProductID

Seek Predicates

Seek Keys[1]: Prefix: [AdventureWorks2017].[Sales].
[SalesOrderDetail].ProductID = Scalar Operator((772))

Now, create a covering index with the following script.

```
CREATE NONCLUSTERED INDEX [IX_CoveringIndex_ProductID_SalesOrderDetail]

ON [AdventureWorks2017].[Sales].[SalesOrderDetail]

( [ProductID],[ModifiedDate] )

INCLUDE ([CarrierTrackingNumber] ,[OrderQty] ,[ProductID],

[UnitPrice],[LineTotal]

)
```

Rerun the select statement, and we get an Index Seek operator. It does not use a key lookup operator.

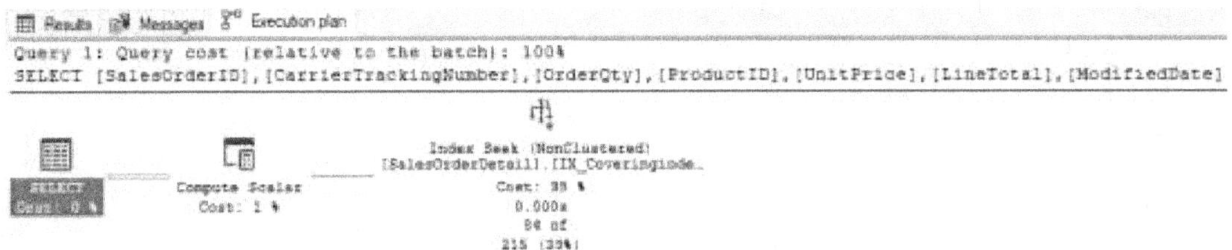

Here the query uses only 5 logical reads in the message tab, while previously, we had 687 logical reads. The query also finishes in 180ms as compared to 296ms of the previous execution.

```
(84 rows affected)
Table 'SalesOrderDetail'. Scan count 1, logical reads 5,
physical reads 0, page server reads 0, read-ahead reads 0,
 page server read-ahead reads 0, lob logical reads 0,
lob physical reads 0, lob page server reads 0, lob read-ahead reads 0,
 lob page server read-ahead reads 0.

(1 row affected)

 SQL Server Execution Times:
   CPU time = 15 ms,  elapsed time = 180 ms.
```

TempDB configuration for Azure SQL Database and Azure SQL Managed Instance

The TempDB is a critical shared database in an SQL Server instance. The right configuration of TempDB ensures your queries can work efficiently. In an Azure SQL database, Azure automatically configures the TempDB.

Azure SQL Database TempDB configuration

- It stores the TempDB files on the local SSD drives for optimal performance.
- Azure SQL Database uses the number of TempDB files according to the number of vCores. For example, for 2Vcores, it configures 4 data files. It supports a maximum of 16 TempDB files.

- You cannot modify the TempDB files configuration, such as the number of files, their auto-growth setting.

Azure SQL Managed Instance TempDB configuration

- It configures 12 TempDB files in a managed instance, independent of the number of vCores.
- Similar to the Azure SQL Database, we cannot modify the TempDB configuration here.

You should refer to maximum tempdb sizes for DTU-based service tiers and V-cores based azure databases from Microsoft docs(**https://docs.microsoft.com/en-us/sql/relational-databases/databases/tempdb-database?view=sql-server-ver15**)

Here, I added a snip for your reference.

tempdb sizes for DTU-based service tiers

Service-level objective	Maximum tempdb data file size (GB)	Number of tempdb data files	Maximum tempdb data size (GB)
Basic	13.9	1	13.9
S0	13.9	1	13.9
S1	13.9	1	13.9
S2	13.9	1	13.9
S3	32	1	32
S4	32	2	64

To check the Azure SQL Database TempDB configuration, execute the following T-SQL.

```
SELECT * FROM SYS.dm_io_virtual_file_stats(2,null) A INNER JOIN

TEMPDB.sys.database_files B ON A.file_id = B.FILE_ID
```

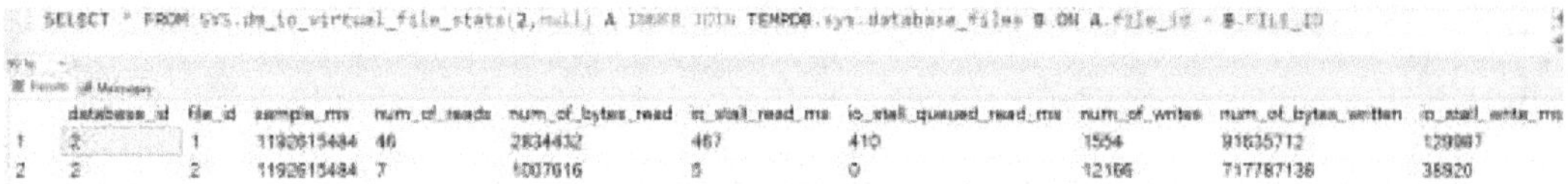

```
SELECT * FROM SYS.dm_io_virtual_file_stats(2,null) A INNER JOIN TEMPDB.sys.database_files B ON A.file_id = B.FILE_ID
```

	database_id	file_id	sample_ms	num_of_reads	num_of_bytes_read	io_stall_read_ms	io_stall_queued_read_ms	num_of_writes	num_of_bytes_written	io_stall_write_ms
1	2	1	1192615484	46	2834432	467	410	1554	91835712	129087
2	2	2	1192615484	7	1007616	5	0	12166	717787136	35920

Similarly, for the managed instance, use the following T-SQL script.

SELECT files.physical_name, files.name, stats.num_of_writes,

(1.0*stats.io_stall_write_ms/stats.num_of_writes) AS avg_write_stall_ms,

stats.num_of_reads,

(1.0*stats.io_stall_read_ms/stats.num_of_reads) as avg_read_stall_ms

FROM sys.dm_io_virtual_file_stats(2, NULL) as stats

INNER JOIN master.sys.master_files AS files

ON stats.database_id = files.database_id

AND stats.file_id = files.file_id

WHERE files.type_desc = 'ROWS'

Max Degree of Parallelism

We can limit the number of processors for parallel query execution in all versions of SQL Server. It can affect individual query performance. SQL Server can do parallel execution for DDL, DML, online alter column, parallel stats collection, cursors.

In the below table, we get a MAXDOP recommendation for SQL Server instances.

Server configuration	Number of processors	Guidance
Server with single NUMA node	Less than or equal to 8 logical processors	Keep MAXDOP at or below # of logical processors
Server with single NUMA node	Greater than 8 logical processors	Keep MAXDOP at 8
Server with multiple NUMA nodes	Less than or equal to 16 logical processors per NUMA node	Keep MAXDOP at or below # of logical processors per NUMA node
Server with multiple NUMA nodes	Greater than 16 logical processors per NUMA node	Keep MAXDOP at half the number of logical processors per NUMA node with a MAX value of 16

- You can configure the MAXDOP at the instance level using the sp_configure in the Azure SQL Managed Instance.
- Azure SQL Database does not support configuration at the instance level. Therefore, you can use database scoped operations for it.

  - Check the current configuration of MAXDOP using the sys.database_scoped_configuration.

SELECT * FROM sys.database_scoped_configurations

WHERE name='MAXDOP'

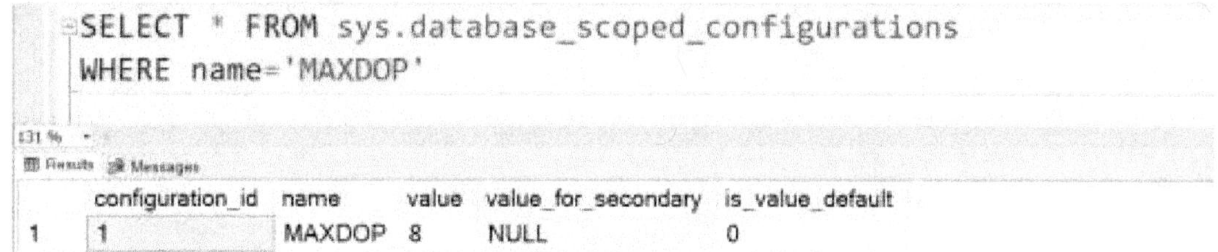

```
SELECT * FROM sys.database_scoped_configurations
WHERE name='MAXDOP'
```

	configuration_id	name	value	value_for_secondary	is_value_default
1	1	MAXDOP	8	NULL	0

  - Modify MAXDOP using the ALTER DATABASE SCOPED CONFIGURATION statement. For example, in the below query, set MAXDOP to 4 for Azure SQL Database.

ALTER DATABASE SCOPED CONFIGURATION SET MAXDOP = 4 ;

Lab 11: Use Query Store feature to resolve the Performance issue

In this lab, we will use the Query Store for identifying and troubleshooting performance issues in the Azure SQL Database query.

By default, Azure SQL Database has a query store configured. Therefore, it does not require additional configuration.

For the lab session, create the table with sample data, a non-clustered index and a stored procedure to select data based on the column [SearchString1] from the script URL specified below.

Copy the script from the URL https://github.com/AzureDP300/AzureDP300/blob/main/Chapter8/Script27.sql

I executed a stored procedure and captured its actual execution plan. It uses an index seek and key lookup to fetch data.

```
EXEC GetDataSearchString1 @SearchString1='Random'
```

131 %

Results Messages Execution plan

Query 1: Query cost (relative to the batch): 100%
SELECT * FROM dbo.DemoTable WHERE SearchString1 = @SearchString1

SELECT
Cost: 0 %

Nested Loops
(Inner Join)
Cost: 0 %
0.000s
0 of
1 (0%)

Index Seek (NonClustered)
[DemoTable].[IX_DemoTable_Se...
Cost: 50 %
0.000s
0 of
1 (0%)

Key Lookup (Clustered)
[DemoTable].[PK__DemoTabl__3...
Cost: 50 %
0.000s
0 of
1 (0%)

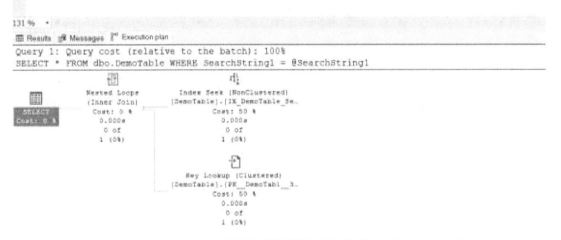

Clear the procedural cache using DBCC FREEPROCCACHE and execute the procedure with argument value **SQL Server.**

DBCC FREEPROCCACHE

GO

EXEC GetDataSearchString1 @SearchString1='SQL Server'

Go

EXEC GetDataSearchString1 @SearchString1='Random'

Go

It uses the clustered index scan for parameter value – SQL Server. If you rerun the procedure with the previous argument value – Random, it uses a clustered index scan.

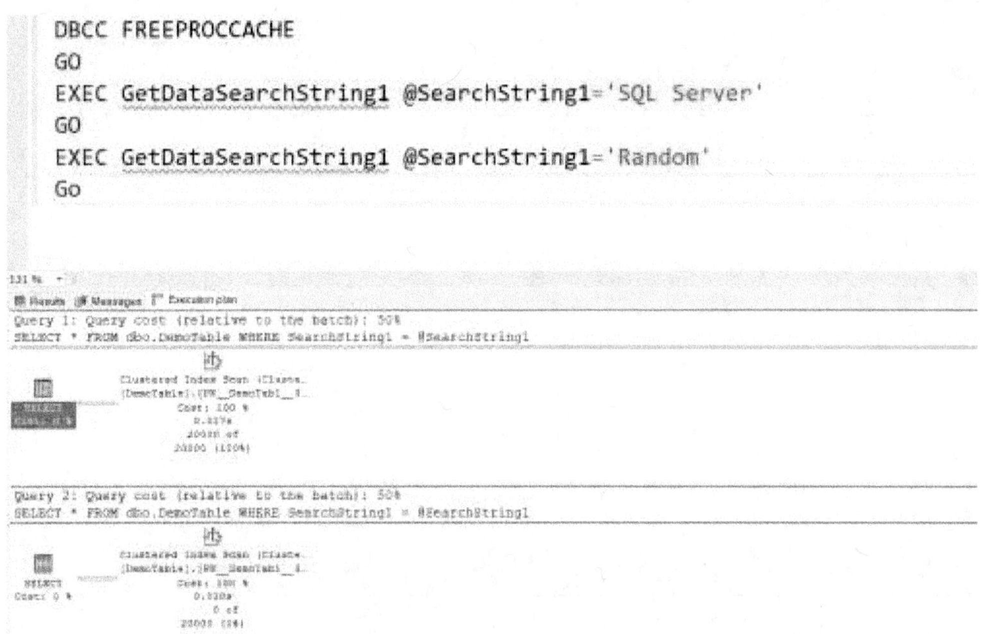

In the Azure SQL Database, navigate to Query Store and Top Resource consuming queries. It opens the query store dashboard, and you can view two different plan ID's for a select statement.

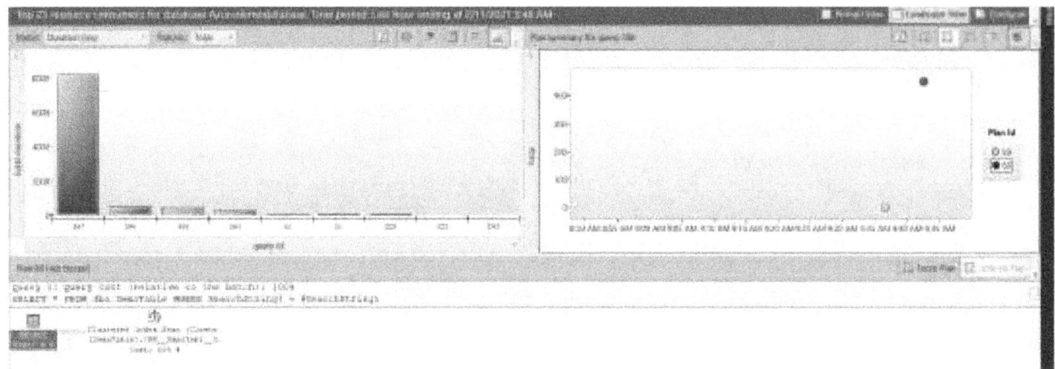

- Plan ID 59: It uses Index seek and key lookup.

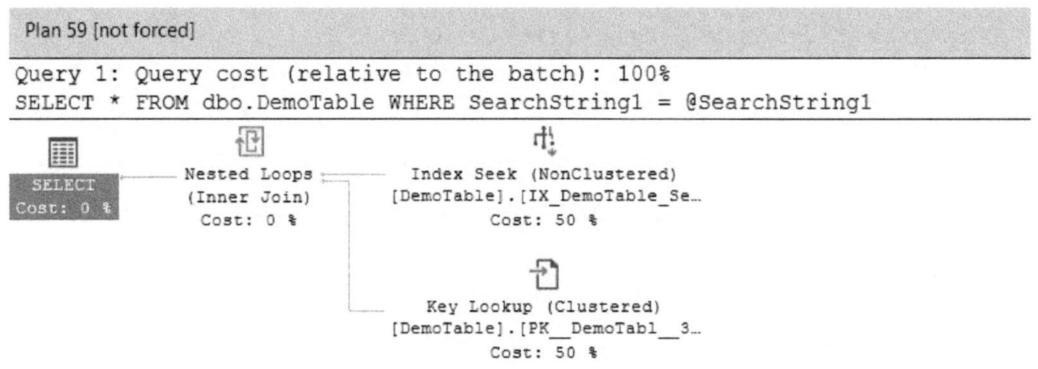

- Plan ID 60 uses the clustered index scan

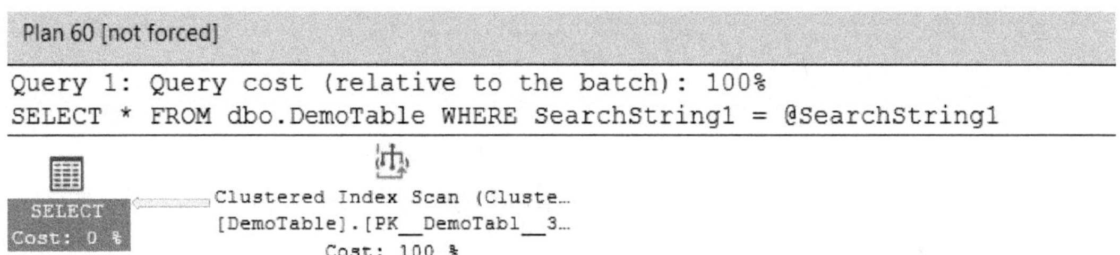

SQL Server cache the stored procedure and reuse it for further executions. View the select statement property, and it shows the parameter runtime value and parameter compiled value. As we can see, the actual plan was optimized for the compiled value SQL Server. Therefore, during the next execution, it uses a clustered index scan for value Random as well.

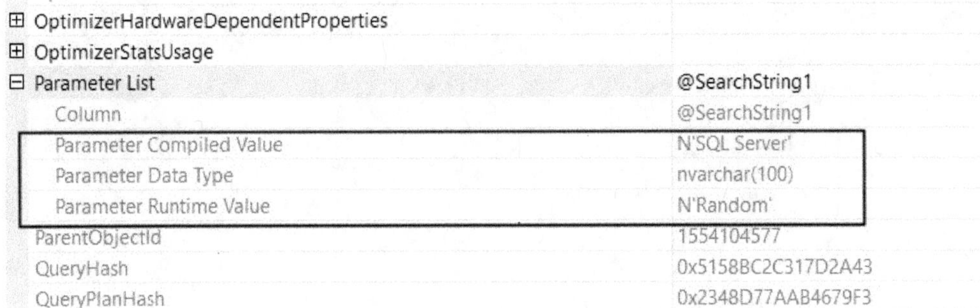

OptimizerHardwareDependentProperties
OptimizerStatsUsage
Parameter List @SearchString1
Column @SearchString1
Parameter Compiled Value N'SQL Server'
Parameter Data Type nvarchar(100)
Parameter Runtime Value N'Random'
ParentObjectId 1554104577
QueryHash 0x5158BC2C317D2A43
QueryPlanHash 0x2348D77AAB4679F3

We can force a query plan using the query store. Select the optimized query plan id and click on Force Plan.

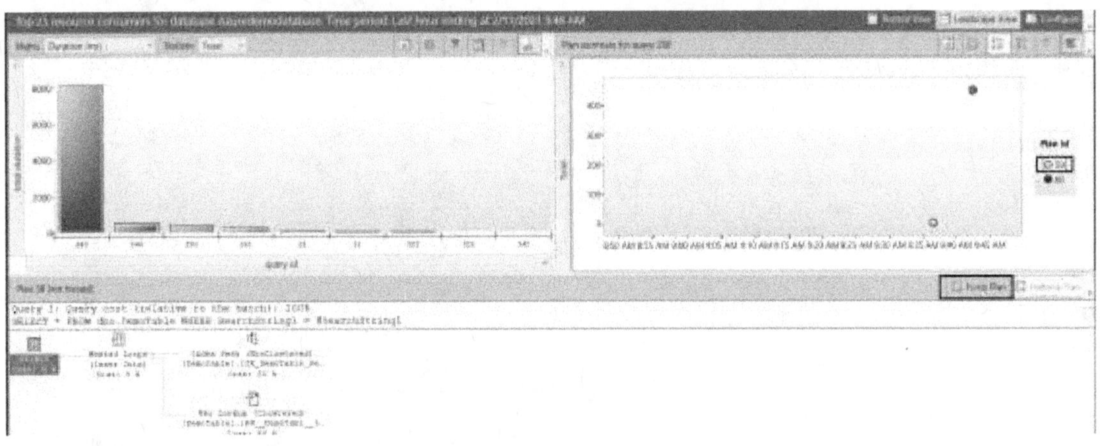

Click on Yes to force a query plan.

Confirmation

Do you want to force plan 59 for query 350?

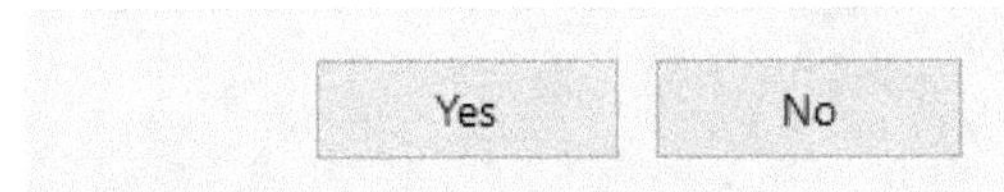

It changes the plan ID status as forced.

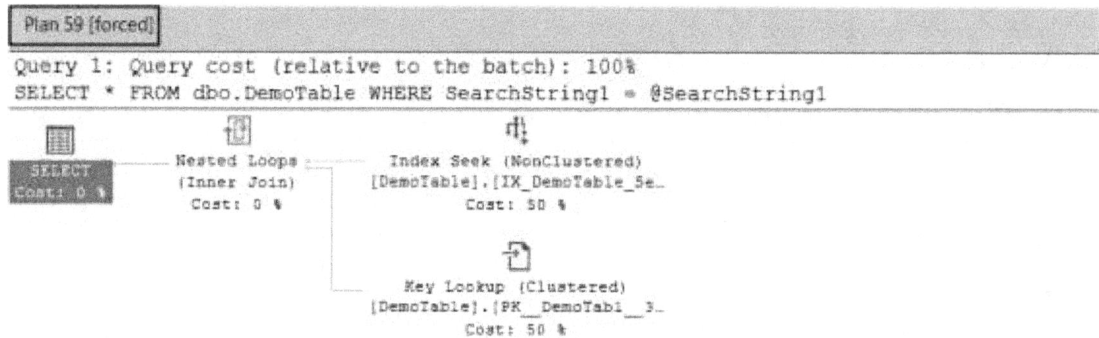

Query with the forced plan:

You can view all queries with a forced plan using a dashboard- Query with the SQL database's forced plan.

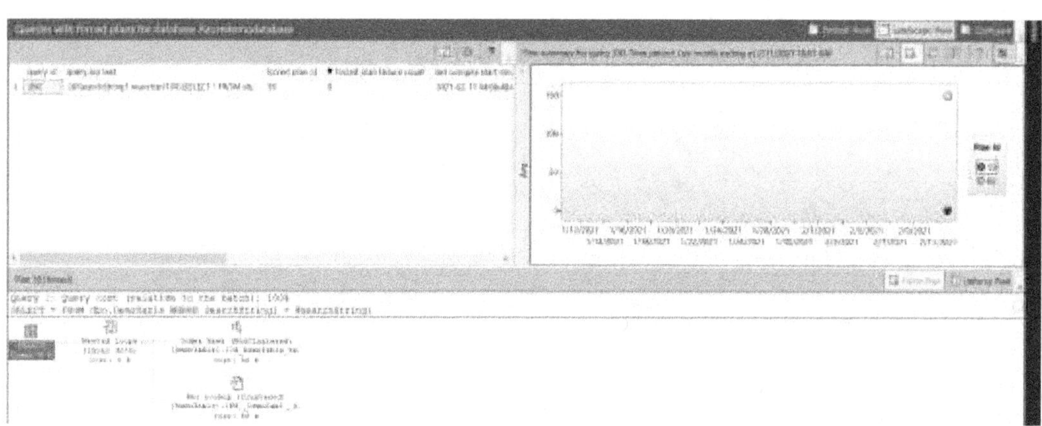

If you re-execute the stored procedure with the argument 'Random', it uses the forced plan as shown below.

```
EXEC GetDataSearchString1 @SearchString1='Random'
Go
```

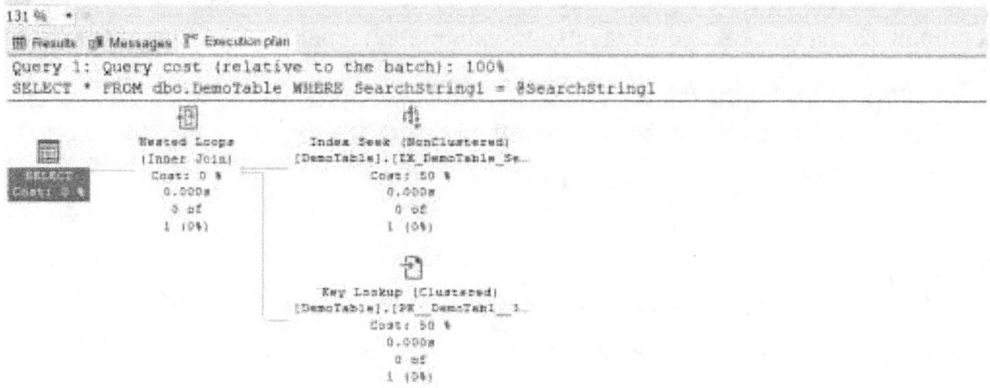

Summary

This chapter focused on optimizing query performance using various methods such as execution plan , lightweight query profiling, SARGAbility, Parameter Sniffing, Column store index, Table partitioning, In-Memory OLTP. The query tuning is almost the same in Azure databases (PaaS, IaaS) or On-premise SQL Server. Therefore, you should monitor the costly queries; optimize them for your workload with a perfect blend of database environment in Azure infrastructure.

Chapter 9 Perform automation of tasks

This chapter introduces the readers to the potential for automating repetitive tasks using the Azure Automation framework. In addition, you will review the other components such as notifications, scheduler, ARM deployment using Automation, and then discover how to create and automate backup and configure alerts using SQL Server Agent jobs.

What you will learn

1. Gain a basic understanding of PowerShell Fundamentals
2. Understand the key difference between Azure PowerShell and AZ CLI
3. Explore Azure Automation framework
4. Access Azure SQL Database using Linked Server on SQL Server
5. Deploy Azure SQL Database using ARM Templates
6. Setup Azure elastic jobs
7. Create scheduled jobs using Azure Logic Apps
8. Run PowerShell scripts using SQL Server Agent jobs
9. Setup and configure alerts for Database maintenance tasks
10. And more...

Are you migrating your infrastructure to the cloud? To get the most value from Microsoft Azure, you need to know how to manage it. You should be able to deploy and configure resources in a quick and repeatable way.

This chapter introduces the Azure management tools and automation extensions:

- Azure CloudShell
- Azure portal
- Azure PowerShell
- Azure CLI
- ARM (Azure Resource Manager) JSON templates
- Azure Automation
- SQL Server Agent jobs
- Azure elastic jobs

- Azure Logic Apps

Azure Cloud Shell

Azure Cloud Shell is an interactive, authenticated, browser-accessible shell for managing Azure resources. It provides the flexibility of choosing the shell experience that best suits the way you work, either Bash or PowerShell.

You can access the Cloud Shell in three ways:

- : Open a browser to

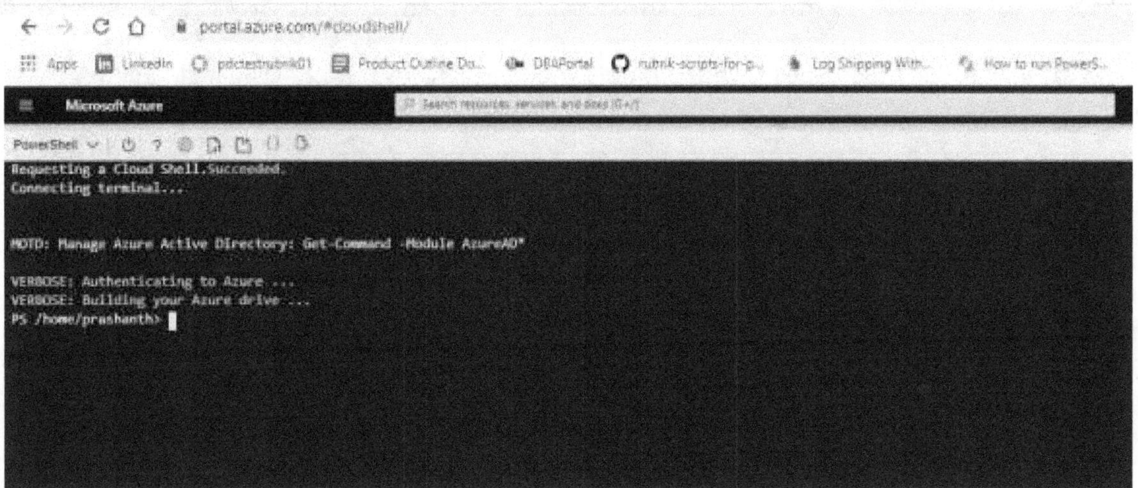

- : Select the Cloud Shell icon on the

On the initial start, Cloud Shell always prompts you to associate new or existing storage, resource group, and file share with persisting files across sessions.

You can associate the details and click create storage to configure the cloud shell.

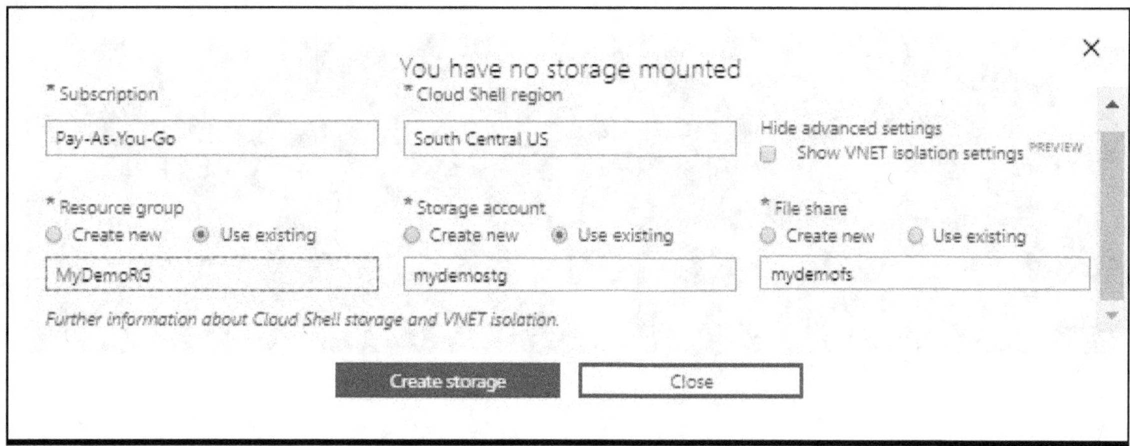

You should now able to access PowerShell or Bash shell

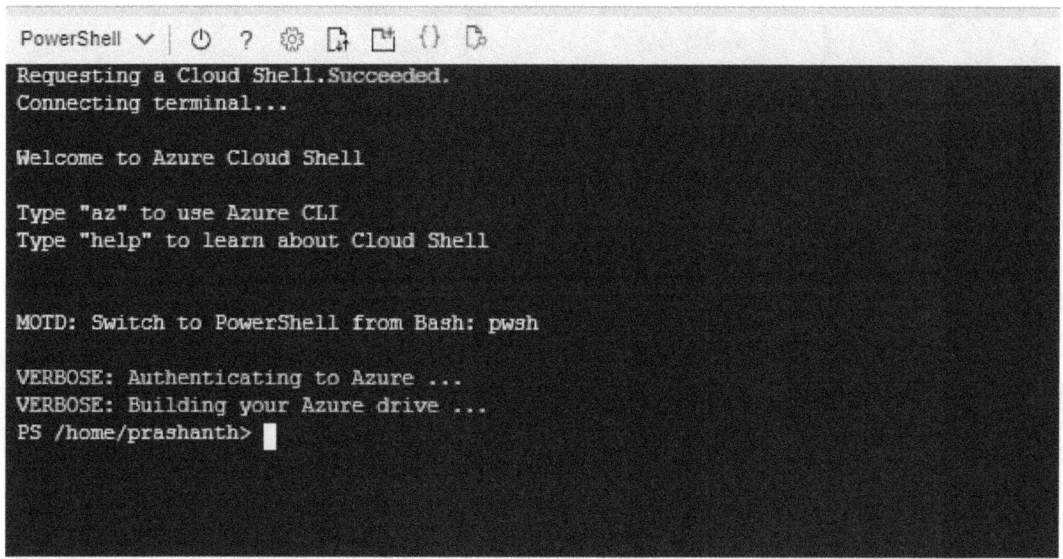

Azure Cloud Shell also offers an integrated graphical text editor based on the open-source Monaco Editor. It is easy to create and edit configuration files by running code.

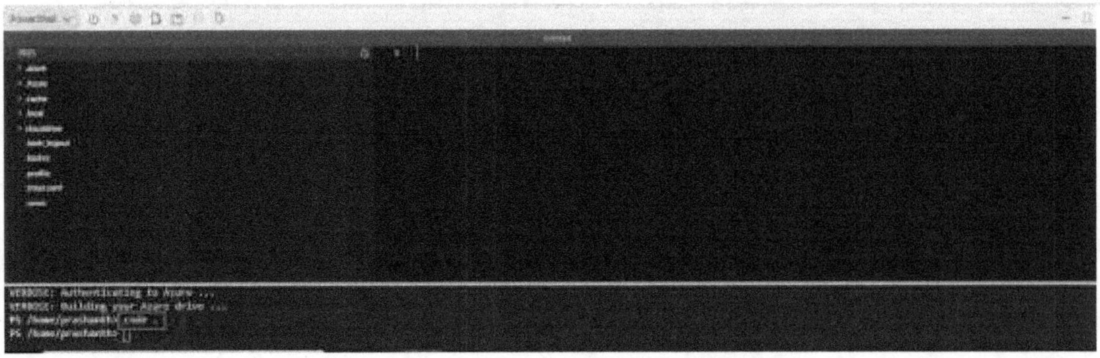

Note: Cloud Shell opens the command prompt, and that command prompt allows you to use the Azure CLI and PowerShell in order to do different things through a command line to Microsoft Azure

Azure CLI overview

It is a cross-platform and command-line CLI interface for provisioning and managing Azure infrastructure. First, it's easy to learn, and it's easy to use. Microsoft started this because they needed a smoother transition to Linux administrators—as they are coming with a bash scripting experience.

In all cases, the portal does not serve well for some things you will need to do repetitively in Microsoft Azure.

- Written and developed in Python
- Simple to use
  - az [group] [subgroup] [command] { parameters}

The syntax is self-intuitive and straightforward. For example, if you want to run a command against the virtual machine and intend to get the disks' details on that virtual machine. The group would be the VM; the subgroup would be the disks; the base command you have to create, delete, show, and list.

- The commands are more intuitive
- az commands are self-explanatory and supports interactive execution

Type in **az interactive** and hit return, and it brings us up to the interactive interface mode of the az cli tool. It is easy to browse group, subgroup, base commands, and traverse through various parameters lists using tab, space-bar and up-and-down arrow keys.

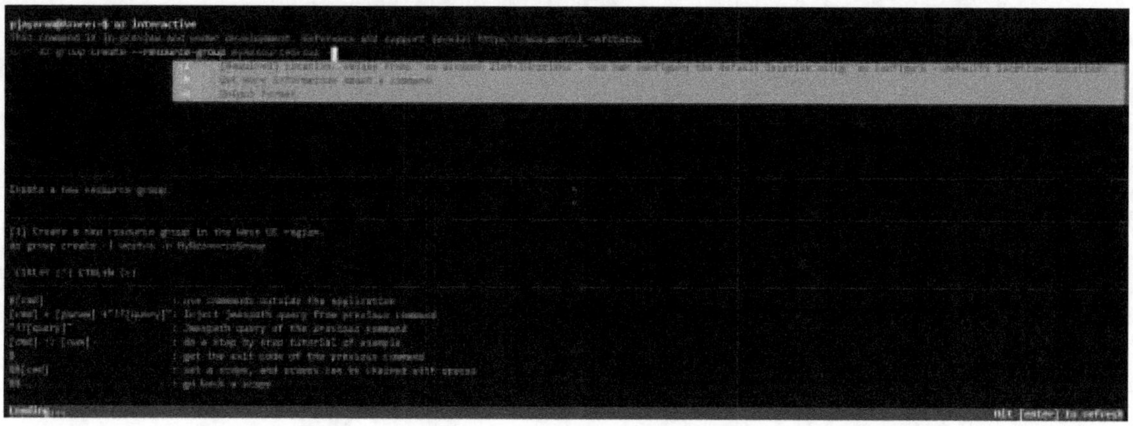

- Advance scripting may require Unix/Linux shell scripting experience

The bash script will create three UbuntuLTS virtual machines (myVM1, myVM2, and myVM3) in the resource group AzureBackupRG_southcentralus_1.

Create three VM instances

for ((i=0; i<3; ++i));

do

az vm create --name myVM$i -g AzureBackupRG_southcentralus_1 --image UbuntuLTS --generate-ssh-keys;

done

```
# Create three VM  machines
for ((i=0; i<3; ++i));
do
az vm create --name myVM$i -g AzureBackupRG_southcentralus_1 --image UbuntuLTS --generate-ssh-keys;
done
```

- Supports JMESPath for query manipulation. The following are the samples:

az>> az storage account list --query [].name --output table

az>> az storage account list --query [].[name,location] --output table

az>> az storage account list --query "[].{Name:name,Location:location}" --output table

az>> az storage account list --query [0:5].[name,location] --output table

```
PS /home/prashanth> az storage account list --query [].name --output table
Result
---------
mydemostg
PS /home/prashanth> az storage account list --query "[].{Name:name}" --output table
Name
---------
mydemostg
PS /home/prashanth>
```

- Supports extensions

You can extend Azure CLI with Groovy, Python, Ruby or any other scripting language

Note: Azure CLI scoped configuration helps to set default values that you intended to use all the time. For example, to bypass entering a resource group name in all your commands—specify the default option.

az configure - -default group="myResourceGroup"

az configure - -default vm="myVM"

Azure PowerShell

PowerShell is a comprehensive command-line interface and scripting language for Windows.

Almost anything you can do with Microsoft Azure, you can do it through PowerShell. Of late, Microsoft has been embracing PowerShell core on Linux and macOS. It becomes an ade-facto toolkit for administrators to manage cross-platforms. It has been around since 2006.

PowerShell is an integrated component with all the windows operating systems. It is one of the core components built on the .Net framework. PowerShell has undergone several iterations and evolutions, and it becomes a powerful tool built with several modules to manage any data platform-and-infrastructure related components.

PowerShell has an in-house set of commands commonly known as cmdlets. These are specialized instructions to run specific operations. The common form of the cmdlet is a combination of a verb and a noun. A verb is the action you want to perform, a noun defines what you want to do. A cmdlet's core is to have a dash between the verb and a noun, an optional parameter and then follow a global parameter.

Why does PowerShell cmdlets so easy to use?

Due to its simple construct, we can use it in the way our mind thinks. In addition to traditional programs and operating system commands (CMD.exe), you can also use PowerShell cmdlets. Anyone can create the cmdlets. The core Microsoft PowerShell team creates the core cmdlets. Still, many other groups and community-based enthusiasts or specialists are also involved in creating the hundreds of cmdlets bundled and shipped to the public repositories. The modules are the functions that take advantage of the facilities built into the .Net framework namespace, and therefore are easy to build and write cmdlets. These cmdlets are the building blocks of PowerShell automation.

PowerShell introduces a powerful new-type of commands called cmdlets (pronounced "command-let") which share a common Verb-Noun syntax. All cmdlets are named in a Verb-Noun pattern, such as Get-Process, Get-Content, Get-Help, Get-AzResourceGroup, Get-VcsUser and Stop-Process

PowerShell automation can be leveraged to build workflows and apps that help you build and manage cloud infrastructures.

To check your PowerShell version, run the command:

$PSVersionTable.PSVersion

```
PS /home/pjayaram> $PSVersionTable.PSVersion

Major  Minor  Patch  PreReleaseLabel BuildLabel
-----  -----  -----  --------------- ----------
7      0      0
```

It is possible to install multiple versions of Azure PowerShell modules. To check the installed Azure PowerShell modules, run the following command:

PS:/>Get-InstalledModule -Name Az -AllVersions | Select-Object -Property Name, Version

```
PS /home/pjayaram> Get-InstalledModule -Name Az -AllVersions | Select-Object -Property Name, Version

Name Version
---- -------
Az   4.4.0
```

To check Azure CLI modules version and extensions, run the following command:

PS:/>az version

```
PS /home/pjayaram> az version
{
  "azure-cli": "2.9.0",
  "azure-cli-command-modules-nspkg": "2.0.3",
  "azure-cli-core": "2.9.0",
  "azure-cli-nspkg": "3.0.4",
  "azure-cli-telemetry": "1.0.4",
  "extensions": {}
}
```

To find the loaded module, run the following the command

PS / > Find-Module -Name Azure,AzureRM,Az

```
PS /home/pjayaram> Find-Module -Name Azure,AzureRM,Az

Version    Name       Repository    Description
-------    ----       ----------    -----------
5.3.0      Azure      PSGallery     Microsoft Azure PowerShell - Service Management
4.4.0      Az         PSGallery     Microsoft Azure PowerShell - Cmdlets to manage resources in Azure. This module is compat…
6.13.1     AzureRM    PSGallery     Azure Resource Manager Module
```

By now, you can say that the use of cmdlets are simple and straightforward.

The history of PowerShell

This table data is important to understand the evolution of PowerShell. The matter of the fact that we still use PowerShell 2.0. It does not mean that you need to use PowerShell 2.0. We are using it all the way up to PowerShell 7.0. I recommend using the latest version of PowerShell. In some cases, the developer's choice or complexity of the process may lead to the use of the legacy version.

Note: The use of different PowerShell versions depends on the preference or choice or perhaps a standard within your company. You should know the available features by version. It may help you to build a more sophisticated automation task.

Using PowerShell, you can automate many mundane and repetitive tasks, and it allows administrators to focus on more important tasks.

PowerShell	Release Date	OS	Features
PowerShell 1.0	November 2006	Windows XP SP2, Windows Server 2003 SP1 and Windows Vista	PowerShell 1.0 started a new revolution to all the administrators. It's a major step to use cmdlets.
PowerShell 2.0	October 2009	Windows 7, Windows Server 2008, Windows XP with SP3, Windows Server 2003 SP2, and Windows Vista SP1	PowerShell v2 made a breakthrough into the scripting language and hosting API. It in-housed more than 240 new cmdlets. Remoting, Background jobs and script debugging is the major breakthrough of this release
PowerShell 3.0	September 2012	PowerShell 3.0 integrated with Windows 8 and with Windows Server 2012. Windows 7	Job scheduling, integration WinRM service for remoting,

		SP1, Windows Server 2008 SP1, and Windows Server 2008 R2 SP 1	Improved code writing IDE environment, intellisense for auto-detection of cmdlets and more
PowerShell 4.0	October 2013	It is an inbuilt feature of Windows 8.1 and with Windows Server 2012 R2, Windows 7 SP1, Windows Server 2008 R2 SP1 and Windows Server 2012	Support for Desired State Configuration (DSC) modules used for build, provision, deploy and manage the configuration of systems.
PowerShell 5.0	February 24, 2016	Windows Management Framework (WMF) 5.0 RTM includes PowerShell 5.0. Windows 7 SP1, Windows 8.1, Windows Server 2012, and Windows Server 2012 R2	Enhancement DSC modules and support to .Net enumerations and classes.
PowerShell 5.1	August 2, 2016	Inbuilt with Windows 10 and Windows Server 2016. And Windows 7 SP1, Windows 8.1, Windows Server 2008 R2 SP1, Windows Server 2012, and	PowerShell 5.1 released in two editions, "Desktop version" and "Core version." It was the last exclusive PowerShell made for the Windows Operating system.

		Windows Server 2012 R2	
PowerShell Core 6+	August 2016	Windows 10,Windows Server 2008 R2 SP1+,Windows Server 2012,Windows Server 2012 R2,Windows Server 2016, Windows Server 2019, Ubuntu 14.04,Ubuntu 16.04, Ubuntu 17.04,DEbian 8.7, CentOS 7, RHEL 7, OpenSUSE 42.2, Fedora 25+, macOS 10.12+	Fully cross-platform support on Windows, Linux and macOS.
PowerShell 7	December 3, 2019	Windows 7, 8.1, and 10 Windows Server 2008 R2, 2012, 2012 R2, 2016, and 2019, macOS 10.13+, Red Hat Enterprise Linux (RHEL) / CentOS 7+, Fedora 29+, Debian 9+, Ubuntu 16.04+, openSUSE 15+, and Alpine Linux 3.8+	PowerShell 7 is the replacement product for PowerShell Core 6.x and Windows PowerShell 5.1—the last supported Windows PowerShell version. The framework optimized for handling structured data such as JSON, CSV, XML, REST APIs, and object models

Note: *Azure PowerShell and Azure CLI both have the older versions—you need to know the parameters, and many of them are already deprecated. It is advised that you give the utmost importance when you're working with the corresponding Azure toolsets. I will also recommend reading online resources and Microsoft documentation to understand each cmdlet's usage and functionality better.*

Az and Az CLI commands

I will walk-through the VM Image data retrieval process using the Az, and Az CLI commands. The following table gives you the details of Az, and Az CLI commands. You can see that Az CLI commands ran within the BASH shell. In addition, it also ran from a PowerShell integrated console. These cmdlets are building blocks for Cloud automation.

Az	Tasks	Az CLI
PS /home/prashanth> Get-AzVMImagePublisher -Location $locName \| Where-Object {$_.PublisherName -like '*WindowsServer*'}|Select-Object PublisherName Note: You can run the Get-AzVMImage only in PowerShell interactive shell. In order to that, type in pwsh in the "$" Bash prompt.And then type in the Get-AzVMImagePublisher cmdlets	List the publisher Name in the specific location	PS /home/prashanth> az vm image list-publishers –l eastus --query "[?starts_with(name, 'MicrosoftWindowsServer')]" Bash: prashanth@Azure:~$ az vm image list-publishers -l eastus --query "[?starts_with(name, 'MicrosoftWindowsServer')]" Note: The output is JSON format. I will discuss more about the formatting part in the upcoming article.
PS /home/prashanth> Get-AzVMImagePublisher -Location eastus | Where-Object {$_.PublisherName -eq 'MicrosoftWindowsServer'}|Select-Object PublisherName,location|Get-AzVMImageOffer Note: The Publisher Name and location are mandatory parameters for Get-AzVMImageOffer. The output PublisherName and location	List the Image offers	>PARAM1='eastus' >PARAM2='MicrosoftWindows Server' az vm image list-offers -l $PARAM1 -p $PARAM2 -o table In the Bash shell, the parameters are declared as PARAM1 and PARAM2 and then passed as parameters to the az vm image list-offers command. Note: In order to run the same command in the PowerShell shell, refer to image Task 2(B).

are then piped to Get-AzVMImageOffer. You can see the details in the image Task 2.		
$locationName='eastus' $publisherName='MicrosoftWindowsServer' $offerName='windowsserver' Get-AzVMImageSku -Location $locationName -PublisherName $publisherName -Offer $offerName | Select-object Skus	List the VMImage SKUs. In this case, we need to type in the location, publisher name, offering to choose the SKU	$locationName='eastus' $publisherName='MicrosoftWindowsServer' $offerName='windowsserver' az vm image list-skus -l $locationName -f $offerName -p $publisherName -o table Note: In this sample, you can see that variables are passed to Az CLI command using PowerShell integrated shell. You can refer to Task(3) image.
Get-AzVMImage -Location "Central US" -PublisherName "MicrosoftWindowsServer" -Offer "windowsserver" -Skus "2016-Datacenter"	List all the versions of the VM Image	$locationName='eastus' $publisherName='MicrosoftWindowsServer' $offerName='windowsserver' $sku='2016-Datacenter' az vm image list -l $locationName -f $offerName -p $publisherName -s $sku

Supported platforms

The below table gives platform details that support Azure PowerShell and Azure CLI modules.

Platform	Azure PowerShell	Azure CLI

Windows	Yes	Yes
Linux	Yes	Yes
macOS	Yes	Yes
CloudShell	Yes	Yes
Container Support	Yes	Yes
Visual Studio Code	Yes	Yes
Open Source	Yes	Yes

Differences between Azure PowerShell and Azure CLI

Azure PowerShell and AZ CLI both are associated with the scripting language.

Azure PowerShell	Azure CLI
A scripting language based on the .Net framework and developed using C#	Developed using Python
The outputs are in the form of objects	The output is in the form of text or strings
Integrated with REST APIs of Azure	Integrated with REST APIs of Azure
Easy to manage cross-platform	Easy to manage cross-platform
Open Source	Open Source
The modules are fully developed and integrated to manage all the Azure cloud resources and services	It is still under development.
Commands are cmdlets that follow a standard naming convention "Verb+Noun" combination	Commands are short, simple and intuitive starts with "az"
Windows Administrators preferred choice	Linux Administrators preferred choice

Azure Automation Account

Microsoft Azure Automation is a framework that simplifies complex and repetitive tasks. It is a service used to create and schedule workflows. We commonly know the workflows as run-books. It is a managed service to automate the entire application life cycle, such as deployment to provisioning and testing to decommissioning.

Azure Automation's engine is built on the PowerShell workflow engine. The Service Management Automation (SMA) framework is compatible with the Windows PowerShell workflows. With a little modification, you will be able to port the Windows PowerShell workflow model and run them in the Azure Automation portal.

What is a runbook?

The run-book is a standard set of operating processes and procedures to run repetitively to serve enterprise tasks. A runbook is the core component for automation that can automate and orchestrate any simple or complex task.

The tasks can include:

1. Resource Management
2. Deployment Management
3. Patching and Upgrade Management
4. Backups Management
5. Error log management
6. Database volume management
7. User and security management

Create Azure automation account

1. Sign in to the Azure Portal at

2. Click Automation Accounts

Azure services

Create a resource
Automation Accounts
Azure SQL
SQL databases
Resource groups
Kubernetes services
Marketplace
Cost Management...
Logic apps

3. Click Add

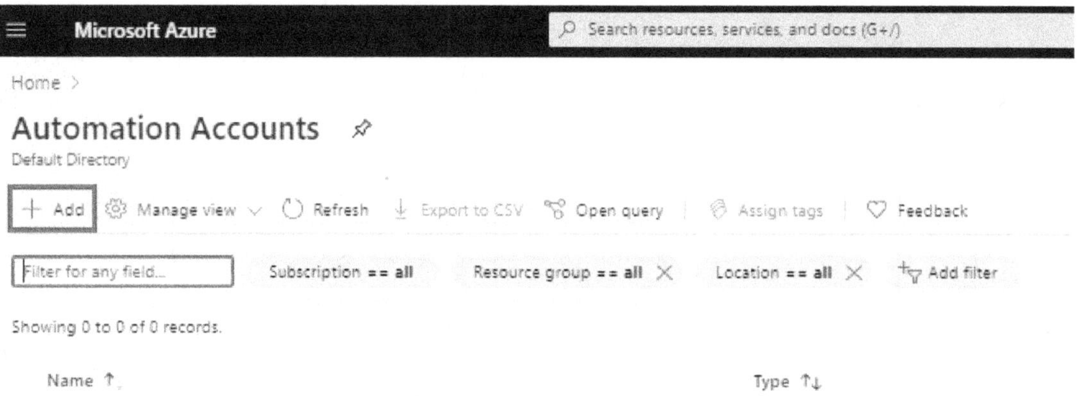

4. Type in the automation account name. The automation account name must be unique per region and resource group.

5. Select the subscription, resource group and location.

6. Next, choose **Create Azure Run As account** to **Yes**. This option simplifies authentication and enables access to internal azure resources.

7. Click Create

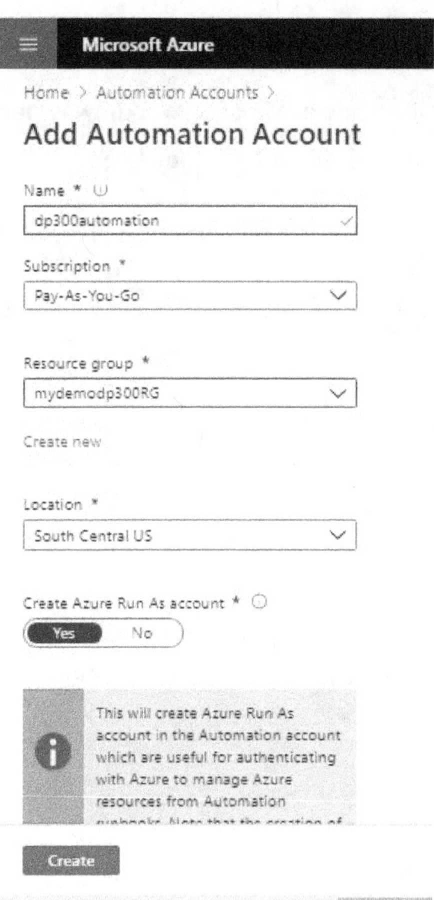

8. Deployment completed. Now, you can see the dp300automation service account created.

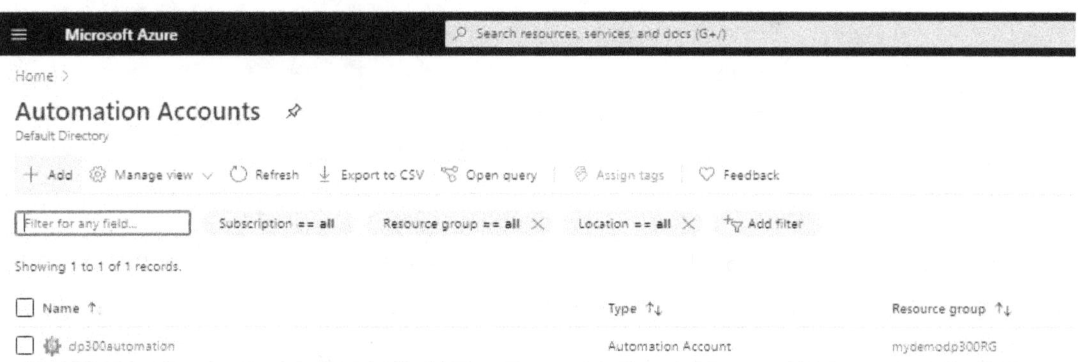

Import a runbook

Importing a runbook is a simple way to onboard the functionality to the automation workflow. When you import a runbook—you get the pre-defined code, written, tested, and made ready to go.

There are several ways to import runbook:

1. Internal company sites—within the internal sites or private repositories within the organization

2. Community sites or Microsoft Script Center

3. Azure Management Portal runbook Gallery

4. Automation GitHub organization

TechNet Script Center is retiring—all the runbooks are moved to Automation GitHub organization

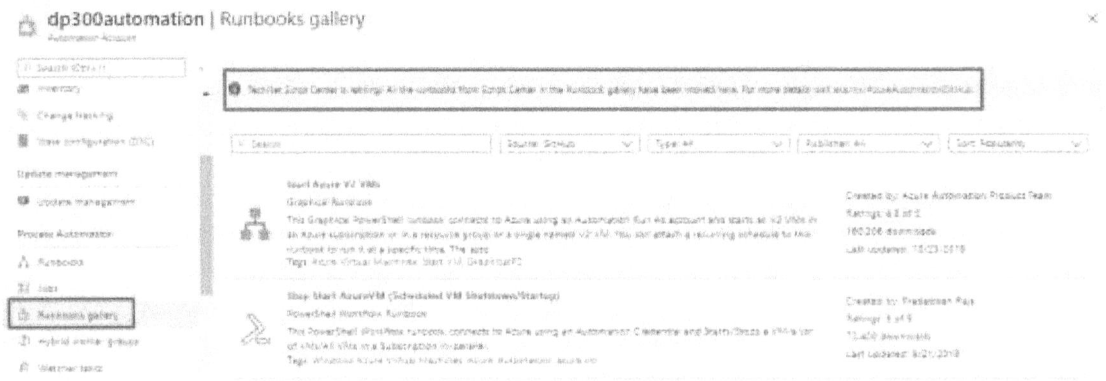

In the search, type the "database" search keyword to list database-related workflow. Next, click the Import button to load the workflow into the automation workspace.

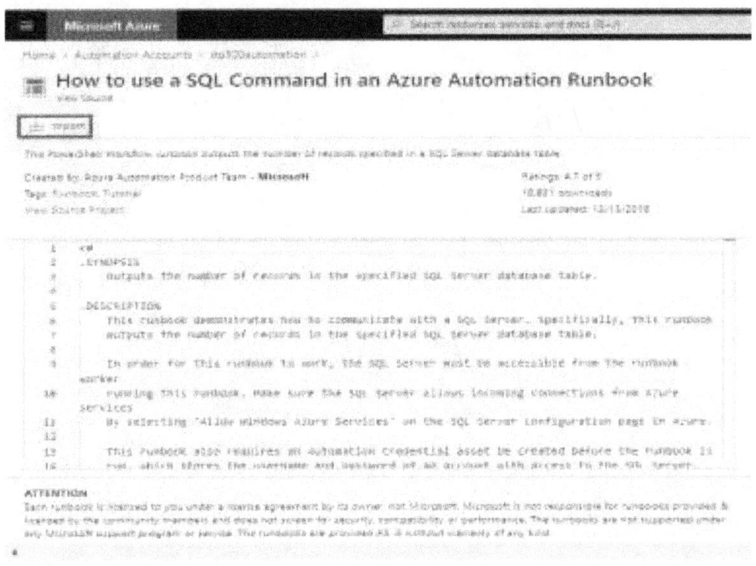

Type in the name and meaning description to load the workflow.

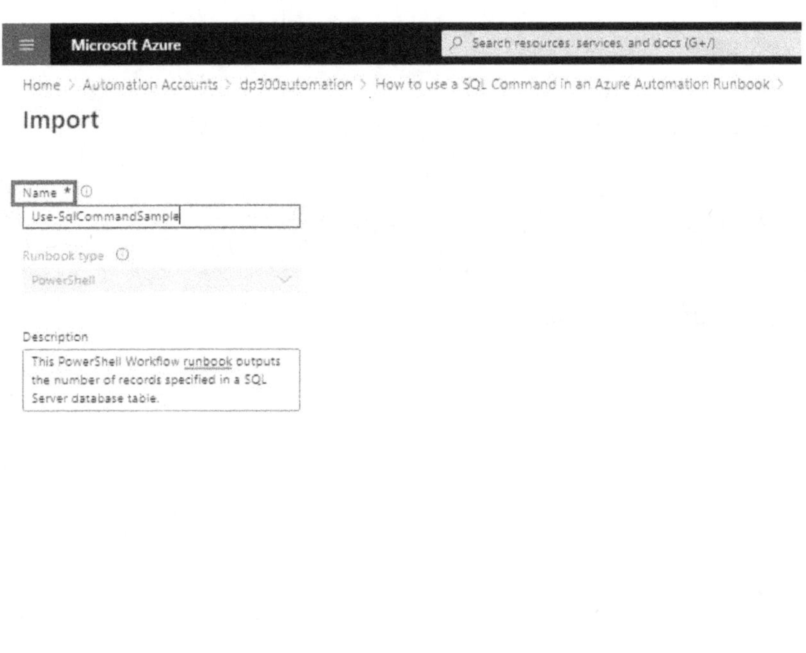

Now, you will see the PowerShell Runbook into the Runbook Process Automation workspace.

How to load PowerShell modules

In this section, you will see how to load the **sqlserver** module from the PowerShell gallery.

1. Browse the link https://www.powershellgallery.com/packages/SqlServer/21.0.17199
2. In the installation option, choose the **Azure Automation** tab.
3. Select **Deploy to Azure Automation.**
4. It will redirect to the Azure portal to authorize your account.

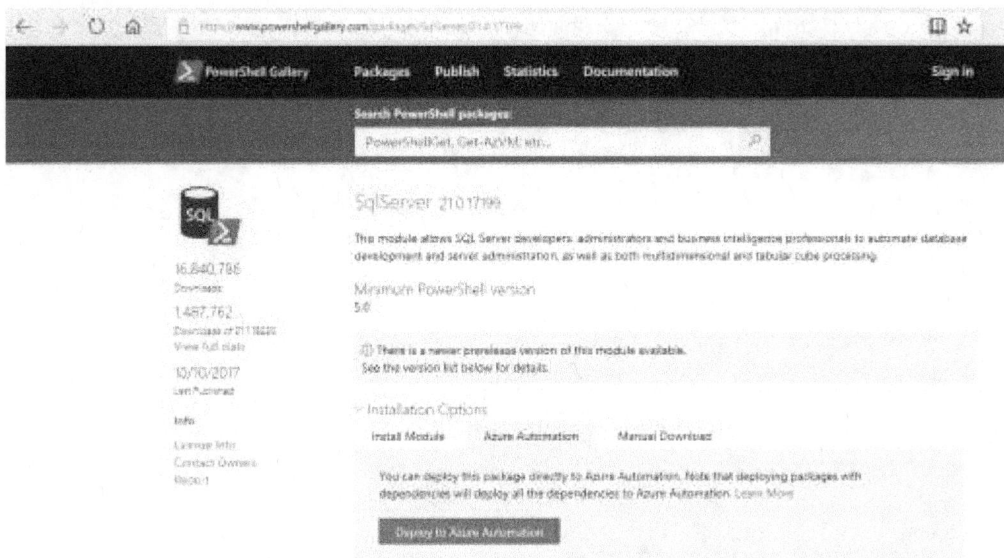

5. Select the module tab and type in sql to check the status of the import operation.

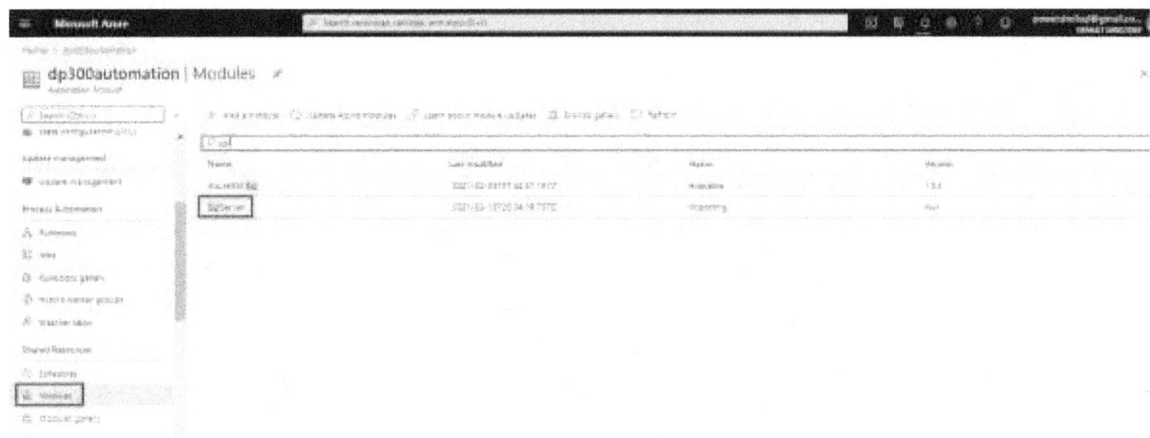

How to create PowerShell workflow

In this section, you will see the steps to create a PowerShell workflow runbook.

1. Open the automation account pane and click **Runbooks**.
2. Click **Create a runbook.**

3. Type in the name, workflow category of the template and description details.
4. Click **Create**

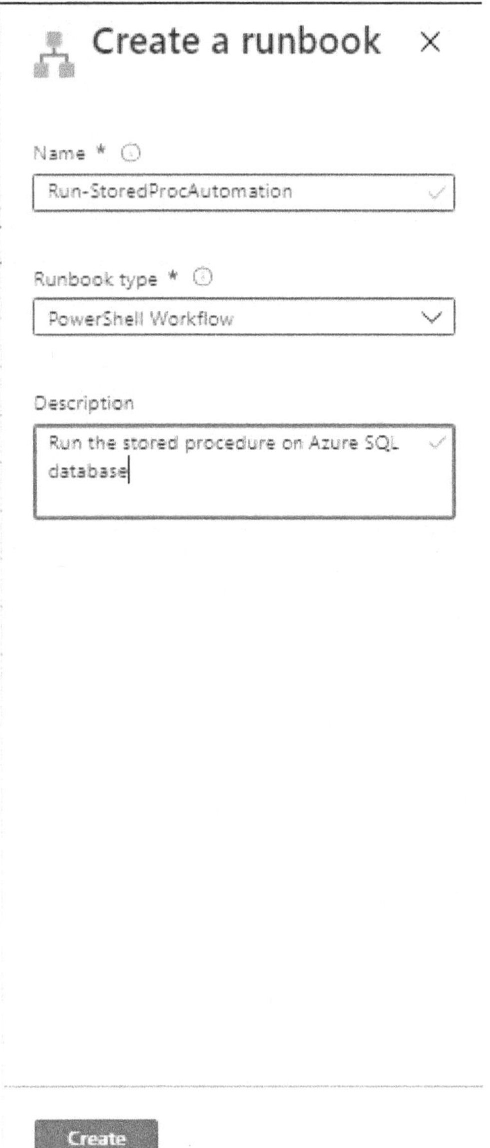

5. Define credentials and variables in the shared resources.

Note: Use credential asset that contains the same User ID and Password for the remote session into Azure SQL databases.

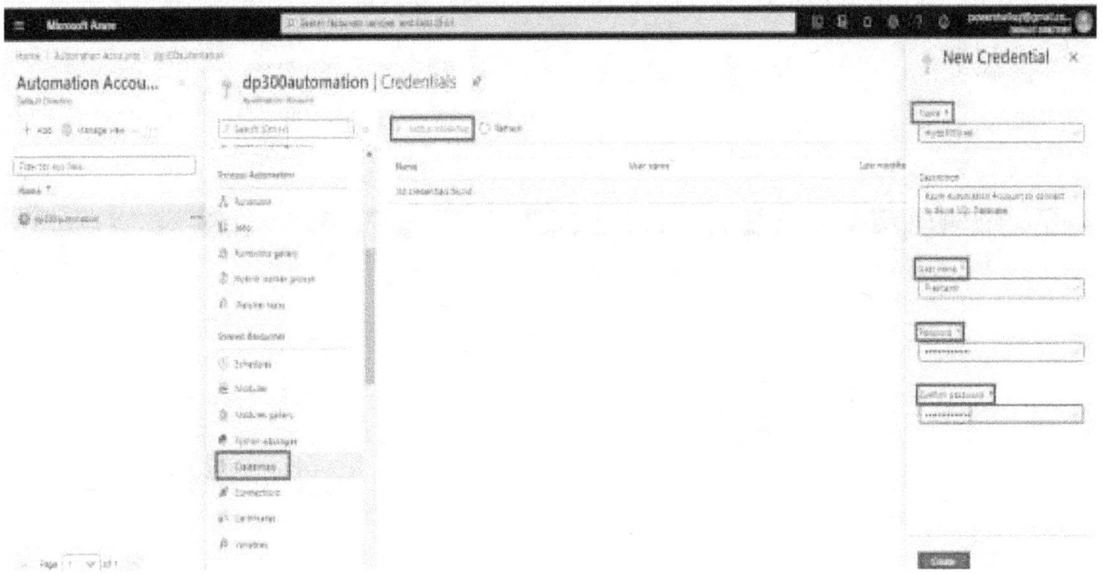

6. The first part of the PowerShell workflow runbook to define some key variables that you will need to set ahead of time.

7. Define Input variables include the Azure connection asset such as server name and database name and PowerShell credential asset.

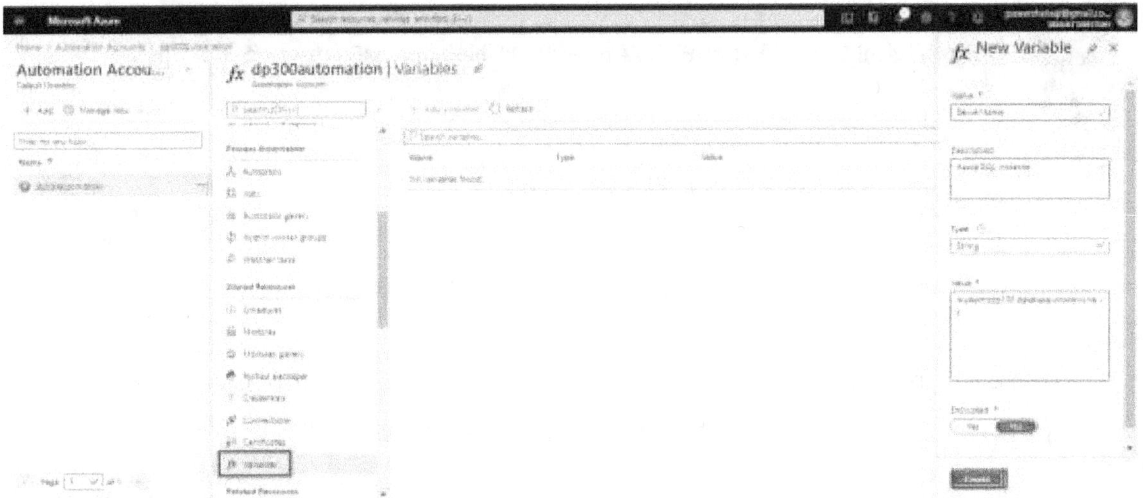

8. The name of the Runbook and workflow must be the same. In this case, it is QuerySP

Note: You should use the same name for both runbook and workflow.

9. Copy and paste the below PowerShell runbook workflow code from the URL

Copy the script from the URL
https://github.com/AzureDP300/AzureDP300/blob/main/Chapter9/Script1.ps1

10. Click the Edit button to test the Runbook.

11. Select the Test pane to test the code.

12. Click the Start button to initiate the test. It is the only enabled option to test the runbook.

13. The Runbook job is created.

14. The status or output is displayed in the result pane.

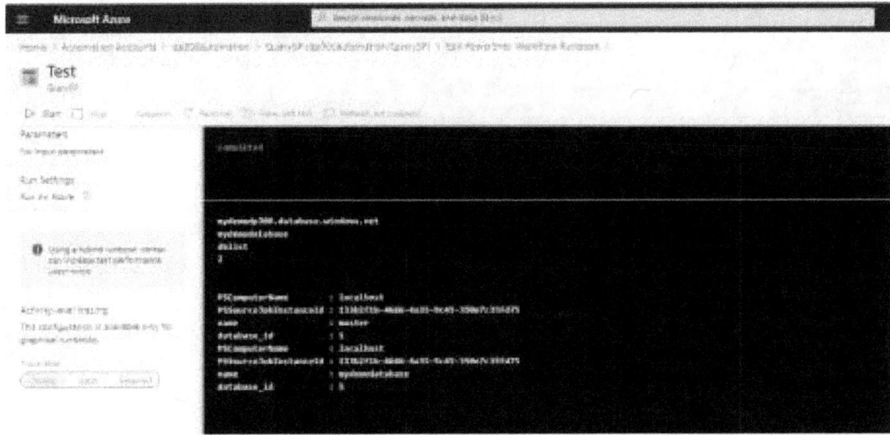

15. Publish the Runbook

Publish the runbook

We have tested the QuerySP runbook and validated the output in the last section. Now, you will see how to commit the draft runbook version. Before you publish a runbook, test it to ensure that you are getting the desired output and it's ready to use.

1. Click Publish to commit the version

2. You will be redirected to the runbooks page, and you can see that the status is set to Published.
3. Click **Start** to execute the published runbook. You will be prompted again, choose "Yes" to start the runbook

4. Now, you will again redirect to a Job pane to view the job status.
5. You can view the complete status of the runbook execution status in the output pane.
6. To check the status, you can keep refreshing the Refresh icon to view the possible status.
7. To view the result, select the output to view the summary.

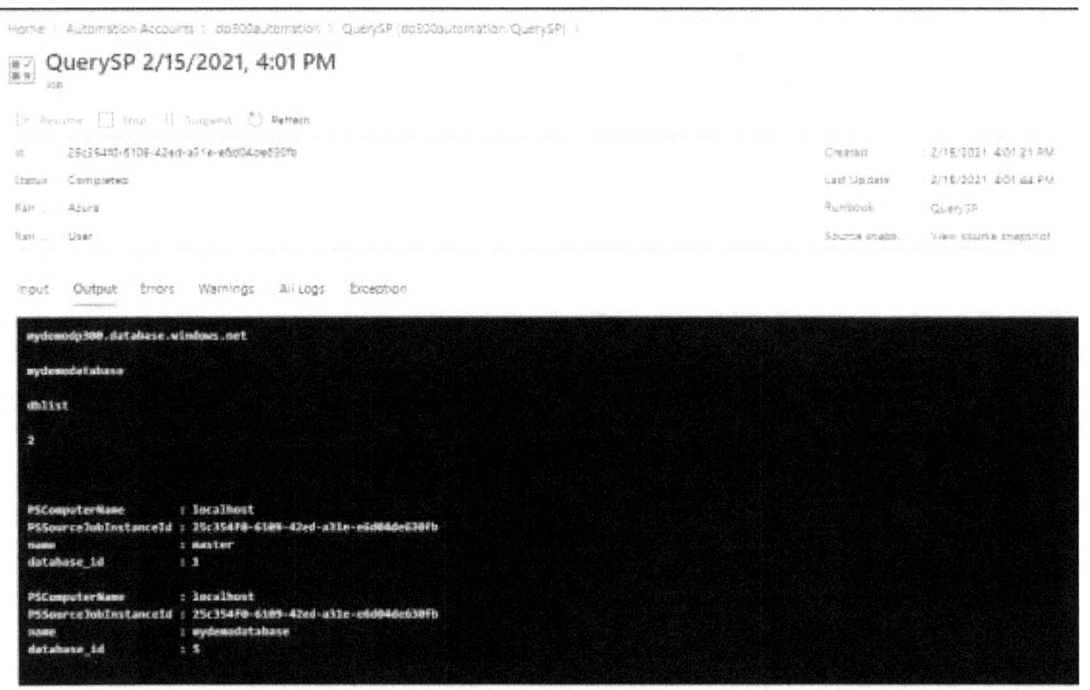

Linked Server to run T-SQL on Azure SQL database

1. To create a linked server, browse the **Object Explorer.**
2. Locate the **Server Objects** folder.
3. Right-click on the Linked Servers folder and choose the **New Linked Server.**
4. Type in the valid **connection name** to the Azure SQL database.
5. Under the **Server type**, choose the **Other data source.**
6. In the Data source, Type in the **target SQL Azure**. Here, we are connecting to mydemodp300.database.windows.net.
7. Enter the **Catalog database** name. Here, we are connecting to mydemodatabase.

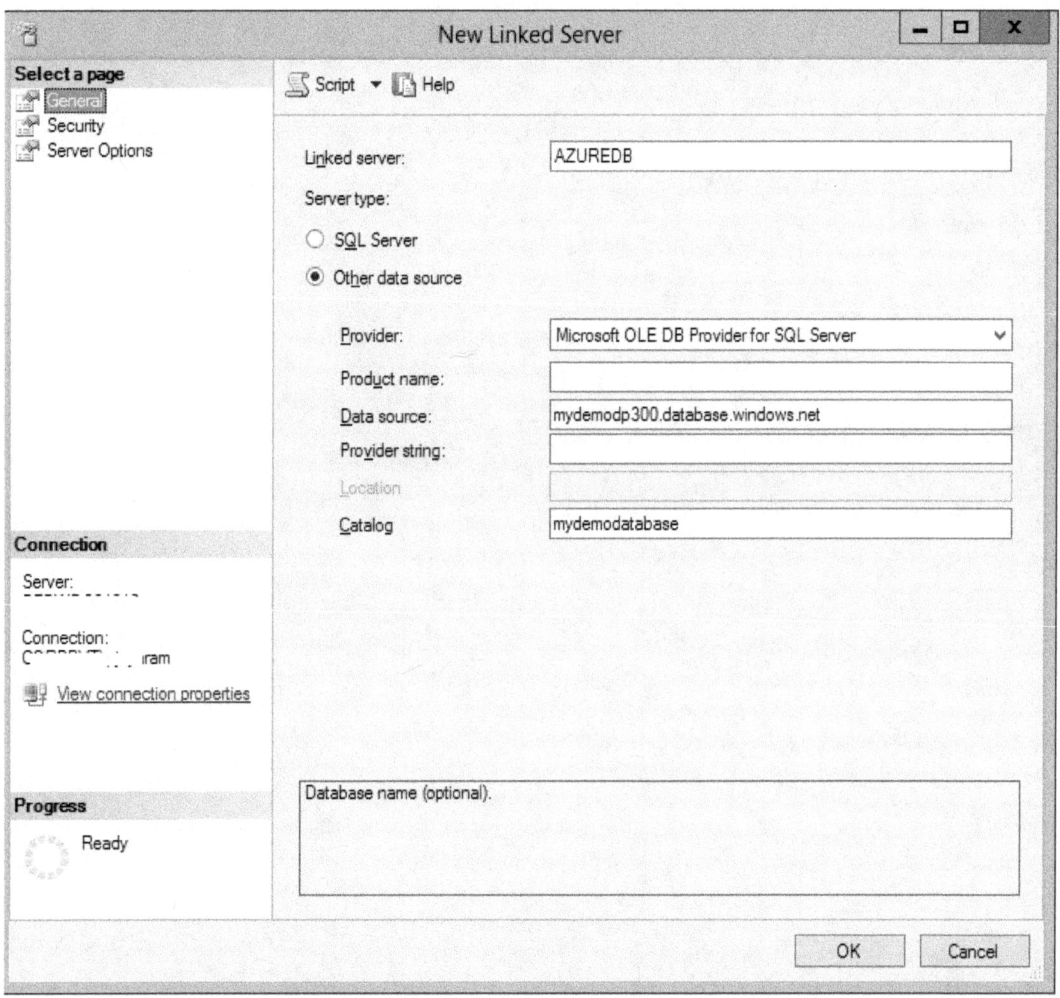

1. Under the **Security tab**, choose Be made using this security context and enter credentials that you use to access the Azure SQL database.

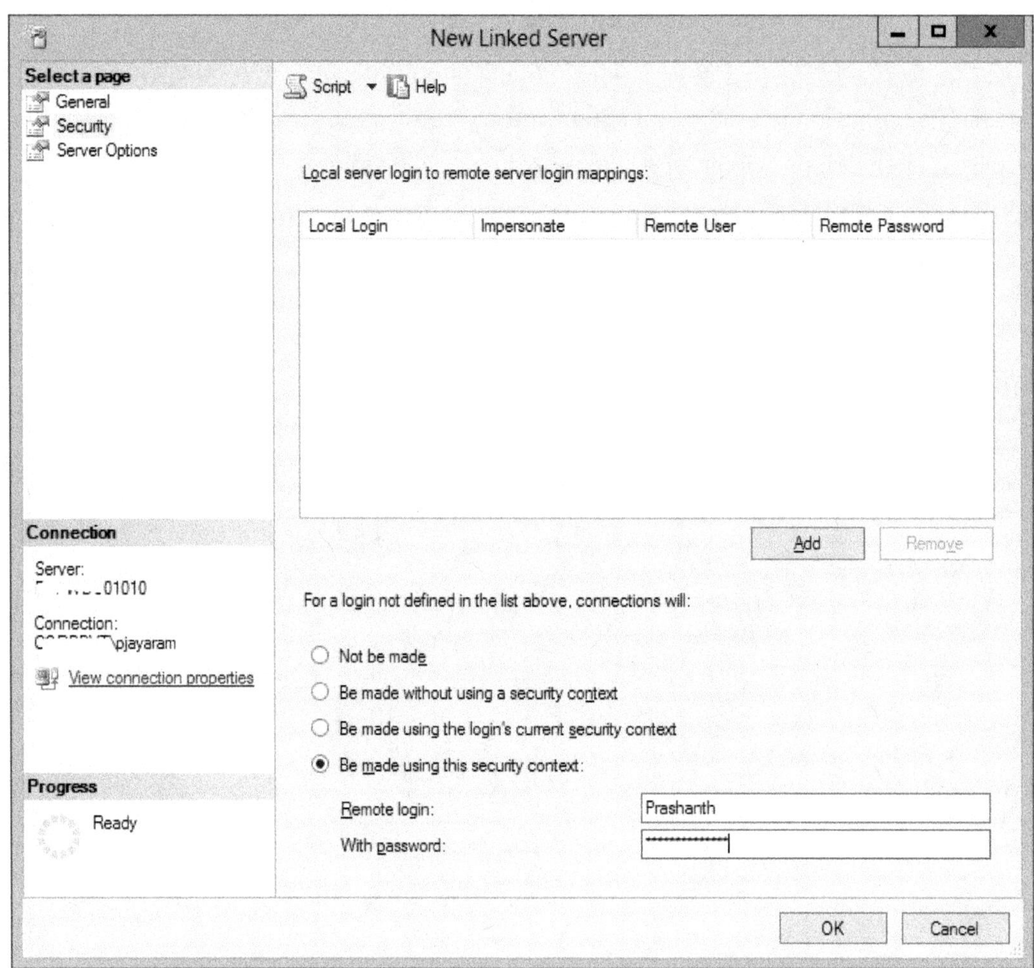

2. Under the Server **Options**, enable RPC and RPC Out (Remote Procedure Call) options that allow remote procedures call using a linked server. By default, these settings are set to false.

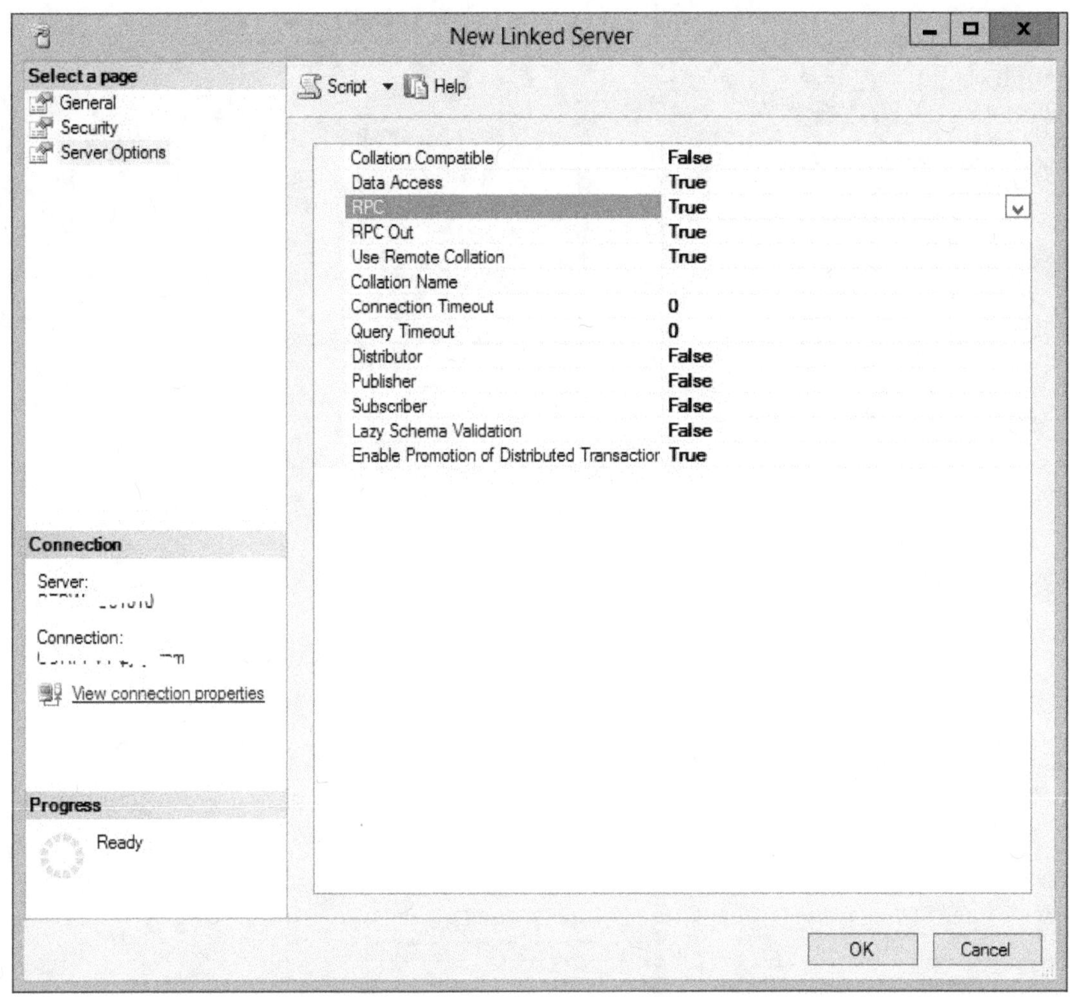

Now, run the stored procedure on the Azure SQL database locally and compare the output against running the same stored procedure remotely using a linked server.

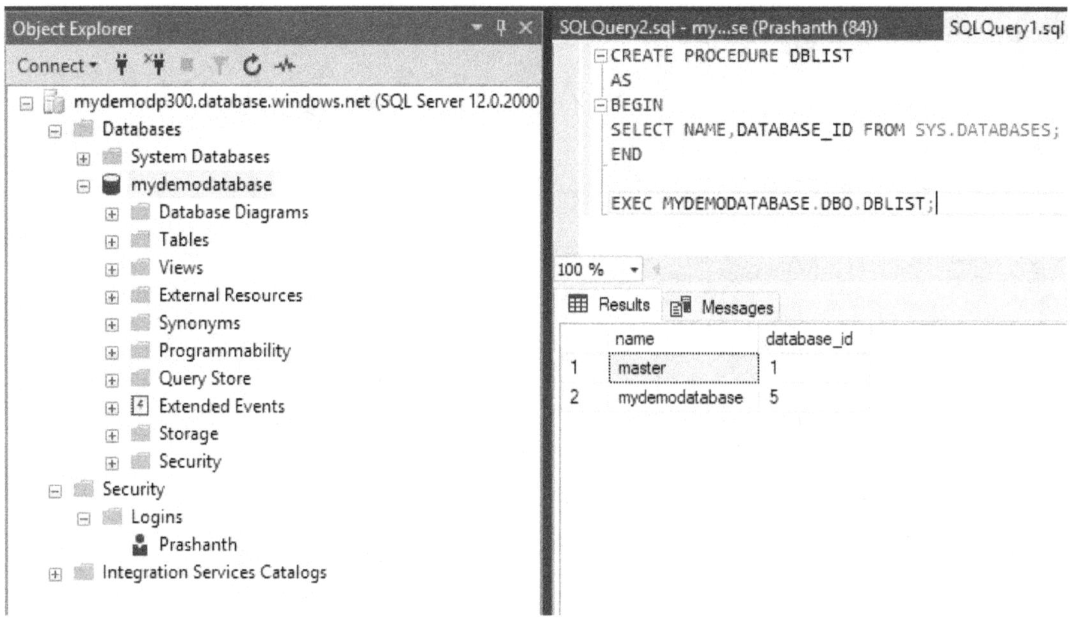

In this way, we can make a remote procedure call using a linked server.

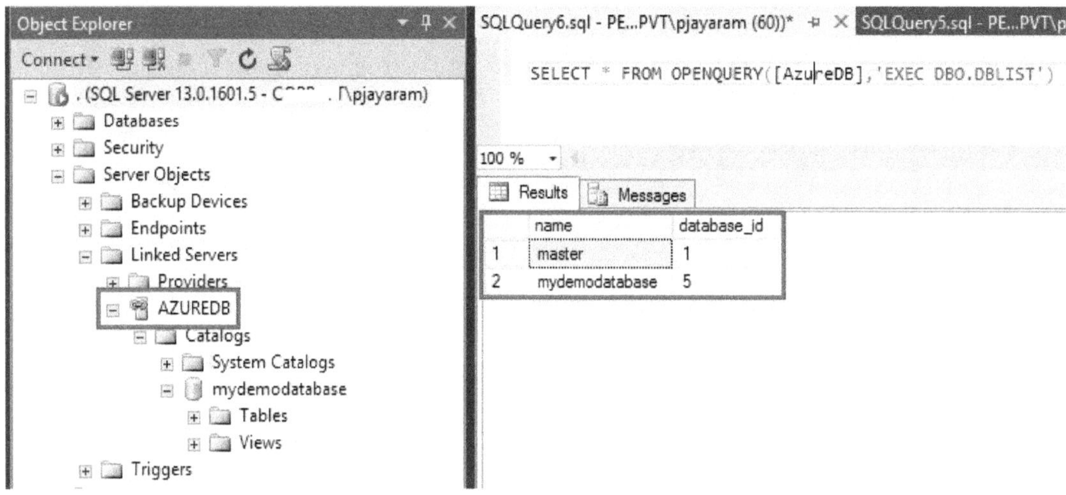

Azure Elastic Jobs

In real-world migration, we see most of the databases are compatible to migrate them to Azure SQL databases. Because of the non-existence of **SQL Server Agent Jobs**, we either opt for SQL on Azure VM or Azure SQL Managed Instance or migrating the jobs to Azure automation. Sometimes, we even manage the jobs using a linked server from an on-premise SQL Server. In addition, Azure bundles with another preview feature of Azure Elastic Database Jobs.

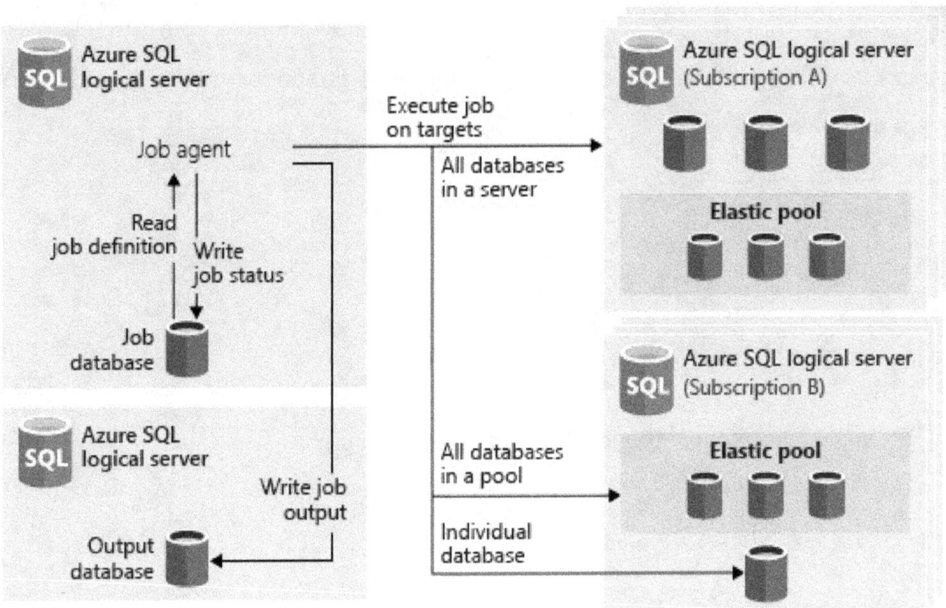

Components

The elastic job components are given below:

Component	Description
Elastic Job agent	The elastic job agent is a resource that allows you to administer Jobs.
Job database	Azure SQL Database captures meta-data related to the jobs. It is like a MSDB database.
Target group	The target group lists the databases to run the job.
Job	It is the basic unit of work, and it comprises one or more job steps. The Job steps are where you specify the T-SQL script to run and other details required to execute the script.

Note: Elastic Jobs feature is currently in public preview. We can still use this feature, and it requires no extra steps to get started after this feature becomes officially available to use.

Elastic jobs

An elastic Job is a powerful tool that can do several automated database maintenance tasks on a set of Azure SQL databases.

- Statistics updates
- Index maintenance
- Data maintenance

The elastic jobs support all the Azure SQL database offerings, such as

- DTU based models—Basic, Standard, and Premium
- VCore based models—Hyperscale and Serverless
- Azure Elastic Pool databases

Note: The only requirement is to configure the Azure SQL database with the service level objective of S0 or above.

When should I use Elastic Jobs?

Elastic Jobs are most suited:

- When you need to run the task regularly on a schedule by targeting one or more Azure SQL databases.
- When you need to run the task across multiple databases targets with multiple schedules

Limitations

There are a couple of limitations to understand before we get into the internals:

- It's still a preview feature from a long time.

- There is a limit to running a number of concurrent jobs.
- Manage jobs using PowerShell or T-SQL.
- You can view the jobs in the portal, but it is not possible to trigger the job.
- We must configure jobs to use the same credentials on all targets. You need to ensure the account must exist in all the target databases.

Configure Elastic job steps

The following are the steps involved in creating an elastic job and scheduling it.

1. Create an Elastic Job agent.
2. Create credentials on the Agent database.
3. Create a target group and members.
4. Create logins on the target master database.
5. Create a user on the target databases.
6. Create job and job steps.
7. Schedule the job .

Create an Elastic Job agent

We can start setting up our elastic job. Before that, we need to set up an Azure SQL database with S1 or above service level objective.

1. Browse the Azure portal and type in the **elastic** keyword in the marketplace search box.
2. Select the **Elastic Job agents**.

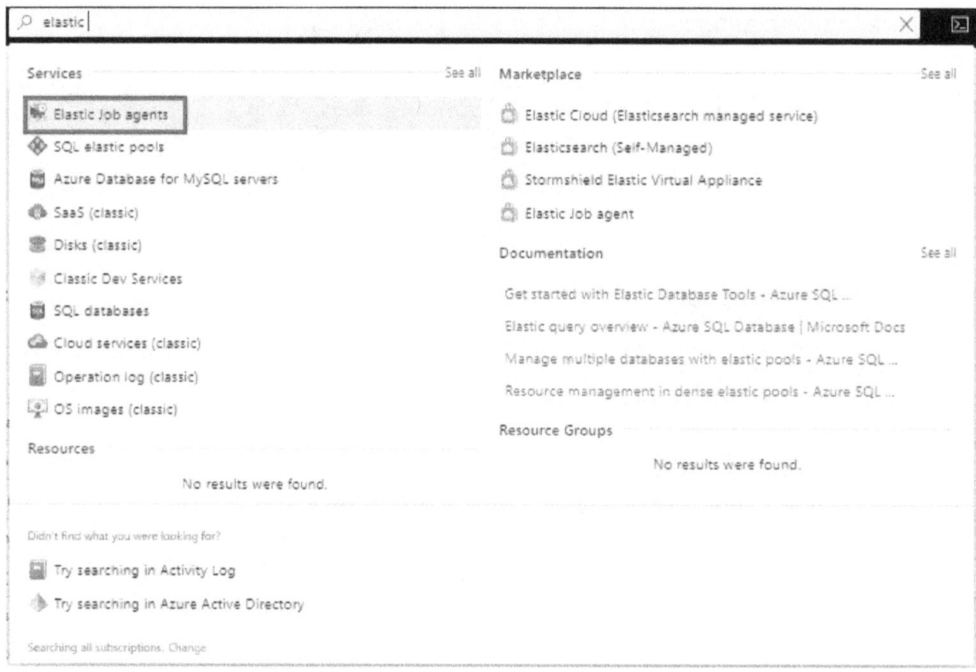

3. Click Add.

4. Type in the name of the elastic job agent.

5. Choose the subscription. In this case, You see that a “Pay-as-you-go” subscription is selected.

6. Select the target database.

7. Click Create.

8. The deployment is in progress. During the process, the Elastic job agent creates meta-data to run the agent jobs from the database.

Once the deployment completes, you can see the elastic job is ready for the configuration.

Creating database scoped credentials on the agent database

Use the credentials to connect with the Azure SQL target to execute the scripts. You need to create two credentials in the elastic job agent database.

```
CREATE MASTER KEY ENCRYPTION BY PASSWORD='elasticdp300@2021';

GO

CREATE DATABASE SCOPED CREDENTIAL elasicJobRun WITH IDENTITY = 'elasticJobUser',

  SECRET = 'elasticdp300@2021';
```

GO

CREATE DATABASE SCOPED CREDENTIAL elasticMaster WITH IDENTITY = 'elasticMasterUser',

SECRET ='elasticdp300@2022';

GO

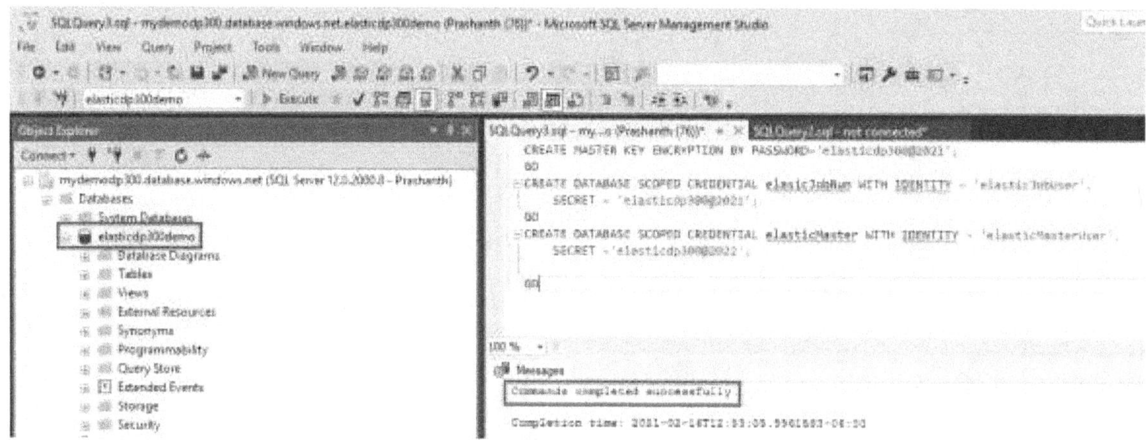

To check the scoped credentials, run the following T-SQL

SELECT * FROM sys. database_scoped_credentials

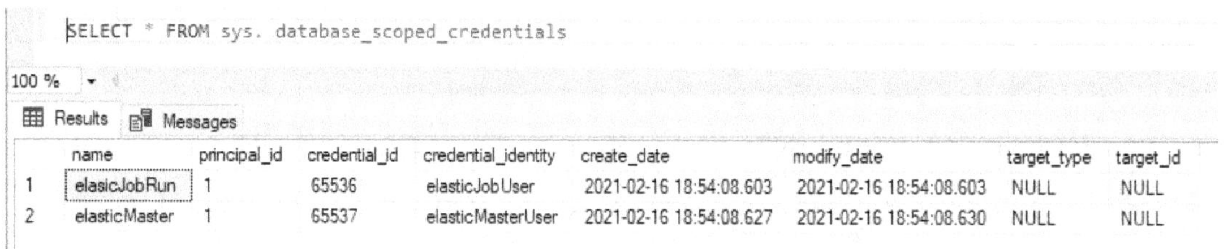

SELECT * FROM sys. database_scoped_credentials

	name	principal_id	credential_id	credential_identity	create_date	modify_date	target_type	target_id
1	elasicJobRun	1	65536	elasticJobUser	2021-02-16 18:54:08.603	2021-02-16 18:54:08.603	NULL	NULL
2	elasticMaster	1	65537	elasticMasterUser	2021-02-16 18:54:08.627	2021-02-16 18:54:08.630	NULL	NULL

Creating a target group and members

The target group lists the databases to run the T-SQL against the list.

EXEC jobs.sp_add_target_group 'DatabaseMaintenanceGroup'

GO

EXEC jobs.sp_add_target_group_member

@target_group_name=N'DatabaseMaintenanceGroup',

@target_type = N'SqlDatabase',

@server_name='mydemodp300.database.windows.net',

@database_name =N'mydemodatabase'

GO

```
EXEC jobs.sp_add_target_group 'DatabaseMaintenanceGroup'
GO
EXEC jobs.sp_add_target_group_member
@target_group_name=N'DatabaseMaintenanceGroup',
@target_type =  N'SqlDatabase',
@server_name='mydemodp300.database.windows.net',
@database_name =N'mydemodatabase'
GO
```

.00 %

Messages

```
Commands completed successfully.

Completion time: 2021-02-16T13:29:07.5646799-06:00
```

Now, let us verify the target group details.

SELECT TOP (1000) [target_id]

,[target_group_name]

,[server_name]

,[database_name]

,[elastic_pool_name]

,[shard_map_name]

,[target_type]

FROM [jobs_internal].[targets]

Results | Messages

	target_id	target_group_name	server_name	database_name	elastic_pool_name	shard_map_name	target_type
1	C8A4EE9F-E24C-43FA-9CBF-054560548D68	DatabaseMaintenanceGroup	NULL	NULL	NULL	NULL	TargetGroup
2	B699AEB5-1D0C-4CDA-BE9D-27F0D9F25B40	NULL	mydemodp300.database.windows.net	mydemodatabase	NULL	NULL	SqlDatabase

Creating logins on target master

Create login for the **elasticmasteruser** and **elasticjobuser** in the target database. Now, change the database context to the master database before executing the T-SQL.

CREATE LOGIN elasticMasterUser

WITH PASSWORD = 'elasticdp300@2022';

GO

CREATE LOGIN elasticJobUser

WITH PASSWORD = 'elasticdp300@2021';

GO

CREATE USER elasticMasterUser

FROM LOGIN elasticMasterUser

Create a user on the target database

Create the user on the target database. You need to ensure you grant enough permission to run the job. Create the user **elasticjobuser** on each target. To run the login script change the database context to the master database. To map the database user, you need to change the database context to the user database again.

CREATE LOGIN elasticJobUser

WITH PASSWORD = 'elasticdp300@2021';

CREATE USER elasticJobUser

FROM LOGIN elasticJobUser

ALTER ROLE db_owner

ADD MEMBER elasticJobUser

Create a job and job step

On the Agent database, create the scripts to run in the job and job steps.

EXEC jobs.sp_add_job @job_name='Run Sample T-SQL', @description='Execute Stored procedure'

EXEC jobs.sp_add_jobstep @job_name='Run Sample T-SQL',

@command=N' EXEC dbo.dblist',

@credential_name='elasicJobRun',

@target_group_name='DatabaseMaintenanceGroup'

Run and monitor the job

To start the job, run sp_start_job on the Agent database.

EXEC jobs.sp_start_job 'Run Sample T-SQL'

To view the job execution status run the following T-SQL.

select * from jobs.job_executions

You can also view the status from the Azure portal. Browse the elastic job service and locate an overview to check the status.

Schedule the job

To schedule a job, you need to understand the different interval types.

1. Once
2. Minutes
3. Hours
4. Days
5. Weeks
6. Months

Now, run the sp_update_job by specifying the interval type on the master or agent database.

```
EXEC jobs.sp_update_job

@job_name='Run Sample T-SQL',

@enabled=1,
```

@schedule_interval_type='Hours',

@schedule_interval_count=1

Create Scheduled Jobs using Logic App

In this chapter, you will understand how to configure a logic app to manipulate the Azure SQL database data using SQL Server connector. You can use this service to automate tasks, processes, or workflows. The SQL Server connector works for **Azure SQL Database, Azure SQL Managed Instance** and SQL Server.

Use-Case: Create a workflow to load the data by executing SP using Logic Apps.

To simulate this use-case, DEMODP300 created in an Azure SQL Database mydemodatabase. In addition, you will see a stored procedure that generates the data for this table.

Create the following objects on the Azure SQL databases. The script will create a base table and a stored procedure. Using Logic Apps, we will trigger a stored procedure execution that will auto-populate the table's data.

CREATE TABLE DEMODP300

(

NAME VARCHAR(200),

DATABASE_ID INT

)

SELECT * FROM DEMODP300;

CREATE PROCEDURE [DBO].[DBLIST]

AS

BEGIN

INSERT INTO DEMODP300

SELECT NAME, DATABASE_ID FROM SYS.DATABASES;

END

SELECT * FROM DEMODP300

Configure Logic Apps

1. Browse the market place to locate Logic apps.

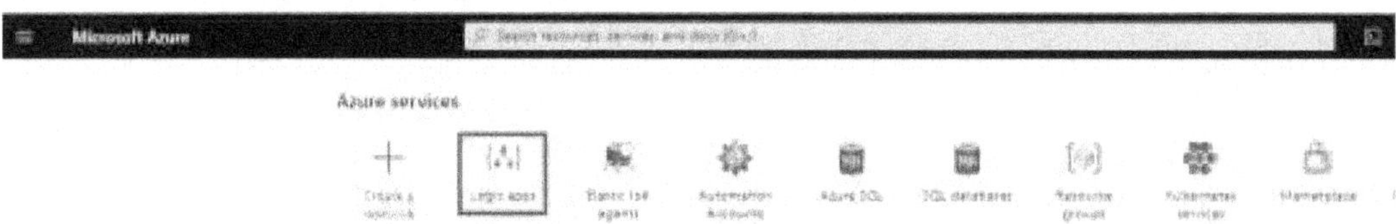

2. Click **Create** to get started.

3. Type in the Logic app name and choose the region.
4. Click Create.

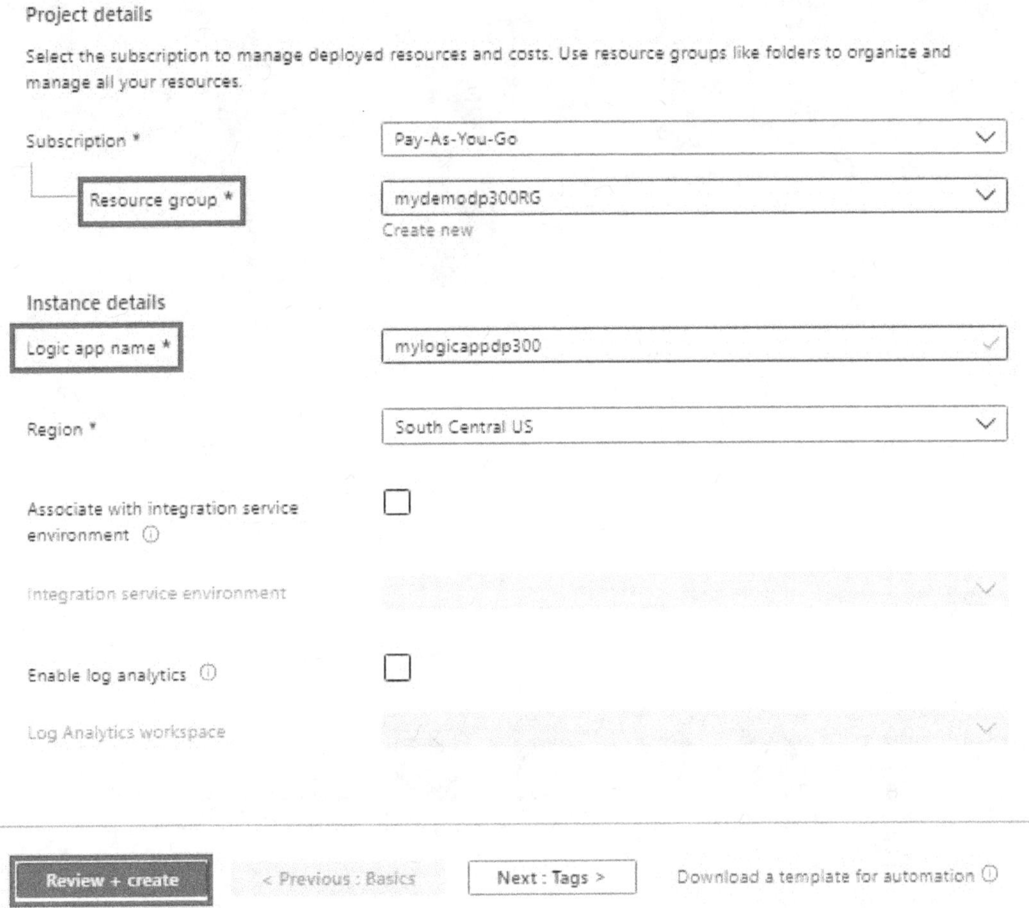

Click on **Go to resource** button when the deployment is complete

Build Logic Apps

The above step should direct you to the **Logic Apps Designer** screen. You will see many pre-built templates but let us choose a **Blank Logic App**.

Logic Apps Designer

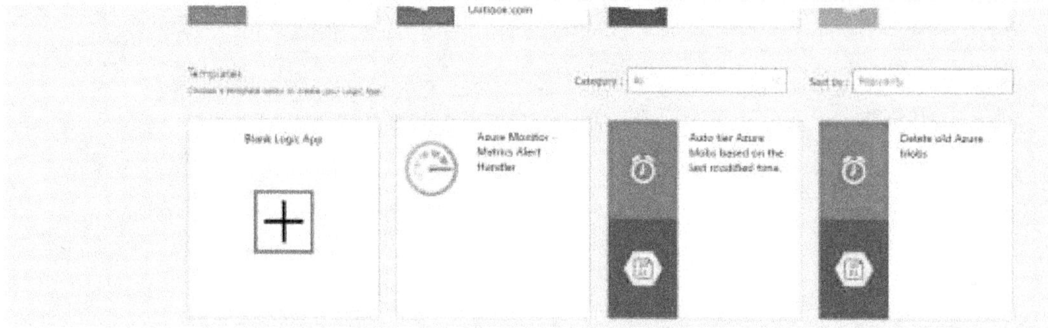

Let us search for a **schedule** to trigger the stored procedure execution.

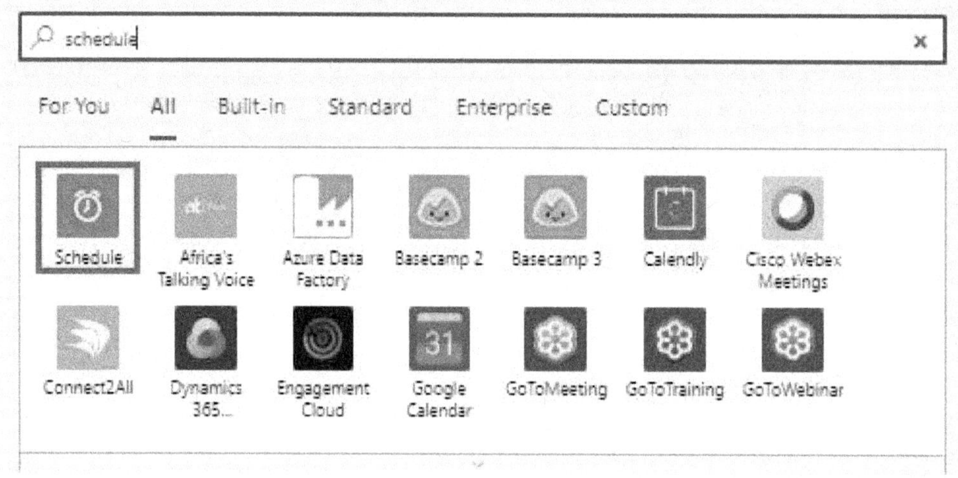

It is like the SQL Server agent schedule in Azure Logic apps. You can choose the schedule of stored procedure execution as per the requirement. Here, the stored procedure is executed with a frequency of 3 minutes. Click New Step.

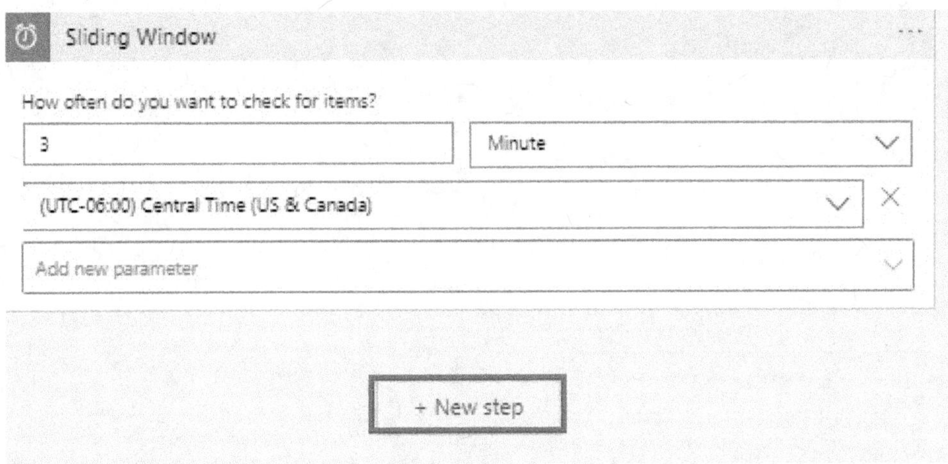

To trigger the job in Azure Logic App, we need to define the schedule event. After you define the schedule, click the next step to add the SQL Server event. Here, you can see that we use the **Execute stored procedure (V2)** event in the **Actions** filter.

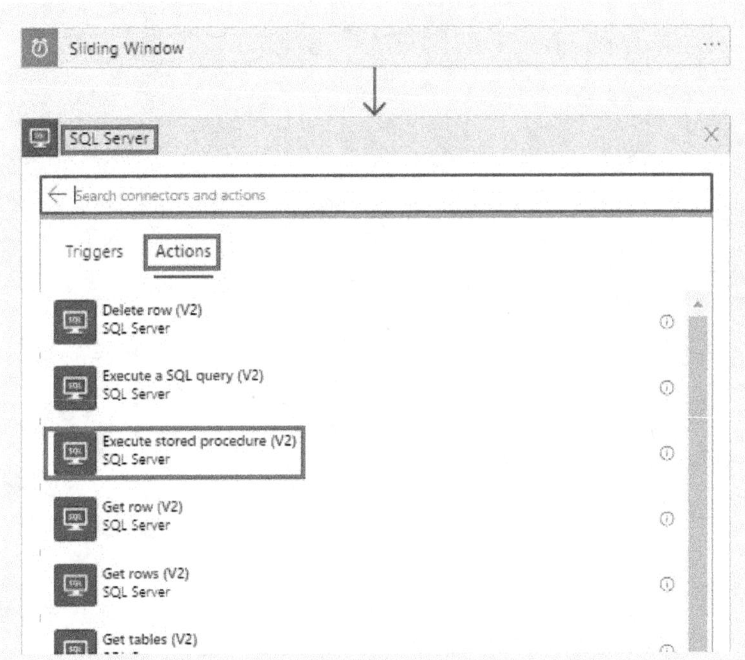

Next, build the server connection to the Azure SQL database. Fill in the details of the target Azure SQL database and click **Create.**

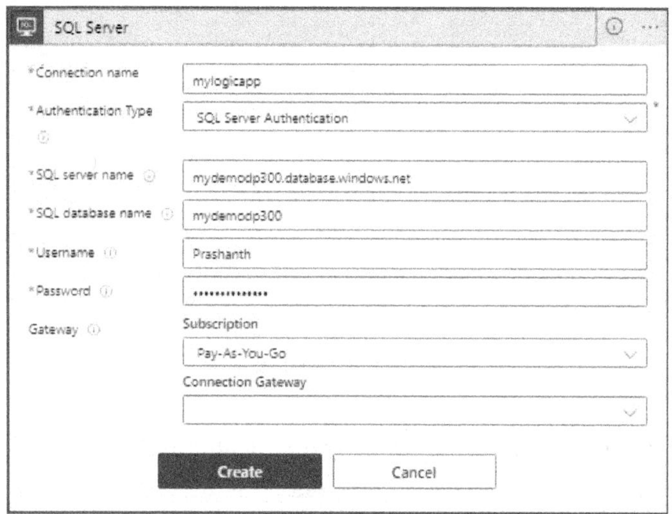

In this sample, we are executing the stored procedure. The job will execute the stored procedure that, in turn, inserts the data into the table.

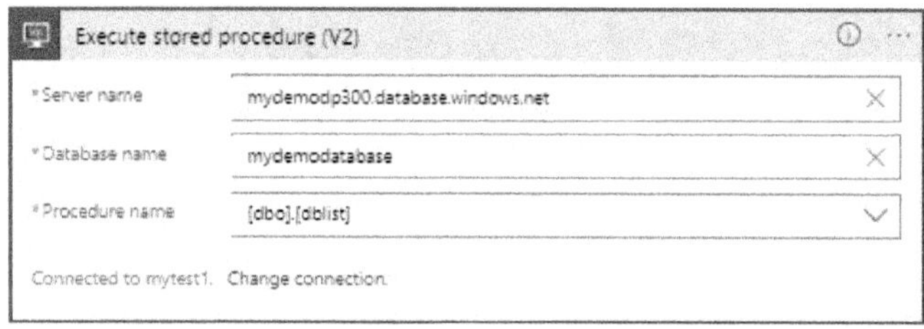

Save the configuration in the Logic Apps Designer window.

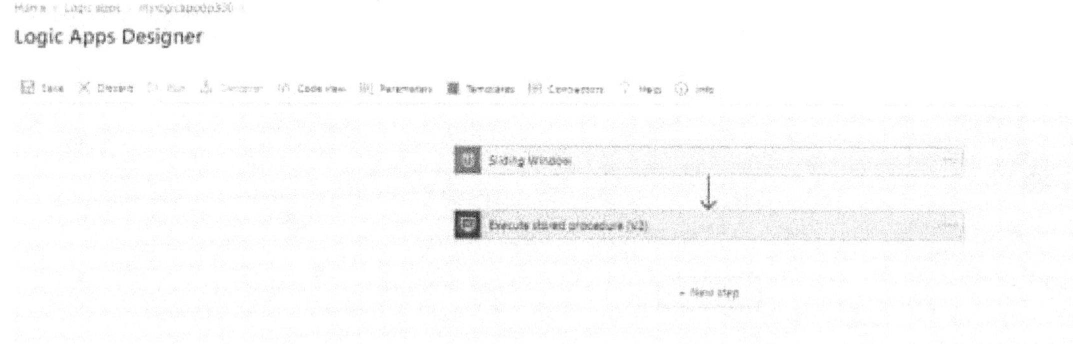

Now, check for the status by manually running the job. You can see a write check mark appear as an indication of the successful execution of the procedure.

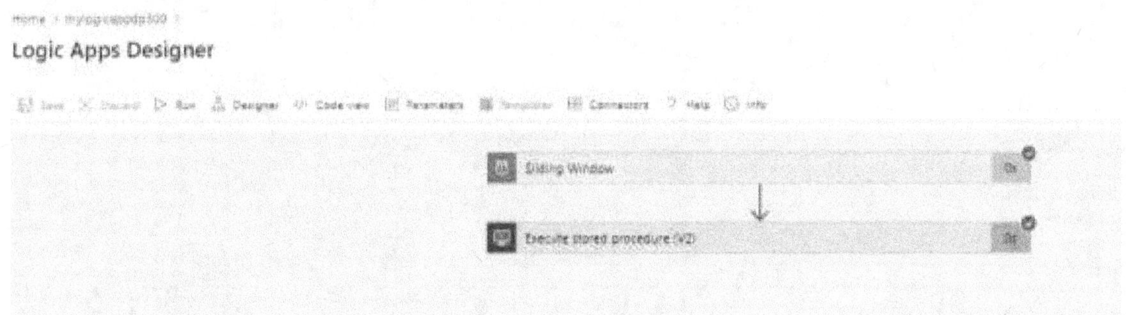

To validate and confirm the job output, query the table. You can see that the Logic App job logs multiple entries.

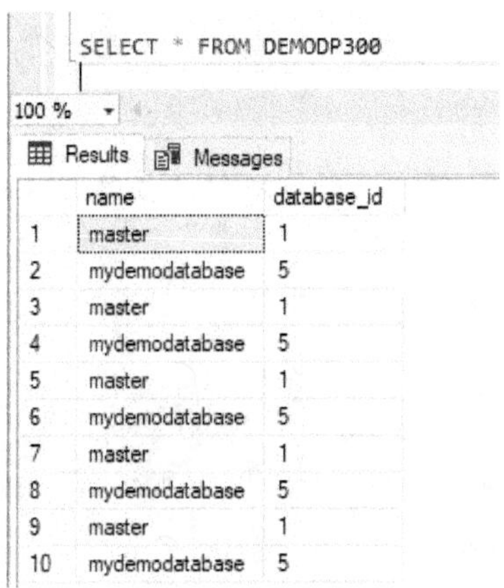

```
SELECT * FROM DEMODP300
```

100 %

Results | Messages

	name	database_id
1	master	1
2	mydemodatabase	5
3	master	1
4	mydemodatabase	5
5	master	1
6	mydemodatabase	5
7	master	1
8	mydemodatabase	5
9	master	1
10	mydemodatabase	5

You can also monitor the status and history from the Logic App Overview menu.

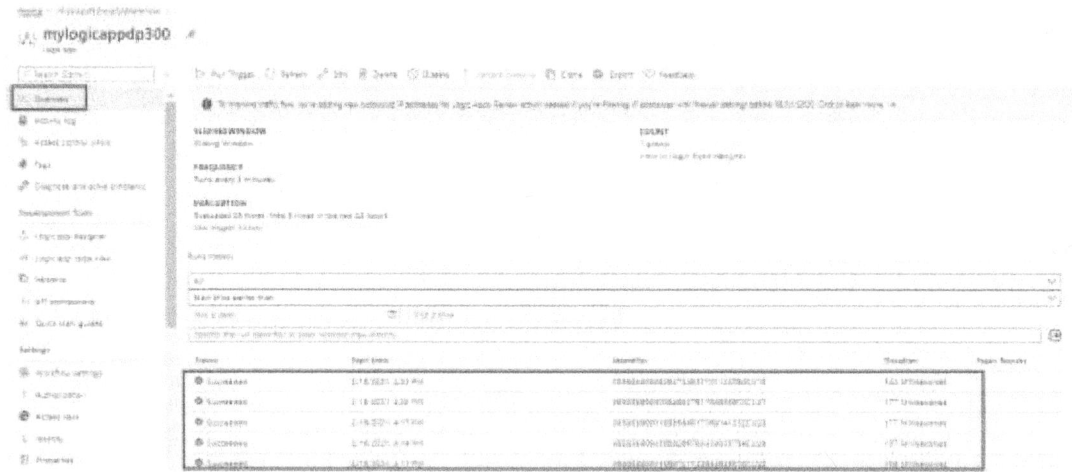

Provisioning an Azure SQL Server and SQL Database Using Azure PowerShell

Azure PowerShell is a set of cmdlets or modules that allows cloud engineers to provision the resources—an application requires running. In this section, you will see how to use Azure PowerShell to provision Azure SQL databases.

Infrastructure-as-code and **Database-as-code** became IT practice managing an application's underlying IT infrastructure through programming. This approach to resource allocation allows developers to monitor and provision resources as opposed to building them manually.

Note: we write the deployment code using Visual Studio Code. I would recommend seeing Chapter 4 to understand the prerequisite to run this deployment. You can also run this deployment using PowerShell ISE, where you have Azure PowerShell modules loaded.

Pre-requisites:

1. To check the Azure PowerShell module, run the following command

```
Get-Module -ListAvailable -Name Az*
```

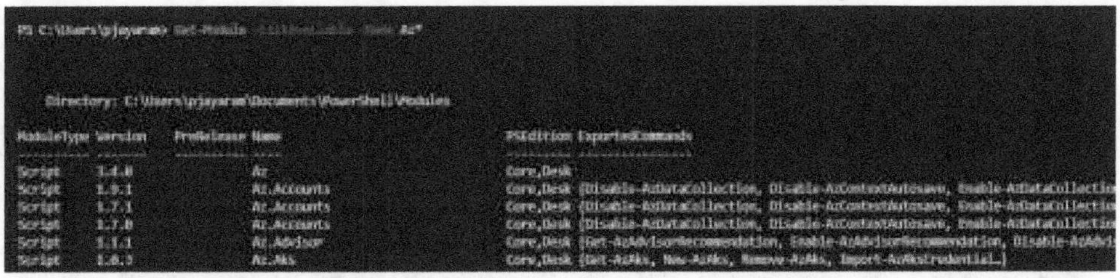

2. Connect to Azure subscription using device authentication—this is to use device code authentication instead of a browser-based authentication.

Connect-AzAccount –UseDeviceAuthentication

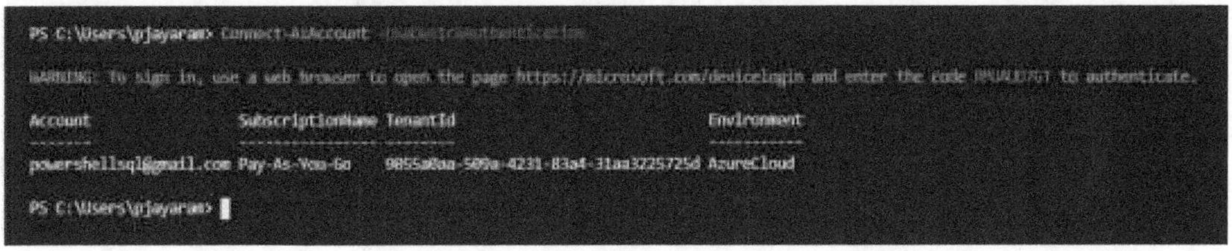

3. To create a profile, run the following command. In this step, you save the current authentication and subscription details in the JSON file. Use this metadata in other PowerShell sessions. This step is useful because it is easy to integrate the profile into the deployment code.

Save-AzContext -Path C:\users\pjayaram\MyAzureProfileDP300.JSON

4. Clear all the security context and load the profile to get into the Azure subscription.

Clear-AzContext

5. Connect to Azure using Profile.

Import-AzContext -Path C:\users\pjayaram\MyAzureProfileDP300.JSON

```
PS C:\Users\pjayaram> Clear-AzContext

Confirm
Remove all accounts and subscriptions in all sessions for the current user?
[Y] Yes [N] No [S] Suspend [?] Help (default is "Yes"):
PS C:\Users\pjayaram> Import-AzContext -Path C:\users\pjayaram\MyAzureProfileDP300.JSON


Account                  SubscriptionName TenantId                             Environment
-------                  ---------------- --------                             -----------
powershellsql@gmail.com Pay-As-You-Go    9055a0aa-509a-4231-83a4-31aa3225725d AzureCloud

PS C:\Users\pjayaram>
```

6. The other way is to use the credential parameter. In this step, you will learn how to use the credential parameter to login and setup azure automation. Here, the Connect-AzAccount cmdlet accepts the credentials to run the session with the specified user context. To do that, declare the variables to hold the values of username and password. You can directly feed values to the cmdlets as well. When you interactively run the script, you can feed the credentials. The real challenge comes when you want to immerse the credentials in your automation.

7. Open the PowerShell ISE or VC code and type in the following commands :

Connect-AzAccount -Credential (Get-Credential)

Note: In the aforementioned method, we cannot run the script unattended. But we can instantiate the credential object using the New-Object System.Management.Automation.PSCredential namespace accepts the username and password parameters. The username is plain text, and the password is a secure string that serves as the password.

8. To convert *SecureString,* run the password along with the ConvertTo-SecureString cmdlet. Let us define the username and password in clear texts.

$username = “powershellsql@gmail.com”
$password="abcd#$@#$@!@#1234"

9. To convert the password into a secure string, run the following ConvertTo-SecureString cmdlet.

$SecurePassword = ConvertTo-SecureString “$password” -AsPlainText -Force

10. Next, we need to pass the parameters to the PSCredential object to prepare the credentials.

$credentials = New-Object System.Management.Automation.PSCredential($username, $SecurePassword)

Note: We can pass the $credentials(PSCredential) object to any cmdlet accepting the -PSCredential parameter. In the following example, you can see the use of–Credential parameter:
\>Get-WmiObject -class Win32_Service –Computer <ServerName> -Credential$credentials

11. Run the below command to login to the Azure Portal:

Connect-AzAccount -Credential $credentials

Prepare the deployment code

In this section, you will see complete systematic detail to build the complete deployment package using a profile.

1. Open the Visual Studio Code.
2. Save the file as AzureSQLDatabase.ps1.
3. Declare the variables.

```
[String] $ResourceGroup,

[String] $Location,

[String] $SQLServer,

[String] $AdminUser,

[String] $AdminUser,

[String] $SQLDatabase,
```

[String] $Edition="Premium",

[String] $Profile="C:\users\pjayaram\MyAzureProfileDP300.JSON"

Import-AzContext -Path $Profile

- *ResourceGroup: The resource group that will host the logical Azure SQL se rver and Azure SQL database.*
- *Location: The location of the resource group*
- *SQLServer: The logical host—a placeholder to Azure SQL database.*
- *AdminUser: Azure SQL Server admin username*
- *AdminPassword: Azure SQL Server admin password*
- *SQLDatabase: Azure SQL database*
- *Edition: Azure SQL Database edition(Basic, Standard, Premium)*
- *Profile: Profile path where you save the current authentication information for use in other PowerShell sessions*

```
C: > Users > pjayaram > Chapter9.ps1
$AdminPassword

Parameter '$AdminPassword' should use SecureString, otherwise this will expose sensitive
information. See ConvertTo-SecureString for more
information. PSScriptAnalyzer(PSAvoidUsingPlainTextForPassword)

Peek Problem (Alt+F8)   Quick Fix... (Ctrl+.)
[String] $AdminPassword,
[String] $SQLDatabase,
[String] $Edition="Basic",
[String] $Profile="C:\users\pjayaram\MyAzureProfileDP300.JSON"
)
Import-AzContext -Path $Profile
```

Note: PSScriptAnalyzer is a static package to analyze code and check the code for PowerShell modules and scripts. In addition, it checks the quality of the PowerShell code by running a set of rules. It bases the rules on PowerShell best practices defined by the PowerShell Team and the community. It also generates diagnostic records (errors-and-warnings) to alert users about code errors and points workable solutions for enhancements or improvements.

By default, the PowerShell extension includes PSScriptAnalyzer. It performs analysis automatically on PowerShell script files being edited using the VS Code.

4. Create the resource group.

```
New-AzResourceGroup -Name $ResourceGroup -Location $Location
```

5. Create Azure SQL Server.

```
New-AzSqlServer -ServerName $SQLServer -ResourceGroupName $ResourceGroup -SqlAdministratorCredentials $credentials -ServerVersion '12.0'
```

6. Create Azure SQL Database.

```
New-AzSqlDatabase -ServerName $SQLServer -ResourceGroupName $ResourceGroup -DatabaseName $SQLDatabase -Edition $Edition -RequestedServiceObjectiveName S1
```

7. Create Firewall rules to Azure resources.

```
New-AzSqlServerFirewallRule -ServerName $SQLServer -ResourceGroupName $ResourceGroup –AllowAllAzureIPs
```

8. Now, Azure SQL Database is up and running. Let’s connect using sqlcmd in CloudShell.

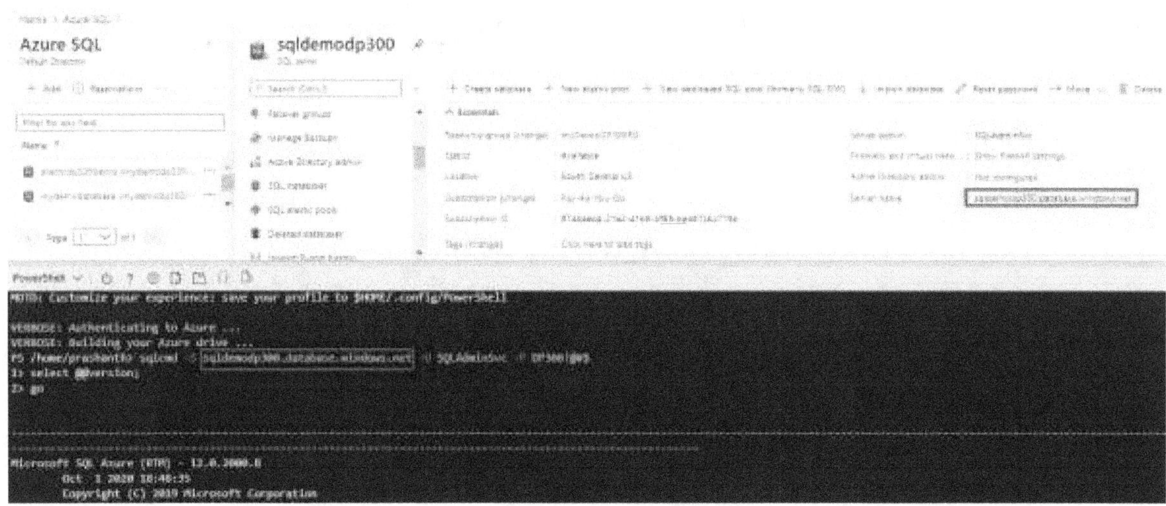

Download the complete code from
https://github.com/AzureDP300/AzureDP300/blob/main/Chapter9/Script2.ps1

Azure Resource Manager Templates

"Faster Time-to-Market" becomes the slogan for my organization—the agile development techniques or methods are only the key to meet this objective. The quick iterative process removed the fine thin-line between operations and development. The release life cycle shortened significantly in recent days. To meet all these challenges, you can adopt the practice of database-as-code and infrastructure-as-code. To implement these practices, use Azure Resource Manager templates.

In this section, we are going to look at ARM (Azure Resource Manager) templates. It is a standardized and pre-defined JSON template used to deploy resources in Microsoft Azure.

The Benefits

1. It is easy and fast, and you can deploy resources quickly.

2. It is customizable to meet specific requirements that you might have for any deployment of any resource.

3. There is a vast library of predefined templates are available for faster deployments.

4. In addition, you can also redeploy current resources configurations. It is not just used for the deployment of new resources, but if you have current resources, you can change those resources through a template.

5. It helps to deploy as many resources required in a quick period.

6. It saves time and meets the standards of your organization. If you need to configure previously deployed resources, JSON templates are for you.

Deploy template steps

Deploying templates is always much faster than manually provisioning the databases. It ensures that we use the same build each time. We can build a template from an existing resource, or we can modify a template as required. In addition, Azure Quickstart Templates several samples to help you get started.

There are three steps when you are deploying a template.

1. First, you need to get or create the template from the existing resources. You can create a template before you provision a resource.

2. Second, use Azure Quickstart Templates that are already available.

3. Third, modify the template to meet the requirement and then deploy the template.

How to find a JSON template?

Let us start to find the JSON template that will meet the requirement to create the Azure SQL Database.

1. First, Open the internet browser, type in **Azure Quickstart Templates** and hit enter.

2. Locate the GitHub and click the link—it will redirect you to the GitHub repo.

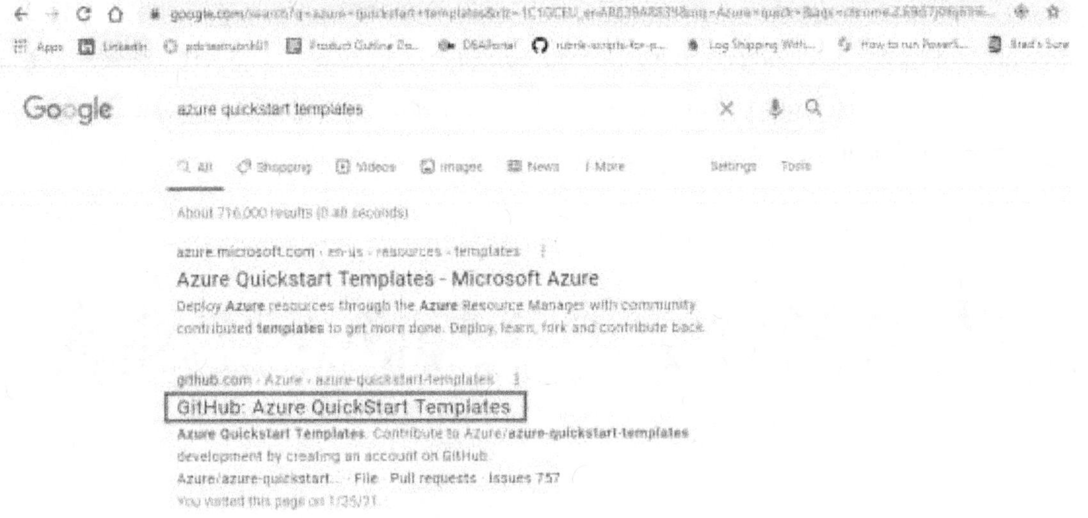

3. Now, select the template. You can see many templates around. It will be challenging to identify the template. Let me simplify it a little further. As you search, you have the specific task that you want to find.

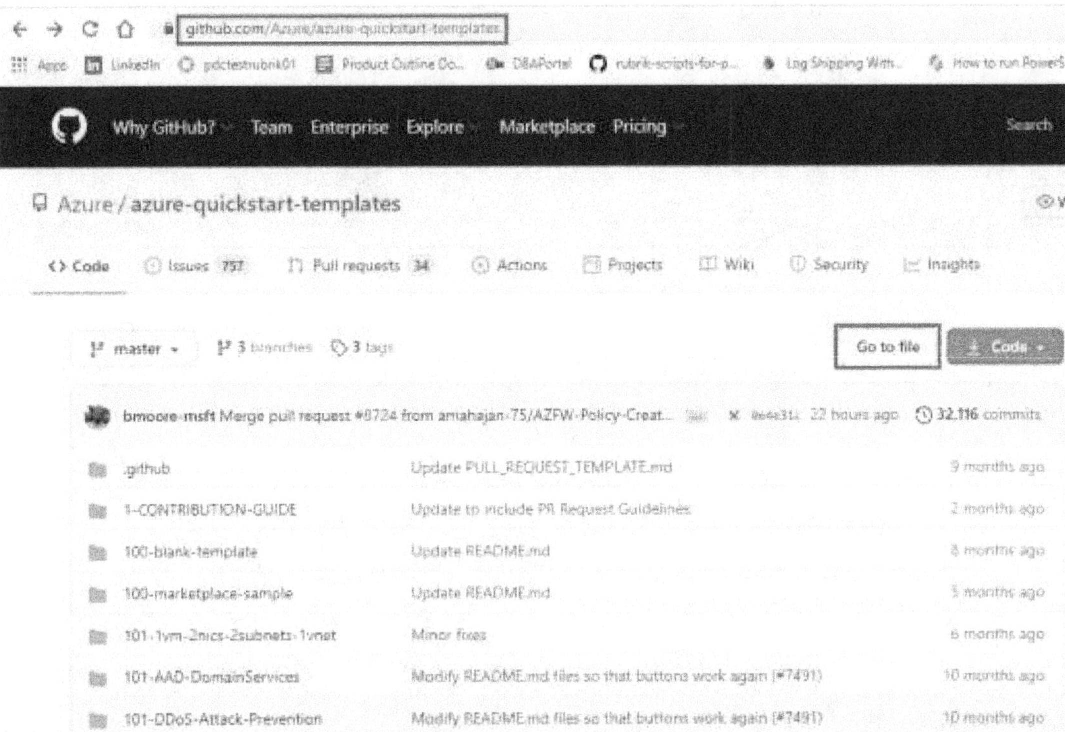

4. Here, you can use the find file option to locate the template you want to use. For example, you are looking at creating an Azure SQL database template. In this case, type in SQL database, and this is going to reduce the number of templates that you need to select from the huge list.

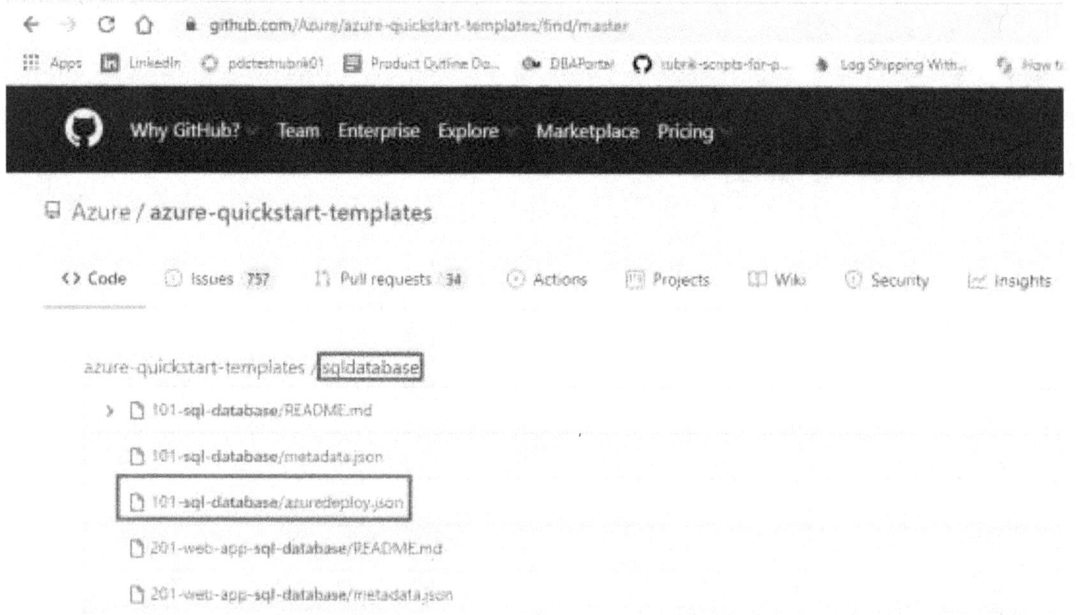

5. The other method is to use the custom template from the marketplace.

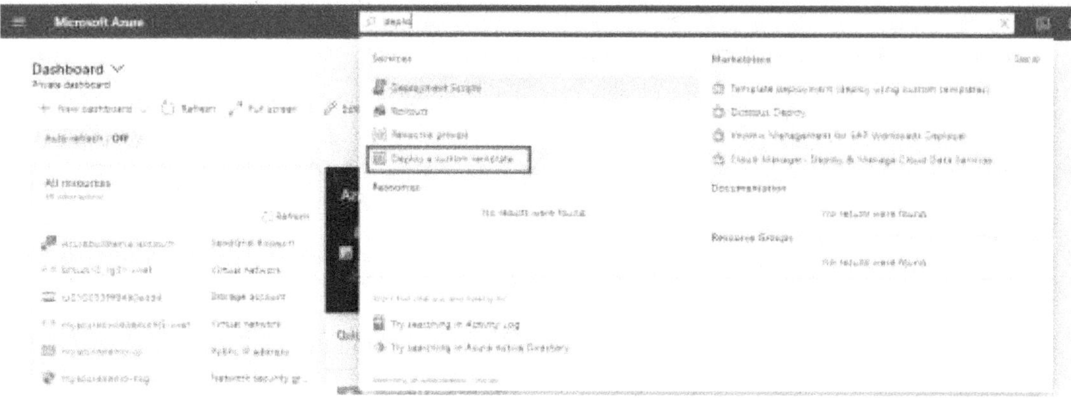

6. Select the Create SQL database template. You also get an option to load directly from the Github repo.

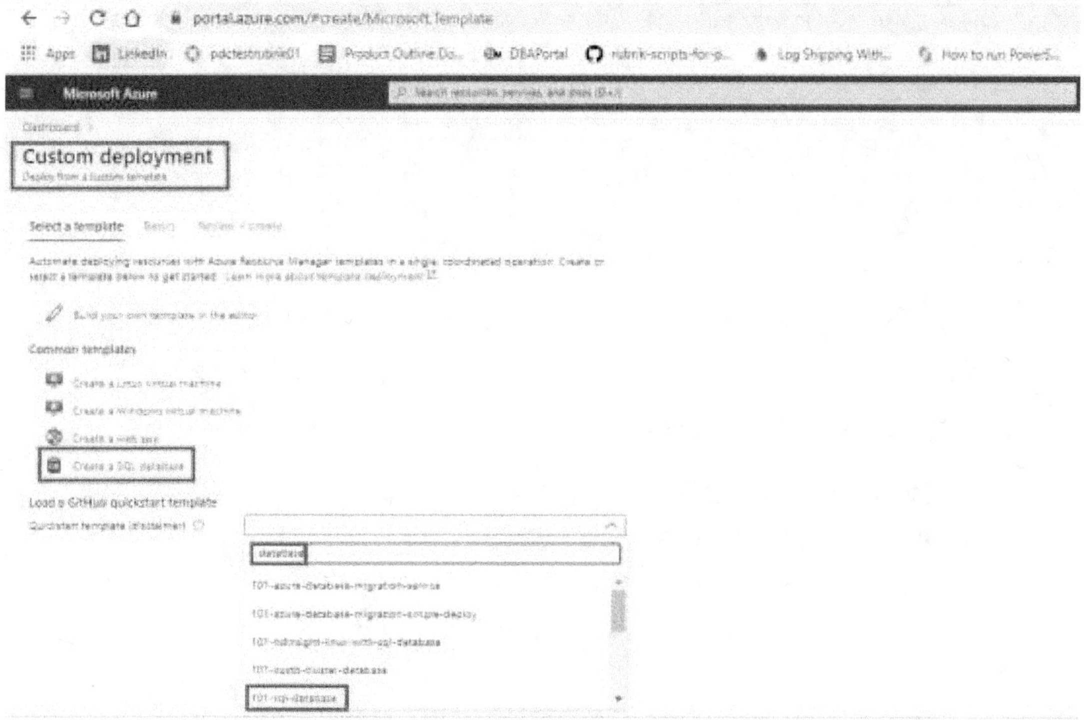

Deploy Azure SQL database using a JSON template

We are now ready to deploy the "Azure SQL Database" template in Microsoft Azure. In the above section, we learnt how to locate the template. Now, open the readme.md where it says deploy to Azure.

1. Click deploy to Azure. This option takes you right into the Azure portal. It sets up the deployment template ready to use.

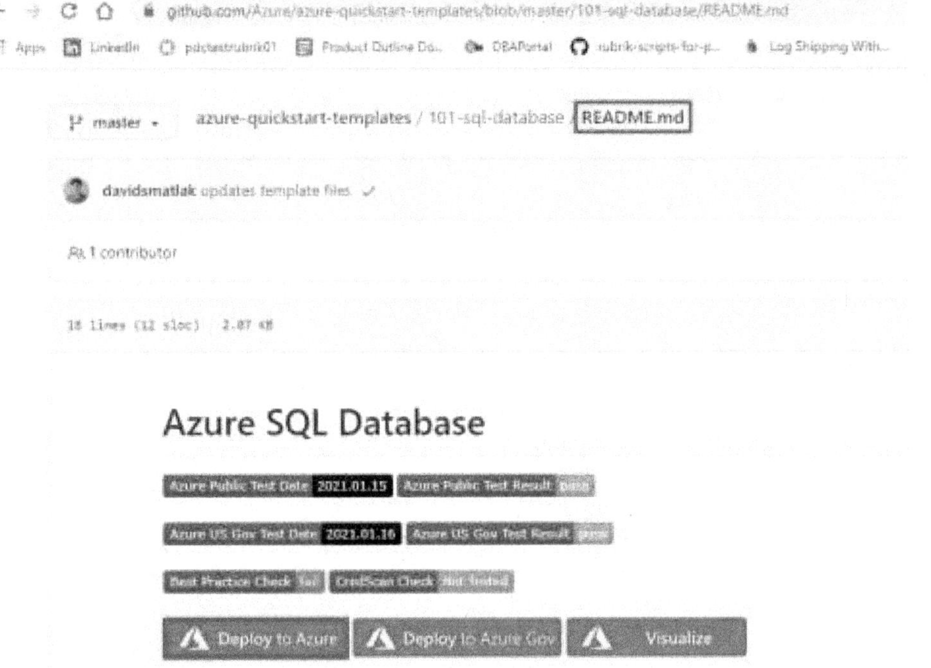

2. Next, let us edit the template to understand more about the template.

A parameter is some information you need to pass to the template to deploy your resource. Think of it this way: if you have a virtual machine, you need the virtual machine's name. You need the resource group the virtual machine is going into and perhaps some other information.

The variable is going to be filled in for you by default if you do not enter anything in there. But a variable, you can go in and make a change if you need to make that change. So that is a look at JSON templates and Microsoft Azure.

For example, you must guarantee to generate unique SQL Server names. In addition, SKUs you may list them in the allowedValues in a drop-down control.

3. Now, Edit the template and modify the parameters as per the requirement.

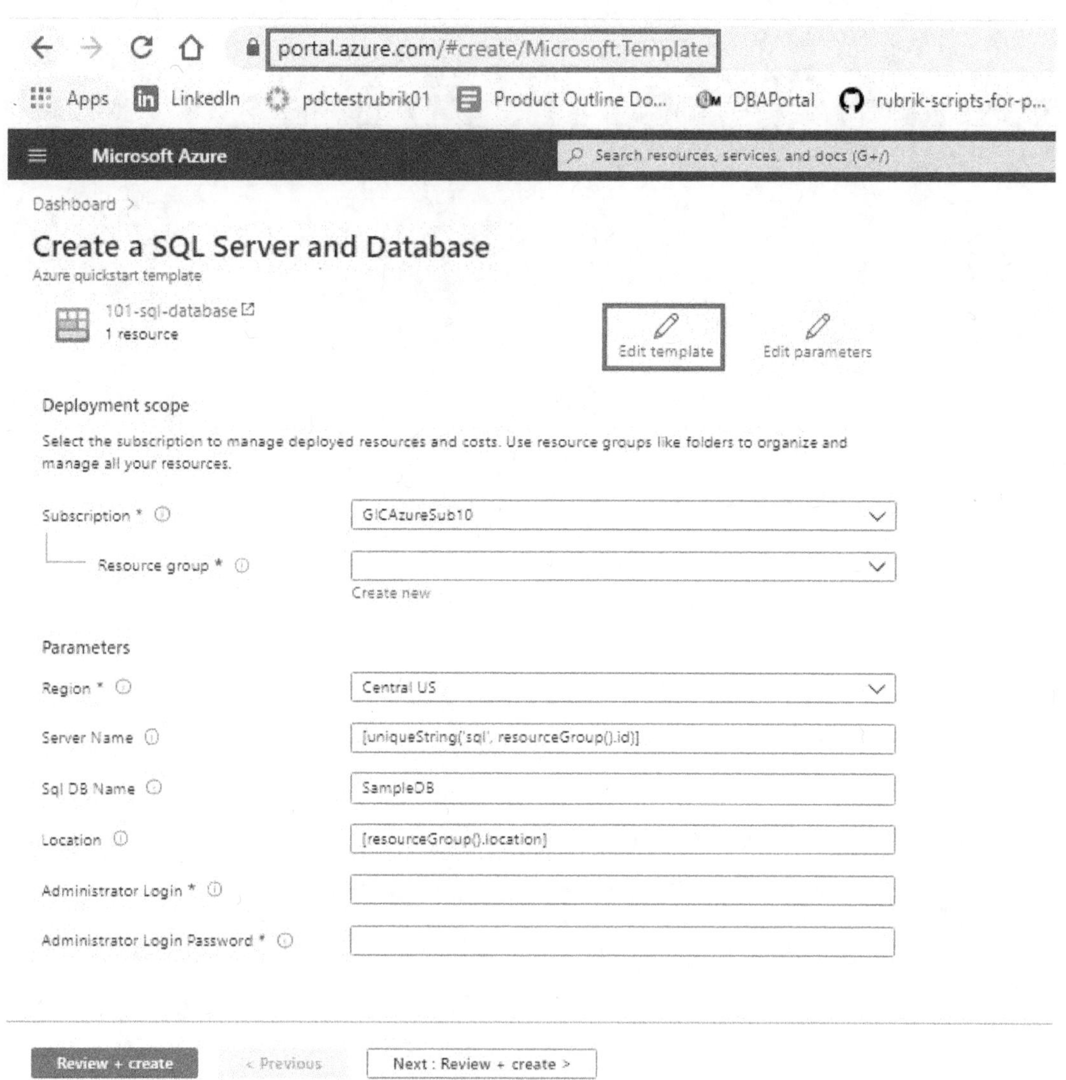

4. Click save the change, if any.

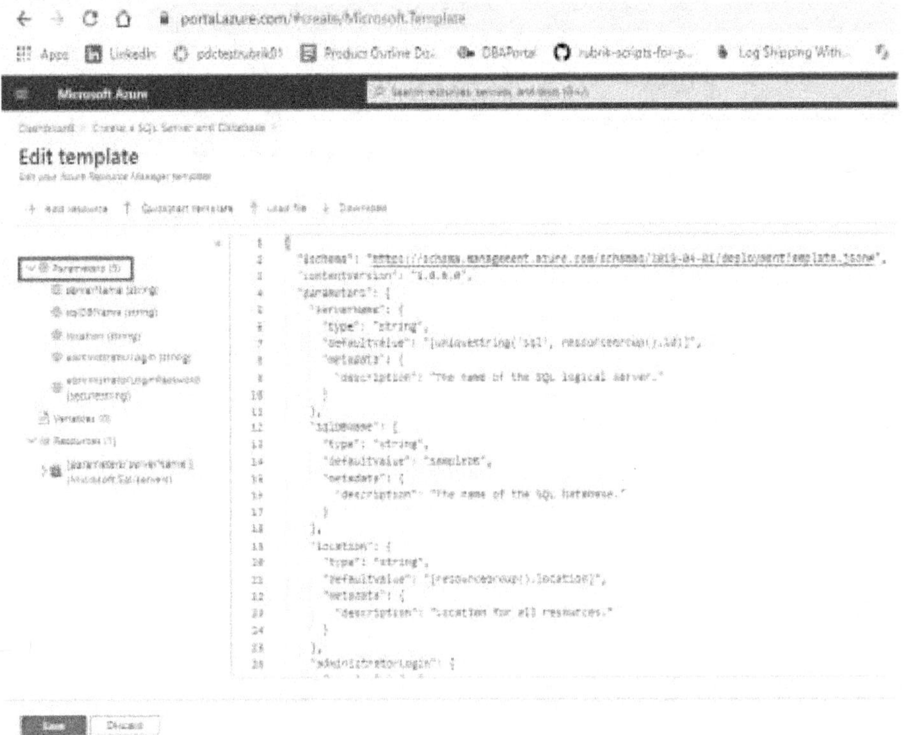

5. Click the Review+Create button to create the Azure SQL database. You can see all the resources are created through the template. It is how you deploy a resource from the template on GitHub or “Custom deployment template” for Microsoft Azure.

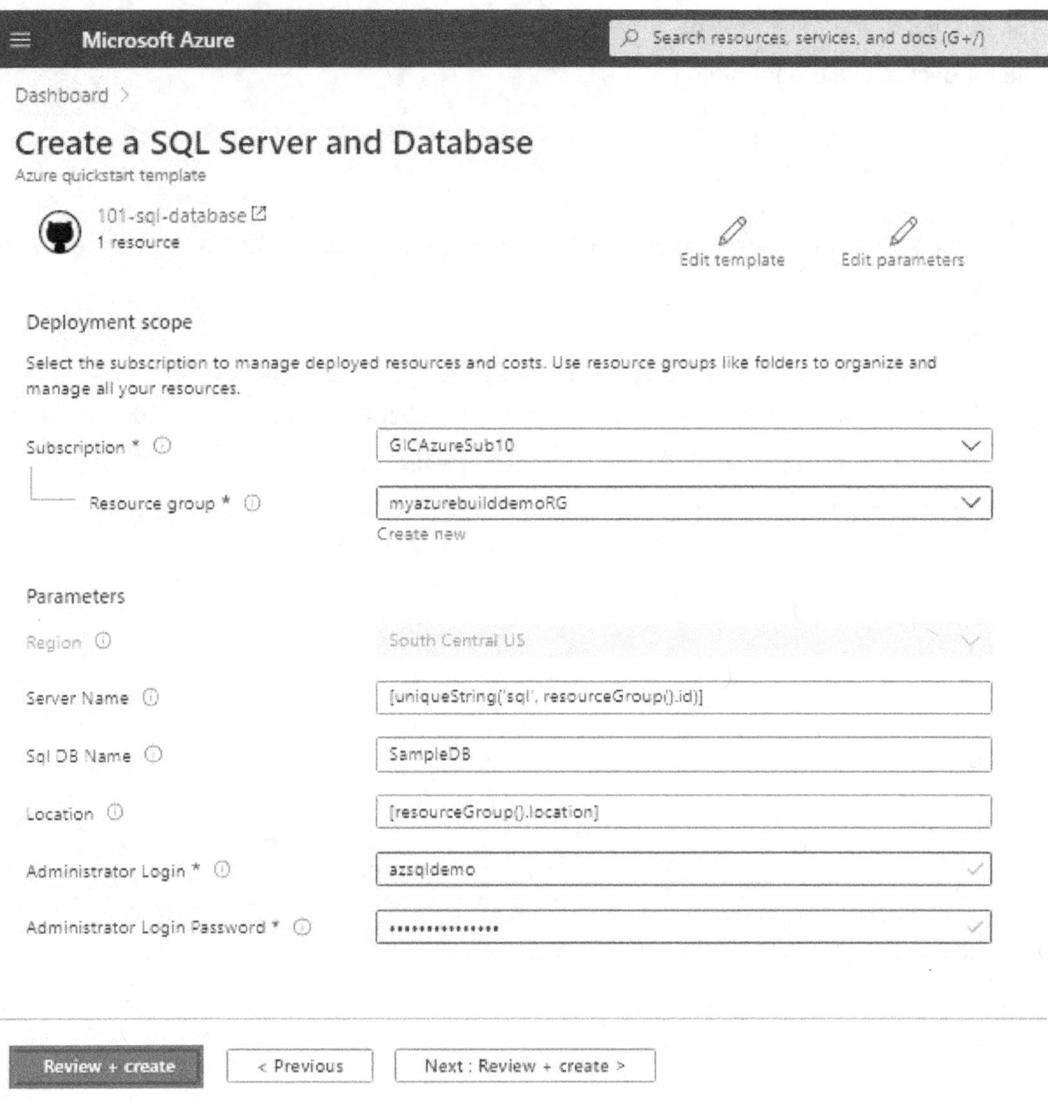

The difference between declarative and imperative programming

It relates the difference between Imperative and Declarative programming and understands how a **program** works vs what a **program** does.

In simple terms, **Imperative programming** is all about how a **program** works but whereas **Declarative programming** is all about what a **program** does.

PowerShell cmdlet is an example of Imperative programming, and ARM templates are the best example for declarative programming.

Deploying an Azure ARM Template using PowerShell

It is easy and simple to deploy the templates. In this section, we deploy the templates using PowerShell.

First, you just need to reference the template file and the parameter file and make the required changes. To deploy, you will use **New-AZResourceGroupDeployment**, cmdlet and provide the resource group name, the template file, and the parameter file.

1. Download the template.

2. In JSON parameter file, modify the parameter **administratorLoginPassword** value from NULL to dp300!@#$

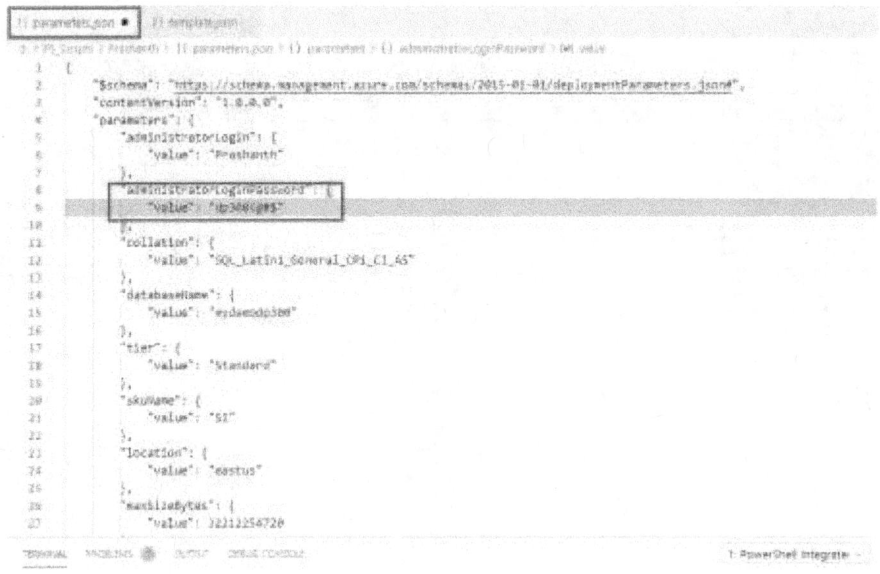

3. In the template.json file, modify the **administratorLoginPassword** from SecureString to String.

```
{} parameters.json   {} template.json ×
d: > PS_Scripts > Prashanth > {} template.json > {} parameters > {} administratorLoginPassword > type
{
    "$schema": "http://schema.management.azure.com/schemas/2014-04-01-preview/deploymentTemplate.json#",
    "contentVersion": "1.0.0.0",
    "parameters": {
        "administratorLogin": {
            "type": "string"
        },
        "administratorLoginPassword": {
            "type": "string"
        },
        "collation": {
            "type": "string"
        },
        "databaseName": {
            "type": "string"
        },
        "tier": {
            "type": "string"
        },
        "skuName": {
            "type": "string"
        },
        "location": {
            "type": "string"
        },
        "maxSizeBytes": {
            "type": "int"
TERMINAL   PROBLEMS   OUTPUT   DEBUG CONSOLE                1: PowerShell Int
```

4. To start the deployment, run the following command. The assumptions are that you are already connected to Azure subscription, and you have the resource group created.

```
New-AzResourceGroupDeployment -Name ExampleDeployment -
ResourceGroupName mydemodp300RG

-TemplateFile D:\PS_Scripts\Prashanth\template.json

-TemplateParameterFile D:\PS_Scripts\Prashanth\parameters.json
```

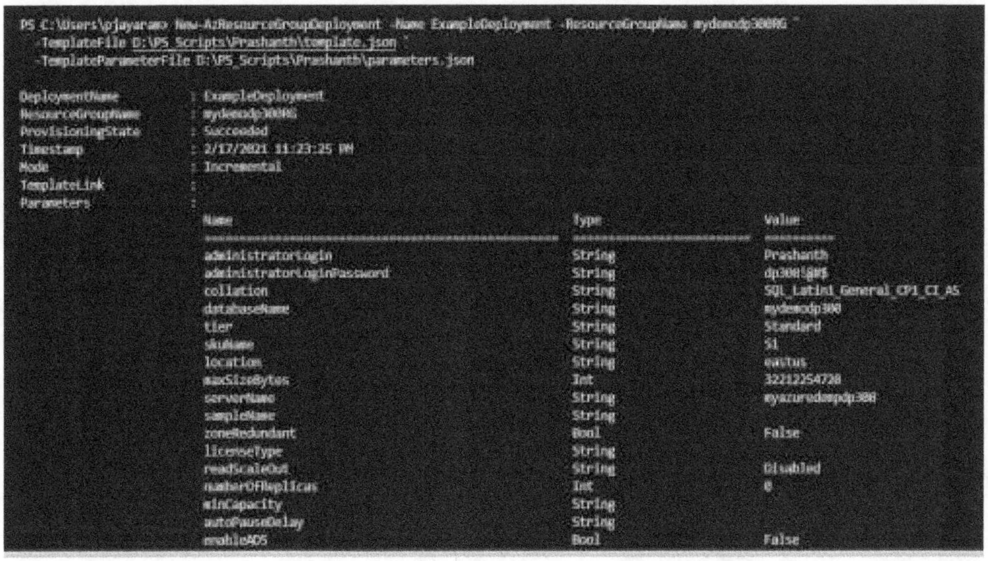

```
PS C:\Users\pjayaram> New-AzResourceGroupDeployment -Name ExampleDeployment -ResourceGroupName mydemodp300RG `
  -TemplateFile D:\PS_Scripts\Prashanth\template.json `
  -TemplateParameterFile D:\PS_Scripts\Prashanth\parameters.json

DeploymentName          : ExampleDeployment
ResourceGroupName       : mydemodp300RG
ProvisioningState       : Succeeded
Timestamp               : 2/17/2021 11:23:25 PM
Mode                    : Incremental
TemplateLink            :
Parameters              :
                          Name                           Type                     Value
                          =============================  =======================  ==========
                          administratorLogin             String                   Prashanth
                          administratorLoginPassword     String                   dp300!@#$
                          collation                      String                   SQL_Latin1_General_CP1_CI_AS
                          databaseName                   String                   mydemodp300
                          tier                           String                   Standard
                          skuName                        String                   S1
                          location                       String                   eastus
                          maxSizeBytes                   Int                      32212254720
                          serverName                     String                   myazuredempdp300
                          sampleName                     String
                          zoneRedundant                  Bool                     False
                          licenseType                    String
                          readScaleOut                   String                   Disabled
                          numberOfReplicas               Int                      0
                          minCapacity                    String
                          autoPauseDelay                 String
                          enableADS                      Bool                     False
```

5. Now, perform the test-connection using **sqlcmd** to check the database connectivity. You see a successful connection and are able to see the database.

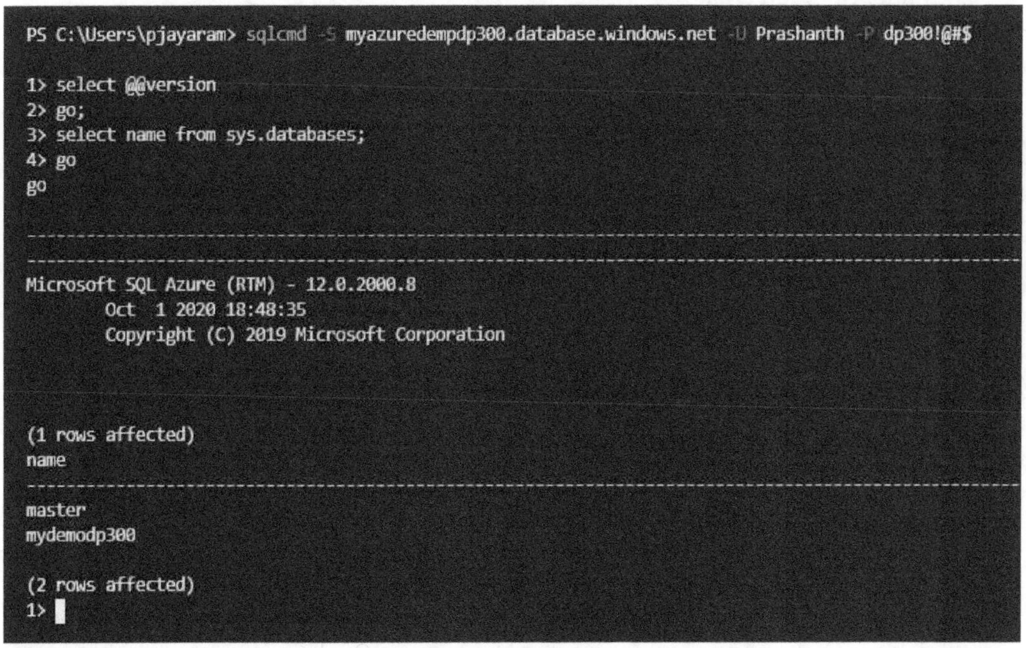

```
PS C:\Users\pjayaram> sqlcmd -S myazuredempdp300.database.windows.net -U Prashanth -P dp300!@#$

1> select @@version
2> go;
3> select name from sys.databases;
4> go
go

------------------------------------------------------------------------------------------
------------------------------------------------------------------------------------------
Microsoft SQL Azure (RTM) - 12.0.2000.8
        Oct  1 2020 18:48:35
        Copyright (C) 2019 Microsoft Corporation


(1 rows affected)
name
------------------------------------------------------------------------------------------
master
mydemodp300

(2 rows affected)
1>
```

Schedule jobs with SQL Server Agent

SQL Server Agent is a scheduler and core component of SQL Server that is responsible for automation and used to administer jobs, operators, alerts, and the SQL Server Agent services.

1. Components of Automatic Administration.

2. Jobs - A job is defined as a series of actions that SQL Server Agent performs to carry out a specific action.

3. Schedules - A schedule defines when the agent job will run. You can set up a job that can run more than one job at the same schedule.

4. Alerts - An alert is an action taken to respond to a specific event automatically.

5. Operators - An operator is an individual responsible for the maintenance of SQL Instances.

Note: SQL Server notifies operators using alerts through:

- E-mail
- Pager (through email)
- net sendSQL

SQL Server Agent must configure to use the credentials of an account that is a member of the **sysadmin** fixed server role in SQL Server to manage all its functions.

I always recommend using **SQL Server Management Studio** to **configure the alerts**—it provides an easy, graphical way to manage and configure the alerting system.

Note: SQL Managed instance does not support **Enabling** and **disabling** SQL Server agent job. By default, in the SQL Managed Instance, SQL Agent is always running.

1.1.7 SQL Server Agent roles

SQL Server has the following **msdb fixed database roles**, which give administrators to control granular level access to SQL Server agent jobs.

- **SQLAgentUserRole**
- **SQLAgentReaderRole**

- **SQLAgentOperatorRole**

	SQLAgentUserRole				SQLAgentReaderRole				SQLAgentReaderRole			
Job Action Items	Operators	Local Jobs(Owner)	Job Schedules(Owner)	Proxy	Operators	Local Jobs	Job Schedules	Proxy	Operators	Local Jobs	Job Schedules	Proxy
Create or Modify or Delete	N	Y	Y	N	N	Y	N	Y	N	N	Y	N
View Jobs	Y	Y	Y	Y	Y	Y	Y	Y	Y	Y	Y	Y
View properties	N	Y	Y	N	N	Y	Y	Y	Y	Y	Y	Y
Enable or Disable	N	Y	Y	NA	N	Y	N	Y	N	N	Y	N
Execute or Start or Stop	NA	Y	NA	NA	N	Y	N	Y	N	N	Y	N
Job History	NA	Y	NA	NA	NA	Y	N	NA	NA	NA	Y	N
Delete Job History	NA	Y	NA	NA	NA	Y	Y	NA	NA	NA	Y	Y
Attach/Detach	NA	NA	Y	NA	NA	N	N	NA	NA	NA	Y	N

Multi-Server Automation

In a real-world scenario, you manage multiple SQL Server instances, and you need to run some T-SQL code, backup jobs, maintenance job, SQL management jobs, etc... across SQL Server estate. We can do it in multiple ways. It is possible to run the SQL Server Agent Job script on multiple SQL Server instances servers using PowerShell or sqlcmd by traversing across the instances. Here, you can see an administrative overhead to manage, deploy, and redeploy the code.

In addition, you have a multi-server administration option to manage SQL Server agent jobs and maintenance plans. IT is helpful when you need to manage the same job across a huge SQL Server estate.

Configure Multi-server automation

In Object Explorer, connect to an instance of the Microsoft SQL Server Database Engine, and then expand that instance.

1. Right-click SQL Server Agent, select Multi-Server Administration.
2. Click Make this a Master.
3. The Master Server Wizard guides you through making a master server and adding target servers.
4. From the Master Server Operator page, configure an operator for the master server to send notifications to operators by using e-mail or pagers, SQL Server Agent must be configured to send an email.
5. To send notifications to operators by using net send, the Messenger service must run on the server where SQL Server Agent resides.
   - Email addressSets: the email address for the operator.
   - Pager addressSets: the pager email address for the operator.
   - Net send addressSets: the net send address for the operator.
6. From the Target Server page, select target servers for the master server.
   - Registered ServersLists: the servers registered in Microsoft SQL Server Management Studio that are not already target servers.
   - Target ServersLists: the servers that are target servers.
   - >:Move the selected server to the target server list.
   - >>:Move all servers to the target server list.
   - <:Remove the selected server from the target server list.
   - <<:Remove all servers from the target server list.
   - Add connection: Add a server to the target server list without registering the server.
   - ConnectionChange: the connection properties for the selected server.

7. From the Master, Server Login Credentials page, specify if you want to create a new login for the target server and assign its rights to the master server.

8. Create a new login if necessary and assign it rights to the MSXCreate a new login on the target server if the login specified does not already exist.

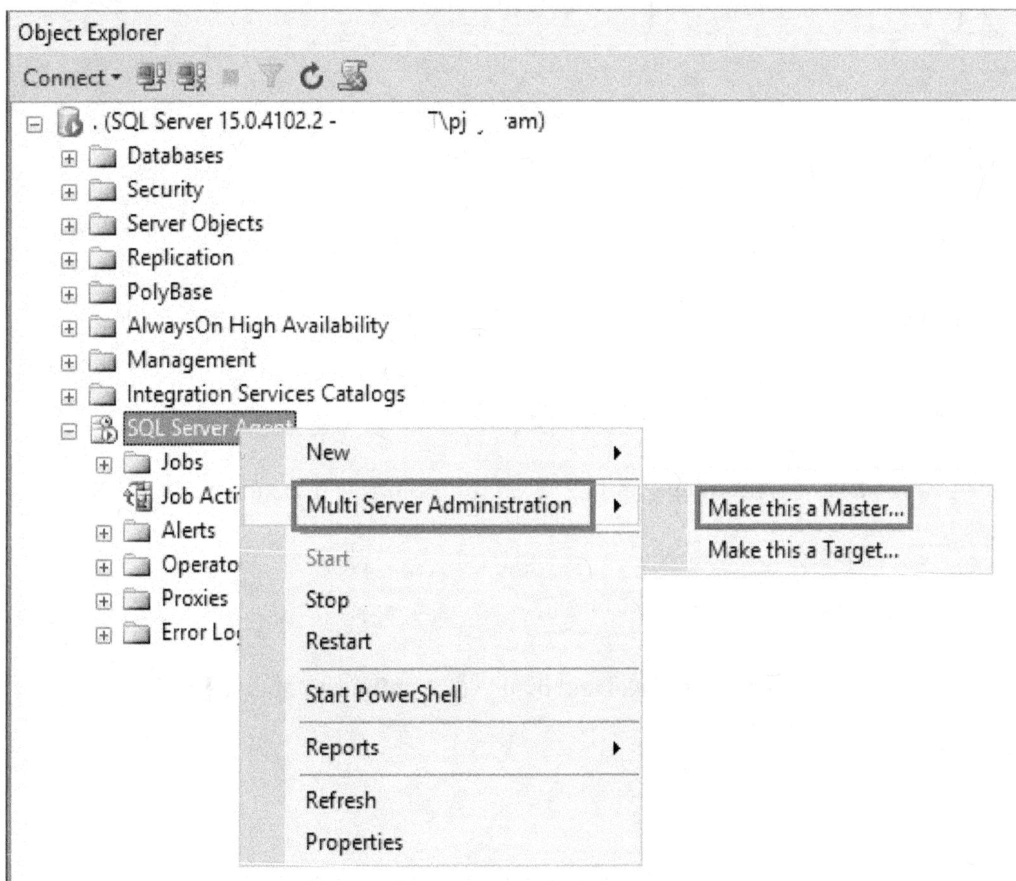

Configure notifications for task success/failure/non-completion

It is easy to configure Database Mail in SQL Server so that you get important notifications right away:

1. Send alerts for high severity errors, monitor performance counters, configuration change and corruption.
2. Automatically send notifications when the agent jobs finish or fail.

Here are the steps:

1. Configure Database Mail.
2. Create an Operator.
3. Create a SQL Server job.
4. Enable notification in SQL Server Agent.
5. Delete the job after it completes the execution.

Configure Database Mail

Let us start. The prerequisite is to have a properly configured mail server.

Note: You can try with localhost, but you need to configure Microsoft IIS or SMTP mail server. In an enterprise organization, this practice restricts configuring mail servers locally. You need to get the details from the Windows administrator.

1. Open **SQL Server Management Studio (SSMS)** and connect to the **Database Engine.**

2. Expand **Management**

3. Right-click on **Database Mail** and then click **Configure Database Mail.**

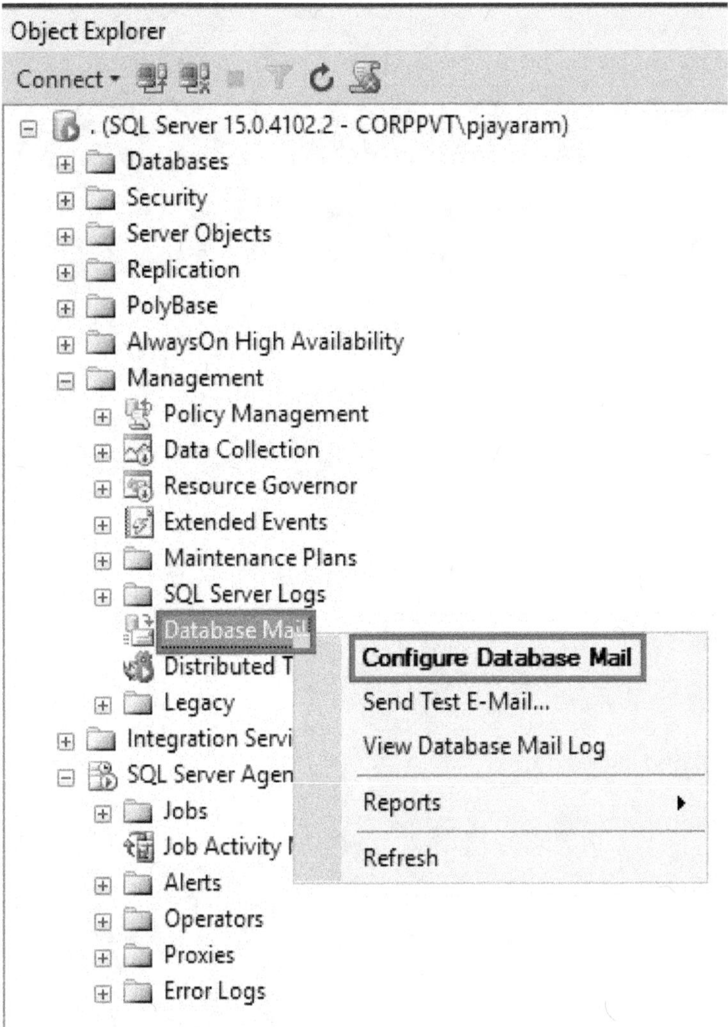

4. Click next on the Wizard.

5. Select the default "**Set up Database Mail by performing the following tasks**" and click **Next.**

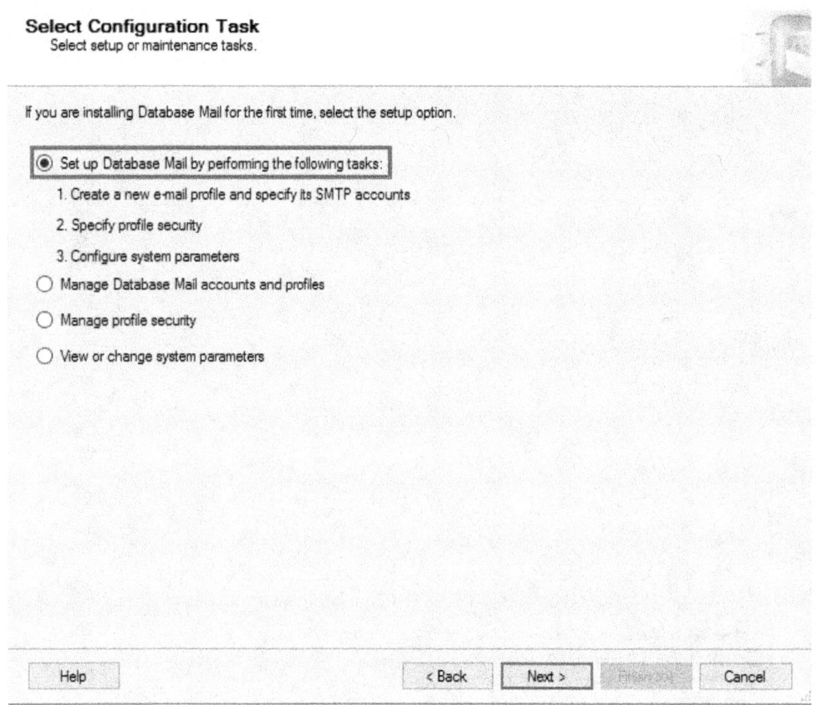

6. Type in **Profile** name and click **Add**.

7. Next, fill out the below details and click **OK.**

   a. *Email address*

   b. *Display name*

   c. *Reply email*

   d. *Server name*

   e. *SMTP Authentication*

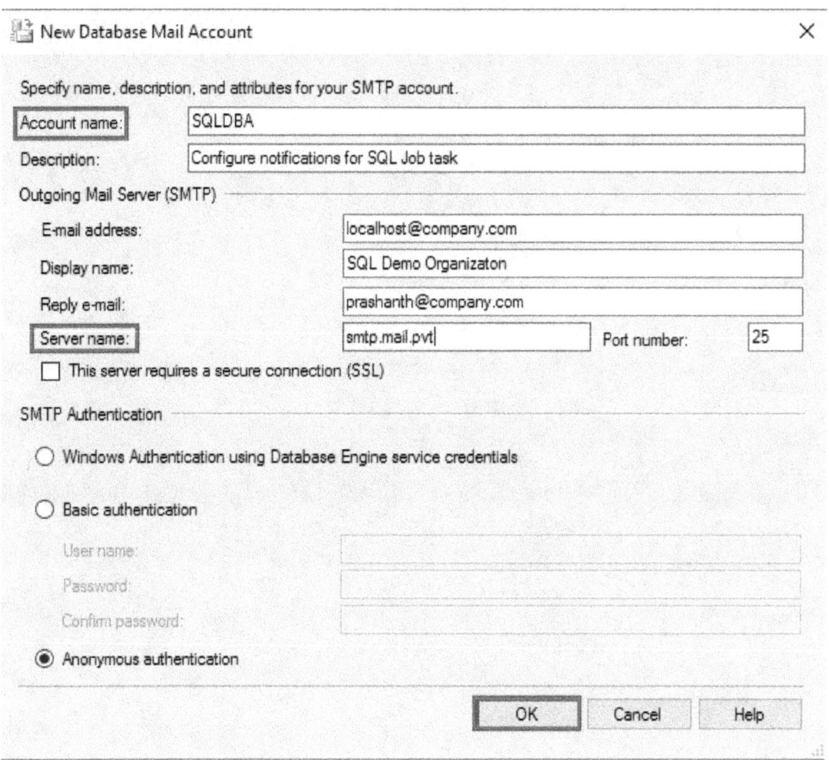

8. Now, make the profile to Public and click next until you reach the finish.

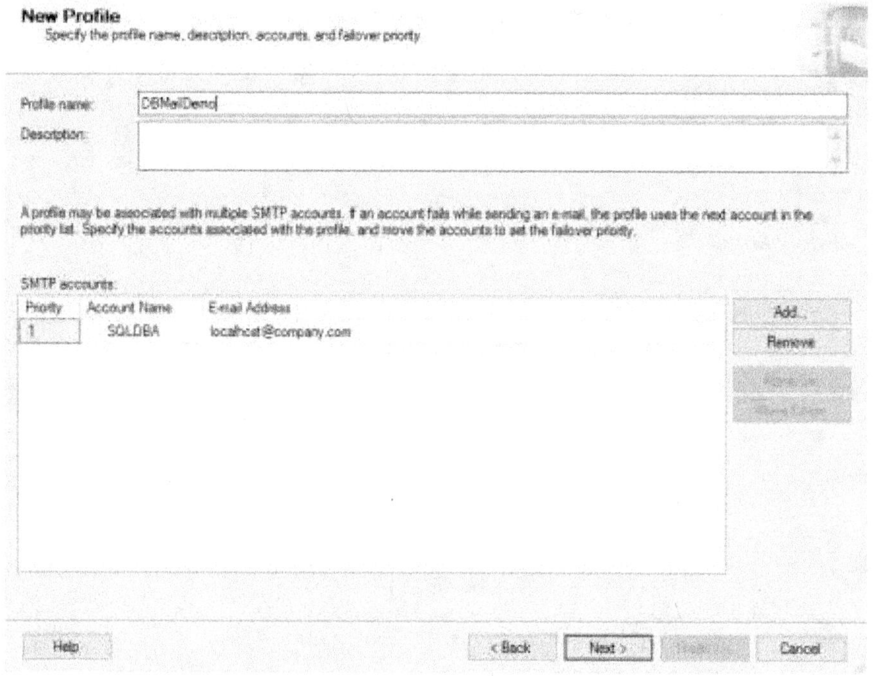
New Profile
Specify the profile name, description, accounts, and failover priority
Profile name:
DBMailDemo
Description:
SMTP accounts:
Priority
Account Name
E-mail Address
1
SQLDBA
localhcat@company.com
Add...
Remove
Help
< Back
Next >
Cancel

9. Click Next.

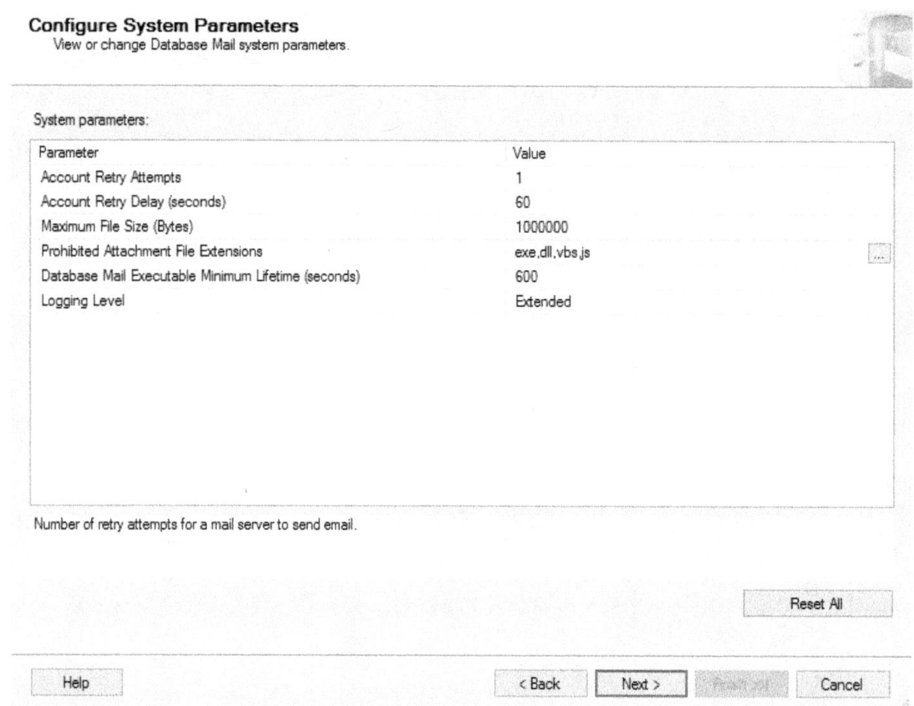
Configure System Parameters
View or change Database Mail system parameters.
System parameters:
Parameter
Value
Account Retry Attempts
1
Account Retry Delay (seconds)
60
Maximum File Size (Bytes)
1000000
Prohibited Attachment File Extensions
exe,dll,vbs,js
Database Mail Executable Minimum Lifetime (seconds)
600
Logging Level
Extended
Number of retry attempts for a mail server to send email.
Reset All
Help
< Back
Next >
Cancel

10. Test the database mail configuration.

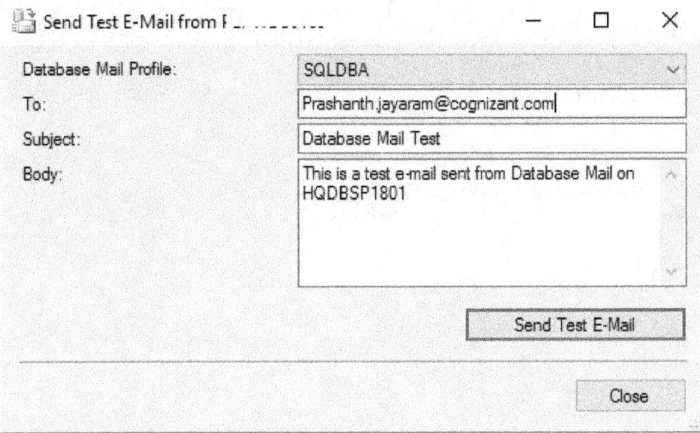

Configure Operator

In this section, you will see how to configure the operator.

1. Browse **SQL Server Agent**

2. Right-click **Operators** and create **New Operator…**

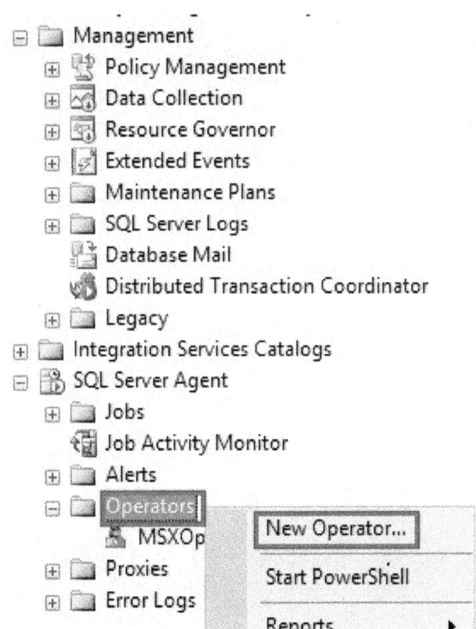

3. Enter the recipient email address and click OK.

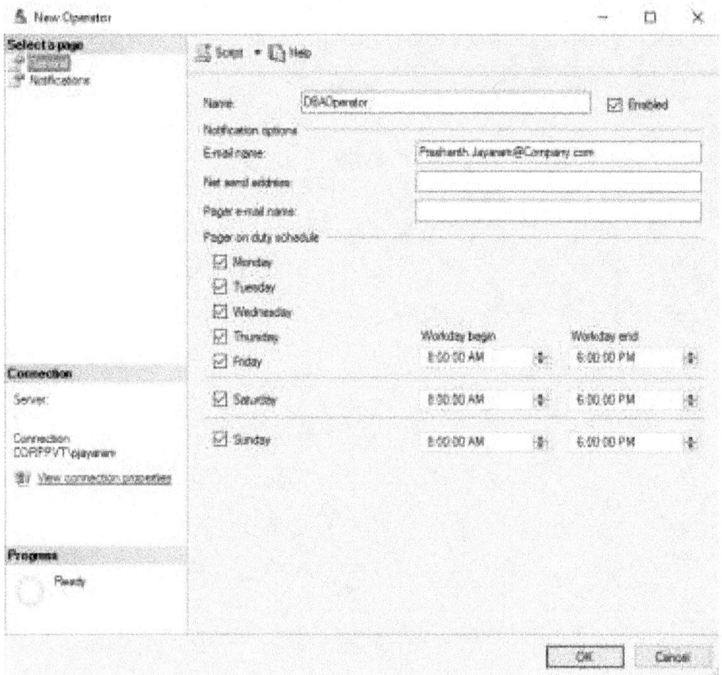

4. Enable the notify email option on the notification tab.

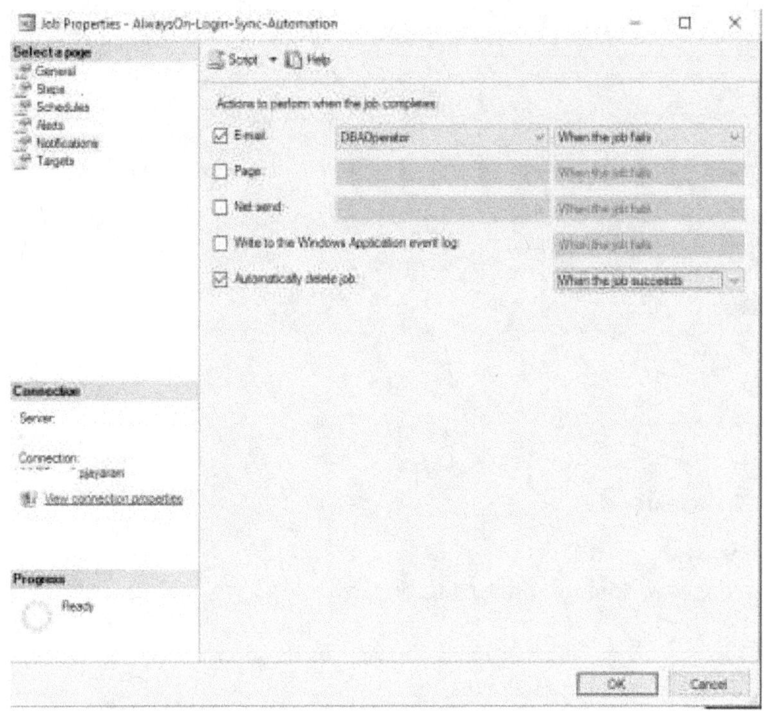

Configure Maintenance jobs to send alerts

Database systems need regular maintenance in order to perform them at the optimum level. Some of the tasks include backups, index maintenance, space management and updating statistics.

Note: We combine multiple maintenance tasks in one maintenance plan. The best practice would be to create a maintenance plan for each type of task—possibly for a specific database on your server. For example, you might create a maintenance plan to backup system databases and other maintenance plans to backup user databases. In addition, have another maintenance plan for special handling of one very large user database backup.

In this section, you will see how to send alerts upon completion of the backup operation.

1. Open SQL Server Management Studio.
2. Locate the Management folder and Maintenance plan.

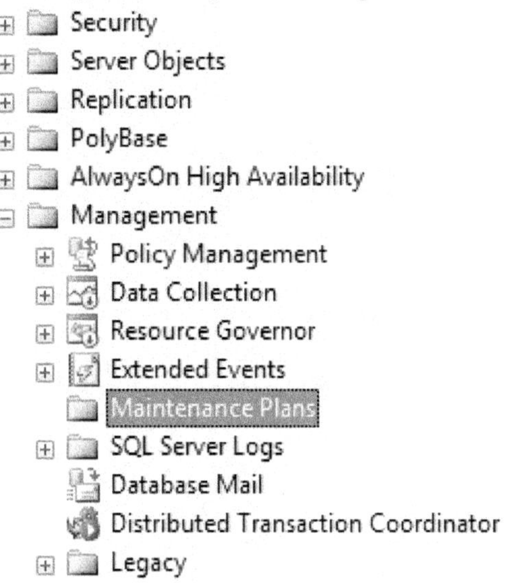

3. Right-click and select **New Maintenance Plan Wizard.**
4. Type in the name of the Maintenance plan.
5. Select the schedule as per the requirement.

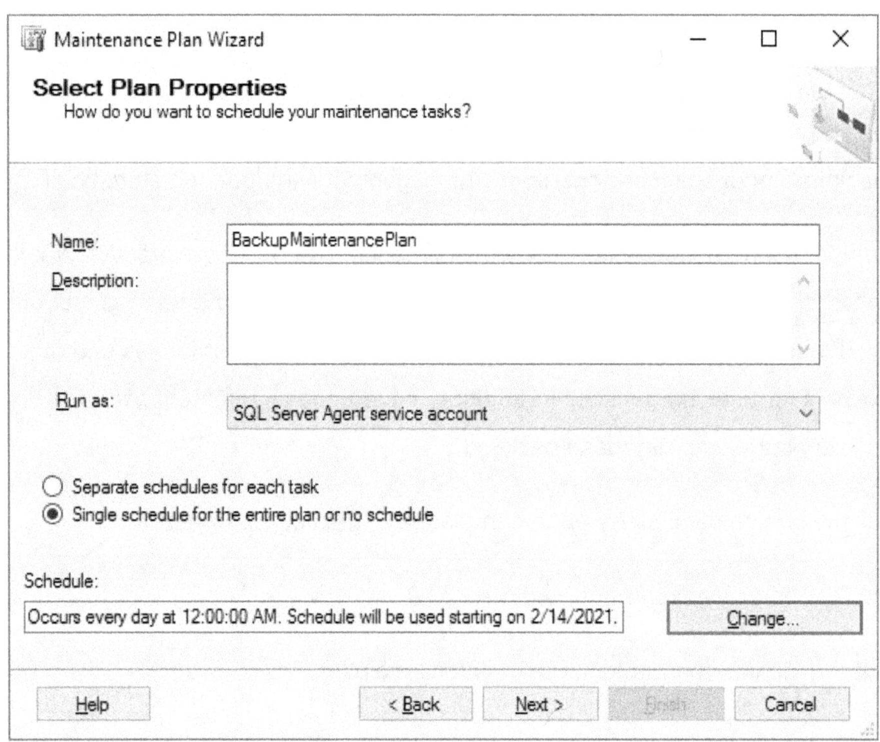

6. Choose Maintenance Tasks. In this case, select **Backup Up Database (Full)** task.

7. Click **Next.**

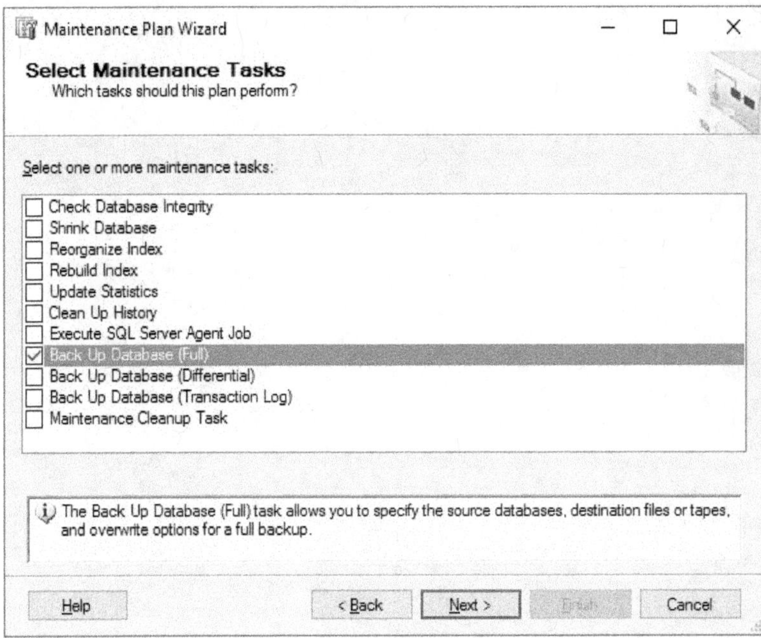

8. Leave the default in the Select Maintenance Task Order.

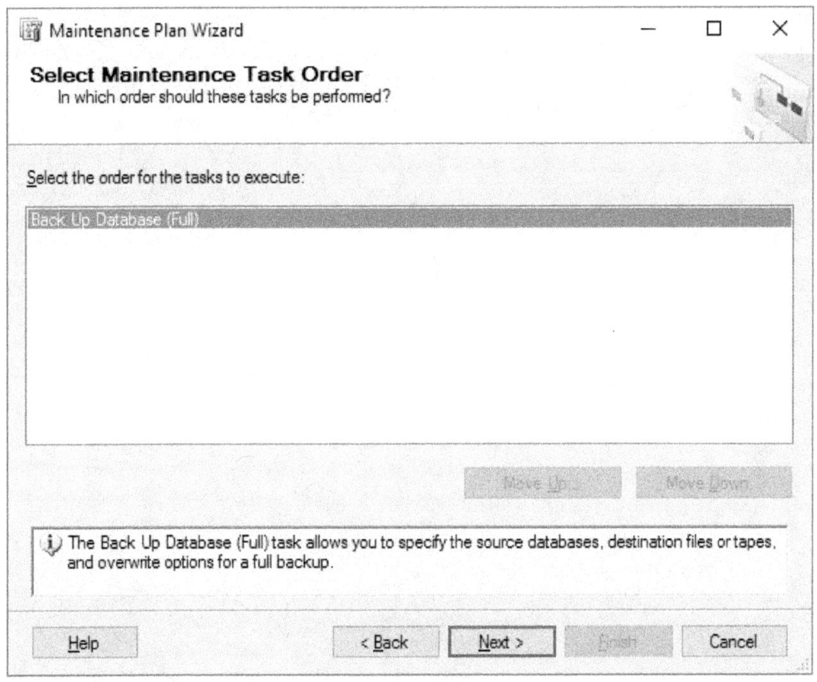

9. Select the specified user database that you intend to initiate the full database backup.

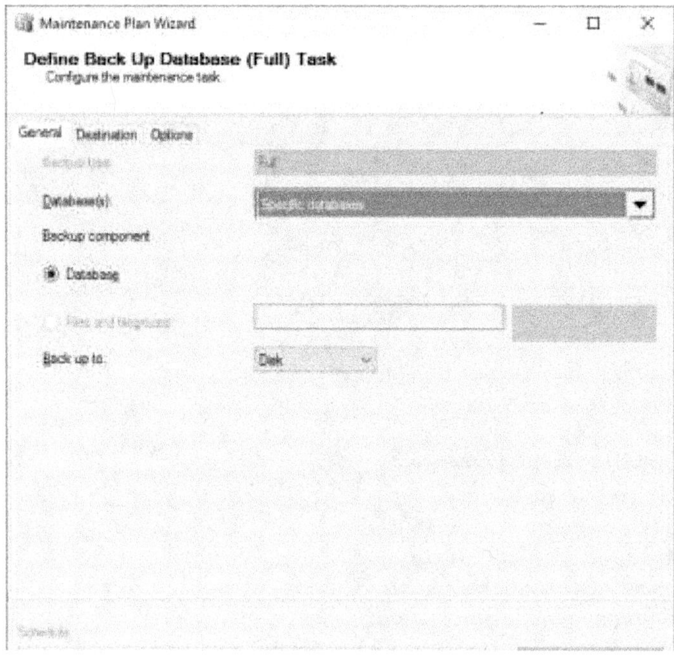

10. In the Select Report Options, Select the Email report and select the operator.

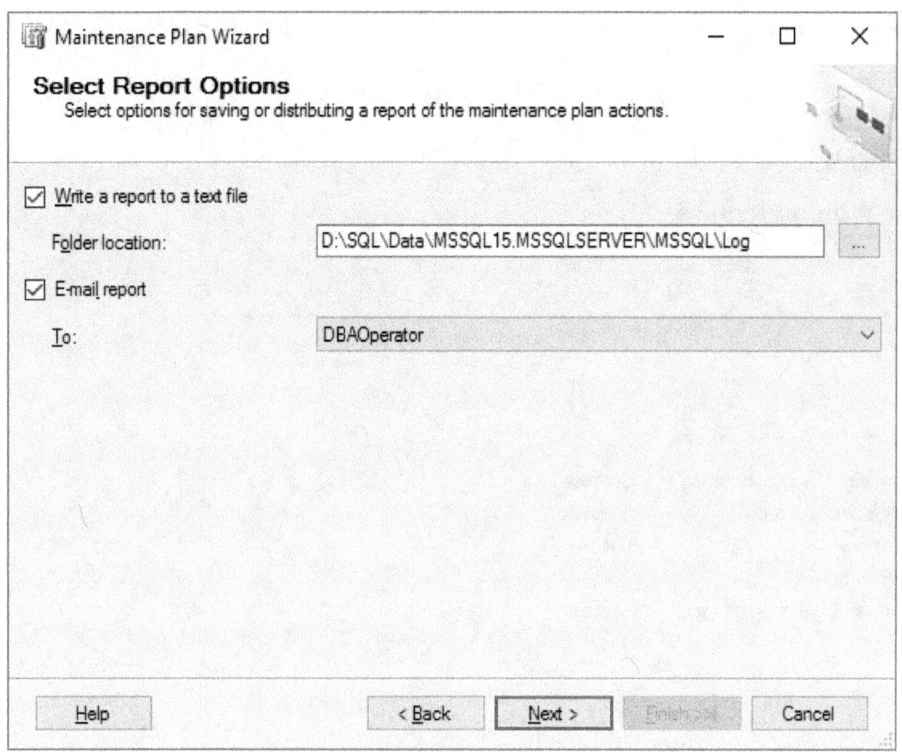

11. Validate the steps and configuration options and click Finish.

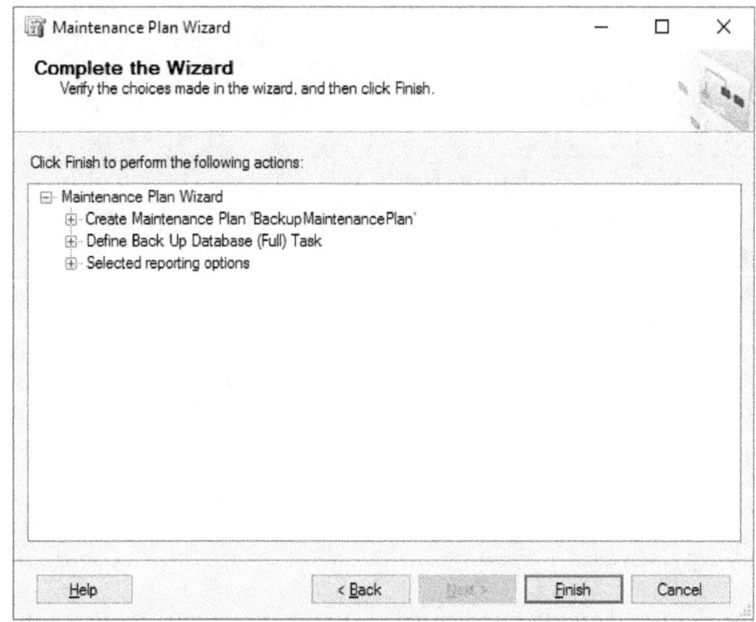

12. You can view the status and progress of each step. It will create maintenance jobs in SQL Server Agent.

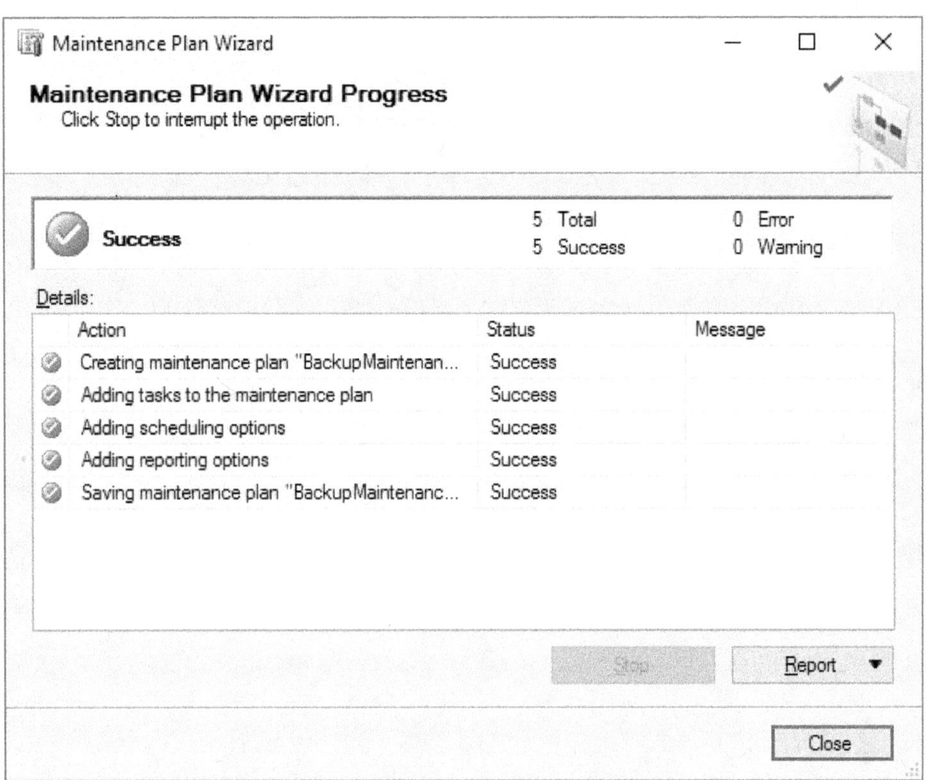

13. To verify, locate the job in the SQL Server Agent job and initiate the job.

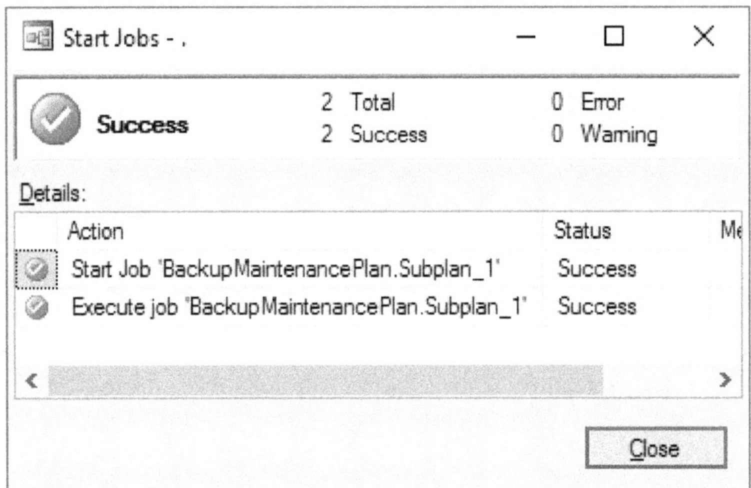

Use-case: How to set up an alert in SQL Server Agent jobs

You have SQL Server on an Azure virtual machine named SQL1. It has an agent job to back up all databases. You add a user named dbadmin1 as a SQL Server Agent operator. You need to ensure that dbadmin1 receives an email alert if a job fails.

Which three actions should you perform in sequence?

Solution:

Step 1: Enable the email settings for the SQL Server Agent.

To send a notification in response to an alert, you must first configure SQL Server Agent to send mail.

Step 2: Create a job alert -

Step 3: Create a job notification

Example:

```
-- adds an e-mail notification for the specified alert (Test Alert)

-- This example assumes that Test Alert already exists

-- and that Prashanth is a valid operator name.

USE msdb

GO

EXEC dbo.sp_add_notification -

@alert_name = N'Test Alert',

@operator_name = N'Prashanth',

@notification_method = 1 ;
```

GO –

https://docs.microsoft.com/en-us/sql/ssms/agent/notify-an-operator-of-job-status
https://docs.microsoft.com/en-us/sql/ssms/agent/assign-alerts-to-an-operator

Run PowerShell script steps in SQL Server Agent

Use SQL Server Agent to run and schedule PowerShell scripts using PowerShell Job Step or Command Prompt Job Step.

Prerequisite:

1. Load SQLServer module.

Run the following command in your PowerShell session to install the SqlServer module for all users.

```
Install-Module -Name SqlServer
Import-Module SqlServer
```

2. Configure Proxy account.

To create a credential, locate the security context, and create credentials. SQL Server Agent proxy account uses the credential to hold the meta-data of Windows account.

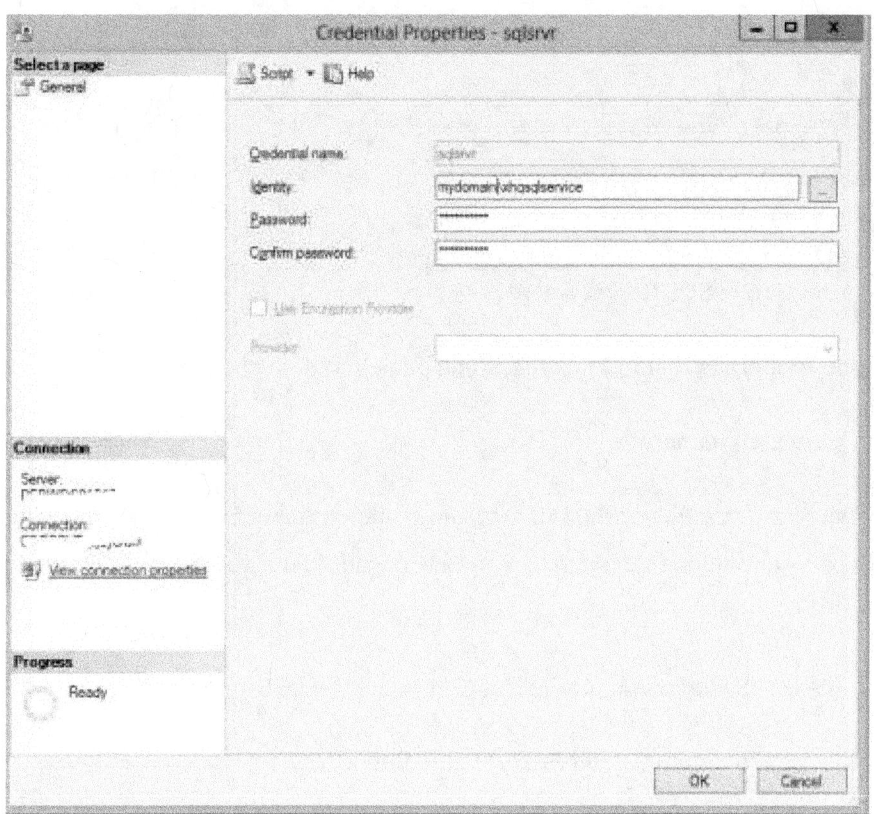

Now, you can see the credential.

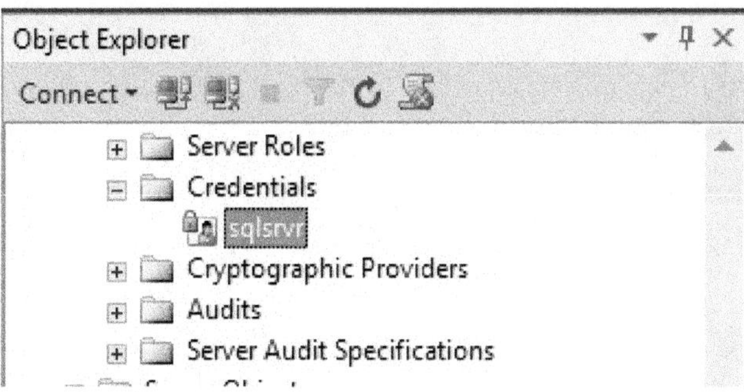

1. In **Object Explorer**, Expand **SQL Server Agent**.
2. Right-click the **Proxies** folder and select **New Proxy**.
3. On the **New Proxy Account** dialog box, on the **General** page, enter the proxy account's name in the **Proxy name** box.
4. Choose the **Credential.**

5. Under **Active to the following subsystems**, select the PowerShell subsystem for this proxy.

6. On the **Principals** page, grant access to the proxy account.

1.1.8 Create a PowerShell Job Step

1. Create a new job in **SQL Server Agent.**

2. In the **Job Properties** dialog, click the **Steps** page and then click **New**.

3. Type in a job **Step name**.

4. In the **Type** list, click **PowerShell** or **Operating system (CmdExec)**. The following command is just an example to highlight the syntax you want to use to run the PowerShell commands.

Powershell.exe -file D:\PS_Scripts\AzureMetrics\Get-AzureMaxDBSize.ps1

5. Select the proxy account "**Cloud Proxy**" in the **Run as** option.

6. In the **Command** box, enter the PowerShell script.

7. Click the **Advanced** page to decide the further course of action.

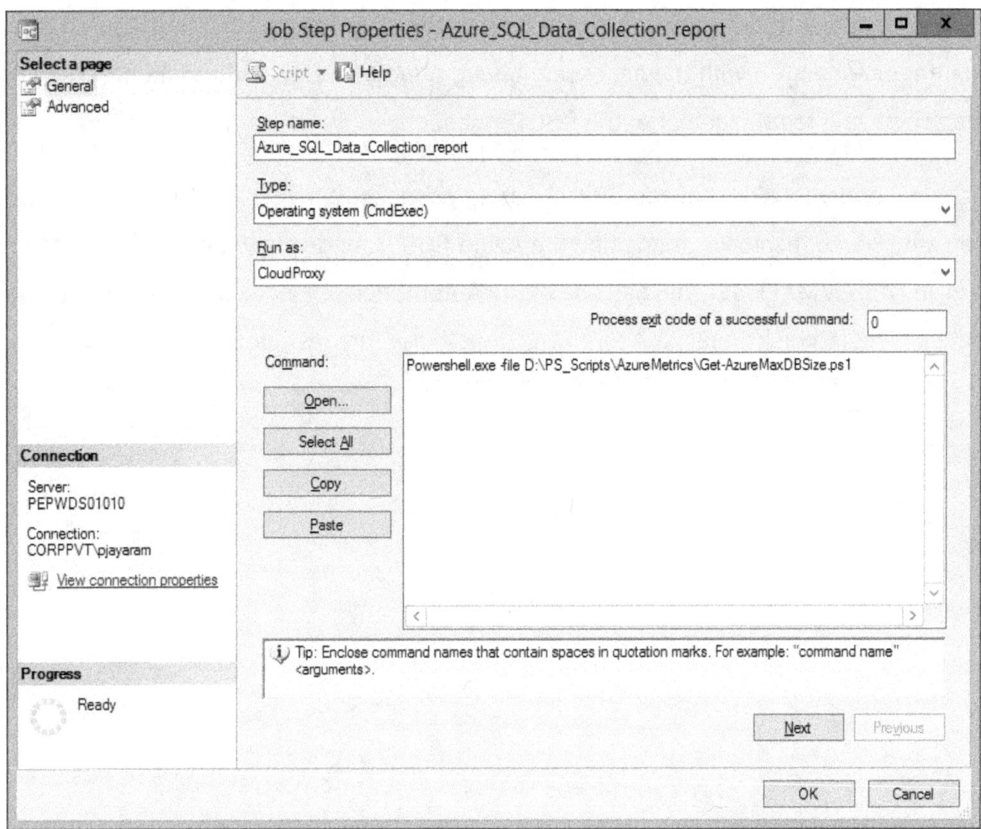

Note: Each SQL Server Agent job step that runs PowerShell with SQL Server module launches a process that consumes approximately 20 MB of memory. Running large numbers of concurrent Windows PowerShell job steps can hurt the performance of the server.

Summary

As you decide to move from on-premise to the cloud, you need to consider a couple of things for automation.

As you have seen, building and managing Azure databases is so simple. This chapter introduced you to the automation framework, available tools and design and implementation procedures that give you the necessary building blocks to experiment with automation.

You also explored advanced topics such as Azure Automation, ARM templates, and Azure Logic Apps. This chapter provides you with the necessary background to create and run the SQL Server agents job and schedule it to run against Azure SQL Database.

Automation is a key and vital skill that the DBA needs to possess. Whether it is deploying Azure resources in an automated fashion or managing the Azure SQL Managed Instance or SQL Server's maintenance in an Azure VM. Finally, you can use Azure Automation or Elastic Jobs or Azure Logic Apps to execute scheduled tasks against Azure SQL and other Azure resources.

Chapter 10 Plan and implement high availability and disaster recovery environments in Azure

Organizations need to plan high availability and disaster recovery solutions for business continuity.

- **High Availability**: High availability refers to automatic fault detection and correction measures to maximize your critical databases and applications availability.
- **Disaster recovery:** Disaster recovery refers to the process for recovering infrastructure after a natural disaster such as Earthquake, Datacenter power outages, and human-induced disaster such as accidentally dropping a database, or a VM.

The Business continuity refers to policies, procedures and mechanisms that enable the infrastructure to continue server user requests in case of any planned outages or disruptive events.

This chapter discusses high availability and disaster recovery for Azure SQL Databases and Azure SQL Managed Instances. By the end of this chapter, you will acquire knowledge on the following topics

- Built-in high availability features for Azure SQL Databases and Azure SQL Managed Instances.
- Disaster recovery solutions in Azure using the geo-recovery and failover groups.
- Backup storage redundancy.
- Azure Backup for SQL VMs.
- PaaS deployments High availability and disaster recovery options.

Recovery Time Objective (RTO) and Recovery Point Objective(RPO)

RPO and RTO play a vital role in defining the HADR strategy or data protection plan. Here, RPO refers to maximum allowable tolerance for data loss. It answers the question, "Up to what point application can tolerate the volume of data lost". Similarly, RTO defines the maximum allowable downtime in an infrastructure. It defines the answer, "How much time did it take to recover infrastructure after a disruption?”

For example, your Azure database experiences an outage at 9:00 AM, and you have an RPO of 10 minutes. The business expectation would be to make the database available with a maximum of 10 minutes of data loss.

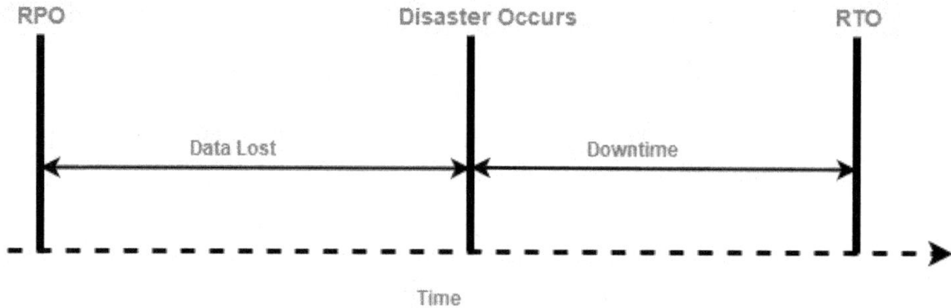

We need to define the RPO and RTO at the individual component as well as the infrastructure level. For example, if you recover the database in 10 minutes, but it is not in sync with application servers for 30 minutes, then the overall downtime (RTO) would be 30 minutes.

The following table lists the SLA percentage and allowed downtime.

SLA Percentage	Daily downtime	Weekly Downtime	Monthly Downtime	Yearly Downtime
99.9	1 minute 26 seconds	10 minutes and 5 seconds	43 minutes and 50 seconds	8 hours, 45 minutes and 57 seconds
99.95	43 seconds	5 minutes and 2 seconds	21 minutes and 55 seconds	4 hours, 22 minutes and 58 seconds
99.99	9 seconds	1 minute	4 minute and 23 seconds	52 minutes and 36 seconds
99.999	Less than 1 seconds	6 seconds	26 seconds	5 minute and 16 seconds
99.9999	Less than 1 seconds	Less than 1 seconds	3 seconds	32 seconds
99.99999	Less than 1 seconds	Less than 1 seconds	Less than 1 seconds	3 seconds
99.999999	Less than 1 seconds	Less than 1 seconds	Less than 1 seconds	Less than 1 seconds

The Azure service SLA is different for each offered service. For example,

- Azure SQL Database:
    - Business-critical and premium tier with Zone Redundant deployment: minimum 99.995%
    - Business-critical and premium tier without Zone Redundant deployment: 99.99%
    - Basic, Standard, Hyperscale tier with two or more replicas: 99.99%
    - Azure SQL Database hyperscale with one replica: 99.95%
    - Azure SQL Database hyperscale with zero replicas: 99.9%
- Azure Site Recovery: 99.9% availability
- Azure SQL Managed Instance:99.99% for both the Business Critical tier and the General Purpose tiers.

You can refer to URL **https://azure.microsoft.com/en-in/support/legal/sla/summary/** for SLA summary of Azure Services.

Explore high availability and disaster recovery options

Azure offers both Infrastructure-as-a-Service and Platform-as-a-Service solutions for databases. In a PaaS offering (Azure SQL Database), Azure offers an inbuilt solution and needs to configure it as per your requirements. However, in an IaaS offering, you configure databases similar to an on-premise infrastructure. The only difference is that you leverage Azure cloud infrastructure for database deployments.

SQL Server HADR Features for Azure Virtual Machine

If we use the IaaS platform for SQL Server configuration, we can configure existing SQL Server HADR features.

- Windows Failover clustering:
- SQL Server Always On Availability Groups
- Log Shipping

Windows Failover clustering

In the on-premise Windows Failover Clustering, users connect to a virtual server name or IP address. This virtual server connects to the active failover instance. Therefore, auto-failover triggers and application to connect to the old passive instance with minimal downtime if the active instance goes down. In a high-level, WSFC works like the following image.

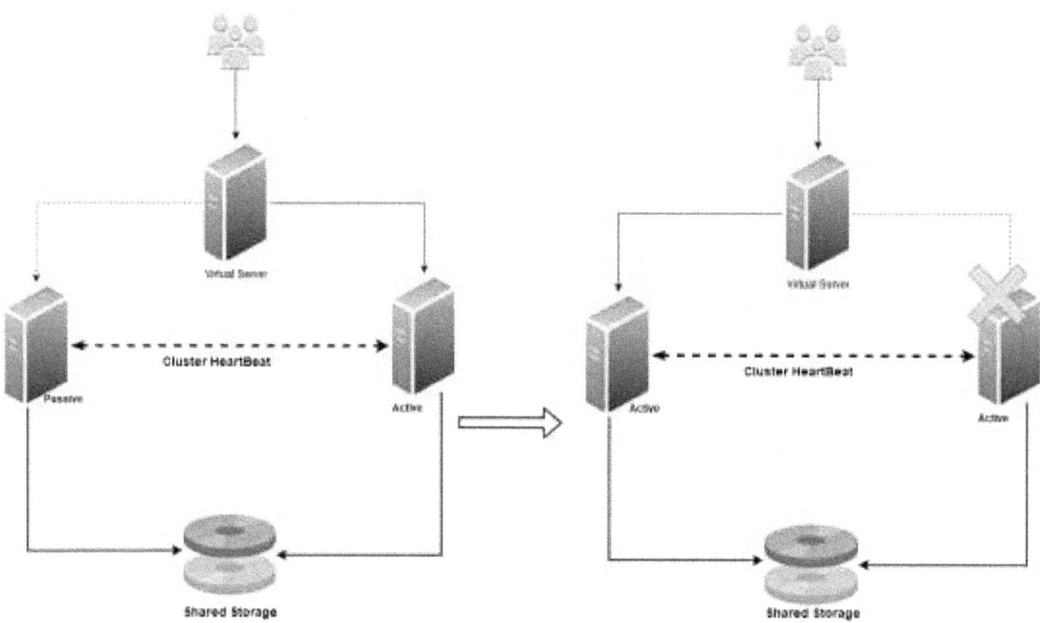

SQL Server Always On Availability Groups

The concept for SQL Server Always On Availability Group is the same in on-premise infrastructure as well on Azure. However, there is a difference - Azure uses an internal load balancer(ILB) for ensuring the application can connect to the failover cluster unique name. It maps the public IP address and port number to the virtual machine private IP address for the incoming and outgoing traffic.

The following points summarize the requirements for a two-node SQL Server AG in Azure.

- Two SQL Server instances in a single domain and Azure availability set.
- File share for cluster witness.
- Azure AD domain account.
- Azure Firewall for following ports:

- Port 1433: SQL Server default port.
- Port 5022:AG endpoint.
- Port 59999 or any specific port: Availability group load balancer IP address.
- Port 58888 or any specific port: It is a cluster load balance IP address.

- Enable failover clustering feature on primary and secondary replica nodes.
- Configure Windows Server Failover Clustering(WSFC) on both servers.
- Configure the cluster quorum. You can choose a file share witness or cloud witness in Windows Server 2016.
- Enable SQL Server always on the feature from SQL Server Configuration Manager
- Create the availability group.
- Create an Azure load balancer: Azure requires a load balancer for holding the IP address for the availability group listener and WSFC.

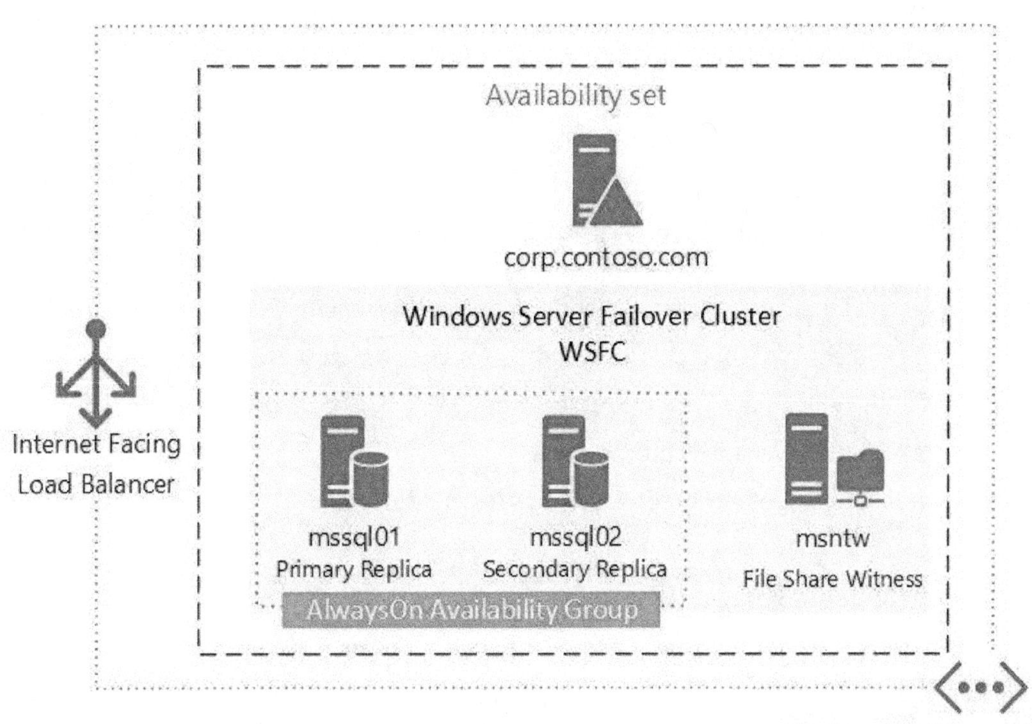

To configure the load balancer, go to Azure portal, resource group, click on Add and search for the load balancer.

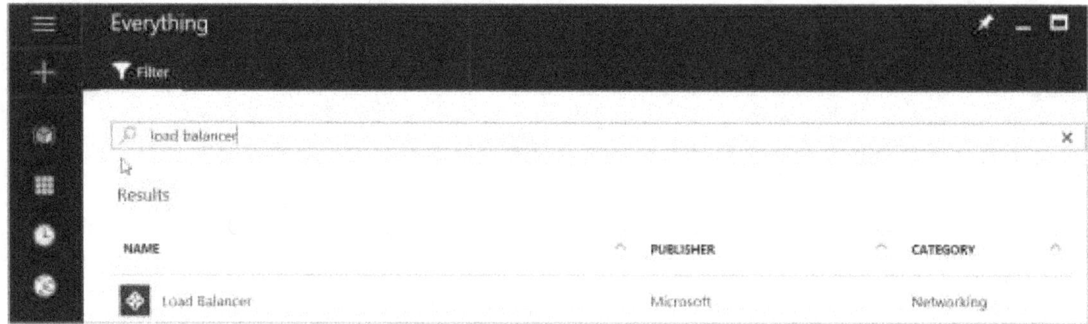

In the load balancer configuration, enter the following parameters.

- Load balancer name
- Load balancer type: Internal
- Virtual network name
- VM subnet
- IP address assignment: Static
- IP address: Select the available address range in the subnet.
- Location: Select your VM location.

Add a backend pool for the availability group listener

In this step, we need to create a backend pool and set the load balancing rules. For this requirement, In the Azure portal, Select your load balancer and select backend pools. Enter the backend pool name and select both virtual machines under the Target network IP configurations.

- Create the availability group listener .
- Validate availability group failover and synchronization.

Configure the health probe

The health probe informs the load balancer about nodes health and status to accept traffic or request.

Configure Load balancing rules

The load balancing rules combine the health probe and backend pools.

Explore the high availability and disaster recovery solution for IaaS

In this section, we discover multiple combinations for deploying HADR solutions in Azure for IaaS. Before we proceed further, let's explore the practical terms - Availability Sets, Availability Zones and Azure Site Recovery.

Availability Sets:

The availability set provides logical grouping capabilities so that VM resources are isolated from each other. Azure ensures that the virtual machines within a specific availability set are spanned across multiple physical servers, storage units, compute racks, network switches. In case of any undesired failure, only a few VMs are impacted, and your infrastructure is available. It provides high availability protection from hardware failures in a datacenter.

- **Update Domains(UD):** It is a local grouping of Azure hardware resources on which you can perform maintenance simultaneously.
- **Fault Domains(FD):-** It provides a logical grouping of Azure hardware such as networking, Power supplies.

The below figure shows three virtual machines in an availability set.

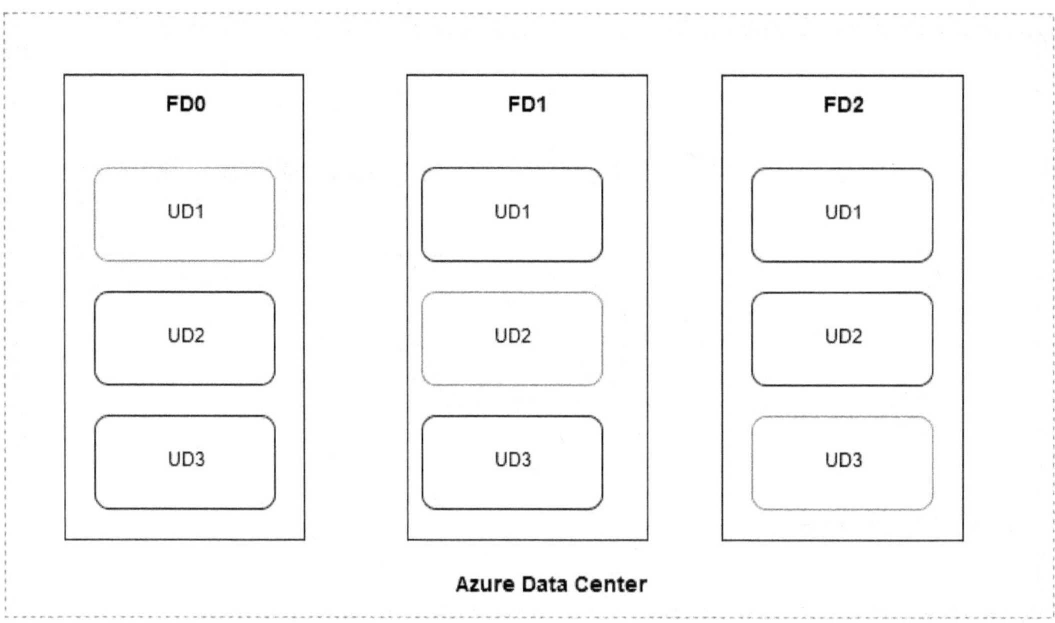

These availability sets do not protect against operating system or database-level failures. Therefore, we require additional resources such as Always On or Failover Clustering.

Availability zones

The availability zones safeguard against the data centre failures. Azure provides multiple availability zones in an Azure region with low network latency(less than 1ms).

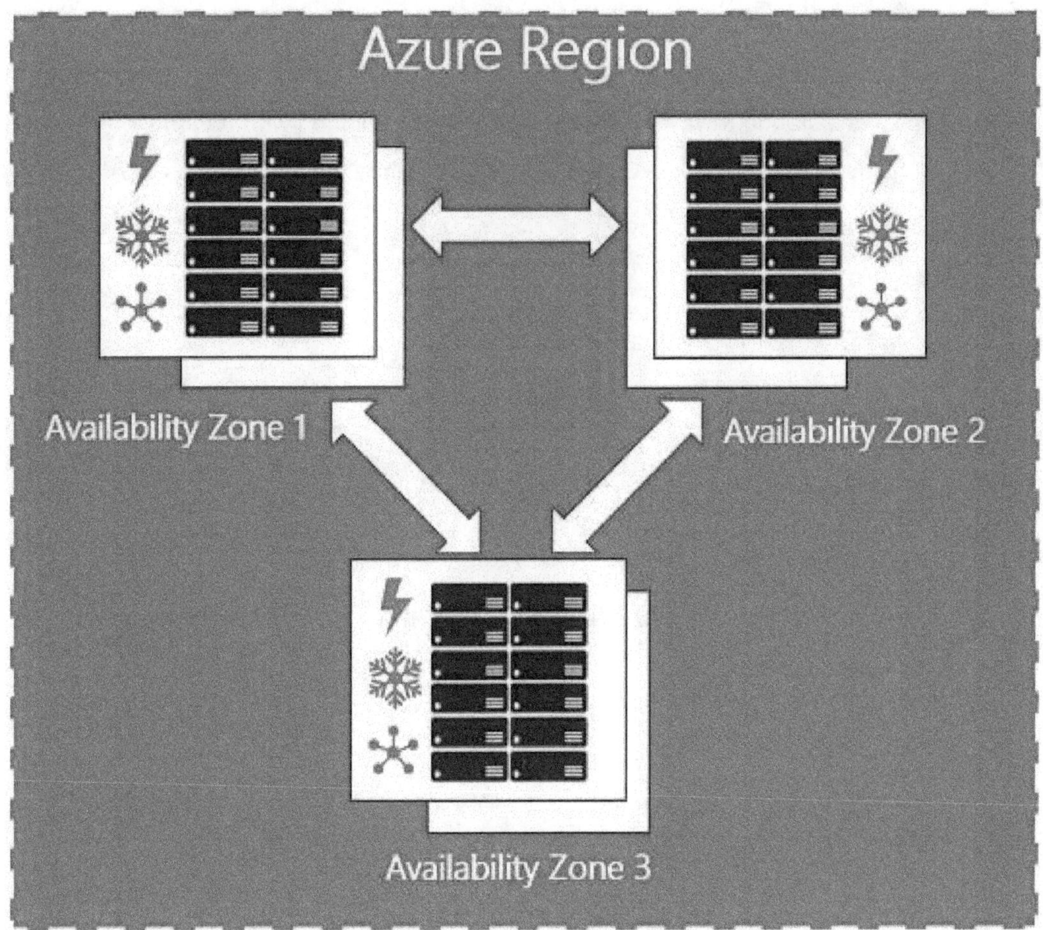

Azure Site Recovery

Azure Site Recovery replicates a virtual machine from one Azure Region to Another Azure region. It creates a disaster recovery mechanism and safeguards you against the failover of the Azure region. It provides a two hours monthly RTO. It might not be suitable for a critical database. Therefore, we are required to configure additional DR solutions.

Single Region SQL Server Always On Availability Group

In this architecture, we deploy SQL Server Always On Availability Groups similar to an on-premise SQL infrastructure.

- You configure multiple VM's with running SQL Server. Each SQL Server VM receives its database storage.
- It is a standard way of implementing an HA solution with minimal complexity.
- You can maintain RPO and RTO with minimal (asynchronous AG) or zero loss (synchronous AG).

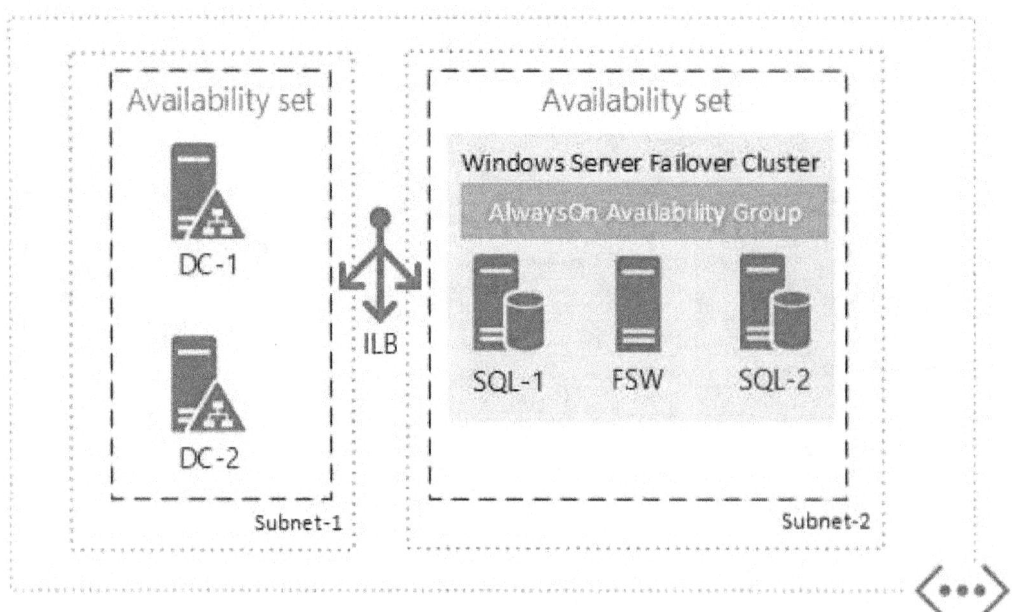

Hybrid SQL Server Always On availability group

We can achieve both high availability and disaster recovery using the hybrid availability group. It spans across multiple data centres. As shown below, in the primary DC, AG uses synchronous replicas to provide zero data loss if the primary goes down.

The AG also maintains two additional copies of data in another reason with asynchronous configuration. You can failover from primary DC to secondary DC in case of any issue on the primary site.

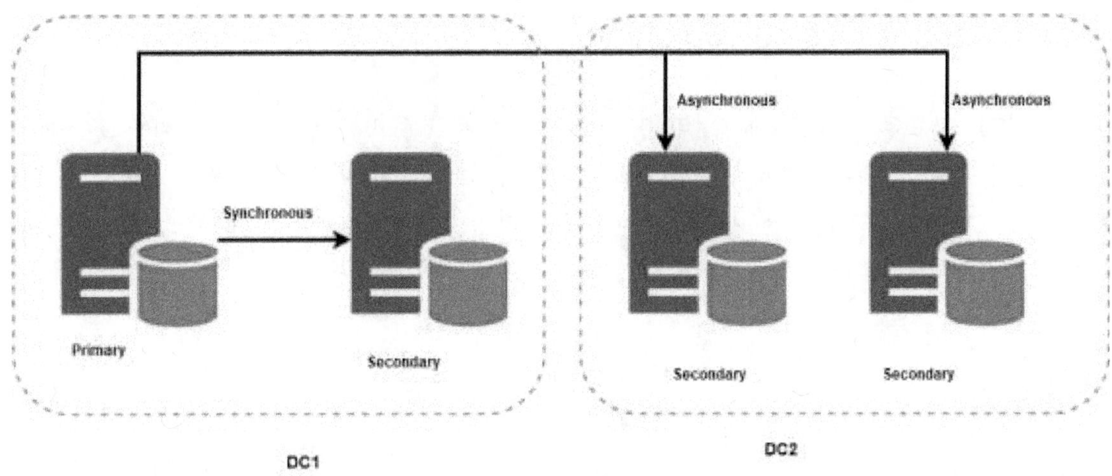

Distributed availability group

The distributed availability group configures separate WSFC for primary and secondary data centres for HADR capabilities. The active replica of secondary DC receives a copy of data from the primary DC active instance. It forwards data to its corresponding secondary replica. Therefore, the primary AG of the secondary replica is known as Forwarder.

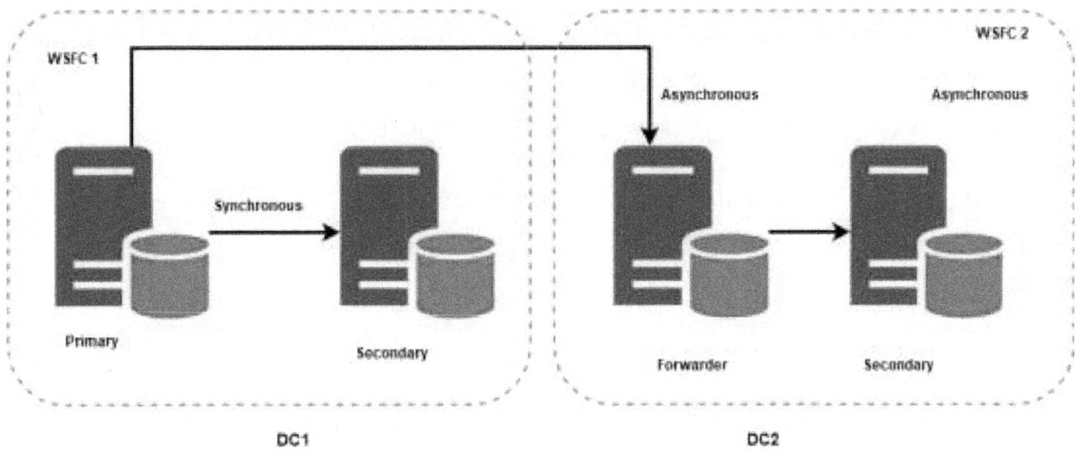

In this architecture, both DCs have separate AD DS and DNS. It safeguards in case the primary WSFC goes down. The secondary DC forwarder can take the role of primary AG after failover and serves user requests. This architecture is available with standard and enterprise edition of SQL Server.

Disaster recovery using Log shipping

Log shipping provides a standby copy of the database in another instance. This instance can be in the same or different data centre. The data loss depends on the backup job frequency, backup copy from primary to secondary site and log backup restoration. It is a feasible and quickly implemented solution without any additional configurations such as FCI, AG.

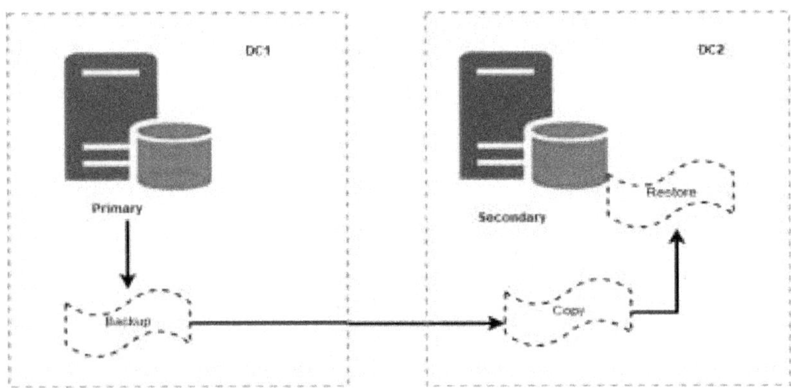

Azure Site Recovery

Azure Site Recovery replicates virtual machines to another specified region. It is suitable for DR solutions where you do not want to configure the DR solution at the SQL Server level. In the VM configuration, we can configure the target region for Azure Site recovery.

We have East US as the source region and West US 2 as the target region in the below image.

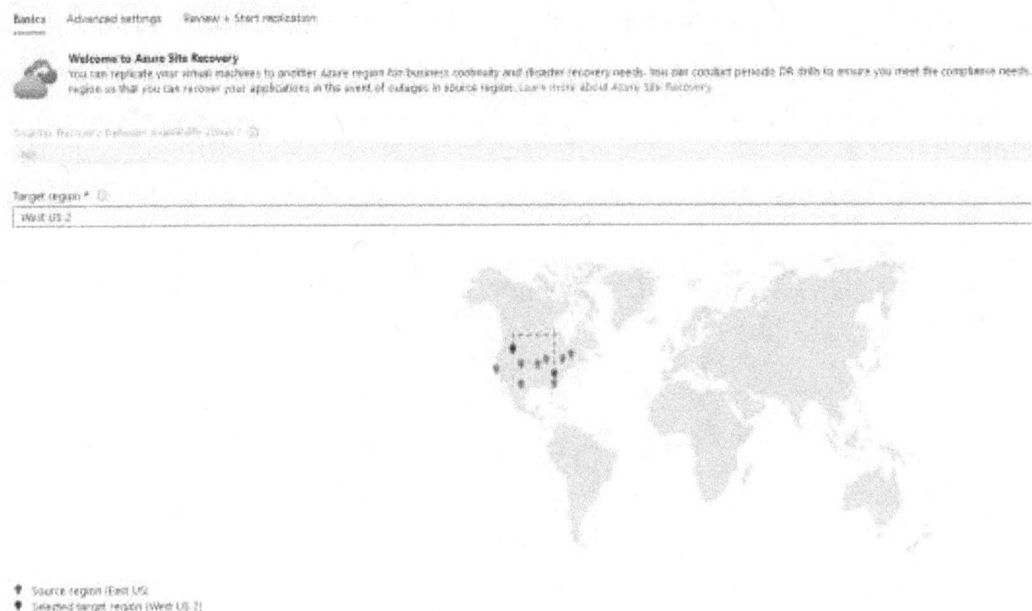

PaaS deployments High availability and disaster recovery options

Azure provides the following PaaS deployments for SQL Server.

- Azure SQL Database
- Azure SQL Database Managed instances

Azure SQL Database and Managed instances depend on the service tier and its underlying architecture model. According to the latest updates(reference:https://azure.microsoft.com/en-us/support/legal/sla/sql-database/v1_5/), Azure PaaS offers the following SLA as per their service tier.

Azure SQL Database is a fully managed relational database with built-in regional high availability and turnkey geo-replication to any Azure region. It includes intelligence to support self-driving features such as performance tuning, threat monitoring, and vulnerability assessments and provides fully automated patching and updating of the code base.

- Azure SQL Database Business Critical or Premium tiers configured as Zone Redundant Deployments have an availability guarantee of at least 99.995%.
- Azure SQL Database Business Critical or Premium tiers not configured for Zone Redundant Deployments, General Purpose, Standard, or Basic tiers, or Hyperscale tier with two or more replicas have an availability guarantee of at least 99.99%.
- Azure SQL Database Hyperscale tier with one replica has an availability guarantee of at least 99.95% and 99.9% for zero replicas.
- Azure SQL Database Business Critical tier configured with geo-replication has a guarantee of Recovery point objective (RPO) of 5 sec for 100% of deployed hours.
- Azure SQL Database Business Critical tier configured with geo-replication has a guarantee of Recovery time objective (RTO) of 30 sec for 100% of deployed hours.

It has the following high availability architectural models:

- Standard availability model
- Premium availability model

Standard availability model

Azure basic, standard and General purpose tiers use the standard availability architecture. In this architecture, we have separate compute and storage resources. In the following image(reference: https://docs.microsoft.com/en-us/azure/azure-sql/database/high-availability-sla), we see separate compute and storage layers.

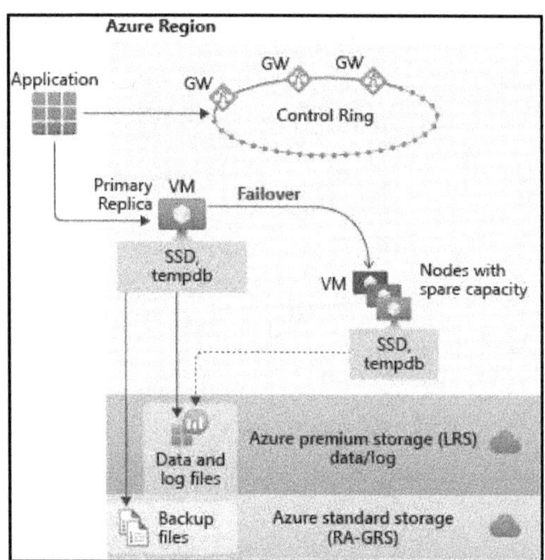

- The compute node has a local SSD for storing the TempDB database. It can failover to another VM with spare capacity. It is a stateless compute layer, and it runs the SQL Server process.
- It stores the data and log files in the Azure blob storage in the second stateful data layer. This storage has an inbuilt data redundancy feature for preserving data and log files.

In case of any failure on the stateless compute later, Azure moves the SQL Server process to another stateless compute node and attaches the data, log files from the Azure Blob Storage. It ensures 99.99% availability of Azure PaaS databases.

General Purpose service tier zone redundant availability

In the Zone redundant availability for general purpose service tier, you can leverage Azure Availability Zones for replicating databases to multiple physical locations. These database copies are in the same Azure region.

- Database MDF and LDF files are stored in the Azure zero-redundant storage. It synchronizes data copies across three physically-isolated Azure AZs.
- The stateless compute layer runs the TempDB and model database on the SSD. It also contains a buffer pool, column store pool and plan cache. In case of any issues, it can failover to another node with spare capacity.

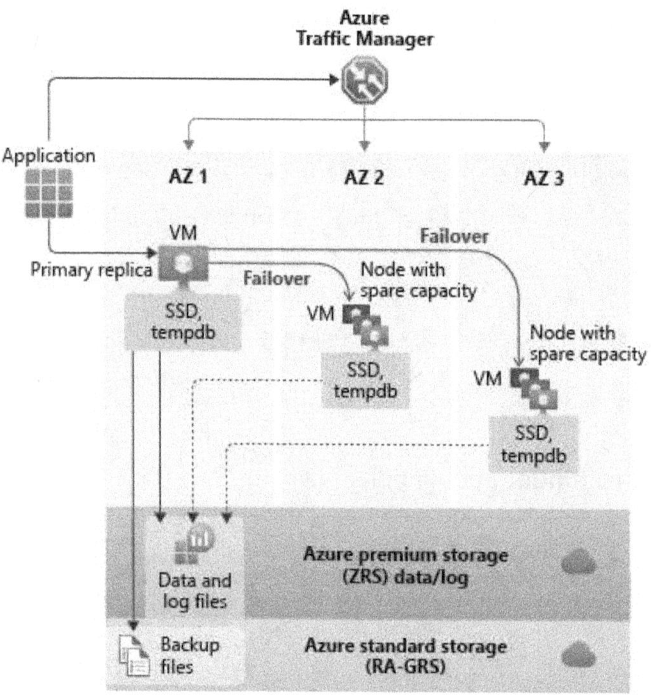

Premium availability model locally redundant availability

The premium availability model for premium and business-critical service tier integrates SQL Server process and storage for a single node.

As per the following architecture diagram, we note the following.

- It integrates the SQL Server process and storage in a single node. Further, it establishes HA by replicating both compute and storage to additional nodes.
- SQL database MDF and LDF files are stored in an SSD storage. It can failover to secondary replicas using the Always On Availability Group.
- The Azure cluster has a single primary replica, and it serves applications for all read-write requests.
- If due to any reason, the primary replica goes down; the secondary replica becomes a new primary and starts responding to application requests.
- Azure creates another secondary replica so that the cluster has enough quorum votes.

- In the premium availability model, you can also redirect read-only connections to the one secondary replica. It allows offloading workload, such as reporting queries, without any extra cost.

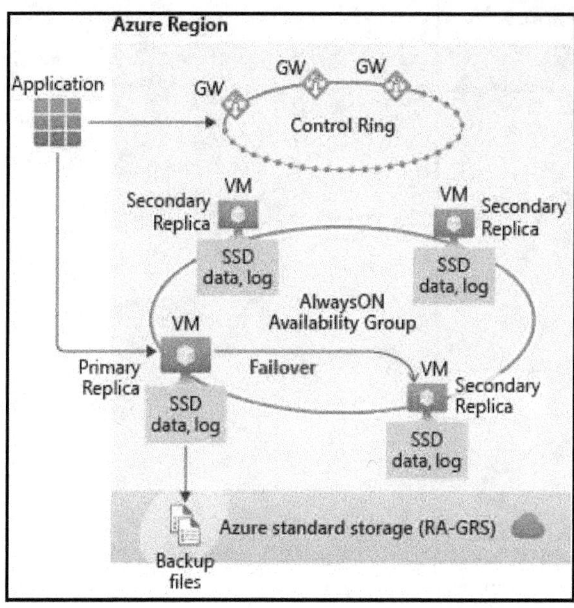

1.1.9 Premium and Business Critical service tier with zone redundant availability

In the premium and business service tier, we can utilize different availability zones in the same region. It uses the cluster of nodes for replicating data to different AZ in the same region. Each AZ has a duplicate of the control ring, and the Azure Traffic Manager (ATM) controls the routing to a specific gateway ring. It enables replicas to automatically failover to different AZ in case of any zone level outage.

We can enable zone redundant configuration without any extra cost for both premium and business-critical service tier.

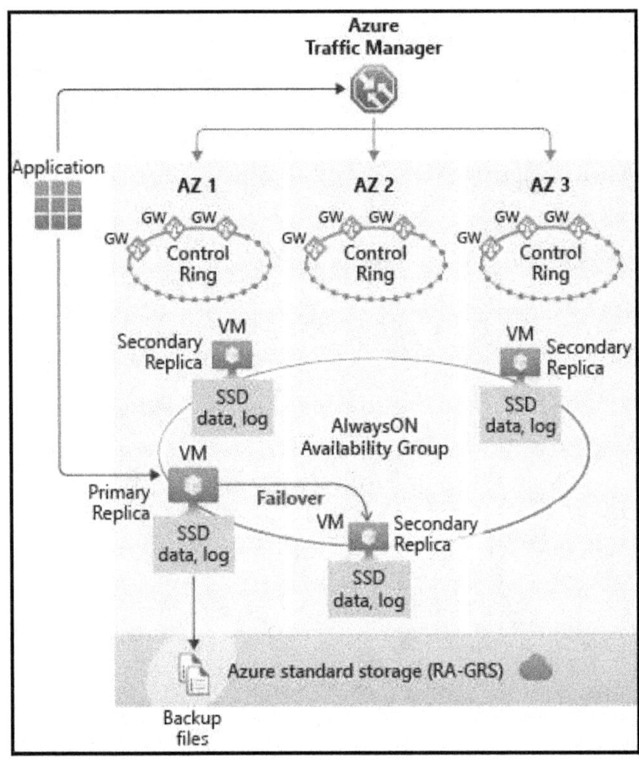

Note: This feature is an application for Azure SQL Database only. We cannot use it for Azure SQL managed instances.

In the database service tier configuration, Azure wizard gives you an option- Would you like to make this database Zone redundant. The default configuration does not configure it.

Note: It is a preview feature and supported in few Azure regions. Current supported Azure regions are:

- West US 2
- North Europe
- East US
- East US 2
- Southeast Asia
- Australia East
- West Europe

Note: Always check Azure documentation before planning the zone redundant feature in your region.

Active geo-replication for Azure SQL databases

Active geo-replica for Azure SQL databases uses SQL Server Always On Availability Group technology for replicating data to a maximum of four secondary replicas asynchronously. It can replicate data to a maximum of four readable replicas in the same or different Azure region.

The azure traffic manager can forward the read-only connections to the secondary replicas to reduce the primary site's workload.

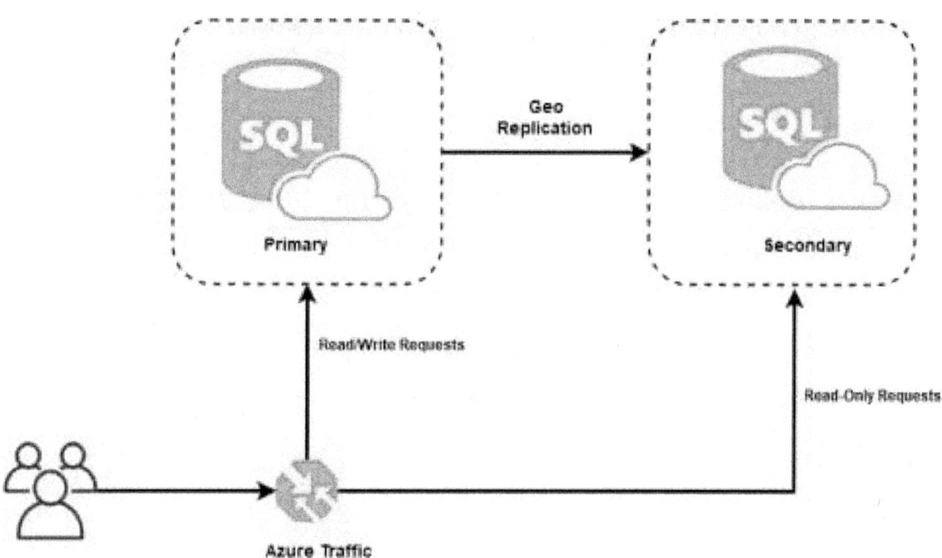

It enables business continuity for the Azure SQL database in case of disaster to a specific Azure region. It requires a manual failover to the secondary database. After the DB failover, it automatically links the secondary replicas with the new primary. It is similar to the SQL AG asynchronous mode that commits transactions on the primary replica without committing to the secondary replica. Therefore, the secondary database copy might have a latency (lag) from the primary replica. However, Azure guarantees data consistency for secondary database copy as well.

It has the following benefits for an Azure SQL Database.

- It offers automatic asynchronous data replication to secondary replicas.

- The replicas can be in the same or different region.
- You can add up to four secondary replicas and use them for read-only operations.
- It supports both planned and unplanned failover.

Note:

1. Once you failover to a secondary database configured using active-geo replication, its endpoint changes for the new primary replica. Therefore, you need to make changes in the application connection string to connect to the new primary.
2. You can force a synchronization using the sp_wait_for_database_copy_sync stored procedure. You can use it to ensure your changes are replicated to the secondary replica.
3. This feature is not supported by Azure Managed SQL instances.

Auto-failover groups

The auto-failover groups enable you to replicate automatically and failover a group of SQL databases for the Azure SQL Managed Instances. You can do manual or automatic failover using the user-defined policy. It requires all databases participating in an auto-failover in a single server, and they failover to a single server only. It safeguards you from a catastrophic failure or other unplanned events in the Azure SQL database or Azure Managed Instance.

It uses the following use terms.

- **Failover group**: It is a group of the database between the primary and secondary SQL Server. Azure considers the failover group as a single unit. Azure replicates data asynchronously between the primary to the secondary database. These primary and secondary servers must be in a different region.
- **Initial Seeding:** Once we add databases in a failover group, Azure starts the initial data seed. It is an expensive operation and takes longer depending upon database size and network link speed. It is similar to the automatic seeding feature in SQL Server Always On Availability Groups. It can usually replicate up to 500 GB per hour for Azure SQL database and up to 360 GB per hour in Azure SQL Managed Instance.
- **DNS zone:** Azure automatically generates a unique ID once you deploy a new Azure SQL Managed Instance. The secondary instance should share the same DNS zone.

Note: Azure SQL Database does not require a DNS zone ID.

- **Read-write listener**: It is a DNS CNAME that always points to the primary server. Azure automatically configures it during failover group configuration, and it allows read-write traffic to the current primary server even after a failover.
- **Read-only listener**: It is also a DNS CNAME that points to the secondary server. You can use it to send read-only queries to the secondary replica.
- **Automatic failover policy**: Azure automatically configures a default failover policy for automatic failover. Azure initiates a failover in case of a failure on the primary replica. You can turn off automatic failover if you want failover process control by the application.

Note: You can initiate a manual failover anytime, and it is independent of the automatic failover policy.

- **Planned failover**: Users can perform a planned failover for activities such as DR drills, failover tests. It performs full data synchronization between primary and secondary replica databases before the secondary database can take over the primary role.
- **Unplanned failover:** If the primary server is not accessible, Azure automatically initiates an automatic failover for a role change. It might result in data loss because the primary and secondary servers do not synchronize during the failover process. If the primary comes up after the failover, it acts as a secondary replica and receives the pending transactions.
- **Grace period with data loss hours**: We can control the data synchronization duration before initiating an automatic failover. For example, if you specify a grace period of 1 hour, then automatic failover happens after one hour in an outage. During the grace period, if the primary server is available, Azure does not perform any failover.

In the below diagram, we get a typical configuration for an auto-failover group for Azure SQL Databases. It has multiple SQL databases in a failover group in a primary and secondary region. The Read-write listener points to the primary logical SQL Server while the read-only listener points to the secondary SQL Server.

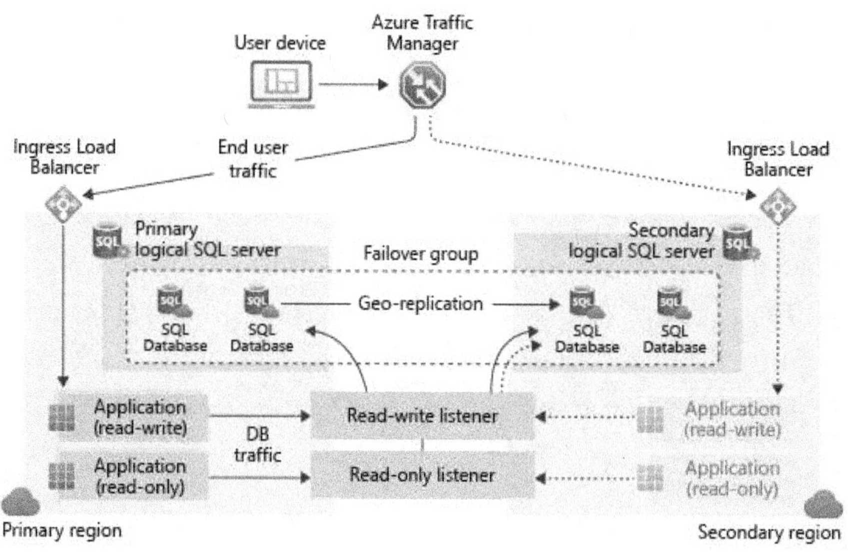

Similarly, the Azure SQL Managed instance configures the failover group for the primary and secondary region. As shown, both primary and secondary instances are in the same DNS zone.

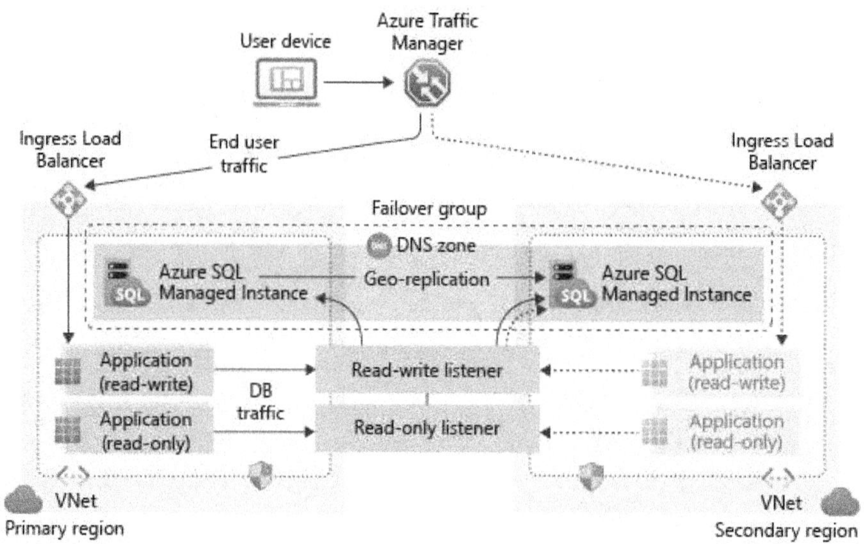

Difference between Active-Geo Replication and Auto-failover groups

Feature	Active Geo-Replication	Auto-failover Groups
Automatic failover	No	Yes
Managed instance support	No	Yes
Multiple replicas	Yes	No
Supports read-scale	Yes	Yes
Failover multiple databases simultaneously	No	Yes
Update connecting string after failover	Yes	No
Can be in the same region as the primary	Yes	No

Backup and restore databases

Backups play a vital role in infrastructure availability and disaster recovery. This section explores backup options available with Azure SQL Database, SQL Managed instance and SQL Server on Azure VM.

Backup and restore SQL Server running on Azure virtual machines

SQL Server on Azure VM is similar to an on-premise SQL Server. It has all supported backups – Full, differential and transaction log backup for satisfying your backup requirements. A typical SQL Server involves the combination of these backups for ensuring RPO requirement.

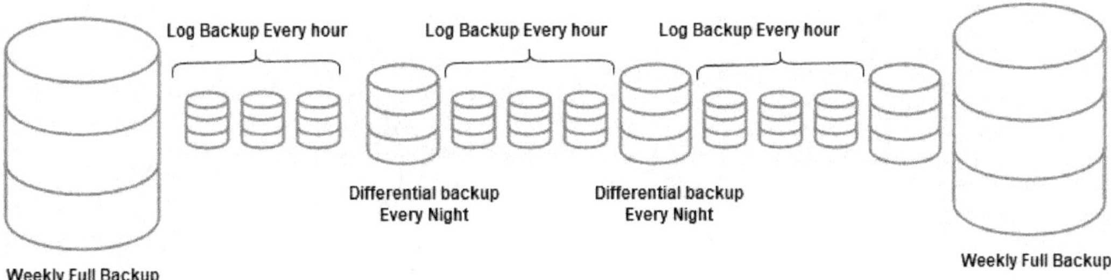

- **Full Backup:** A full database backup is a complete database backup.

Scenario 1 : Only Full Backup

- Works in Simple, Bulk-logged and Full recovery Model
- It takes a lot of space (depending upon your database size)
- Recovery is easy using full backup
- You can recovery data up to the time of backup.

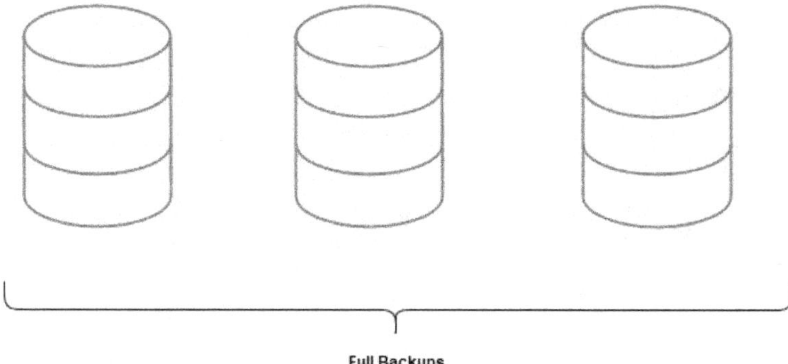

- **Differential backup**

The differential database backup is a *superset* of the last full backup, and it contains all changes performed since the last full backup. The differential backup size depends upon the number of transactions. If you have performed a large number of transactions or your recent full backup was very old, its size might be more prominent.

Scenario 2 : Full + Differential Backup

- Differential backups takes modified extents backups since last full backup.
- It takes less space than full backup however it always references last full backup.
- It is suitable for scenario that can tolerate some data loss.
- You always require last full backup for restoring a differential backup

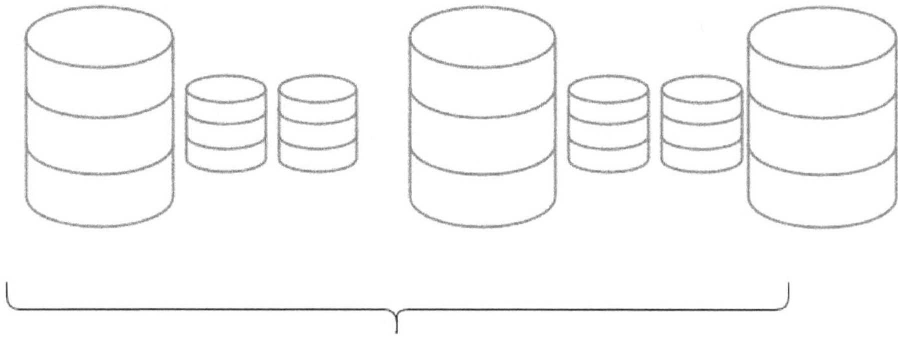

- **Transaction log backup**

The transaction log backup enables you for a point-in-time recovery with almost zero data loss. It is an incremental backup that means you need to restore all transaction log backups since the last full or differential backup for a particular point-in-time recovery.

Scenario 3 : Full + Differential Backup + Transaction Log Backup

- You can perform point-in-time recovery with almost zero data loss.
- This scenario is suitable for production databases.
- For database restore, you require last full backup, recent differential backup and all log backups (till restoration point) performed after the differential backup.
- It works with Full and Bulk-logged recovery model.

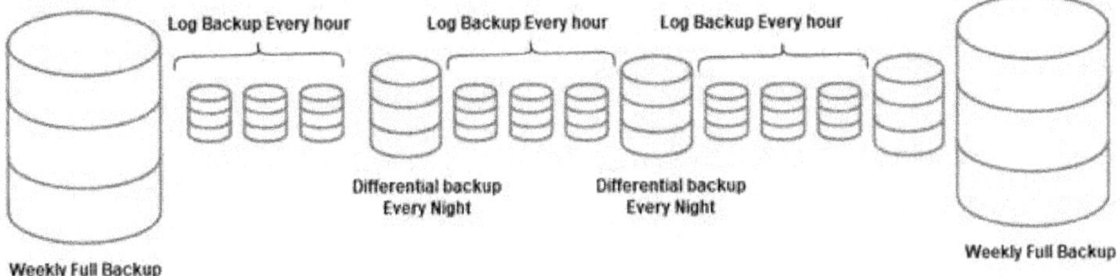

1.1.10 Backup a SQL Server virtual machine

This section is a guide for available backup and restores options for SQL Server running on the Azure VM. The databases are stored in the Azure storage that maintains three copies of the Azure VM disk. It guarantees protection against storage level corruption. However, it is best to take regular backups for protection against accidental data deletion, insertion or update.

Azure provides the following backup and restores options for IaaS.

- Automated backup
- Manual backup for SQL VM
- Database backup (Backup to URL)

1.1.11 Automated Backup

- It allows you to configure and schedule regular backups for databases hosted on a SQL Server VM.
- It is available for SQL Server standard and enterprise edition.

- It supports SQL Server versions 2014,2016, and 2017.
- It takes encrypted database backup in the Azure storage account.
- The backup retention period is up to 30 days.

Automated Backup V2 for SQL Server 2016 onwards

Starting from SQL Server 2016, you can customize database backups using the Automated Backup V2. The automated backup V2 depends on a SQL Server IaaS agent extension for automation and managing the administrative tasks.

Once you configure a new virtual machine, navigate to SQL Server settings and enable the automated backup.

Note: By default, automated backup V2 is disabled.

On this page, you get the following backup configuration options.

- Retention period: Up to 30 days
- Storage account: Configure the azure storage container in which we want to take database backups.
- Encryption: It enable or disable backup encryption. If you enable backup encryption, Azure stores the certificate in the Azure storage account.
- Password: If we enable backup encryption, we need to specify the password for the encryption key.
- System database backups: In these advanced settings, we can choose to take system database backups (excluding TempDB).
    - System databases should be in full recovery model for a transaction log backup.
    - You cannot take a transaction log backup for the master database.
- Backup schedule: Manual or automated. By default, it uses an automated backup schedule depending upon the log growth.
- Full backup frequency: If you choose manual backup, configure the full backup frequency.
- Full backup start time: It is the start time of full backup depending upon the backup frequency.

- Full backup time window: It is the duration of the time-window during which full backup will occur.
- Log backup frequency: Specify the transaction log backup frequency.

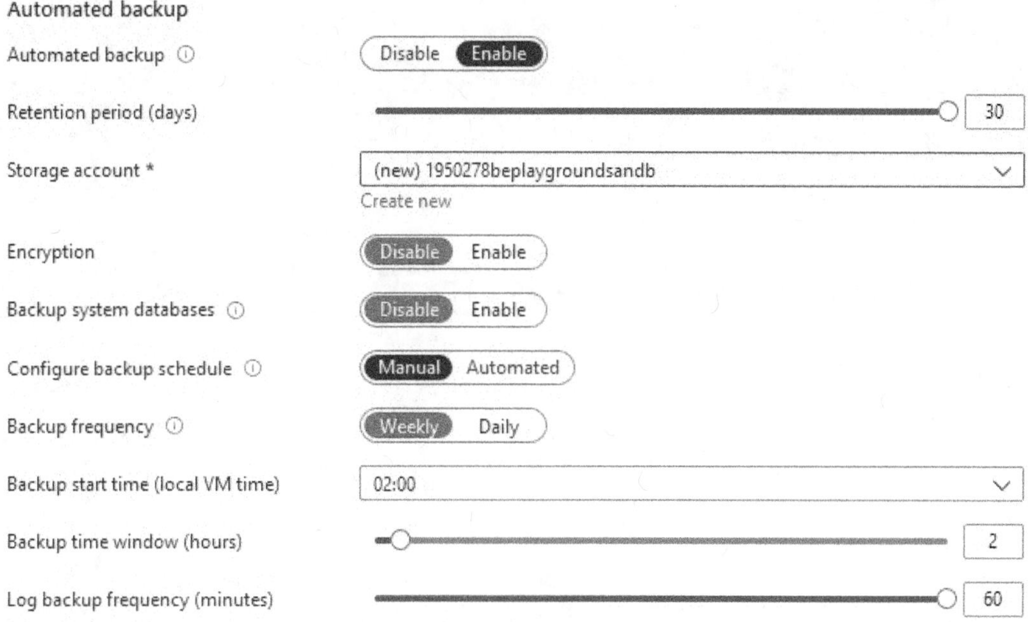

Scenario 1: Weekly full backup

Suppose we configure the Automated backup V2 as per the following configuration.

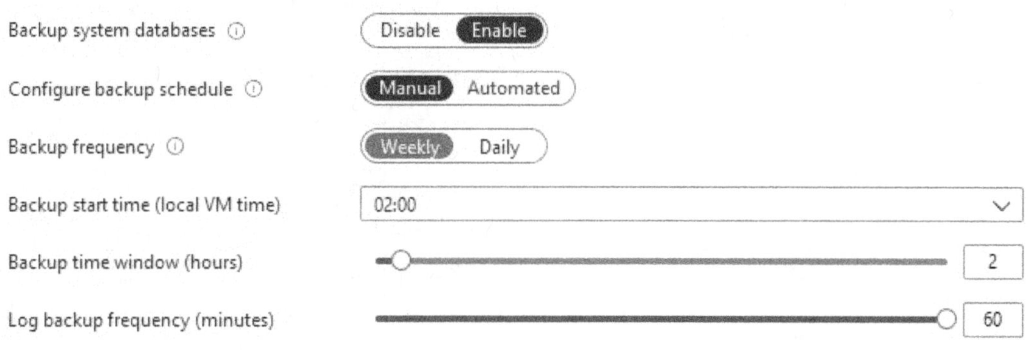

- Backup system databases: Enable
- Backup schedule: Manual

- Full backup frequency: Weekly
- Full backup start time: 02:00
- Full backup time window: 2 hour

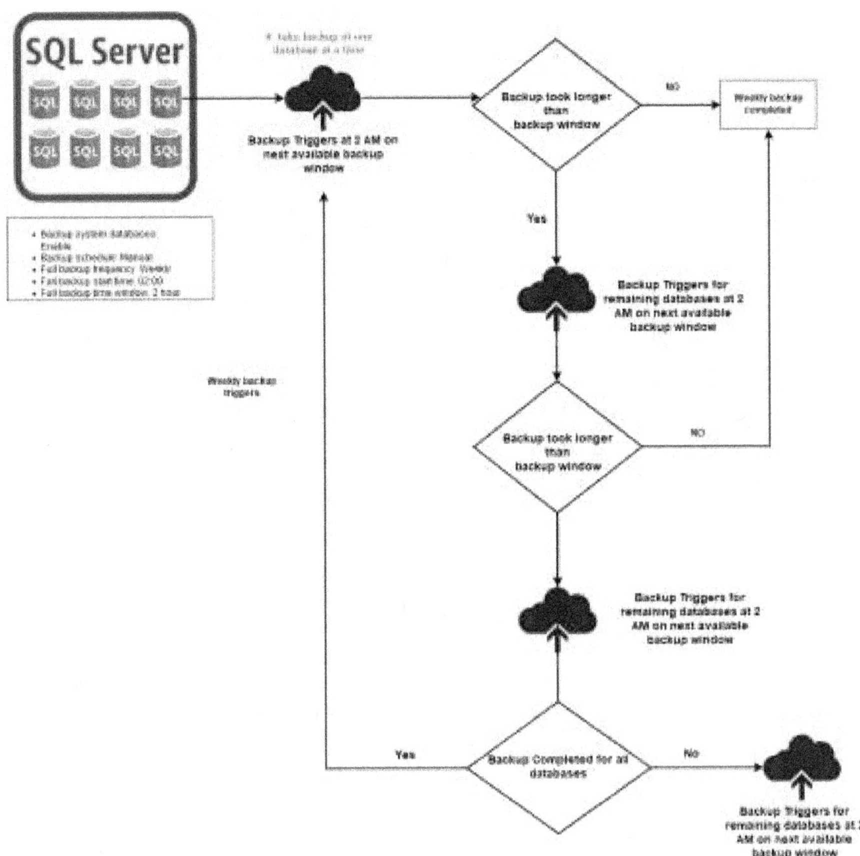

In the above scenario, Automated backup V2 starts at the next available backup window. It takes backup for a single database at a time. If the database's backup completes within the specified full backup window, Azure moves to the next database and takes backup. If the backup window finishes, Automated backup tries backing up the remaining database the next day at the same backup start time. This process continues until all databases have a weekly full backup.

Scenario 2: Daily full backup

In this scenario, suppose we defined a daily backup frequency. The backup starts at 2 AM daily.

Backup system databases	Disable / Enable
Configure backup schedule	Manual / Automated
Backup frequency	Weekly / Daily
Backup start time (local VM time)	02:00
Backup time window (hours)	7
Log backup frequency (minutes)	60

It takes a database backup and moves to the next database within the specific backup window.

Note: You should use a sizable backup time window in case you configure a full daily backup.

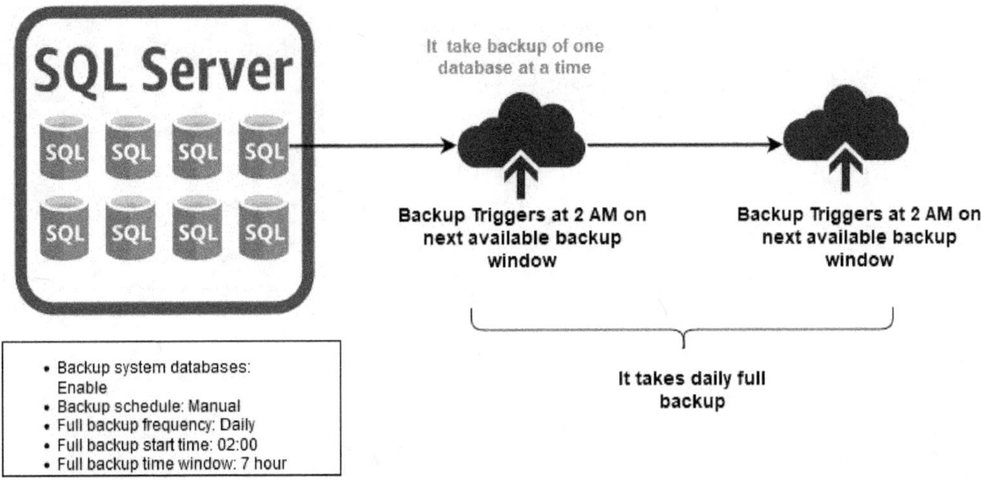

SQL Server
SQL
It take backup of one database at a time
Backup Triggers at 2 AM on next available backup window
Backup Triggers at 2 AM on next available backup window
It takes daily full backup
• Backup system databases: Enable
• Backup schedule: Manual
• Full backup frequency: Daily
• Full backup start time: 02:00
• Full backup time window: 7 hour

Azure Backup for SQL VMs

Azure Backup is an enterprise-level backup capability for SQL Server running on Azure VM. The Recovery service vault manages it.

- Zero infrastructure backup: Users do not manage backup or storage locations.
- Pay-As-You-Go: It provides a Pay-as-you-go billing model.
- Central backup management and monitoring.
- Create policies for backup and retention: We can define custom policies and retention periods for a group of servers.
- It defines 15 minutes RPO using transaction log backups.
- It provides support for SQL Server Always On Availability Groups.
- It enables point in time restore.

- Customize reports and alerts.

The high-level architecture for Azure Backup for SQL Server running in Azure VM is as below.

- It uses the **AzurebackupWindowsWorkload** extension for configuring backup and restore.
- Azure configures the account **NT SERVICE\AzureWLBackupPluginSvc** in SQL Server with sysadmin permissions. It is a virtual service account that does not require any password management.
- Azure uses the **NT AUTHORITY\SYSTEM** account with public access for database discovery.
- It sends data directly to the Azure recovery service vault. Therefore, we don't require any intermediate location.

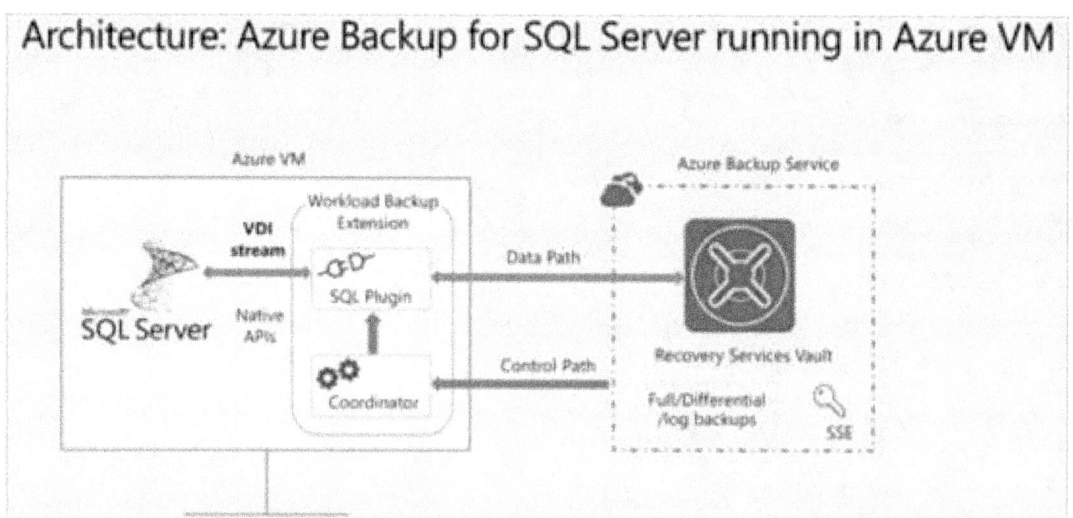

Manual backup – Backup To URL

Starting from SQL Server 2012 SP1 CU2, Azure allows you to take backup and restore these backups directly from the Azure Storage container.

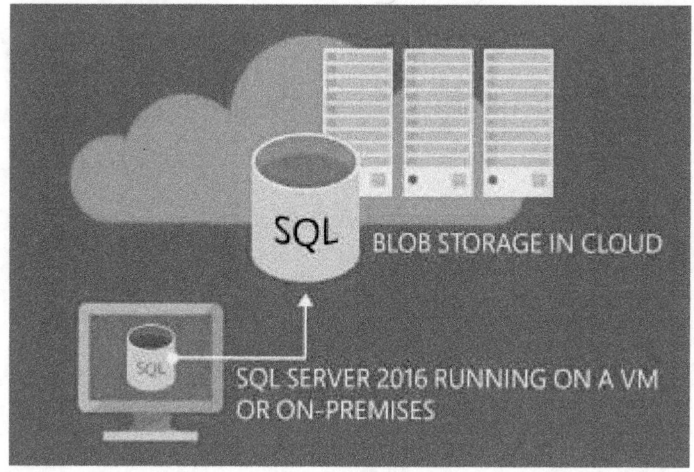

In an on-premise SQL Server, we take backup to the disk or TAPE. Similarly, Azure allows directly taking backup to your Azure Storage container.

Backup to block blob vs page blob

Azure Blob Storage provides block or page blob storage for database backups.

- Block blob storage: it is suitable for backups, streaming contents, documents or binary data.
- Page Blob: It is suitable for random read and writes operation. It is useful for a scenario such as an index and sparse data structure.
- Block blob storage cost is less in comparison to the page blob.

Note: it is recommended to use block blob storage for SQL Server 2016 or later.

We can configure the backups using two ways.

- Storage account access keys
- Shared Access Signature

A shared access signature is a preferred and safe way for authorized blob access compared to the storage access key.

Microsoft Azure Blob Storage service components

To configure a database backup on the Azure blob storage, Azure requires the following components.

- Azure Storage account
- Blob container
- Blob
- Blob URL: Azure allows blob accessibility using the URL format. By default, it uses the following format: https://<storage account>.blob.core.windows.net/<container>/<blob>.

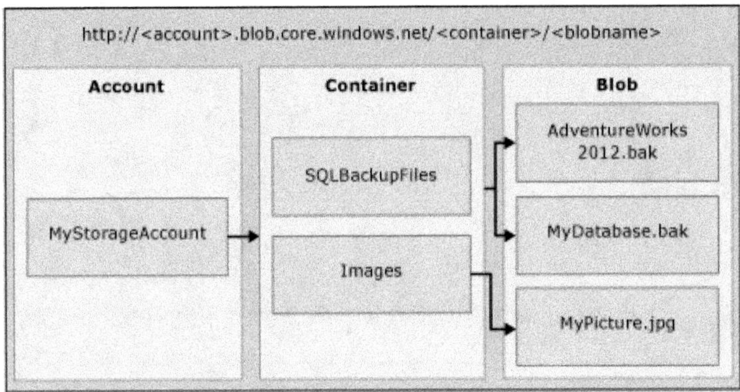

Decision matrix

Microsoft provides the following decision matrix that summarizes each backup's capabilities and restored option for SQL Server virtual machines in Azure.

Option	Automated Backup	Azure Backup for SQL	Manual backup
Requires additional Azure service		✓	
Configure backup policy in Azure portal	✓	✓	
Restore databases in Azure portal		✓	
Manage multiple servers in one dashboard		✓	
Point-in-time restore	✓	✓	✓
15-minute Recovery Point Objective (RPO)	✓	✓	✓
Short-term backup retention policy (days)	✓	✓	
Long-term backup retention policy (months, years)		✓	
Built-in support for SQL Server Always On		✓	
Backup to Azure Storage account(s)	✓ (automatic)	✓ (automatic)	✓ (customer managed)
Management of storage and backup files		✓	
Backup to attached disks on the VM			✓
Central customizable backup reports		✓	
Consolidated email alerts for failures		✓	
Customize monitoring based on Azure Monitor logs		✓	
Monitor backup jobs with SSMS or Transact-SQL scripts	✓	✓	✓
Restore databases with SSMS or Transact-SQL scripts	✓		✓

Backup and restore for an Azure SQL Database

In the PaaS Azure SQL Database, backup and restore requirements are different from the IaaS Azure SQL. It automatically takes database backup as per the following criteria.

- Full database backup – Once a week
- Differential backup: Every 12 hours
- Transaction log backup: Every 5-10 minutes. The frequency depends upon the compute size and database activity.

These database backups are stored in a geo-redundant (RA-GRS) blob, and it is replicated to a paired data center. It safeguards Azure SQL Database backups from a single data centre.

- Azure automatically schedules and takes a full backup once the database is configured.
- Backup retention depends on the service tier.
  - Basic: Max. 7 days retention
  - Standard and Premium Tier: Max. 35 days

These default retention periods might not be suitable enough for a production database. Therefore, we can configure the long-term backup retention policy for a retention period of up to 10 years.

- Azure stores backup copies automatically in different blob storage asynchronously.
- It does not have any impact on the source database.

Understand Long-term retention period policy

Azure SQL Database uses the following parameters for configuring LTR policy.

Frequency	LTR Policy keyword
Weekly	W
Monthly	M
Yearly	Y
Week of the Year	WeekofYear

LTR policy examples:

- W=0, M=0, Y=5, WeekofYear=12: This policy takes the 12th-week full backup and stores it with 5-year retention.
- W=6, M=0, Y=0: This policy stores weekly backup for 6 weeks.
- W=0, M=4, Y=0: This policy stores the first full backup each month for 4 months.
- W=3, M=10, Y=4, WeekofYear=41: It stores each weekly full backup for 3 weeks. The 1st full backup of each month is stored for 10 months. Along with this, the backup on the 52nd week of the year is stored for four years.

In the Azure portal, navigate to the Azure SQL Server dashboard and click on Configure policies and Long-term Retention Configurations.

Configure policies

SQL server

Point In Time Restore Configuration

7 Days

Long-term Retention Configurations

Weekly LTR Backups

How long would you like weekly backups to be kept?

0 Week(s)

Monthly LTR Backups

How long would you like the first backup of each month to be kept?

0 Week(s)

Yearly LTR Backups

Which weekly backup of the year would you like to retain?

Week 1

How long would you like this annual backup to be kept?

0 Week(s)

Apply Cancel

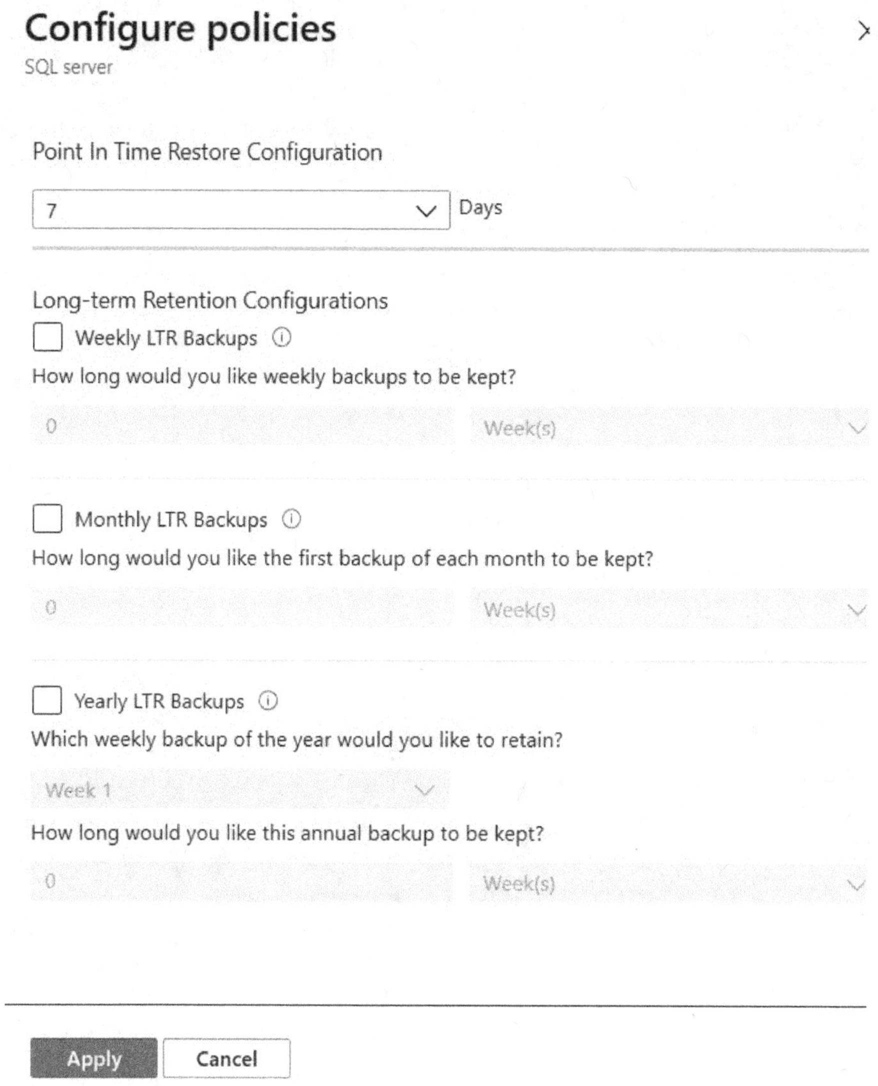

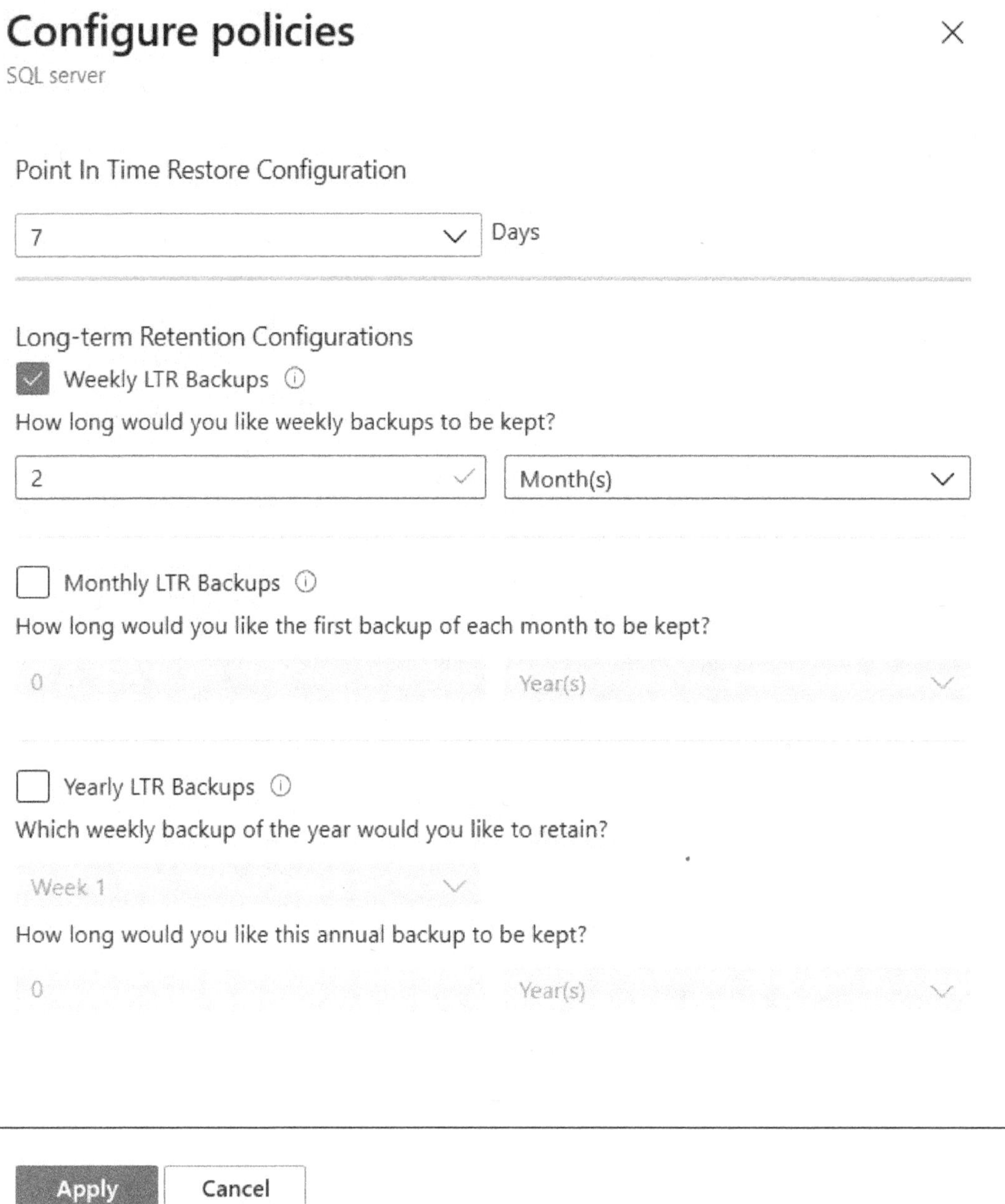

Backup storage redundancy for SQL Database and SQL MI on Azure

As we explained earlier, the Azure Database provides two types of automated backups.

- Short-term backups: The backup retention period is up to 35 days depending on the service tier.

- Long-term backup: You can configure a long-term retention policy for storing backup up to 10 years.

By default, Azure uses geo-redundant blogs that replicate data to another paired region to protect against unplanned events such as hardware failures, network or power outages, and natural disasters. You can configure database backups in the following ways for both the short term.

- Locally-redundant
- Zone-redundant
- Geo-redundant

Locally-redundant storage(LRS)

The locally-redundant storage maintains three copies of data within a single datacenter.

- It provides at least 99.999999999% (11 nines) durability over a given year.
- It is the lowest-cost redundancy option.
- It protects from drives or server rack failures. The data synchronization is synchronous for all data copies. It returns a successful write operation once data is written to all three replicas.

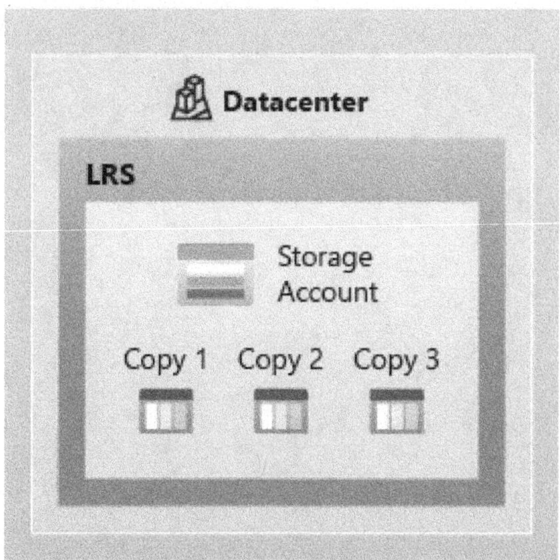

Note:

- It maintains all data copies in a single data center region; therefore, the locally-redundant storage does not protect if any disaster – Fire or flooding occurs in a data center.
- If you require data in the same region due to compliance purposes and require data residency capabilities, you can use the lowest-cost LRS.

Zone-redundant storage (ZRS)

The Zone-redundant storage replicates data across three availability zones in the primary region. These availability groups have independent power, networking configuration.

- The ZES provides the durability of at least 99.9999999999% (12 9's) over a given year.
- Data is accessible for both read and write operations if an availability zone is unavailable.
- The data synchronization is synchronous for all data copies. It returns successful write operation once data is written to all three replicas across three availability zones.
- It is recommended to use ZRS data that requires high availability, durability and consistency.

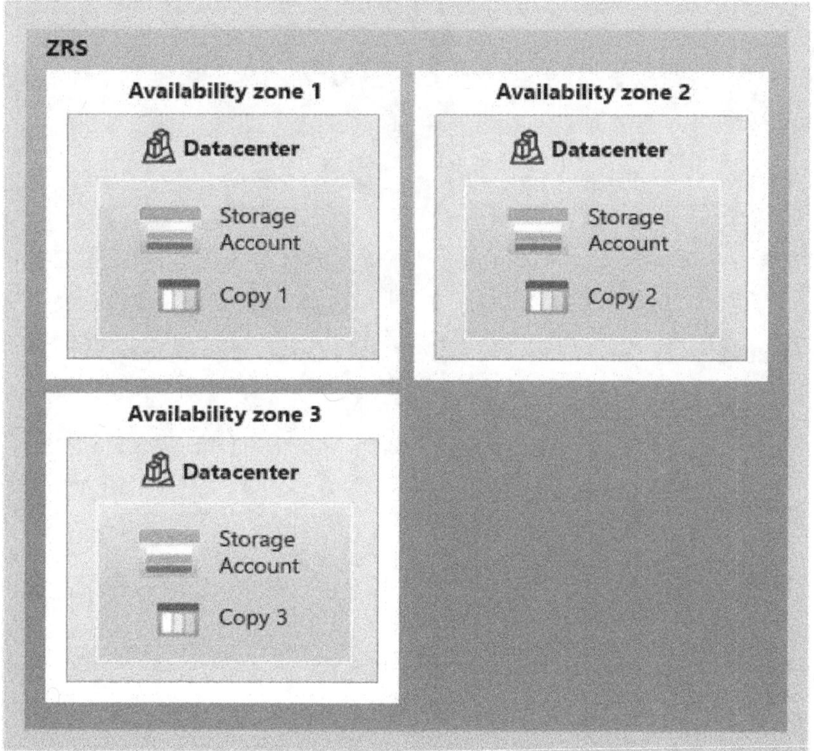

Note:

- ZRS does not protect against disaster at the Azure region level.
- You should refer to **Services support by region before planning ZRS usage. (https://docs.microsoft.com/en-us/azure/availability-zones/az-overview)**

Geo-redundant storage (RA-GRS)

- The Geo-redundant storage replicates data three times within a single physical location in the primary region. The data copy in a primary region is synchronous.
- It replicates data to the secondary region asynchronously. The secondary region is located hundreds of miles away from the primary region.
- It provides 99.99999999999999% (16 9's) durability over a given year.

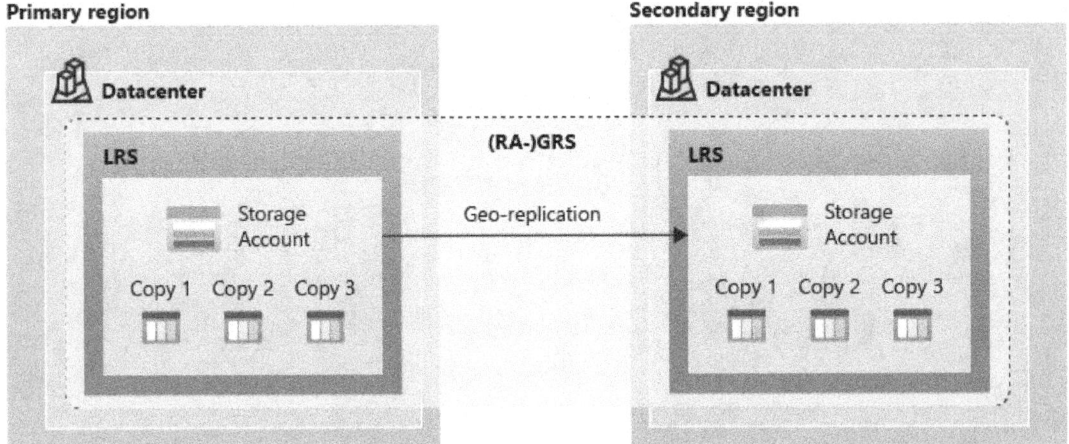

- It is recommended for a disaster recovery option for the production workloads due to its durability.

Geo-zone-redundant storage(GZRS)

The Geo-zone-redundant storage Is a combination of the ZRS and GRS.

- It replicates data to three availability zones in the primary region.
- It also replicates data to the secondary region.
- It offers the durability of at least 99.99999999999999% (16 9's) for a given year.

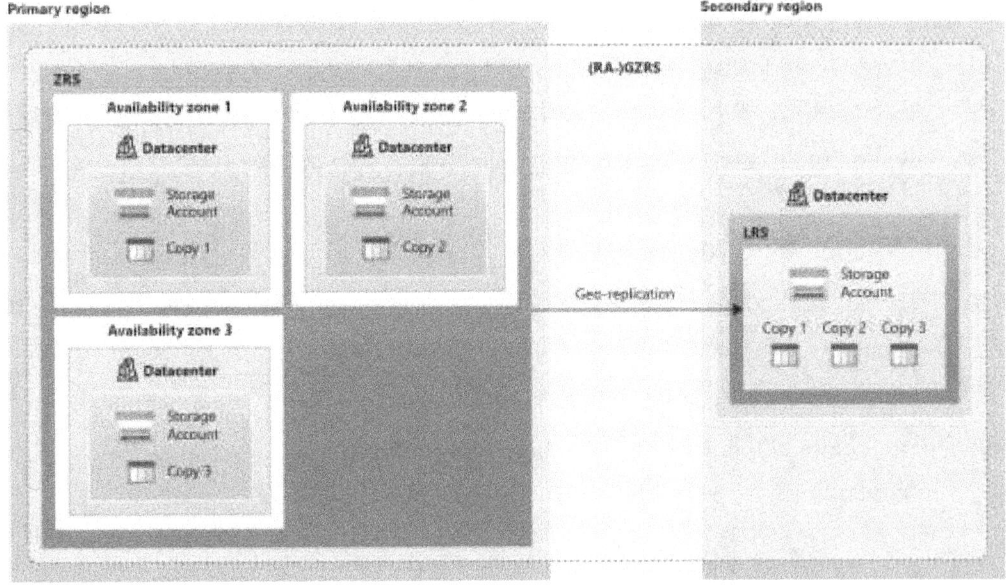

Note:

- It is supported only for general-purpose V2 storage accounts.
- It is supported in specific regions.
    - Europe North
    - Europe West
    - Asia Southeast
    - US East 2
    - US West 2
    - Japan East
    - UK South
    - US Central
    - US East

Data redundancy options comparisons

Microsoft documents provide a high-level summary for different redundancy options of Azure storage.

Durability and availability parameters

Durability and availability parameters

The following table describes key parameters for each redundancy option:

Durability and availability parameters

Parameter	LRS	ZRS	GRS/RA-GRS	GZRS/RA-GZRS
Percent durability of objects over a given year	at least 99.999999999% (11 9's)	at least 99.9999999999% (12 9's)	at least 99.99999999999999% (16 9's)	at least 99.99999999999999% (16 9's)
Availability for read requests	At least 99.9% (99% for cool access tier)	At least 99.9% (99% for cool access tier)	At least 99.9% (99% for cool access tier) for GRS At least 99.99% (99.9% for cool access tier) for RA-GRS	At least 99.9% (99% for cool access tier) for GZRS At least 99.99% (99.9% for cool access tier) for RA-GZRS
Availability for write requests	At least 99.9% (99% for cool access tier)	At least 99.9% (99% for cool access tier)	At least 99.9% (99% for cool access tier)	At least 99.9% (99% for cool access tier)
Number of copies of data maintained on separate nodes	Three copies within a single region	Three copies across separate availability zones within a single region	Six copies total, including three in the primary region and three in the secondary region	Six copies total, including three across separate availability zones in the primary region and three locally redundant copies in the secondary region

Durability and availability by outage scenario

Outage scenario	LRS	ZRS	GRS/RA-GRS	GZRS/RA-GZRS
A node within a data center becomes unavailable	Yes	Yes	Yes	Yes
An entire data center (zonal or non-zonal) becomes unavailable	No	Yes	Yes[1]	Yes
A region-wide outage occurs in the primary region	No	No	Yes[1]	Yes[1]
Read access to the secondary region is available if the primary region becomes unavailable	No	No	Yes (with RA-GRS)	Yes (with RA-GZRS)

Configure backup storage redundancy

By default, it uses geo-redundant backups storage for both Azure SQL Database, and Azure SQL Managed Instances.

Note:

- Azure allows configuring backup storage redundancy during Managed instance creation. You cannot change it later.
- The Zone-redundant storage option is available in specific regions.
- The backup storage redundancy for Azure SQL Database is in public preview. This preview is available in the Brazil South. It is in the generally availability phase for Southeast Asia Azure region.
- The hyperscale tier for Azure SQL Database does not support configuring the backup storage redundancy.
- Azure backup redundancy is applicable only for backups taken after configuring the redundancy.
- It takes up to 48 hours for any changes to be applicable.

You can choose the backup storage redundancy option in the supported regions in the Azure SQL database, as shown below.

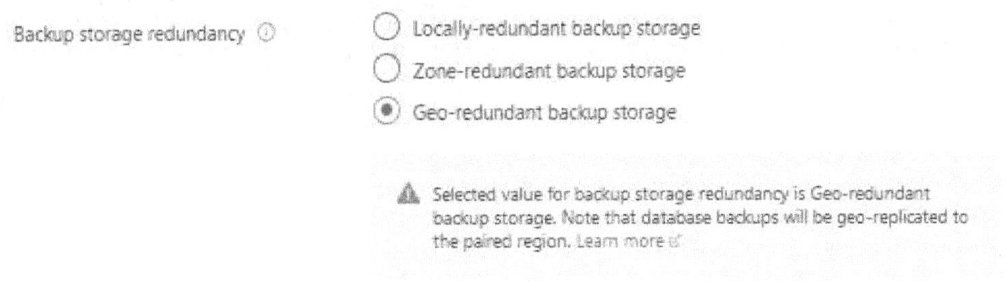

Backup storage redundancy

Locally-redundant backup storage
Zone-redundant backup storage
Geo-redundant backup storage

Selected value for backup storage redundancy is Geo-redundant backup storage. Note that database backups will be geo-replicated to the paired region. Learn more

Lab 12: Configure an Azure SQL Database Geo-Replication using Azure portal

In the Azure Services, click on SQL Databases and launch the dashboard.

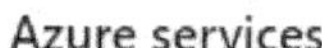

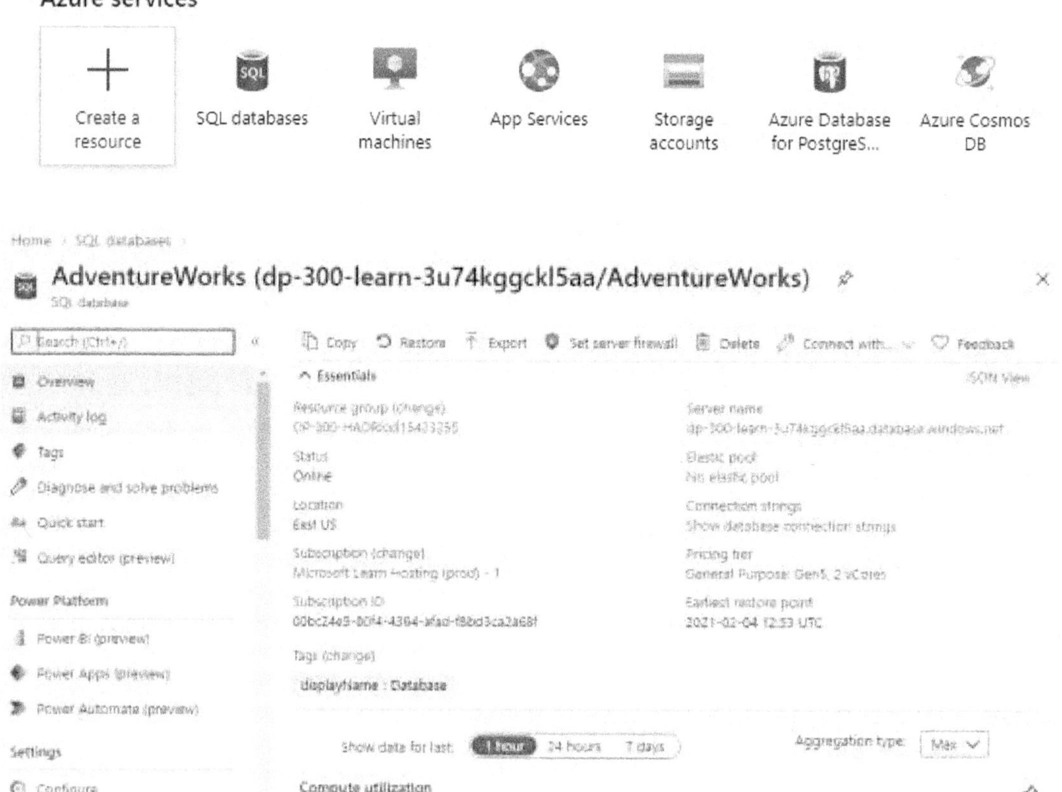

In the left-hand side menu, click on Geo-Replication. The geo-replication page lists the primary region(blue hexagon) where your Azure SQL Database is configured.

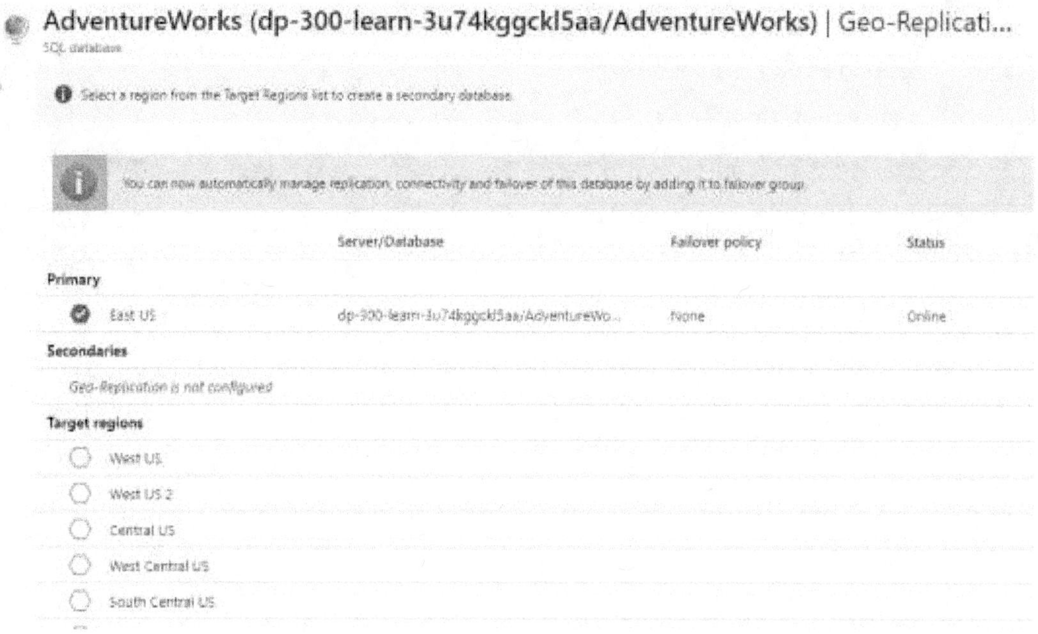

In the target regions, select a region for your secondary SQL Server. Here, I click on West US 2. it opens to create the secondary blade.

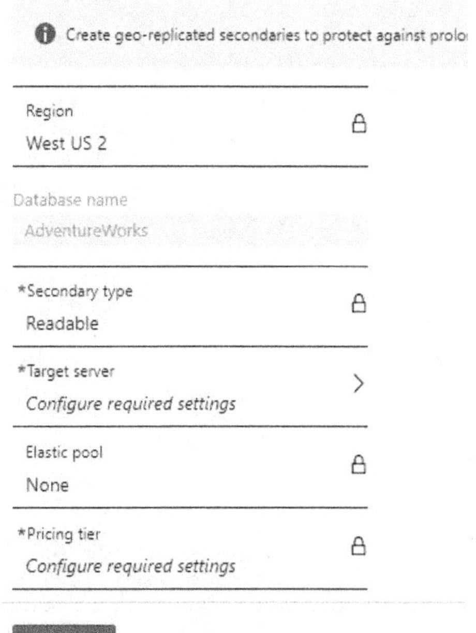

On this page, click on the target server and enter the following details.

- Secondary SQL Server name
- Server admin login
- password

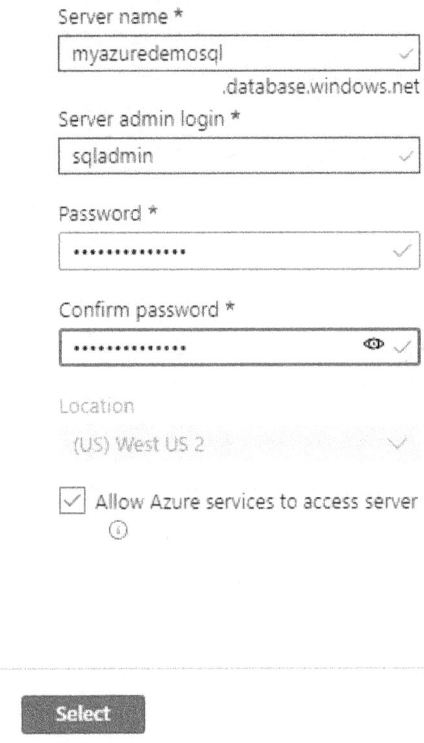

Click on Select, and it takes you on the create the secondary page.

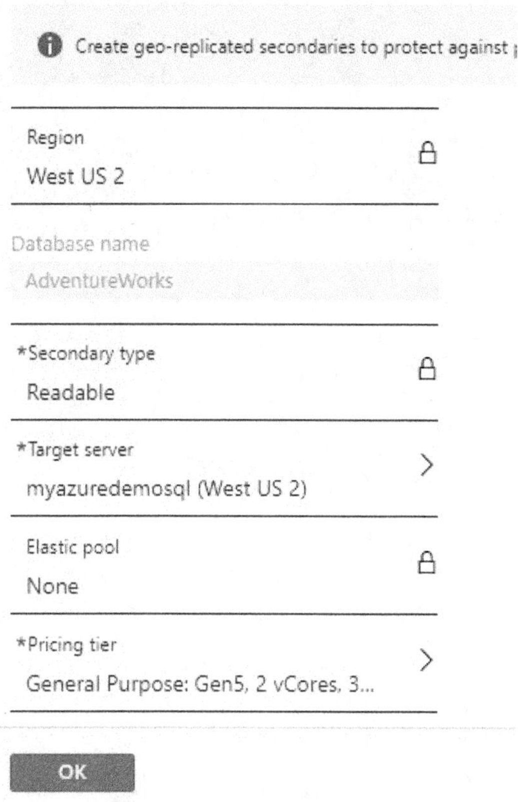

Verify your configuration and click on Ok to start the deployment. It starts creating a secondary SQL Server and database. You can view the status in the notification bar.

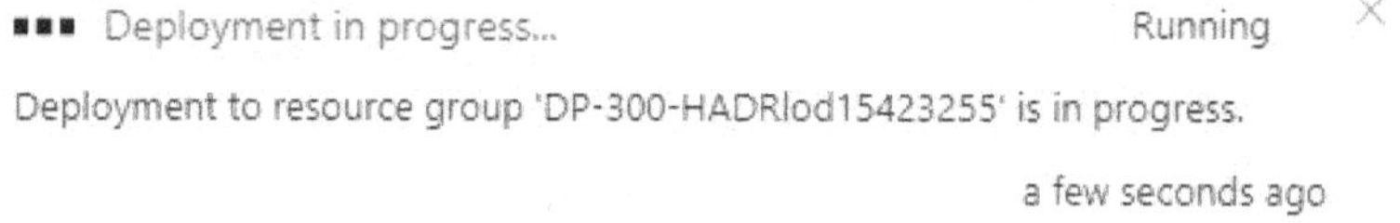

During the deployment, it starts the initial seeding. As stated earlier, it might take time depending upon your database size and network bandwidth.

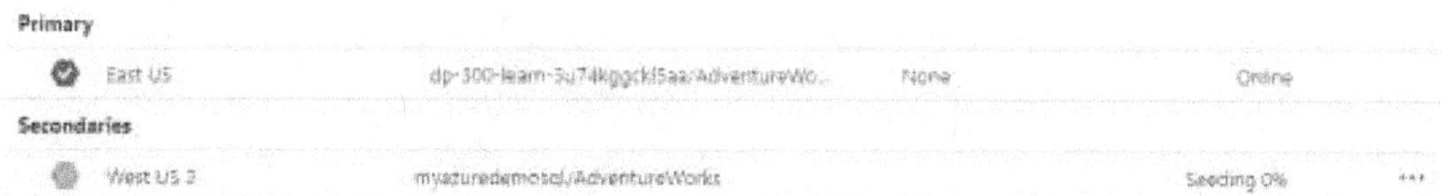

It synchronizes the database after the initial seeding, and its status changes to Readable.

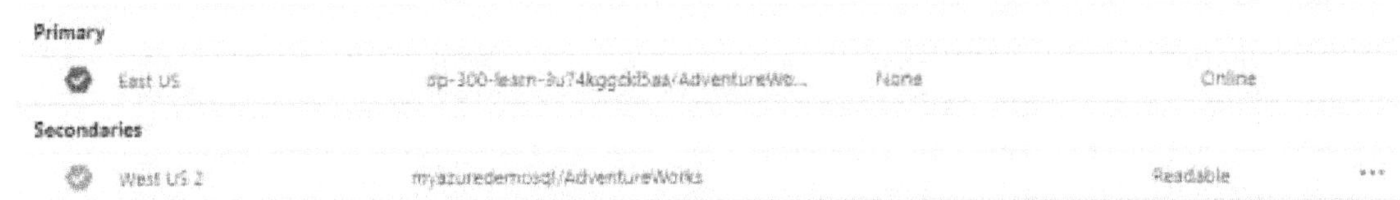

You can refresh the Azure console for SQL Databases, and it displays both the primary and secondary role of databases.

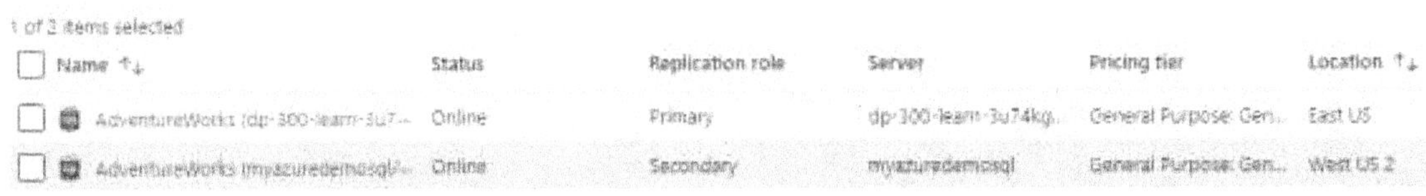

Name
Status
Replication role
Server
Pricing tier
Location
Online
Primary
East US
Online
Secondary
myazuredemosql
West US 2

1.1.12 Initiate a forced failover in Geo-replication

To initiate a forced failover, click on the secondary server, and it gives options.

- Forced failover
- Stop Replication.

Home > AdventureWorks (dp-300-learn-3u74kggckl5aa/AdventureWorks) >

West US 2

Secondary database

Forced Failover Stop Replication

Region

West US 2

Database name

AdventureWorks

Click on Forced failover, and it gives a warning before initiating a failover. It lists out the current primary and new primary database as well.

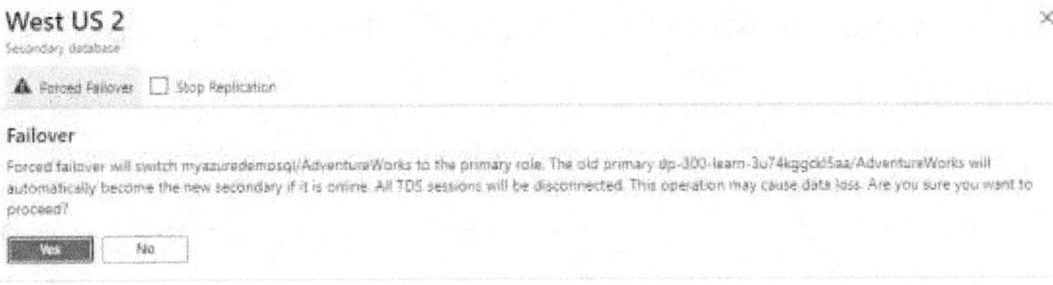

Click on Yes. In the notification panel, it displays a request submitted message for failover to the secondary server,

Request submitted for failover replication 7:12 AM

Request submitted for failover replication to secondary server: myazuredemosql, secondary database: AdventureWorks

During the failover, the primary status changes to **Pending** and secondary status as **Failover**.

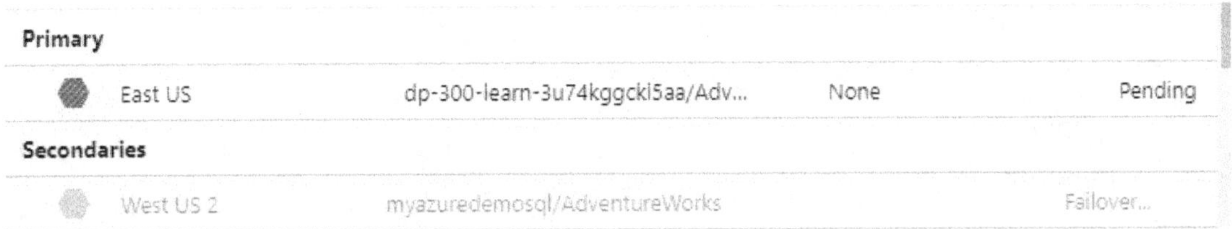

Primary			
East US	dp-300-learn-3u74kggckl5aa/Adv...	None	Pending
Secondaries			
West US 2	myazuredemosql/AdventureWorks		Failover...

It will take a few minutes for failover to the secondary replica. Once the process completes, you can verify the role switch.

	Server/Database	Failover policy	Status
Primary			
West US 2	myazuredemosql/AdventureWorks	None	Online
Secondaries			
East US	dp-300-learn-3u74kggckl5aa/AdventureWorks		Readable

Lab 13: Configure an Azure SQL Database auto-failover groups using Azure portal

In this activity, we configure auto-failover groups for the Azure SQL database. Suppose we have an Azure database [labazuresqldemo] in the East US region. We require an auto-failover group configuration so that the database can failover automatically in any disaster in the East US region.

Step1: In the Azure portal (https://portal.azure.com) and open the [myazuresqldemo1 Azure SQL Server overview page.

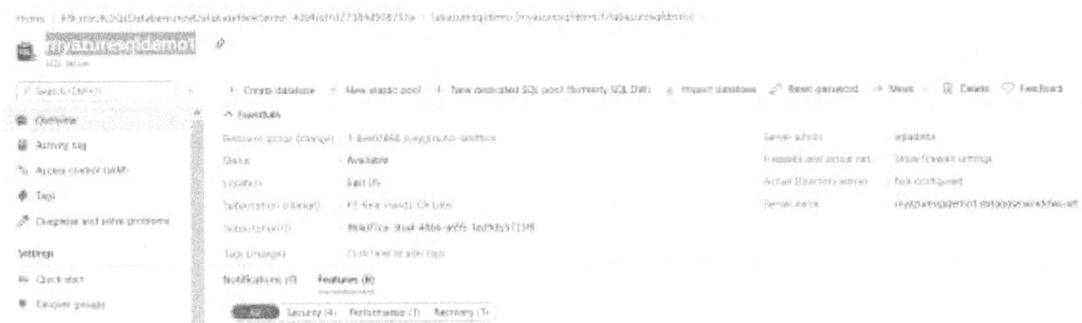

Click on the failover groups in the settings section. As we can see, there are no failover groups defined for this Azure server.

Step 2: Click on Add group and give the following inputs.

- Failover group name: Enter a name for the failover group.
- Secondary server: It is the Azure SQL Server name in the secondary region. It hosts the secondary databases.
- Read/write failover policy: Azure has an automatic failover policy. You can change it manually if required.
- Read/write grade period in hours: By default, the grace period is 1 hour. Leave it as it is.

- The database within the group: Select the Azure databases to add to the failover group.

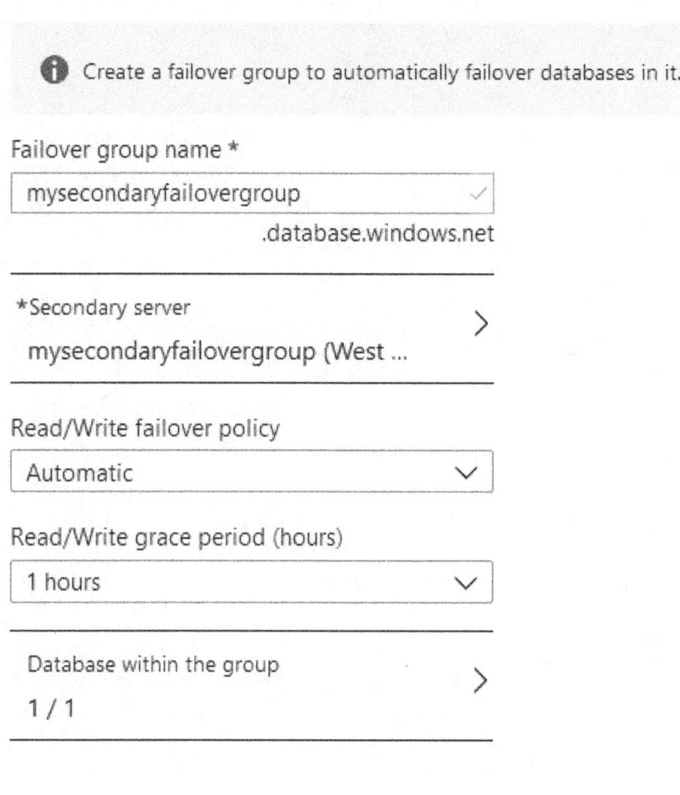

Click on Create, and it starts provisioning the secondary server with a failover group. It shows the failover group details along with primary, secondary servers.

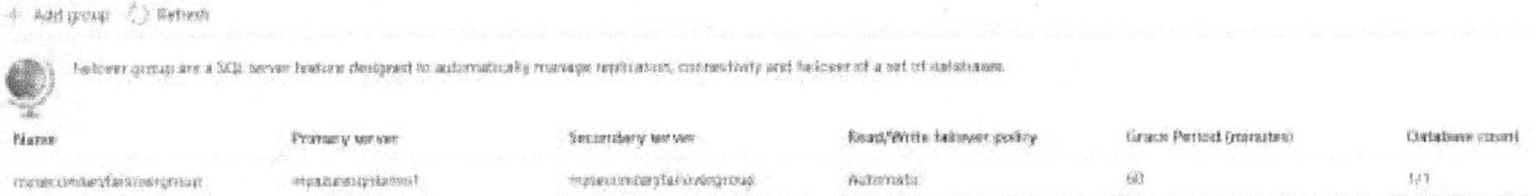

Click on the failover group. It gives a map view of your failover group configuration.

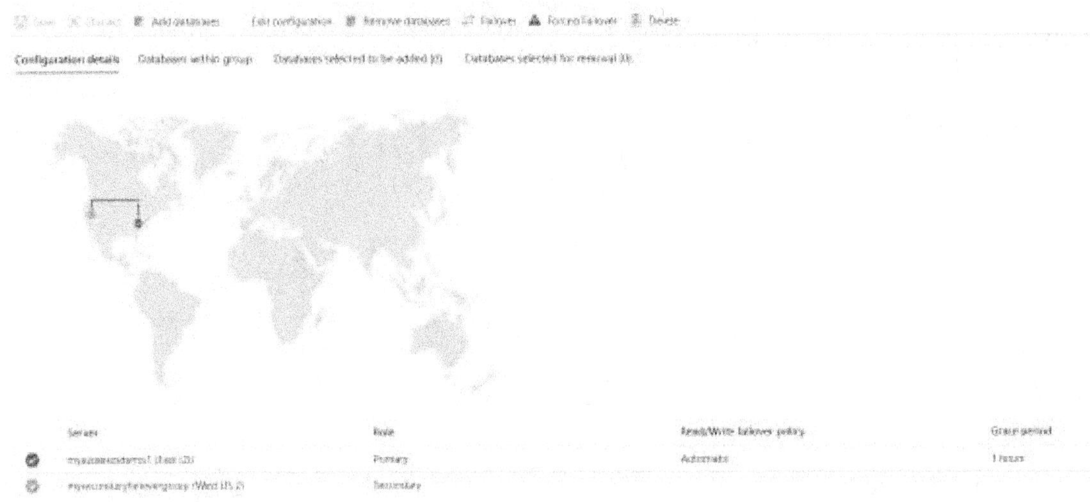

Scroll down to view the Read-write and Read-only listener endpoints.

Read/write listener endpoint

mysecondaryfailovergroup1.database.windows.net

Read-only listener endpoint

mysecondaryfailovergroup1.secondary.database.windows.net

In the map view, click on Databases within the group.

- Primary server East US: Online status
- Secondary server West US 2: Readable

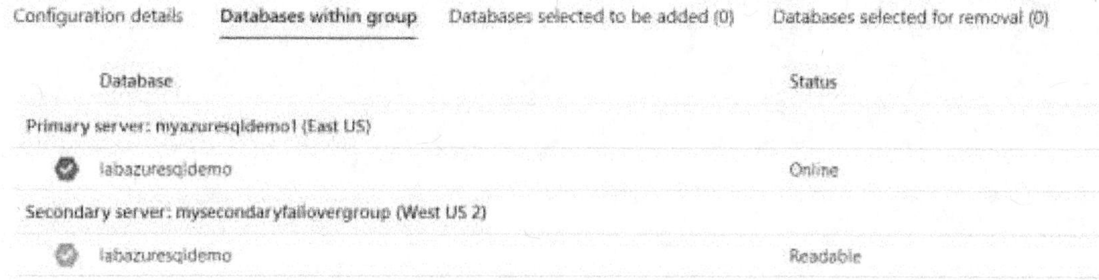

Initiate a manual failover for auto-failover groups

In this section, we initiate a manual failover for the configured failover group.

Click on Failover and get a warning message – This will switch all secondary databases *to the primary role. All TDS sessions will be disconnected. All new TDS sessions will be automatically re-routed to the secondary server, becoming the primary server.*

Click on Yes.

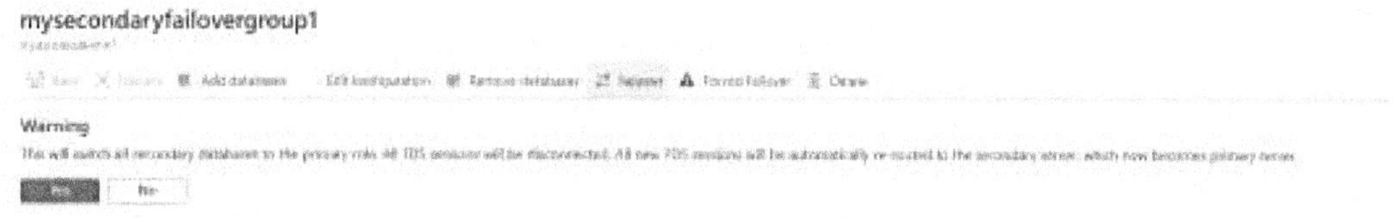

It begins the failover group failover.

Failover group failover in progress 8:54 AM

Failover group failover in progress for failover group: mysecondaryfailovergroup1, old secondary server: mysecondaryfailovergroup

During the failover process, you get a dotted line between the primary and secondary region.

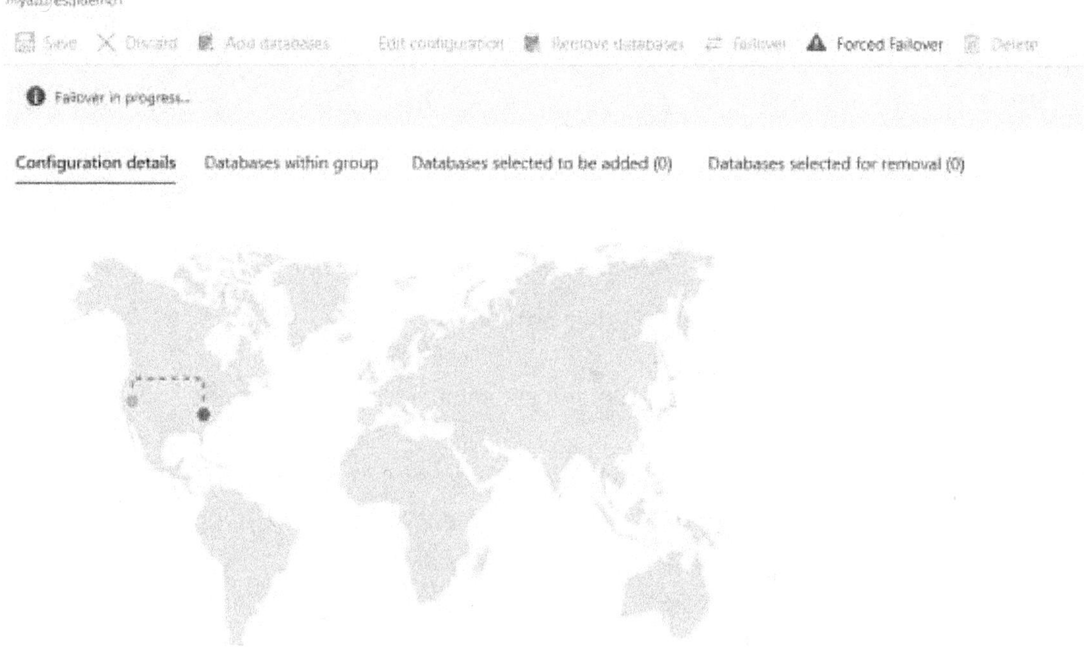

Once failover is successful, you get a notification as well.

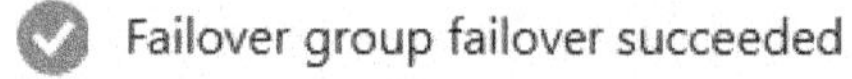

Failover group failover succeeded for failover group: mysecondaryfailovergroup1, old secondary server: mysecondaryfailovergroup

a few seconds ago

We can verify the primary and secondary region after failover.

Before failover:

- Primary region: East US
- Secondary region: West US 2

After Failover

- Primary Region: West US 2
- Secondary Region: East US

Lab 14: Configure an Azure SQL Database geo-replication using Azure CLI

In this lab, we use Azure CLI for implementing the following tasks.

- Create a primary resource group in the West US 2 region.
- Create a secondary resource group in the East US region.
- Deploy an Azure SQL Server and SQL database in the primary region with the basic service tier.
- It establishes Active Geo-replication from primary to the secondary database.

Copy the script from **https://github.com/AzureDP300/AzureDP300/blob/main/Chapter10/Script1.ps1**

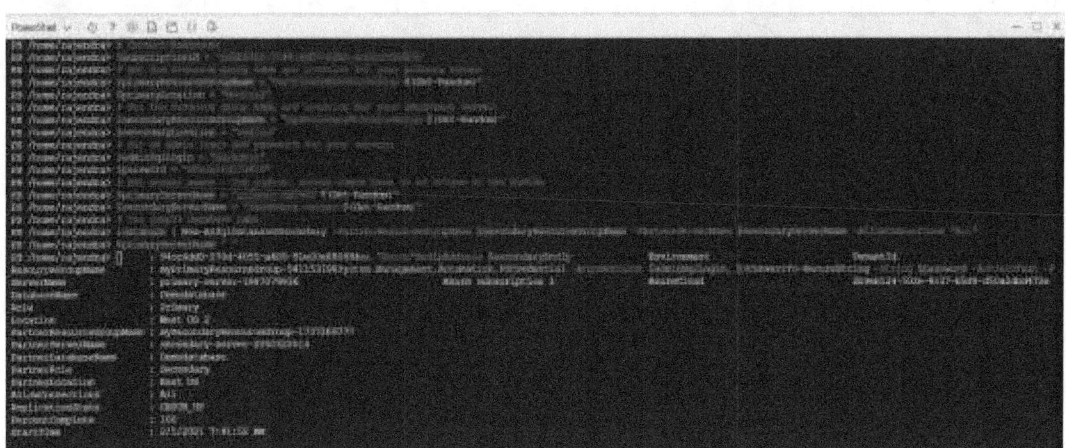

In the Azure portal, open the primary resource group and Azure database. In the geo-replication, you can verify the primary and secondary replica.

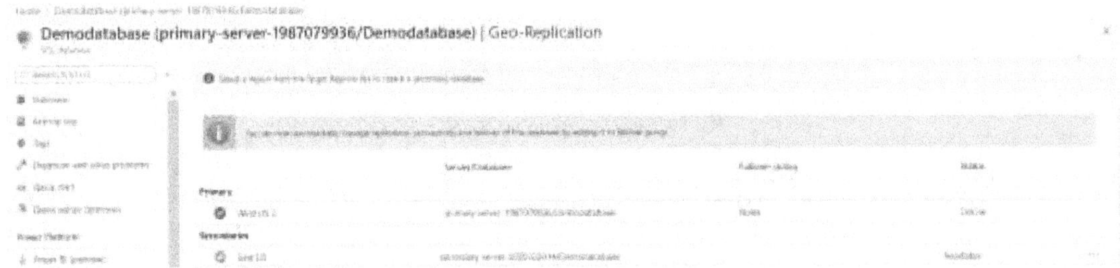

The below script initiates a manual failover and monitors the geo-replication configuration after the failover.

Copy the script from
https://github.com/AzureDP300/AzureDP300/blob/main/Chapter10/Script2.ps1

Once the above script executes, you can verify new primary and secondary resources.

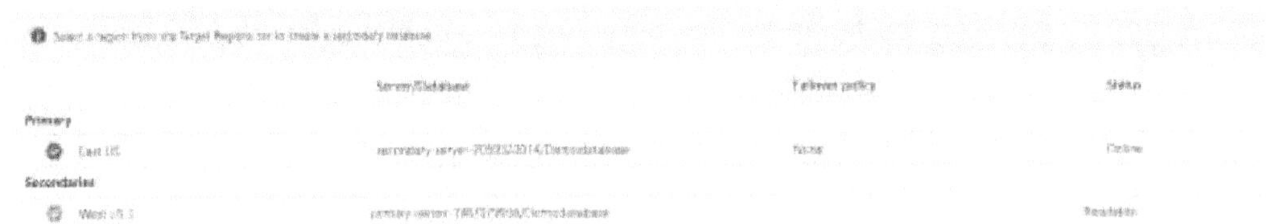

The following script removes the geo-replication link post failover and cleans up both primary and secondary resources.

Note: Execute the cleanup deployment only if you want to drop primary and secondary resource groups and Azure SQL Server database inside it.

Copy the script from
https://github.com/AzureDP300/AzureDP300/blob/main/Chapter10/Script3.ps1

Lab 15: Configure auto-failover group using Azure CLI

In this lab, we use Azure CLI to implement an auto-failover group, initiate failover, and verify using the Azure CLI.

- Creates a primary and secondary SQL Server in East US and West US, respectively.
- Configure auto-failover group from primary to secondary.

Copy the script from
https://github.com/AzureDP300/AzureDP300/blob/main/Chapter10/Script4.ps1

You can verify the failover group in the Azure portal.

- Primary Location: East US
- Secondary location: West US

The below script initiates a failover and confirms the role of the secondary (new primary).

Copy the script from **https://github.com/AzureDP300/AzureDP300/blob/main/Chapter10/Script5.ps1**

```
PS /home/rajendra>
PS /home/rajendra> echo "Confirming role of $failoverServer is now primary..." # note ReplicationRole property
Confirming role of sqlsecondary-664789961 is now primary...
PS /home/rajendra> az sql failover-group show --name $failover --resource-group $resource --server $server
```

Refresh the Azure portal and verify that failover is successful.

- Primary Location: West US
- Secondary location: East US

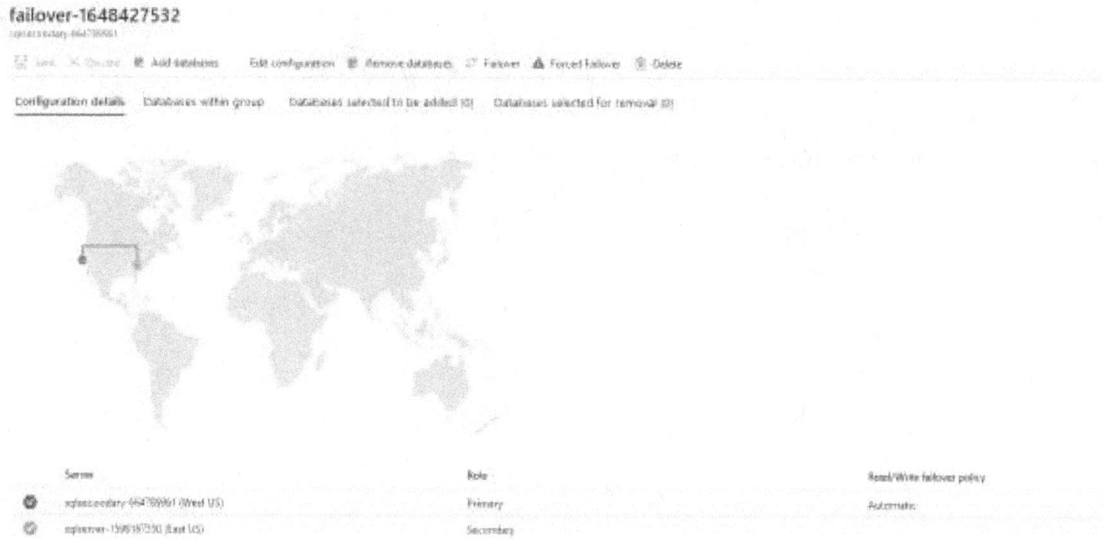

Once you have deployed the failover group and validated, you can clean up resources to save recurring costs.

Note: You should only remove resources if those are not in use.

az group delete --name $resource

Azure requires confirmation before proceeding with resource deletion.

```
PS /home/rajendra> az group delete --name $resource
Are you sure you want to perform this operation? (y/n): y
PS /home/rajendra>
```

Lab 15: Backup database to URL

In this lab, we require a storage account and container. For this demo, I have created a [azuresqlbackup] container in the [azurebackupstoragedemo] storage account.

We can use the storage account access key and shared access signature for backup to URL, as discussed earlier.

Backup to URL using Storage account access key

In the storage account settings, click on access keys. On the access key page, note down the access key.

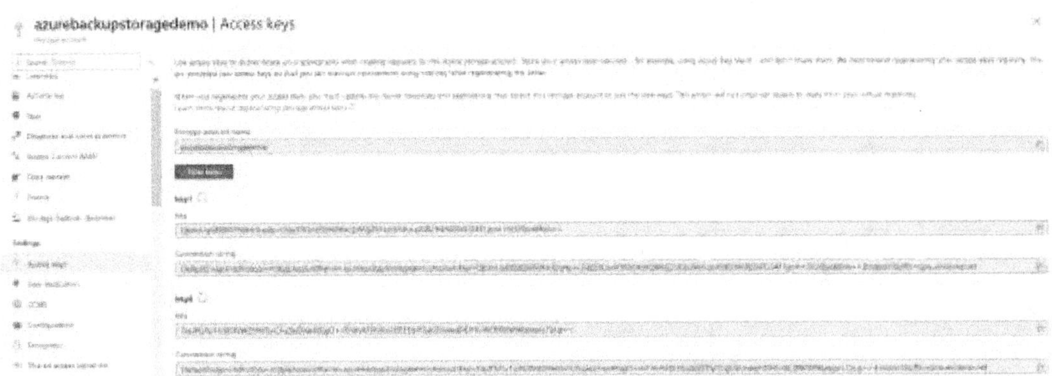

Now, connect to the SQL Instance in SSMS and create a credential. This query uses the following arguments.

- Credential name: Specify a credential name. Here, we specify DBbackupToURL.
- WITH IDENTITY: In this argument, specify the storage account name.
- SECRET: Enter the access key you obtained from the access key page.

CREATE CREDENTIAL DBbackupToURL WITH IDENTITY = 'azurebackupstoragedemo'

,SECRET = 'QbJmUq6B5BSIFRdNxTpq4p+GlibZDUoHD0fx0KmQWVjjZ0Fzo3IMLos/iD82HkNBJMCG4F1pxm +5tCl5po6BxA=='

To take a database backup, we specify the blob URL along with the credential name.

The below query uses the following arguments.

- blob URL: https://azurebackupstoragedemo.blob.core.windows.net/azuresqlbackup/AdventureWorks2017.bak
- Credentials: Credential name DBbackupToURL

BACKUP DATABASE [AdventureWorks2017] TO

URL = 'https://azurebackupstoragedemo.blob.core.windows.net/azuresqlbackup/AdventureWorks2017.bak'

WITH credential='DBbackupToURL', FORMAT,

NAME = N'AdventureWorks2017-Full Database Backup',

NOREWIND, NOUNLOAD, COMPRESSION, STATS = 10

GO

Execute the script, and it stores the full backup in the blob storage container.

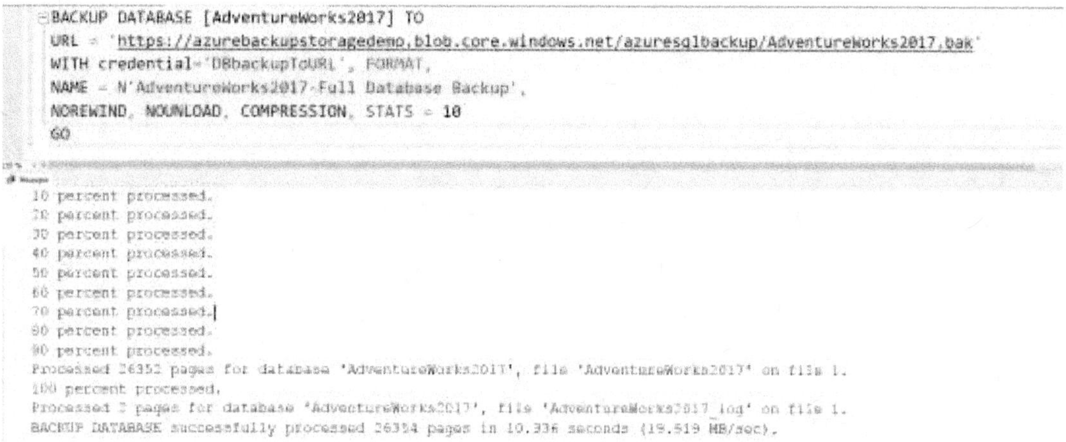

```
BACKUP DATABASE [AdventureWorks2017] TO
URL = 'https://azurebackupstoragedemo.blob.core.windows.net/azuresqlbackup/AdventureWorks2017.bak'
WITH credential='DBbackupToURL', FORMAT,
NAME = N'AdventureWorks2017-Full Database Backup',
NOREWIND, NOUNLOAD, COMPRESSION, STATS = 10
GO
```

```
10 percent processed.
20 percent processed.
30 percent processed.
40 percent processed.
50 percent processed.
60 percent processed.
70 percent processed.
80 percent processed.
90 percent processed.
Processed 26352 pages for database 'AdventureWorks2017', file 'AdventureWorks2017' on file 1.
100 percent processed.
Processed 2 pages for database 'AdventureWorks2017', file 'AdventureWorks2017_log' on file 1.
BACKUP DATABASE successfully processed 26354 pages in 10.336 seconds (19.919 MB/sec).
```

Backup to URL using shared access signature

The shared access signature provides secure and delegated access for Azure Storage account resources. Navigate to Shared Access Signature in the Storage account.

On this page, give the following inputs.

- Allowed resource type: Container and object
- Allowed permissions
- Start and expiry date: Select a start and expiry date for the Shared access signature key.

Note: Be careful in configuring the expiry date, the backup does not work if the shared access signature is expired.

- Allowed IP address: You can specify an IP address range for access.
- Allowed protocols: HTTPS only
- Preferred routing: Basic

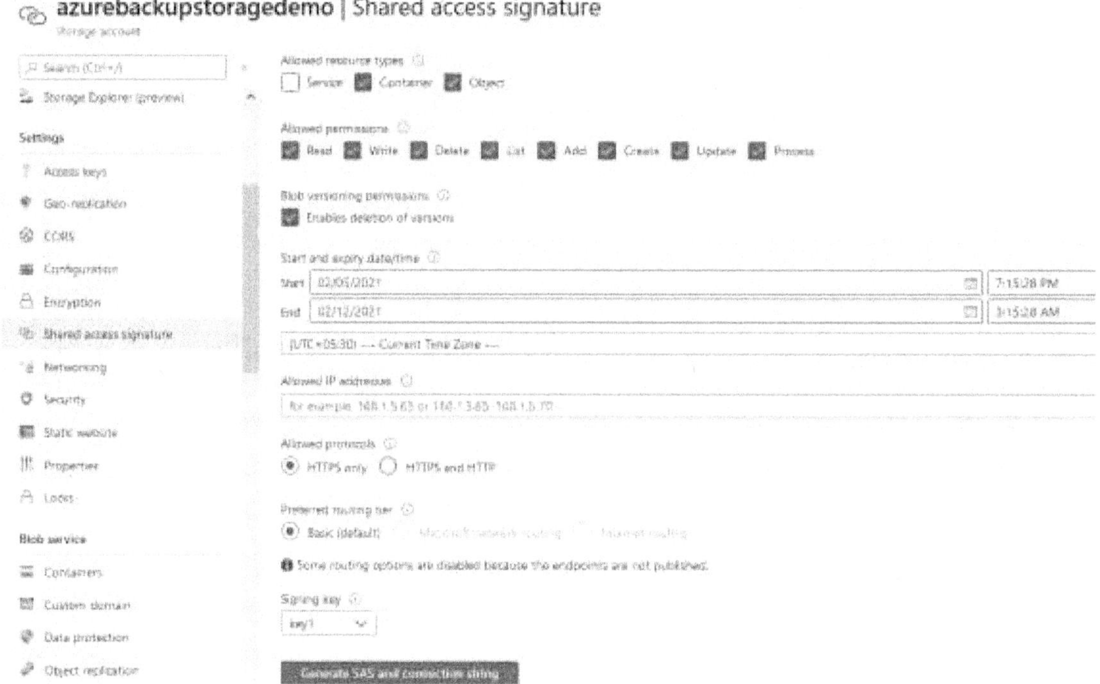

Click on Generate SAS and connection string. It generates the connecting string, blob service URL. Note-down the SAS token from this page.

Connect to the SQL Server and create a credential with the following information.

- Credential Name: Enter the blob container URL in brackets.
- IDENTITY: Shared Access Signature
- SECRET: Enter the SAS token that we obtained from the Shared Access Signature.

This token contains a leading question mark (?), remove it before creating the credential.

CREATE CREDENTIAL

[https://azurebackupstoragedemo.blob.core.windows.net/azuresqlbackup]

WITH IDENTITY='Shared Access Signature'

,SECRET = 'sv=2019-12-12&ss=bfqt&srt=co&sp=rwdlacupx&se=2021-02-09T20:17:32Z&st=2021-02-05T12:17:32Z&spr=https&sig=CtKNrime11gemjObuNmQ8Q6F2GfUx%2BG%2BnoLZ7jVi2K0%3D'

To take database backup using a shared access signature, we do not need to specify the credential name. Specify the blob container URL and execute the script.

BACKUP DATABASE [AdventureWorks2017] TO

URL = 'https://azurebackupstoragedemo.blob.core.windows.net/azuresqlbackup/AdventureWorks2017.bak'

It takes database backup, as shown below.

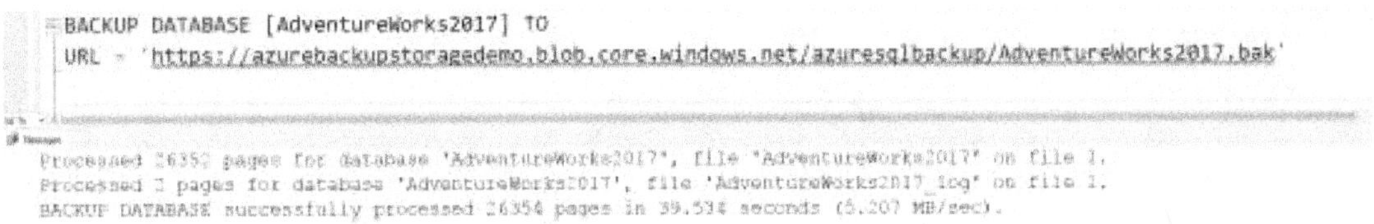

```
BACKUP DATABASE [AdventureWorks2017] TO
URL = 'https://azurebackupstoragedemo.blob.core.windows.net/azuresqlbackup/AdventureWorks2017.bak'
```

```
Processed 26352 pages for database 'AdventureWorks2017', file 'AdventureWorks2017' on file 1.
Processed 2 pages for database 'AdventureWorks2017', file 'AdventureWorks2017_log' on file 1.
BACKUP DATABASE successfully processed 26354 pages in 39.534 seconds (5.207 MB/sec).
```

You can connect to the Azure storage account and navigate to the blob container. It has the database backup file.

Lab 16: Configure automatic backup V2 for existing VM

In this lab, we will configure automatic backup V2 for existing SQL VM using the Azure CLI.

Step1: Verify the SQL Server IaaS extension.

Azure automatically installs an IaaS extension for taking automatic backup V2 for a SQL Server VM. Launch Azure CLI and enter the following command with VM and Azure resource group name.

$vmname = "myazuresqlvm"

$resourcegroupname = "azuresql"

(Get-AzVM -Name $vmname -ResourceGroupName $resourcegroupname).Extensions

This command returns the **SqlIaaSAgent** extension version and provision state as Succeeded.

```
VERBOSE: Authenticating to Azure ...
VERBOSE: Building your Azure drive ...
PS /home/rajendra>
PS /home/rajendra>
PS /home/rajendra>
PS /home/rajendra> (Get-AzVM .Extensions

ForceUpdateTag                  :
Publisher                       : Microsoft.SqlServer.Management
VirtualMachineExtensionType     : SqlIaaSAgent
TypeHandlerVersion              : 2.0
AutoUpgradeMinorVersion         : True
EnableAutomaticUpgrade          :
Settings                        : {AutoPatchingSettings, KeyVaultCredentialSettings, ServerConfigurationManagementSettings, SqlManagement…}
ProtectedSettings               :
ProvisioningState               : Succeeded
InstanceView                    :
Id                              : /subscriptions/
Name                            : SqlIaasExtension
Type                            : Microsoft.Compute/virtualMachines/extensions
Location                        : centralindia
Tags                            :
```

Step 2: Fetch current automated backup configuration.

This command fetches the current automated backup configuration. We do not have enabled automated backup for SQL Server on VM. Therefore, it returns the status as Enable: False.

(Get-AzVMSqlServerExtension -VMName $vmname -ResourceGroupName $resourcegroupname).AutoBackupSettings

Step 3: Configure Automated Backup v2.

In this section, we configure an automated backup for our existing Azure Storage account. It applies the following backup policy.

- Backup retention period: 10 days
- Log backup frequency: every 30 minutes
- Weekly full backup
- Full backup start time: 20:00
- Full backup window: 2 hours

Copy the script from
https://github.com/AzureDP300/AzureDP300/blob/main/Chapter10/Script6.ps1

```
PowerShell
PS /home/rajendra> $region = "[illegible]"
PS /home/rajendra> $storage_accountname = "[illegible]"
PS /home/rajendra> $storage_resourcegroupname = $azuresql
PS /home/rajendra> $resourcegroupname = "[illegible]"
PS /home/rajendra>
PS /home/rajendra> $storage =Get-AzStorageAccount -ResourceGroupName $resourcegroupname `
>>     -Name $storage_accountname -ErrorAction SilentlyContinue
PS /home/rajendra>
PS /home/rajendra>
PS /home/rajendra>  $autobackupconfig = New-AzVMSqlServerAutoBackupConfig -Enable `
>>     -RetentionPeriodInDays 10 -StorageContext $storage.Context `
>>     -ResourceGroupName "[illegible]" -BackupSystemDbs `
>>     -BackupScheduleType Manual -FullBackupFrequency Weekly `
>>     -FullBackupStartHour 20 -FullBackupWindowInHours 2 `
>>     -LogBackupFrequencyInMinutes 30
PS /home/rajendra>
PS /home/rajendra> Set-AzVMSqlServerExtension -AutoBackupSettings $autobackupconfig `
>>     -VMName $vmname -ResourceGroupName $resourcegroupname

RequestId IsSuccessStatusCode StatusCode ReasonPhrase
--------- ------------------- ---------- ------------
                         True         OK OK

PS /home/rajendra>
PS /home/rajendra>
```

Step 4: Verify the automated backup configuration.

In this step, we verify the automated backup configuration performed in the previous step.

$vmname = "myazuresqlvm"

$resourcegroupname = "azuresql"

(Get-AzVMSqlServerExtension -VMName $vmname -ResourceGroupName $resourcegroupname).AutoBackupSettings

```
PS /home/rajendra> (Get-AzVMSqlServerExtension -VMName $vmname -ResourceGroupName $resourcegroupname).AutoBackupSettings

Enable                  : True
EnableEncryption        : False
RetentionPeriod         : 10
StorageUrl              : https://azurebackupstoragedemo.blob.core.windows.net/
StorageAccessKey        :
Password                :
BackupSystemDbs         : True
BackupScheduleType      : Manual
FullBackupFrequency     : WEEKLY
FullBackupStartTime     : 20
FullBackupWindowHours   : 2
LogBackupFrequency      : 30
```

Lab 17: Configure SQL Server Backup in Azure VMs

This lab configures the recovery service vault for SQL Server backup on Azure VM.

In the Azure portal, search for Recovery Vault Services.

No recovery services vaults to display

A disaster recovery and data protection strategy keeps your business running when unexpected events occur. Get started by creating a Recovery Services vault.

Learn more about Backup   Learn more about Site Recovery

Create recovery services vault

Click on Create recovery service vault. In the recovery service vault configuration page, enter the following information.

- Resource group
- Vault name
- Region

Create Recovery Services vault

Preview

*Basics Tags Review + create

Project Details

Select the subscription and the resource group in which you want to create the vault.

Subscription * Azure subscription 1

Resource group * azuresql

Create new

Instance Details

Vault name * azurevmbackup

Region * Central India

Verify recovery service vault configuration.

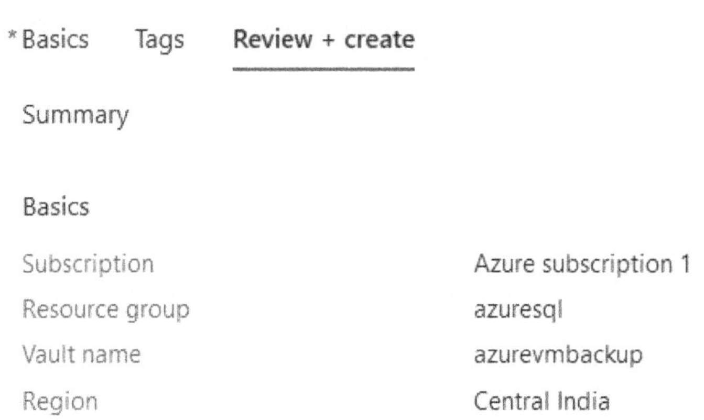

Once resources are deployed, go to the recovery service vault overview page.

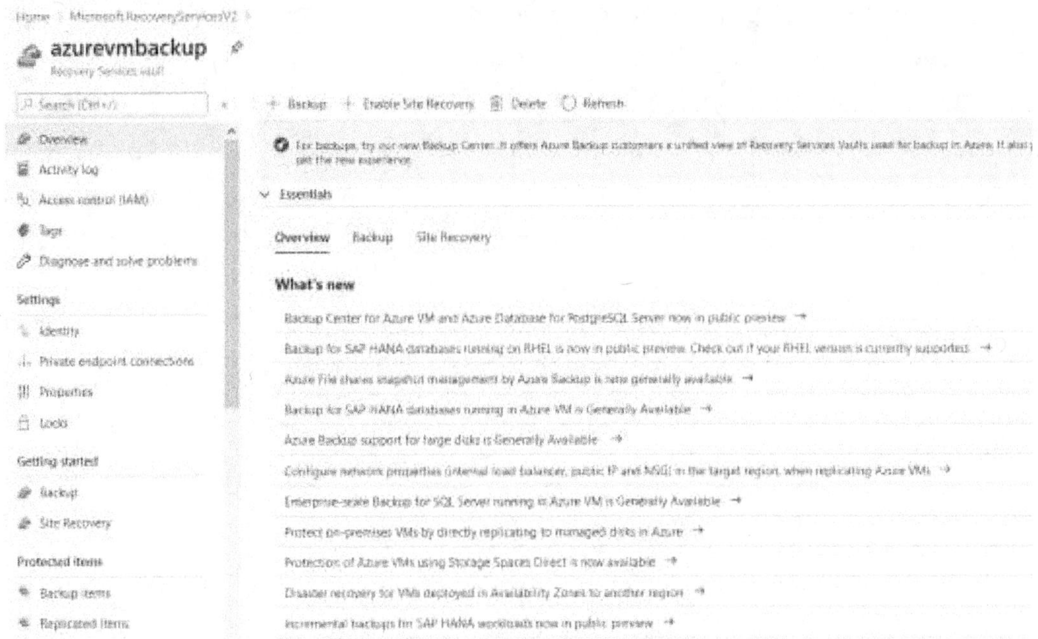

Configure a backup in the default recovery service vault policy

Click on Backup and answer the following questions.

- Where is your workload running? – Azure
- What do you want to backup? – Virtual machine

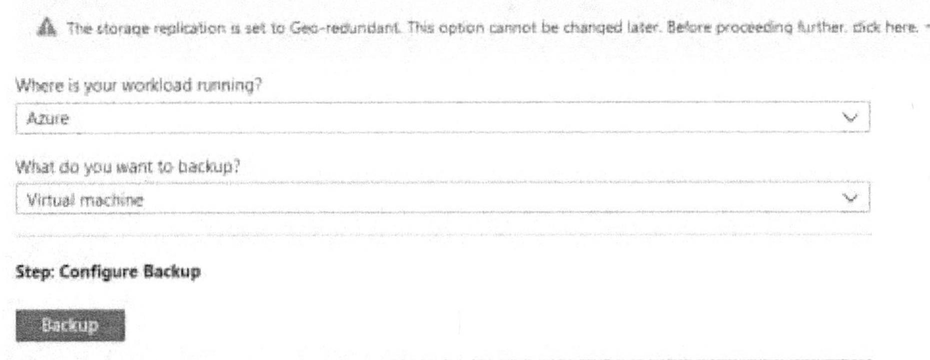

Click on Backup. In the backup configuration, select the default policy and search the virtual machine you want to backup.

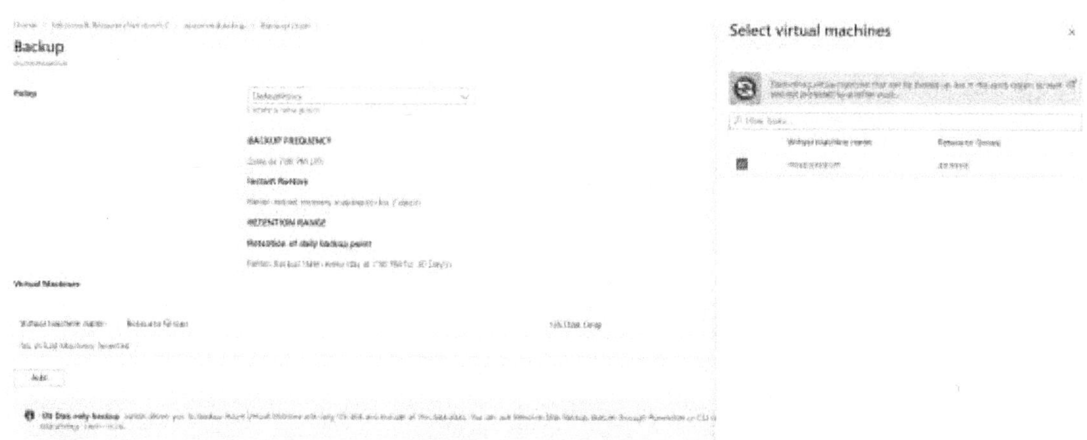

It lists out the virtual machine you have selected.

Home > Microsoft.RecoveryServicesV2 > azurevmbackup > Backup Goal >

Backup

azurevmbackup

Policy

DefaultPolicy

Create a new policy

BACKUP FREQUENCY

Daily at 7:00 PM UTC

Instant Restore

Retain instant recovery snapshot(s) for 2 day(s)

RETENTION RANGE

Retention of daily backup point

Retain backup taken every day at 7:00 PM for 30 Day(s)

Virtual Machines

Virtual machine name	Resource Group	OS Disk Only
myazuresqlvm	azuresql	☐

Add

OS Disk only backup option allows you to backup Azure Virtual Machine with only OS disk and exclude all the data disks. You can use Selective Disk Backup feature through and pricing- Learn more.

Enable Backup

Click on Enable Backup. It configures the recovery vault service backup policy on the selected virtual machine. To verify, go to the virtual machine overview page and click on Backup. In the backup dashboard, you get the recovery service vault name and applied backup policy.

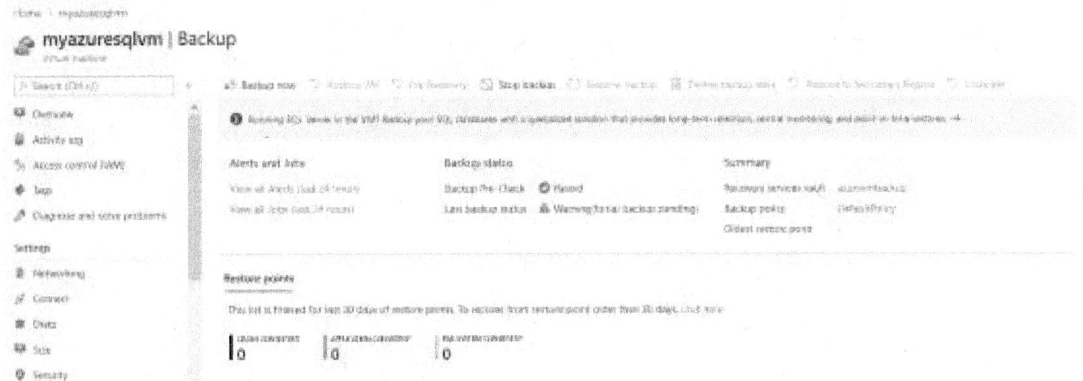

Create a custom backup policy in the recovery service vault

In the previous step, we applied a default policy for SQL Server on Azure VM. To create a custom policy, in the recovery service vault, click on Backup policies.

It lists all available backup policies.

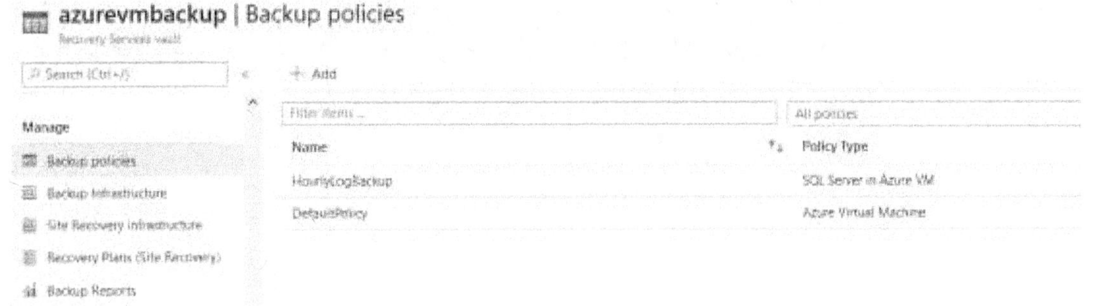

Click on Add to configure a custom backup policy. In the next step, select the policy type. Here, we choose SQL Server in Azure VM.

Home > Recovery Services vaults > azurevmbackup >

Add

Policy Type

Azure Virtual Machine

Azure File Share

SQL Server in Azure VM

SAP HANA in Azure VM

Enter a policy name and define the full, differential and log backup frequency, retention period.

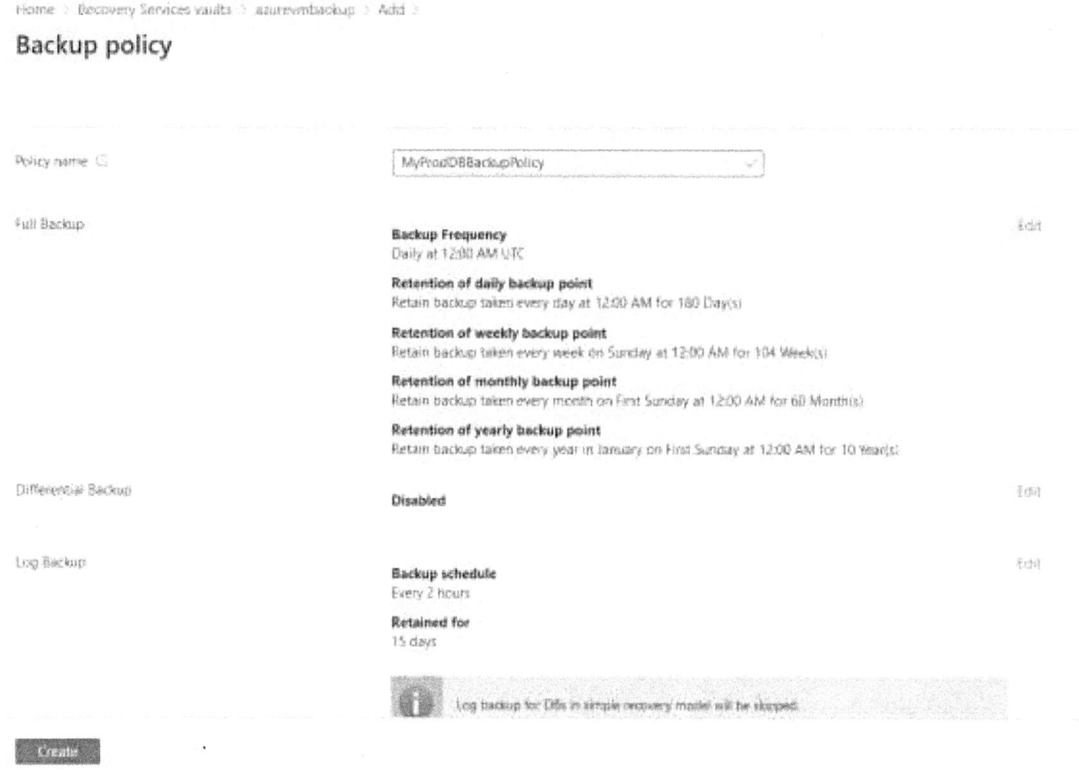

Click on Create, and you get a custom policy configured. You can apply this policy to SQL Server on VM, similar to a default policy.

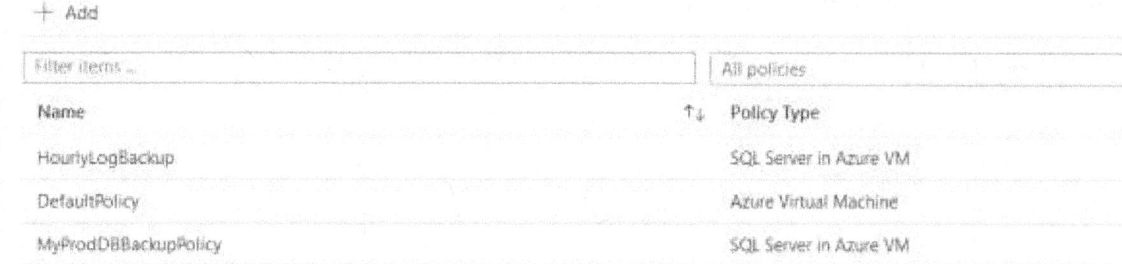

Lab 18: Configure LTR policy for Azure SQL Database using Azure CLI

In this lab, we configure a long-term retention policy for the Azure SQL Database using Azure CLI.

In the following code, specify the following parameters.

- $serverName: Azure SQL Server name
- $resourceGroup: Azure resource group in which Azure SQL Database exists
- $dbname: Azure SQL Database name.

It configures a LTR policy with WeeklyRetention =10 weeks, YearlyRetention=7 years, WeekofYear=15.

Copy the script from
https://github.com/AzureDP300/AzureDP300/blob/main/Chapter10/Script7.ps1

It returns the configured LTR policy in the output.

```
PowerShell
PS /home/rajendra> $subId = "[illegible]"
PS /home/rajendra> $serverName = "azuredemosqldemo"
PS /home/rajendra> $resourceGroup = "MyAzureLabSQL"
PS /home/rajendra> $dbName = "Azuredemodatabase"
PS /home/rajendra> $server = Get-AzSqlServer -ServerName $serverName -ResourceGroupName $resourceGroup
PS /home/rajendra>
PS /home/rajendra> Set-AzSqlDatabaseBackupLongTermRetentionPolicy -ServerName $serverName -DatabaseName $dbName `
>>     -ResourceGroupName $resourceGroup -WeeklyRetention P10W -YearlyRetention P7Y -WeekOfYear 15

ResourceGroupName : MyAzureLabSQL
ServerName        : azuredemosqldemo
DatabaseName      : Azuredemodatabase
WeeklyRetention   : P10W
MonthlyRetention  : PT0S
YearlyRetention   : P7Y
WeekOfYear        : 15
Location          :
```

Refresh Azure console and verify the LTR configuration.

You can also view the existing LTR policy using the following code.

$ltrPolicies = Get-AzSqlDatabaseBackupLongTermRetentionPolicy -ServerName $serverName -DatabaseName $dbName -ResourceGroupName $resourceGroup

```
PS /home/rajendra> $ltrPolicies = Get-AzSqlDatabaseBackupLongTermRetentionPolicy -ServerName $serverName -DatabaseName $dbName `
>>     -ResourceGroupName $resourceGroup
PS /home/rajendra> $ltrPolicies

ResourceGroupName : MyAzureLabSQL
ServerName        : azuredemosqldemo
DatabaseName      : Azuredemodatabase
WeeklyRetention   : P10W
MonthlyRetention  : PT0S
YearlyRetention   : P7Y
WeekOfYear        : 15
Location          :
```

Remove LTR policy: To remove the LTR policy from a specific Azure SQL Database, run the following code with the argument **-RemovePolicy**.

Set-AzSqlDatabaseBackupLongTermRetentionPolicy -ServerName $serverName -DatabaseName $dbName -ResourceGroupName $resourceGroup -RemovePolicy

```
PS /home/rajendra> Set-AzSqlDatabaseBackupLongTermRetentionPolicy -ServerName $serverName -DatabaseName $dbName `
>>     -ResourceGroupName $resourceGroup -RemovePolicy

ResourceGroupName : MyAzureLabSQL
ServerName        : azuredemosqldemo
DatabaseName      : Azuredemodatabase
WeeklyRetention   : PT0S
MonthlyRetention  : PT0S
YearlyRetention   : PT0S
WeekOfYear        : 0
Location          :
```

As shown below, the LTR policy does not exist now. It gives a default retention period of 7 days as per the basic service tier.

Summary

The HADR planning and implementation are essential for business continuity and high resiliency of database infrastructure. In this article, we explored various HADR solutions for both PaaS and IaaS deployment models such as Active geo-replication, Auto-failover groups, automated backup, data redundancy option, backup storage redundancy, Backup to URL, Automated backup V2.

Chapter 11 Perform administration using T-SQL and PowerShell.

In this chapter, you will learn how to monitor and administer the Azure SQL Database using T-SQL and PowerShell.

What you will learn

1. Learn how to manage Azure SQL Database using T-SQL.
2. Understand T-SQL compatibility.
3. Explore administration tasks using T-SQL and PowerShell.
4. Create an Azure SQL database.
5. Change Azure SQL service tier.
6. Monitor database performance using extended events and DMVs.
7. Configure Automatic Tuning.
8. Protect Azure SQL Server using Locks.
9. Manage Security using T-SQL.
10. Check data integrity.
11. Perform query execution using MFA authentication with PowerShell.
12. And more...

Azure SQL database and SQL on Azure VM or SQL Server on-premise fully support Transact-SQL features. In other words, the core T-SQL constructs and components such as data types, operators, and string, arithmetic, logical, and cursor functions work identically in all SQL flavours. However, the underlying design isolates query execution components and master databases; thus, it exhibits a few T-SQL differences in DDL (data-definition language) and DML (data manipulation language).

T-SQL query elements and some features and syntax are partially supported. The primary reason is that the database is self-contained and does not require performing server-level activities, operating system components, or managing file system configuration.

Overview of Azure SQL database

The core functionality of CREATE DATABASE command still exits on most of the relational database system. On a similar note, the base command still holds good for the Azure SQL database. Because of its architectural design, the CREATE DATABASE syntax and semantics can take multiple forms in Azure SQL compared with on-premises SQL Server or SQL on Azure VM.

Use CREATE DATABASE T-SQL statement to create an Azure SQL database or elastic pool database.

1. With the T-SQL statement, you need to specify the mandatory option database name.

2. The other option includes collation, max size, edition, service objective, and the new database's elastic pool, if applicable.

3. You can create the database in an Azure elastic pool.

4. It also allows creating a copy of the database on another Azure SQL database server.

5. CREATE DATABASE on Azure SQL database is a deployment process. During the database creation, a new deployment will create a dedicated instance and host the database. In addition, the meta-data information is stored in a control plan.
6. By default, when you create a database, the following features are turned on:

    a. Query Store
    b. Auto-create statistics
    c. Auto-update statistics
    d. Snapshot isolation
    e. Read committed snapshot
    f. FULL recovery
    g. Checksum
    h. TDE
    i. ADR (Accelerated Database Recovery)

j. Stale page detection

7. The CREATE DATABASE is an asynchronous operation but can be tracked with the DMV.

```
select * from sys.databases;
```

Create a database in Azure SQL using T-SQL

This section will see a few examples of creating an Azure SQL database using CREATE DATABASE T-SQL statement.

The basic T-SQL syntax of creating a database in Azure SQL Server

```
CREATE DATABASE <DBName>;
```

If no option or parameters are specified, then the CREATE DATABASE command will execute to create a database on the Azure SQL Server with the default configuration. i.e. you will see the Azure SQL database created with the database edition General Purpose with service objective Gen5, 2 vCores, and database size property set to 32 GB.

Create a database with the options

This example will see creating an Azure SQL Database with a basic edition. To create a database in the specific edition, run the following T-SQL

```
CREATE DATABASE <DATABASENAME>
(EDITION = 'Basic');
```

The above T-SQL creates an Azure SQL database with a basic edition. In the sample T-SQL, you see you don't specify the max size option, then the default value of 2 GB is allocated in the basic edition.

The different available editions in the Azure SQL database:

1. Basic
2. Standard
3. Premium
4. General Purpose
5. Hyper-Scale
6. Business Critical

Create an elastic pool database

To create an elastic pool database, you must have the elastic pool exists before running the T-SQL. The following T-SQL creates an elastic database with the name demodp300.

```
CREATE DATABASE demodp300

 ( SERVICE_OBJECTIVE = ELASTIC_POOL ( name = dempdp300pool) ) ;
```

Copy Azure SQL Database

Use **AS COPY OF** clause in CREATE DATABASE statement to create a copy from the existing database to a different server.

Note: It is not possible to change the new database's edition when you copy with AS COPY OF clause. You can only change the service objective of the new database.

In the following example, you will create a database from a copy of an existing database within the same Azure SQL Server.

```
CREATE DATABASE <TargetdatabaseName>
```

```
AS COPY OF <SourceDatabaseName>
```

In the above sample, the target database will retain the properties of the source database. You can change the service objective using the following T-SQL.

```
CREATE DATABASE <TargetDatabaseName>
 AS COPY OF <SourceDatabaseName>
 (SERVICE_OBJECTIVE = 'S1' ) ;
```

In this example, create a copy of a database from an existing database on another server. You need to specify the server name along with the database name using object dot notation. If dp300 is the server name and database dempdp300, you need to specify the dp300.demodp300 as the database source name.

```
CREATE DATABASE NewDemodp300
 AS COPY OF dp300.demodp300
 (SERVICE_OBJECTIVE = 'S1' );
```

Change the Service Tier using T-SQL

1. Open SQL Server Management Studio and connect to the Azure SQL database. Change the session context of the specific database

2. To get the current database tier, run the following query :

```
SELECT * FROM sys.database_service_objectives
```

3. The sys.database_service_objectives DMV returns the current Azure SQL Database edition and the service objective or the performance level.

4. To check the status of an ongoing operation, set the user session context to the master database and run the following T-SQL

```
SELECT * FROM sys.dm_operation_status
WHERE resource_type_desc='database' AND major_resource_id='mydemodp300'
```

5. Next, change the edition from S0 to S2 using Alter database T-SQL.

```
ALTER DATABASE ToyStore MODIFY (Edition='Standard', Service_objective='S0')
```

6. To validate the service objective, run the following T-SQL

```
SELECT * FROM sys.database_service_objectives
```

Performance monitoring using extended events T-SQL

Azure SQL database does not support SQL profiler, but whereas SQL Managed Instance supports SQL profiler. The other alternatives are DMVs (Dynamic Management Views), extended events, or monitor using Azure SQL analytics.

Extended Events (xEvents) are a powerful, lightweight, powerful tool used to perform troubleshooting and, indeed, the best way to troubleshoot Azure SQL Databases performance events. It is easy to troubleshoot a specific issue by configuring extended events.

In the Azure SQL database, we capture the extended events in two ways. First, using ring buffers—directly use the memory. It is directly proportional to memory consumption and may inject memory pressure into the database. In addition, the other limitation is difficult to share the data. Second, the other alternative is the use of a file. It works pretty well for on-premise SQL Server, but whereas for Azure SQL database, you must rely on a storage account to create blob storage.

The overall steps for creating and capturing extended events from an Azure DB are going to be as follows

1. Create a container in the blob storage

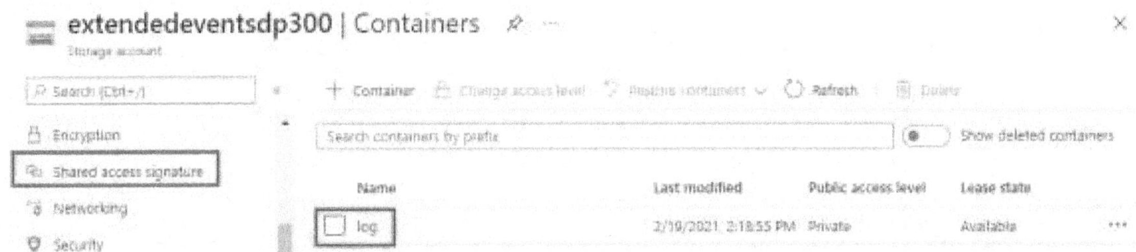

2. Create a master encryption key using T-SQL. Change the user session context to the user database.

```
CREATE MASTER KEY ENCRYPTION BY PASSWORD = 'mydem0dp3000#!@#$'
```

3. Create database scoped credentials using a shared access signature to access the storage account. You can see that SAS token generated with FULL permission **sp=racwdl** (Read, Access, Create, Write, Delete and List) in the following T-SQL

```
CREATE DATABASE SCOPED CREDENTIAL

 [https://extendedeventsdp300.blob.core.windows.net/log]

   WITH

     IDENTITY = 'SHARED ACCESS SIGNATURE',

     SECRET = 'sp=racwdl&st=2021-02-19T20:17:56Z&se=2021-02-
20T04:17:56Z&sv=2020-02-10&sr=c&sig=SDFSfTF1BD177q7OQDmS84aFo%3D'
```

4. Configure extended events using the following T-SQL. You can see that you need
   a. Database_name, here, mydemodp300.
   b. Filename – Container URL followed by a file

```
CREATE EVENT SESSION [LongRunningQueries]

ON DATABASE ADD EVENT sqlserver. sql_statement_completed

(

    ACTION

            ( sqlserver.database_name, sqlserver.query_hash,
sqlserver.query_plan_hash, sqlserver.sql_text, sqlserver.username )

WHERE

  (

    [sqlserver].[database_name] = N'mydemodp300'

    AND duration > 1000

  )

) ADD TARGET package0.event_file (

  SET

    filename = 'https://extendedeventsdp300.blob.core.windows.net/log/logdata.xel'
)

      WITH (MAX_MEMORY = 50 MB, MAX_DISPATCH_LATENCY = 3 SECONDS) ;

GO
```

5. Run the events.

The extended event session **LongRunningQueries** will gather the events based on the action sql_statement_completed.

```
ALTER EVENT SESSION [LongRunningQueries]
```

ON DATABASE STATE = START;

6. Finally, view the log file in the container

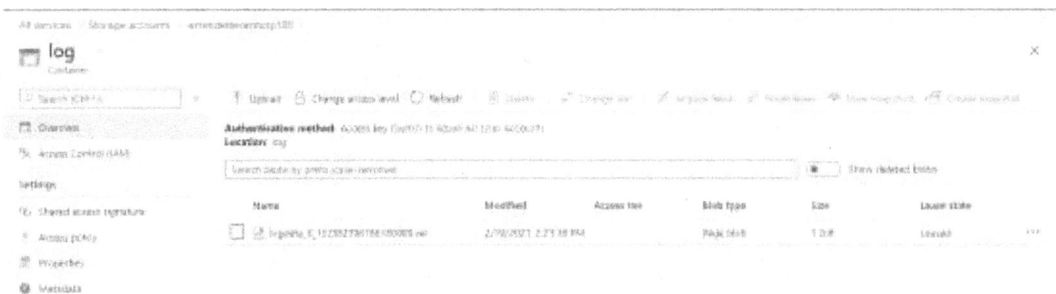

7. Let us read the XEL file from an Azure blob storage account. You can use the **sys.fn_xe_file_target_read_file** function. This function requires a total of four arguments.

a. *Path* – the path of the XEL file(s)

b. *mdpath* – the metadata file path

c. *initial_file_name* – specify the first file to read. Please keep it to NULL, will read all files

d. *initial_offset* – Used to specify the last offset

```
SELECT event_data = convert(xml, event_data)

FROM sys.fn_xe_file_target_read_file(

'https://extendedeventsdp300.blob.core.windows.net/log/logdata_0_132582396786180000.xel',null, null, null);
```

How to use SSMS to read extend events log files

To Read the extended event log file through SSMS, follow the below steps.

1. Download the extended event log files.

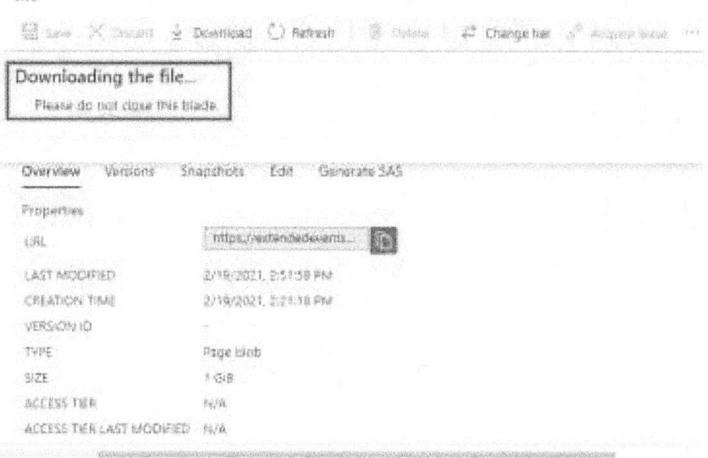

2. Open SSMS and select the **File** menu.
3. Go to the **Open** pop-out menu and select **Merge Extended Event Files...**

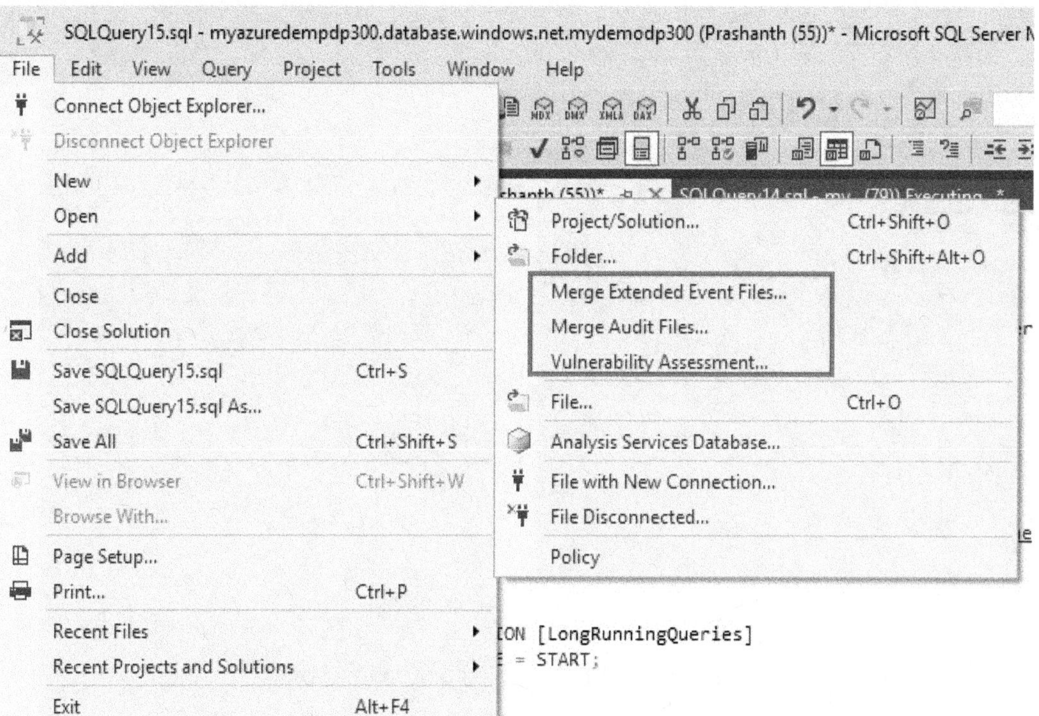

4. Browse and add the related extended event log file.
5. Click Ok.

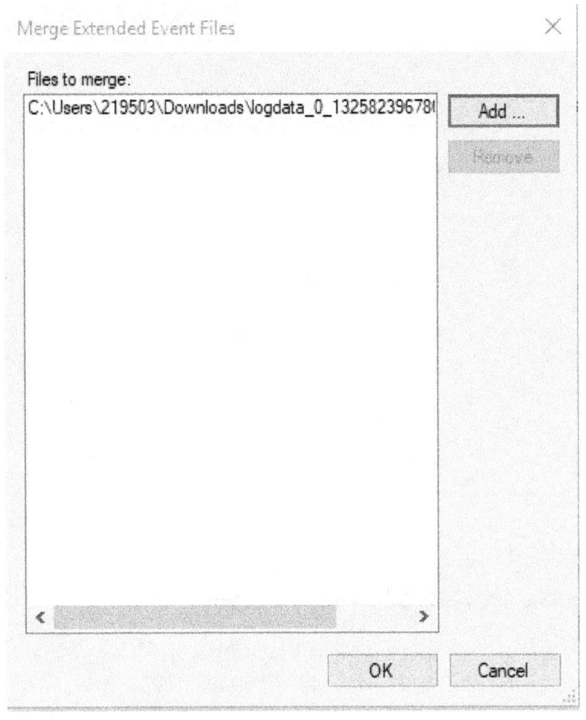

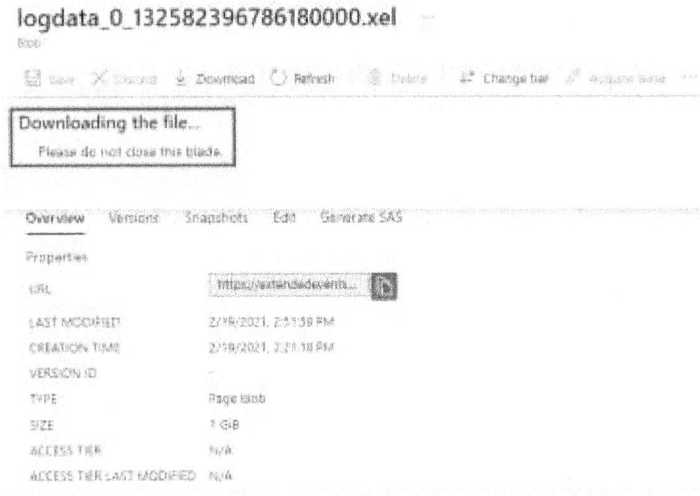

6. Now, you can view the extended log file content in SSMS.

Displaying 9 Events

name	timestamp
sql_statement_completed	2021-02-19 14:48:32.9181733
sql_statement_completed	2021-02-19 14:48:33.1437851
sql_statement_completed	2021-02-19 14:48:33.4690264
sql_statement_completed	2021-02-19 14:48:33.5240944
sql_statement_completed	2021-02-19 14:48:38.5487640
sql_statement_completed	2021-02-19 14:50:16.8558442
sql_statement_completed	2021-02-19 14:50:17.8506515
sql_statement_completed	2021-02-19 14:51:56.0052142
sql_statement_completed	2021-02-19 14:54:21.4320895

Event:sql_statement_completed (2021-02-19 14:48:33.5240944)

Details

Field	Value
offset_end	528
page_server_reads	0
parameterized_plan...	0x
physical_reads	0
query_hash	15691091958178926927
query_plan_hash	16974521995267805500
row_count	113
spills	0
sql_text	SELECT SCHEMA_NAME(xproc.schema_id) AS [Schema], xpro...
statement	SELECT SCHEMA_NAME(xproc.schema_id) AS [Schema], xpro...
username	Prashanth
writes	0

1.1.13 How to list the extended events, targets and actions

To find the available extended events, actions, and targets, you can run the following T-SQL:

```
SELECT
    o.object_type,
    p.name        AS [package_name],
    o.name        AS [db_object_name],
    o.description  AS [db_obj_description]
```

```
FROM
  sys.dm_xe_objects  AS o
  INNER JOIN sys.dm_xe_packages AS p  ON p.guid = o.package_guid
WHERE
  o.object_type in
    (
    'action',  'event',  'target'
    )
ORDER BY
  o.object_type,
  p.name,
  o.name
```

Dynamic Managed views in Azure SQL

Microsoft Azure SQL Database and Azure SQL Managed Instance partially support three categories of dynamic management views.

1. Database-related dynamic management views.
2. Execution-related dynamic management views.
3. Transaction-related dynamic management views.

Note Server-scoped dynamic management views and functions. These require VIEW SERVER STATE permission on the server.

Database-scoped dynamic management views and functions. These require VIEW DATABASE STATE permission on the database.

How to determine the databases with compute utilization over 75% last days

Azure SQL Database, a dynamic management view sys.resource_stat comes to the rescue. This DMV returns CPU usage and storage data for an Azure SQL Database.

Copy the script from
https://github.com/AzureDP300/AzureDP300/blob/main/Chapter11/Script1.sql

How to measure resource consumption of a database using sys.dm_db_resource_stats

The **sys.dm_db_resource_stats** is a database-scoped view that shows recent resource consumption data relative to the configured service tier. The metrics collection process runs every 15 seconds to record average CPU percentage, I/O, log writes, and memory consumption and maintain the metrics for 1 hour. The metrics provide a more granular level of data for initial analysis and troubleshooting.

In this example, the following query shows the average, maximum resource consumption data for the current database in the past hour.

Copy the script from
https://github.com/AzureDP300/AzureDP300/blob/main/Chapter11/Script2.sql

How to configure automatic tuning using T-SQL

Automatic tuning is a database feature to address the following performance issues:

1. Provide insight into potential query performance problems.
2. Recommend solutions.
3. Automatically fix identified problems.

Manage automatic tuning in two ways:

Manual method to take corrective measures when there is a:

1. performance issue
2. Automatic method where the database engine automatically fixes the performance issues. The automatic tuning feature enables Azure SQL to identify the potential performance issue caused by query regressions. In Azure SQL Database, this feature creates necessary indexes and drops unused indexes.

It is easy to configure Automatic Tuning options at the database level or the logical host level. To view automatic tuning options through the catalog view **sys.database_automatic_tuning_options**

Automatic index management

In Azure SQL Database, a good index design is vital for the optimal performance of the database. Automatic index tuning helps to optimize the indexes.

1. The automatic tuning feature identifies the indexes that could improve T-SQL query performance in the read operation. In addition, it identifies redundant indexes or unused indexes that are no longer in use, and it is an excellent candidate to remove the index.
2. In manual index management, DBA manually query DMV, sys.dm_db_missing_index_details, view the index details and fine-tune them to perform better.

1.1.14 How to enable automatic tuning using T-SQL

You enable automatic tuning for Azure SQL Database in using the ALTER DATABASE T-SQL statement. To enable automatic tuning on the database via T-SQL, connect to the database and execute the following query:

```
ALTER DATABASE <DBNAME> SET AUTOMATIC_TUNING = AUTO | INHERIT | CUSTOM
```

If the automatic tuning option is AUTO, it will apply Azure Defaults; INHERIT will use the parent server's configuration; CUSTOM will manually configure the tuning option.

To configure individual automatic tuning options via T-SQL, connect to the database and execute the query such as this one:

```
ALTER DATABASE <DBNAME> SET AUTOMATIC_TUNING (FORCE_LAST_GOOD_PLAN = ON, CREATE_INDEX = ON,DROP_INDEX = OFF)
```

How to Enable, Modify and Disable change tracking

The following example enables change tracking for the specific database and sets the retention period to 5 days.

```
ALTER DATABASE <database_name>
SET CHANGE_TRACKING = ON
(AUTO_CLEANUP = ON, CHANGE_RETENTION = 5 DAYS);
```

The following example shows how to change the retention period to 9 days.

```
ALTER DATABASE <database_name>
SET CHANGE_TRACKING (CHANGE_RETENTION = 9 DAYS);
```

The following example shows how to disable change tracking for the specific database.

```
ALTER DATABASE <database_name>
```

How to recover the deleted Azure SQL Databases

It is easy to recover the deleted Azure SQL Database. The deleted databases are kept intact by design as per the service level tiers or the retention settings.

To recover the deleted database:

1. Open the Azure Portal
2. Browse the Azure SQL Server
3. Scroll down to locate Deleted databases
4. Perform the recovery

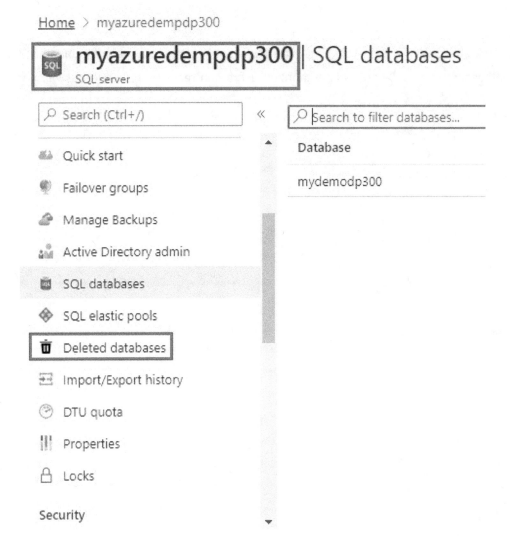

Lab 19: How to protect the accidental deletes of logical Azure SQL Server?

Azure does not protect the Azure SQL Server. The deletion of Azure SQL Server knowingly and unknowingly may cost a lot. There are a couple of ways to protect the Azure SQL Server.

1. Read-only lock
2. Update lock

Read-only lock

It is better to lock the resources to ensure that extra steps are in place to protect the underlying Azure SQL databases. In a read-only lock, authorized users can read the resource but will not modify it.

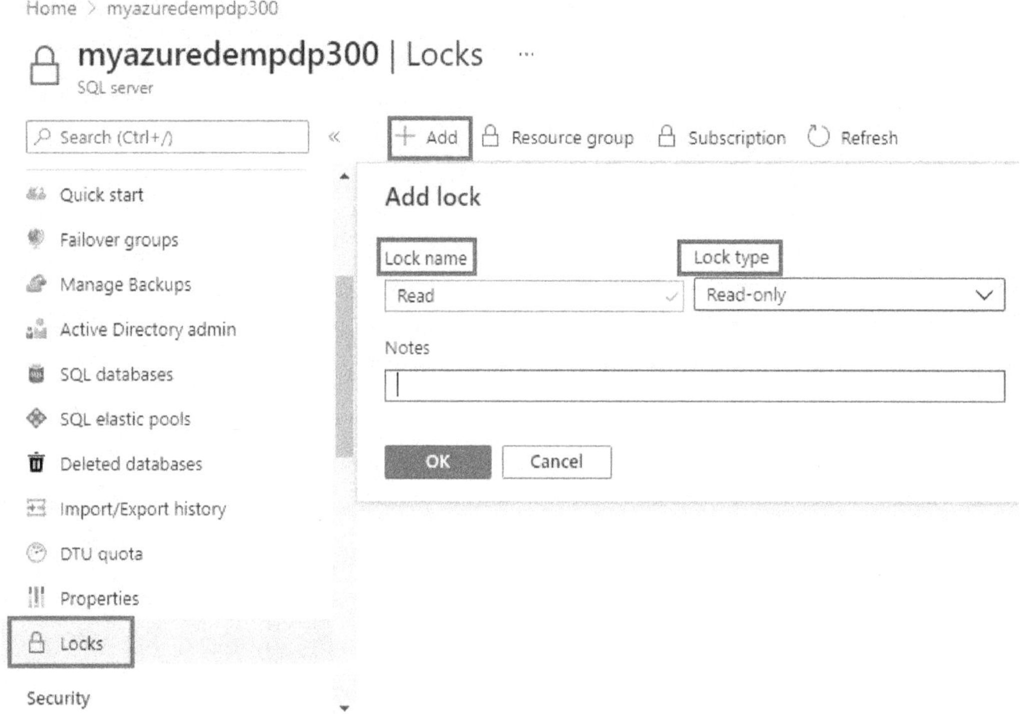

a. In the Azure portal, locate the Azure SQL Server on the left blade, scroll down and locate **Locks**.

b. Click **Add**

c. Type in **Lock Name**

d. Select the **Lock Type**

e. Click **Ok**

2. Now, let us try to delete the Azure SQL Server. Locate the Azure SQL Server and click Delete.
3. Type the server name.
4. Click **Delete.**

Are you sure you want to dele...
Warning! Deleting myazuredempdp300 is irreversible. The action you're about to take can't be undone. Going further will delete it and all the items in it permanently.
TYPE THE SERVER NAME
myazuredempdp300
Affected items
Database name
Location
Pricing tier
mydemodp300
eastus
Standard S0: 10 DT
Delete
Cancel

5. You see a dialogue box appear like below, stating the resource is locked.

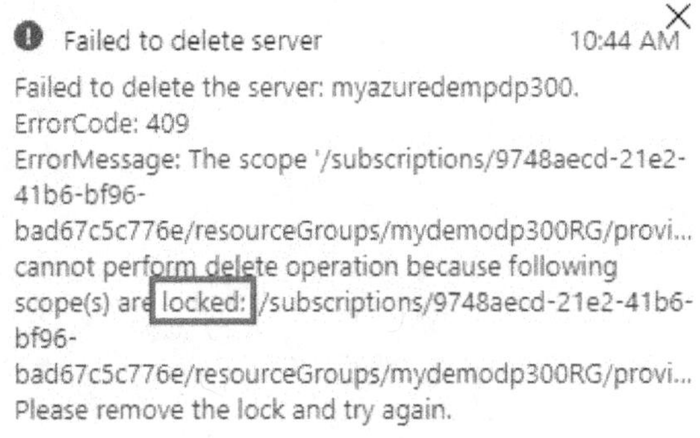

6. In the next example, you try to update the Azure SQL Database service tiers from S0 to S1. However, due to the existence of locks, you are not allowed to make any changes.

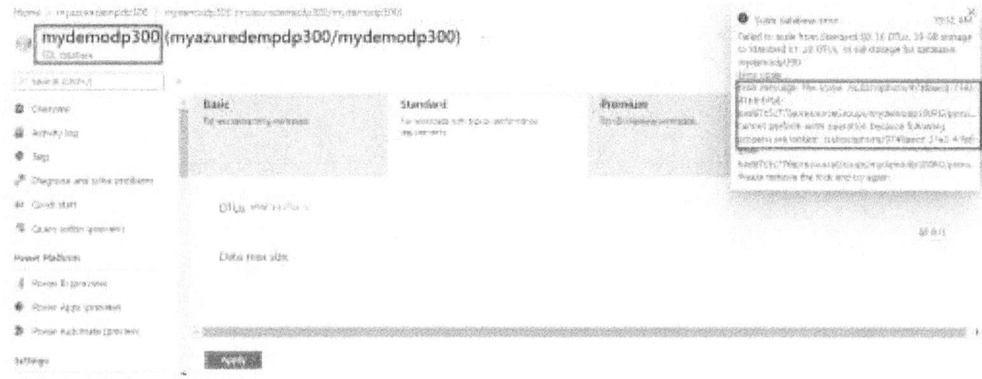

Delete lock

A delete lock, authorized users will be able to read and modify the resource but will not delete it.

1. Open Azure portal
2. Click **Add**
3. Type **lock Name** and choose **Delete** as Lock type
4. Click **Ok**

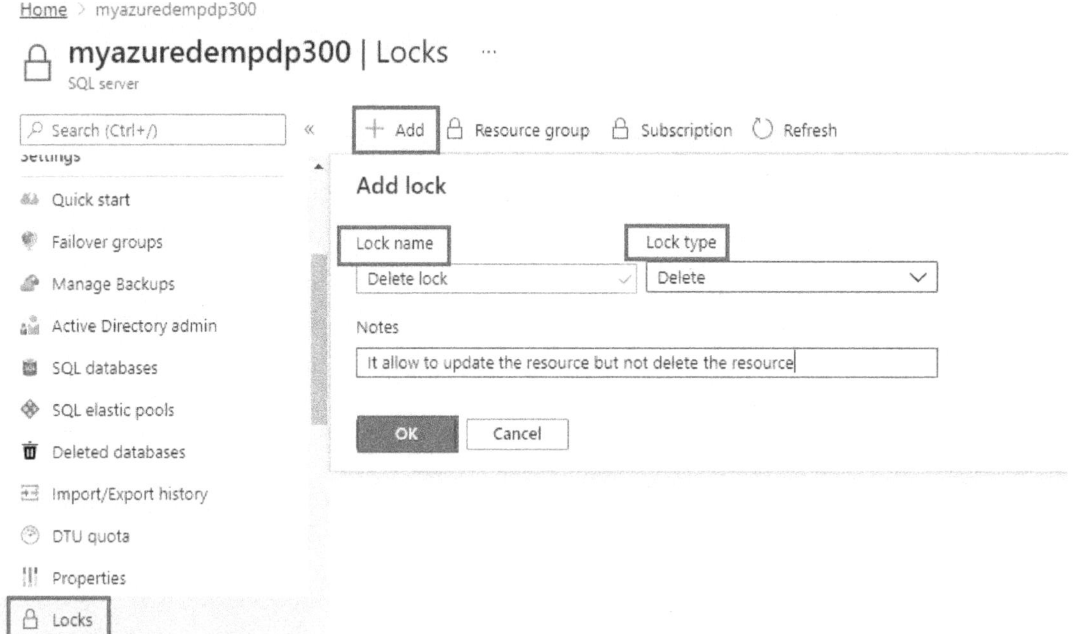

7. Next, try to delete the Azure SQL Server or Azure SQL database. You see a dialogue box appear like below, stating the resource is locked.

Failed to delete server 11:06 AM

Failed to delete the server: myazuredempdp300.
ErrorCode: 409
ErrorMessage: The scope '/subscriptions/9748aecd-21e2-41b6-bf96-bad67c5c776e/resourceGroups/mydemodp300RG/provi... cannot perform delete operation because following scope(s) are locked: '/subscriptions/9748aecd-21e2-41b6-bf96-bad67c5c776e/resourceGroups/mydemodp300RG/provi... Please remove the lock and try again.

5. Now, let us update the database service tiers from S0 and S1 using T-SQL. You can see that database service tiers updated from S0 to S1 without exception.

```
SELECT * FROM sys.database_service_objectives

ALTER DATABASE mydemodp300 MODIFY (Edition='Standard', Service_objective='S1')

GO

WAITFOR DELAY '00:00:20'

GO

SELECT * FROM sys.database_service_objectives

GO
```

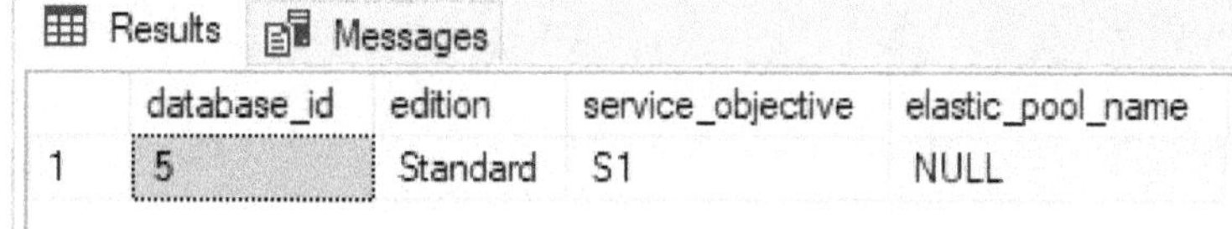

Results | Messages

	database_id	edition	service_objective	elastic_pool_name
1	5	Standard	S1	NULL

The lock-type read-only or delete in the Azure SQL database has no impact on the DML or DDL operations. The locks at the resource level are to protect from unintentional deletion of the resources.

You need owner privileges to set these locks

Lab 20: Configure LTR (Long Term Retention) for Azure SQL Server

The organization has applications to meet various backup SLAs (Service Level Agreement). To meet the regulatory, compliance, or other business requirements to retain database backups beyond the 35 days, use the long-term retention (LTR) feature. It is possible to store the specified Azure SQL Database, and SQL Managed full backups in Azure Blob storage with a retention period of up to 10 years.

1. In the **Azure** portal, locate the **Azure SQL Server** instance and then click Manage Backups...
2. In the **Configure** policies pane, select the retention period, weekly, monthly or yearly backups.
3. Click Apply.

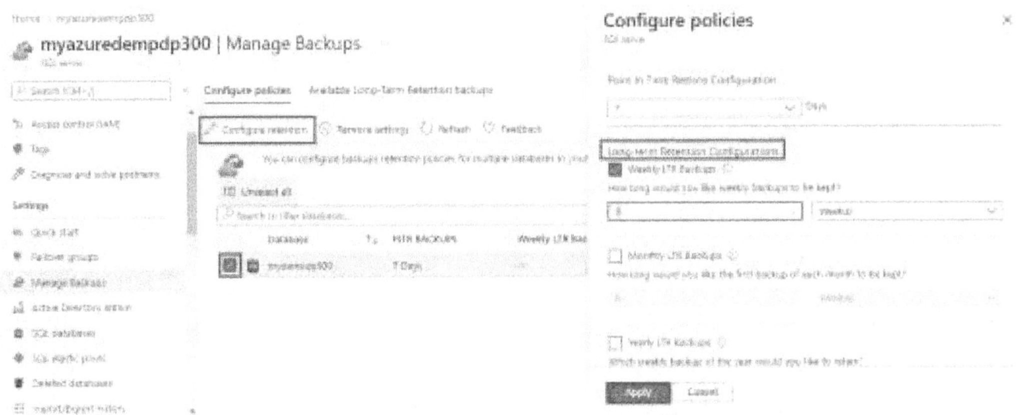

6. You can see the progress in the notification tab

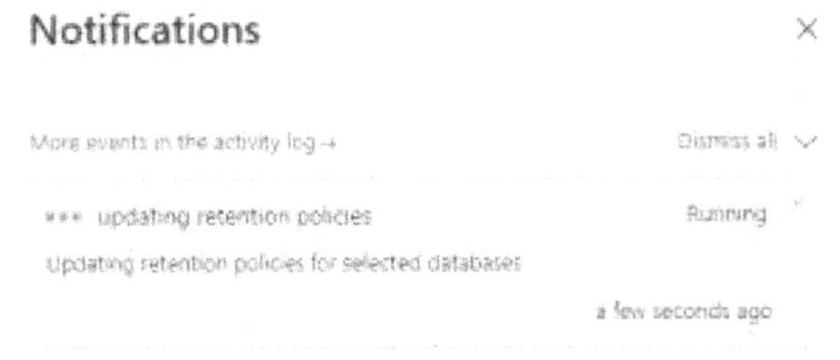

7. Now, you can see the list of the database in the **Available Long-Term Retention backups.**

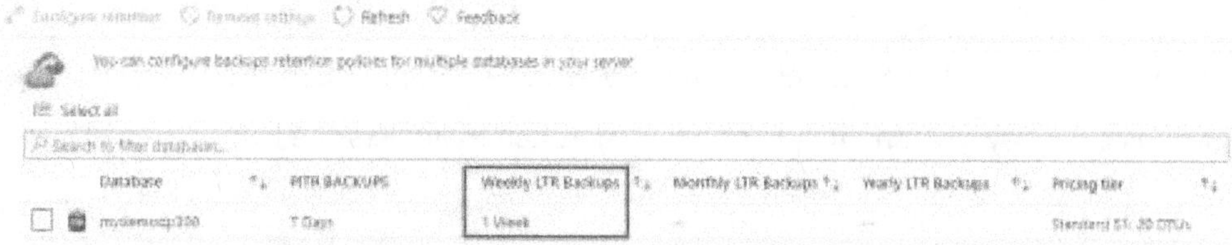

How to view backups using Azure PowerShell

To view the backups that are retained for a specific database with an LTR policy.

1. In the Azure portal, select your server and then click **Manage Backups**. On the **Available backups** tab, choose the database to which you want to see available backups.
2. In this example, you can view the list using Azure PowerShell cmdlet Get-AzSqlDatabaseLongTermRetentionBackup

```
$subId = "9748aecd-21e2-41b6-bf96-asdcd"
$serverName = "myazuredempdp300"
$resourceGroup = "mydemodp300RG"
$dbName = "myazuredempdp300"

#set the context to specified SubscriptionId
Get-AzSubscription -SubscriptionId $subId |Set-AzContext

$server = Get-AzSqlServer -ServerName $serverName -ResourceGroupName $resourceGroup
Get-AzSqlDatabaseLongTermRetentionBackup -Location $server.Location -ServerName $serverName -DatabaseName $dbName
```

Backup SQL Server databases to Azure Blob Storage Account using T-SQL

BACKUP DATABASE and RESTORE DATABASE commands integrated with CREDENTIAL and URL clause. The credential stores the authentication and authorization details to connect to the Azure Blob storage account. The URL (Uniform Resource Locator)—Blob storage are accessible using URL format https://<storageaccount>.blob.core.windows.net/<Container Name>

SQL Server on Azure VM or SQL Server on On-premise can either use the Azure storage account along with access key to authenticate or use SAS token to access the URL.

Note: SQL MI (Managed Instance) databases use service-managed keys, and it is not possible to export them to the other instances. Therefore, you cannot execute BACKUP DATABASE ... WITH COPY_ONLY. To restore the database backup on SQL MI, use automatic backup or use the customer-managed key.

By design, Managed Instance has a higher internal database version than any SQL Server version. Because of this, you cannot restore the database on the SQL Server target.

If the database size is too huge, such as 1 TB, you need to stripe the backup files into multiple files as SQL Managed instances cannot support a more than 195 GB backup stripe size.

In this example, you will see how to use the **Access key.** The Access key is the secret key to the storage account. To find the access key:

1. Browse the storage account
2. Click on **Settings**
3. Select **Access keys**.
4. To the right, copy **key1**, the access key.
5. Save this Access key information

6. Create the credentials

```
IF NOT EXISTS (SELECT * FROM sys.credentials WHERE name = 'mydemodp300')

CREATE CREDENTIAL mydemodp300cred

WITH IDENTITY='mydemodp300',
SECRET='9ZqCm8BvCjijcsuA01oN6OoeP0lKa+iSY7bWP7XUSCbTfM6oGUElkylsdOJq2ACuJQ
UlwYUMJkXUUt4Rp1NV8A=='
```

7. Prepare the T-SQL to backup the database to the URL.
   a. List the blob storage account service and the access key.
   b. Initiate a full database backup of the mydemodp300 database to the blob storage (URL+Storage+Container+filename).

```
BACKUP DATABASE mydemodp300

TO URL =
'https://extendedeventsdp300.blob.core.windows.net/log/mydemodp300_full_02202021.bak'

  WITH CREDENTIAL = 'mydemodp300cred'
```

,COMPRESSION,STATS = 5;

Manage Security using T-SQL

Azure SQL Database security administration is similar to security management of on-premises instances or SQL on Azure VM. Managing security at the database-level is almost the same, with a key difference in the available parameters. The auto-scale feature of Azure SQL Databases adopts a different server-level administration strategy.

Azure SQL Database Admin account

When you set up a logical SQL instance, you need to create a login account called the SQL Database admin account.

This account connects to Azure SQL instances using SQL authentication method where you tend to pass username and password. This administrator account has the highest privilege on the logical Azure SQL Server and all the user databases.

Azure SQL admin account limitation

1. You can have only one SQL admin account. You cannot create an additional SQL login with full administrative permissions in SQL Database.
2. Permissions on this account cannot be restricted.
3. It is not possible to change the Azure SQL Admin once you deploy.
4. You are allowed only to reset the password.
5. The roles dbmanager and loginmanager do not apply to SQL Managed Instance.

Azure SQL special accounts

SQL Database provides two additional administrative roles to access the master database to create the database using the dbmanager role and manage the logins using the loginmanager role.

Dbmanager role

Administrative accounts can create new databases. You must create a user in the master database, and add the user to the **dbmanager** role will enable the user can create the database. The user can be a contained database user or a user created as SQL Server login in the master database.

1. Connect to the master database using SQL admin account
2. Create a SQL authentication login using the CREATE LOGIN statement.
3. CREATE LOGIN Prashanth WITH PASSWORD = '<strong_password>';
4. In the master database, create a user by using the CREATE USER statement.
5. CREATE USER Prashanth FROM LOGIN Prashanth;
6. Add the user Prashanth to the **dbmanager** database role by using the ALTER ROLE statement.
7. ALTER ROLE dbmanager ADD MEMBER Prashanth;
8. If necessary, configure the server-level firewall to allow the new user to connect.

Now, the newly created user can connect to the master database and create new databases and become the database owner.

Login managers

You can repeat the same above steps to create a login and user and add a user to the **loginmanager** role to enable a user to create new logins in the master. Microsoft recommends using contained database users that authenticate at the database-level instead of using users based on logins.

The dbmanager allows the user to create Azure SQL databases, and the loginmanager, as the name suggests, will enable you to create a new login.

Azure Active Directory administrator

You can configure one Azure Active Directory account as an administrator. It can be an individual Azure AD User or an Azure AD Group containing several Azure AD Users. It is optional to configure an Azure AD administrator. I prefer to configure Azure AD administrator if you want to use Windows Authentication for Azure AD accounts to connect to SQL Database.

Configure the firewall using T-SQL

Using the Azure portal, you can configure the server-level firewall. In addition, you can use **sp_set_firewall_rule** T-SQL to configure the additional server-level-firewall settings. It allows the logins to connect to Azure SQL databases and all user databases.

The logical host, Azure SQL server, uses firewall rules to connect the Azure SQL servers and all the databases. It is possible to define server-level and database-level firewall settings for the master or user databases in the Azure SQL server logical server to allow access to the database.

Manage server-level firewall rules through Transact-SQL

The server-level firewall rules can be selected, created, updated, or deleted in the query window. SQL Server administrator or Azure Active Directory administrator can create a server-level firewall rule using Transact-SQL.

1. Open SSMS and launch a query window.
2. Connect to the master database.
3. To check the rules, run the following T-SQL

SELECT * FROM sys.firewall_rules ORDER BY name;

1. Next, add a firewall rule.
2. EXECUTE sp_set_firewall_rule @name = N'mydemodp300rule', @start_ip_address = '192.167.1.10', @end_ip_address = '192.167.1.20'
3. To delete a server-level firewall rule, execute the sp_delete_firewall_rule stored procedure.
4. EXECUTE sp_delete_firewall_rule @name = N'mydemodp300rule'

Database-level firewall rules

Only a database user with db_owner permission or a user with CONTROL permission can create a database-level firewall rule.

To create a new database rule or update an existing database-level firewall rule, run the sp_set_database_firewall_rule stored procedure

1. After creating a server-level firewall for your IP address, launch a query window through the Classic Portal or through SQL Server Management Studio.
2. Create a database-level firewall rule.
3. EXEC sp_set_database_firewall_rule @name = N'mydemodp300dbrule', @start_ip_address = '192.167.1.16', @end_ip_address = '192.167.1.18'
4. To delete an existing database-level firewall rule, run the following T-SQL

EXEC sp_delete_database_firewall_rule @name = N'mydemodp300dbrule'

Create a database role that owns a fixed database role

In this example, you will create a database role **securitygroup** that owns the db_securityadmin fixed database role.

```
CREATE ROLE secuitygroup AUTHORIZATION db_securityadmin;
GO
```

Azure SQL Database security management

The following table summarizes the security management difference between on-premises SQL Server and Azure SQL Database.

	On-premises or SQL on Azure VM	**Azure SQL Database**
SQL Server Admin	SA	Setup admin account during the installation of Azure SQL Database
Admin accounts	You can create multiple SYSADMIN accounts	You can have only one SQL admin account
Windows Administrator account	You can create multiple windows AD groups or individual Windows identities	You can have only one Azure active directory identities group or individual AD account
Manage server-level security	Browse SSMS, locate the Security folder and perform the operation	Browse master database using SSMS and via Azure portal
Windows Authentication	Active Directory authentication	Azure Active Directory identities add them as external users
Modify the admin accounts	It is possible to change the sysadmin accounts and reset the password	It is not possible to change the Azure SQL Admin once you deploy. You are allowed only to reset the password
Fixed server-level security role to create logins	securityadmin	Create loginmanager, a database role in the master database
Manage logins using T-SQL	CREATE LOGIN, ALTER LOGIN and DROP LOGIN in the master database	The same set of the on-premise command run with CREATE LOGIN, ALTER LOGIN, and DROP LOGIN with a set of parameter limitation and you must be connected to the **master** database
Logins synchronization in HA	Manual(Always On)	Manual(Geo-Replication)
View all logins	You can query sys.server_principals	Query sys.sql_logins in the master database
Fixed Server role for creating databases	**Dbcreator**	**create dbmanager, a** database role in the **master** database
Command to create a database	CREATE DATABASE	CREATE DATABASE with a set of limitation in the parameter usage
To list all the databases	Query sys.databases	Query sys.databases, and you must connect to the master database

How to view the roles and permissions in Azure SQL server instance

To view logins on your Azure SQL Database server, use the master database and query sys.sql_logins views. To list all the logins and databases on your Azure SQL Database server, run the following SQL.

Copy the script from
https://github.com/AzureDP300/AzureDP300/blob/main/Chapter11/Script3.sql

Data Integrity in Azure SQL Database

Azure SQL databases, by default, the page CHECKSUM option is enabled for database consistency checks. CHECKSUM is calculated and stored at the page level (not at each row-level), providing high-level data integrity.

You can run DBCC CHECKDB to check the database consistency errors. No repair option is available.

```
-- Check the current database.

DBCC CHECKDB;

GO

-- Check the mydemodp300 database without nonclustered indexes

DBCC CHECKDB (mydemodp300, NOINDEX);

GO

--Checking the current database, suppressing informational messages

DBCC CHECKDB WITH NO_INFOMSGS,PHYSICAL_ONLY;

GO
```

----Checking the current database, with informational messages

DBCC CHECKDB WITH ALL_ERRORMSGS,PHYSICAL_ONLY;

GO

```
----Checking the current database, with informational messages
DBCC CHECKDB WITH ALL_ERRORMSGS,PHYSICAL_ONLY;
GO

100 %

Messages
DBCC results for 'mydemodp300'.
CHECKDB found 0 allocation errors and 0 consistency errors in database 'mydemodp300'.
DBCC execution completed. If DBCC printed error messages, contact your system administrator.

Completion time: 2021-02-22T16:43:20.5852554-06:00
```

1. Azure SQL Database engineering team build automation to perform tests on database backup periodically. If automation does not fix the problem, they will work directly with the customer to seamless the data restoration process.

2. The automatic page repair feature uses SQL Server database mirroring and availability groups to fix and repair the pages automatically.

3. The Azure engineering team handles the data corruption incidents with the highest-severity and highest-priority—24x7 support model takes integrity with the highest importance to minimize unavailability and minimize data loss.

Query Azure SQL Database with AD Universal MFA Authentication using PowerShell

This section provides a PowerShell program that connects to Azure SQL Database. The program uses interactive mode authentication, which supports Azure AD Multi-Factor Authentication.

Use ADO.NET objects.

1. As ADO.NET is an integral part of the .NET framework, PowerShell can access .NET objects; no additional objects reference require executing a database query.
2. Browse Azure SQL Database.
3. Locate **Connection strings** under the **settings** option.
4. Copy the connection string **ADO.NET (Active Directory password authentication).**

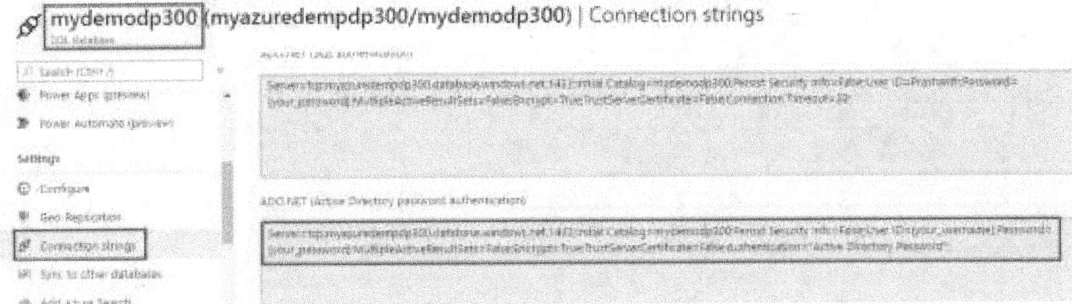

5. Open the PowerShell ISE and copy and paste the below PowerShell script.

    a. Build the connection string

    b. Prepare the query

    c. Load the data

    d. Display the data

6. Change the script as per your connection setting.

Copy the script from
https://github.com/AzureDP300/AzureDP300/blob/main/Chapter11/Script4.ps1

```
#define the connection string
$SqlConnection.ConnectionString = "Data Source=TCP:mydemodb3001d.database.windows.net,1433;Initial Catalog=Analytics;
User ID=pjayaram@domain.com;Password=thanvitha@2021
;MultipleActiveResultSets=False;Connect Timeout=30;Encrypt=True;TrustServerCertificate=False;
Authentication='Active Directory Password';Application Name='MyTest'"
#Prepare the query
$SqlQuery = 'SELECT TOP(10) * FROM [dbo].[device]'
# Build a connection to Azure SQL database.
$SqlConnection = New-Object System.Data.SqlClient.SqlConnection
#Represents a Transact-SQL statement or stored procedure to execute against a SQL Server database.Next, let us set up
$SqlCmd = New-Object System.Data.SqlClient.SqlCommand
$SqlCmd.CommandText = $SqlQuery
$SqlCmd.Connection = $SqlConnection
#Use SqlCommand of the SqlConnection object to add $Query data to the CommandText property.
$SqlAdapter = New-Object System.Data.SqlClient.SqlDataAdapter
$SqlAdapter.SelectCommand = $SqlCmd
$DataSet = New-Object System.Data.DataSet

#the SqlDataAdapter class creates an in-memory table fill a dataset with the data that are extracted from the SQL serv
$SqlAdapter.Fill($DataSet)
#Display the result
$DataSet.Tables[0] |Format-Table -AutoSize
```

```
   ID Uuid                                 UserIdName         UserIdId LocationGroupIdName UserName EnrollmentStatus IsSuperv
   -- ----                                 ----------         -------- ------------------- -------- ---------------- --------
 5501 e8a718c2-940f-4b7b-9bfd-213319146500 Jose J Pelayo         19209 FL iPad             03234556 Enrolled         0
 5676 0030cae3-61e5-4d8f-b3d0-ca00fa8a6947 Anthony Battaglia      6906 PBC Fanny           01170477 Enrolled         0
 5847 d1996eb6-05e9-4605-86fe-27c0d73a59c6 Dustin Finn            5317 Corporate           01168562 Enrolled         0
 6037 b24c30fa-1ae4-4625-9872-ef6a3a60f45b Sean Nelson           16568 PBC Fanny           01144144 Enrolled         0
 6366 4a6fe349-da8f-40ae-a703-0da2ccbbc27d Alina Osipova         45707 FL iPad             71048723 Enrolled         0
 6940 9fac9051-26f0-44f5-8787-a0534890fb3a Ulises Miranda         9223 FL iPad             03346762 Enrolled         0
10829 1c8bb598-93ec-4cb5-945f-0bc7f6754cf3 Chen-Fang  Wu         16907 PBC Delivery        10113935 Enrolled         0
11431 02eedb86-ed51-44dd-9ae2-972e085bc80f George Guzzarde       14417 PBC Briefcase       11010480 Enrolled         0
11435 95512558-3f5a-4ce1-9b52-ded6c909eb69 Janine Johnson        14416 PBC Briefcase BYOD  11012290 Enrolled         0
12127 bedcac53-c046-431e-81ff-c30ee05a7b70 Brett Shelhimer        6364 FL iPad             03240563 Enrolled         0
```

How to report free database space in Azure SQL Database

Understanding the following, storage space quantities are essential to manage the space on Azure SQL Database.

1. Data space used -The space used to store data in 8 KB pages.
2. Data space allocated - The formatted file space made available for storing data.
3. Data space allocated but unused -The difference between the data space allocated and data space used.
4. Data max size - The maximum space that a database can grow and used for storing data.

Note: Azure SQL Database does not automatically shrink data files to reclaim unused allocated space. However, it automatically shrinks log files since that operation does not affect database performance.

There are different methods to get the data:

1. Azure Portal
2. Query master database using sys.resource_stats
3. Query individual user database using sys.database_files

Data storage using Azure Portal

1. Browse the Azure Portal to locate the Azure SQL Server.
2. Go to Azure SQL database and click Overview.
3. Scroll down to the overview blade to see the database data storage.

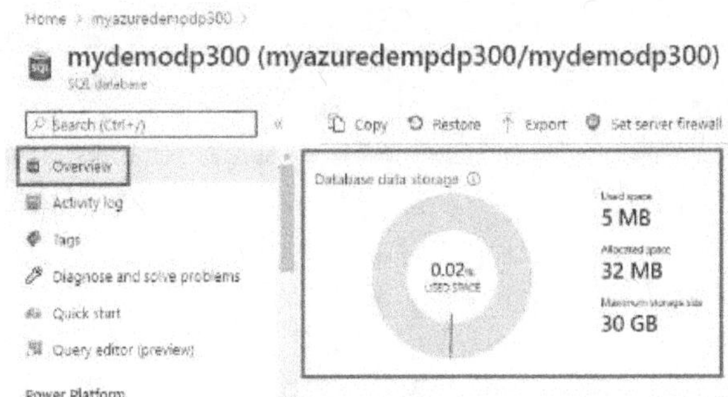

Data storage details using T-SQL

Query sys.resource_stats view on master database to get data space usage details:

```
-- Connect to master

SELECT  top 1 storage_in_megabytes AS DatabaseDataSpaceUsedInMB

FROM sys.resource_stats

WHERE database_name = 'mydemodp300'

ORDER BY end_time DESC
```

Query the individual database using sys.database_files

Copy the script from
https://github.com/AzureDP300/AzureDP300/blob/main/Chapter11/Script5.sql

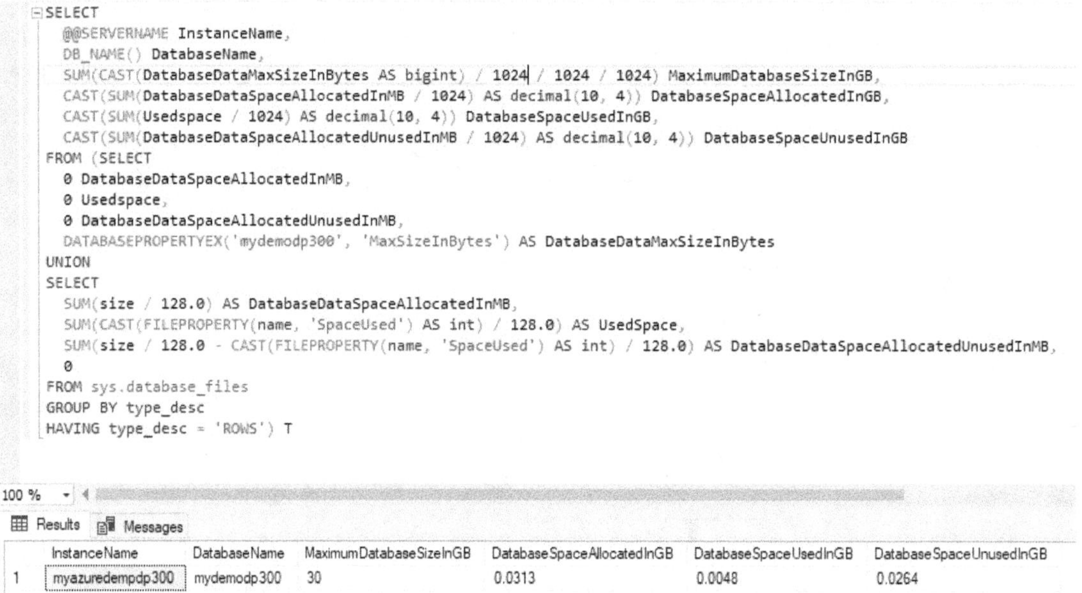

SELECT
@@SERVERNAME InstanceName,
DB_NAME() DatabaseName,
SUM(CAST(DatabaseDataMaxSizeInBytes AS bigint) / 1024 / 1024 / 1024) MaximumDatabaseSizeInGB,
CAST(SUM(DatabaseDataSpaceAllocatedInMB / 1024) AS decimal(10, 4)) DatabaseSpaceAllocatedInGB,
CAST(SUM(Usedspace / 1024) AS decimal(10, 4)) DatabaseSpaceUsedInGB,
CAST(SUM(DatabaseDataSpaceAllocatedUnusedInMB / 1024) AS decimal(10, 4)) DatabaseSpaceUnusedInGB
FROM (SELECT
0 DatabaseDataSpaceAllocatedInMB,
0 Usedspace,
0 DatabaseDataSpaceAllocatedUnusedInMB,
DATABASEPROPERTYEX('mydemodp300', 'MaxSizeInBytes') AS DatabaseDataMaxSizeInBytes
UNION
SELECT
SUM(size / 128.0) AS DatabaseDataSpaceAllocatedInMB,
SUM(CAST(FILEPROPERTY(name, 'SpaceUsed') AS int) / 128.0) AS UsedSpace,
SUM(size / 128.0 - CAST(FILEPROPERTY(name, 'SpaceUsed') AS int) / 128.0) AS DatabaseDataSpaceAllocatedUnusedInMB,
0
FROM sys.database_files
GROUP BY type_desc
HAVING type_desc = 'ROWS') T
100 %
Results
Messages
InstanceName
DatabaseName
MaximumDatabaseSizeInGB
DatabaseSpaceAllocatedInGB
DatabaseSpaceUsedInGB
DatabaseSpaceUnusedInGB
1
myazuredempdp300
mydemodp300
30
0.0313
0.0048
0.0264

Accelerated Database Recovery (ADR)

Accelerated Database Recovery (ADR) is a database recovery solution that significantly improves database availability, especially in the presence of long-running transactions. ADR is currently available for Azure SQL Database; Azure SQL Managed Instance; Azure Synapse Analytics database, and SQL Server on Azure VMs starting with SQL Server 2019.

1. With ADR, you can see a fast and consistent database recovery. The long-running transactions do not impact the database's overall recovery time.
2. It enables a fast and consistent database recovery process irrespective of the number of active transactions and transaction sizes.
3. It supports instant transaction rollback.
4. The transaction log is dynamically managed and aggressively truncated, which prevents it from growing out of control.

Note: By default, ADR is enabled in Azure SQL Database and Azure SQL Managed Instance. It is not possible to disable ADR for either product is not supported. ADR is off by default in SQL Server 2019 or SQL on Azure VM.

Summary

In this chapter, you learnt how to manage and administrate Azure SQL database using T-SQL, PowerShell and Azure Portal. To manage SQL on Azure requires you not only to understand how to manage efficiently using Portal but also to learn other methods.

Given this, you must ensure to know how to use the available tools to help you find and configure SQL on Azure. This chapter helps you to take a step closer to manage Azure database infrastructure for better performance.

Chapter 12 Unified Azure SQL management

Azure SQL is a modern platform that provides simple discovery, creation, and management by unifying SQL Server offerings in Azure.

- The unified management experience eliminates the complexity of managing diverse collections of Azure SQL resources.
- It provides seamless lift-and-shift migrations.
- Modernization of existing applications in building modern cloud services.

Azure SQL or SQL virtual machines in the Azure marketplace help you quickly locate the intended resource based on the needs with simple navigation and guided experience to see all the resources.

The unified experience suite helps discover the SQL resources quickly, and it is a great user experience to browse the traditional SQL resources.

The unified, central view offers an overview and manages all Azure SQL resources.

Automatic SQL VM resource provider registration

The registration process will register all available SQL VMs with the SQL VM resource provider in an automatic lightweight-mode subscription. In addition, it will also register any SQL VMs deployed to the subscription in the near future. This process does not restart the SQL Server service.

Microsoft recommends upgrading all SQL VMs to **full-mode** to take full advantage of SQL unified features.

To unblock the entire feature, you need to register SQL VM with the SQL IaaS Agent extension. This process requires a restart of the SQL Server service.

Registering SQL Server on Azure virtual machines (VMs) with the SQL VM resource provider has several advantages:

1. Automatic Monitoring
2. Automatic Patching
3. Automated Backup
4. Unlocking licensing edition flexibility

5. Build High Availability

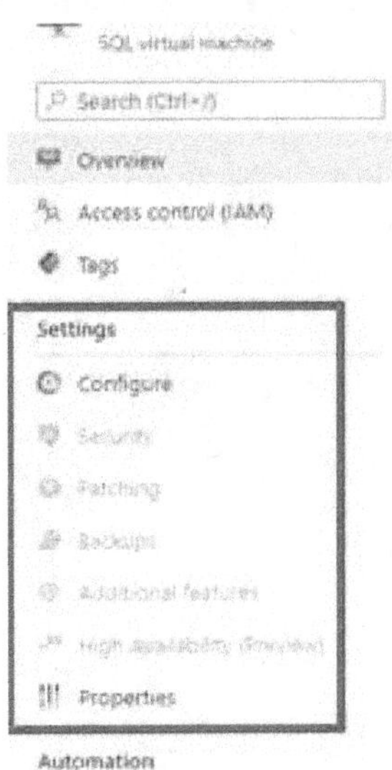

The capabilities provided will expand over time, as Microsoft will continue to add new benefits over time.

Pre-requisites:

To register SQL Server VM with the extension, you will need:

- An Azure subscription
- To check the role, browse the subscription, go to access control (IAM) and select Roles. You must have a Contributor role

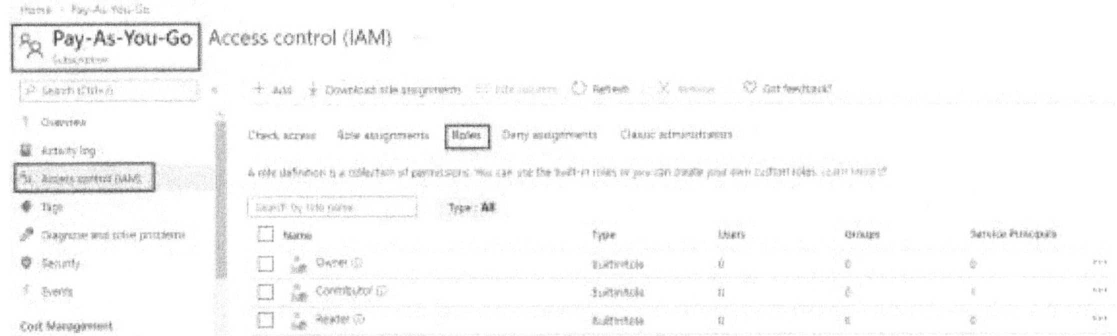

- An Azure Resource Model with Windows Server 2008 R2 (or later) virtual machine with SQL Server.

Enable automatic registration

To enable automatic registration of SQL Server VMs in the Azure portal, follow these steps:

1. login to Azure portal.
2. Browse **SQL virtual machines** resource page.
3. Select **Automatic SQL Server VM registration** to open the **Automatic registration** page.

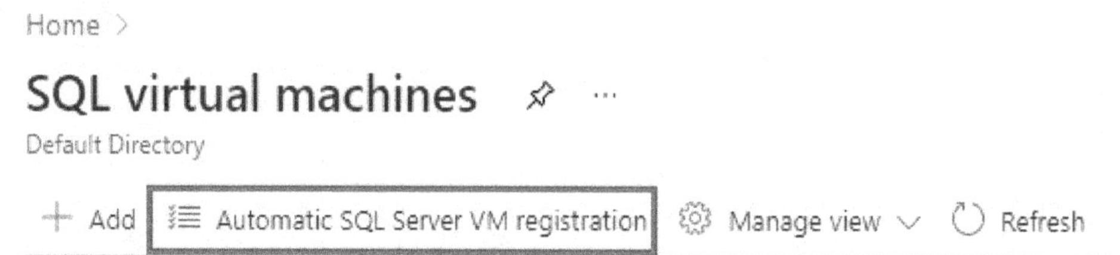

4. Choose the subscription.
5. To accept the terms and conditions, click, **I accept**.
6. Select **Register** to enable the feature and SQL Server VMs with the SQL IaaS Agent extension.
7. It will not restart the SQL Server service on any of the VMs.

Automatic SQL Server VM registration

SQL virtual machine

Registering SQL Server on Azure virtual machines (VMs) with the SQL VM resource provider has several advantages including monitoring and manageability capabilities (such as automated patching and automated backup), as well as unlocking licensing and edition flexibility. The capabilities provided will expand over time as Microsoft will continue to add new benefits over time. Learn more

Automatic SQL VM resource provider registration

The automatic registration of a subscription will register all currently available SQL VMs with the SQL VM resource provider in lightweight mode as well as any SQL VMs deployed to the subscription in the future. This process does not restart the SQL Server service. Manually upgrading to full manageability mode is recommended to take advantage of the full feature set. Learn more

Subscription *

EULA

I accept the terms in the agreement *

By clicking "I accept", I confirm that I have authority to enter into agreements on behalf of the above subscription ID, and I consent to allow Microsoft to access SQL Server environment information on all Azure Virtual Machines belonging to the above subscription ID. Furthermore, I permit Microsoft to register all SQL Server instances with the SQL VM resource provider as described here. Learn more

To learn more about SQL Server data processing and privacy controls, please see the SQL Server Privacy Supplement. Learn more

Register Cancel

Register SQL Server VM with SQL IaaS Agent Extension

You automatically register SQL Server with the extension when you deploy a SQL Server on Azure VM via Azure Marketplace image.

However, in most cases, SQL Server is built using a custom image or provision of an Azure virtual machine from a custom VHD. In such a case, you must register your SQL Server VM with the SQL IaaS Agent extension to unlock full feature benefits and manageability.

To register SQL Server VM with SQL IaaS Agent extension, you must first register your subscription with **Microsoft.SqlVirtualMachine** provider. You can register the extension using Azure Portal:

1. Log in to the Azure portal
2. **Locate All Services**
3. Go to **Subscriptions, list the subscription and go to extensions**
4. Type in **SQL** to bring up the SQL related extensions

5. Select **Register**, **Re-register**, or **Unregister** for the **Microsoft.SqlVirtualMachine** provider

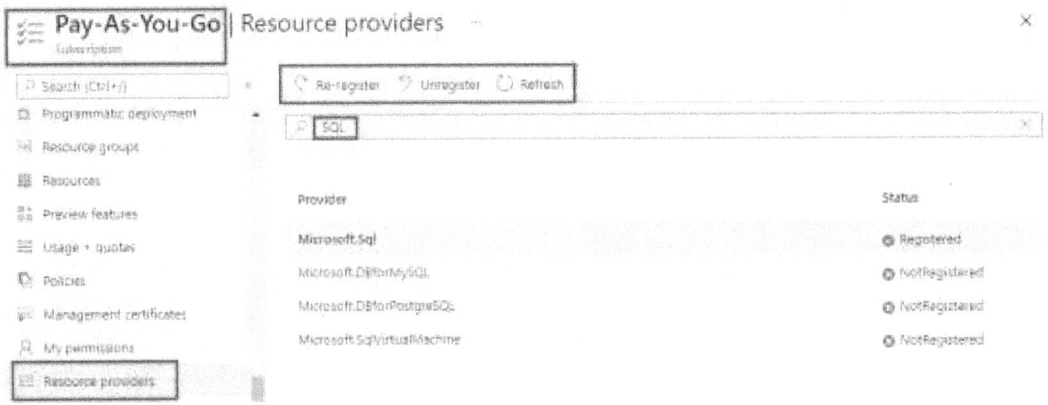

Update SQL on Azure VM to Full mode using Azure Portal

To upgrade the full mode using the Azure portal, follow these steps:

1. Sign in to the Azure portal.
2. Go to SQL virtual machines resource.
3. Select SQL Server VM and click **Overview**.
4. Click **Only license type, and edition updates are available with the SQL IaaS extension** message.

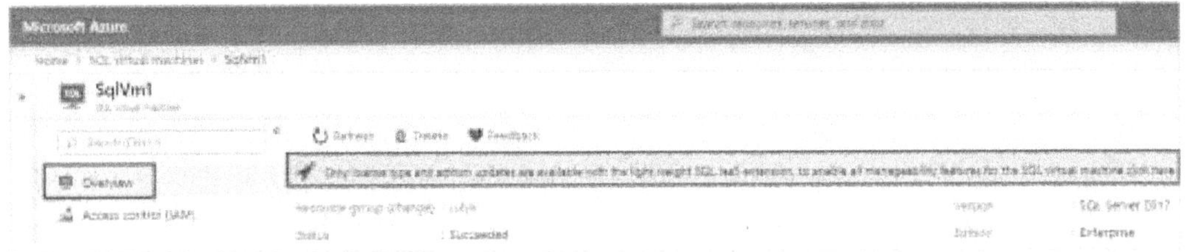

5. Select **I agree to restart the SQL Server service on the virtual machine** check box, and then **Confirm** to upgrade SQL Server to full mode.

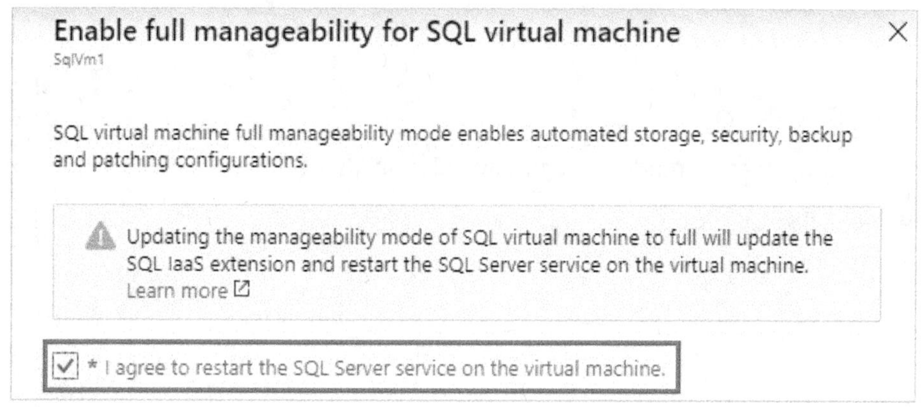

Update SQL on Azure VM to Full mode using PowerShell

To register your SQL Server VM in full mode, run the following Azure PowerShell command:

Get the existing Compute VM

$vm = Get-AzVM -Name <vm_name> -ResourceGroupName <resource_group_name>

Register with SQL IaaS Agent extension in full mode

Update-AzSqlVM -Name $vm.Name -ResourceGroupName $vm.ResourceGroupName -SqlManagementType Full

After the update, restart the SQL Server service.

Verify registration status using PowerShell

To view SQL Server VM registration with the extension status, run the following cmdlet:

Get the existing Compute VM

Get-AzVM -Name <vm_name> -ResourceGroupName <resource_group_name>

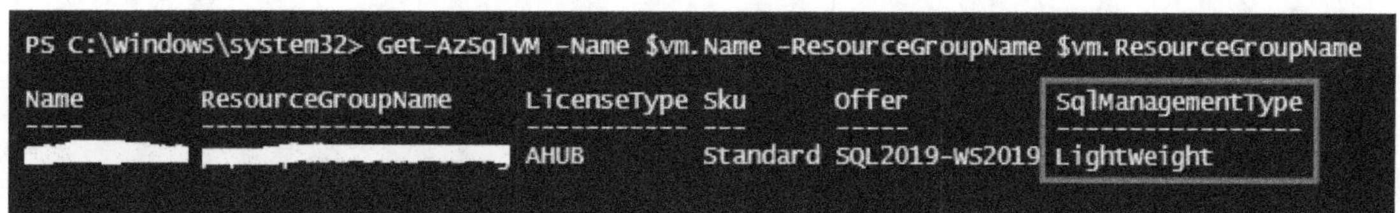

Look into the future.

Azure SQL engineering team already making several significant advancements to build on the unified foundation suite.

Feature	Full Mode	Lightweight Mode
Central portal management of SQL Server VMs	Yes	Yes
Automate the backup schedule	Yes	No
Automated patching for important Windows and SQL Server Security updates.	Yes	No
Azure Key Vault integration for SQL Server VM	Yes	No
Graphical representation of disk utilization in the portal	Yes	No
Flexible licensing transitioning from various supported models	Yes	Yes
Flexible version or edition upgrade Process	Yes	No

Summary

This chapter covered the Unified Azure SQL management using the SQL Server IaaS agent extension using Azure portal, Azure PowerShell and Azure CLI. We also looked at the future roadmap to build on the unified foundation suite.

As the company business grows, it is the database administrator's responsibility to keep track of the data storage and retrieval speed to provide your clients' best performance. Suppose the system administrator starts complaining about the physical limitation in the hosting machines resources or the time it takes to purchase new resources. In that case, it is the best time to take the idea of moving the SQL workload to Microsoft Azure to the next management meeting.

Planning

Before the discussion with the management team, you should be prepared and ready for any question. It can be achieved by performing a comprehensive study. The study includes the current site problems and limitations, a plan for the design and implementation phases of the migration process, and the benefits that the company will gain from moving that workload to Azure from all performance business growth handling and cost.

In addition, you need to have a look at the cloud solutions that can be used to replace the current on-premises site. It includes learning the features available in each service, and each service's pros and cons to identify which service meets your requirements.

Before choosing the suitable Microsoft Azure database service that meets your requirements, you need to specify the suitable Azure platform. Microsoft Azure provides two high-level platform options: Infrastructure as a Services, also known as IaaS and Platform as a Service, also known as PaaS. The platform choice specifies the Azure services that can be used and the control you can have over that platform's services.

For example, choosing the IaaS database platform, such as SQL Server on Azure Virtual Machine, you are renting the IT infrastructure servers and virtual machines from the cloud provider. It includes storage, networks, and operating systems. With this platform, you are still responsible for and have control over the Operating System layer and all layers over the OS, including installing the services, the operating system patching, and so on.

On the other hand, the PaaS database platform, Azure SQL Database, Azure SQL Managed Instance(transactional SQL workload), Azure Cosmos DB (No-SQL transactional workload), and Azure Synapse Analytics (for analytical workload) provides you with the ability of building, testing, and deploying your applications without worrying about the underlying infrastructure management. In other words, you are not responsible for installing an operating system or patching the machine with the latest security and system updates.

Migration tools

Microsoft Azure supports several migration assistant tools that can be used to provide guidance steps for the migration process and assess the existing environment for any changes that should be performed before migrating the SQL workload to Microsoft Azure.

The **Azure Database Migration Guide** provides us with a comprehensive guide for designing and implementing the database workload migration process and migration assistance tools and programs. It includes the pre-migration steps, such as discovering the current workload and listing the required transformation and conversion steps to meet the target schema.

It also provides us with the steps that should be performed during the migration process, such as databases migrating and synchronizing, and post-migration tasks, such as connecting the application to the new target database and testing all its functionalities performance.

It can be accessed by browsing the https://datamigration.microsoft.com/ address, then select the data source and target from the list of supported data sources:

- Microsoft SQL Server
- Oracle
- DB2
- MySQL
- PostgreSQL
- MongoDB
- Cassandra
- MariaDB
- Access
- SAP ASE
- Microsoft Azure Table Storage:

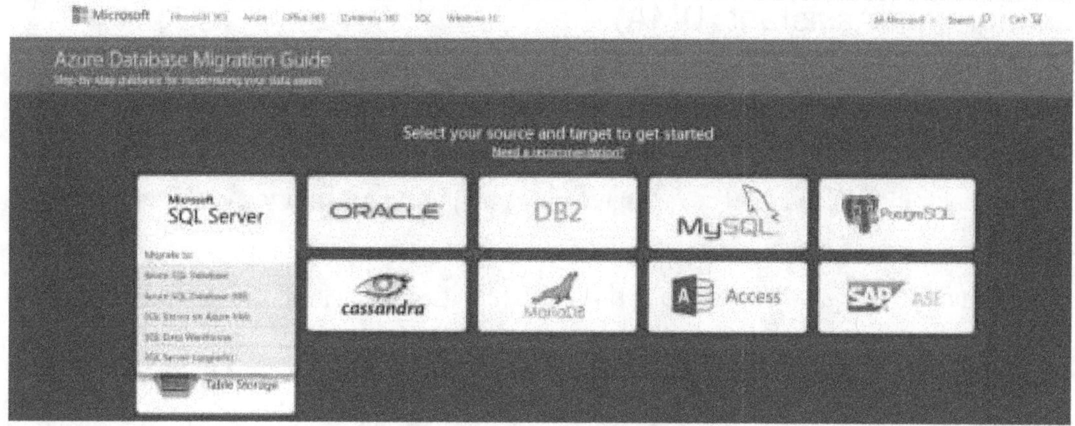

Microsoft Assessment and Planning Toolkit

The **Microsoft Assessment and Planning Toolkit** is used to check whether the current environment is ready to be migrated to the new on-prem or cloud environment by providing the required inventory, assessment, and reporting resources that help in the migration process.

To use the Microsoft Assessment and Planning Toolkit, you need to download it from the Microsoft Download page, install it to the machine and create an inventory database to store the collected information. Once you have the inventory created, you need to go through the Inventory and Assessment Wizard to initiate the discovery process, then review the returned changes that should be performed before migrating to the required data source:

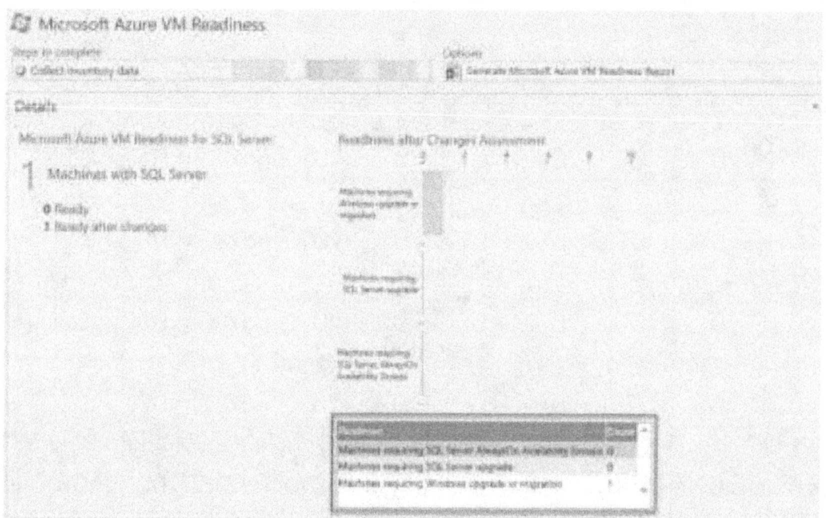

Data Migration Assistant (DMA)

The **Data Migration Assistant (DMA)** is used to check for any compatibility issue that may affect the database functionality when migrating the databases to a new SQL Server version or Azure SQL Database. It helps identify the current version features that are not supported in the target version or in the cloud, the new features in the new version you can take advantage of, and the recommendations that may enhance the performance and the reliability in the target version.

After providing all the useful information, the Data Migration Assistant helps in migrating the on-premises current version. It can migrate any SQL Server installed on a Windows machine with version 2005 and later, to a newer database platform version, SQL Server instance installed on Windows or Linux with version 2012, or to Azure SQL Database.

You need to download the Data Migration Assistant from the Microsoft Download center and install it on your machine. Once installed, you need to create a new assessment project to confirm it does not have migration blockers. You will be required to specify whether to check for database compatibility, features parity and the benefits from the new features. In addition, you need to specify the data source that will be checked using the Data Migration Assistant tool for any migration blockers.

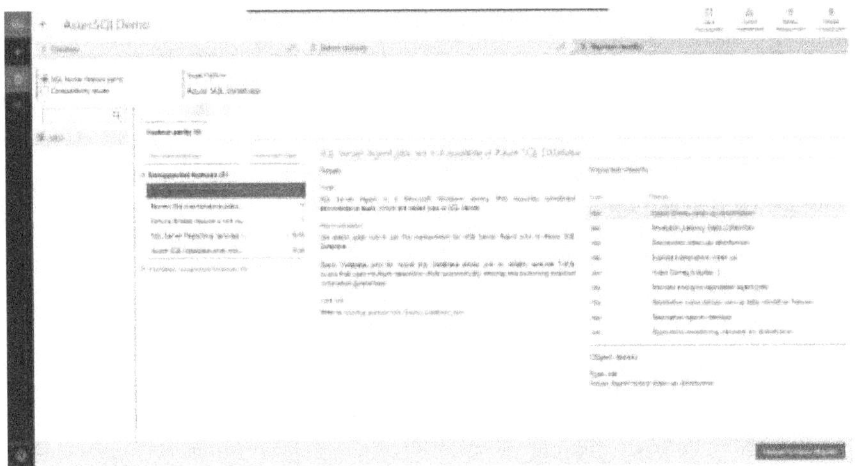

The Azure Database Migrate service allows us to perform online or offline database migration from a large scale of database sources, including SQL Server, MySQL, Oracle, DB2, MongoDB and PostgreSQL, to Microsoft Azure Data platform using the Azure Portal and with minimal downtime.

It generates the assessment reports and provides pre-migration steps using a built-in copy of the Database Migration Assistant tool.

To use the Azure Database Migrate service to migrate the databases to Microsoft Azure, you need to perform the following:

- Register Microsoft.DataMigration resource provider under your subscription,
- Create a new Azure Database Migration Service instance using the Azure Portal,
- Create a new migration project.

In the migration project, you will be requested to provide the following:

- The source type,
- Whether to perform online or offline data migration,
- The data source connection string,
- The target connection string,

After providing the required information, you should map the source and target databases and configure the different migration settings. The migration process status can be easily monitored within the Azure Portal:

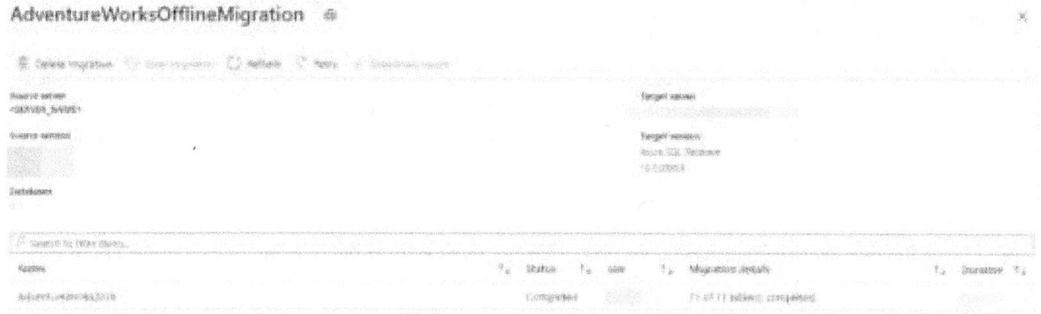

Azure Migrate Service

Azure Migrate Service is used to assess and migrate on-premises virtual machines with its infrastructure, applications, and database to Microsoft Azure. It provides a recommendation for the destination Azure Virtual machine's size to migrate to and the estimated monthly cost for running your virtual machine in Azure. Also, it helps in migrating the virtual machine to Azure with high confidence.

Azure Migrate Service consists of built-in tools that are used to perform the assessment and migration process. It includes the following:

- The Server Assessment tool to discover and assess on-premises VMS,
- The Server Migration to migrate the VM servers,
- The Data Migration Assistant to identify any migration blocking issue,
- The Azure Database Migration Service to migrate the on-premises databases to Microsoft Azure Database platform,
- The Web App Migration Assistant used to assess on-premises websites,
- The Azure Data Box to migrate large amounts of offline data to Microsoft Azure.

The Azure Migrate Service tool can be used to migrate the databases from On-premises to Microsoft Azure by creating a new project, using Azure Portal, and select the tools that will be used to assess or migrate the database:

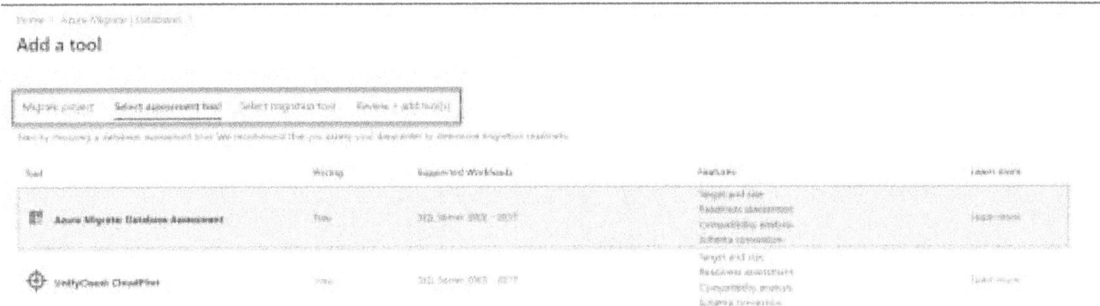

Migrate to a SQL Server instance on an Azure VM

After specifying the Azure database target service and the tool that will be used for assessment and migration, you need to specify the migration strategy based on the confirmed downtime. Make sure that you already performed all compatibility and assessment checks.

If you plan to migrate your on-premises database to a SQL Server instance on an Azure Virtual Machine, you can perform an offline database migration by:

- Taking a compressed database backup from the on-premises SQL Server database,
- Copying it to the Azure VM or set the Azure Blob Container URL as the backup target,
- Restoring it to the SQL Server instance hosted in the Azure VM.

Other options that can be used to migrate a database to a SQL Server instance hosted on an Azure VM includes:

- Detaching the database from the on-premises SQL Server instance, copying it directly to the VM or an Azure Blob Storage, and attaching it to the VM SQL instance.
- Converting the on-premises physical machine to Hyper-V VHD, uploading that VHD to Azure Blob storage, and deploying the VHD as a new Microsoft Azure VM.

If the migration process should be performed with the minimum possible downtime, you can configure an Always On Availability Group in the on-premises SQL Server instance. After that, you need to add the target Azure VM as a replica, then perform a failover to make the SQL Server instance hosted in the Azure VM as the primary replica.

An alternative method is to configure a SQL Server Transactional Replication with the on-premises SQL Server instance as the publisher and the SQL Server instance hosted in the Azure VM as the subscriber. Once the two databases are synchronized, the replication site can be disabled.

Migrate to an Azure SQL Database

If you plan to migrate your on-premises databases to an Azure SQL Database, you need to select the migration method that meets your migration requirements. Make sure that you already perform all compatibility and assessment checks ahead.

If this is not a business-critical database migration process that tolerates downtime, you can use the Data Migration Assistant tool. This tool helps in assessing the on-premises SQL Server database for any compatibility or migration blocking issue. It helps also fix these blockers and migrate the consistent database to a single or pooled Azure SQL Database.

Also, you can use the BACPAC method. In this method, you import the on-premises SQL Server database into the Azure SQL Database using a BACPAC file that is generated from the source database and stored in an Azure Blob Storage.

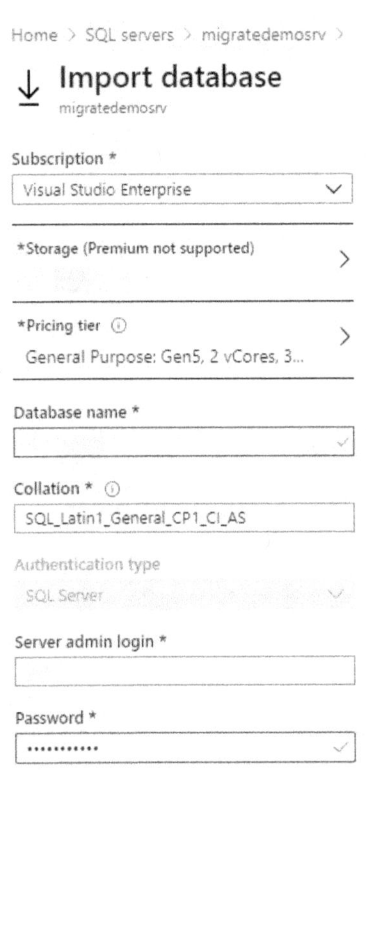

If your database migration to Azure SQL Database is business-critical and cannot tolerate downtime, you can use the SQL Server Transactional Replication. You need to configure the on-premises database as a publisher, the Azure SQL Database as a subscriber, then disable the replication after the two databases are in sync state.

Migrate to an Azure SQL Database Managed Instance

If you plan to migrate your database to the Azure PaaS database platform, you need to migrate your database to an Azure SQL Database Managed Instance. In this way, you will take advantage of all PaaS benefits, such as SQL Server Agent jobs and cross-database queries, without performing many changes to the on-premises SQL Server database.

After using the assessment tools to identify any migration blocker, you can choose the appropriate migration method based on the available downtime. If you are migrating a business-critical database, migrate your database to the Azure SQL Database Managed Instance using the Azure Database Migration Service.

If your database migration can tolerate downtime, you can use the Backup and Restore method. In this method, a backup is taken from the on-premises SQL database with the Azure Blob Storage URL as the backup target and restored to the Azure SQL Database Managed Instance from that blob storage.

Refer to link **https://github.com/AzureDP300/AzureDP300/blob/main/Chapter14/RefLinks.html** for detailed information on Database Migration to Azure database platforms

Summary

This chapter converts the various SQL Migrations to Microsoft Azure using the Microsoft Assessment and Planning toolkit (MAP), Data Migration Assistant (DMA), Azure Migrate Service. We also covered the migration of SQL Server to Azure VM, Azure SQL Database and Azure SQL Managed Instance.

Chapter 14 Practice tests with direct and scenario related questions

The Administering Relational Databases on Microsoft Azure certificate exam measures your intermediate-level knowledge on seven main areas. This includes:

- How to plan and implement data platform resources, with relative questions weight in the exam up to 20%
- How to implement a secure environment, with relative questions weight in the exam up to 20%
- How to monitor and optimize operational resources, with relative questions weight in the exam up to 20%
- How to optimize query performance, with relative questions weight in the exam up to 10%
- How to perform automation of tasks, with relative questions weight in the exam up to 15%
- How to plan and implement a High Availability and Disaster Recovery (HADR) environment, with relative questions weight in the exam up to 20%
- How to perform administration by using T-SQL, with relative questions weight in the exam up to 15%

Before you start preparing for this course, it is recommended to have basic knowledge in:

- Operating system and virtualization concepts, such as Virtual Machines, virtual networking, and virtual hard disks
- The SQL Server Network configurations, such as TCP/IP, DNS, virtual, VPNs, firewalls, and in-transit encryption
- SQL Server database creation, management, and configuration
- Performing different administration tasks and querying using T-SQL language
- SQL Server table and index types and structures

Certificate Candidate

With most large companies moving their data to the cloud, it is the best time for the database administrators to validate their knowledge in the Microsoft Azure data platform.

The Administering Relational Databases on Microsoft Azure exam is designed as an intermediate level exam for the relational database administrators and data management specialists interested in starting their journey in administering the relational databases hosted in Microsoft Azure.

To become an Azure Database Administrator, you need to have the proper skills to implement and manage the different aspects of the data platform solutions that are built on Microsoft Azure data services and the on-premises Microsoft SQL Server, including the databases availability, security, performance monitoring and optimization.

Study Guidelines

Plan and Implement Data Platform Resources

In this module, you will be measured in the skills below:

- Deploy resources by using manual methods:

Measured Skills	Useful Links
Create SQL Server on a virtual machine in the Azure portal	https://docs.microsoft.com/en-us/azure/azure-sql/virtual-machines/windows/sql-vm-create-portal-quickstart
Create SQL Server on a Windows virtual machine with Azure PowerShell	https://docs.microsoft.com/en-us/azure/azure-sql/virtual-machines/windows/sql-vm-create-powershell-quickstart
Create SQL Server VM using an ARM template	https://docs.microsoft.com/en-us/azure/azure-sql/virtual-machines/windows/create-sql-vm-resource-manager-template?tabs=CLI
Create an Azure SQL Database single database	https://docs.microsoft.com/en-us/azure/azure-sql/database/single-database-create-quickstart?tabs=azure-portal

Create a single database in Azure SQL Database using an ARM template	https://docs.microsoft.com/en-us/azure/azure-sql/database/single-database-create-arm-template-quickstart
Elastic pools help you manage and scale multiple databases in Azure SQL Database	https://docs.microsoft.com/en-us/azure/azure-sql/database/elastic-pool-overview
Create a managed instance of SQL Managed Instance	https://docs.microsoft.com/en-us/azure/azure-sql/managed-instance/instance-create-quickstart
Use PowerShell to create a managed instance	https://docs.microsoft.com/en-us/azure/azure-sql/managed-instance/scripts/create-configure-managed-instance-powershell
Create an Azure SQL Managed Instance using an ARM template	https://docs.microsoft.com/en-us/azure/azure-sql/managed-instance/create-template-quickstart?tabs=azure-powershell
Deploy Azure SQL Managed Instance to an instance pool	https://docs.microsoft.com/en-us/azure/azure-sql/managed-instance/instance-pools-configure
Deploy MariaDB, MySQL, and PostgreSQL on Azure	https://docs.microsoft.com/en-us/learn/modules/deploy-mariadb-mysql-postgresql-azure/

Recommend an appropriate database offering based on specific requirements:

Measured Skills	**Useful Links**
What is Azure SQL?	https://docs.microsoft.com/en-us/azure/azure-sql/azure-sql-iaas-vs-paas-what-is-overview
What is Azure SQL Database?	https://docs.microsoft.com/en-us/azure/azure-sql/database/sql-database-paas-overview
What is Azure SQL Managed Instance?	https://docs.microsoft.com/en-us/azure/azure-sql/managed-instance/sql-managed-instance-paas-overview
SQL Server on Azure VM.	https://docs.microsoft.com/en-us/azure/azure-sql/virtual-machines/windows/create-sql-vm-resource-manager-template?tabs=CLI
An overview of Azure SQL Database and SQL Managed Instance security capabilities	https://docs.microsoft.com/en-us/azure/azure-sql/database/security-overview

Configure resources for scale and performance:

Measured Skills	Useful Links
Scaling out with Azure SQL Database	https://docs.microsoft.com/en-us/azure/azure-sql/database/elastic-scale-introduction
Scale elastic pool resources in Azure SQL Database	https://docs.microsoft.com/en-us/azure/azure-sql/database/elastic-pool-scale
Tune applications and databases for performance in Azure SQL Database and Azure SQL Managed Instance	https://docs.microsoft.com/en-us/azure/azure-sql/database/performance-guidance
Performance guidelines for SQL Server on Azure Virtual Machines	https://docs.microsoft.com/en-us/azure/azure-sql/virtual-machines/windows/performance-guidelines-best-practices
Storage and SQL Server capacity planning	https://docs.microsoft.com/en-us/sharepoint/administration/storage-and-sql-server-capacity-planning-and-configuration
Sharding pattern	https://docs.microsoft.com/en-us/azure/architecture/patterns/sharding

Evaluate a strategy for moving to Azure:

Measured Skills	Useful Links
Perform a SQL Server migration assessment with Data Migration Assistant	https://docs.microsoft.com/en-us/sql/dma/dma-assesssqlonprem?view=sql-server-ver15
Assess the readiness of a SQL Server data estate migrating to Azure SQL Database using the Data Migration Assistant	https://docs.microsoft.com/en-us/sql/dma/dma-assess-sql-data-estate-to-sqldb?view=sql-server-ver15
Supported version & edition upgrades	https://docs.microsoft.com/en-us/sql/database-engine/install-windows/supported-version-and-edition-upgrades-2017?view=sql-server-ver15
Migrating SQL workloads to Microsoft Azure: Planning the jump	https://github.com/AzureDP300/AzureDP300/blob/main/Chapter13/ReferenceLinks.html
Migrating SQL workloads to Microsoft Azure: Services Selection	https://github.com/AzureDP300/AzureDP300/blob/main/Chapter13/ReferenceLinks.html

Migrating SQL workloads to Microsoft Azure: Guidance and Assessment Tools	https://github.com/AzureDP300/AzureDP300/blob/main/Chapter13/ReferenceLinks.html
Migrating SQL workloads to Microsoft Azure: Assessment and Migration Tools	https://github.com/AzureDP300/AzureDP300/blob/main/Chapter13/ReferenceLinks.html

Implement a migration or upgrade strategy for moving to Azure:

Measured Skills	Useful Links
Migrate SQL Server to Azure SQL Database offline using DMS	https://docs.microsoft.com/en-us/azure/dms/tutorial-sql-server-to-azure-sql
Migrate SQL Server to a single database or pooled database in Azure SQL Database online using DMS	https://docs.microsoft.com/en-us/azure/dms/tutorial-sql-server-to-azure-sql
Manage rolling upgrades of cloud applications by using SQL Database active geo-replication	https://docs.microsoft.com/en-us/azure/azure-sql/database/manage-application-rolling-upgrade
Upgrade to a Different Edition of SQL Server	https://docs.microsoft.com/en-us/sql/database-engine/install-windows/upgrade-to-a-different-edition-of-sql-server-setup?view=sql-server-ver15
Migrating SQL workloads to Microsoft Azure: Databases Trip to SQL Server on Azure VM	https://github.com/AzureDP300/AzureDP300/blob/main/Chapter13/ReferenceLinks.html
Migrating SQL workloads to Microsoft Azure: Databases Trip to Azure SQL Database	https://github.com/AzureDP300/AzureDP300/blob/main/Chapter13/ReferenceLinks.html
Migrating SQL workloads to Microsoft Azure: Databases trip to Azure SQL Database Managed Instance	https://github.com/AzureDP300/AzureDP300/blob/main/Chapter13/ReferenceLinks.html

Implement a Secure Environment

In this module, you will be measured in the skills below:

Configure database authentication by using platform and database tools:

Measured Skills	Useful Links
Configure and manage Azure AD authentication with Azure SQL	https://docs.microsoft.com/en-us/azure/azure-sql/database/authentication-aad-configure?tabs=azure-powershell
Configure database authorization by using platform and database tools	https://docs.microsoft.com/en-us/dotnet/framework/data/adonet/sql/authorization-and-permissions-in-sql-server
Authorization and Permissions in SQL Server	https://docs.microsoft.com/en-us/dotnet/framework/data/adonet/sql/authorization-and-permissions-in-sql-server

Implement security for data at rest:

Measured Skills	Useful Links
Transparent data encryption for SQL Database, SQL Managed Instance, and Azure Synapse Analytics	https://docs.microsoft.com/en-us/azure/azure-sql/database/transparent-data-encryption-tde-overview?tabs=azure-portal
Configure Always Encrypted by using Azure Key Vault	https://docs.microsoft.com/en-us/azure/azure-sql/database/always-encrypted-azure-key-vault-configure?tabs=azure-powershell
Get started with SQL Database dynamic data masking with the Azure portal	https://docs.microsoft.com/en-us/azure/azure-sql/database/dynamic-data-masking-configure-portal
Create and encrypt a Windows virtual machine with the Azure portal	https://docs.microsoft.com/en-us/azure/virtual-machines/windows/disk-encryption-portal-quickstart

Implement security for data in transit:

Measured Skills	Useful Links

Secure a database in Azure SQL Database	https://docs.microsoft.com/en-us/azure/azure-sql/database/secure-database-tutorial
Configure Always Encrypted by using the Windows certificate store	https://docs.microsoft.com/en-us/azure/azure-sql/database/always-encrypted-certificate-store-configure
Install and configure an on-premises data gateway	https://docs.microsoft.com/en-us/azure/analysis-services/analysis-services-gateway-install?tabs=azure-portal

Implement compliance controls for sensitive data:

Measured Skills	Useful Links
Data Discovery & Classification	https://docs.microsoft.com/en-us/azure/azure-sql/database/data-discovery-and-classification-overview
Auditing for Azure SQL Database and Azure Synapse Analytics	https://docs.microsoft.com/en-us/azure/azure-sql/database/auditing-overview
Track Data Changes (SQL Server)	https://docs.microsoft.com/en-us/sql/relational-databases/track-changes/track-data-changes-sql-server?view=sql-server-ver15
SQL Vulnerability Assessment helps you identify database vulnerabilities	https://docs.microsoft.com/en-us/azure/azure-sql/database/sql-vulnerability-assessment

Monitor and Optimize Operational Resources

In this module, you will be measured in the skills below:

Monitor activity and performance:

Measured Skills	Useful Links
Establish a Performance Baseline	https://docs.microsoft.com/en-us/sql/relational-databases/performance/establish-a-performance-baseline?view=sql-server-ver15
Sources of monitoring data for Azure Monitor	https://docs.microsoft.com/en-us/azure/azure-monitor/platform/data-sources

Query Performance Insight for Azure SQL Database	https://docs.microsoft.com/en-us/azure/azure-sql/database/query-performance-insight-use
Monitoring and performance tuning in Azure SQL Database and Azure SQL Managed Instance	https://docs.microsoft.com/en-us/azure/azure-sql/database/monitor-tune-overview#sql-database-resource-monitoring
Intelligent Insights using AI to monitor and troubleshoot database performance (preview)	https://docs.microsoft.com/en-us/azure/azure-sql/database/intelligent-insights-overview

Implement performance-related maintenance tasks:

Measured Skills	Useful Links
Automating Azure SQL Database index maintenance using Elastic Job Agents	https://github.com/AzureDP300/AzureDP300/blob/main/Chapter13/ReferenceLinks.html
Update Statistics Task	https://docs.microsoft.com/en-us/sql/relational-databases/maintenance-plans/update-statistics-task-maintenance-plan?view=sql-server-ver15
Enable automatic tuning in the Azure portal to monitor queries and improve workload performance	https://docs.microsoft.com/en-us/azure/azure-sql/database/automatic-tuning-enable

Identify performance-related issues:

Measured Skills	Useful Links
Monitoring performance by using the Query Store	https://docs.microsoft.com/en-us/sql/relational-databases/performance/monitoring-performance-by-using-the-query-store?view=sql-server-ver15
Resolve and Troubleshoot SQL Blocking chains with root sessions	https://github.com/AzureDP300/AzureDP300/blob/main/Chapter13/ReferenceLinks.html
Get details of SQL Server Database Growth and Shrink Events	https://github.com/AzureDP300/AzureDP300/blob/main/Chapter13/ReferenceLinks.html
Considerations for the “autogrow” and “autoshrink” settings in SQL Server	https://support.microsoft.com/en-us/help/315512/considerations-for-the-autogrow-and-autoshrink-settings-in-sql-server

Set the AUTO_CLOSE Database Option to OFF	https://docs.microsoft.com/en-us/sql/relational-databases/policy-based-management/set-the-auto-close-database-option-to-off?view=sql-server-ver15

Configure resources for optimal performance:

Measured Skills	Useful Links
Storage configuration for SQL Server VMs	https://docs.microsoft.com/en-us/azure/azure-sql/virtual-machines/windows/storage-configuration
tempdb Database	https://docs.microsoft.com/en-us/sql/relational-databases/databases/tempdb-database?view=sql-server-ver15
Manage the size of the transaction log file	https://docs.microsoft.com/en-us/sql/relational-databases/logs/manage-the-size-of-the-transaction-log-file?view=sql-server-ver15
How to determine proper SQL Server configuration settings	https://support.microsoft.com/en-in/help/319942/how-to-determine-proper-sql-server-configuration-settings
Resource governance in Azure SQL Database	https://azure.microsoft.com/en-in/blog/resource-governance-in-azure-sql-database/'

Configure a user database for optimal performance:

Measured Skills	Useful Links
ALTER DATABASE SCOPED CONFIGURATION	https://docs.microsoft.com/en-us/sql/t-sql/statements/alter-database-scoped-configuration-transact-sql?view=sql-server-ver15
Manage compute in Azure Synapse Analytics data warehouse	https://docs.microsoft.com/en-us/azure/synapse-analytics/sql-data-warehouse/sql-data-warehouse-manage-compute-overview
Intelligent query processing in SQL databases	https://docs.microsoft.com/en-us/sql/relational-databases/performance/intelligent-query-processing?view=sql-server-ver15

Optimize Query Performance

In this module, you will be measured in the skills below:

Review query plans

Measured Skills	Useful Links
SQL Server Execution Plans types	https://github.com/AzureDP300/AzureDP300/blob/main/Chapter13/ReferenceLinks.html
How to Analyze SQL Execution Plan Graphical Components	https://github.com/AzureDP300/AzureDP300/blob/main/Chapter13/ReferenceLinks.html
SQL Server Query Store – Overview	https://github.com/AzureDP300/AzureDP300/blob/main/Chapter13/ReferenceLinks.html
Force query execution plan using SQL Server 2016 Query store	https://github.com/AzureDP300/AzureDP300/blob/main/Chapter13/ReferenceLinks.html

Evaluate performance improvements:

Measured Skills	Useful Links
Monitoring Microsoft Azure SQL Database and Azure SQL Managed Instance performance using dynamic management views	https://docs.microsoft.com/en-us/azure/azure-sql/database/monitoring-with-dmvs
SQL Server index design basics and guidelines	https://github.com/AzureDP300/AzureDP300/blob/main/Chapter13/ReferenceLinks.html
Gathering SQL Server indexes statistics and usage information	https://github.com/AzureDP300/AzureDP300/blob/main/Chapter13/ReferenceLinks.html
Maintaining SQL Server indexes	https://github.com/AzureDP300/AzureDP300/blob/main/Chapter13/ReferenceLinks.html
Tracing and tuning queries using SQL Server indexes	https://github.com/AzureDP300/AzureDP300/blob/main/Chapter13/ReferenceLinks.html
Hints (Transact-SQL) – Query	https://docs.microsoft.com/en-us/sql/t-sql/queries/hints-transact-sql-query?view=sql-server-ver15

Review the database table and index design:

Measured Skills	Useful Links
Data Matching	https://docs.microsoft.com/en-us/sql/data-quality-services/data-matching?view=sql-server-ver15
Description of the database normalization basics	https://docs.microsoft.com/en-us/office/troubleshoot/access/database-normalization-description
Improve the performance of your Azure SQL Databases using Index Advisor	https://azure.microsoft.com/en-in/blog/optimize-database-performance-using-index-advisor-7/
Data types (Transact-SQL)	https://docs.microsoft.com/en-us/sql/t-sql/data-types/data-types-transact-sql?view=sql-server-ver15
Database Files and Filegroups	https://docs.microsoft.com/en-us/sql/relational-databases/databases/database-files-and-filegroups?view=sql-server-ver15
Horizontal, vertical, and functional data partitioning	https://docs.microsoft.com/en-us/azure/architecture/best-practices/data-partitioning
Enable Compression on a Table or Index	https://docs.microsoft.com/en-us/sql/relational-databases/data-compression/enable-compression-on-a-table-or-index?view=sql-server-ver15

Perform Automation of Tasks

In this module, you will be measured in the skills below:

Create scheduled tasks:

Measured Skills	Useful Links
Schedule a Job	https://docs.microsoft.com/en-us/sql/ssms/agent/schedule-a-job?view=sql-server-ver15
How-to: Multi Server administration with master and target SQL Agent jobs	https://github.com/AzureDP300/AzureDP300/blob/main/Chapter13/ReferenceLinks.html
Reporting and alerting on job failure in SQL Server	https://github.com/AzureDP300/AzureDP300/blob/main/Chapter13/ReferenceLinks.html

Evaluate and implement an alert and notification strategy:

Measured Skills	Useful Links
Respond to events with Azure Monitor Alerts	https://docs.microsoft.com/en-us/azure/azure-monitor/learn/tutorial-response
Create alerts for Azure SQL Database and Azure Synapse Analytics using the Azure portal	https://docs.microsoft.com/en-us/azure/azure-sql/database/alerts-insights-configure-portal
Enable tracking and alerting for critical changes	https://docs.microsoft.com/en-us/azure/cloud-adoption-framework/manage/azure-server-management/enable-tracking-alerting
Event Notifications	https://docs.microsoft.com/en-us/sql/relational-databases/service-broker/event-notifications?view=sql-server-ver15

Manage and automate tasks in Azure:

Measured Skills	Useful Links
Azure SQL database deployment	https://docs.microsoft.com/en-us/azure/devops/pipelines/targets/azure-sqldb?view=azure-devops&tabs=yaml
Automated backups – Azure SQL Database & SQL Managed Instance	https://docs.microsoft.com/en-us/azure/azure-sql/database/automated-backups-overview?tabs=single-database
Automatic tuning in Azure SQL Database and Azure SQL Managed Instance	https://docs.microsoft.com/en-us/azure/azure-sql/database/automatic-tuning-overview
Automated Patching for SQL Server on Azure virtual machines (Resource Manager)	https://docs.microsoft.com/en-us/azure/azure-sql/virtual-machines/windows/automated-patching
Administer Servers by Using Policy-Based Management	https://docs.microsoft.com/en-us/sql/relational-databases/policy-based-management/administer-servers-by-using-policy-based-management?view=sql-server-ver15

Plan and Implement a High Availability and Disaster Recovery (HADR) Environment

In this module, you will be measured in the skills below:

Recommend a HADR strategy for a data platform solution:

Measured Skills	Useful Links
Overview of business continuity with Azure SQL Database	https://docs.microsoft.com/en-us/azure/azure-sql/database/business-continuity-high-availability-disaster-recover-hadr-overview
Understanding and leveraging Azure SQL Database's SLA	https://azure.microsoft.com/en-in/blog/understanding-and-leveraging-azure-sql-database-sla/
Business continuity and HADR for SQL Server on Azure Virtual Machines	https://docs.microsoft.com/en-us/azure/azure-sql/virtual-machines/windows/business-continuity-high-availability-disaster-recovery-hadr-overview
Always On availability groups: a high-availability and disaster-recovery solution	https://docs.microsoft.com/en-us/sql/database-engine/availability-groups/windows/always-on-availability-groups-sql-server?redirectedfrom=MSDN&view=sql-server-ver15
Always On Failover Cluster Instances (SQL Server)	https://docs.microsoft.com/en-us/sql/sql-server/failover-clusters/windows/always-on-failover-cluster-instances-sql-server?redirectedfrom=MSDN&view=sql-server-ver15
About Log Shipping (SQL Server)	https://docs.microsoft.com/en-us/sql/database-engine/log-shipping/about-log-shipping-sql-server?redirectedfrom=MSDN&view=sql-server-ver15
SQL Server Backup and Restore with Microsoft Azure Blob Storage Service	https://docs.microsoft.com/en-us/sql/relational-databases/backup-restore/sql-server-backup-and-restore-with-microsoft-azure-blob-storage-service?redirectedfrom=MSDN&view=sql-server-ver15

Test a HADR strategy by using platform, OS and database tools:

Measured Skills	Useful Links
Perform a planned manual failover of an Always On availability group (SQL Server)	https://docs.microsoft.com/en-us/sql/database-engine/availability-groups/windows/perform-a-planned-manual-failover-of-an-availability-group-sql-server?view=sql-server-ver15
Restore your Azure SQL Database or failover to a secondary	https://docs.microsoft.com/en-us/azure/azure-sql/database/disaster-recovery-guidance

Perform backup and restore a database by using database tools:

Measured Skills	Useful Links
BACKUP (Transact-SQL)	https://docs.microsoft.com/en-us/sql/t-sql/statements/backup-transact-sql?view=sql-server-ver15
RESTORE Statements (Transact-SQL)	https://docs.microsoft.com/en-us/sql/t-sql/statements/restore-statements-transact-sql?view=sql-server-ver15
Restore a SQL Server Database to a Point in Time (Full Recovery Model)	https://docs.microsoft.com/en-us/sql/relational-databases/backup-restore/restore-a-sql-server-database-to-a-point-in-time-full-recovery-model
Manage Azure SQL Database long-term backup retention	https://docs.microsoft.com/en-us/azure/azure-sql/database/long-term-backup-retention-configure

Configure DR by using platform and database tools:

Measured Skills	Useful Links
SQL Replication: Basic setup and configuration	https://github.com/AzureDP300/AzureDP300/blob/main/Chapter13/ReferenceLinks.html
configure Azure Site Recovery for a database offering	https://docs.microsoft.com/en-us/azure/site-recovery/site-recovery-sql

Configure HA using platform, OS and database tools:

Measured Skills	Useful Links
Configuring a SQL Server AlwaysOn High Availability Group	https://github.com/AzureDP300/AzureDP300/blob/main/Chapter13/ReferenceLinks.html
Join a secondary database to an Always On availability group	https://docs.microsoft.com/en-us/sql/database-engine/availability-groups/windows/join-a-secondary-database-to-an-availability-group-sql-server?view=sql-server-ver15
Configure and manage quorum	https://docs.microsoft.com/en-us/windows-server/failover-clustering/manage-cluster-quorum
Configure a listener for an Always On availability group	https://docs.microsoft.com/en-us/sql/database-engine/availability-groups/windows/create-or-configure-an-availability-group-listener-sql-server?view=sql-server-ver15

Perform Administration by Using T-SQL

In this module, you will be measured in the skills below:

Examine system health:

Measured Skills	Useful Links
Monitoring Microsoft Azure SQL Database and Azure SQL Managed Instance performance using dynamic management views	https://docs.microsoft.com/en-us/azure/azure-sql/database/monitoring-with-dmvs
System Dynamic Management Views	https://docs.microsoft.com/en-us/sql/relational-databases/system-dynamic-management-views/system-dynamic-management-views?view=sql-server-ver15
DBCC CHECKDB (Transact-SQL)	https://docs.microsoft.com/en-us/sql/t-sql/database-console-commands/dbcc-checkdb-transact-sql?view=sql-server-ver15

Monitor database configuration by using T-SQL:

Measured Skills	Useful Links
Get details of SQL Server Database Growth and Shrink Events	https://github.com/AzureDP300/AzureDP300/blob/main/Chapter13/ReferenceLinks.html
How to determine free space and file size for SQL Server databases	https://github.com/AzureDP300/AzureDP300/blob/main/Chapter13/ReferenceLinks.html
Change the Configuration Settings for a Database	https://docs.microsoft.com/en-us/sql/relational-databases/databases/change-the-configuration-settings-for-a-database?view=sql-server-ver15

Perform backup and restore a database by using T-SQL:

Measured Skills	Useful Links
Prepare a secondary database for an Always On availability group	https://docs.microsoft.com/en-us/sql/database-engine/availability-groups/windows/manually-prepare-a-secondary-database-for-an-availability-group-sql-server?view=sql-server-ver15

Transaction Log Backups (SQL Server)	https://docs.microsoft.com/en-us/sql/relational-databases/backup-restore/transaction-log-backups-sql-server?view=sql-server-ver15
RESTORE Statements (Transact-SQL)	https://docs.microsoft.com/en-us/sql/t-sql/statements/restore-statements-transact-sql?view=sql-server-ver15
BACKUP (Transact-SQL)	https://docs.microsoft.com/en-us/sql/t-sql/statements/backup-transact-sql?view=sql-server-ver15

Manage authentication by using T-SQL:

Measured Skills	Useful Links
Certificate Management (SQL Server Configuration Manager)	https://docs.microsoft.com/en-us/sql/database-engine/configure-windows/manage-certificates?view=sql-server-ver15
Principals (Database Engine)	https://docs.microsoft.com/en-us/sql/relational-databases/security/authentication-access/principals-database-engine?view=sql-server-ver15

Manage authorization by using T-SQL:

Measured Skills	Useful Links
Permissions (Database Engine)	https://docs.microsoft.com/en-us/sql/relational-databases/security/permissions-database-engine?view=sql-server-ver15
CREATE ROLE (Transact-SQL)	https://docs.microsoft.com/en-us/sql/t-sql/statements/create-role-transact-sql?view=sql-server-ver15

Chapter 15 Q&A

As any exam, after completing the study material, you need to make sure that you are prepared well for the exam. To be familiar with the dynamically changing Microsoft exams format, it is highly recommended to check the Microsoft official link: https://docs.microsoft.com/en-us/learn/certifications/certification-exams#exam-formats-and-question-types

This chapter will show the number of questions you can use to measure the required skills before taking the exam.

1. Microsoft Office 365 is an example of?

   a) Infrastructure as a Service

   b) Platform as a Service

   c) Software as a Service

Answer C: Software as a Service

2. Which cloud model provides the greatest degree of ownership and control?

   a) Hybrid

   b) Private

   c) Public

Answer B: Private

3. Which cloud model provides the greatest degree of flexibility?

   a) Public

   b) Private

   c) Hybrid

Answer C: Hybrid

4. Which of the following describes Platform as a Service (PaaS)?

   a) Users are responsible for purchasing, installing, configuring, and managing their own software—operating systems, middleware, and applications.

   b) Users create and deploy applications quickly without having to worry about managing the underlying infrastructure.

   c) Users pay an annual or monthly subscription.

Answer B: Users create and deploy applications quickly without having to worry about managing the underlying infrastructure.

5. Which of the following requires the most user management of the cloud services?

   a) Infrastructure as a Service

   b) Platform as a Service

   c) Software as a Service

Answer A: Infrastructure as a Service

6. Which of the following ensures data-residency and compliance needs are met for customers who need to keep their data and applications close?

   a) Geographies
   b) Regions
   c) Zones

Answer A: Geographies

7. As a best practice, all resources that are part of an application and share the same lifecycle should exist in the same?

   a) Availability set
   b) Region
   c) Resource group

Answer C: Resource group

8. Microsoft Azure datacenters are organized and made available by?

   a) Geographies
   b) Regions
   c) Zones

Answer B: Regions

9. An Azure SQL Database Managed Instance represents what kind of cloud service:

   a) Platform as a Service (PAAS)
   b) Infrastructure as a Service (IAAS)
   c) Software as a Service (SAAS)

Answer A: Platform as a Service (PAAS)

10. One of the following is NOT an Azure SQL Database deployment option:

   a) Availability Zones
   b) Serverless
   c) Elastic Pools

Answer A: Availability Zones

11. If you are planning to migrate a set of databases that use distributed transactions from on-premises SQL Server, the target database platform that you will use in Microsoft Azure is:

a) Azure SQL Database

b) Azure SQL Managed Instance

c) Azure SQL For MySQL

Answer B: Azure SQL Managed Instance

12. The best option to host the new cloud database that you expect to grow to 40 TB is:

a) Azure SQL Database Serverless

b) Azure SQL Database Single Database

c) Azure SQL Database Hyperscale

Answer C: Azure SQL Database Hyperscale

13. The best option to host your new database in the cloud for testing purposes that will be used less than 5 hours a day and is expected to be 20 GB in size, is

a) Azure SQL Database Serverless

b) Azure SQL Database Single Database

c) Azure SQL Database Hyperscale

Answer A: Azure SQL Database Serverless

14. The type of data that can have its own schema defined at query time:

a) Structured data

b) Unstructured data

c) Semi-structured data

Answer B: Unstructured data

15. The Microsoft Azure data platform technology that is a globally distributed, multi-model database that can offer sub-second query performance and low latency:

a) Azure SQL Database

b) Azure Synapse Analytics

c) Microsoft Azure Cosmos DB

Answer C: Microsoft Azure Cosmos DB

16. Which role works with services such as Cognitive Services, Cognitive Search, and the Bot Framework?

    a) Azure Database Administrator
    b) Data Engineer
    c) Data Scientist
    d) AI Engineer

Answer D: AI Engineer

17. Which role works in designing, implementing, management, monitoring, securing, and maintaining data-related solutions?

    a) Azure Database Administrator
    b) Data Engineer
    c) Data Scientist
    d) AI Engineer

Answer B: Data Engineer

18. Which role works in provisioning, managing, and maintaining the relational database services provided by Microsoft Azure?

    a) Azure Database Administrator
    b) Data Engineer
    c) Data Scientist
    d) AI Engineer

Answer A: Azure Database Administrator

19. An Azure SQL Database Managed Instance represents what kind of cloud service?

    a) Platform as a Service (PAAS)
    b) Infrastructure as a Service (IAAS)
    c) Software as a Service (SAAS)

Answer A: Platform as a Service (PAAS)

20. Which of the following is NOT a valid reason for migrating your database into an IaaS environment?

a) Your applications need to run older versions of SQL Server, such as SQL Server 2016.

b) You want Azure to manage all the upgrades, patching and server configuration.

c) You need to use other SQL Server services with your application, such as SQL Server Analysis Services

d) (SSAS), Integration Services (SSIS) and Reporting Services (SSRS)

Answer B: You want Azure to manage all the upgrades, patching and server configuration.

21. Which of the following is NOT an Azure SQL Database deployment option?

a) Availability Zones

b) Serverless

c) Elastic Pools

Answer A: Availability Zones

22. Which version of SQL Server does compatibility level 100 equate to?

a) SQL Server 2008

b) SQL Server 2014

c) SQL Server 2019

Answer A: SQL Server 2008

23. What does Microsoft guarantee if you upgrade versions of SQL Server but maintain the same compatibility level, on similar hardware?

a) Execution Plan Shape

b) Elapsed time of queries

c) Syntax compatibility

Answer A: Execution Plan Shape

24. Where do you change the compatibility level settings?

a) The individual database properties page

b) The server settings page

c) Using a trace flag through the Configuration Manager

Answer A: The individual database properties page

25. How do you get access to a private preview?

    a) Gain access directly from Microsoft

    b) Check a box in the Azure Portal

    c) File a support case

Answer A: Gain access directly from Microsoft

26. What type of storage offers the lowest latency in Azure?

    a) Ultra Disk

    b) Premium Disk

    c) Standard SSD

Answer A: Ultra Disk

27. Which tool would you use to assess and migrate your databases from an on-premises SQL Server to an Azure VM?

    a) Microsoft Assessment and Planning Toolkit

    b) Database Experimentation Assistant

    c) Data Migration Assistant

Answer B: Data Migration Assistant

28. To reduce the cost of an Azure SQL Server VM you intend to run full time for 3 years, which option should you choose?

    a) Azure Reserved VM Instances

    b) Availability Set

    c) Pay as You Go Licensing

Answer A: Azure Reserved VM Instances

29. You need to migrate a set of databases that use distributed transactions from on-premises SQL Server.

    a) Which of the following options should you choose?

    b) Azure SQL Managed Instance

    c) Azure SQL Database

    d) Azure SQL Database Hyperscale

Answer B: Azure SQL Managed Instance

30. You are building a new cloud database that you expect to grow to 50 TB. Which is the best option for your database?

    a) Azure SQL Database Hyperscale

    b) Azure SQL Database Managed instance

    c) Azure SQL Database Serverless

Answer A: Azure SQL Database Hyperscale

31. You are building a database for testing purposes that will be used less than 8 hours a day and is expected to be 20 GB in size. What is your most cost-effective option?

    a) Azure SQL Database Serverless

    b) Azure SQL Database Elastic Pools

    c) Azure SQL Database Managed instance

Answer A:Azure SQL Database Serverless

32. You are deploying a mission critical MySQL database to support an e—commerce site which depends on low latency. What should you configure your application to do in order to handle transient errors?

    a) Connection resiliency

    b) Secure Socket Layer (SSL)

    c) An Azure Virtual Network

Answer A: Connection resiliency

33. Which of the following is a benefit of Azure Database for PostgreSQL?

    a) Automatic Query Tuning

    b) Managed automated backups

    c) Automated cross-region disaster recovery

Answer B: Managed automated backups

34. What's the process to upgrade a major version of Azure Database for MySQL?

    a) The Service performs the update for you

    b) Create a dump and restore to a server at the higher version

    c) Change the version of the server in the portal

Answer B: Create a dump and restore to a server at the higher version

35. Which protocol is used by Azure Active Directory for Authorization?

    a) Kerberos

    b) LDAP

    c) OAuth

Answer C:OAuth

36. Which database stores the information about logins in SQL Server?

    a) master

    b) model

    c) msdb

Answer A: master

37. Which role allows users to create users within a database

    a) db_datareader

    b) db_accessadmin

    c) db_securityadmin

Answer C: db_securityadmin

38. Which permission allows the user to perform any option against a database object?

    a) Control

    b) Delete

    c) View Definition

Answer A: Control

39. Which database object can be granted insert access?

    a) Functions

    b) Tables

    c) Procedures

Answer B:Tables

40. What feature allows a user to execute a stored procedure even if she does not have permission to access the tables referenced in the stored procedure?

a) Ownership chaining

b) Principle of least privilege

c) Granular security

Answer A: Ownership chaining

41. Which security object is required in order to enable transparent data encryption?

a) Credential

b) Master Key

c) Login

Answer B: Master Key

42. Which feature prevents members of the sysadmin role from viewing the values of data in a table?

a) Always Encrypted

b) Dynamic Data Masking

c) Transparent Data Encryption

Answer A: Always Encrypted

43. Which is a valid location for Always Encrypted keys?

a) Azure Key Vault

b) Azure Automation

c) Azure Blob Storage

Answer A: Azure Key Vault

44. Which feature provides a private IP address for an Azure SQL Database?

a) Network Endpoints

b) Private Link

c) Database Firewall

Answer B: Private Link

45. Which technique can be used to create database firewall rules in Azure SQL Database?

a) Running a PowerShell script

b) Running a Azure CLI script

c) Executing a T-SQL statement

Answer C: Executing a T-SQL statement

46. Which features allow for ExpressRoute connectivity to Azure SQL Database?
    a) Private Link
    b) Network Endpoints
    c) Linked Server

Answer A: Private Link

47. Which of the following threats is analyzed by Advanced Threat Protection?
    a) Weak passwords
    b) Open Firewall rules
    c) SQL Injection

Answer C: SQL Injection

48. Which attack type is commonly associated with dynamic SQL?
    a) SQL Injection
    b) Brute Force
    c) Data Exfiltration

Answer A: SQL Injection

49. Which Intelligent Insights option provides SQL Insights?
    a) Log Analytics
    b) Azure Storage
    c) Event Hub

Answer A: Log Analytics

50. Which Performance Monitor counter reflects how long SQL Server expects to retain data in memory?
    a) Page Life Expectancy
    b) Processor Queue Length
    c) Paging File Usage

Answer A: Page Life Expectancy

51. If you want to see the sizes of your SQL Server Databases running in an Azure VM which tool should you use?

a) The SQL VM Resource Provider

b) Azure Monitor

c) Intelligent Insights

Answer A: The SQL VM Resource Provider

52. Which isolation level should you choose if you want to prevent users reading data from blocking users writing data?

a) Serializable

b) Read Committed Snapshot Isolation

c) Repeatable Read

Answer B: Read Committed Snapshot Isolation

53. Which DMV shows sessions holding locks?

a) sys.dm_os_wait_stats

b) Sys.dm_tran_locks

c) Sys.dm_exec_requests

Answer: B: Sys.dm_tran_locks

54. Which Query Store catalog view provides the Query ID to allow for query tracking?

a) Sys.query_store_plan

b) Sys.query_store_runtime_statistics

c) Sys.query_store_queries

Answer C: Sys.query_store_queries

55. Which type of storage should be used in conjunction with Azure VMs for SQL Server data files?

a) Table Storage

b) Blob Storage

c) Disk Storage

Answer C: Disk Storage

56. Which of the following can be limited using Resource Governor?

a) Buffer pool allocation

b) Write IOPs

c) Recompilation

Answer B:Write IOPs

57. Which is an option from the SQL Server Resource Provider for Azure VMs?

a) Storage configuration

b) Changing Max Degree of Parallelism

c) Maintenance Plans

Answer A: Storage configuration

58. Which intelligent query processing feature allows for faster calculations of a large number of rows?

a) Batch Mode on Row Store

b) Approximate Count Distinct

c) Interleaved Execution

Answer A: Batch Mode on Row Store

59. Which component of resource governor allows you to configure limits on system resources?

a) Workload Groups

b) Classifier Functions

c) Resource Pools

Answer C: Resource Pools

60. Which database setting affects the way the query optimizer generates execution plans?

a) Recovery Model

b) Optimize for Ad-Hoc Workloads

c) Compatibility Level

Answer C: Compatibility Level

61. Which platform supports automatic index management?

a) Azure SQL Managed Instance

b) Azure SQL Database

c) SQL Server in an Azure VM

Answer B: Azure SQL Database

62. Which of the following actions triggers automatic plan choice activity to occur?

a) An execution plan recompilation

b) An execution plan change that has caused an estimated CPU gain of 10 seconds

c) A new index is created

Answer B: An execution plan change that has caused an estimated CPU gain of 10 seconds

63. Which DVM shows the status of a plan updated by automatic tuning?

a) sys.dm_db_tuning_recommendations

b) sys.dm_db_automatic_tuning_options

c) sys.dm_exec_query_plan_stats

Answer A: sys.dm_db_tuning_recommendations

64. Which type of execution plan is stored in the plan cache?

a) Estimated execution plan

b) Actual execution plan

c) Live Query Stats

Answer A: Estimated execution plan

65. Which DMV should you use to find index utilization?

a) sys.dm_db_index_usage_stats

b) sys.dm_db_missing_index_details

c) sys.dm_exec_query_plan_stats

Answer A: sys.dm_db_index_usage_stats

66. Which of the following wait types would indicate excessive CPU consumption?

a) SOS_SCHEDULER_YIELD

b) RESOURCE_SEMAPHORE

c) PAGEIOLATCH_SH

Answer A: SOS_SCHEDULER_YIELD

67. What type of database design should you use for a data warehouse when you want to reduce the data volume of your dimensions?

a) Snowflake schema

b) Star Schema

c) 3rd normal form

Answer A: Snowflake schema

68. What is the minimum number of rows you need to bulk insert into a columnstore index?

a) 102,400

b) 1,000,000

c) 1000

Answer A: 102,400

69. Which compression type offers the highest level of compression?

a) Columnstore Archival

b) Page Compression

c) Row Compression

Answer A: Columnstore Archival

70. What type of index is best used on a data warehouse fact table?

a) Clustered Columnstore

b) Nonclustered Columnstore

c) Clustered b-tree

Answer A: Clustered Columnstore

71. Which DMV provides information about server level wait statistics?

a) sys.dm_db_index_physical_stats

b) sys.dm_os_wait_stats

c) sys.dm_exec_session_wait_stats

Answer C: sys.dm_os_wait_stats

72. Which DMV can you use to capture the last Actual Execution Plan for a given query?

a) sys.dm_exec_cached_plans
b) sys.dm_exec_query_plan
c) sys.dm_exec_query_plan_stats

Answer C: sys.dm_exec_query_plan_stats

73. What language are ARM templates written in?

a) JSON
b) C#
c) T-SQL

Answer A: JSON

74. If you want to pass in the region for a resource group deployment which option should you include in your template?

a) Parameter
b) Variable
c) Output

Answer A: Parameter

75. Which element of a template allows for you to build dependencies into resources?

a) dependsOn
b) concat
c) apiVersion

Answer A: dependsOn

76. What has to be configured before the SQL Server Agent can send e-mail?

a) a mail profile
b) An agent job
c) An alert

Answer A: a mail profile

77. Which system database stores SQL Server Agent jobs and their information?

a) MSDB
b) Master
c) Model

Answer A: MSDB

78. Which operation recalculates the statistics on an index?

    a) Rebuild

    b) Reorganize

    c) Shrinking a file group

Answer A: Rebuild

79. Which Extended Events target only writes to memory and is not persisted?

    a) Ring Buffer

    b) Target File

    c) Event Tracing for Windows

Answer A: Ring Buffer

80. Where do you implement a filter in your Extended Event Session?

    a) On the Event

    b) On the Storage Target

    c) On a Global Field

Answer A: On the Event

81. Which scenario can you troubleshoot using Extended Events?

    a) A server restart

    b) A long running query

    c) A failed backup

Answer B: long running query

82. What is the unit of execution for your Azure Automation Account?

    a) Runbook

    b) Schedule

    c) Container

Answer A: Runbook

83. What scope can Azure Policy be deployed to?

    a) Tenant

    b) Subscription

c) User

Answer B: Subscription

84. What is the name for the scope of SQL Elastic Job?

    a) Target Group

    b) Management Group

    c) Resource Group

Answer A: Target Group

85. What is RPO?

    a) The number of nodes in a cluster

    b) The point to which data needs to be recovered after a failure

    c) A partial database restore

Answer B: The point to which data needs to be recovered after a failure

86. What is a hybrid solution?

    a) A solution that has resources both in Azure as well as on premises or in another cloud provider

    b) A solution that uses two different database engines e.g. MySQL and SQL Server

    c) A solution that spans two different versions of SQL Server

Answer A: solution that has resources both in Azure as well as on premises or in another cloud provider

87. What is available after failover with database-level protection in SQL Server?

    a) Logins, Databases, and SQL Server Agent Job

    b) Databases and SQL Server Agent jobs

    c) Whatever is in the databases; anything outside must be dealt with manually

Answer C: Whatever is in the databases; anything outside must be dealt with manually

88. What component in Azure needs to be configured for the listener in an AG to work properly?

a) The NIC
b) The NSG
c) A load balancer

Answer :C load balancer

89. How should you create a WSFC in Azure for AGs and FCIs?

a) Wizard in Failover Cluster Manager
b) PowerShell
c) WMI

Answer B: PowerShell

90. What Azure feature lets you test disaster recovery without bringing down your production system?

a) ASR
b) Azure SQL Database
c) Azure Load Balancer

Answer A: ASR

91. What feature is not available with Azure SQL Database Managed Instance?

- Failover group
- Secondary replica that is readable
- Active geo-replication

Answer C: Active geo-replication

92. What do Temporal Tables allow you to do with Azure SQL Database?

- Recover deleted data
- Scale out reads
- Temporarily process additional data

Answer A: Recover deleted data

93. What setting for auto-failover groups must you change if you need to ensure a low RPO?

- RPOZero
- AlwaysBeInSync

- GracePeriodWithDataLossHours

Answer C: GracePeriodWithDataLossHours

94. How does backup to URL in SQL Server or Azure SQL Server Database Managed Instance store the backup file?

    a) As a URL
    b) As a blob
    c) As a pointer

Answer B: As a blob

95. Which platforms can a PaaS database backup from Azure be restored to?

    a) Microsoft SQL Server
    b) PostgreSQL
    c) MySQL
    d) All of the above
    e) None of the above

Answer E: None of the above

96. What is the cost for backup storage for both Azure Database for MySQL and Azure Database for PostgreSQL?

    a) Free up to the size of the database
    b) Double the cost of the service
    c) Half the cost of the service

Answer A: Free up to the size of the database

97. Assume that you have an Azure SQL Database that contains a table that has 7 billion rows. This table is loaded nightly by using a batch process. Which type of compression provides the greatest space reduction for that database?

    a) page compression
    b) row compression
    c) columnstore compression
    d) columnstore archival compression

Answer D: columnstore archival compression

98. You have a Microsoft SQL Server 2019 instance in an on-premises datacenter. The instance contains a 4-TB database named DB1.

You plan to migrate DB1 to an Azure SQL Database managed instance.

What should you use to minimize downtime and data loss during the migration?

a) distributed availability groups

b) database mirroring

c) log shipping

d) Database Migration Assistant

Answer D: Database Migration Assistant

99. You have a resource group named dp300RG that contains an Azure SQL Database server named DevDB1. DevDB1 contains an Azure SQL database named DB1. The schema and permissions for DB1 are saved in a Microsoft SQL Server Data Tools (SSDT) database project.

You need to populate a new resource group named db300RG2 with the DB1 database and an Azure SQL Server named TestServer1. The resources in db300RG2 must have the same configurations as the resources in dp300RG.

Which four actions should you perform in sequence? To answer, move the appropriate actions from the list of actions to the answer area and arrange them in the correct order.

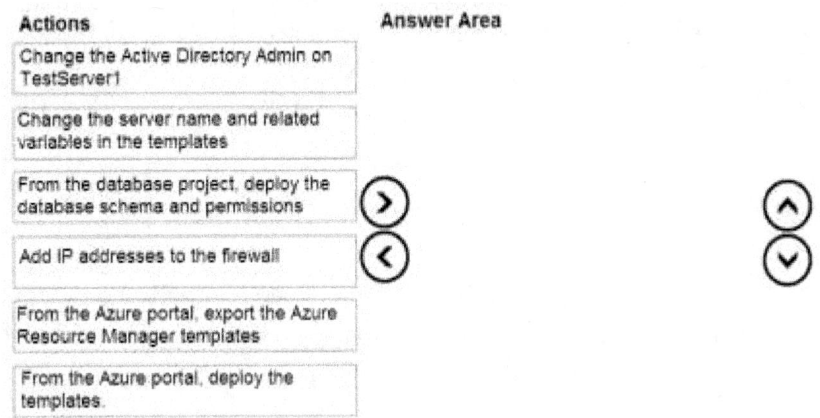
Actions
Answer Area
Change the Active Directory Admin on TestServer1
Change the server name and related variables in the templates
From the database project, deploy the database schema and permissions
Add IP addresses to the firewall
From the Azure portal, export the Azure Resource Manager templates
From the Azure portal, deploy the templates.

Answer :

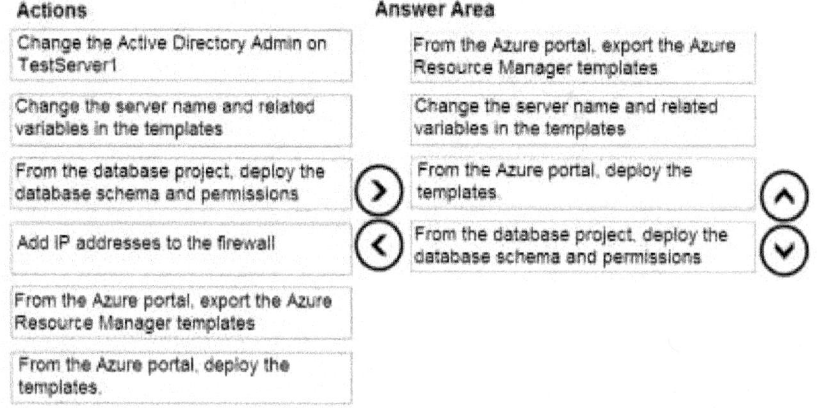
Actions
Change the Active Directory Admin on TestServer1
Change the server name and related variables in the templates
From the database project, deploy the database schema and permissions
Add IP addresses to the firewall
From the Azure portal, export the Azure Resource Manager templates
From the Azure portal, deploy the templates.
Answer Area
From the Azure portal, export the Azure Resource Manager templates
Change the server name and related variables in the templates
From the Azure portal, deploy the templates.
From the database project, deploy the database schema and permissions

100. You have a new Azure SQL database. The database contains a column that stores confidential information. You need to track each time values from the column are returned in a query. The tracking information must be stored for 365 days from the date the query was executed.

Which three actions should you perform? Each correct answer presents part of the solution.

NOTE: Each correct selection is worth one point.

a) Turn on auditing and write audit logs to an Azure Storage account.
b) Add extended properties to the column.
c) Turn on Advanced Data Security for the Azure SQL server.
d) Apply sensitivity labels named Highly Confidential to the column.

Turn on Azure Advanced Threat Protection (ATP).

Answer

- **Turn on auditing and write audit logs to an Azure Storage account.**
- **Turn on Advanced Data Security for the Azure SQL server.**
- **Apply sensitivity labels named Highly Confidential to the column.**

101. You have an Azure virtual machine named VM1 on a virtual network named VNet1. Outbound traffic from VM1 to the internet is blocked.

You have an Azure SQL database named SqlDb1 on a logical server named SqlSrv1.

You need to implement connectivity between VM1 and SqlDb1 to meet the following requirements:

⇨Ensure that all traffic to the public endpoint of SqlSrv1 is blocked.

⇨Minimize the possibility of VM1 exfiltrating data stored in SqlDb1.

What should you create on VNet1?

a) a VPN gateway

b) a service endpoint

c) a private link

d) an ExpressRoute gateway

Answer C: private link

102. You have a Microsoft SQL Server database named DB1 that contains a table named Table1. The database role membership for a user named User1 is shown in the following image:

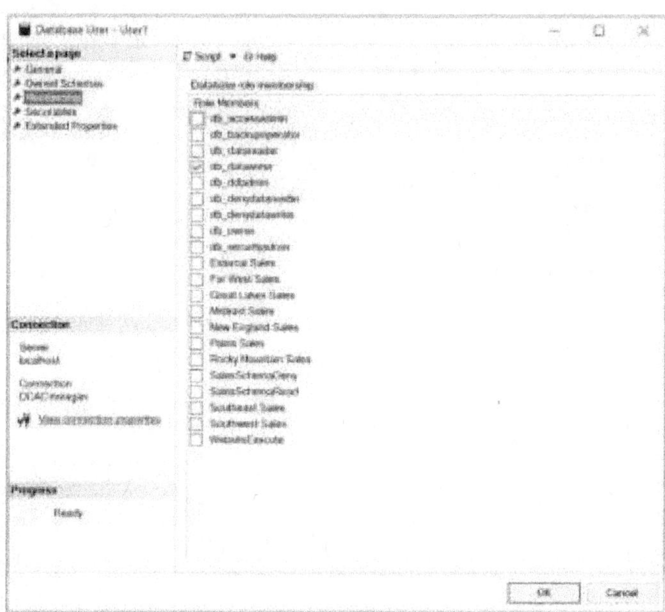

Use the drop-down menus to select the answer choice that completes each statement based on the information presented in the graphic.

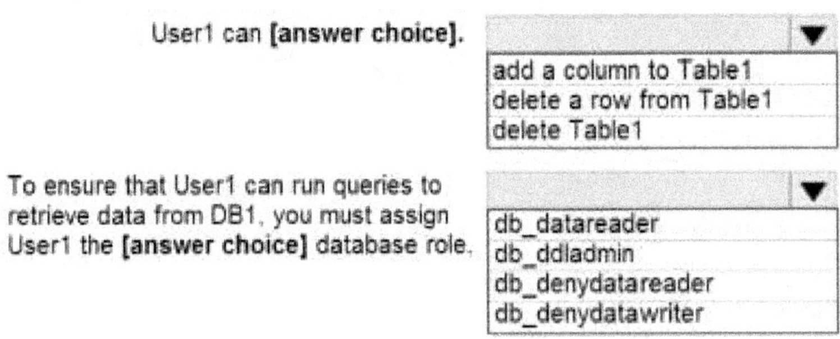
Answer Area
User1 can [answer choice].
add a column to Table1
delete a row from Table1
delete Table1
To ensure that User1 can run queries to retrieve data from DB1, you must assign User1 the [answer choice] database role.
db_datareader
db_ddladmin
db_denydatareader
db_denydatawriter

Answer: Box 1: delete a row from Table1. Box 2: db_datareader

103. You have a new Azure SQL database named DB1 on an Azure SQL server named AzSQL1.

The only user who was created is the server administrator.

You need to create a contained database user in DB1 who will use Azure Active Directory (Azure AD) for authentication.

Which three actions should you perform in sequence? To answer, move the appropriate actions from the list of actions to the answer area and arrange them in the correct order.

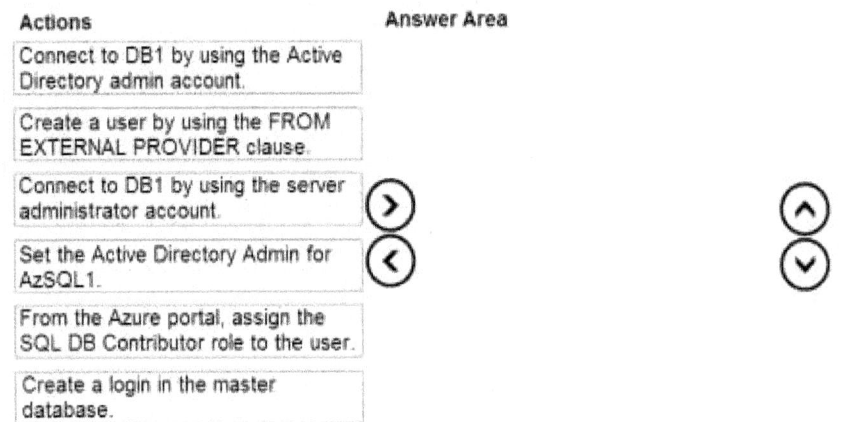
Actions
Answer Area
Connect to DB1 by using the Active Directory admin account.
Create a user by using the FROM EXTERNAL PROVIDER clause.
Connect to DB1 by using the server administrator account.
Set the Active Directory Admin for AzSQL1.
From the Azure portal, assign the SQL DB Contributor role to the user.
Create a login in the master database.

Answer :

Actions	Answer Area
Connect to DB1 by using the Active Directory admin account.	Set the Active Directory Admin for AzSQL1.
Create a user by using the FROM EXTERNAL PROVIDER clause.	Connect to DB1 by using the Active Directory admin account.
Connect to DB1 by using the server administrator account.	Create a user by using the FROM EXTERNAL PROVIDER clause.
Set the Active Directory Admin for AzSQL1.	
From the Azure portal, assign the SQL DB Contributor role to the user.	
Create a login in the master database.	

104. You have an Azure SQL database that contains a table named Customer. Customer has the columns shown in the following table.

Customer_ID	Customer_Name	Customer_Phone
11001	Contoso, Ltd.	555-555-0173
11002	Litware, Inc.	555-505-3124
11003	ADatum Corporation	555-689-4312

You plan to implement a dynamic data mask for the Customer_Phone column. The mask must meet the following requirements:

- The first six numerals of each customer's phone number must be masked.
- The last four digits of each customer's phone number must be visible.
- Hyphens must be preserved and displayed.

How should you configure the dynamic data mask? To answer, select the appropriate options in the answer area.

Answer Area

Exposed Prefix: [dropdown]
0
1
3
5

Padding String: [dropdown]
x
xxxxxx
xxx-xxx
xxx-xxx-
x[3]-x[3]

Exposed Suffix: [dropdown]
0
1
3
5

Answer A: Box 1: 0 , Box 2: xxx-xxx , Box 3: 5

105. You have an Azure SQL database that contains a table named Employees. Employees contain a column named Salary.

You need to encrypt the Salary column. The solution must prevent database administrators from reading the data in the Salary column and must provide the most secure encryption.

Which three actions should you perform in sequence? To answer, move the appropriate actions from the list of actions to the answer area and arrange them in the correct order.

Actions

- Encrypt the Salary column by using the randomized encryption type.
- Create a column encryption key.
- Enable Transparent Data Encryption (TDE).
- Encrypt the Salary column by using the deterministic encryption type.
- Apply a dynamic data mask to the Salary column.
- Create a column master key.

Answer Area

Answer :

Actions	Answer Area
Encrypt the Salary column by using the randomized encryption type.	Create a column master key.
Create a column encryption key.	Create a column encryption key.
Enable Transparent Data Encryption (TDE).	Encrypt the Salary column by using the randomized encryption type.
Encrypt the Salary column by using the deterministic encryption type.	
Apply a dynamic data mask to the Salary column.	
Create a column master key.	

106. You have SQL Server on an Azure virtual machine that contains a database named DB1. DB1 contains a table named CustomerPII.

You need to record whenever users query the CustomerPII table.

Which two options should you enable? Each correct answer presents part of the solution.

- server audit specification
- SQL Server audit
- database audit specification
- a server principal

Answer B: SQL Server audit

database audit specification

107. You have an Azure virtual machine based on a custom image named VM1.

VM1 hosts an instance of Microsoft SQL Server 2019 Standard.

You need to automate the maintenance of VM1 to meet the following requirements:

⇨Automate the patching of SQL Server and Windows Server.

⇨Automate full database backups and transaction log backups of the databases on VM1.

⇨Minimize administrative effort.

What should you do first?

- ➢ Enable a system-assigned managed identity for VM1
- ➢ Register VM1 to the Microsoft.Sql resource provider
- ➢ Install an Azure virtual machine Desired State Configuration (DSC) extension on VM1
- ➢ Register VM1 to the Microsoft.SqlVirtualMachine resource provider

Answer B: Register VM1 to the Microsoft.SqlVirtualMachine resource provider

108. You receive numerous alerts from Azure Monitor for an Azure SQL database.

You need to reduce the number of alerts. You must only receive alerts if there is a significant change in usage patterns for an extended period.

Which two actions should you perform? Each correct answer presents part of the solution.

NOTE: Each correct selection is worth one point.

a) Set Threshold Sensitivity to High

b) Set the Alert logic threshold to Dynamic

c) Set the Alert logic threshold to Static

d) Set Threshold Sensitivity to Low

e) Set Force Plan to On

Answer

B - Set the Alert logic threshold to Dynamic

D- Set Threshold Sensitivity to Low

109. You have an Azure SQL database named sqldb1. You need to minimize the amount of space by the data and log files of sqldb1. What should you run?

a) DBCC SHRINKDATABASE

b) sp_clean_db_free_space

c) sp_clean_db_file_free_space

d) DBCC SHRINKFILE

Answer A: DBCC SHRINKDATABASE

110. You have an Azure SQL Database server named sqlsrv1 that hosts 10 Azure SQL databases.

The databases perform slower than expected.

You need to identify whether the performance issue relates to the use of tempdb on sqlsrv1.

What should you do?

- ➢ Run Query Store-based queries
- ➢ Review information provided by SQL Server Profiler-based traces
- ➢ Review information provided by Query Performance Insight
- ➢ Run dynamic management view-based queries

Answer D: Run dynamic management view-based queries

111. You are building an Azure virtual machine.

You allocate two 1-TiB, P30 premium storage disks to the virtual machine. Each disk provides 5,000 IOPS.

You plan to migrate an on-premises instance of Microsoft SQL Server to the virtual machine. The instance has a database that contains a 1.2-TiB data file. The database requires 10,000 IOPS.

You need to configure storage for the virtual machine to support the database.

Which three objects should you create in sequence? To answer, move the appropriate objects from the list of objects to the answer area and arrange them in the correct order.

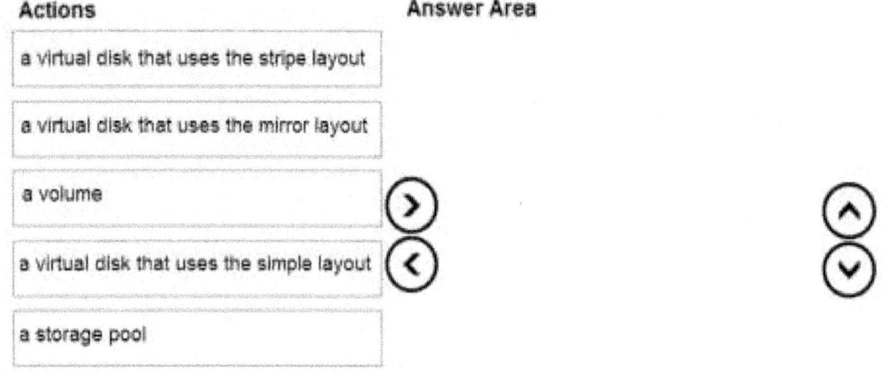

Actions
Answer Area
a virtual disk that uses the stripe layout
a virtual disk that uses the mirror layout
a volume
a virtual disk that uses the simple layout
a storage pool

Answer :

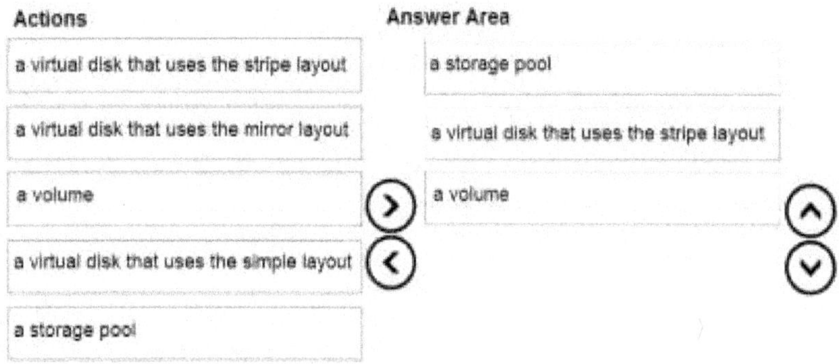

112. You have an Azure SQL database named sqldb1.

You need to minimize the possibility of Query Store transitioning to a read-only state.

What should you do?

- ➢ Double the value of Data Flush interval
- ➢ Decrease by half the value of Data Flush Interval
- ➢ Double the value of Statistics Collection Interval
- ➢ Decrease by half the value of Statistics Collection interval

Answer D: Decrease by half the value of Data Flush Interval

113. You have SQL Server 2019 on an Azure virtual machine that runs Windows Server 2019. The virtual machine has 4 vCPUs and 28 GB of memory.

You scale up the virtual machine to 16 vCPUSs and 64 GB of memory.

You need to provide the lowest latency for tempdb.

What is the total number of data files that tempdb should contain?

- 2
- 4
- 8
- 64

Answer C: 8

114. You have an Azure SQL database named db1. You need to retrieve the resource usage of db1 from last week. How should you complete the statement? To answer, select the appropriate options in the answer area.

Answer Area

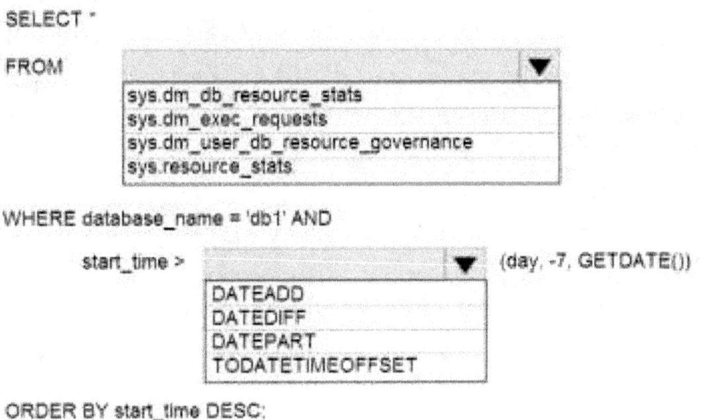

Answer : Box1: sys.dm_db_resource_stats. Box2: DATEADD.

115. You have SQL Server on an Azure virtual machine. You review the query plan shown in the following image:

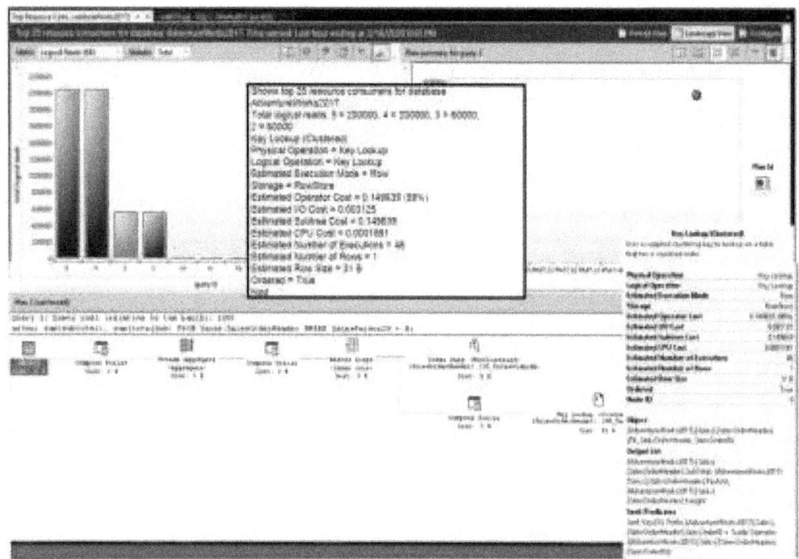

For each of the following statements, select yes if the statement is true. Otherwise, select no.

Answer Area

Statements	Yes	No
You will reduce the I/O usage and the query execution time if you force the query plan.	○	○
You will increase the I/O usage and the query execution time if you create a new index on the SalesOrderHeader table.	○	○
You will reduce the I/O usage and the query execution time if you include the SubTotal, TaxAmt, and Freight columns in the PK_SalesOrderHeader_SalesOrderID index.	○	○

Answer : No, No, Yes.

116. A data engineer creates a table to store employee information for a new application. All employee names are in the US English alphabet. All addresses are locations in the United States. The data engineer uses the following statement to create the table.

```
CREATE TABLE dbo.Employee
(
    EmployeeID        INT IDENTITY(1,1) PRIMARY KEY CLUSTERED NOT NULL,
    FirstName         VARCHAR(100) NOT NULL,
    LastName          VARCHAR(100) NOT NULL,
    Title             VARCHAR(100) NULL,
    LastHireDate      DATETIME NULL,
    StreetAddress1    VARCHAR(500) NOT NULL,
    StreetAddress2    VARCHAR(500) NOT NULL,
    StreetAddress3    VARCHAR(500) NOT NULL,
    City              VARCHAR(200) NOT NULL,
    StateName         VARCHAR(20) NOT NULL,
    Salary            VARCHAR(20) NULL,
    PhoneNumber       VARCHAR(20) NOT NULL
)
```

You need to recommend changes to the data types to reduce storage and improve performance.

Which two actions should you recommend? Each correct answer presents part of the solution.

a) Change Salary to the money data type.
b) Change PhoneNumber to the float data type.
c) Change LastHireDate to the datetime2(7) data type.
d) Change PhoneNumber to the bigint data type.
e) Change LastHireDate to the date data type.

Answer

A: Change Salary to the money data type.

E: Change LastHireDate to the date data type.

117. You have an Azure SQL database. You identify a long running query.

You need to identify which operation in the query is causing the performance issue.

What should you use to display the query execution plan in Microsoft SQL Server Management Studio (SSMS)?

a) Live Query Statistics

b) an estimated execution plan

c) an actual execution plan

d) Client Statistics

Answer A: Live Query Statistics

118. You have a version-8.0 Azure Database for MySQL database.

You need to identify which database queries consume the most resources.

Which tool should you use?

- Query Store
- Metrics
- Query Performance Insight
- Alerts

Answer A: Query Store

119. You have SQL Server on an Azure virtual machine that contains a database named DB1.

You have an application that queries DB1 to generate a sales report.

You need to see the parameter values from the last time the query was executed.

Which two actions should you perform? Each correct answer presents part of the solution.

a) Enable Last_Query_Plan_Stats in the master database

b) Enable Lightweight_Query_Profiling in DB1

c) Enable Last_Query_Plan_Stats in DB1

d) Enable Lightweight_Query_Profiling in the master database

e) Enable PARAMETER_SNIFFING in DB1

Answer:

B: Enable Lightweight_Query_Profiling in DB1

C: Enable Last_Query_Plan_Stats in DB1

120. You have SQL Server on an Azure virtual machine that contains a database named Db1.

You need to enable automatic tuning for Db1.

How should you complete the statements? To answer, select the appropriate answer in the answer area.

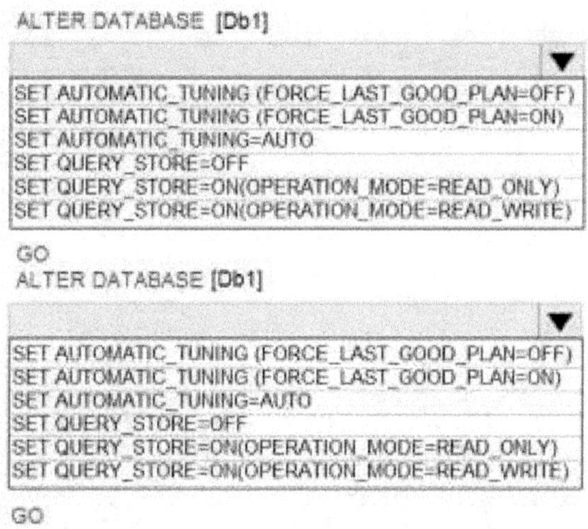

Answer: **Box1 - SET QUERY_STORE = ON (OPERATION MODE = READ_WRITE) Box2 - SET AUTOMATIC_TUNNING (FORCE_LAST_GOOD_PLAN = ON)**

121. You deploy a database to an Azure SQL Database managed instance.

You need to prevent read queries from blocking queries that are trying to write to the database.

Which database option should set?

a) PARAMETERIZATION to FORCED
b) PARAMETERIZATION to SIMPLE
c) Delayed Durability to Forced

d) READ_COMMITTED_SNAPSHOT to ON

Answer D:READ_COMMITTED_SNAPSHOT to ON

122. You have an Azure SQL database.

You discover that the plan cache is full of compiled plans that were used only once.

You run the select * from sys.database_scoped_configurations Transact-SQL command and receive the results shown in the following table.

configuration_id	name	value	is_value_default
1	LEGACY_CARDINALITY_ESTIMATION	0	1
2	QUERY_OPTIMIZER_HOTFIXES	0	1
3	OPTIMIZE_FOR_AD_HOC_WORKLOADS	0	1
4	ACCELERATED_PLAN_FORCING	1	1

You need to relieve the memory pressure.

What should you configure?

a) LEGACY_CARDINALITY_ESTIMATION

b) QUERY_OPTIMIZER_HOTFIXES

c) OPTIMIZE_FOR_AD_HOC_WORKLOADS

d) ACCELERATED_PLAN_FORCING

Answer C: OPTIMIZE_FOR_AD_HOC_WORKLOADS

123. You have SQL Server on an Azure virtual machine named SQL1.

SQL1 has an agent job to back up all databases.

You add a user named dbadmin1 as a SQL Server Agent operator.

You need to ensure that dbadmin1 receives an email alert if a job fails.

Which three actions should you perform in sequence? To answer, move the appropriate actions from the list of actions to the answer area and arrange them in the correct order.

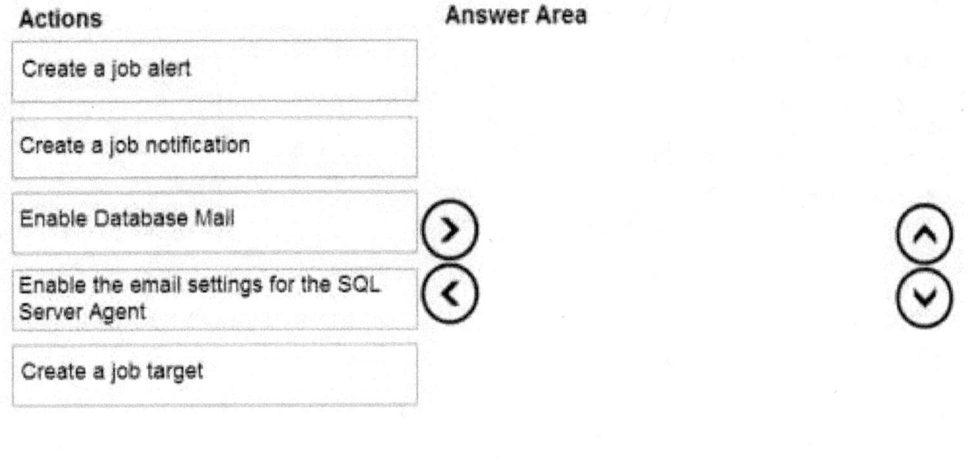
Actions
Answer Area
Create a job alert
Create a job notification
Enable Database Mail
Enable the email settings for the SQL Server Agent
Create a job target

Answer:

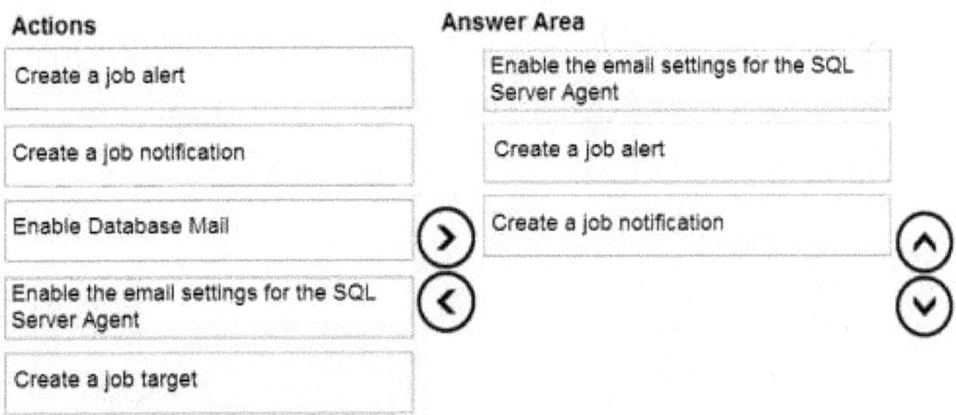
Actions
Answer Area
Create a job alert
Create a job notification
Enable Database Mail
Enable the email settings for the SQL Server Agent
Create a job target
Enable the email settings for the SQL Server Agent
Create a job alert
Create a job notification

124. You need to apply 20 built-in Azure Policy definitions to all new and existing Azure SQL Database deployments in an Azure subscription. The solution must minimize administrative effort. Which three actions should you perform in sequence? To answer, move the appropriate actions from the list of actions to the answer area and arrange them in the correct order.

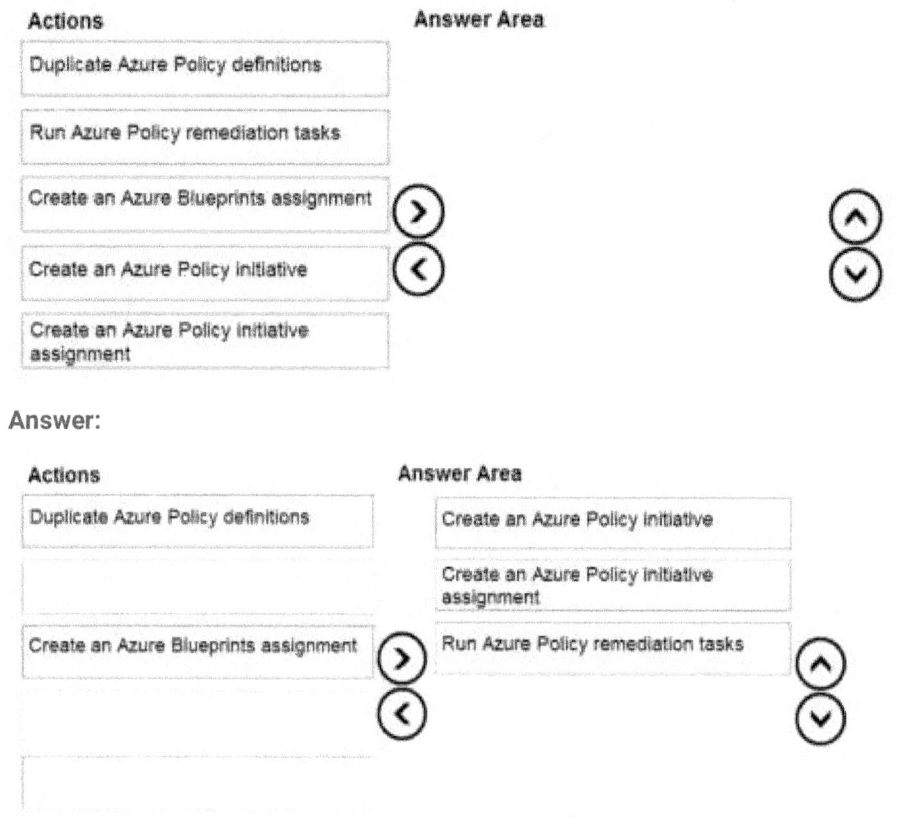

125. You have an Azure SQL Database managed instance named SQLMI1. A Microsoft SQL Server Agent job runs on SQLMI1.

You need to ensure that an automatic email notification is sent once the job completes.

What should you include in the solution?

a) From SQL Server Configuration Manager (SSMS), enable SQL Server Agent
b) From SQL Server Management Studio (SSMS), run sp_set_sqlagent_properties
c) From SQL Server Management Studio (SSMS), create a Database Mail profile
d) From the Azure portal, create an Azure Monitor action group that has an Email/SMS/Push/Voice action

Answer C: From SQL Server Management Studio (SSMS), create a Database Mail profile

126. You have an Azure SQL database named Sales.

You need to implement disaster recovery for Sales to meet the following requirements:

⇨During normal operations, provide at least two readable copies of Sales.

⇨Ensure that Sales remains available if a datacenter fails.

Solution: You deploy an Azure SQL database that uses the Business Critical service tier and Availability Zones.

Does this meet the goal?

a) Yes
b) No

Answer A: Yes.

127. You have an Azure SQL database named Sales.

You need to implement disaster recovery for Sales to meet the following requirements:

⇨During normal operations, provide at least two readable copies of Sales.

⇨Ensure that Sales remains available if a datacenter fails.

Solution: You deploy an Azure SQL database that uses the General Purpose service tier and failover groups.

Does this meet the goal?

a) Yes
b) No

Answer B: No

128. You have two Azure SQL Database servers named Server1 and Server2. Each server contains an Azure SQL database named Database1.

You need to restore Database1 from Server1 to Server2. The solution must replace the existing Database1 on Server2.

Solution: From the Azure portal, you delete Database1 from Server2, and then you create a new database on Server2 by using the backup of Database1 from Server1.

Does this meet the goal?

a) Yes

b) No

Answer A: Yes

129. You have two Azure SQL Database servers named Server1 and Server2. Each server contains an Azure SQL database named Database1.

You need to restore Database1 from Server1 to Server2. The solution must replace the existing Database1 on Server2.

Solution: You run the Remove-AzSqlDatabase PowerShell cmdlet for Database1 on Server2. You run the Restore-AzSqlDatabase PowerShell cmdlet for

Database1 on Server2.

Does this meet the goal?

a) Yes

b) No

Answer A: Yes

130. You have two Azure SQL Database servers named Server1 and Server2. Each server contains an Azure SQL database named Database1.

You need to restore Database1 from Server1 to Server2. The solution must replace the existing Database1 on Server2.

Solution: You restore Database1 from Server1 to the Server2 by using the RESTORE Transact-SQL command and the REPLACE option.

Does this meet the goal?

a) Yes

b) No

Answer: Yes

131. You have an Always On availability group deployed to Azure virtual machines. The availability group contains a database named DB1 and has two nodes named SQL1 and SQL2. SQL1 is the primary replica.

You need to initiate a full backup of DB1 on SQL2. Which statement should you run?

a) BACKUP DATABASE DB1 TO URL='https://mystorageaccount.blob.core.windows.net/mycontainer/DB1.bak' with (Differential, STATS=5, COMPRESSION);

b) BACKUP DATABASE DB1 TO URL='https://mystorageaccount.blob.core.windows.net/mycontainer/DB1.bak' with (COPY_ONLY, STATS=5, COMPRESSION);

c) BACKUP DATABASE DB1 TO URL='https://mystorageaccount.blob.core.windows.net/mycontainer/DB1.bak' with (File_Snapshot, STATS=5, COMPRESSION);

d) BACKUP DATABASE DB1 TO URL='https://mystorageaccount.blob.core.windows.net/mycontainer/DB1.bak' with (NoInit, STATS=5, COMPRESSION);

Answer : B

BACKUP DATABASE DB1 TO URL='https://mystorageaccount.blob.core.windows.net/mycontainer/DB1.bak' with (COPY_ONLY, STATS=5, COMPRESSION);

132. You plan to move two 100-GB databases to Azure.

You need to dynamically scale resources consumption based on workloads. The solution must minimize downtime during scaling operations.

What should you use?

a) An Azure SQL Database elastic pool
b) SQL Server on Azure virtual machines
c) an Azure SQL Database managed instance
d) Azure SQL databases

Answer: A An Azure SQL Database elastic pool

133. You plan to move two 100-GB databases to Azure.

You need to dynamically scale resources consumption based on workloads. The solution must minimize downtime during scaling operations.

What should you use?

a) An Azure SQL Database elastic pool
b) SQL Server on Azure virtual machines
c) an Azure SQL Database managed instance
d) Azure SQL databases

Answer A: An Azure SQL Database elastic pool

134. You have 10 Azure virtual machines that have SQL Server installed.

You need to implement a backup strategy to ensure that you can restore specific databases to other SQL Server instances. The solution must provide centralized management of the backups.

What should you include in the backup strategy?

Automated Backup in the SQL virtual machine settings

- ➢ Azure Backup
- ➢ Azure Site Recovery
- ➢ SQL Server Agent jobs

Answer A:Azure Backup

135. You need to recommend an availability strategy for an Azure SQL database. The strategy must meet the following requirements:

⇨ Support failovers that do not require client applications to change their connection strings.

⇨Replicate the database to a secondary Azure region.

⇨Support failover to the secondary region.

What should you include in the recommendation?

a) failover groups
b) transactional replication
c) Availability Zones
d) geo-replication

Answer A: failover groups

136. You have SQL Server on an Azure virtual machine that contains a database named DB1. DB1 is 30 TB and has a 1-GB daily rate of change.

You backup the database by using a Microsoft SQL Server Agent job that runs Transact-SQL commands. You perform a weekly full backup on Sunday, daily differential backups at 01:00, and transaction log backups every five minutes.

The database fails on Wednesday at 10:00.

Which three backups should you restore in sequence? To answer, move the appropriate backups from the list of backups to the answer area and arrange them in the correct order.

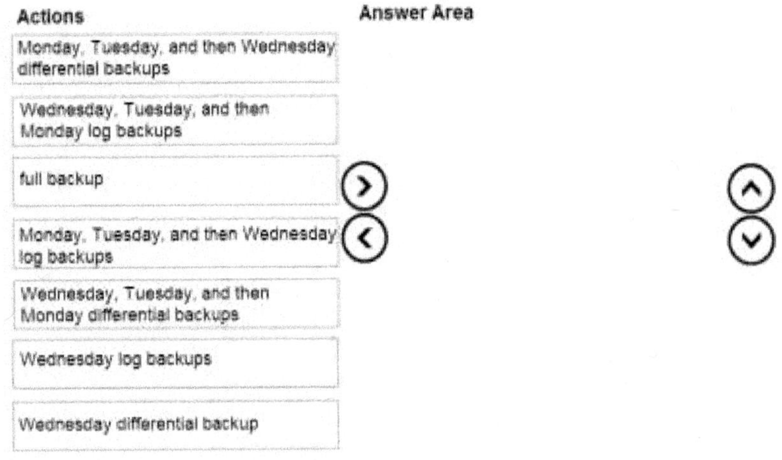

Answer :

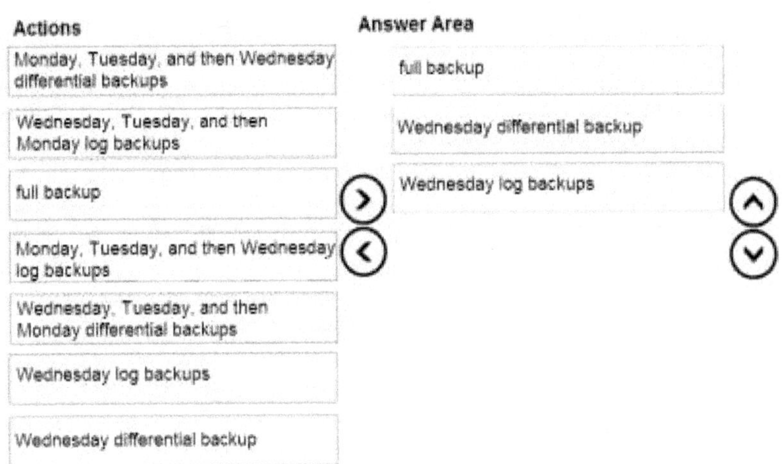

137. You are building a database backup solution for a SQL Server database hosted on an Azure virtual machine.

In the event of an Azure regional outage, you need to be able to restore the database backups. The solution must minimize costs.

Which type of storage accounts should you use for the backups?

a) locally-redundant storage (LRS)
b) read-access geo-redundant storage (RA-GRS)

c) zone-redundant storage (ZRS)
d) geo-redundant storage

Answer C: geo-redundant storage (ZRS)

138. You have SQL Server on Azure virtual machines in an availability group.

You have a database named DB1 that is NOT in the availability group.

You create a full database backup of DB1.

You need to add DB1 to the availability group.

Which restore option should you use on the secondary replica?

a) Restore with Recovery
b) Restore with Norecovery
c) Restore with Standby

Answer B: Restore with Norecovery

139. You are planning disaster recovery for the failover group of an Azure SQL Database managed instance.

Your company's SLA requires that the database in the failover group become available as quickly as possible if a major outage occurs.

You set the Read/Write failover policy to Automatic.

What are two results of the configuration? Each correct answer presents a complete solution.

a) In the event of a datacenter or Azure regional outage, the databases will fail over automatically.
b) In the event of an outage, the databases in the primary instance will fail over immediately.

c) In the event of an outage, you can selectively fail over individual databases.

d) In the event of an outage, you can set a different grace period to fail over each database.

e) In the event of an outage, the minimum delay for the databases to failover in the primary instance will be one hour.

Answer

A: In the event of a datacenter or Azure regional outage, the databases will fail over automatically.

E: In the event of an outage, the minimum delay for the databases to failover in the primary instance will be one hour.

140. You have an Azure SQL database named DB1.

You need to ensure that DB1 will support automatic failover without data loss if a datacenter fails. The solution must minimize costs.

Which deployment option and pricing tier should you configure?

A) Azure SQL Database Premium

B) Azure SQL Database serverless

C) Azure SQL Database managed instance Business Critical

D) Azure SQL Database Standard

Answer A: Azure SQL Database Premium

141. You have an Azure SQL database named Sales.

You need to implement disaster recovery for Sales to meet the following requirements:

⊸During normal operations, provide at least two readable copies of Sales.

⊸Ensure that Sales remains available if a datacenter fails.

Solution: You deploy an Azure SQL database that uses the General Purpose service tier and geo-replication.

Does this meet the goal?

a) Yes

b) No

Answer: No

142. You have an Azure SQL database named DB3.

You need to provide a user named DevUser with the ability to view the properties of DB3 from Microsoft SQL Server Management Studio (SSMS) as shown in the image below:

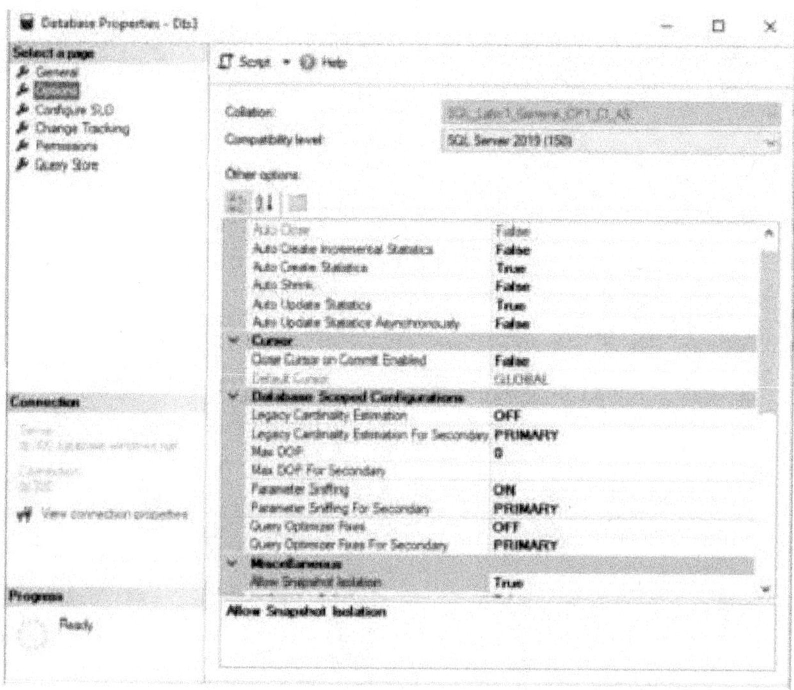

Which Transact-SQL command should you run?

a) GRANT SHOWPLAN TO DevUser

b) GRANT VIEW DEFINITION TO DevUser

c) GRANT VIEW DATABASE STATE TO DevUser

d) GRANT SELECT TO DevUser

Answer C: GRANT VIEW DATABASE STATE TO DevUser

143. You have SQL Server on an Azure virtual machine that contains a database named DB1.

The database reports a CHECKSUM error.

You need to recover the database.

How should you complete the statements? To answer, select the appropriate options in the answer area.

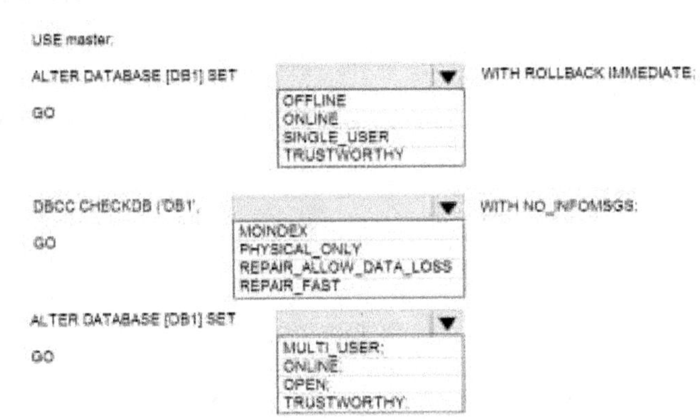

Answer Area
USE master;
ALTER DATABASE [DB1] SET
WITH ROLLBACK IMMEDIATE;
GO
OFFLINE
ONLINE
SINGLE_USER
TRUSTWORTHY
DBCC CHECKDB ('DB1',
WITH NO_INFOMSGS;
GO
NOINDEX
PHYSICAL_ONLY
REPAIR_ALLOW_DATA_LOSS
REPAIR_FAST
ALTER DATABASE [DB1] SET
GO
MULTI_USER;
ONLINE;
OPEN;
TRUSTWORTHY

Answer:

Box 1: SINGLE_USER

Box 2: REPAIR_ALLOW_DATA_LOSS

Box 3: MULTI_USER

144. You have an Azure SQL Database managed instance named sqldbmi1 that contains a database named Sales.

You need to initiate a backup of Sales.

How should you complete the Transact-SQL statement? To answer, select the appropriate options in the answer area.

Answer Area

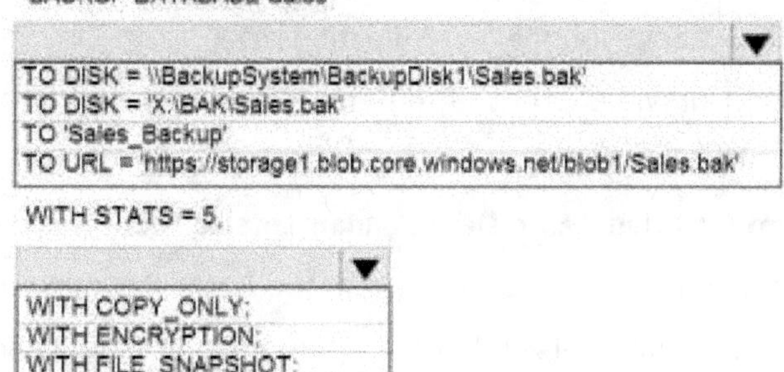
BACKUP DATABASE Sales
TO DISK = '\\BackupSystem\BackupDisk1\Sales.bak'
TO DISK = 'X:\BAK\Sales.bak'
TO 'Sales_Backup'
TO URL = 'https://storage1.blob.core.windows.net/blob1/Sales.bak'
WITH STATS = 5,
WITH COPY_ONLY;
WITH ENCRYPTION;
WITH FILE_SNAPSHOT;
WITH NO_TRUNCATE

Answer

Box 1: TO URL = 'https://storage1.blob.core.windows.net/blob1/Sales.bak'

Box 2: WITH COPY_ONLYssssss

What is the next step

After completing this course and becoming a Microsoft Certified Azure Database Administrator Associate, you need to think about your next certifications step.

In the data field, Microsoft provides you with different roles that can be the next step for the database administrators. This includes:

- **Microsoft Certified Azure Data Fundamentals:** This certificate is for beginners in the Azure data platforms. If you already finish the Azure Database Administrator course, no need for a data fundamentals certificate. For more information about the exam required to gain that certificate, check the certificate site: https://docs.microsoft.com/en-us/learn/certifications/azure-data-fundamentals/.
- **Microsoft Certified Azure Data Engineer Associate**: Azure Data Engineers are responsible for designing, implementing, management, monitoring, securing, and maintaining data-related solutions. For more information about the exams required to gain that certificate, check the certificate site: https://docs.microsoft.com/en-us/learn/certifications/azure-data-engineer/.
- **Microsoft Certified Data Analyst Associate:** Data Analysts are responsible for designing and building data models by transforming them into a format that can be easily analyzed and visualized. For more information about the exams required to gain that certificate, check the certificate site: https://docs.microsoft.com/en-us/learn/certifications/data-analyst-associate/.
- **Microsoft Certified Azure Data Scientist Associate**: Data Scientists are responsible for applying the different machine learning techniques to solve business-related problems by training, evaluating, and deploying these machine learning models. For more information about the exams required to gain that certificate, check the certificate site: https://docs.microsoft.com/en-us/learn/certifications/azure-data-scientist/.
- **Microsoft Certified Azure AI Engineer Associate:** AI Engineers are responsible for using the Cognitive Services, the Azure Machine Learning Service, and Knowledge Mining to design and implement different types of AI solutions, such as language and speech processing solutions. For more information about the exams required to gain that certificate, check the certificate site: https://docs.microsoft.com/en-us/learn/certifications/azure-ai-engineer/.

www.ingramcontent.com/pod-product-compliance
Lightning Source LLC
LaVergne TN
LVHW081506050326
832903LV00025B/1399

* 9 7 9 8 7 0 6 1 2 8 0 2 9 *